Second Edition

Fingerprints and Other Ridge Skin Impressions

INTERNATIONAL FORENSIC SCIENCE
AND INVESTIGATION SERIES
Series Editor: Max Houck

Forensic Examination of Hair
James R. Robertson
ISBN 9780748405671 • 1999

Forensic Examination of Fibres, 2nd edition
J. Robertson and M. Grieve
ISBN 9780748408160 • 1999

Forensic Examination of Glass and Paint: Analysis and Interpretation
B. Caddy
ISBN 9780748405794 • 2001

Forensic Speaker Identification
P. Rose
ISBN 9780415271827 • 2002

Bitemark Evidence
B. J. Dorion
ISBN 9780824754143 • 2004

The Practice of Crime Scene Investigation
J. Horswell
ISBN 9780748406098 • 2004

Fire Investigation
N. Nic Daéid
ISBN 9780415248914 • 2004

Forensic Computer Crime Investigation
Thomas A. Johnson
ISBN 9780824724351 • 2005

Analytical and Practical Aspects of Drug Testing in Hair
Pascal Kintz
ISBN 9780849364501 • 2006

Nonhuman DNA Typing: Theory and Casework Applications
Heather M. Coyle
ISBN 9780824725938 • 2007

Chemical Analysis of Firearms, Ammunition, and Gunshot Residue
James Smyth Wallace
ISBN 9781420069662 • 2008

Forensic Science in Wildlife Investigations
Adrian Linacre
ISBN 9780849304101 • 2009

Scientific Method: Applications in Failure Investigation and Forensic Science
Randall K. Noon
ISBN 9781420092806 • 2009

Forensic Epidemiology
Steven A. Koehler and Peggy A. Brown
ISBN 9781420063271 • 2009

Ethics and the Practice of Forensic Science
Robin T. Bowen
ISBN 9781420088939 • 2009

Introduction to Data Analysis with R for Forensic Scientists
James Michael Curran
ISBN: 9781420088267 • 2010

Forensic Investigation of Explosions, Second Edition
A. Beveridge
ISBN 9781420087253 • 2011

Firearms, the Law, and Forensic Ballistics, Third Edition
Tom Warlow
ISBN 9781439818275 • 2011

The Neuroscience of Handwriting: Applications for Forensic Document Examination
Michael P. Caligiuri and Linton A. Mohammed
ISBN 9781439871409 • 2012

Forensic Metrology: Scientific Measurement and Inference for Lawyers, Judges, and Criminalists
Ted Vosk and Ashley F. Emery
ISBN 9781439826195 • 2015

Fingerprints and Other Ridge Skin Impressions, Second Edition
C. Champod, C. Lennard, P. Margot, and M. Stoilovic
ISBN 9781498728935 • 2016

Second Edition

Fingerprints and Other Ridge Skin Impressions

CHRISTOPHE CHAMPOD
University of Lausanne
Switzerland

CHRIS LENNARD
Western Sydney University
Australia

PIERRE MARGOT
University of Lausanne
Switzerland

MILUTIN STOILOVIC
Optimum Technology
Australia

CRC Press
Taylor & Francis Group
Boca Raton London New York

CRC Press is an imprint of the
Taylor & Francis Group, an **informa** business

CRC Press
Taylor & Francis Group
6000 Broken Sound Parkway NW, Suite 300
Boca Raton, FL 33487-2742

© 2016 by Taylor & Francis Group, LLC
CRC Press is an imprint of Taylor & Francis Group, an Informa business

Printed and bound in India by Replika Press Pvt. Ltd.

Printed on acid-free paper
Version Date: 20160120

International Standard Book Number-13: 978-1-4987-2893-5 (Hardback)

Library of Congress Cataloging-in-Publication Data

Names: Champod, Christophe, author.
Title: Fingerprints and other ridge skin impressions / Christophe Champod, Chris Lennard, Pierre Margot, Milutin Stoilovic.
Description: Second edition. | Boca Raton, FL : CRC Press, 2016. | Series: International forensic science & investigation series ; 27
Identifiers: LCCN 2015044800 | ISBN 9781498728935 (alk. paper)
Subjects: LCSH: Fingerprints. | Fingerprints--Identification. | Criminal investigation. | Forensic sciences.
Classification: LCC HV6074 .F564 2016 | DDC 363.25/8--dc22
LC record available at http://lccn.loc.gov/2015044800

Visit the Taylor & Francis Web site at
http://www.taylorandfrancis.com

and the CRC Press Web site at
http://www.crcpress.com

Contents

Preface to the Second Edition...xi
Preface to the First Edition xiii
Authors..xix

Chapter 1   Friction Ridge Skin and Prints...1

    1.1   Structure of the Skin 1
    1.2   Morphogenesis of Friction Ridge Skin: Primary Dermal
          Ridge Development 3
    1.3   Factors Affecting the General Pattern and the Configuration of Minutiæ........6
    1.4   Morphogenesis of Friction Ridge Skin: Secondary Dermal Ridge
          Development and Dermal Papillae...12
    1.5   Other Features than Major Epidermal Papillary Lines on Friction
          Ridge Skin..14
    1.6   Abnormal Friction Ridge Skin 17
    1.7   Summary of the Stages of Friction Ridge Skin Morphogenesis 19
    1.8   Relationship with Permanency and Alterations 20
    1.9   Relationship with Selectivity..27
    References 28

Chapter 2   Friction Ridge Identification Process 33

    2.1   Analysis 39
          2.1.1   Purpose of the Analysis...39
          2.1.2   Factors Considered during Analysis 43
          2.1.3   Documentation of the Analysis 45
          2.1.4   Quality Metrics for Marks..50
          2.1.5   Decisions Reached Following Analysis 51
          2.1.6   Variability in the Conclusions Reached Following
                  the Analysis Phase...53
    2.2   Search Heuristics to Facilitate the Comparison 56
          2.2.1   Predicting the Finger Number of the Hand at the Source
                  of a Mark 56
          2.2.2   Predicting the Source Area of the Finger or the Palm......................65
          2.2.3   Predicting Gender and Other Characteristics of the Donor.............67
    2.3   Comparison 67
    2.4   Evaluation 70
          2.4.1   The Weight to Be Assigned to the Observations................70
          2.4.2   Decisions Reached Following Evaluation 77
                  2.4.2.1   Identification 78
                  2.4.2.2   Exclusion...96
                  2.4.2.3   Inconclusive 97
          2.4.3   Left, Touched or Handled: The Hierarchy of Propositions...............99
          2.4.4   Reliability of the Evaluation Process 102

2.5   Verification 104
2.6   How Many Similarities Are Required for an Identification? 105
        2.6.1   Historical Milestones 105
        2.6.2   Current Views and Practices 106
                 2.6.2.1   Predetermined Minimum Number of Minutiæ:
                            An Empirical Standard 106
                 2.6.2.2   No Predetermined Numerical Standard:
                            A Holistic Approach 108
2.7   Probability Models Applied to Fingermarks 111
2.8   An LR-Based Reporting Scheme 114
References 116

Chapter 3   Chemistry, Light, and Photography 127

3.1   Standard Weights and Measures 127
3.2   Chemistry Theory 128
3.3   Light Theory 133
        3.3.1   Introduction 133
        3.3.2   Wave Theory 133
        3.3.3   Particle Theory 134
        3.3.4   White Light and Colored Light 135
        3.3.5   Spectral Sensitivity of the Human Eye 136
        3.3.6   Absorption and Reflection of Light 137
        3.3.7   Polarization of Light 138
        3.3.8   Photoluminescence 139
        3.3.9   Optical Filters 140
        3.3.10   Absorption Mode 144
        3.3.11   Diffused Reflection Mode 148
        3.3.12   Episcopic Coaxial Illumination 149
        3.3.13   Photoluminescence Mode 150
        3.3.14   Polarized Light Examinations 152
        3.3.15   Ultraviolet Illumination Techniques 153
3.4   Forensic Light Sources 155
        3.4.1   Conventional Light Sources 155
        3.4.2   LED-Based Light Sources 156
        3.4.3   FLS Requirements 158
3.5   Photography 160
        3.5.1   Introduction 160
        3.5.2   Basic Image Formation and Capture 160
        3.5.3   Digital Cameras 162
                 3.5.3.1   Image Sensors 162
                 3.5.3.2   Digital Single-Lens Reflex Camera 164
                 3.5.3.3   Camera Lenses 165
                 3.5.3.4   Camera Settings 165
                 3.5.3.5   Sensitivity and Noise 167
                 3.5.3.6   Choosing a Digital Camera 168
                 3.5.3.7   Photography in the Luminescence Mode 168
3.6   Digital Imaging 169
        3.6.1   Introduction 169
        3.6.2   Data Compression and File Formats 170

		3.6.3	Image Processing Techniques	171
		3.6.4	Legal Requirements	173
	3.7		Hyperspectral Imaging	175
	References			177

Chapter 4 Fingermark Detection and Enhancement 179

4.1	Types of Fingermarks	179
	4.1.1	Visible Fingermarks	179
	4.1.2	Latent Fingermarks	179
4.2	Surface Characteristics	182
	4.2.1	Porous Surfaces	183
	4.2.2	Nonporous Surfaces	184
	4.2.3	Semiporous Surfaces	185
4.3	Optical Detection Techniques	185
	4.3.1	Absorption	185
	4.3.2	Luminescence	185
	4.3.3	Diffused Reflection	186
	4.3.4	Ultraviolet Imaging	187
	4.3.5	Near-Infrared Imaging	188
	4.3.6	Visible Hyperspectral Imaging	189
4.4	Detection Techniques for Porous Surfaces	190
	4.4.1	Ninhydrin	190
		4.4.1.1 General	190
		4.4.1.2 Ninhydrin Formulations	193
		4.4.1.3 Secondary Metal Salt Treatment	195
	4.4.2	Ninhydrin Analogs	198
	4.4.3	Diazafluorenone	200
	4.4.4	Indanedione	203
	4.4.5	Other Amino Acid Reagents	207
	4.4.6	Physical Developer	208
	4.4.7	Lipid Stains	211
		4.4.7.1 Oil Red O	211
		4.4.7.2 Nile Red	213
	4.4.8	Recommended Detection Sequence	214
4.5	Detection Techniques for Nonporous Surfaces	216
	4.5.1	Fingerprint Powders	216
	4.5.2	Powder Suspensions	218
		4.5.2.1 Small Particle Reagent	218
		4.5.2.2 Thick Powder Suspensions	219
	4.5.3	Cyanoacrylate Fuming	221
		4.5.3.1 Conventional Cyanoacrylate Fuming	221
		4.5.3.2 Portable Fuming Systems	225
		4.5.3.3 Vacuum Cyanoacrylate Fuming	225
		4.5.3.4 Enhancement of CA-Developed Marks	226
	4.5.4	Vacuum Metal Deposition	231
	4.5.5	Recommended Detection Sequence	235
4.6	Nanoparticle-Based Detection Methods	236
	4.6.1	Nanopowders	236
	4.6.2	Multimetal Deposition	237
	4.6.3	Single-Metal Deposition	238

          4.6.4   Quantum Dots 239

          4.6.5   Silica-Based Nanocomposites 240

          4.6.6   Health and Safety Concerns 241

    4.7   Miscellaneous Techniques 241

          4.7.1   Iodine–Benzoflavone 241

          4.7.2   Dimethylaminocinnamaldehyde 243

          4.7.3   Ruthenium Tetroxide 245

          4.7.4   Silver Nitrate 246

          4.7.5   Sudan Black 247

    4.8   Novel Approaches to Fingermark Detection 248

          4.8.1   Upconverters 248

          4.8.2   Immunology: Antibodies and Aptamers 250

          4.8.3   Mass Spectrometric Imaging 251

    4.9   Fingermark Detection on Semiporous Surfaces 252

    4.10   Fingermark Detection on Human Skin 254

          4.10.1   General 254

          4.10.2   Powdering 255

          4.10.3   Transfer Techniques 255

          4.10.4   Iodine Fuming 256

          4.10.5   Cyanoacrylate 257

          4.10.6   Ruthenium Tetroxide 258

          4.10.7   Fingermarks in Blood on Skin 258

          4.10.8   Recommended Detection Sequence 259

    4.11   Fingermark Detection on Adhesive Surfaces 260

          4.11.1   Gentian Violet 261

          4.11.2   Powder Suspensions 262

          4.11.3   Cyanoacrylate Fuming 264

          4.11.4   Miscellaneous Techniques 264

          4.11.5   Recommended Detection Sequence 264

    4.12   Fingermark Detection on Thermal Paper 266

    4.13   Fingermark Detection on Fabrics 267

    4.14   Fingermark Detection on Firearms and Cartridge Cases 268

          4.14.1   Cyanoacrylate Fuming 269

          4.14.2   Gun Blue 269

          4.14.3   Miscellaneous Techniques 270

          4.14.4   Recommended Detection Sequence 271

    4.15   Enhancement of Fingermarks in Blood 272

          4.15.1   Optical Techniques 273

          4.15.2   Protein Stains 274

          4.15.3   Diaminobenzidine 277

          4.15.4   Miscellaneous Techniques 277

          4.15.5   Recommended Detection Sequence 278

    4.16   Fingermark Detection at the Crime Scene 280

    4.17   Effects of Fingermark Detection Techniques on Subsequent
        Forensic Analyses 281

          4.17.1   Document Examination 281

          4.17.2   DNA Profiling 282

          4.17.3   Recovery and Analysis of Explosive Residues 286

    4.18   Standards for Fingermark Detection Research 288

4.19 Health and Safety Considerations 290
    4.19.1 Hazardous Substances...290
    4.19.2 Light Sources...292
References 293

Chapter 5 Issues Related to the Exploitation of Fingerprints and Fingermarks 315

5.1 Terminology 315
5.2 Use of Fingerprints..318
    5.2.1 Print-to-Print Comparison...319
    5.2.2 Trace-to-Record or Trace-to-Print Comparison.........................319
    5.2.3 Trace-to-Trace Comparison...320
    5.2.4 Combining Evidence Types..321
    5.2.5 Identification Decision in Other Forums than the Court 321
5.3 Relevance..321
5.4 Age Estimation of Marks 322
5.5 Forged and Fabricated Fingerprint Evidence 327
    5.5.1 Forgeries Committed by Law Enforcement Personnel 328
    5.5.2 Forgeries Committed by Criminals...328
    5.5.3 Detection of Forged Marks 329
5.6 Errors..331
    5.6.1 Error Types...333
    5.6.2 Quality Assurance..333
        5.6.2.1 Fingerprint Examiner 334
        5.6.2.2 Processes..336
        5.6.2.3 The Product..336
References 337

Chapter 6 Conclusions 343

6.1 Fingermark Detection...343
6.2 Fingerprint Identification..344
References 346

Appendix A: Statistical Data for General Fingerprint Patterns, Ridge Widths, and Gender 347

Appendix B: Statistical Data on Minutiæ 359

Appendix C: Fingermark Detection Sequences 365

Appendix D: Reagent Preparation and Application..373

Appendix E: Abbreviations..415

Index..421

Preface to the Second Edition

We initially thought that a new edition was a simple matter of updating the previous edition; however, we soon had to admit that far-reaching changes for the professions—both in the detection and identification processes—needed a thorough treatment. The general outline and subdivision found in the first edition is retained, and, as with the first edition, our focus is on fundamental issues (whether in the identification process, the detection processes, the semantics, or ongoing research). Indeed, valuable books and chapters go into the details of current detection procedures, whereas we have kept an outline of what would be widely applicable methods that would help detect a large majority of ridge impressions, while keeping paragraphs dedicated to future and potential developments. Over the 13 years since the first edition, the scientific literature in this area has exploded (over 1,000 publications) and the related professions have been shaken by errors, challenges by courts and other scientists, and changes of a fundamental nature related to previous claims of infallibility and absolute individualization. This implies fundamental changes in the way training, identifying, and reporting should be conducted. We address these questions with a definite view of where the profession has to go and what efforts and research should help develop the field over the next few years. We propose solutions that were already watermarked in the previous edition but with a full development of probabilistic and decision theories that will support the identification process. The mask is down, and this should lead to heated debates in the near future as many practitioners have not yet realized the earth-shattering nature of the changes. This is a book, we hope, that will prepare the reader for the challenges ahead.

We are also pleased to announce that we have a website for the book where you can access additional resources such as Bayesian networks, comparison tools, and updated reagent formulations. The website address is http://esc-app.unil.ch/blogs/forsi/.

Such a venture would not have been possible without the contributions of many colleagues and researchers from the University of Lausanne whom we acknowledge. They are Alexandre Anthonioz, Andy Bécue, Alex Biedermann, Marco de Donno, Nicole Egli Anthonioz, Aline Girod, Tacha Hicks Champod, Sébastien Moret, Eric Sapin, Franco Taroni, Romain Voisard, and Céline Weyermann. Also, there have been numerous other colleagues from around the world who have had a strong influence on our work over the past years and have helped us shape our thinking on relevant issues. Conscious that it is hard to be exhaustive, we thank Yossi Almog, JoAnn Buscaglia, Toni Cantu, Itiel Dror, Heidi Eldridge, Ian Evett, Jean-Christophe Fondeur, Austin Hicklin, Anil Jain, Terry Kent, Glenn Langenburg, Didier Meuwly, Cédric Neumann, Michio Okajima, Robert Ramotowski, James Robertson, Claude Roux, Xanthe Spindler, David Stoney, the members of the Scientific Working Group on Friction Analysis, Study and Technology, and the members of the International Fingerprint Research Group.

Finally, we dedicate this book to our families for their unquestioning love and support.

Lausanne, Canberra, and Sydney

Preface to the First Edition

Our aim with this book was to place, under the same roof, two distinct but intertwined aspects of the use of fingerprinting for personal identification and criminal investigation: (1) the aspects associated with the visualization, detection, and recording of friction ridge skin impressions and (2) the issues regarding the identification or individualization of unknown marks when compared with known prints. In 1978, Robert Olsen (1978) published one of the rare books where both aspects were covered with equal weight. Two of us published an overview of fingerprint detection techniques, putting significant emphasis on detection sequences (Margot and Lennard 1994); however, the identification process was only briefly covered. In recent years, we have all been involved in various research projects on fingerprint detection techniques as well as identification issues. We have tried to reflect these dual aspects through our mandate to regularly update the forensic community on the field for the triennial Interpol Forensic Science Symposiums in Lyon (Margot and Lennard 1993; Champod and Margot 1997, 1998; Meuwly and Margot 2001). We have observed a field that is in rapid progress on both detection and identification issues, and in light of the recent debate on the admissibility of fingerprint evidence in US courts, we have decided to bring together both sides of this discipline within the same volume and to give them the evenhanded critical analysis they deserve. Our chapters are arranged as follows:

In Chapter 1, we give a brief overview of the current state of knowledge on the morphogenesis of friction ridge skin. Our objective is to embed the identification process on a firm ground of understanding of biological uniqueness. We are particularly grateful here to Prof. Michio Okajima, who has shared with one of us his time, extensive knowledge, and photographic material during a wonderful summer afternoon in Tokyo in 1996.

In Chapter 2, we investigate the nature of the identification process. We have tried to step beyond the well-known ACE-V protocol, which does not completely fulfill the requirements—as described by van Koppen and Crombag (2000)—of (1) a fully articulated descriptive model, (2) a detailed and systematic account of the variation of the features, and (3) a transparent decision model. Consequently, we put some effort into making explicit the available knowledge, with special emphasis on the documented selectivity of fingerprint features. We have also made a deliberate attempt to reconcile the two main approaches to the identification process: an approach based on an empirical numerical standard (a predefined number of points) and a holistic approach. We believe that most of the antagonism of this debate fades away when an appropriate perspective is adopted on the concept of identification standards: a sound professional framework founded on a sound corpus of scientific data, high standards of quality management, proficiency testing, performance monitoring, and blind testing.

Chapter 3 presents the knowledge of chemistry, optics, and photography that is necessary to develop skills and understanding in detection techniques. We felt that it was important to draw special attention to the use of filters, optical enhancement techniques, and also digital image processing. Following the creation of the School of Forensic Science (Institut de Police Scientifique) at the University of Lausanne in 1909, Prof. R. A. Reiss taught pioneer forensic scientists to maximize and secure the recovery of evidential marks through the expert use of photographic techniques (Reiss 1903). The importance of the recording process can never be overstressed.

In Chapter 4, the major fingerprint detection techniques are reviewed according to the type of surface encountered. The chapter starts with information regarding the composition of fingermark residue, allowing an understanding of the nature of the components targeted by the detection techniques and the added value of detection sequences as opposed to a single treatment. It is not intended to provide an exhaustive account of all optical, physical, or chemical techniques that have been proposed in the literature, but rather to provide a consistent and optimized set of techniques that have shown good potential in operational casework.

Chapters 5 and 6 bring the book to its conclusion. They provide the reader with an insight into fingerprint-related matters such as age determination, forgeries, and the management of errors. We also made an attempt at setting a standard nomenclature. In developing this book, we have made some choices that the reader needs to be aware of. First, we decided to give no account of the history of the use of fingerprinting in criminal investigation. We consider that the chapter from John Berry and the relevant section in David Ashbaugh's book are very complete accounts for fingerprint examiners (Ashbaugh 1999; Berry and Stoney 2001). In addition, recent publications have covered these historical aspects and brought to the table important sociological perspectives (Cole 1998, 1999, 2001), reaffirmed the contribution of Dr. Henry Faulds (Beavan 2001), and documented the essential development of the method in India during the nineteenth century and its influence in Britain (Sengoopta 2003). Although the reader will find significant material in the aforementioned references, we strongly felt the need to complement this view by presenting a European perspective that remains largely unknown and poorly documented. Among the active forensic scientists during the transition period between anthropometry (Bertillon) and dactyloscopy (Faulds, Galton, Henry, and Vucetich), little credit is generally given to Dr. Edmond Locard and Prof. R. A. Reiss. Locard (who later became head of the forensic science laboratory in Lyon) heralded from the famous medicolegal school of Lyon under the direction of Prof. A. Lacassagne. This group of researchers pioneered the optimization of detection techniques for bloodstains and fingermarks (Florence 1885; Coutagne and Florence 1889; Florence 1889; Frécon 1889). The early work of Galton became well known in France in 1891 through the publication of De Varigny (1891). Locard (1903) was immediately impressed by the simplicity and efficiency of dactyloscopy but was still hesitant to replace bertillonage. A thesis by France's Yvert (1904) gave Locard all the arguments necessary to push dactyloscopy forward. Locard then engaged himself in the review of all the systems of personal identification available at that time, covering Bertillon's anthropometry as well as the various dactyloscopic systems proposed worldwide (Locard 1909). This first book by Locard is a key contribution in the development of fingerprint science, providing a fair and comparative assessment of anthropometry and the dactyloscopic systems of Vucetich, on the one hand, and Galton-Henry, on the other hand. By 1909, Locard was convinced of the superiority of fingerprinting over anthropometry as a worldwide means of personal identification (Locard 1909). The between-user variability of recorded measurements was indeed one of the weakest points of anthropometry. The main debate at that time revolved around the efficiency of the classification system. Bertillon's system offered a versatile means of classifying hundreds of thousands of cards, whereas, at that time, fingerprints suffered from a lack of standardization. That view was held by Bertillon himself, followed by R. A. Reiss (1909a,b,c). There was no doubt that fingermarks offered a fantastic tool for criminal investigation (as Faulds first suggested), but the application of fingerprinting as the only record for personal identification was initially viewed with skepticism. Bertillon is often portrayed as a dogmatic opponent to the development of fingerprint identification. We believe that the reality is more subtle. Bertillon, in fact, embraced fingerprints very early and recorded fingerprints on the anthropometric cards from 1894. Around 1900, Bertillon worked on the development of easy and efficient detection techniques for revealing fingermarks at crime scenes. Indeed, Bertillon is known for one of the first identifications, that of a murderer, based on marks secured with powder at the crime scene; the Scheffer case (October 10, 1902) is known as the earliest conviction (March 15, 1903) for homicide in Europe that relied on fingerprint evidence (Sannié 1950). In 1903, Bertillon produced a classification system very close to the Vucetich system, and he suggested using fingerprints as a subsidiary (to anthropometry) classification system. Bertillon did indeed publish the now-infamous prints modified to display what could be viewed as 16 points in agreement (Bertillon 1912), but this publication was never intended by Bertillon to be a warning or a barrier against fingerprint evidence (Champod et al. 1993). Bertillon was forward looking, and despite his strong character and dedication to his anthropometric system, he contributed enormously to the development of fingerprinting as a new tool for identification purposes. The slow development of dactyloscopy is certainly due to the lack of international standardization regarding a classification system, whereas Bertillon's system was applied uniformly in the identification bureaus. This state of affairs was deplored by all the main actors during the sixth conference on criminal anthropology in Turin, Italy, in 1906, but we had to wait until the first conference devoted to police judiciaire in Monaco in 1914 to see some international resolution toward standardization (Roux 1926). (The proceedings of this meeting were published much later due to the First World War.) It is fair to say that international exchanges are still not fully optimized today. Although it is difficult to cover the development of fingerprinting in all countries, the work of Heindl (1927), a famous German dactyloscopist, deserves a special mention here. Heindl's book remains the most complete reference for its time (Heindl 1927).

The second option chosen for this book was to avoid a chapter on the development and use of automatic fingerprint identification/recognition systems. Nowadays, these systems are used operationally as very successful and decisive sorting devices, but they have no impact on the identification process itself. In other words, the identification of an unknown fingermark remains unaffected by whether or not the potential corresponding prints have been put forward to the fingerprint expert through a *standard* police inquiry or following a search within a database of millions of fingerprint records. Of course, this is not to say that automatic techniques have no impact on fingerprint matters; they represent decisive tools for the criminal justice system, moving fingerprint bureau practices from a few "cold hits" a week to dozens a day. In addition, we believe that automated processes will contribute significantly to the validation of the field in the very near future. Interested readers should refer to the historical accounts by Foote (1974) and Moore (1991). Surveys describing relevant research and the implementation of automated systems have recently been published, respectively, by Peterson (1996) and by Jain and Pankanti (2001), and recent books and dissertations portray a very active research community (Hong 1998; Jain et al. 1999b; Prabhakar 2001; Bazen 2002; Maltoni et al. 2003). Fingerprint technology cannot be separated from other biometric systems that are receiving very close attention nowadays (Jain et al. 1999a), and in the future, we will undoubtedly see the development of integrated systems combining multiple characteristics (e.g., fingerprints, DNA, face, and voice).

Finally, we express our gratitude to all those who have provided assistance and advice in the elaboration of this book. Our special thanks to Alexandre Anthonioz, David Ashbaugh, Les Bush, Nicole Egli, Eric Sapin (author of the photographs illustrating Section 3.6), Kasey Wertheim, and James Robertson.

Our thanks also to our respective families for their patience and understanding while this book was being put together.

Lausanne, Switzerland and Canberra, Australia

REFERENCES

Ashbaugh, D. R. (1999), Chapter 2: History of friction ridge identification, *Qualitative–Quantitative Friction Ridge Analysis—An Introduction to Basic and Advanced Ridgeology*, Boca Raton, FL: CRC Press, pp. 11–60.

Bazen, A. M. (2002), *Fingerprint Identification—Feature Extraction, Matching and Database Search*, Enschede, the Netherlands: Twente University Press.

Beavan, C. (2001), *Fingerprints—The Origins of the Crime Detection and the Murder Case That Launched Forensic Science*, New York: Hyperion.

Berry, J. and Stoney, D. A. (2001), The history and development of fingerprinting, in *Advances in Fingerprint Technology*, 2nd ed., eds. H. C. Lee and R. E. Gaensslen, Boca Raton, FL: CRC Press, pp. 1–40.

Bertillon, A. (1912), Notes et observations médico-légales—les empreintes digitales, *Archives d'anthropologie criminelle, de médecine légale et de psychologie normale et pathologique*, 27, 36–52.

Champod, C., Lennard, C., and Margot, P. A. (1993), Alphonse Bertillon and dactyloscopy, *J. Forensic Ident.*, 43, 604–625.

Champod, C. and Margot, P. A. (1997), Marks and impressions, in *Proceeding of the 11th Interpol Forensic Science Symposium*, Lyon, France: Forensic Sciences Foundation Press, pp. 161–182.

Champod, C. and Margot, P. A. (1998), Fingermarks, shoesole impressions, ear impressions and toolmarks: A review (Sept. 1995–Aug. 1998), in *Proceeding of the 12th Interpol Forensic Science Symposium*, Lyon, France: Forensic Sciences Foundation Press, pp. 303–331.

Cole, S. (1998), Witnessing identification: Latent fingerprinting evidence and expert knowledge, *Soc. Stud. Sci.*, 28, 687–712.

Cole, S. (1999), What counts for identity? The historical origins of the methodology of latent fingerprint identification, *Sci. Context*, 12, 139–172.

Cole, S. (2001), *Suspect Identities: A History of Fingerprinting and Criminal Identification*, Cambridge, MA: Harvard University Press.

Coutagne, H. and Florence, A. (1889), Les empreintes dans les expertises judiciaires, *Arch. anthrop. crim. et des sciences pénales*, 4, 25–56.

De Varigny, H. (1891), Les empreintes digitales d'après Galton, *Revue Scientifique*, 17, 557–562.

Florence, A. (1885), *Les taches de sang, leur signification en médecine judiciaire*, PhD thesis No. 256, Faculté de médecine, Lyon, France.

Florence, A. (1889), Les taches de sang, leur signification, leur importance en médecine judiciaire, *Arch. anthrop. crim et des sciences pénales*, 19.

Foote, R. D. (1974), Fingerprint identification: A survey of present technology, automated applications and potential for future development, *Criminal Justice Monograph*, Vol. 5, No.2, Institute of Contemporary Corrections and the Behavioral Sciences, Sam Houston State University, Huntsville, TX.

Frécon, A. (1889), *Des empreintes en général*, PhD Thesis, Imprimerie Storck, Bibliothèque d'anthropologie criminelle et des sciences pénales, Lyon, France.

Heindl, R. (1927), *System und Praxis der Daktiloskopie*, 3rd ed., Berlin and Leipzig, Germany: Walter de Gruyter & Co., Vereinigung Wissenschaftlichen Verleger.

Hong, L. (1998), *Automatic personal identification using fingerprints*, PhD thesis, Michigan State University, Computer Science and Engineering, Chicago, IL.

Jain, A. K., Bolle, R., and Pankanti, S. (eds.) (1999a), *Biometrics—Personal Identification in Networked Society*, Norwell, MA: Kluwer Academic Publishers.

Jain, A. K. and Pankanti, S. (2001), Automated fingerprint identification and imaging systems, in *Advances in Fingerprint Technology*, 2nd ed., eds. H. C. Lee and R. E. Gaensslen, Boca Raton, FL: CRC Press, pp. 275–326.

Jain, L. C., Halici, U., Hayashi, I., Lee, S. B., and Tsutsui, S. (1999b), *Intelligent Biometric Techniques in Fingerprint and Face Recognition*, Boca Raton, FL: CRC Press.

Locard, E. (1903), La dactyloscopie: Identification des récidivistes par les empreintes digitales, *Mém. Acad. Sci. Lyon*, 7(3ème série), 147–161.

Locard, E. (1909), *L'identification des récidivistes*, Paris, France: A. Maloine.

Maltoni, D., Maio, D., Jain, A. K., and Prabhakar, S. (2003), *Handbook of Fingerprint Recognition*, New York: Springer-Verlag.

Margot, P. and Lennard, C. (1994), *Fingerprint Detection Techniques*, 6th revised edition Lausanne, Switzerland: Institut de Police Scientifique et de Criminologie, Université de Lausanne.

Margot, P. and Lennard, C. J. (1993), Traces et empreintes: Le point sur les nouvelles techniques, *Revue Internationale de Police Criminelle*, 48(441), 10–18.

Meuwly, D. and Margot, P. A. (2001), Fingermarks, shoesole and footprint impressions, tire impressions, ear impressions, toolmarks, lipmarks and bitemarks: A review (September 1998–August 2001), in *Proceeding of the 13th Interpol Forensic Science Symposium*, D1, eds. R. E. Tontarski, Washington DC: US Department of Justice, pp. 1–52.

Moore, R. T. (1991), Automatic fingerprint identification systems, in *Advances in Fingerprint Technology*, eds. H. C. Lee and R. E. Gaensslen, New York: Elsevier Science Publishing Co., Inc., pp. 163–191.

Olsen, R. D. (1978), *Scott's Fingerprint Mechanics*, Springfield, IL: Charles C. Thomas.

Peterson, J. L. (1996), The status of AFIS systems worldwide: Issues of organizations, performance and impact, in *Proceedings of the International Symposium on Fingerprint Detection and Identification*, eds. J. Almog and E. Springer, Ne'urim, Israel, June 26–30, 1995: Israel National Police, pp. 233–254.

Prabhakar, S. (2001), *Fingerprint classification and matching using a filterbank*, PhD thesis, Michigan State University, Computer Science and Engineering, Chicago, IL.

Reiss, R. A. (1903), *La photographie judiciaire*, Paris, France: C. Mendel.

Reiss, R. A. (1909a), Les méthodes modernes d'identification de criminels, *Wissen und Leben*, 15 Janvier, 338–345.

Reiss, R. A. (1909b), Les méthodes modernes d'identification de criminels II. La fiche dactyloscopique, *Wissen und Leben*, 1 février, 385–389.

Reiss, R. A. (1909c), Les méthodes modernes d'identification de criminels III. Le portrait parlé, *Wissen und Leben*, 15 février, 439–452.

Roux, J. A. (1926), *Actes du premier congrès de police judiciaire internationale*, Paris, France: Marchal et Billard, G. Godde succ.

Sannié, C. (1950), Alphonse Bertillon et la dactyloscopie. L'affaire Scheffer, *Revue internationale de police criminelle*, 5(41), 255–262.

Sengoopta, C. (2003), *Imprint of the Raj—How Fingerprinting Was Born in Colonial India*, London, U.K.: Macmillan.

van Koppen, P. J. and Crombag, H. F. M. (2000), Oren, lippen en vingers: De waarde van oud en nieuw identificatiebewijs, *Modus*, 9(4), 28–32, 75, 6–12.

Yvert, A. (1904), *L'identification par les empreintes digitales palmaires (la dactyloscopie)*, Thèse de doctorat, A. Storck et Cie Ed., Lyon, France: Université de Lyon.

Authors

Christophe Champod received his MSc and PhD (*summa cum laude*), both in forensic science, from the University of Lausanne, Switzerland, in 1990 and 1995, respectively. He remained in academia until holding the position of assistant professor in forensic science. From 1999 to 2003, he led the Interpretation Research Group of the Forensic Science Service (United Kingdom) before returning to Switzerland to take up a full professorship position at the School of Criminal Justice (ESC; Ecole des sciences criminelles), University of Lausanne. He is currently in charge of education and research on identification methods and maintains an activity as an expert witness in these areas. He is a member of the Steering Committee for the International Fingerprint Research Group (IFRG) and a past member of Scientific Working Group on Friction Analysis, Study and Technology, and since 2014, he has been an invited member of the Friction Ridge Subcommittee (part of the Physics and Pattern Evidence Scientific Area Committee) of the Organization for Scientific Area Committees. In 2015, he received the European Network of Forensic Science Institutes (ENFSI) Distinguished Forensic Scientist Award for his contribution to forensic science. His research is devoted to the inferential aspects associated with forensic identification techniques. The value to be attached to fingerprint evidence is at the core of his interests.

Chris Lennard holds a PhD in chemistry (forensic science) from the Australian National University, Canberra—awarded for research into amino acid–specific reagents for fingermark detection on paper substrates. He took up a postdoctoral position with the School of Forensic Science at the University of Lausanne, Switzerland, in 1986 and became an associate professor in criminalistics at that university in 1989. He returned to Australia in 1994 to work for Forensic Services, Australian Federal Police (AFP), initially as laboratory services coordinator (1994–2002) and then as forensic operations support manager (2002–2006). In this latter role, he was the chief scientist, responsible for coordinating research and development across the organization's forensic science portfolio. In 2006, he moved to the University of Canberra and took up the role of professor of forensic studies (head of discipline). After eight years in that position, he relocated to Sydney in 2014 to run the forensic science program at Western Sydney University at their Hawkesbury Campus, Richmond. Over his career, he has maintained a strong interest and involvement in fingerprint-related research, particularly with respect to fingermark detection and enhancement techniques, with an extensive publication record in this area. He is a Steering Committee member for the IFRG, and he played a major role in the establishment of IFRG guidelines for the assessment of fingermark detection techniques.

Pierre Margot fell early into the cauldron of forensic science by earning a combined degree in forensic science and criminology from the University of Lausanne, Switzerland, in 1974. A short spell in the United Kingdom attracted him to pursue an MSc followed by a PhD in forensic science at Strathclyde University in Glasgow. Postdoctoral research led him from Salt Lake City (United States) in forensic toxicology at the Center for Human Toxicology (University of Utah), to the Federal Institute of Technology (EPFL) in Lausanne (research in chromatography), and then to the Australian National University in Canberra (Australia) to pursue research and development in dactyloscopy. He returned to Switzerland in 1986 to take up a professorial position at the University of Lausanne. He was the fourth professor occupying what was the first academic chair in forensic science, created in 1909. One of his major contributions is the creation of a research center where more than 60 PhD theses have been completed over the last 20 years, with a full commitment to further develop this center as a key contributor in areas that include forensic intelligence, investigative science, and the provision of solid and measurable evidence in court. His group has published more than 220 peer-reviewed papers in forensic science within the last 10 years. His contributions to forensic science have been internationally acclaimed, with major awards such as the Douglas M. Lucas Medal of the American Academy of Forensic Sciences, a doctorate honoris causa at the University of Québec in Trois-Rivières (Canada), accession to the French-speaking Pantheon of Criminalistics, and an ENFSI Distinguished Contributor Award. He is an associate editor of *Forensic Science International*, the major scientific journal in forensic science.

Milutin Stoilovic received his bachelor's and master's degrees at Belgrade University. In June 1980, he immigrated to Australia. From September 1980 till December 1989, he worked at the Australian National University in Canberra and was involved in fingermark detection research and the application of light sources in forensic science. His innovative work on the development of a forensic light source led to the eventual commercialization of the Polilight. In August 1990, he joined the Australian Federal Police (AFP), where, among other duties, he continued to research fingermark detection methods and optical enhancement techniques. He was involved in designing and evaluating a vacuum metal deposition unit that was built in Melbourne by the company Dynavac, specifically for the AFP. He has conducted numerous workshops on advanced fingerprint detection and enhancement and the application of optical methods for various forensic science disciplines. He has authored or coauthored more than 40 articles in this field. He retired from the AFP in 2008.

1 Friction Ridge Skin and Prints

The aim of this chapter is to provide a summary of the basic elements of friction ridge skin morphogenesis and their relationship to friction ridge skin variability. More extensive accounts for fingermark examiners can be found in the literature (Ashbaugh 1999; Bush 2002; Wertheim and Maceo 2002; Maceo 2011; Wertheim 2011). These contributions, with their associated references, constitute the essential material required to gain an understanding of the biological basis for friction ridge pattern variability. They complement and extend the work undertaken by earlier pioneers such as Wilder and Wentworth (1932) and Cummins and Midlo (1961).

Two cornerstones to the use of fingerprints as a means of personal identification are the overall permanence (a.k.a. persistency, durability, or reproducibility) and the high selectivity (a.k.a. discrimination) of friction ridge skin. It is thanks to these two attributes, and to the fact that fingerprints can be classified with relative ease, that the technique imposed itself over precedent identification methods based on anthropometric measurements. Both of these foundations—permanence and selectivity—have been challenged and confirmed through 100 years of fingerprint identification practice and their scientific foundations lie within biological research.

Unless examiners have a good understanding of friction ridge skin morphogenesis (the biological development of form), the basic tenet for individuality is, unfortunately, often resolved by using standard, shallow statements such as "nature never repeats itself" (McRoberts 1996). We strive to avoid a justification for individualization that only revolves around the tautological argument that every entity in nature is unique. The permanence and selectivity of friction ridge skin should be fully understood from a biological perspective and then applied in assessing fingermark comparisons.

1.1 STRUCTURE OF THE SKIN

Skin is an essential organ of the human body. Finger, palm, and sole areas of the epidermis display a series of friction ridges taking various forms and shapes. These volar areas of the skin are known to display friction ridge skin. Depending on the surface considered, we generally refer to them as fingerprints, palm prints, and soleprints. It is postulated that the essential function of having friction ridge skin is to increase grip.

The skin is usually divided into two distinct layers. The outer layer (Figure 1.1), called the epidermis, is a stratified epithelium of five sublayers, listed as follows from bottom to top:

1. Basal generating layer (*stratum germinativum*)
2. Spinous layer (*stratum spinosum*)
3. Granular layer (*stratum granulosum*)
4. Transitional hyalin layer (*stratum lucidum*)
5. Horny cornified layer (*stratum corneum*)

The layers of the epidermis are named on the basis of microscopic shape of the keratinocyte cells that constitute them. The layer under the epidermis is called the dermis and is 15–40 times thicker than the epidermis and constitutes the primary mass of the skin. The cornified layer exposed to the environment is made up of 15–20 layers of flat dead cells that are regularly shed through abrasion and replaced by keratinization. All these cells originate from initial cuboidal-shaped cells formed

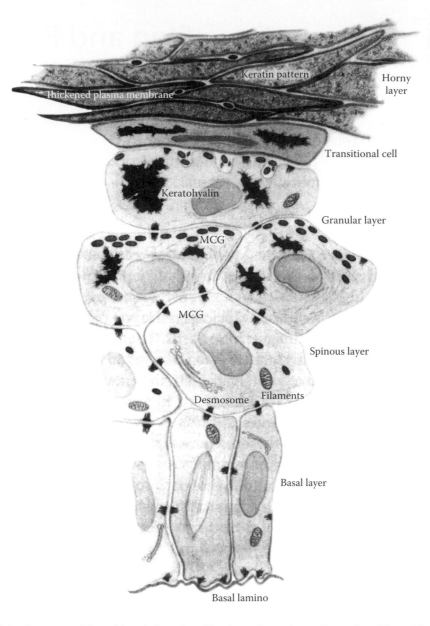

FIGURE 1.1 Structure of the epidermis from basal lamina to horny layer. (Reproduced from Montagna, W. and Parakkal, P.F., *The Structure and Function of Skin*, 3rd ed., Academic Press, London, U.K., 1974. With permission.)

on the basal layer (cells just above the basal lamina) that migrate through the epidermal layers up to the horny layer. The cells move upward simultaneously with surrounding cells. The basal cells do not migrate and remain firmly attached to the generating layer. During this process, cells change shape, reduce their activity, and take up keratin (a water-repellent protein). All cells of the epidermis therefore originate from the basal layer at the interstice between the dermis and the epidermis. As we will explain in more details later, permanency of the friction ridge pattern is largely due to this generative process, whereby the cells constituting the epidermis (and thus its shapes) are produced on the inner protected basal layer just above the dermis. Only damage to the basal layer will result in permanent scars on the epidermis.

1.2 MORPHOGENESIS OF FRICTION RIDGE SKIN: PRIMARY DERMAL RIDGE DEVELOPMENT

The morphogenesis of friction ridge skin starts during the very first weeks of gestation. In fact, we can only speak of estimated gestational age (EGA). The hand starts to develop from 5 to 6 weeks EGA. The first fingers appear around 6–7 weeks. At that time, volar pads appear on the palm (interdigital pads first, followed by thenar and hypothenar pads). Volar pads are transient swellings of mesenchymal tissue under the epidermis on the volar surfaces of the fetus. Volar pads appear on each finger at 7–8 weeks (Figure 1.2). These pads remain visible until 10 weeks, when the growth of the hand overtakes the pads, rendering them not visible by week 16 EGA. This phenomenon is often described as the "regression" stage of the volar pads. It is between weeks 11 and 20 that the major development of friction ridge skin occurs. The volar pads provide the bedding for that development.

At around 10 weeks EGA, cells on the basal layer start to proliferate. Prior to ridge development, the embryonic epidermal surface—the periderm—is three or four cell layers thick and smooth on its outer surface (Figure 1.3). The location of the initial proliferations seems coincident with sweat gland development, but it could also be associated with the arrangement of superficial dermal nerves (Merkel cell clusters and Meissner corpuscles) organized in an approximately two-dimensional hexagonal grid that orchestrates the spacing and general arrangement of the papillary ridges (Dell and Munger 1986). These cells, each associated with a sweat gland, multiply rapidly and fuse into ridges called "ledges" (Hale 1952). These ridges, called primary dermal ridges (PDRs), are still immature and will start to mature by developing downward within the dermis. Individual dermal ridges are not yet differentiated on the areas surrounding these focal areas; rather, the dermis presents a primordial crepe-like appearance (Figure 1.3). The latter is predictive of the basic orientation of the ridge structure to be manifested there later (Okajima and Newell-Morris 1988).

The first obvious manifestation of friction ridge skin is primary ridges on the dermis with fully formed minutiæ (ridge endings or bifurcations). The configuration can be viewed as a series of ridge units (each associated with a sweat pore) that have fused together into ridges of various lengths—lengths being defined by the number of ridge units between two minutiæ, the smallest ridge being a single ridge unit.

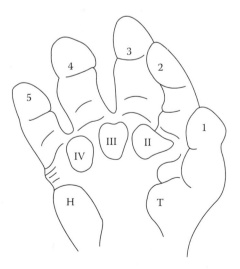

FIGURE 1.2 Volar pads as they appear on the surface of the hand. The first to appear are the second, third, and fourth interdigital pads (II to IV), followed by the apex finger pads. (Reproduced from Ashbaugh, D.R., in *Qualitative-Quantitative Friction Ridge Analysis—An Introduction to Basic and Advanced Ridgeology*, CRC Press, Boca Raton, FL, 1999. Figure 2.20. With permission.)

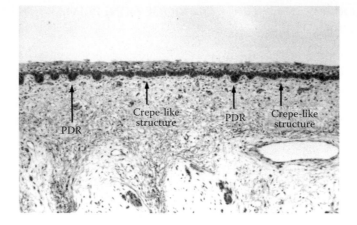

FIGURE 1.3 Cross-sectional view of the skin of a fetus at the initial stages of primary ridge development, showing the primary dermal ridge and the crepe-like structure. (Image obtained from M. Okajima, Tokyo, Japan. With permission.)

When the surface of the dermis is examined at its various stages of development, ridges start to be visible from the apex of the volar pad (core of the fingerprint), the distal periphery (tip of the finger), and the distal interphalangeal flexion crease area. These three fronts of ridges develop at different speeds until they ultimately converge to fully cover the glabrous dermal surface (Figures 1.4 through 1.6). Such pattern development may follow the molecular mechanism proposed by (Turing 1952), called the reaction–diffusion system, which can develop periodic patterns from an initially homogeneous state. Many models—as will be discussed later—have since been proposed in mathematical biology to account for patterning phenomena in morphogenesis based on this mechanism, and a computer model has been used to generate fingerprint patterns.

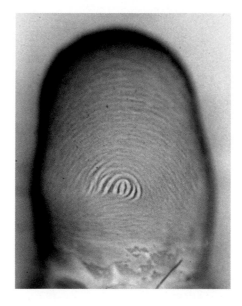

FIGURE 1.4 Image of the dermal surface of the index finger of a fetus (11 weeks estimated gestational age). Note the initial development of the ridges on the apex of the finger. Dark staining indicates primary ridges. (Image obtained from M. Okajima, Tokyo, Japan. With permission.)

FIGURE 1.5 Dermal surface of the index finger of a fetus (11 weeks estimated gestational age), showing the development of ridges from various development fronts. Dark staining indicates primary ridges. (Image obtained from M. Okajima, Tokyo, Japan. With permission.)

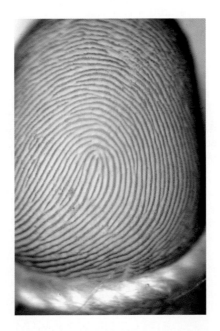

FIGURE 1.6 Dermal surface of the index finger of a fetus (14 weeks estimated gestational age), showing the final friction ridge pattern. (Image obtained from M. Okajima, Tokyo, Japan. With permission.)

1.3 FACTORS AFFECTING THE GENERAL PATTERN AND THE CONFIGURATION OF MINUTIÆ

The general pattern taken by the ridges is dependent on the following interrelated factors (Bonnevie 1924; Cummins 1926; Penrose and Loesch 1969; Babler 1987):

- Shape (symmetry) and size of the volar pads (Penrose hypothesized that the flow of the ridges follows the lines of curvature of the skin on the volar pad) (Penrose and O'Hara 1973); research in mathematical biology confirmed this hypothesis (Smith 1979; Mardia et al. 1992)
- Timing between the regression of the volar pads and the onset of primary ridge formation
- Relative speed of the development fronts
- Bone morphology (Babler 1991)

It is important to recognize that the basic form of the general pattern is established before the initial development of the PDR (Figure 1.7). Wertheim (2011), based on Wertheim and Maceo (2002), provided detailed examples of the various general patterns associated with the behavior of the aforementioned variables, with didactic animations at the following website (accessed January 31, 2016): http://www.clpex.com/animation.htm.

Symmetrical pads will tend to develop into whorls; displaced laterally volar pads will lead to result in loops (to the right or to the left depending on the leaning of the pad). Very weakly elevated pads will produce arches. The pattern size that can be measured by the distance between the core of the pattern and the delta(s) depends on the overall size of the pad at the moment where friction ridges started to develop. The timing of the onset of volar pad regression and the timing of the onset of primary ridge formation are critical factors affecting the overall size of the fingerprint pattern. Hence, timing and symmetry control of the volar pads, both conditioned on the aforementioned interrelated factors, are driving the overall ridge flow.

Recent work by Kücken (2004, 2007) and Kücken and Newell (2004, 2005) in relation to the formation of the general patterns of friction ridge skin brings a very comprehensive

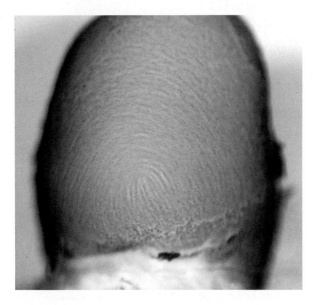

FIGURE 1.7 Dermal surface of the index finger of a fetus (11 weeks estimated gestational age), showing the initial development of dermal ridges in the center as well as the crepe-like appearance on the other regions setting the general pattern. (Image obtained from M. Okajima, Tokyo, Japan. With permission.)

bibliographical resource and new insights on the morphogenesis of friction ridge skin. They conclude that the general pattern is due to a buckling (folding) process in a cell layer of the epidermis. Growth forces due to expansion of the basal layer of the epidermis and the shrinkage of the volar pad create mechanical compressive stress in the basal layer. These mechanical forces lead to buckling. The stress distribution obtained by these mechanisms can be calculated using finite element simulations.

Relative frequencies of general pattern types have been extensively studied in various populations (Mavalwala 1977) and in relation to chromosomal deficiencies and diseases (Wertelecki et al. 1979; Loesch 1983; Plato et al. 1991; Durham et al. 2000). This research area (often without a direct relationship to forensic science) is named *dermatoglyphics*. Most of the research effort in dermatoglyphics has been focused on studying general patterns and ridge counts, but it also offers very good insight into the morphogenesis process as well.

The general patterns taken by the ridges offer substantial discrimination power, but the main contribution to selectivity stems from the configuration of the minutiæ (types and relative position). It is well documented that the general pattern taken by friction ridges is indirectly inherited (Ökrös 1965; Holt 1968; Slatis et al. 1976; Chakraborty 1991) and later we shall address the specific case of twins.

In addition, valuable research has been carried out looking at minutiæ distributions for diagnostic and genetic study. Correlations between the presence or absence of pattern area and the number of minutiæ have also been investigated (Loesch 1973). Dankmeijer and coworkers (1980) confirmed that the number of minutiæ was correlated to the finger number and pattern type, but again no bilateral difference was noted. It was also observed that the number of minutiæ is correlated to the total finger ridge counts (Banerjee and Sarkar 1983b). From these results, it appears that the number of minutiæ is a hereditary trait because of its relationship with the general pattern. Dermatoglyphic studies on the various types of minutiæ are limited, but they tend to show that the frequency of bifurcation (forks) depends on the sex and the digit number, hence suggesting the existence of a genetic role (Okajima 1970, 1977). Data collected in India (Banerjee and Sarkar 1983a) have shown that the fork index (number of bifurcations in relation to the other minutiæ) is slightly higher on prints from males compared to prints from females, slightly higher on whorls compared to ulnar or radial loops and, finally, also depends on the finger number. Nevertheless, the ability of the fork index to predict sex, finger number, or the general pattern is very modest. The number of minutiæ, however, tends to be uncorrelated to the frequency of bifurcations (forks) (Okajima and Usukara 1984). It was also shown that the ridge ending is the more frequent type of minutiæ, followed by the bifurcation. Then come the other more complex minutiæ types such as the island, the enclosure, or the connecting ridge (Banerjee and Sarkar 1983b).

The study by Sarkar (2004, 2005) represents the most extensive data acquisition dealing with minutiæ from a dermatoglyphic perspective. Based on a sample of 2010 fingerprints from 201 males and 2020 fingerprints from 202 females, the author concludes on the following trends in relation to minutiæ that confirm and expand on previous studies (generally carried out on much smaller sized populations):

- A larger number of minutiæ is observed on the thumb followed by the ring finger, while minimum occurrence manifests on the index or little finger.
- The mean count of minutiæ is significantly higher on males than on females. The mean count is significantly higher for whorls than for loops.
- Ridge endings, out of eight minutiæ types considered, show a preponderance over the other types, and the least frequently occurring minutia is the connecting ridge. Two minutiae types, ridge endings and bifurcations together, represent more than 80% of the total number of minutiæ, while the remaining six types represent only about 20%.
- The correlations for familial combinations except parent–parent are positive and most of them are statistically significant. The values of correlation for bifurcations and ridge

endings are similar to each other and are on a par with correlation values for total minutiæ count, but higher than those of other minutiæ types.

- Two minutia types, bifurcations and ridge endings, along with the total minutiæ count have strong hereditary significance. They are presented as useful predictors in filiation analyses. These results are in line with those of Ökrös (1965), whereas both Steffens (1965) and Newman (1930) assigned much less heredity predicting ability to minutiæ but worked on much smaller populations.

It is worth elaborating now on the special case of twins, especially because historically the fact that fingerprints from twins can be easily distinguished has given dactyloscopy the gold status of absolute discriminating power not yet fully achieved by DNA profiling techniques (Cole 2007). The dermatoglyphics literature offers a rich corpus of research studying fingerprints from twins in the context of assessing whether the individuals were monozygotic (MZ) or dizygotic (DZ) based on the patterns observed on fingers, palms, or soles. That was indeed before the era of DNA analysis. The distance between sets of fingerprints from two individuals is generally measured using homolateral comparisons between the hands of each individual, accounting for the general pattern classification and the total ridge count. For palms, the interdigital deltas and the deltas observed in the thenar or hypothenar areas are used to develop a set of distance measurements. A comprehensive bibliographical review is offered by Ducommun (2011, 2013). From that body of research, we note the following main tendencies and we will refer here only to a restricted set of authors:

- The level of correspondence between general patterns on the fingers from twins tends to decrease as we move from MZ twins to DZ twins and ultimately unrelated individuals. This effect is more pronounced when quantitative variables such as ridge counts are used rather than qualitative variables such as general pattern classifications (Peña et al. 1973).
- MZ twins and DZ twins have different homolateral and bilateral behaviors that permit a differentiation with a fair degree of confidence (Newman 1928; MacArthur 1938). However, there remains an overlap between the populations almost regardless of the metric used (Reed et al. 1977). Nevertheless, when a large set of dermatoglyphic variables are used to characterize both fingerprints and palms, discriminant analysis allows perfect distinction between MZ and DZ twins (Colletto et al. 1987).

Ducommun (2013) brought additional insight into the relationship between twins' fingerprints only (whereas most of the dermatoglyphic research considered palms as well). A specific metric to reflect the distance (homolateral and bilateral) between fingerprints of individuals has been proposed. It accounts for the general patterns, their relative frequency, and ridge counts when applicable. Based on a corpus of 238 pairs of MZ twins whose fingerprints had been classified according to the NCIC classification (see Appendix A), Ducommun shows that, considering such a metric computed on data from 10 fingers only, it is possible to predict whether two individuals are twins or unrelated with an error rate of about 11%.

We turn now to the minutiæ on the prints from twins. It has always been observed that prints from twins can be readily distinguished by visual examination of the relative arrangement of minutiæ even if the general pattern may show some correspondence at first sight. However, from this discrimination capability, we should not infer that minutiæ between twins are distributed both in numbers and arrangements in the same way as between unrelated individuals. Indeed, Okajima indicated that the total count of minutiæ and also the fork index do show a high correlation among twins (Okajima 1966, 1967; Okajima and Usukara 1984). These two trends (number of minutiæ and fork index) have been confirmed by Anthonioz (1998) and Chopard (2004) using semi-automatic methods. In addition, they confirmed the hypothesis postulated by Steffens (1965) that combined minutiae (such as enclosures, islands, and connecting ridges) are also under some genetic influence.

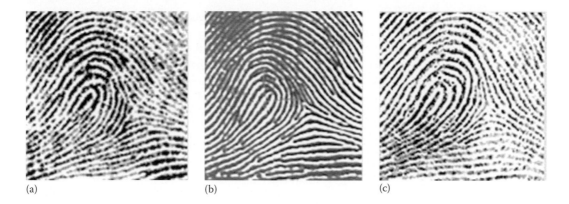

(a) (b) (c)

FIGURE 1.8 Images (a) and (c) are prints from twins that show the level of closeness that may be observed. Image (b) is an unrelated person chosen to be as close as possible to (a and c). (Images courtesy of Wisconsin Department of Justice-State Crime Laboratory Bureau, Madison, WI.)

In the forensic science literature, the proximity between twins in terms of number of minutiæ and their arrangement was first reported by Lin et al. (1982). And, to put the community at rest, they also published the closest prints observed between twins to stress upon the fact that close examination will readily allow them to be distinguished. Additional cases have been made available to the practitioners (e.g., Figure 1.8). Hence, even if elements of the general pattern of friction ridge skin are close between MZ twins, "developmental noise," not under genetic control, causes variations within their fingerprints (Arrieta et al. 1991).

Additional evidence of the proximity between fingerprints from twins compared to unrelated individuals comes from the advances in automatic fingerprint recognition systems. When fingerprints from twins are submitted to pairwise comparisons that take advantage of systems that are based essentially on the relative positioning of minutiæ, all studies have shown that the fingerprints can be distinguished. However, the accuracy of comparisons between prints from twins will be slightly lower than for the transactions involving prints from unrelated individuals (Jain et al. 2002; Han et al. 2005; Srihari et al. 2008; Liu and Srihari 2009; Sun et al. 2010; Tao et al. 2012). Ducommun (2013) showed on 238 pairs of MZ twins that, with an automatic extraction and matching system applied across the 10 fingers, it is possible to correctly distinguish MZ twins from pairs of unrelated individuals with an error rate of about 8%. The use of automatic systems and measurement of accuracy have further demonstrated that, even though full prints from twins will be readily distinguished by a fingerprint expert, their minutiæ tend to show a level of closeness that should not be ignored. Hence, fingerprint examiners should not claim that the minutiæ arrangements are as different between twins as they are between unrelated individuals.

The exact "random" process governing minutiæ formation is still largely unknown. Hale (1952) suggested that, due to the growth of the surface, ridges separate and create room for the formation of new ridges. It is postulated that ridge endings are formed when a new ridge is formed between two existing ridges, with bifurcations resulting from ridge units developing on the side of a host ridge. Alternatively, minutiæ and the full ridge structure might be formed at the outset of the proliferation but remain transient until becoming clearly visible through the maturation on the dermis. Very little research was available to articulate more precisely the stochastic process of minutiæ generation. It is only recently that Kücken and Champod (2013) proposed a specific model for the morphogenesis of minutiæ that is based on the link between the Merkel cells and the epidermal stress distribution. The role of Merkel cells had already been suggested previously in the biological literature (e.g., Moore and Munger 1989) and adopted by forensic scientists (Bush 2011; Wertheim 2011). Merkel cells rearrange from a random initial configuration into roughly parallel ridges along the lines of smallest compressive stress. They serve as the initial

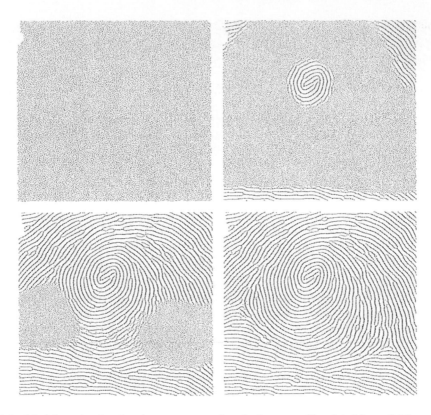

FIGURE 1.9   Model results showing the emergence of a whorl pattern. (Reprinted from *J. Theor. Biol.*, 317, Kücken, M. and Champod, C., Merkel cells and the individuality of friction ridge skin, 229–237, Copyright 2013, with permission from Elsevier.)

induction for the formation of primary ridges. Using a model invoking short-range attraction and long-range repulsion between Merkel cells, simulations of the production of friction ridges can be run from the initial seeds of Merkel cells to the completed and stabilized full fingerprint pattern. Figure 1.9 is the example of a whorl generated in this fashion.

Only a change in the random initial configurations of the Merkel cells, keeping all other parameters of the model constant, will lead to different arrangements of minutiæ (Figure 1.10).

FIGURE 1.10   Model results for the exact same parameters but for different random initial configurations of Merkel cells. General ridge direction and the flow of the pattern are preserved, but the location of the defects (or minutiæ) is significantly different. (Reprinted from *J. Theor. Biol.*, 317, Kücken, M. and Champod, C., Merkel cells and the individuality of friction ridge skin, 229–237, Copyright 2013, with permission from Elsevier.)

Even minute initial disturbances have an effect on the friction ridge skin configuration (not so much in terms of the general pattern, but on the specific arrangements taken by the minutiæ). It is postulated that it is this sensitivity that is at the core of selectivity with respect to the topology of friction ridge skin.

One must keep in mind that the model proposed remains a model and is not the perfect generator of natural friction ridge areas. When simulations are qualitatively compared to fingerprints, deviations from reality have been noted such as an overproduction of bifurcations compared to ridge endings and a disproportionate number of specific minutiæ combinations. The model is compatible with morphogenesis studies, but certainly there are additional parameters that condition the production and arrangements of minutiæ.

The compatibility with morphogenesis studies is what distinguishes the earlier research from research in the biometric area to computer-generated fingerprints (Cappelli 2009). Such synthetic images are used for developing, optimizing, and testing fingerprint recognition systems. The input of the simulator is a class of general pattern, its associated orientation field, and average density of minutiæ. Using Gabor filtering techniques applied iteratively from minutiæ seeds, a fingerprint image is produced with clearly identified minutiæ (as shown in Figure 1.11). The image can be further rendered by additional factors that will affect image quality (e.g., position on the capturing device, elastic distortion of the finger, background noise). Generated samples of images of this type are well suited to benchmarking algorithms on the same test sets or assessing minutiæ detection algorithms.

FIGURE 1.11   Image of a left loop generated without the addition of noise using the program SFinGe Demo v. 4.1 (Synthetic Fingerprint Generator) developed by the Biometric System Laboratory of the University of Bologna, available online at http://biolab.csr.unibo.it/home.asp (accessed February 6, 2016). For illustration purposes, the location of the core (orange circle), delta (green circle), ridge endings (in red), and bifurcations (in blue) have been indicated.

1.4 MORPHOGENESIS OF FRICTION RIDGE SKIN: SECONDARY DERMAL RIDGE DEVELOPMENT AND DERMAL PAPILLAE

Although the general pattern and minutiæ are fully determined by the PDR development, which is set very early in the development process, the PDRs continue to develop within the dermis until 15–16 weeks EGA. Their size and progression within the dermis are fully related to the development of the size of the fetus (assessed by the crown-to-rump length) (Babler 1987). At that time (16 weeks), the pattern is permanently set. In a cross section of the skin (Figure 1.12), we can see the downward penetration of PDRs within the dermis, with a proliferation of cells under a groove being the initial manifestation of a sweat gland.

Between 15 and 17 weeks EGA, secondary ridges start to develop between primary ridges and mature until 24 weeks (Babler 1991). Secondary ridges increase the surface area of attachment to the dermis (Figure 1.13). Primary ridges do not develop any further in the dermis at that time (24 weeks).

Further maturation leads to the formation of bridges between the apex of PDRs and secondary ridges, cordoning off sections of dermal ridges referred to as papillae pegs (Hale 1952) also known as "dermal papillae." Their differentiation is composed of microridges and compartments that develop with advancing age. The papillae are formed for the purpose of increasing the anchorage, exchange, and surface area at the dermal–epidermal interface. Some of them will accommodate the insertion of Meissner corpuscles (allowing the detection of tactile stimuli) (Okajima 1979).

Scanning electron microscopy (SEM) photographs (Figure 1.14) illustrate this development of papillae on both sides of the PDR. Pores can be seen at the bottom of the primary ridges roughly in their center. The shapes of the ridges will be tuned by the locations and size of the papillae.

Research has shown that dermal papillae evolve with age, tending to multiply in order to anchor the skin structure and to maintain the tactile apparatus (Figure 1.15) (Okajima 1979; Misumi and Akiyoshi 1984).

Flexion creases share exactly the same principles of morphogenesis (Ashbaugh 1991b; Kimura 1991; Bali 1994; Ashbaugh 1999). Their development starts between 7 and 9 weeks EGA. They are associated with the boundaries of the volar pads.

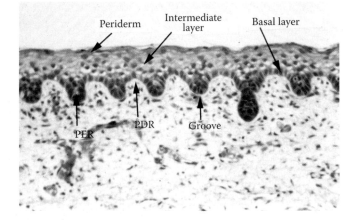

FIGURE 1.12 Cross-sectional view of the skin of a fetus at the initial stages of primary ridge development. PER stands for "primary epidermal ridge." PDR stands for "primary dermal ridge." "Groove" is the term used by Okajima to denote the penetration into the dermis, the term "ridge" being reserved for the friction surface of the dermis. The proliferation of cells under the second dermal groove from the right is the precursor of a sweat gland. (Image obtained from M. Okajima, Tokyo, Japan. With permission.)

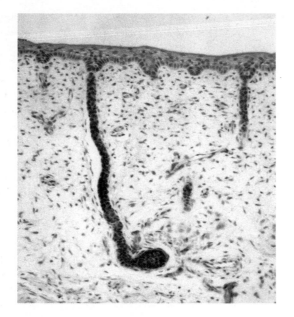

FIGURE 1.13 Cross-sectional view of the skin of a fetus at the final stages of primary and the initial secondary dermal ridge development. The sweat duct connecting the groove of the primary dermal ridge and the eccrine gland is clearly visible. (Image obtained from M. Okajima, Tokyo, Japan. With permission.)

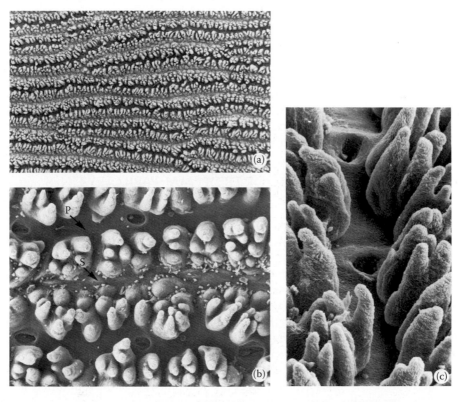

FIGURE 1.14 Views of (a) low magnification (22×) scanning electron microscopy (SEM) view of the plantar dermis following the removal of the epidermis, (b) SEM (130×) of the primary (P) and secondary (S) dermal ridges, and (c) SEM (260×) showing two pores surrounded by the papillae. (Reproduced from Kawabe, T. et al., *Anat. Rec.*, 211, 142, 1985. With permission.)

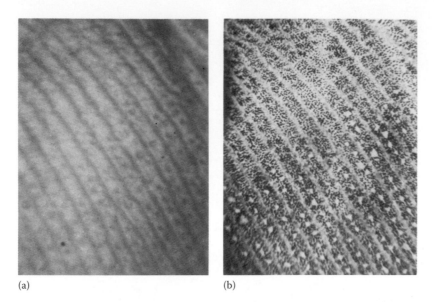

(a)   (b)

FIGURE 1.15 Views of (a) the epidermal surface (ridges on a dark background) of an 82-year-old man with orifices for sweat gland ducts and (b) the dermal surface of the same volar section. (Reproduced from Okajima, M., Dermal and epidermal structures of the volar skin, in *Dermatoglyphics—Fifty Years Later,* W. Wertelecki, C.C. Plato, and N.W. Paul, eds., Vol. XV (6), Alan R. Liss, New York, 1979, pp. 179–198. With permission.)

At 24 weeks EGA, the development of the dermis is finalized. The epidermis is gradually formed by cell development from the dermis into five layers (as shown in Figure 1.1). The friction ridge pattern in its final stage is a projected image of the structure on the dermis. The primary deeply formed dermal grooves correspond to the ridges on the epidermis, and the furrows coincide with the secondary dermal ridges. The dermal papillae are therefore arranged in a double row (parallel to the primary ridge) and define the shape and form of the epidermal friction ridge. Each sweat duct on the epidermis is connected to an eccrine sweat gland via a canal of cells.

1.5   OTHER FEATURES THAN MAJOR EPIDERMAL PAPILLARY LINES ON FRICTION RIDGE SKIN

Between major ridges, small additional ridges are often observed. These *incipient ridges* (also called secondary or subsidiary ridges (Ashbaugh 1992)) follow the same development process but, due to timing constraints, remain only partially developed. These ridges have received some attention from a dermatoglyphic perspective (Wendt 1956; Penrose and Plomley 1969). Wendt (1956) indicates that about 40% of individuals will present incipient ridges, with a dominance on the thumb followed by the other fingers and more occurrence on male subjects compared to female subjects. Stücker et al. (2001) recently confirmed these trends. Wendt (1956) also reported on the hereditary tendency of incipient ridges following studies among family members and pairs of twins. Incipient ridges are without pores and are lower in height compared to regular ridges. Hence, incipient ridges may be more or less recorded on marks and prints depending on the pressure applied by the finger on the surface. Figure 1.16 gives an example of inked impressions taken with different pressures leading to different recordings when it comes to incipient ridges.

White lines are fine secondary creases, shallow grooves of different length, width, and direction, that can often be observed on areas of friction ridge skin. They are surface phenomena without any anchoring on the dermis. A buckling of the epidermis surface with its papillary lines is the cause.

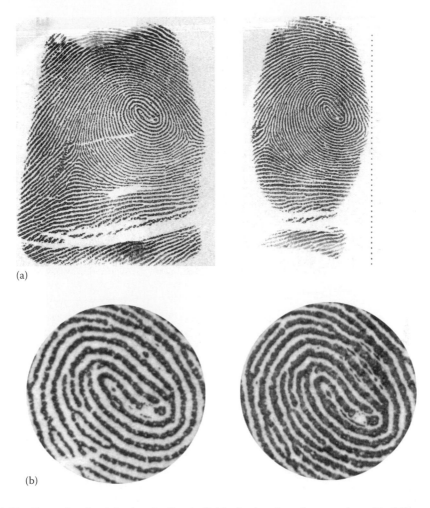

(a)

(b)

FIGURE 1.16 Example of a right thumb of an individual printed on the same day with different pressures between the rolled print (a) obtained with light pressure and the slap print (b) obtained with heavier pressure. Not only the recording of incipient ridges has changed due to the pressure, but also the white line fully visible in the rolled print is not apparent on the second print.

This creates a linear depression on the surface. The epidermal ridges, though, continue to run through the so-formed furrow of the white line. Hence, if the papillary surface is inked and applied on paper, the white lines will appear as straight lines across the dark ridges. But, despite the broken appearance of the ridges on the print, the papillary ridges on the friction skin are not interrupted at all; they simply follow across the depression of the crease (Figure 1.17).

If the depth of the crease (forming the white line) is reduced by increasing the pressure upon application, the white line visible in the print tends to diminish, showing the continuous ridges coming into contact with the surface (Figure 1.18).

The research of Wendt (1956) is one of the only systematic studies on white lines. He reports a lower rate of occurrence of these for female prints (about 20%) compared to male prints (about 40%). White lines will often affect the ring finger and rarely the index. They are linked with the physical build of the person (lower rates are reported for athletics and higher rates for endomorphs). The examination of prints from twins has led to the conclusion that their occurrence is not conditioned by genetic factors. They are more due to external factors such as age and activity (see the section on permanency).

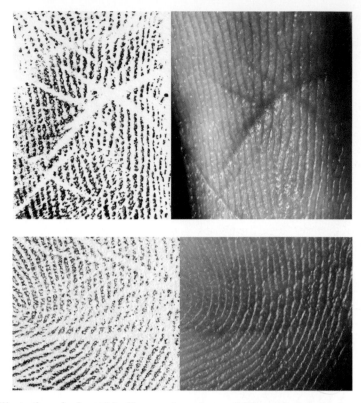

FIGURE 1.17   Illustration of a few white lines on the palm as visible on the inked print and its appearance on the epidermal surface itself. The papillary ridges are going across the white lines.

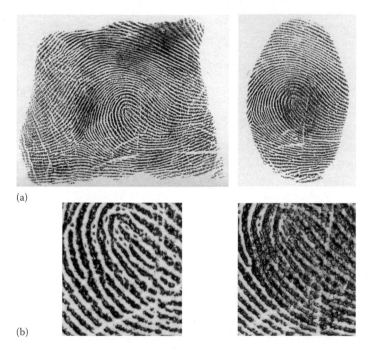

(a)

(b)

FIGURE 1.18   Example of a left thumb of an individual printed on a given day. (a) The rolled impression showing two white lines below the core. (b) The slap impression inked subsequently with heavier pressure applied on the core. This leads to the partial disappearance of the white lines.

1.6 ABNORMAL FRICTION RIDGE SKIN

Some medical disorders may affect the regular morphogenesis of friction ridge skin. Forensic science practitioners refer to these prints as "abnormal" prints (Haylock 1987). Congenital malformations have been extensively described by David (1973), Cummins (1967), and Schaumann and Alter (1976). As a full account of all disorders that may affect the ridge patterns is beyond our scope, we limit the discussion here to some examples only. The following can affect all or part of the friction ridge skin surface:

- *Ridge aplasia*: An absence of friction ridges over the entire volar surface. A genetic mutation causing aplasia has recently been identified (Nousbeck et al. 2011).
- *Ridge dysplasia*: A disassociation of ridges that can be broken up into short ridges or curved segments (Figure 1.19). It can be so extensive that the general pattern or flow of the ridges cannot be seen.
- *Ridge hypoplasia*: The ridges are not absent but very reduced in height.
- *Ridges off the end*: The ridges at the tip of the finger, instead of running transversely, are vertical and run vertically off the end of the fingertips (Figure 1.20). They are also called *cuspal* patterns.

All of these congenital conditions can be inherited.

Flexion creases can also show evidence of congenital malformation. The most well-known is the Simian creases (a merge of the distal and proximal palmar creases leading to a single transverse flexion palmar crease) often observed when the individual is suffering from autosomal trisomies such as

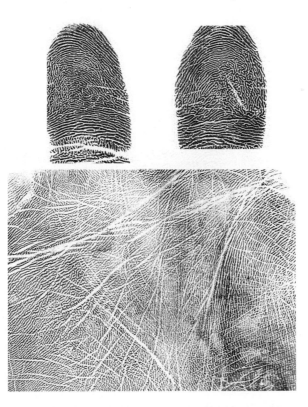

FIGURE 1.19 Example of an individual showing partial dysplasia on his palm. In this case, only the two thumbs are heavily affected by dysplasia, whereas the other fingers have regular friction ridges. (Image courtesy of D. Clark, Western Identification Network, Cordova, CA.)

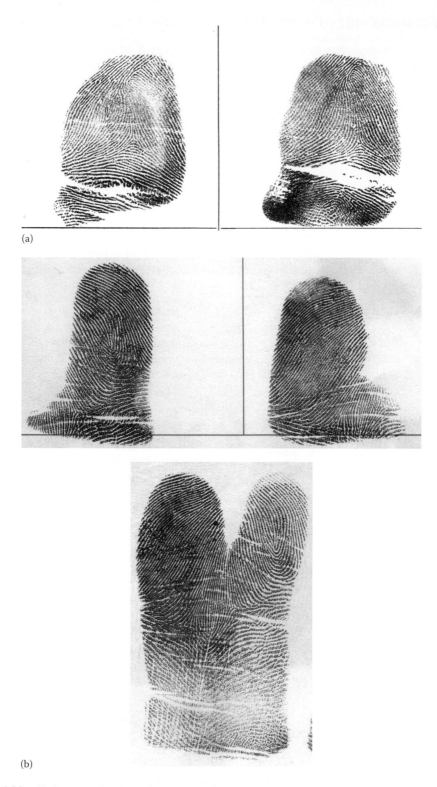

(a)

(b)

FIGURE 1.20   (a) An example of two fingerprints of an individual showing ridges off the end on some of his fingers. (b) A case of ridges off the end on two fingers. It is linked to a syndactyly as evidenced in the plain impressions corresponding to the two fingers. (Images courtesy of A. Glaeser, AFIS-DNA Services Bern, Switzerland.)

Down syndrome (Trisomy 21). Down syndrome also impacts on the general patterns with a marked increase of ulnar loops compared to the other types of general patterns and small total ridge counts.

Forensic science practitioners may see these unusual patterns on occasions and Samischenko (2001) compiled an atlas of his observations over decades of practice in Russia. The publication also includes cases of hand malformations such as polydactylia, syndactylia, and hand deformity (also covered in Schaumann and Alter 1976).

1.7 SUMMARY OF THE STAGES OF FRICTION RIDGE SKIN MORPHOGENESIS

Okajima (1975a,b, 1982) presented a series of useful sketches to summarize the friction ridge skin morphogenesis process (Figures 1.21 through 1.23). These sketches show that the friction ridge skin on the epidermal surface is the consequence of a constant proliferation of cells from a basal

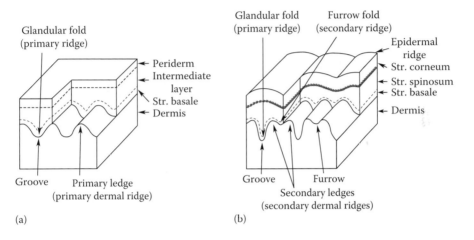

FIGURE 1.21 Diagrams illustrating ridge differentiation: (a) Primary development and (b) secondary development. (Reproduced from Okajima, M., A methodological approach to the development of epidermal ridges on the dermal surface of fetuses, in *Progress in Dermatoglyphic Research,* C.S. Bartsocas, ed., Vol. 84, Alan R. Liss, New York, 1982, pp. 175–188. With permission.)

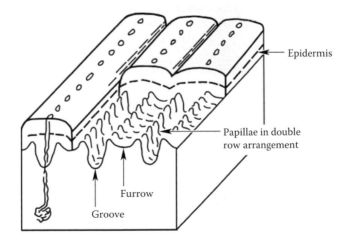

FIGURE 1.22 Diagram of the final dermal surface, illustrating the dermal papillae and the corresponding mirror-image epidermal development. (Reproduced from Okajima, M., Technical aspects of dermatoglyphic examination in primates, in *Contemporary Primatology: Proceedings of the Fifth International Congress of Primatology,* S. Kondo, M. Kawai, and A. Ehara, eds., S. Karger, New York, 1975b, pp. 49–53. With permission.)

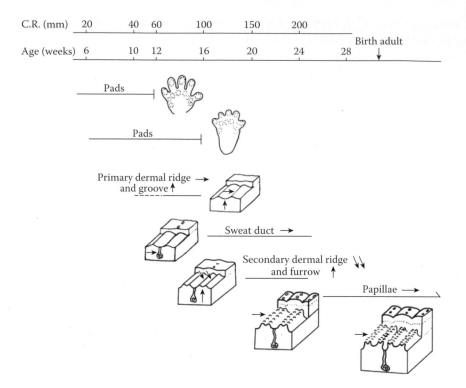

FIGURE 1.23 Diagrammatic representation of dermal ridge morphogenesis based on published studies. C.R. is crown rump. (Reproduced from Okajima, M., Development of dermal ridges in the fetus, *J. Med. Genet.*, 12, 243, 1975a. With permission.)

generating layer, a blueprint, on the very top of the dermis. The configuration of the ridges (with the minutiæ) mimics the configuration defined by the dermal primary and secondary ridges, as a mirror image. On the epidermis, the ridges will display sweat ducts (pores) spaced almost evenly—but to varying degrees—along the ridges. Each pore corresponds originally to a ridge unit associated with a sweat gland. The shape and structure translated on the surface by each ridge unit depends on the shape and structure on the dermis that is obtained following the maturation process. The forms of the pores and ridge edges add to the selectivity of friction ridge skin.

1.8 RELATIONSHIP WITH PERMANENCY AND ALTERATIONS

The relationship between the friction ridge arrangement of the dermis and the friction ridge skin on the epidermis is the basis for the permanency of the fingerprint pattern. Early anecdotal evidence of permanency can be found in the work of Herschel (1916) used by Galton (1888, 1892) and Welker (1898). However, a detailed knowledge of the structure of the skin provides an understanding as to why the fingerprint pattern is reproduced to the exact image of the dermis. Superficial damage to the epidermis will have no bearing on the pattern (if we allow its restoration), with visible scars only being acquired when the dermis is damaged.

A skin cell regeneration process induces permanence of the epidermal friction ridge skin where cells on the basal layer of the dermis are constantly produced to regenerate the epidermis. A chapter written by Maceo (2011) is an essential reference here. These cells, called keratinocytes, start at the basal layer of the epidermis and migrate upward from the basal layer to the *stratum corneum* (the outermost skin layer). Over a period of four weeks, the cells undergo progressive differentiation (keratinization, cornification), gradually flattening out as they move toward the surface. When reaching

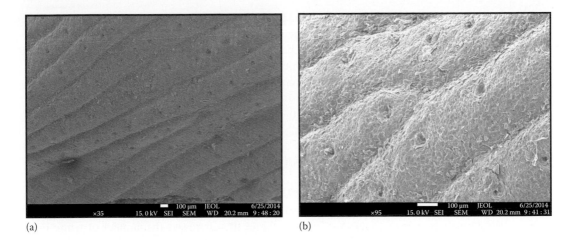

(a)   (b)

FIGURE 1.24 Scanning electron microscope micrographs of the surface of friction ridge skin after detachment of the *stratum corneum*. The remaining surface exhibits lines with arrangements similar to the friction ridges: (a) at 35× magnification and (b) at 95× magnification. (Reproduced from Lopes Mizokami, L., Estudo morfológico comparativo das superfícies epidérmica e dérmica: perspectivas na identificação necro-papiloscópica, Universidade de Brasília, Brasília, Brazil, 2014. With permission.)

the *stratum corneum*, the cells are shed. The epidermal surface is then constantly shedding cells through desquamation. Figure 1.24 illustrates the very rough surfaces of the epidermal skin.

The basal keratinocytes are tightly linked to the basal layer with hemidesmosomes. The keratinocytes on the basal layer undergo cell division (mitosis) that produces the upper layer of cells that will move up to the surface. These new cells are attached together with desmosomes that act as a molecular glue and that imparts its tight and solid structure to the formation. Cell membranes between these keratinocytes may also be very tightly fused together at places (called focal tight junctions). Fine regulation of the production of cells maintains the structure and ensures that more epidermal cells are generated for the epidermal ridges compared to the valleys. The cell-to-cell attachments ensure that the cells move toward the surface in concert. Hence, due to this constant regeneration process, the friction ridge skin on the epidermis constantly and permanently reflects the blueprint image on the dermis.

Permanence of the friction ridge skin arrangements is extremely high when it comes to the papillary line arrangements (the main papillary lines, their flow, and the relative positioning of the minutiæ). This is what is often described as the persistence of the fingerprint pattern. From birth to adolescent or adult age, the friction ridge skin pattern will grow in size. The growth essentially leads to an isotropic rescaling (Gottschlich et al. 2011; Hotz et al. 2011), but with some nonlinear distortion, due in part to the capturing process (Schneider 2010). It is then possible to associate fingerprints from infants with their fingerprints some years later (toddlers, adolescents, or adults) without much difficulty even for an AFIS system (Gottschlich et al. 2011; Richards 2011; Schumacher 2013; Jain et al. 2014).

However, the friction ridge skin is not absolutely permanent in all of its aspects. The level of permanency will depend on the level of detail considered. This is explored further in the next few paragraphs.

Little is known regarding the aging of the surface of the dermis. One key observation made by Chacko and Vaidya (1968) and Okajima (1975b) is that papillae tend to further differentiate as the age of the individual increases and also with exposure to sheering stress. An increased number of papillae improve the adhesion between the dermis and the epidermis. However, it is suggested that this increased number of papillae has no bearing on the epidermal structure of the skin (Misumi and Akiyoshi 1984). A recent study on pores suggests that the number of pores does not significantly vary with the age. However, the size gradually increases, and the position and shape of pores changes (Nagesh et al. 2011).

Regular physical activity heavily involving the friction ridge surface (either by friction or contact with liquids) leads to ridge hypoplasia, where ridges are reduced in height and appear "worn-off" (Schaumann and Alter 1976). This reduction in height is generally reversible after the activity had stopped. However, age is a factor promoting hypoplasia that is not reversible. Hypoplasia impacts on the height of the ridges and the relative difference between the fully developed epidermal ridges and the incipient ridges. Hence, we observe an increased prevalence of incipient ridges with age as shown by Wendt (1956) and confirmed by Stücker et al. (2001). In addition, they showed that, during the course of a lifetime, new incipient ridges could develop (although never disappear). It is postulated that this development corresponds to a compensation for the degenerative change (loss of tactile sensitivity) that occurs with age or activity. An example of recordings made 15 years apart is provided in Figure 1.25.

White lines are not permanent (Almandos 1930), as shown in Figure 1.26. However, they are durable over long periods of time. They can also be promoted by external factors such as extensive contact with chemicals or water. Age is also a factor that increases the number of white lines (Aznar 1933).

One obvious case of potential alteration of the friction ridge skin pattern is scarring due to wounds. The morphology of the epidermal friction ridges will be altered only if the basal keratinocyte cells are damaged. Otherwise, when the wound is not affecting the dermis, the cells will gradually regenerate to reconstitute the exact initial pattern. In other words, surface alterations will be gradually healed as a result of the usual cell generative process. The healing mechanisms have been fully described by Maceo (2005, 2011). When the dermis is affected, keratinocyte cells on the

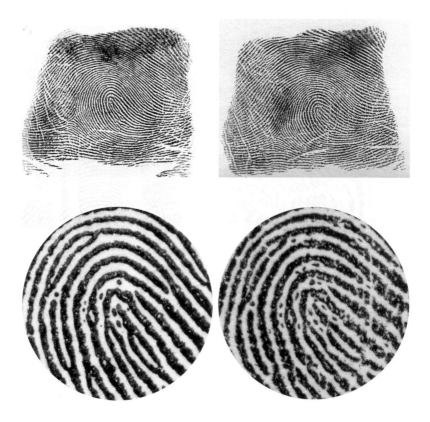

FIGURE 1.25 Example of a right thumb of an individual printed twice but 15 years apart. The central part of the fingerprint is magnified to show how incipient ridges may show up or not depending on how the finger was applied to the paper and, presumably, the age difference.

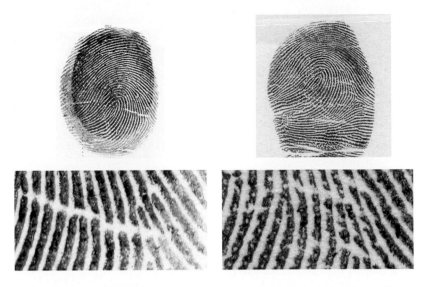

FIGURE 1.26 Example of a left thumb of an individual printed with 15 years apart. The white line has disappeared and cannot be perceived in the more recent print on the right (on the print itself or by examining the finger directly.)

basal layers will start to divide, creating new cells to compensate for the missing components and to cover the wound. During this proliferation, the upper layers of cells are pinched together causing the puckering effect around the scar that is visible once healed (Figures 1.27 and 1.28). Once the basal layer is reconstructed, the production of keratinocyte cells starts again to reconstitute the epidermis. The original friction ridges on the dermis at that point before the damage are not reconstituted nor are the potentially damaged sweat gland connections and associated pores. The new blueprint for

FIGURE 1.27 A scar on a thumb. The scar is located to the upper left of the core. An enlargement is provided on the left with the print on the top and what is visible directly on the finger in the image that follows.

FIGURE 1.28 Example of an arch print taken before and after a deep scar. The cut in the dermis is now apparent on the epidermis. Note the specific puckering effect of the ridges around the scar. (Images obtained from A. Torres, King County Regional AFIS, Seattle, WA. With permission.)

the epidermal structure will now be based on the keratinocyte basal layer cells that proliferated to fully cover the wound. The persistence of these formations follows, then, the same principles as described before.

Very often, scarring is due to cuts, but it can also be caused by heat (numerous cases are reported in Samischenko [2001]), the use of abrasive material, or the exposure to chemicals (see the case reported by Gibbs [2012]). Alteration of the friction ridge skin is most of the time unintentional but in some circumstances it can be intentional. As discussed as early as 1935 (Cummins 1935), intentional fingerprint alterations mainly serve the purpose of defeating fingerprint identification measures in an attempt to hide criminal records, escape detection at borders, and escape deportation measures. A few historical cases have been publicized (Anonymous 1974; Wertheim 1998). A well-known case is that of John Dillinger, killed in 1934, who had the core of his fingerprints mutilated by cuts and the use of acids in an attempt to escape detection. The Federal Bureau of Investigation (FBI's Criminal Justice Information Services Division—Latent and Forensic Support Unit 2015) recently confirmed that voluntary alterations, either self-inflicted or with surgical assistance, are used to defeat identification efforts. The FBI reported on the discovery of 412 fingerprint records in their AFIS system with clear indications of deliberate alterations. The most used techniques to alter the fingerprint patterns are vertical cuts (leaving a heavy scar), the removal of a vertical slice from the core of the fingerprints, Z-cuts (fully explained by Wertheim (1998)), or the use of heat or chemicals to burn the fingertips. A telling example is provided in Figure 1.29.

The intimate relationship between the basal layer and the epidermis is not only the key to permanency but also offers a means to access the original pattern of friction ridges when the epidermis is not readily legible. For example, in cases of disaster victim identification, if the regeneration techniques allowing restoration of the epidermis fail, that layer is removed to take advantage of the image on the dermis. Plotnick and Pinkus (1958) showed how the double papillary rows on each side of the dermal primary ridge precisely follow the ridge pattern of each corresponding epidermal ridge. Figure 1.30 shows such a case taken from Uhle and Leas (2007).

Some medical conditions affecting the individual after birth may also have an impact on the friction skin. Coeliac disease can cause changes in ridges that vary between moderate epidermal ridge atrophy and actual loss of visible ridges (David et al. 1973). Diseases causing histopathological changes in the junction between the epidermis and dermis will have noticeable impact

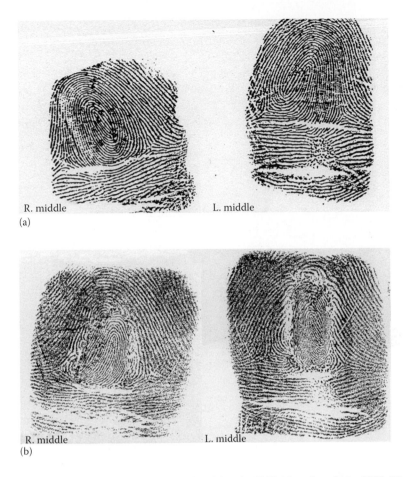

(a)

R. middle   L. middle

(b)

R. middle   L. middle

FIGURE 1.29 Example of an individual fingerprinted first in 1998 (a) and again in 2003 (b), with just the middle fingers shown. The fingerprints have been altered by placing the core of the right middle into the core of the left middle. This type of "musical chairs" affected all of the individual's fingers. (Images obtained from C. Grice, State of Connecticut Forensic Science Laboratory, Meriden, CT. With permission.)

FIGURE 1.30 Recording of an epidermal fingerprint on the left and its corresponding dermal print on the right. (Reproduced from Uhle, A.J. and Leas, R.L., *J. Forensic Ident.*, 57, 358, 2007. With permission.)

on the ridges. Hand or fingertip eczema, verruca vulgaris (warts), and psoriasis are common examples fully documented by Dolezel et al. (2012) and Drahansky et al. (2012) in the context of biometric systems (Figure 1.31).

The pathological changes have an impact on the recognition capability when carried out either by an expert or by automatic biometric systems. For example, hand dermatitis, a pathology observed with a median incidence rate of 5–6 cases per 1000 persons, can cause either fingerprint dystrophy on part or all of the area of the fingers or abnormal (much broader) white lines (Lee et al. 2013). Lee and

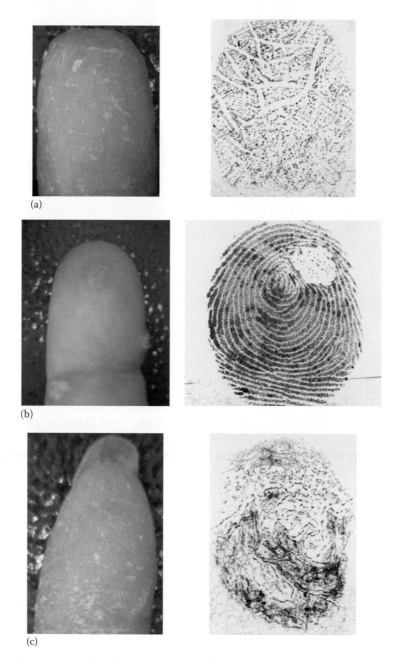

(a)

(b)

(c)

FIGURE 1.31 Three cases of skin diseases: (a) a severe form of fingertip eczema, (b) a verruca vulgaris (wart), and (c) a case of psoriasis. On the left, the finger as observed under white light. On the right, the associated fingerprint as recorded on an optical livescan system. (Images courtesy of M. Drahansky Brno, Czech Republic.)

coworkers reported that, on average, 41% of patients showing these stigmata on their fingerprints failed the biometric verification process (Lee et al. 2015). Chemotherapy treatments can also be the cause of a lack of fingerprints, hence preventing these patients from being enrolled in or recognized by biometric systems (Wong et al. 2009; Al-Ahwal 2012; Chavarri-Guerra and Soto-Perez-de-Celis 2015).

Although operational practice has shown that the papillary patterns on hands and feet are extremely stable and subject to limited changes (apart from scars), it was Yoon and Jain (2015) who provided empirical and statistical evidence of the capacity of AFIS systems to successfully deal with time differences (in years) between enrolments. The number of subjects studied (15,597) and the number of 10-print cards for each subject (5 minimum, with an average of 8) were the largest ever tested. Their study shows that although the time between the two sets of acquired fingerprints and the age of subjects have some impact on the matching performance, the main driver is the quality of the fingerprint recordings.

1.9 RELATIONSHIP WITH SELECTIVITY

In this chapter, we covered the sum of stochastic processes dictating, in turn, the general pattern, the configuration of ridges (with their minutiæ), and their shapes and structures. This is the basis of the selectivity of friction ridge skin. By selectivity we mean the discrimination capability that these patterns offer to distinguish between individuals. We have here the fundamental premise of what most examiners refer to as the *individuality* of friction ridge skin. Ashbaugh (1991a, pp. 82–83) summarized this premise in the following way:

> The friction ridges are constructed of ridge units. The number of ridge units that make up a ridge is established at random. Where one ridge starts and stops, the factors that designate its length are completely dependent on differential growth. The location of the ridge unit where a branching develops is also established at random. Due to the plethora of genetic and physical variances the ridge units are subjected to during ridge formation and the number of units involved, the paths of friction ridges are unique to that area of friction skin.

The ridge units are not only subjected to differential growth factors while developing into rows, but they are also subjected to varying growth factors in relation to their shapes. Therefore, ridge units may vary in shape, size, alignment, and whether they link to the next ridge unit or not. For example, some units are thinner than others, some have bulges on one side, and some misalign with the next ridge unit or fail to develop to maturity. Friction ridge surfaces are three-dimensional and, due to the variables along the friction ridge surface, they are specific, even in a very small area. Various forces through differential growth also establish the location of the pore opening on a ridge unit. The placement of pore openings on the friction ridge is another factor that enhances the selectivity of friction skin. The number of variables involved and their joint impact on the arrangement of friction ridge skin is such that chance duplication is considered to be extremely small.

In this chapter, the terminology "unique" or "uniqueness" of friction ridge skin is avoided for reasons that will become clear in the next chapters. We prefer to avoid this terminology even if we do accept the common use of "friction ridge skin is unique." Uniqueness is a concept that has seen semantic extensions that may not be warranted. Indeed it is not rare to hear an examiner testifying in court that individualization has been established because fingerprints are *unique*. Indeed, what we want to avoid is a systematic and imperceptible transition from "friction ridge skin is unique" to "*every mark* from friction ridge skin is unique" in the sense that it can be associated with certainty to the individual at its source. Again, the mark itself will be unique and we can safely posit that no two marks will ever appear the same. However, our ability to link a mark back to its source is not a function of the *uniqueness* but a function of the balance between the reproducibility and the selectivity of the features that are apparent in the mark. Saying that a specific area of friction ridge skin is unique is a statement of the obvious; it does not tell us much about our ability to record features in one of its marks, left under uncontrolled conditions, and subsequently compare this mark against controlled prints taken at a different time.

REFERENCES

Al-Ahwal, M. S. (2012), Chemotherapy and fingerprint loss: Beyond cosmetic, *Oncologist*, 17, 291–293.

Almandos, R. (1930), Las lineas blancas dactiloscopicas, *Revue Internationale de Criminalistique*, 2, 652–661.

Anonymous. (1974), "Cutting up" with fingerprints, *Ident. News*, 24, 5.

Anthonioz, A. (1998), *Etude des minuties sur les surfaces papillaires des jumeaux univitellins*, Séminaire IPSC (4ème année), Université de Lausanne, Institut de Police Scientifique et de Criminologie, Lausanne, Switzerland.

Arrieta, M. I., Martinez, B., Criado, B., Salazar, L., Lobato, N., and Lostao, C. M. (1991), Fluctuating asymmetry in quantitative dermatoglyphic traits: Twins and singletons, *Hereditas*, 115, 31–35.

Ashbaugh, D. R. (1991a), Ridgeology—Modern evaluative friction ridge identification, *Fingerprint Whorld*, 17, 14–16.

Ashbaugh, D. R. (1991b), Palmar flexion crease identification, *J. Forensic Ident.*, 41, 255–273.

Ashbaugh, D. R. (1992), Incipient ridges and the clarity spectrum, *J. Forensic Ident.*, 42, 106–114.

Ashbaugh, D. R. (1999), *Qualitative-Quantitative Friction Ridge Analysis—An Introduction to Basic and Advanced Ridgeology*, Boca Raton, FL: CRC Press.

Aznar, B. (1933), Sur l'origine des lignes blanches dactyloscopiques, *Revue Internationale de Criminalistique*, 5, 481–483.

Babler, W. J. (1987), Prenatal development of dermatoglyphic patterns: Associations with epidermal ridge volar pad and bone morphology, *Coll. Antropol.*, 11, 297–303.

Babler, W. J. (1991), Embryologic development of epidermal ridges and their configurations, in *Dermatoglyphics—Science in Transition* (Vol. 27 (2)), eds. C. C. Plato, R. M. Garruto, B. A. Schaumann, and N. W. Paul, New York: Wiley-Liss, pp. 95–112.

Bali, R. S. (1994), *Anthropology of Crease Morphogenesis: A Scientific Analysis*, New Dehli, India: Concept Publishing Company.

Banerjee, A. R. and Sarkar, N. C. (1983a), Distribution of fork-index within the area of finger ball pattern, in *Anthropology in Indian Context*, ed. I. J. S. Bansal, New Delhi, India: Today and Tomorrow's Printers and Publishers, pp. 25–29.

Banerjee, A. R. and Sarkar, N. C. (1983b), Distribution of epidermal ridge minutiae within the area of finger-ball pattern and their significance in identification, *J. Ind. Acad. Sci.*, 22, 12–38.

Bonnevie, K. (1924), Studies on papillary patterns of human fingers, *J. Genet.*, 15, 1–111.

Bush, L. (2002), Golden hands and silver feet, Technical Report, Australian Federal Police, Canberra, Australian Capital Territory, Australia.

Bush, L. (2011), Human fingerprints—A combination of nerves and skin, Personal communication, Canberra, Australian Capital Territory, Australia.

Cappelli, R. (2009), Synthetic fingerprint generation, in *Handbook of Fingerprint Recognition*, 2nd ed., eds. D. Maltoni, D. Maio, A. K. Jain, and S. Prabhakar, London, U.K.: Springer Verlag, pp. 271–302.

Chacko, L. W. and Vaidya, M. C. (1968), The dermal papillae and ridge patterns in human volar skin, *Cells Tissues Organs*, 70, 99–108.

Chakraborty, R. (1991), The role of heredity and environment on dermatoglyphic traits, in *Dermatoglyphics—Science in Transition* (Vol. 27 (2)), eds. C. C. Plato, R. M. Garruto, B. A. Schaumann, and N. W. Paul, New York: Wiley-Liss, pp. 151–191.

Chavarri-Guerra, Y. and Soto-Perez-de-Celis, E. (2015), Loss of fingerprints, *N. Engl. J. Med.*, 372, e22.

Chopard, F. (2004), *Fréquence et apparition des minuties chez les jumeaux univitellins*, Séminaire de 4ème année, Université de Lausanne Ecole des sciences criminelles, Institut de police scientifique, Lausanne, Switzerland.

Cole, S. A. (2007), Twins, Twain, Galton, and Gilman: Fingerprinting, individualization, brotherhood, and race in pudd'nhead wilson, *Configurations*, 15, 227–265.

Colletto, G. M. D. D., Kolya, M., and Zimberknopf, S. (1987), Diagnosis of twin zygosity by dermatoglyphic index, *Brasil. J. Genet.*, 10, 289–299.

Cummins, H. H. (1926), Epidermal ridge configurations in developmental defects, with particular references to the ontogenetic factors which condition ridge direction, *Am. J. Anat.*, 38, 89–151.

Cummins, H. H. (1935), Attempts to alter and obliterate fingerprints, *J. Crim. Law. Criminol.*, 25, 982–991.

Cummins, H. H. (1967), Finger prints: Normal and abnormal patterns, *Fingerprint Ident. News*, 49(5), 3–31.

Cummins, H. H. and Midlo, C. (1961), *Fingerprints, Palms and Soles*, 2nd ed., New York: Dover Publications, Inc.

Dankmeijer, J., Waltman, J. M., and De Wilde, A. G. (1980), Biological foundations for forensic identifications based on fingerprints, *Acta Morphol. Neerl.-Scand.*, 18, 67–83.

David, T. J. (1973), Congenital malformations of human dermatoglyphs, *Arch. Dis. Child.*, 48, 191–198.

David, T. J., Ajdukiewicz, A. B., and Read, A. E. (1973), Dermal and epidermal ridge atrophy in celiac sprue, *Gastroenterology*, 64, 539–544.

Dell, D. A. and Munger, B. L. (1986), The early embryogenesis of papillary (sweat duct) ridges in primate glabrous skin: The dermatotopic map of cutaneous mechanoreceptors and dermatoglyphics, *J. Comp. Neurol.*, 244, 511–532.

Dolezel, M., Drahansky, M., Urbanek, J., Brezinova, E., and Tai-hoon, K. (2012), Chapter 12—Influence of skin diseases on fingerprint quality and recognition, in *New Trends and Developments in Biometrics*, eds. J. Yang and S. J. Xie, InTech, http://dx.doi.org/10.5772/51992.

Drahansky, M., Dolezel, M., Urbanek, J., Brezinova, E., and Tai-hoon, K. (2012), Influence of skin diseases on fingerprint recognition, *J. Biomed. Biotechnol.*, 2012, Article ID 626148.

Ducommun, M. (2011), *Caractéristiques papillaires chez les jumeaux—revue de la littérature et analyse statistique*, BSc project, Université de Lausanne, Ecole des sciences criminelles, Lausanne, Switzerland.

Ducommun, M. (2013), *Analyse statistique des empreintes digitales des jumeaux univitellins*, MSc thesis, Université de Lausanne, Ecole des sciences criminelles, Lausanne, Switzerland.

Durham, N. M., Fox, K., and Plato, C. C. (eds.) (2000), *The State of Dermatoglyphics: The Science of Finger and Palm Prints* (Vol. 2), New York: E. Mellen Press.

FBI's Criminal Justice Information Services Division—Latent and Forensic Support Unit. (2015), Altered fingerprints: A challenge to law enforcement identification efforts, FBI Law Enforcement Bulletin, http://leb.fbi.gov/2015/may/forensic-spotlight-altered-fingerprints-a-challenge-to-law-enforcement-identification-efforts?utm_campaign=email-Immediate&utm_content=427661 (last accessed January 29, 2016).

Galton, F. (1888), Personal identification and description II, *Nature*, June 28, 201–202.

Galton, F. (1892), *Finger Prints*, London, U.K.: Macmillian & Co.

Gibbs, P. (2012), Metamorphosis of friction ridge skin, *J. Forensic Ident.*, 62, 191–193.

Gottschlich, C., Hotz, T., Lorenz, R., Bernhardt, S., Hantschel, M., and Munk, A. (2011), Modeling the growth of fingerprints improves matching for adolescents, *IEEE Trans. Inf. Forensic Secur.*, 6, 1165–1169.

Hale, A. R. (1952), Morphogenesis of volar skin in the human fetus, *Am. J. Anat.*, 91, 147–181.

Han, Y., Ryu, C., Moon, J., Kim, H., and Choi, H. (2005), A study on evaluating the uniqueness of fingerprints using statistical analysis, in *Information Security and Cryptology—ICISC 2004* (Vol. 3506), eds. C. S. Park and S. Chee, Berlin, Germany: Springer, pp. 467–477.

Haylock, S. E. (1987), Abnormalities in dermatoglyphics, *Fingerprint Whorld*, 12, 71–75.

Herschel, W. J. (1916), *The Origin of Finger-Printing*, London, U.K.: Humphrey Milford/Oxford University Press.

Holt, S. B. (1968), *The Genetics of Dermal Ridges*, ed. I. Newton Kugelmass, Springfield, IL: Charles C. Thomas.

Hotz, T., Gottschlich, C., Lorenz, R., Bernhardt, S., Hantschel, M., and Munk, A. (2011), Statistical analyses of fingerprint growth, in *BIOSIG 2011—Proceedings of the International Conference of the Biometrics Special Interest Group,* Lecture Notes in Informatics, Darmstadt, Germany, pp. 11–20.

Jain, A. K., Kai, C., and Arora, S. S. (2014), Recognizing infants and toddlers using fingerprints: Increasing the vaccination coverage, in *2014 IEEE International Joint Conference on Biometrics* (IJCB), Clearwater, FL, pp. 1–8.

Jain, A. K., Prabhakar, S., and Pankanti, S. (2002), On the similarity of identical twin fingerprints, *Pattern Recognit.*, 35, 2653–2663.

Kawabe, T. T., Maccallum, D. K., and Lillie, J. H. (1985), Variation in basement membrane topography in human thick skin, *Anat. Rec.*, 211, 142–148.

Kimura, S. (1991), Embryologic development of flexion creases, in *Dermatoglyphics—Science in Transition* (Vol. 27 (2)), eds. C. C. Plato, R. M. Garruto, B. A. Schaumann, and N. W. Paul, New York: Wiley-Liss, pp. 113–129.

Kücken, M. and Champod, C. (2013), Merkel cells and the individuality of friction ridge skin, *J. Theor. Biol.*, 317, 229–237.

Kücken, M. and Newell, A. C. (2004), A model for fingerprint formation, *Europhys. Lett.*, 68, 141–146.

Kücken, M. and Newell, A. C. (2005), Fingerprint formation, *J. Theor. Biol.*, 235, 71–83.

Kücken, M. U. (2004), *On the Formation of Fingerprints*, PhD, The University of Arizona, Graduate Interdisciplinary Program in Applied Mathematics, Tucson, AZ.

Kücken, M. U. (2007), Models for fingerprint pattern formation, *Forensic Sci. Int.*, 171, 85–96.

Lee, C. K., Chang, C., Johar, A., Puwira, O., and Roshidah, B. (2013), Fingerprint changes and verification failure among patients with hand dermatitis, *JAMA Dermatol.*, 149, 294–299.

Lee, C. K., Chang, C. C., Johar, A., Othman, P., and Baba, R. (2015), Fingerprint verification prediction model in hand dermatitis, *Int. J. Dermatol.*, 54, 765–770.

Lin, C. H., Liu, J. H., Osterburg, J. W., and Nicol, J. D. (1982), Fingerprint comparison I: Similarity of finger-
    prints, *J. Forensic Sci.*, 27, 290–304.
Liu, Y. and Srihari, S. N. (2009), A computational discriminability analysis on twin fingerprints, in *Third
    International Workshop on Computational Forensics*, The Hague, the Netherlands: Springer-Verlag,
    pp. 43–54.
Loesch, D. Z. (1973), Minutiae and clinical genetics, *J. Ment. Defic. Res.*, 17, 97–105.
Loesch, D. Z. (1983), *Quantitative Dermatoglyphics: Classification, Genetics and Pathology*, Oxford, U.K.:
    Oxford University Press.
MacArthur, J. W. (1938), Reliability of dermatoglyphics in twin diagnosis, *Hum. Biol.*, 10, 12–35.
Maceo, A. V. (2005), The basis for the uniqueness and persistence of scars in the friction ridge skin, *Fingerprint
    Whorld*, 31, 147–161.
Maceo, A. V. (2011), Chapter 2: Anatomy and physiology of adult friction ridge skin, in *The Fingerprint
    Sourcebook*, ed. A. McRoberts, Washington, DC: National Institute of Justice http://www.ncjrs.gov/
    pdffiles1/nij/225322.pdf (last consulted January 29, 2016).
Mardia, K. V., Li, Q., and Hainsworth, T. J. (1992), On the Penrose hypothesis on fingerprint patterns, *J. Math.
    Appl. Med. Biol.*, 9, 289–294.
Mavalwala, J. (1977), *Dermatoglyphics: An International Bibliography*, Chicago, IL: Mouton Publishers.
McRoberts, A. L. (1996), Nature never repeats itself, *The Print*, 12, 1–3.
Misumi, Y. and Akiyoshi, T. (1984), Scanning electron microscopic structure of the finger print as related to
    the dermal surface, *Anat. Rec.*, 208, 49–55.
Montagna, W. and Parakkal, P. F. (1974), *The Structure and Function of Skin*, 3rd ed., London, U.K.: Academic
    Press.
Moore, S. J. and Munger, B. L. (1989), The early ontogeny of the afferent nerves and papillary ridges in human
    digital glabrous skin, *Dev. Brain Res.*, 48, 119–141.
Nagesh, K. R., Bathwal, S., and Ashoka, B. (2011), A preliminary study of pores on epidermal ridges: Are
    there any sex differences and age related changes? *J. Forensic Leg. Med.*, 18, 302–305.
Newman, H. (1930), The finger prints of twins, *J. Genet.*, 23, 415–446.
Newman, H. H. (1928), Studies of human twins. I. Methods of diagnosing monozygotic and dizygotic twins,
    Biol. Bull., 55, 283–297.
Nousbeck, J., Burger, B., Fuchs-Telem, D., Pavlovsky, M., Fenig, S., Sarig, O., Itin, P., and Sprecher, E. (2011),
    A mutation in a skin-specific isoform of *SMARCAD1* causes autosomal-dominant adermatoglyphia,
    Am. J. Hum. Genet., 89, 302–307.
Okajima, M. (1966), Anthropologische und erbbiologische Untersuchung der Minutiae bei Deutschen und
    Japanern—Ihre Häufigkeit in calcanearen Teil der Fussabdrücke, *Z. Morph. Anthropol.*, 58, 1–37.
Okajima, M. (1967), Frequency of epidermal-ridge minutiae in the calcar area of japanese twins, *Am. J. Hum.
    Genet.*, 19, 660–673.
Okajima, M. (1970), Frequency of forks in epidermal-ridge minutiae on the finger print, *Am. J. Phys.
    Anthropol.*, 32, 41–48.
Okajima, M. (1975a), Technical aspects of dermatoglyphic examination in primates, in *Contemporary
    Primatology: Proceedings of the Fifth International Congress of Primatology,* Nagoya, Japan, August
    21–24, 1974, eds. S. Kondo, M. Kawai and A. Ehara, New York: S. Karger, pp. 49–53.
Okajima, M. (1975b), Development of dermal ridges in the fetus, *J. Med. Genet.*, 12, 243–250.
Okajima, M. (1977), Epidermal-ridge minutia in the hallucal area, *Mitteilungen der Anthropologischen
    Gesellschaft in Wien*, 57, 135–139.
Okajima, M. (1979), Dermal and epidermal structures of the volar skin, in *Dermatoglyphics—Fifty Years Later*
    (Vol. XV (6)), eds. W. Wertelecki, C. C. Plato and N. W. Paul, New York: Alan R. Liss Inc., pp. 179–198.
Okajima, M. (1982), A methodological approach to the development of epidermal ridges on the dermal surface
    of fetuses, in *Progress in Dermatoglyphic Research* (Vol. 84), ed. C. S. Bartsocas, New York: Alan R.
    Liss Inc., pp. 175–188.
Okajima, M. and Newell-Morris, L. (1988), Development of dermal ridges on the volar skin of fetal pigtailed
    macaques (*Macaca nemastrina*), *Am. J. Anat.*, 183, 323–337.
Okajima, M. and Usukara, K. (1984), Quantitative and genetic features of epidermal ridge minutiae on the
    palm of twins, *Hum. Hered.*, 34, 285–290.
Ökrös, S. (1965), *The Heredity of Papillary Patterns*, Budapest, Hungary: Akadémiai Kiadó.
Peña, H. F., Salzano, F. M., and Callegari, S. M. (1973), Dermatoglyphics in twins, *Acta Genet. Med. Gemellol.*,
    22, 91–98.
Penrose, L. S. and Loesch, D. (1969), Dermatoglyphic sole patterns: A new attempt at classification, *Hum.
    Biol.*, 41, 427–448.

Penrose, L. S. and O'Hara, P. T. (1973), The development of epidermal ridges, *J. Med. Genet.*, 10, 201–208.

Penrose, L. S. and Plomley, N. J. B. (1969), Structure of interstitial epidermal ridges, *Z. Morph. Anthropol.*, 61, 81–84.

Plato, C. C., Garruto, R. M., Schaumann, B. A., and Paul, N. W. (eds.) (1991), *Dermatoglyphics—Science in Transition* (Vol. 27 (2)), New York: Wiley-Liss.

Plotnick, H. and Pinkus, H. (1958), The epidermal vs. The dermal fingerprint: An experimental and anatomical study, *AMA Arch. Derm.*, 77, 12–17.

Reed, T., Norton, J. A., and Christian, J. C. (1977), Sources of information for discriminating MZ and DZ twins by dermatoglyphic patterns, *Acta Genet. Med. Gemellol.*, 26, 83–86.

Richards, C. (2011), An interesting case of resizing fingerprints, *Fingerprint Whorld*, 37, 102–104.

Samischenko, S. S. (2001), *Atlas of the Unusual Papilla Patterns*, Moscow, Russia: Jurisprudencia.

Sarkar, N. C. (2004), *Finger Ridge Minutiae: Classification, Distribution and Genetics*, Kolkata, India: Anthropological Survey of India.

Sarkar, N. C. (2005), Genetics of epidermal ridge minutiae, *Int. J. Anthropol.*, 20, 51–62.

Schaumann, B. and Alter, M. (1976), *Dermatoglyphics in Medical Disorders*, New York: Springer-Verlag.

Schneider, J. K. (2010), Quantifying the dermatoglyphic growth patterns in children through adolescence, National Institute of Justice, www.ncjrs.gov/pdffiles1/nij/grants/232746.pdf (last accessed January 29, 2016).

Schumacher, G. (2013), Fingerprint recognition for children, Joint Research Centre: Institute for the Protection and Security of the Citizen, Luxembourg, Europe. http://publications.jrc.ec.europa.eu/repository/handle/JRC85145 [Last accessed January 29, 2016].

Slatis, H. M., Katznelson, M. B.-M., and Bonné-Tamir, B. (1976), The inheritance of fingerprint patterns, *Am. J. Hum. Genet.*, 28, 280–289.

Smith, C. A. B. (1979), Note on the forms of dermatoglyphic patterns, in *Dermatoglyphics—Fifty Years Later* (Vol. XV (6)), eds. W. Wertelecki, C. C. Plato and N. W. Paul, New York: Alan R. Liss Inc., pp. 43–52.

Srihari, S. N., Srinivasan, H., and Fang, G. (2008), Discriminability of fingerprints of twins, *J. Forensic Ident.*, 58, 109–127.

Steffens, C. (1965), Vergleichende Untersuchungen der Minutien der Fingerbeerenmuster bei Familien und eineiigen Zwillingspaaren, *Anthropologischer Anzeiger, J. Biol. Clin. Anthropol.*, 29, 234–249.

Stücker, M., Geil, M., Kyeck, S., Hoffman, K., Rochling, A., Memmel, U., and Altmezer, P. (2001), Interpapillary lines—The variable part of the human fingerprint, *J. Forensic Sci.*, 46, 857–861.

Sun, Z., Paulino, A. A., Feng, J., Chai, Z., Tan, T., and Jain, A. K. (2010), A study of multibiometric traits of identical twins, in *Proceedings of the SPIE 7667, Biometric Technology for Human Identification VII*, Orlando, FL, pp. 776670T-1-12.

Tao, X., Chen, X., Yang, X., and Tian, J. (2012), Fingerprint recognition with identical twin fingerprints, *PLoS ONE*, 7, e35704.

Turing, A. M. (1952), The chemical basis of morphogenesis, *Philos. Trans. R. Soc. Lond. B*, 237, 37–72.

Uhle, A. J. and Leas, R. L. (2007), The boiling technique: A method for obtaining quality postmortem impressions from deteriorating friction ridge skin, *J. Forensic Ident.*, 57, 358–382.

Welker, H. (1898), Die Dauerhaftigkeit des Desseins der Riefchen und Fältchen der Hände, *Archiv für Anthropologie—Zeitschrift für Naturgeschichte und Urgeschichte des Menschen*, 25, 29–32.

Wendt, G. G. (1956), Zwillingsuntersuchungen über Zwischenlinien und weisse Linien im Abdruck der menschlichen Fingerbeere, *Acta Genet.*, 6, 143–155.

Wertelecki, W., Plato, C. C., and Paul, N. W. (eds.) (1979), *Dermatoglyphics—Fifty Years Later* (Vol. XV (6)), New York: Alan R. Liss Inc.

Wertheim, K. (1998), An extreme case of fingerprint mutilation, *J. Forensic Ident.*, 48, 466–477.

Wertheim, K. (2011), Chapter 3: Embryology and morphology of friction ridge skin, in *The Fingerprint Sourcebook*, ed. A. McRoberts, Washington, DC: National Institute of Justice, http://www.ncjrs.gov/pdffiles1/nij/225323.pdf [Last accessed January 29, 2016].

Wertheim, K. and Maceo, A. (2002), The critical stage of friction ridge and pattern formation, *J. Forensic Ident.*, 52, 35–85.

Wilder, H. H. and Wentworth, B. (1932), *Personal Identification—Methods for the Identification of Individuals Living or Dead*, 2nd ed., Chicago, IL: The Fingerprint Publishing Association.

Wong, M., Choo, S.-P., and Tan, E.-H. (2009), Travel warning with capecitabine, *Ann. Oncol.*, 20, 1281–1286.

Yoon, S. and Jain, A. K. (2015), Longitudinal study of fingerprint recognition, *Proc. Natl. Acad. Sci. USA*, 112, 8555–8560.

2 Friction Ridge Identification Process

Friction ridge identification procedures have been widely discussed in the literature and in other forums. Traditional literature coverage of the issues has been provided by Cowger (1983), Grieve (1988, 1990), Ashbaugh (1999), Wertheim (2000), and SWGFAST (2013a). The Internet is also a valuable source of information regarding the identification process. Edward German's site (http://www.onin.com/fp, last accessed January 29, 2016) is a reference on these matters, covering the basic concepts and a discussion of some known cases of erroneous identifications.

The approach taken for this chapter aims at describing the inferential process and disclosing, as much as possible, the underpinning data that help fingerprint examiners in reaching conclusions. The exact nature of their conclusions—in fact, their decisions—will be detailed.

This chapter covers all stages of the examination, with a perspective that is in contrast with traditional accounts given in the fingerprint-related literature. At first, the examiners will probably find the approach and content as going against all that they have been exposed to in the past and during their training. As we proceed through this chapter, we gradually introduce a formal model to deal with uncertainty and decisions. Specific information boxes have been included to provide the theoretical background that will assist readers who are unfamiliar with probability and decision theory. We also introduce probabilistic tools in the form of Bayesian networks to carry out complex calculations and expose the inferential concepts associated with the identification process. Each phase of the comparison process is covered from analysis through to comparison, evaluation, and verification. Then, we discuss the classic question "how many similarities are required to identify?" and present the future perspectives of statistical models to help examiners in their probabilistic assignments. We conclude with a case example that demonstrates a new reporting scheme. The paradigm shift proposed throughout this chapter will question the necessity or adequacy for examiners to decide upon identification and provide a definite and categorical opinion as to identity of sources. The change we are advocating will be gradual and will go through steps. A middle ground, as suggested by Lennard (2013), will probably continue to have opinions/decisions made by the examiner but have, at the very least, mathematical models that can support this opinion and, if required in court, be used to indicate evidential weight (in a way that would be more refined, and less likely to be misinterpreted, than the terminology typically used by practitioners).

Allow us to be very clear at the outset. We are not suggesting transforming the endeavor into a statistical exercise. Probabilities and statistics are used solely to (1) structure the inference and (2) help the examiner assign weights to their observations. Examiners remain absolutely central to the whole process; they can simply be supported by the new concepts that we will gradually introduce in the next sections. We are not expecting fingerprint examiners to immediately jump from their current practice to the principles espoused here. However, we hope to show that there is a fully structured way to proceed with inference in the fingerprint area that, we firmly believe, will impact on the future of this profession.

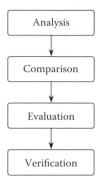

FIGURE 2.1 ACE-V methodology in a simple flow diagram.

Useful protocols and flow charts have been published as step-by-step descriptions of the comparative identification process (Smith et al. 1993; Olsen and Lee 2001). The most extensive process map was recently published by the NIST/NIJ Expert Working Group on Human Factors in Latent Print Analysis (2012). These protocols will serve as a reference for this chapter. The aim of this chapter is to encapsulate the detailed procedure within the generic methodology or protocol known as "ACE-V" as adopted by (Ashbaugh 1991a) in the early 1990s, reinforced by Tuthill (1994), and subsequently by Tuthill and George (2002).

The Royal Canadian Mounted Police (RCMP) should be recognized as the organization that developed and adopted the ACE-V protocol for forensic comparisons (Huber 1959, 1972), from fingerprints to footwear impression examinations (Cassidy 1980) and questioned document examination (Huber and Headrick 1999). ACE-V is a useful mnemonic acronym that stands for analysis, comparison, evaluation, and verification (Figure 2.1). Although not originally named that way, pioneers in forensic science were already applying such a protocol (Heindl 1927; Locard 1931).

An initial critical analysis can be attributed to Clark (2002), followed by the evaluation by Haber and Haber (2008). The most thorough and balanced analysis of ACE-V is attributed to Langenburg (2012). Many of his recommendations have been adopted here. ACE-V is the acronym used by the most contemporary fingerprint examiners to describe their examination process. This is certainly due, at least in part, to the first *Daubert* hearing in the United States (*U.S. v. Mitchell*, U.S. District Court for the Eastern District of Pennsylvania, Criminal No. 96-00407) where, for the first time, the fingerprint profession was challenged on the methodological soundness of the discipline (Epstein 2002). The ACE-V protocol is now referred to in standards (SWGFAST 2013a), regulatory documents (Forensic Science Regulator 2015a,b), or reports from expert groups (Interpol 2004; Expert Working Group on Human Factors in Latent Print Analysis 2012).

The ACE-V methodology provides the descriptive phases of the examination process to communicate how an analyst compares fingerprints. It is a protocol that does not, in itself, give details as to how the inference is conducted. Most authors stay at this descriptive stage and leave the inferential or decision component of the process to "training and experience" without giving any more guidance as to how examiners arrive at their decisions. As rightly highlighted in the NRC report (National Research Council 2009, pp. 5–12): "ACE-V provides a broadly stated framework for conducting friction ridge analyses. However, this framework is not specific enough to qualify as a validated method for this type of analysis." Some have compared the steps of ACE-V to the steps of standard hypothesis testing, described generally as the "scientific method" (Wertheim 2000; Triplett and Cooney 2006; Reznicek et al. 2010; Brewer 2014). We agree that ACE-V reflects good forensic practice and that there is an element of peer review in the verification stage (as we shall see later); however, draping ACE-V with the term "scientific method" runs the risk of giving this acronym more weight than it deserves.

This chapter has the ambition to describe the ACE-V process but also to thoroughly explain how conclusions are reached, taking full advantage of probability and decision theory. It will be built on ACE-V but goes into much more detail where required, to provide the foundations upon which conclusions are reached. It will also highlight the limitations. The fingerprint field has been subject to recent and necessary scrutiny by commentators and scholars. We cannot refer to all published papers here, but we recommend the review carried out by Lawless et al. (2009) in the context of the Fingerprint Inquiry in Scotland, the conclusions of the 2009 NRC report (National Research Council 2009) and the review of its follow-up actions (Champod 2015). Professor Mnookin sums up one legitimate demand with this snappy call*: "show me the data." This chapter aims to provide our humble answer to this call. But let us first agree with the definition of *data*. Here, we adopt the definition that has been recently used for the development of the ENFSI (European Network of Forensic Science Institutes) guidelines for evaluative reporting (Willis 2015, p. 19):

> The term "data" refers to the technical and empirical knowledge associated with a given trace type. It is used to refer to general (empirical) observations, such as the occurrence of DNA profiles among members of a relevant population or the expected number of glass fragments transferred on garments as a result of breaking glass. Such data can take, for example, the structured form of scientific publications, databases, or internal reports or, in addition to or in the absence of the above, be part of the expert knowledge built upon experiments conducted under controlled conditions (including case-specific experiments), training and experience.

This means that a broad spectrum of knowledge will constitute the data. Precedence will be given to published and documented research, but expert judgment will not and should not be dismissed when it can be assessed through adequate proficiency testing. Our aim is to adopt an all-encompassing approach and not to focus only on one source of knowledge.

ACE-V is presented here as a linear process, requiring the examiner to start with the analysis phase before proceeding with the comparison phase in order to avoid knowledge of the print impacting on the assessment of the mark. Some authors have proposed a more recurring process of ACE-V (Vanderkolk 2004).

For this chapter, we distinguish and constantly refer to the three levels of information that can be recorded from a mark or a print: level 1, level 2, and level 3 as proposed by Ashbaugh (1999). Table 2.1 provides a short definition for each level.

Note that some practitioners are suggesting a distinction between three levels according to the magnification required to visualize the features (Wertheim 2000). Level 1 features are visible without magnification, level 2 features require 5× to 10× magnification, whereas the visualization of level 3 features benefits from higher magnification. Hence, depending on its size and clarity, features of a scar may fall into level 1, 2, or 3. Vanderkolk (2011) and the glossary of SWGFAST (2013b) are inspired by the latter approach.

In our view, the convention used to divide between categories of features has no significant impact on the following discussion. It is, however, important that fingerprint practitioners clarify the meaning of the terms when they use them either in discussion, statements, or in court.

These three levels are illustrated in Table 2.2. Figure 2.2 shows Mairs' family tree of transitional fingerprint patterns (Mairs 1933a).

---

* http://projects.nfstc.org/ipes/presentations/Mnookin_show-me-data.pdf (last accessed February 6, 2016).

TABLE 2.1

Definition of the Three Levels of Friction Ridge Skin Features

Level	Definition
Level 1	Level 1 refers to the overall pattern formed by the flow of papillary ridges on the papillary surface. Traditionally, the general pattern formed on the fingertips has been classified into generic classes. However, it is not required to assign a class to a ridge flow to qualify it as a level 1 feature. The flow itself, without any assigned conventional class, represents what can be referred to as level 1. For example, impressions of phalanges or tips of the fingers will present elements of ridge flow.
	Various classification schemes were developed in the early days of dactyloscopy, aimed at offering a classification system to enable a 10-print card search. The most widespread classification systems are by Galton (1892), Henry (1900) and Vucetich (1904) distinguishing typically between arches (and tented arches), loops, and whorls. An account of the various historical classification systems is given in Hutchins (2011).
	In this book, we use the Galton–Henry classification published by the FBI (United States Department of Justice and Federal Bureau of Investigation 1984).
	We have to recognize, however, that any partitioning scheme is a simplification of the continuum of papillary flow patterns that fingerprints may possess, as emphasized by Mairs (1933a,b) (Figure 2.2). This continuum is also recognized among the computer scientists who are developing automated fingerprint identification systems (AFIS). After devoting much effort to mimicking a discrete fingerprint classification system based on a small number of classes, scientists are now focusing their efforts on capturing the full spectrum of general forms (Maltoni et al. 2009).
	In addition to the forms taken by the flow of the ridges, some measurements can be classed as level 1 features, such as ridge counting and ridge tracing. Both of these measures were implemented within classification systems to increase the discriminative power of the systems. They are well described, for example, in Moenssens (1971) or the FBI's manual on fingerprint science (United States Department of Justice and Federal Bureau of Investigation 1984). We will refer to ridge counting and ridge tracing on a regular basis in this chapter.
	The general flow of papillary ridges on the palm has been subject of classification attempts (Alexander 1973; Coppock 2007) and to an important publication of Tietze and Witthuhn (2001). The latter indeed allows examiners to gain an understanding of the various flow structures that friction skin ridges form in palmar areas. Examiners can use this knowledge to quickly locate unknown palm marks.
Level 2	Level 2 refers to major ridge path deviations, also known as minutiæ, points of identification, or Galton characteristics. Basic forms are ridge endings, bifurcations, and dots (Olsen 1981). Additional types of minutiæ (combinations of the basic minutiæ) have been identified in the literature as being more specific than their basic components. For these features, the nomenclature in the literature is not standardized (Saviers 1987, 1989), and it is safer to work with illustrations. The lengths of ridges, defined by the distances between pairs of minutiæ connected by a ridge, will also fall under the umbrella of level 2 features. The same applies to the relative arrangements of ridges when ridges are considered in sequence, piled up one after the other.
	Occasional features such as warts, scars, creases, and wrinkles are sometimes referred to as level 2. The same holds for incipient, or subsidiary ridges (Ashbaugh 1992) and flexion creases (Ashbaugh 1991b).
Level 3	Level 3 refers to intrinsic or innate ridge formations: the alignment and shape of each ridge unit, pore shape, and relative pore positions are level 3 features. The early description of pores shapes comes from Locard between 1912 and 1913 (1912a,b, 1913). Shapes of edges have been proposed for consideration by examiners by Chatterjee (1962). Both authors indicated that these features varied between individuals in number, position, shape, and size. It is important to indicate upfront that there is no clear consensus among practitioners, especially in relation to the reproducibility and perceived contribution of such features when available in agreement in a given comparison (Anthonioz et al. 2008). Between 5% and 10% of marks will show legible third-level detail (Liddle 2001).

TABLE 2.2

Illustrations of the Three Levels of Friction Ridge Skin Features

Level	Illustration
Level 1	Mairs' family tree is illustrated in Figure 2.2; basic general patterns are as follows:

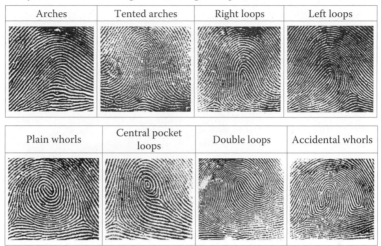

Arches	Tented arches	Right loops	Left loops

Plain whorls	Central pocket loops	Double loops	Accidental whorls

Images taken from the Royal Canadian Mounted Police, Fingerprint Manual, Chapter 2—Pattern type. With permission.

Level 2 — Ridge endings, bifurcations, and dots are the basic minutiæ (ridges are shown in black):

Images taken from Champod, C., Reconnaissance automatique et analyse statistique des minuties sur les empreintes digitales, PhD thesis, Université de Lausanne, Institut de Police Scientifique et de Criminologie, Lausanne, Suisse, 1996.

All other types are combinations of bifurcations and ridge endings; here, for example, from left to right: a lake (or enclosure), a hook (or spur), a double bifurcation, a bridge and opposed bifurcations.

Images taken from Champod, C., Reconnaissance automatique et analyse statistique des minuties sur les empreintes digitales, PhD thesis, Université de Lausanne, Institut de Police Scientifique et de Criminologie, Lausanne, Suisse, 1996.

Below are illustrations of wrinkles, creases and warts, and scars:

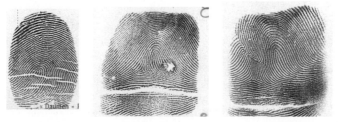

(Continued)

TABLE 2.2 (*Continued*)

Illustrations of the Three Levels of Friction Ridge Skin Features

Level	Illustration
Level 3	Inked impression showing a succession of pores and specific edge features (friction ridges are in black ink):

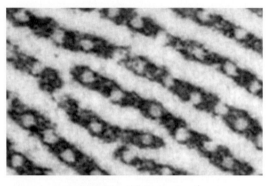

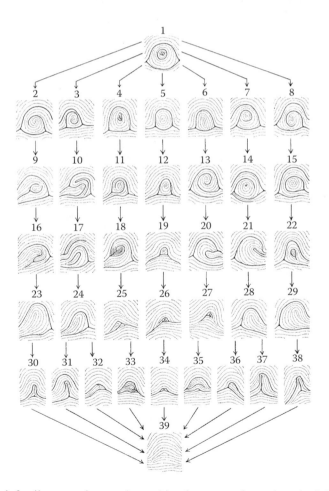

FIGURE 2.2 Mairs' family tree of general transitional patterns from the whorl (1) to the arch (39). (Reproduced from Mairs, G.T., *Finger Print Ident. Mag.*, 15, 16, 1933a. With permission.)

2.1 ANALYSIS

2.1.1 PURPOSE OF THE ANALYSIS

"Analysis" comes from the Greek word for "breaking up." It is finding and classifying complex elements into simple descriptive elements. It is a phase of observation, detection, and data collection. This step calls for an analysis of the recovered mark to assess the presence of ridge formations and their reproducibility and specificity. The analysis concludes with a decision regarding the suitability of the mark in the subsequent comparison phase. Analysis is essentially an information-gathering phase from the mark itself that terminates with a decision by the examiner regarding how this mark will be used in the forensic process. As Heidi Eldridge put it, "analysis entails an observation task, an assessment task, and a decision task" (personal communication, 2014).

The analysis should be focused solely on the mark in order to determine, without being informed by a reference print, what information is visible and reliable, taking into account the clarity of the image and considering the effects of pressure, distortion, substrate, and development techniques. An example of marks left by the same finger is shown in Figure 2.3 to illustrate how the result may vary from mark to mark as a function of substrate, detection techniques, and deposition.

During the analysis phase, it is expected that examiners will observe and characterize (break-up) all the features that are visible in the mark, with an assessment of their reality and the conditions (favorable or adverse) under which the mark has been left. In addition, examiners will assign to the features a level of confidence that translates their expectation to observe them in that form and

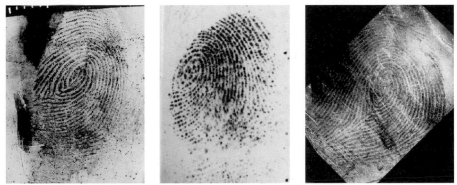

Mark detected on a sheet of plastic   Mark detected on a sheet of paper   Mark detected on the adhesive side of a tape

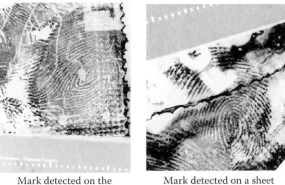

Mark detected on the adhesive side of a tape   Mark detected on a sheet of plastic

FIGURE 2.3 Series of marks left by the same finger at different times, on various surfaces and detected with different techniques. Note the distortion of the core across these marks.

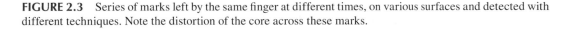

configuration in a good quality print from the actual donor. Langenburg (2012) refers to this assessment as the robustness of the features. We will use the term *reproducibility* of the features to be aligned with Chapter 1. Indeed, in Chapter 1, we discussed extensively how reproducible ridge skin features are over time and in prints obtained under controlled conditions. With marks, the concept is simply extended to encompass additional variables due to uncontrolled conditions under which marks are left, the range of substrates on which they are deposited, and, finally, the various means used to visualize or detect them. It is the result of the *within-source* variability observed over a series of depositions of different marks from the same area of friction ridge skin.

Assessment of reproducibility first requires the examiner to make observations on the mark and then to assign confidence to the observed features. When an examiner assigns high confidence to a feature, it expresses that its reproducibility is high and that there is a high expectation to observe this feature in the corresponding print. Conversely, if the examiner assigns low confidence to a feature, there is a higher chance the feature will not be represented in the print as seen on the mark. Confidence is intrinsically linked to the concept of *tolerances* that will need to be taken into account during the comparison phase. These tolerances must allow for the mechanisms and constraints of the deposition process. They represent the boundaries that the examiner will have to allow for when considering a potential correspondence. It means that, if a feature or a set of features is said to be with low tolerances, the examiner will expect, upon comparison, to observe these features in the print with the same precise configuration and shape. The tighter the tolerances, the less opportunities are available for a print from a difference source to fall within them. The expectation is then that, in comparison, the compared images will be visually indistinguishable (or nearly so) if they are coming from the same source. Conversely, a feature or set of features labeled with high tolerances means that there are more opportunities for multiple configurations and shapes to be successfully considered as being within the defined limits used to declare a correspondence. In this case, the examiner's expected range of visual similarities among prints is larger. Reproducibility is dictated by the tolerances and reflects, overall, the confidence that the examiner will put on the observed features in their capacity to be reproduced in the corresponding print.

An illustrated example is provided in Figure 2.4. The mark on the left will have high tolerances (low confidence in observed features) due to the lack of clarity of the ridges and their dotted appearance, whereas the mark on the right, in the area above the core, will have very low tolerances (high confidence in observed features). For the latter, the features (minutiæ, their positioning, and the visible pores) must be in very close correspondence in a good quality print from the same source.

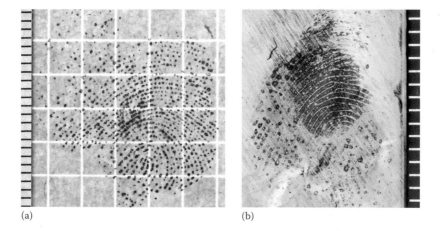

(a)   (b)

FIGURE 2.4   (a) High tolerances have a dotted appearance typical of marks detected with DFO on paper. (b) Low tolerances have been detected on aluminum foil with cyanoacrylate.

When the features visible on the mark have been identified and their tolerances understood, the examiner would then assess the mark's intrinsic value, i.e., its capacity to discriminate between prints from different individuals. Langenburg (2012) refers to this as the *specificity* of the features. The question is, how distinctive (or discriminative) are the features given the tolerances previously identified? Or, how much discrimination will these features provide when searched against a set of prints? Specificity is then related to the *between-source* variability, how features in marks will vary when they are left by different sources of friction ridge skin.

These three concepts—*reproducibility, specificity,* and *tolerances*—are intimately linked. A set of reproducible features means low tolerances and higher specificity compared to the same set of features but with limited reproducibility (meaning high tolerances) that will have a lower specificity. During the comparison phase, it will be assessed whether or not the print features fall within the tolerances set during the analysis. All things being equal, lower reproducibility translates to lower specificity because one must consider a wider "window" of configurations that may correspond to a given set of features. Generally, these tolerances cannot be adjusted after the comparison, meaning after consideration of the potential source print. It is of paramount importance to set these parameters based on the examination of the mark alone, so as to avoid post-hoc rationalization of differences. As we shall see later in this chapter, the documentation of the tolerances set during the analysis phase is the only way to hold the examiner accountable for them during the comparison phase.

Many fingerprint practitioners will indirectly assess reproducibility and specificity by referring to the *quality* and the *quantity* of features (Vanderkolk 1999). Quality refers to the clarity of the mark, whereas quantity refers to the number of features in the mark (all levels considered). Generally, poor quality and quantity means low reproducibility and low specificity. Conversely, high quality and quantity describes marks with high reproducibility and high specificity. We shall see that these intertwined concepts impact directly on the decisions that follow from the analysis phase.

To sum up, the analysis of a mark comes down to addressing the following two generic probabilistic questions ($Q1_a$ and $Q2_a$—subscript a used to denote analysis):

$Q1_a$ What is my expectation to observe the features seen on the mark in the corresponding print (i.e., a print from the friction ridge skin that is the source of the mark)?

$Q2_a$ What is my expectation to observe the features seen on the mark in a print from an unknown individual (i.e., a print from friction ridge skin that is not the source of the mark)?

We have used the term "expectation" because, at this stage, no print has been compared to the mark. It is a typical process called *case pre-assessment* in other areas of forensic science. The responses to the aforementioned two key questions ($Q1_a$ and $Q2_a$), when taken as a ratio of two probabilities, give what forensic scientists refer to as the likelihood ratio (see Box 2.1). It represents here the expected value or expected strength of support the findings will bring to the proposition of common source *should* the corresponding print be compared against the mark. In the analysis phase, the print is hypothesized (hence the *should*). The concept will remain the same in the comparison stage but, at that later point, a print (allegedly from the same source as the mark) *is* available.

A small digression on the meaning of probability is required here, because we will continue to assign probabilities in the rest of this chapter. We view probabilities as an expression of degrees of belief in a subjective tradition (Box 2.2). It means that probabilities are assigned based on some knowledge and not systematically calculated. Let us focus on $Q2_a$ and refer back to Figure 2.4 to illustrate the concept. For the mark on the right, detected with cyanoacrylate, $Q2_a$ is asking for the probability of observing these features (about 8 level 2 features, combined with clear incipient ridges and pores). Without resorting to any statistical study, an examiner, based on his knowledge and experience, will know that the probability of finding such features in the print of an unknown person is very low (some may even claim that it is impossible). A number between 0 and 1 can be assigned to this probability. In this case, *our* probability is of the order of 1 in a billion. We use the term "our" to qualify this probability to make explicit that it is our assignment and that it may differ from one examiner to the other

BOX 2.1   CASE PRE-ASSESSMENT, LIKELIHOOD RATIO AND WEIGHT OF EVIDENCE

Case pre-assessment is a generic procedure developed by Cook et al. (1998a) to approach forensic cases. It seeks to specify and anticipate potential findings prior to performing any comparisons in order to assess the potential value associated with each of these findings as well as the probability with which these results may be obtained. The reader will find a full description of the approach in the publication by Jackson and Jones (2009). When applied to friction ridge skin impressions, pre-assessing a mark means to explore how it can contribute to the assessment of the source (*who left the mark?*) or potentially to the assessment of the activities (*what activities led to the deposited mark?*). The distinction between source and activity is addressed later in Section 2.4.3. Here, we concentrate on the issue of source only.

If we denote the features of the recovered mark with the letter y and the features in the potential corresponding print with the letter x, the likelihood ratio following analysis (LR_a) is formally developed as follows:

$$LR_a = \frac{Pr(y|x, H_p, K)}{Pr(y|H_d, K)} = \frac{Q1_a}{Q2_a}$$

This likelihood ratio takes the form of two conditional probabilities. These two probabilities, forming LR_a, can be phrased as the two questions $Q1_a$ and $Q2_a$, they are sometimes referred to the *numerator* (at the top) and the *denominator* (at the bottom) of the likelihood ratio.

Pr stands for probability. The event for which we want to assign a probability is before the vertical bar (|), here y. What is after the vertical bar (|) is what is known or given, here (x, H_p, H_d, K). They will condition the assigned probabilities of y. Because we have information that will condition our probabilities, we talk about conditional probabilities and the vertical (|) make the distinction between what is known (on its right) and what is under assessment (on its left).

In the aforementioned expression, H_p represents the proposition that the mark and the print are from the same source (the prosecution hypothesis) and H_d represents the proposition that the mark and the print originated from different sources (the defense hypothesis). K represents knowledge that is critical to the assignment of these probabilities, such as the nature of the substrate, the observation of disturbing factors (distortion, slippage, multiple appositions, etc.). It is important to stress that not all the case information is relevant when considering K. Indeed, a lot of investigative information (about the suspect's criminal history, whether he confessed to the alleged crime or not, the other forensic evidence pointing to him, etc.) has nothing to do with the consideration of the mark and the print. To avoid any unnecessary bias on the examiner's judgments, it is important to focus only on the information that has a bearing on the assessment of the forensic observations; hence, there is a focus on information that is task relevant while shielding the examiner from all unwanted information. The document prepared by the Human Factors Subcommittee of the US National Commission on Forensic Science is helpful here: http://www.justice.gov/ncfs/file/641676/download (last accessed January 29, 2016).

The LR_a represents the weight of the information content, often coined weight of evidence, that we can expect from the mark (y) if we obtain a fully legible print (x) to compare against.

A LR_a of 1 means that the probability of finding the features observed in the mark in the comparison print is the same regardless of whether or not the print and the mark are from the same source. Obviously, in this case, the mark has no capacity to provide guidance regarding the source issue. For example, a mark in the form of a smudge will fall into this category. The corresponding finger (at the source of the smudge) or another finger (not at its source) will both produce a similar smudge. As soon as features can be observed in the mark, the mark will offer a capacity to guide as to its source. Let us say that a blurred arch is observed as a mark. If the comparison print is an arch, then $Q1_a = 1$, and $Q2_a$ will be proportional to the rarity of an arch in the population (here set to 0.05 or 5%). The expected likelihood ratio will then be $1/0.05 = 20$. This means that, if the correct corresponding print is compared against that mark, we expect that it will provide some support for the proposition that the mark is coming from that source. The amount of support is directly proportional to the likelihood ratio. Here, the likelihood ratio of 20 means that the observations regarding the mark (an arch) are 20 times more likely in the corresponding source print rather than in a print from an unknown source. In a nutshell, the rarer the features observed in the mark the stronger the expected likelihood ratio will be. If the features are declared impossible to find in a print from an unknown person ($Q2_a = 0$), the ratio will be infinite. That is the strongest information that can be obtained.

The term *weight of evidence* (WoE) is sometimes used for the logarithm (base 10) of the likelihood ratio. Hence, a likelihood ratio of 1 has a weight of 0, a ratio of 1000 a weight of 3, and so on. The concept of weight of evidence expressed this way is due to Turing and Good following their work during the Second World War on decoding Enigma (Good 1985). In this book, when we use the expression "value of the findings," this refers to the likelihood ratio (LR); when the term "weight" is used, it refers to WoE that equals $\log_{10}(\text{LR})$.

The following illustration captures the aforementioned concepts, showing the minimum and maximum values for the expected likelihood ratio and its conversion into weight of evidence.

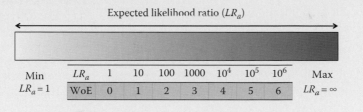

depending on the knowledge that has conditioned that assessment. It is expected, however, that a group of peer examiners will be somewhat consistent (or calibrated) in their assignments. We explore later how such an informed assignment can also be guided by structured data when available.

2.1.2 Factors Considered during Analysis

To inform responses to these two questions ($Q1_a$ and $Q2_a$), the fingerprint examiner will explore the following factors during analysis:

- Is it a mark left by an area of friction ridge skin?
- Where was the mark found? What does it tell us with respect to the anatomical position of the hand at its source? Does it indicate a particular finger?
- What method was used to enhance the mark (e.g., optical, physical, or chemical techniques) and how do they impact on the appearance of the ridges?
- Did the substrate on which the mark was detected affect its appearance?
- How might the medium of the mark affect its appearance (e.g., heavy sebaceous secretion or blood)?
- What is the contrast of the ridges (dark on a light background or reverse)? Is this contrast uniform for the whole area of the mark?
- Do we see signs of distortion or movements (different signs may be apparent in one single mark)?
- Do we see signs of multiple appositions (e.g., double taps), or superimposed marks?
- How does the clarity or lack of clarity affect the tolerances that will be allowed when checking the print from the putative source?

BOX 2.2   PROBABILITIES: A SUBJECTIVE DEFINITION

This concept of subjective probability, as it applies to forensic science, is defined in the ENFSI guidelines for evaluative reporting. We quote *verbatim* (Willis 2015, p. 16 and 23):

PROBABILITY, CONDITIONAL

Probability is a concept by which one can express uncertainties (about an event or, more generally, an unknown state of affairs). The laws of probability define the values that probability can take and how probabilities combine (Aitken and Taroni 2004). Among forensic practitioners and other members of the judicial area at large, it is useful to view probabilities as conditioned on the information available to the individual who makes a probability assignment (i.e., all probabilities are conditional). Probabilities may be estimated from numerical data (where available and known as an objective probability) or stated as a personal degree of belief (known as a subjective probability) (Taroni et al. 2001).

PROBABILITY, SUBJECTIVE

Your subjective probability is the measure for your belief in the occurrence of an event. A number between 0 and 1 represents this measure. The laws of probability apply to these probabilities just as they apply to calculated probabilities. A measure of belief might be obtained by doing thought experiments, and possibly further informed by ad hoc small-scale physical experiments. Expert knowledge elicitation is a more technical approach to obtain subjective probabilities (O'Hagan et al. 2006; Lindley 2014). Further reference about subjective probability is given in Taroni et al. (2001). Forensic practitioners often experience difficulty in assigning and justifying probabilities when the assignments are based on expert knowledge. However, likelihood ratios can be informed by subjective probabilities using expert knowledge. These probability assignments shall still be expressed by a number between 0 and 1 rather than by an undefined qualifier (such as frequent, rare, etc.). Such personal probability assignment is not arbitrary or speculative, but is based on a body of knowledge that should be available for auditing and disclosure. The forensic practitioner should not mislead the recipient of expert information as to the basis of the personal assignment, and the extent to which the assignment is supported by scientific research. Forensic practitioners should consider exploring the sensitivity of the likelihood ratio to different probabilities by examining the effect of assigning different probabilities according to their personal uncertainties.

- Does the mark show a ridge flow that allows limiting the area of friction ridge to consider and its orientation on the surface (e.g., a specific ridge flow, the visibility of a core, a delta, a ridge count, a ridge tracing between two deltas, a classifiable general pattern, an anatomical sequence, a specific hand or finger)?
- What features can be observed across all three levels of details?
- What is the specificity of the friction ridge features that are observed on the mark, considering the tolerances set before and possible location and orientation?

Addressing the aforementioned reproducibility question requires a deep knowledge of the factors affecting the transition from the three-dimensional friction skin structure to a mark (most of the time, a two-dimensional outcome). Ashbaugh (1999, p. 172) refers to this transition as the "clarity bridge." It is essential to realize that the transfer process from a three-dimensional organ to a two-dimensional mark necessarily results in a loss of information. Tackling these issues requires that the examiner possesses a detailed knowledge of the circumstances under which the mark has been secured. The observed mark will depend not only upon the friction ridge skin that came into contact with the receiving surface, but also upon the medium (latent, bloody, other contaminants), the surface (smooth, rough, contaminated), the contact pressure, the duration of contact, distortion, and the fingerprint detection techniques employed. Little has been published on this topic (Singh 1963), with assessment relying heavily on the examiner's experience. However, Ashbaugh (1999) has presented numerous cases that will help any examiner with this process. Recently, researchers have presented qualitative results on the deformation of fingerprints when deposited (Maceo 2009), the reproducibility of level 3 features during applications (Richmond 2004) or the effect of blood on marks (Langenburg 2008; Praska and Langenburg 2013).

Very few systematic studies have explored the reproducibility of third-level detail. A call for such reproducibility studies has followed the Mayfield case (Budowle et al. 2006). Indeed, the report by the OIG showed that some examiners who wrongly associated the questioned mark to the print of Brandon Mayfield falsely relied on third-level detail perceived to be of significance (United States Department of Justice and Office of the Inspector General—Oversight and Review Division 2006). These features were lacking reproducibility as shown by the comparison of the different exemplars of Mayfield's fingerprints available to the FBI. The first source of material to study and confirm the reproducibility of such features is then the multiple sets of inked impressions from the putative source that may have been taken at different times. The assessment of reproducibility by practitioners has shown to vary from examiner to examiner (Anthonioz et al. 2008). Pore dimensions have been studied using inked impressions left on different substrates (Gupta et al. 2007). It has been confirmed that pore surface area measurements are subject to a high variability from print to print. The lack of reproducibility limits their usage in the identification process. The analysis was then extended to pores visible in marks detected using cyanoacrylate fuming and ninhydrin, reaching the same conclusion that pore area is not reproducible in latent marks (Gupta et al. 2008). In this regard, a word of caution had already been voiced by Faulds (1913, p. 636):

> "[...] where a finger-print pattern is doubled the pores always agree in position but rarely in shape or size."

The studies devoted to the evaluation of the reproducibility of third-level detail are sparse and further research would certainly be welcome. However, the available data (e.g., Richmond 2004) indicate that only relative pore positions along the ridge (not their size or shape) and the specific shape of minutiæ are reproducible under casework circumstances.

Quantitative research with regard to the effect of force or distortion is in the early stages in forensic science (Sheets et al. 2014; Fieldhouse 2015), whereas it has received more attention in the biometric area (e.g., Cappelli et al. 2001; Bazen and Gerez 2002; Ross et al. 2004). An illustration of the range of distortion that can be obtained when a finger is applied and moved on the flat surface of an optical live scan device is shown in Figure 2.5.

Addressing the specificity question requires consideration of the weighted values, rarity and discriminating strength of features and their configurations with neighboring features while giving due allowance for tolerances. This is similar to what will be addressed following the comparison stage should a corresponding print have been obtained. The essential difference between the assessment done in the analysis phase and the assessment done in the comparison phase is that, in the first, we envisage a comparison with a pristine print from the donor, whereas, in the second, the comparison will be done with the print as recorded. Often the actual print will not be pristine and may present a level of complexity that may even call for an analysis of the print itself. We will leave the full discussion on specificity for the comparison stage.

2.1.3 Documentation of the Analysis

To assist the documentation of the features during analysis, GYRO—green, yellow, red, orange— has been suggested as a convention for marking minutiæ or other features (Langenburg and Champod 2011). GYRO allows the examiner to assign confidence levels regarding the existence of

FIGURE 2.5   The central print was from a finger that was inked and rolled on paper. The side prints were taken on an optical livescan device. The livescan acquisitions were made with the finger moving on the flat glass surface to initiate distortion. (Images courtesy of M. Kæhr, Fribourg, Switzerland.)

a feature: green for high confidence, yellow for medium confidence, and red for low confidence. The link with the corresponding levels of tolerances associated with the features is clear. Orange is reserved for minutiæ that have been observed after the comparison with a known print in an iterative process. Its implementation is easily achieved with any image processing software. A few dedicated software options are also available, among them the widely used ULW (Universal Latent Workstation, version 6.4.1; https://www.fbibiospecs.cjis.gov/Latent/PrintServices [last accessed January 29, 2016]), that offers the possibility to annotate a large range of features, the Extended Feature Sets (EFS), according to the ANSI/NIST standard (American National Standards Institute and National Institute of Standards and Technology 2011; Chapman et al. 2013; Noblis Inc. 2013). ULW can be used to distinguish features that have a high level of certainty from features that are less clear. PiAnoS (Picture Annotation System, currently in version 4) is a generic interface to annotate, take case notes and conduct forensic comparison work, separating the analysis from the comparison phase. In addition, it offers specific tools (1) to capture the level of confidence for the minutiæ observations and (2) to review cases processed through a group of examiners. PiAnoS is an open-source software package developed by the University of Lausanne and available from https://ips-labs.unil.ch/pianos/.

The examiner should annotate the mark accordingly, displaying, when visible, the flow of the ridges, the minutiæ, and the level 3 features. This process may be seen as time-consuming, and it is acknowledged that some quicker analysis may be carried out on marks of high clarity, but this process is essential for all poor-quality marks. An example of annotations in PiAnoS is shown in Figure 2.6.

SWGFAST (2013a) is requiring more extensive documentation in cases qualified as complex. The level of complexity is assessed by the dual consideration of the quantity of minutiæ against the overall quality of the mark as illustrated in the following graph (Figure 2.7), based on a consensus of collective experience among SWGFAST members.

According to SWGFAST, a mark falling in the B area is considered as complex and will require extensive documentation of the relevant features used as a basis for a conclusion. A standard for documentation

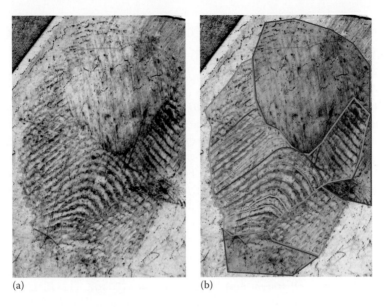

(a)   (b)

FIGURE 2.6 (a) The mark without annotation. (b) The annotations given by the fingerprint examiners. The overall quality of the friction ridge areas is assessed using a three-color scheme (green for good legibility of the ridges, orange for medium and red for poor – not to be confused with the colors used for minutiae in the GYRO system). The ridges are traced (the colors have no specific meaning). The minutiæ are then indicated with an assignment of the confidence to be given to their type (square for a likely bifurcation, round for a likely ridge endings and triangle when the type of minutiæ cannot be reasonably assigned but ridge flow and numbers of ridges indicate the presence of a minutia).

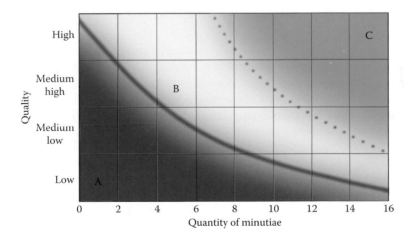

FIGURE 2.7 Graph taken from Scientific Working Group on Friction Ridge Analysis, Study and Technology (SWGFAST) (2013a), Standards for Examining Friction Ridge Impressions and Resulting Conclusions, version 2.0. with permission.

has also been issued by SWGFAST (2010) and guidance provided by Maceo (2011b). Recommendations to document more extensively complex cases have also been made by Interpol (2004), the NIST Expert Working Group on Human Factors in Latent Print Analysis (2012), and in two reports concluding investigations into now infamous cases of erroneous fingerprint identifications (United States Department of Justice and Office of the Inspector General—Oversight and Review Division 2006; Campbell 2011). We refer to specific cases at multiple points in this chapter as such cases have triggered operational changes in fingerprint practices. A quick summary of these cases is provided in Box 2.3.

BOX 2.3   NOTORIOUS CASES THAT CHANGED FINGERPRINT PRACTICE

THE MAYFIELD CASE IN THE UNITED STATES

In May 2004, Brandon Mayfield, an Oregon attorney, was arrested by the FBI in the context of an investigation of terrorist attacks on commuter trains in Madrid, Spain. The arrest was based on the identification by the FBI of a fingermark detected on a plastic bag of detonators recovered from a car near the scene of the bombings. The mark had been searched in the IAFIS system and subsequently identified to Brandon Mayfield. The identification was confirmed by three FBI examiners and a court-appointed expert. A few weeks after the arrest, the Spanish National Police (SNP) informed the FBI that they had, in fact, identified the mark to an Algerian national named Daoud. The case received significant attention from the media and the legal and forensic communities (Rudin and Inman 2004; Wax and Schatz 2004). It showed that fingerprint evidence was not as absolute as we may have thought. The U.S. Department of Justice, Office of the Inspector General (OIG), launched a review into the FBI's handling of the case and provided an assessment of the causes of the misidentification (United States Department of Justice and Office of the Inspector General—Oversight and Review Division 2006). The FBI also conducted reviews that have been published (Stacey 2004; Budowle et al. 2006; Smrz et al. 2006). We mention here several factors that contributed to the misattribution, which are discussed more thoroughly later in the chapter: a set of coincidences between the print of Mayfield and the print of Daoud that qualifies them as close non-matches; the fact that the print had been obtained from a search against millions of prints; a verification stage that had been carried out by examiners knowing the conclusions reached by the first examiner; and an unquestioning reliance on features qualified as level 3 features.

THE MCKIE CASE IN THE UNITED KINGDOM: THE SCOTTISH FINGERPRINT INQUIRY

In 1997, during the trial of Mr David Asbury for the murder of Miss Marion Ross, Ms Shirley McKie, one of the police officers, did not accept that she had left a fingermark at the crime scene. However, fingerprint examiners of the then Scottish Criminal Records Office (SCRO) identified that mark (known as "Y7") to her left thumb. She was subsequently charged with perjury. Shirley McKie challenged the identification (verified by three experts of SCRO according to their protocols) and called upon other experts to refute the claimed identification. Shirley McKie was found not guilty, but the fingerprint evidence remained a matter of dispute and controversy across the national and international fingerprint community for the next decade. In 2008, Sir Anthony Campbell was appointed to hold a public inquiry into the matter. The full Fingerprint Inquiry Report has been published (Campbell 2011) and all associated documents are available in the public domain. The ultimate conclusion of the report regarding the mark Y7 has been expressed as follows by Sir Anthony Campbell (p. 459): "The fact that there remains no satisfactory explanation of the Rosetta reinforces the conclusion that SCRO were in error in identifying Y7 as having been made by Ms McKie judged by (1) the standard of the day and (2) the source materials then available to them." [...] "I could not accept a non-numeric finding of identification because the number of level two characteristics that might be in agreement is small, such level three detail as has been mentioned is unreliable and the Rosetta is an unexplained difference. That gives my conclusion on the fingerprint evidence in isolation but, as with any source of evidence, it ought properly to be assessed in the light of the evidence as a whole. The absence of any evidence that Ms McKie went beyond the porch at the entrance to the house has to be factored in. That is consistent with a conclusion that the mark was not made by her. Having reviewed the evidence as a whole my conclusion is that the mark Y7 was misidentified and was not made by Ms McKie."

A large series of recommendations were made in the report in response to recognized risks factors, among them: a culture of 100% certainty, leading to a perceived state of infallibility; an examination process that was heavily conditioned by the print to inform the observations on the mark; a verification process that amounted to a ratification of a known conclusion of a colleague; contextual information from the police, which may have subconsciously influenced the conclusions; and the peer-pressure of experienced examiners, more senior in the hierarchy, whose decisions could not be challenged. The paper by Cole and Roberts (2012) complements well the official inquiry report.

R. v SMITH [2011] EWCA CRIM 1296 IN ENGLAND

The Court of Appeal quashed the conviction of Peter Smith for the murder of Mrs Linda Owen on the ground that the defense was severely disadvantaged by the decision of the lower court not to allow them to call their own fingerprint examiner, Ms Tweedy. Apart from this procedural but decisive aspect, the Court of Appeal was exposed to a series of conflicting testimonies from both prosecution and defense fingerprint experts. No agreement could be reached regarding, for example, the initial assessment of the value of the mark, its quality, the exact nature of the ridges and furrows and their associated features, and the mechanisms, whereby the mark had been left (single touch or double touch). The Court of Appeal concluded its ruling with some critical observations regarding the presentation of the fingerprint evidence they received. The Court was surprised by the absence of contemporaneous documentation made at the time of examination, by the limited quality and depth of the reports submitted, and of the presentation made at trial. The Court invited the relevant bodies to "examine as expeditiously as possible the issues we [the Court] have identified, to assess the position and to ensure that there are common quality standards enforced through a robust and accountable system."

In operational agencies, the systematic classification of marks according to their complexity is in its early days. Some may comply with the aforementioned SWGFAST guidance, others may use thresholds based on the number of minutiæ. In Switzerland, for example, if 12 or more reproducible minutiæ are annotated on the mark in the analysis stage, the mark is declared as non-complex; below 12, the mark will be declared as complex. In the Netherlands, an observation between 10 and 12 reproducible minutiæ defines a complex mark. Below 10 minutiæ, the mark is not retained for further identification purposes.

A last word on documentation: It should be performed systematically at the time of examination and not *a posteriori* upon request or when the conclusions are disputed. It seems trivial to reiterate that case notes should be made and be contemporaneous to the analysis/examination as part of any good scientific practice; however, common fingerprint practice suggests otherwise (e.g., the recent *R. v Smith* [2011] EWCA Crim 1296 case in England, see Box 2.3). We cannot overemphasize the absolute requirement of establishing contemporaneous notes in complex cases; otherwise, there is an impossibility (1) to comply with the requirements of ISO 17025 (clause 4.13.2) regarding technical records (Forensic Science Regulator 2015b) and (2) to investigate cases of misattributions and to learn from them (Champod 2009a). Cases in the United States where courts have rejected fingerprint evidence due to a lack of proper documentation are currently sparse (see *State of New Hampshire v. Richard Langill*, 05-S-1129, Rockingham, SS Superior Court 2007 but reversed by the Supreme Court of New Hampshire, *State of New Hampshire v. Richard Langill*, No. 2007-300, or *People v. Safford*, 392 Ill. App. 3d at 223), but we expect that number to increase in the future. Documentation is, in our view, an essential component of the right to a fair trial.

2.1.4   QUALITY METRICS FOR MARKS

Hicklin et al. (2013) studied the process of analysis including local and overall assessments of clarity. This endeavor was based on a survey of examiners, where the participants were asked to assess the quality of 70 marks (Hicklin et al. 2011) detailing the perceived quality of various areas of the mark. Standardization of the process is proposed and an interface presented (Hicklin et al. 2013). This work paves the way for automated methods to measure the quality (or information content) of marks. The quality metrics developed by Hicklin and colleagues are now part of the tools available in ULW (see Figure 2.8 for an example). Such tools can also be adapted to comparatively assess fingermark detection techniques (Pulsifer et al. 2013).

Yoon et al. (2012, 2013) made another significant contribution with a dedicated algorithm to inform an AFIS systems of the quality of a mark as measured by the clarity of the ridges and the total number of minutiæ detected in the mark. Kellman et al. (2014) have also shown the possibility of using metrics characterizing the image of the mark to predict expert performance and assess fingerprint comparison difficulty. Such research opens the possibility of automatically distinguishing between complex marks and non-complex marks.

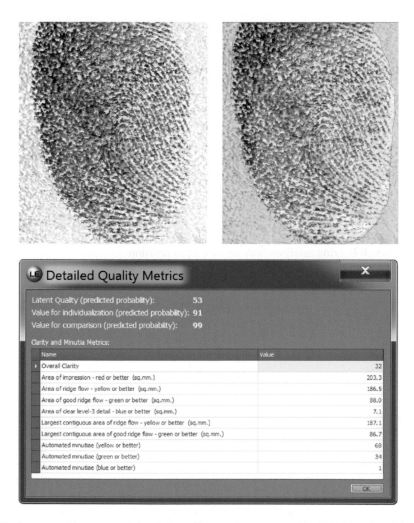

FIGURE 2.8 Image quality map and detailed quality metrics computed by ULW (version 6.4.1). ULW puts the highest quality areas in blue, followed by green, yellow, and red.

2.1.5 Decisions Reached Following Analysis

At the end of the analysis, the fingerprint examiner makes a decision regarding the "suitability" of the mark. It is a decision by the examiner regarding the capacity of the mark to be compared against known prints (a limited number of 10-print forms or using AFIS). In some instances, the analysis stage concludes that there is sufficient data to be able to identify a source when the corresponding source is available. There is no standard as to whether or not the conclusion of an analysis should relate only to the capacity to identify or also to the capacity to be compared against known prints—hence allowing marks to be used for exclusion even if they would not have the quality required to identify.

Practice can vary significantly between agencies and even practitioners. This is due to a lack of clear definition of the term suitability. Broadly speaking, two approaches can be distinguished and have been described by SWGFAST (2013a) as follows:

> *Approach #1* is commonly referred to as "of value for identification": Only impressions of value for identification are compared. If a mark cannot be individualized when presented with the correct (corresponding) exemplars from the same source as the mark, then the mark is deemed "no value." Under this approach, two decisions are then possible: (1) *Suitable for identification* (aka *value for identification*—VID) and (2) *No Value* (NV). The label "No Value" refers thus only to a mark's potential to identify. Marks allowing potential exclusion but failing the identification threshold will be qualified as "No Value" in this approach.
>
> *Approach #2* is commonly referred to as "of value for comparison": Impressions of value for identification (and possibly for exclusion only) are considered. Three decisions are possible here: (1) *Suitable for identification*; (2) *Suitable only for exclusion* (but not for identification) (a.k.a. *value for exclusion only*—VEO); (3) *No Value*. The second option "suitable only for exclusion" indicates that the mark is not expected to be identified but has sufficient features to allow an exclusion or an association of a strength that is less than an identification. The term "No Value" is reserved for marks of a quality that is insufficient either to associate or to exclude.

The term "suitable for identification" indicates, under both approaches, that the mark is or may be identifiable. Practice has shown that most examiners will mean "is," but it is important to recognize that the conclusion following analysis may be subject to revision.

The choice between each approach is a matter of organizational policy. Generally, agencies with a large number of submissions tend to adopt approach #1 as it will reduce the number of marks that should be further compared. The choice is governed by considerations such as input, output, backlogs, and resources. Other agencies may adopt approach #2, or both, with the selection based on the nature of the crime investigated. For example, for volume crime (typically burglaries), it may be decided that it is more cost-effective to take approach #1 and consider approach #2 in serious crimes only.

There is no standard regarding the assessment of the quality of features observed in a mark and its overall value. There is currently no value standard. In some countries, typically when a numerical standard for identification is in force (notably in the Netherlands, France, Spain, and Italy), the numerical threshold—the minimum number of minutiæ required for an identification—may be used to filter the marks at this stage. However, we will explore later how variable the counts of minutiæ can be between examiners, leading to variation in the value determination. When no numerical standard is in place, there is no set standard defined to decide upon the quality of a mark. The assessment is then left to the examiner who will exercise a holistic judgment based on the intrinsic features displayed by the mark at hand. Likewise, it is not customary among fingerprint practitioners to weigh individually and explicitly the features identified during the analysis phase. In other words, the contribution of features will be assessed globally, without detailing their individual contributions (statistically or otherwise). Leaving that assessment to the expert is unsatisfactory. We think that the profession needs to develop systematic methods to measure quality. Hicklin et al. (2013) proposed dedicated algorithm to measure the quality of marks. These efforts should be pursued.

We have outlined before the two pre-assessment questions ($Q1_a$ and $Q2_a$) that should be addressed during the analysis stage, leading to an expected likelihood ratio (LR). In general, practitioners do not formalize this so precisely. However, there is benefit in making the process more transparent, because it does help to identify the factors that influence the decision-making process.

Later in this chapter, we will introduce decision theory as the framework to fully articulate decisions made by fingerprint examiners at the end of the evaluation phase. The decisions made here, following the analysis phase, do not differ. The critical point is that these decisions are influenced not only by the perceived value of the mark (the expected LR following that pre-assessment) but also by numerous forces under which the fingerprint examiner is operating (societal values, available manpower, type of crime, etc.). It means that every decision made by examiners is not informed solely by a consideration of the mark, but is also influenced (or modulated) by their societal and organizational values.

There are two steps toward the decision following analysis. The first is an assessment of the expected weight that can be assigned to the mark through the joint consideration of reproducibility and specificity. The second is a decision-making step that considers this expected weight and the other factors outlined above. Gittelson et al. (2013) presented a formal treatment of the complex decision-making at hand. A schematic representation of the process is provided in Figure 2.9. One key element is that the decisions are made accounting for two factors: (1) the expected weight and (2) an assessment the benefits or losses (called *utilities*) associated with each decision.

Given an expected LR assigned to a mark (through the consideration of reproducibility and specificity), a first decision is made as to whether or not the mark will be considered of value for comparison, hence kept in the subsequent comparison process, or classified as no value (NV). How

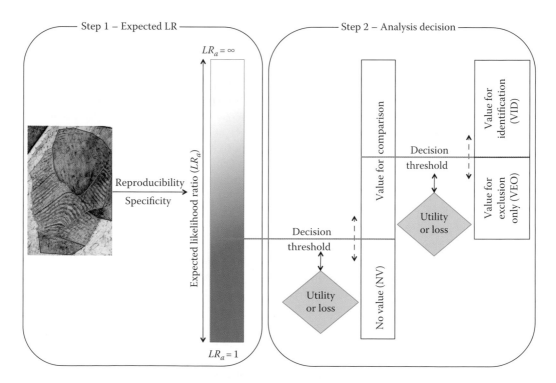

FIGURE 2.9 Schematic representation of the decision process in the analysis phase.

the threshold is set will depend on the resources of the laboratory and the efforts that we are prepared to invest for the expected return (expected LR). It may also depend on other factors such as the seriousness of the case under investigation (e.g., a murder versus a petty crime). Then, in a second decision stage, the marks labeled "value for comparison" will be classified as either VID or VEO. The utility or loss will come into play and has an impact on the conclusion of identification after the evaluation stage of ACE-V. This process is discussed in detail at that stage in the chapter. Also, note that in the aforementioned scheme, we have avoided introducing the initial triage that may occur at the detection phase (typically when the fingerprint examiners are not carrying out the detection of marks, a task taken up by laboratory practitioners). Earwaker et al. (2015) have shown, as expected, that the quality of the triage made by laboratory practitioners was dependent on the nature or seriousness of the case. Once again, it shows that suitability decisions are based on a large number of factors in addition to the quality of the marks themselves.

We are not suggesting that the examiner should avoid making a decision at the analysis stage, but we want to highlight that there is more than the actual mark that has a bearing on the decisions made at this point.

2.1.6 Variability in the Conclusions Reached Following the Analysis Phase

Langenburg (2004, 2012) showed that fingerprint examiners performed better than novices at the task of observing and annotating minutiæ. As also shown by Schiffer and Champod (2007), the number of minutiæ detected by an examiner increases with training. However, the variability between experts in their decisions may still be important, especially when the marks have a limited number of minutiæ. Inconsistency starts to increase for marks below 7–8 minutiæ. This threshold number of 7–8 minutiæ to decide whether the mark will be of value or not is a rule of thumb observed in other studies (Neumann et al. 2013; Ulery et al. 2014) as shown in Figure 2.10.

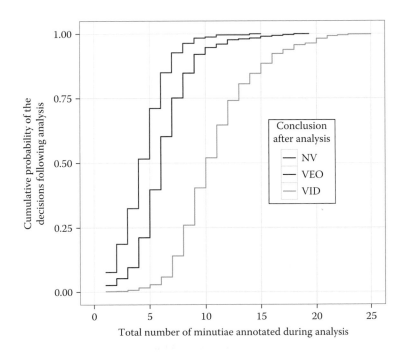

FIGURE 2.10 Cumulative distribution for each decision reached following analysis (VID, VEO, NV) as a function of the number of annotated minutiæ in the analysis phase. In total, 146 experts made 1522 decisions on 15 marks (working under approach #2).

It is interesting to note that the range between 8 and 12 minutiæ is the historical range used by Locard (1914) to define (in French) a *cas limite* (limit case) that will require consultation with one or more additional experts. Variation was not only observed between experts but also for the same expert when asked to reproduce the analysis in different sessions. Hence, we have both intra-observer and inter-observer variations. In the study by Langenburg (2012), a group of Dutch examiners was significantly more conservative in their annotation (less minutiæ reported) and more consistent as a group compared to the other examiners (mainly originating from the United States). The United States and the Netherlands are operating on two distinct philosophies when it comes to the examination process. American experts tend to have an "annotate everything—sort it out later" approach and the criteria for suitability are entirely left to the subjective assessment of the examiner. In contrast, the training in the Netherlands is highly structured and requires examiners to annotate only the features that will be used in comparison (and only these features will have a say in the comparison process), and a 10–12 point rule is applied to retain a mark as identifiable. Different policies imply different utility functions, hence different decisions. Early results from China tend to show a similar trend as in the United States (Liu et al. 2015).

Ulery et al. (2011) also showed, with a large experiment involving 169 examiners largely from the United States, that examiners may differ in their decisions regarding value of marks when looking at the same mark (unanimity was reached in only 43% of marks classified as VID). They also noted intra-examiner inconsistency: 147 marks were presented twice to the same examiner and examiners changed from VID to VEO 8% of the time and from VID to NV in 1% of instances. Looking in-depth into the reproducibility (inter-examiner) and repeatability (intra-examiner) of conclusions reached following analysis, Ulery et al. (2012) indicated that "Much of the variability appears to be due to making categorical decisions in borderline cases." It is indeed on the marks for which the examiners did not reach a consensus decision on value and qualified them as difficult or very difficult, where lack of reproducibility was observed. When forced to make a decision between VID, VEO, or NV in these borderline case, it becomes almost a random assignment. It shows the limit of forcing examiners to choose among fixed categories when the strength to be assigned to a mark would be better expressed by a continuum. That is where the concept of a likelihood ratio is powerful.

How value judgments are carried out has been studied in the so-called white-box studies. These studies use the quantity of annotated features and the quality map and other features, and assess how these elements are linked to the value judgment (Neumann et al. 2013; Ulery et al. 2013, 2014). Results show that minutiæ count is a good predictor of the value assigned to a particular mark. Hence, examiners are essentially using (explicitly or implicitly) minutiæ counts to determine whether a mark is NV, VEO, or VID.

When focusing only on minutiæ, other studies led to the same conclusion that there is quite an important range of variation between experts (Swofford et al. 2013a,b). This observation is not new: Evett and Williams (1996) made the same observation in the context of the 16-point standard review, but over the years, no efforts have been put into managing such variability. One of the cases used by Neumann et al. (2013) illustrate the extent of variations that may be observed for a complex mark (Figure 2.11).

Finally, none of the above studies showed any significant impact on decisions from variables such as education, number of years of experience, volume of cases processed, age, or gender.

Some of the pragmatic recommendations offered by Dror et al. (2011) have been adapted here. Initially, the analysis of a latent mark should be done in isolation from the comparison print. It is not ruled out to reconsider the analysis after exposure to the comparison print, but, should it occur, it must be clearly and transparently documented and justified. A marking of the level of confidence associated with the annotated features will force examiners to

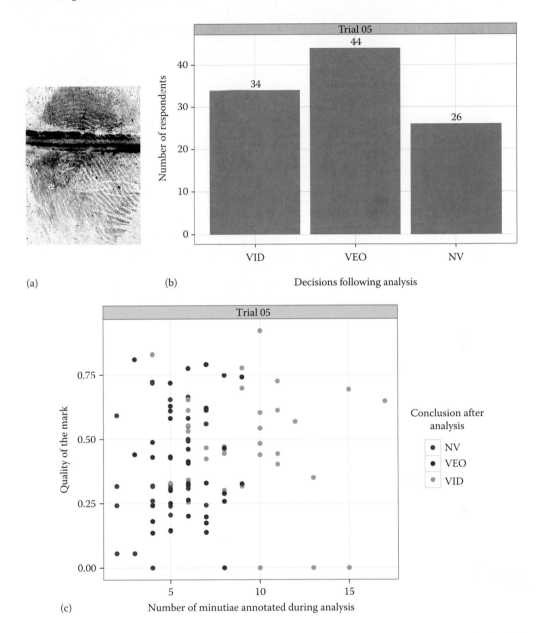

(a)

(b)

(c)

FIGURE 2.11 The mark submitted to the consideration of 104 examiners espousing Approach#2 (a). The distribution of results between the three possible decisions (VID, VEO, and NV) (b). Distribution of the numbers of annotated minutiæ (c).

consider much more critically changes in features marked with high confidence compared to those marked with low confidence. Marks, especially when complex, can be subject to more than one analysis, independently, by different examiners. That consensus can define which features have high confidence and which features have low confidence. As proposed by Langenburg (2012), the use of a consensus set of features established through a defined process in complex cases will help to compensate for the lack of reproducibility observed between examiners.

2.2   SEARCH HEURISTICS TO FACILITATE THE COMPARISON

Before we move to the comparison stage, it is worth exploring how the mark can help in setting priorities to conduct the comparison, either by being able to guide as to the finger number, the hand (right or left), the anatomical position on the friction ridge skin, or the gender of the donor. We refer to these guidance factors as "search heuristics." Some are experienced based; others can find confirmation in structured data. When structured data are available, they provide an ideal conduit for training new examiners without requiring years of experience to build up the body of search heuristics presented below.

This section introduces inference engines in the form of Bayesian networks (BNs) that will also be instrumental in the evaluation phase discussed later. Bayesian networks are briefly presented in Box 2.4.

2.2.1   Predicting the Finger Number of the Hand at the Source of a Mark

Predicting the finger number that is at the source of a mark can be an important contribution to search efficiency either in a manual mode, through a set of 10-print cards, or when an AFIS is employed. In the latter, if the search database can be segmented according to prioritized finger number (or, by extension, general pattern), the accuracy and speed of the searches can increase. For these reasons, developing the capability of fingerprint examiners to predict the finger number is a priority. Not much is available in the published literature, but we can refer to the clues associated with whorls (Brazelle 2015). Most of the clues take advantage of the statistical distributions of fingerprint features on fingers. We will specifically refer to them in this section.

Anatomical positioning of the mark on the object is a first clue that can help guide toward the most likely finger number at the source. The relative positioning of the fingers and the generally constant relative shape of the hand allows often a fair assessment of the anatomical position of the hand at the time of deposition. To carry out that activity, there is a requirement to record marks in their context, both in relation to the touched object and in relation to other marks (legible or not) surrounding the mark of interest.

Another possibility is to take advantage of the relationship between the general patterns of fingerprints and the finger number. Fingerprint practitioners, especially when they carried out manual 10-print classification or manual searches in large files, developed sets of heuristics that are all based on the statistical distribution of general patterns among fingers. For example, ulnar loops are more common than radial loops; i.e., right loops tend to be on the right hand and left loops on the left hand. Some published data are available to examiners for each finger taken individually, for groups of fingers or type of general pattern (e.g., Cummins and Midlo 1961; Cowger 1983; Singh et al. 2005). In some countries, such as India, where the right thumbprint is systematically applied to endorse contracts or official documents, such determination can be decisive in certain cases (Puri 1966). Kapoor and Badiye (2015b) published recent data on the special case of the thumb.

Appendix A provides the statistics for general patterns obtained from the FBI collection in 1993 (according to the NCIC [National Crime Information Center] classification scheme). To our knowledge, these are the only publically available data of this type. Table 2.3 provides a compiled summary of the NCIC data with the relative frequencies of the general patterns as a function of the finger number (from Finger 1 to Finger 10).

The NCIC collected frequency distributions for ridge counts, ridge tracings and patterns among individuals whose fingerprints were taken in booking stations. Such data help determine whether a certain general pattern is rare or common. For example, from aforementioned Table 2.3, we can see how double loops are relatively frequent on the right thumb (9.9%) compared to the right little finger (0.4%). These data can be organized in a database but they are quite difficult to manipulate efficiently to compute the probabilities of interest. Putting such data into practice can be difficult as the tabulated information gives percentages for each general pattern as a function of the finger number, from which it is hard to easily predict the probabilities associated with

BOX 2.4 BAYESIAN NETWORKS: A SHORT INTRODUCTION

The fundamentals of Bayesian networks in forensic science are covered by Taroni et al. (2014). Bayesian networks are influence diagrams that are used for representing and dealing with complex probabilistic problems. We will use a simplified example to introduce them. Let us assume that two marks, both arches, left by the middle and ring fingers of a right hand have been detected. We will focus here only on level 1 features. It is known, and more detailed data are provided in this chapter, that the relative frequencies between general patterns vary as a function of the gender of the donor. Women tend to present a slightly higher rate of arches compared to men. Overall, regardless of the finger number considered, we observe 3% of arches on fingerprints from men and 5% from women. Then, observing two arches is indicative that the donor is a female. The question is "what is the strength of this indication?" In addition, to make the matter more complex, fingers are not independent from each other. The pattern observed on the middle finger will depend on the pattern observed on the ring finger. This probabilistic relationship makes the problem difficult to be tackled with tabulated data as in Table 2.3 while a Bayesian network model will be very efficient. First, we can represent the structure of the relationship between the variables in a Bayesian network as follows:

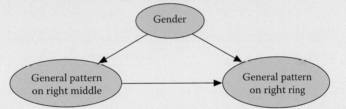

Each node represents a variable. The arrows represent the probabilistic relationships outlined before. That is to say that the general pattern on the right ring will depend on both the gender and the pattern on the right middle, whereas the general pattern on the right middle depends only on the gender.

Behind the structure of the network, each node receives a probability table that can be conditional when arrows are pointing on them. For the two nodes related to general pattern, we have the distribution associated with the general patterns given the state of the "parent" node. Typically, you will get the following conditional probability tables:

General pattern on right middle		
Gender	Male	Female
Arch	0.06354	0.06966
Not an A...	0.93646	0.93034

General pattern on right ring				
General...	Arch		Not an Arch	
Gender	Male	Female	Male	Female
Arch	0.18993	0.25142	0.00627	0.00836
Not an A...	0.81007	0.74858	0.99373	0.99164

The network therefore encapsulates all the probabilistic relationships and updates on probabilities can be very easily calculated. Two examples are given here. In the first case, we make an inference from the cause (gender) to the effects (predicting the general patterns); in the second, we make an inference from the observations of the effects (general patterns) to the cause (predicting the gender). These computations are made using Bayes theorem. We refrain from introducing Bayes theorem at this point and leave it for the section dealing with the identification (see Box 2.5).

We could reproduce these calculations analytically for such a simple network, but here we take advantage of the exact computation offered by Bayesian networks.

Let us say that you know that a male left the mark, then we can instruct the BN that the gender "male" has been observed (hence entered as information and highlighted in red in the following figure). The network will automatically update the probabilities associated with the general pattern for each finger (highlighted in green). Here, we are making an inference going in the same direction as the arrows (hence from cause to effects). The probabilities are shown as percentage probabilities. So, you have a probability of 6.35% of observing an arch on the right middle finger of a male.

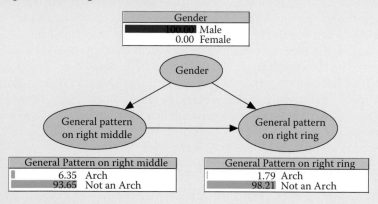

The real benefit from Bayesian networks is when we want to go backwards, hence from effects to cause. Suppose that we make the observation of arches on both impressions and ask what will be the updated probability that the marks have been left by a male? For this type of inference, it is sufficient to enter the observations, called evidence in the BN, for both fingers (known arches, highlighted in red in the following figure) and the network will update the probabilities associated with the two possible states for the gender. It gives:

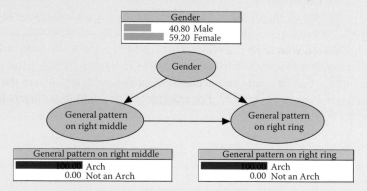

If we initially assumed a 1:1 split between males and females, the observations made on the two marks (two arches) increase the probability that the marks have been left by a female from 50% to 59.2%.

All of the Bayesian networks presented in this book have been developed with Hugin (www.hugin.com). The associated files (.net), provided on the website associated with this book, can be opened using either a demonstration version of Hugin or open-source software such as GeNie (https://dslpitt.org/genie/). User instructions and tutorials to use either Hugin or GeNie are provided on their respective websites. On the website associated with this book, we provide video tutorials with step-by-step demonstrations using the files presented here.

TABLE 2.3

Relative Frequencies of General Patterns according to Finger Number

	Finger 1 RT (%)	Finger 2 RI (%)	Finger 3 RM (%)	Finger 4 RR (%)	Finger 5 RL (%)
Ulnar loops	50.8	34.5	72.5	49.7	82.3
Radial loops	0.4	18.6	1.7	1.2	0.3
Plain whorls	34.8	24.2	14.2	37.0	11.8
Central pockets	1.1	4.4	2.6	8.8	3.6
Double loops	9.9	3.6	1.1	0.9	0.4
Plain arches	2.5	5.7	4.2	1.1	0.7
Tented arches	0.4	8.2	3.3	1.0	0.6
Others	0.1	0.9	0.4	0.3	0.2
Total	100.0	100.0	100.0	100.0	100.0
	Finger 6 LT (%)	Finger 7 LI (%)	Finger 8 LM (%)	Finger 9 LR (%)	Finger 10 LL (%)
Ulnar loops	59.8	39.2	71.0	61.9	86.5
Radial loops	0.5	16.9	1.6	0.4	0.1
Plain whorls	20.2	22.1	13.0	24.1	7.1
Central pockets	1.1	3.8	2.4	8.6	3.2
Double loops	13.1	3.3	1.7	1.7	1.0
Plain arches	4.6	5.8	5.4	1.6	0.9
Tented arches	0.6	8.1	4.4	1.3	1.0
Others	0.2	0.9	0.4	0.3	0.2
Total	100.0	100.0	100.0	100.0	100.0

the finger numbers given a specific general pattern. Bayesian networks are versatile inference engines that can be readily deployed to carry out that task.

These data have been organized in a Bayesian network (Figure 2.12) that is available on the website associated with this book.

Such a network can be used in two ways. The first goes from the causes to the effects. It means that, based on the knowledge of the cause (i.e., the gender or the finger number), you can obtain the probabilities associated with observed effects (i.e., the information associated with general patterns). It allows an examiner to access distributional data in relation to general patterns as a function of the finger considered. For this, only one needs to input the relevant states in the *finger number* node and the *gender* node as in Figure 2.13. For example, on the right little fingers from males, the most observed general pattern is the right loop (82.3%) followed by the plain whorl (11.8%).

The second way is to infer in the opposite direction from the effects (observation associated with general patterns) to the causes (gender or finger number). The Bayesian network will update all probabilities according to Bayes' theorem and provide the posterior probabilities of interest. The next example (Figure 2.14) shows the predictions for the finger number when an inside tracing double loop is observed. As many fingerprint examiners will know through experience, the search has to start on the left thumb (60.7%), followed by the right index (11.7%).

This Bayesian network can be used to explore any type of situation that may be relevant and to confirm known heuristics used by examiners; the difference now is that these trends can be fully characterized statistically. For example

- Clockwise turning plain whorls (inside tracing) are predominantly on the left hand, whereas counterclockwise plain whorls are more frequent on the right hand (odds ratio of about 7:3). When the ridge tracing is "meet," 65% will be on the right hand.
- Central pocket loops follow the same trend, but with an even stronger trend with an odds ratio of about 8:2.

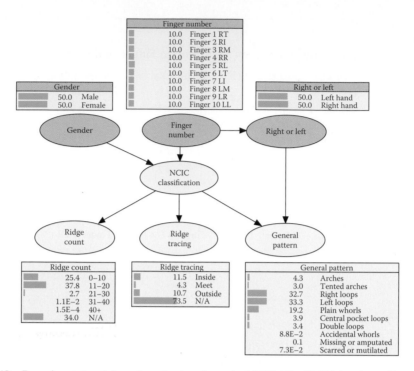

FIGURE 2.12   Bayesian network based on the data from the NCIC. The NCIC data have directly informed the parameters for the node *NCIC classification*.

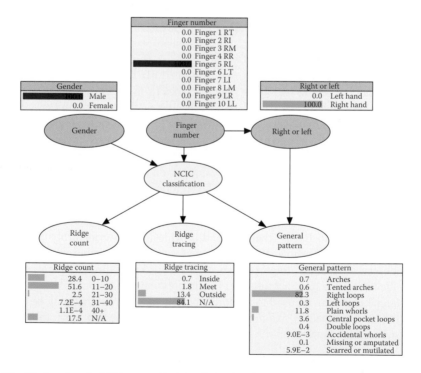

FIGURE 2.13   Updated probabilities on all nodes following the provision of knowledge for the two nodes *gender* and *finger number*. Here, we specified that the *gender* is male and the *finger number* is 5 RL. These inputted values are highlighted in red in the interface. All other probabilities (expressed as percentages with corresponding green bars) have been directly updated based on the specified knowledge.

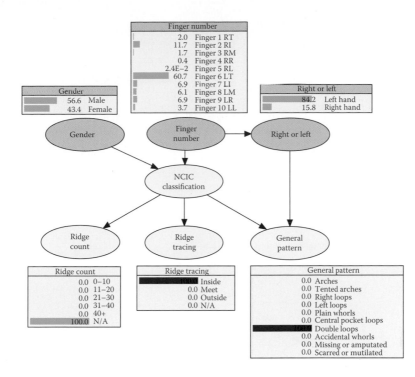

FIGURE 2.14 Updated probabilities on all nodes following the provision of knowledge for the two nodes *general pattern* and *ridge tracing*. For example, we have specified a double loop with an inside tracing (highlighted in red). All other probabilities (expressed as percentages) have been directly updated based on the specified knowledge.

- The odds ratio increases to 85:15 for double loops.
- Right loops should be searched first on the right hand, the converse for left loops (odds ratio about of 94:6). Note the exception of the index that shows a high rate (~5%) of radial loops (left loops on the right hand and right loops on the left).

However, the data provided earlier do not account for the potential dependencies between fingers; hence, the approach will only be appropriate when faced with single marks.

The ability to predict gender is rather weak based on the NCIC classification and considering only one finger. However, there are some instances where the support for a male or a female fingerprint will be high as shown in Figure 2.15.

If there is a need to consider the joint occurrence of multiple fingers of the same hand (in an anatomical sequence, for example), then the aforementioned network is not appropriate because it does not capture the probabilistic dependencies between fingers. It is difficult to obtain data with the full NCIC classification on all fingers for each individual. A 2011 dataset from the Swiss-AFIS/DNA services in Bern (courtesy of A. Glæser) has been made available to us with all fingers classified according to a less selective classification than the NCIC. The following classes are used: whorls, arches, left loops, right loops, amputated, and others (e.g., accidentals). The entire set of 10-print cards (672,423 individuals) has been classified according to this scheme. The classification was facilitated by the auto-classification algorithm of the AFIS system but vetted by fingerprint examiners. The database comprises 84.6% male cards and 15.4% female cards. A Bayesian network capturing the dependency structure across the 10 fingers has been elaborated (Figure 2.16). The dependencies have been informed by the literature (Kücken 2004). Each finger is dependent on the state of its neighbors and, further, there is a dependency between right and left hands. The parameters of the network have been estimated by the expectation-maximization (EM) algorithm

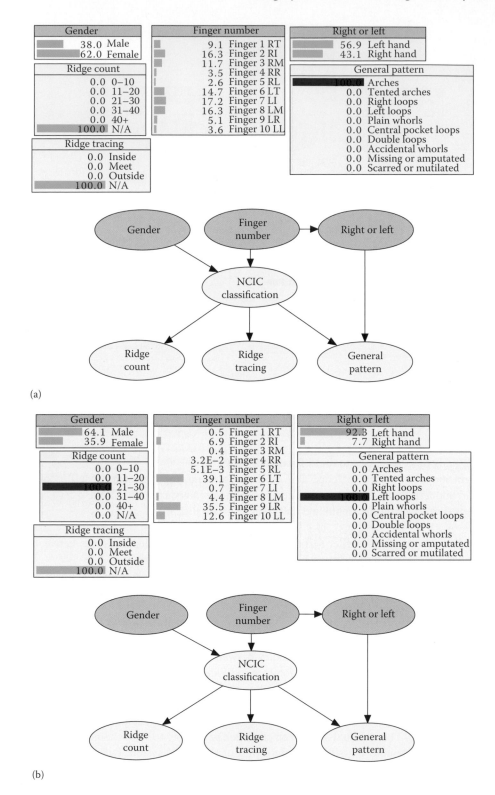

FIGURE 2.15   Updated probabilities in two cases. (a) The first when an arch is observed, lending support for a female donor (62/38). (b) The second when a high-ridge count loop is observed which gives support for a male donor (64.1/35.9).

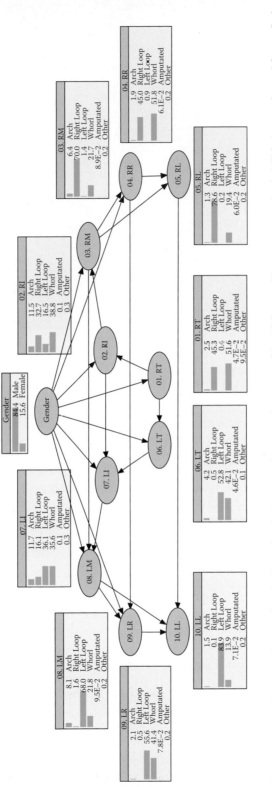

FIGURE 2.16 Bayesian network capturing the dependencies between the general patterns of the 10 fingers. The parameters (probabilities) are estimated from a Swiss-AFIS dataset provided to the authors. (Courtesy of A. Glaeser, AFIS-DNA services, Switzerland.).

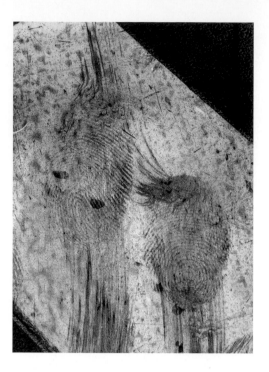

FIGURE 2.17   A lift of two marks potentially in anatomical sequence. (Image courtesy of S. Hafsi, Service forensique de la police cantonale neuchâteloise, Neuchâtel, Switzerland.)

from Hugin Researcher (version 8.2). The algorithm allows Hugin to find the maximum-likelihood estimates for the conditional probabilities based directly on the raw data.

This fully operational network allows the user to explore the joint probabilities for the combination of patterns, hence accounting for the finger-to-finger dependencies. A short example is proposed here in the context of the assessment of simultaneous impressions. Consider the two marks in Figure 2.17—a right loop and a plain whorl. Judging from the anatomical positioning of these marks on the surface, they could originate either from a right hand (middle and ring fingers) or from a left hand (middle and index fingers).

We can define the following events:

$E1$ = finding a right loop on the right middle finger
$E2$ = finding a plain whorl on the right ring finger
$E3$ = finding a right loop on the left middle finger
$E4$ = finding a plain whorl on the left index finger

Exploring the probabilities using the above BN, we can show that

$$Pr(E1, E2) = Pr(E1) \times Pr(E2 | E1) = 0.701 \times 0.433 = 0.304$$

and

$$Pr(E3, E4) = Pr(E3) \times Pr(E4 | E3) = 0.0159 \times 0.169 = 0.0027$$

From the above, we can conclude that the probability of making these observations (a right loop and a plain whorl) is 112 (0.304/0.0027) times more likely of the marks were made by the right middle

FIGURE 2.18 Print of a right loop showing two clusters of minutiæ. The first, above the delta, has all ridge endings creating ridges toward the delta. The second is below the core on the right and, again, shows all ridge endings creating ridges toward the core of the loop and the delta.

and ring fingers rather than the left middle and index fingers. There is no doubt that a clever search would start with the right hand. The above LR of 112 in favor of a right hand will not surprise experienced examiners, but we go here beyond informed judgment and show, using statistical data, how powerful the general pattern can be for the selection of the appropriate fingers.

The direction of minutiæ can also help (when the general pattern is not fully legible). Above the core of loops, minutiæ tend to open (hence create a new ridge) toward the delta (Doak 2004). Hence, a majority of minutiæ pointing to the right suggests a delta on the right, hence a left loop, which is more prevalent on the left hand. If the minutiæ points on the left, it suggests a right hand (odds ratio of about 6:4). For whorls and central pocket loops, the delta closer to the core is acting as the dominant delta, so the same tendencies as for whorls are observed. Whorls with a ridge tracing classified as meet will have a more balanced (1:1) distribution of the directions of minutiæ. For loops, below the delta and opposite the delta, the minutiæ tend to open toward the core (odds ratio of about 8:2), hence providing a way to position the mark. The average ratios provided earlier are based on Champod (1996). The tendencies on loops are illustrated in Figure 2.18. These effects are known in the literature as "pattern forces" (Interpol 2004) in the sense that the general flow of the ridges will constrain the minutiæ arrangement.

The general pattern also offers some capability to predict ethnicity (as their variations were well documented in dermatoglyphic studies) but, apart from very remote and exotic populations, the strength of the prediction is rather limited, whereas the prioritization with regard to finger numbers is more efficient (Swofford 2005).

2.2.2 PREDICTING THE SOURCE AREA OF THE FINGER OR THE PALM

Finally, when a classifiable general pattern is not legible on a mark, the flow of the ridges can provide excellent clues for the positioning on the papillary surface of the source of the mark. Minutiæ have already been discussed in relation to the hand.

Ron Smith and Associates (www.ronsmithandassociates.com) have developed a specialist course entitled "Palm Prints Comparison Techniques" to train examiners in the identification of the major areas of the palm, the flexion creases, the specific ridge flows in each area, and how this knowledge can help in locating and orienting palm marks of small surface area. This course has been extremely successful—taken up and adapted in numerous countries. The book by Tietze and Witthuhn (2001) is also an excellent reference in this context, as is the chapter by Maceo et al. (2013) and the paper by Ray (2012).

Marks left by some parts of fingers have distinctive shapes that provide clues that are useful. Marks left by the very tips of fingers have a drop-like shape depending on the angle of application. The pointy side of the drop (when visible) indicates the core of the finger. Marks left by thumbs, because of the position of the thumb on the hand, will present distinct shapes, with a dominant ridge flow on the right side for the left thumb and on the left side for the right thumb. For double loops, the core pointing downward toward the delta has a more angular shape, whereas the core pointing toward the top of the finger has a more round shape (Pat Wertheim, personal communication 2001). It is the presence of the delta close to the core of one loop that impacts on its overall flow (Figure 2.19).

Friction ridges from phalanges have distinct flows of the ridges that are good indicators of the finger involved. Data from Topper (2011) obtained on the prints of phalanges without wrinkles of 200 individuals (index, middle, and ring fingers only) are illustrated in Figure 2.20. For example, a flow the ridge falling down to the right is a good indicator of a right hand.

FIGURE 2.19   Three double loops. Note, in each fingerprint, the rounded path taken by the ridges above the first left core of the loop and the angular path taken by the ridges close to the second right core.

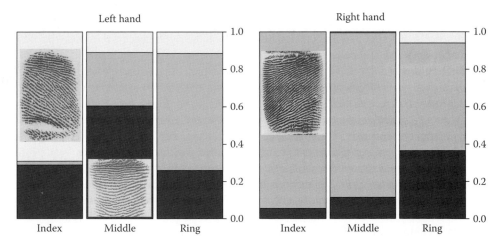

FIGURE 2.20   Distribution of the general flow of the ridges on phalange prints obtained by Topper (2011). Three categories are cumulatively presented to show their relative proportion. The first category (in dark grey) represents ridges that have a horizontal flow (as illustrated on the middle finger of the left hand). The second category (in medium grey) represents flows with a slope of the ridges down on the left (as illustrated on the index finger of the right hand). The third category (in light grey) represents flows with a slope of the ridges down on the right (as illustrated on the index finger of the left hand.)

2.2.3 Predicting Gender and Other Characteristics of the Donor

Dermatoglyphic research has highlighted that fingerprint features such as general patterns, ridge counts, or ridge breadths could be robust predictors for gender and, to some degree, the ethnic population of the individual. For example, Ohler and Cummins (1942) had already shown that the epidermal ridges of females are 10 to 13% narrower than those of males. However, that was mainly based on an analysis of all ten fingers and palm prints. In the context of marks recovered during forensic investigations, the information will be drastically reduced, very often to one partial finger or palm mark that could potentially show a general pattern, ridge count(s) between core and delta(s), or ridge widths. Whether it is possible to infer the gender of the donor based on the ridge widths observed in a single mark is the subject of recent research efforts that we have condensed in the following section.

Acree (1999) paved the way for a series of data acquisition efforts that are summarized in Appendix A. All the counts were carried out diagonally in a square measuring 5 mm × 5 mm, thus obtaining the number of ridges per 25 mm^2. The positioning of the square on the print may differ between studies as well as the type of inking process used (rolled or plain impressions). Many studies have followed the approach of Acree and are summarized in Appendix A. Two studies (Gutiérrez-Redomero et al. 2008; Krishan et al. 2013) also showed that the effect of gender is observed mainly in the sample areas above the core, and it differs between the ulnar and the radial side. The area below the core did not permit a distinction between male and female prints. There is a slight tendency for the density to increase as we move from the thumb to the little finger. Appendix A is focused on fingerprints, but data in relation to palms have been published showing similar trends (Gutiérrez-Redomero and Alonso-Rodríguez 2013).

The question then becomes, "Do these data assist fingerprint practitioners in determining the gender of the donor?" To some degree the answer is yes, but the strength of support provided based on ridge density is rather modest once we account for the uncertainty in the determination of the ridge density in marks. The LRs will typically lie between 1/10 and 10 in favor of a male depending on the ridge density. On the website associated with the book, the reader will find several Bayesian networks constructed with the published data discussed earlier. It has also been shown that males from different geographical origins can be differentiated using ridge density (Gutiérrez-Redomero et al. 2013a,b). The strength of the indication in terms of LRs remains low (mainly between 1/20 and 20 as orders of magnitude). In both cases, we fear that such information may bring more risks than benefits to an investigation, especially if it is reported without all the appropriate caveats.

Finally, it is of interest to indicate some relationship between blood groups (ABO and Rh) and fingerprint patterns (Rastogi and Pillai 2010; Fayrouz et al. 2012; Eboh 2013; Raloti et al. 2013; Deopa et al. 2014; Ekanem et al. 2014). To our knowledge, the use of such data to provide investigative leads in operational casework has never been reported.

2.3 COMPARISON

The analysis phase being complete, it is at this stage only that the print(s) should become available to the examiner. We intentionally leave aside the use of AFIS systems that may help to select a potential print (or a set of prints) to be compared against the mark. Here, we concentrate on the situation where a print is put forward as potentially sharing the same source as the mark.

Normally prints, taken under controlled conditions, should be legible; however, practice has shown that they can also suffer from artifacts that make them complex (in a very similar way as for marks). Inked prints can be smudged, over-inked, illegible, taken with excessive pressure, etc. Electronic digital capture systems (using livescan) can also have their own types of distortion artifacts such as stitching misalignment or ghost images [see the case example by Doak (2010)]. Hence, a detailed analysis of the print itself may be required before embarking on the comparison stage. Generally, if the examiner is not satisfied with the quality of the prints then a request for additional exemplars should be made.

Basically, the comparison process is an iterative comparison, side-by-side, between the unknown mark and a known print, focusing successively on level 1, level 2, and level 3 features (when they have been identified in the mark), and taking into account the tolerances dictated by the quality of the mark. It is briefly detailed by SWGFAST (2013a) and the Expert Working Group on Human Factors in Latent Print Analysis (2012).

As the clarity of the unknown mark is generally inferior to the quality of the known print, when both images are compared (especially when looking at the print then at the mark), our suggestive brain tends to compensate for any differences. Ashbaugh reiterates the capacity of our brain to reconstruct poor-quality images based on our prior representation of reality (Ashbaugh 1991a). Vulnerabilities in perceptual tasks are well-known and have received healthy renewed attention, with cognitive research in forensic science and, in particular, in the field of fingerprint examinations (Busey and Dror 2011). This phenomenon may lead an examiner to believe that some features are concordant between a mark and a print, whereas their visibility can only be ascertained in the print and not in the mark. Knowledge of the known material may provide the examiner with expectations that may distort their judgment on the visibility of features in the mark, leading to inappropriate, expectation-led observations (Nordby 1992). This danger of a reverse reasoning (from the print to the mark and not from the mark to the print) was identified as one of the causes of misidentification in the Mayfield case (United States Department of Justice and Office of the Inspector General—Oversight and Review Division 2006) and the McKie case (Campbell 2011).

To ensure maximum objectivity during the comparison process, the examiner should avoid any prior knowledge of the known print under examination. For that reason, prior completion of the analysis stage is essential; the comparison process should, in theory, be focused primarily on features that have been identified previously, during the independent assessment of the mark. In any case, the comparison should always begin with an observed feature in the mark that serves as a control measure to be tested against the known print. The comparison process should be unidirectional from the mark to the print. Once the print is available, it is not rare that features overlooked during the analysis are now decipherable/visible on the mark. Some practitioners will not use these features, while others will account for them. What is important, in our opinion, is that there should be a possibility to distinguish which features were seen in analysis and which features have benefited from knowledge of the print. The associated documentation should reflect this. GYRO or PiAnoS offer this possibility with color coding.

The process logically flows from general to particular; hence, starting with considerations regarding level 1 features before moving to level 2 and level 3 features. We emphasize that level 2 features cannot be located without elements of a flow of ridges (level 1) and level 3 cannot really be considered without the help of either level 1 or level 2 features. For example, there is little hope conducting a search based on pores only, without any other anchoring features of level 1 or 2.

The process begins with the search on the print for a potential correspondence of features observed and documented previously on the mark. During analysis, clues indicating the anatomical area of interest, the hand or specific finger numbers have been gathered. This information will facilitate and prioritize the search of a potential correspondence on the papillary surface. The examiner will also pay attention to any group of minutiæ or any other configuration (generally of level 2 features) that may serve as a target to search for in the print. A "target group" is typically a cluster of easily recognizable minutiæ or some other distinctive feature, such as a scar, pattern of creases, etc. A target selected close to well-identified level 1 features (such as the core or the delta) to anchor the search makes the process easier. It is advised to choose targets in areas of the friction ridge skin that are less prone to distortion or away from the core (even though their clarity may be outstanding). To help memorization and the search process, the target can be drawn in different orientations. It is then searched on the print giving due consideration to the tolerances defined in the analysis phase.

If the target group is not found on the print, often a second (or a third) target group is selected and searched. The search will continue until the examiner has exhausted all possible searches or is sufficiently satisfied that the printed area of friction skin corresponding to the mark, within tolerance, is not present.

If a corresponding target is found with corresponding relative position, orientation and length of the ridges, the comparative procedure is pursued, adding into the process any new feature observed in the mark. This iterative process is carried out until all ridges visible in the mark have been examined and compared. It is strongly advised to comparatively run ridges (establish the path taken by each friction ridge) and furrows. This means that the examiner shall not only pinpoint minutiæ (or level 2 features), but is also checking that the ridges and valleys are compared in terms of sequence and lengths. During that iterative process, all available areas of the mark should be compared at the various levels identified and within the tolerances defined during the analysis. Note that recent publications are offering computer-assisted methods to raise an alarm, when the pairing of minutiæ is offset compared to expectations. This is based on the expectations of distortion in a known source (Comber 2012; Kalka and Hicklin 2014). These tools are very welcome additions to warn the examiner of potential problems and invite a deeper assessment of proposed minutiæ pairings (or as an additional quality control measure).

The documentation of the comparison process has the same importance as the documentation of the analysis phase. We repeat again that it is an absolute requirement. The extent of documentation can be a function of the quality of the mark, but evidence of what features have been considered should be available for peer review. This recommendation goes further than what SWGFAST (2010) is requiring. There is a widely accepted view among fingerprint examiners that a legible copy of the mark and the print on file is sufficient to meet the documentation requirement, because it allows another examiner to reprocess the case. We do not subscribe to that view for the reasons expressed earlier for the documentation of the analysis phase. As soon as we realize that examiners may vary in their conclusions following the examination of the same mark and print (see Section 2.4.4), the argument that a legible image is sufficient documentation becomes moot.

When the conclusions reached by experts are disputed, the only way to explore the underpinning reasons for the difference of opinions is to go back to the features that were used by the various experts. Unfortunately, when no contemporaneous notes have been taken (of the features actually used), documentation and rationalization is usually prepared upon request during post-hoc inquiries and is unlikely to be insightful or accurate in terms of the examiner's view at the time of the examination. The dispute between experts investigated during the Fingerprint Inquiry in Scotland is a prime example of that difficulty (Champod 2009a). In the final report of that inquiry, Sir Anthony Campbell recommended that the examiner should always take notes at each stage of ACE-V when they are examining marks that they consider to be complex (Campbell 2011) and these notes will include (recommendation 52):

> The characteristics taken into account at the comparison stage including their types and sequence in mark and print; any revision to the initial analysis made at the comparison stage; any differences observed at the comparison stage; the explanation for any differences; any third level detail relied upon in arriving at the conclusion.

The introduction of levels of complexity is a way to reduce the burden of documentation, when it is felt unnecessary. It is acknowledged that, when the mark offers high clarity and quantity of features, it will "speak by itself" and even a layperson will have no difficulty at discerning the features in the mark. Complex marks, on the other hand, will need expertise to be appropriately understood. And that applies, by extension, to the print that may also be "complex" and difficult to read. The difficulty is to design appropriate mechanisms to make the distinction between complex and non-complex comparisons. This triage should not wait for the comparison stage but should have been dealt with in the analysis stage (and the potential analysis of the print if it is of dubious quality).

FIGURE 2.21　Annotation of the correspondence between features in the mark (11 minutiæ marked in correspondence) and features in the print. Features highlighted in red on the mark were observed during the analysis phase. In yellow, three additional minutiæ were added after being observed with the benefit of the print.

Documenting cases when features fall within tolerances is relatively easy and dedicated tools such as PiAnoS are available to examiners (Figure 2.21). Documentation should go beyond minutiæ and cover the complete spectrum of fingerprint features. Differences in appearance should also be indicated.

When the features in the mark are not found in the print or vice versa, the documentation of this finding can at times be more difficult and written notes may suffice, for example: "the general pattern of the mark is a double loop that differs from the arch pattern of the print" or "the target group identified in the analysis of the mark has not been found in the inked prints available."

In this section, we have left the aforementioned comparison process at the stage of information gathered during the comparison. The evaluation of these findings has been reserved for the next stage: the evaluation stage. However, such a distinction may give the misleading impression that the comparison stage can be separated from the evaluation stage. The ACE-V acronym tends also to suggest such a clear-cut distinction between the phases. In reality, the examiner will evaluate on an ongoing basis as they collect information from the comparison stage. An exclusion decision may take place quite early in the comparison process and the examiner will stop the comparison without considering all three levels of detail. For this chapter, both stages have been distinguished to help the structure of the arguments, but both comparison and evaluation are typically conducted simultaneously. This is why Langenburg (2012), in his treatment of the comparison phase, added the examiner's judgments on reproducibility (linked to tolerances) and specificity. We treat these in the evaluation phase.

2.4　EVALUATION

2.4.1　THE WEIGHT TO BE ASSIGNED TO THE OBSERVATIONS

During the comparison between a mark and a print, the examiner faces a set of observations from which an inference concerning the identity of source must be drawn. An exclusion decision logically follows when discrepancies are observed that cannot be explained other than by the hypothesis of different sources. Such discrepancies can be observed at any level of the comparison between the mark and the print. In theory, one significant unexplainable difference is enough for the examiner to declare an exclusion, irrespective of the number of concordances that have been revealed before the difference is noted. In practice, the difficulty lies in defining what a "significant difference" actually is (Thornton 1977). We could define "significant" as being a clear difference that cannot be readily explained other than by a conclusion that the print and mark are from different sources. But it is a circular definition: Is it "significant" if one can cannot resolve it by another explanation than a different source or do we conclude to an exclusion because of the "significant" difference? To qualify a difference as a significant difference is sometimes difficult and, when concordant features have already been observed up to that point, it can be tempting to invoke obscure mechanisms to explain away the differing observations. The decision is even made more difficult because of a few anecdotal cases where differences (such as the observation of an additional full ridge on the mark compared to the print) were observed in an area qualified as reliable or of high quality during the analysis. To our knowledge, these cases often involved thin substrates or foils than can be folded or wrapped around the finger. The mechanical process of leaving a mark may be very complex and lead to the observation of differences that do not find easy explanation even after a thorough analysis. Unfortunately, the number of documented case reports discussing the assessment of differences in a comparison is limited (Puri 1962, 1964; Ferguson 1992). It is only recently that the issue has received more attention (Ray and Dechant 2013). The McKie case is again a good example of the type of issues that may arise. The experts who concluded that the mark at the scene had not been left by the left thumb of Shirley McKie were adamant in claiming that the observed differences were discrepancies, sufficient alone to conclude to an exclusion. On the other side, the experts who supported the identification all maintained that the differences could be reconciled by virtue of deposition mechanisms (multiple touches, movement of the finger at deposition, etc.). Examples of extreme differences—where common source was not disputed—have been presented to justify this approach, such as in the testimony of Leadbetter (2009).

The terms used to discuss differences have varied over the years and can cause confusion (Leo 1998). The terminology is now more or less settled (SWGFAST 2013b). *Dissimilarities* are differences in appearance between two compared friction ridge areas from the same source, whereas *discrepancy* is the observation of friction ridge detail in one impression that does not exist in the corresponding area of another impression. In the United Kingdom, the term *disagreement* is also used for discrepancy and the term *explainable difference* for dissimilarity (Forensic Science Regulator 2015a).

A discrepancy is then a "significant" difference and arises when the compared features are declared to be "out of tolerance" for the examiner, tolerances as defined during the analysis. This ability to distinguish between dissimilarity (compatible to some degree with a common source) and discrepancy (meaning almost *de facto* different sources) is essential and relies mainly on the examiner's experience. The link to the concept of reproducibility is evident. The difference in the comparison phase is that a set of prints from a person of interest (POI) is provided. The first key question (see Section 2.1.1) then becomes (with the *c* here referring to the comparison phase):

$Q1_c$ How probable is it to observe the features in the mark and in the submitted print in correspondence, meaning within tolerances, if these have come from the same source?

When put into this probabilistic framework, it is easier to see that if the assignment of this probability is 0 then it means that significant differences have been highlighted and they are discrepancies. If the probability is 0, an exclusion of common source is the obvious deductive conclusion as long as the set of prints represents all the friction ridges of the person of interest. When the probability moves above 0, the examiner envisages some mechanisms in the deposition of the mark or the print that could lead to the observed features (and their differences), then the exclusion is no longer trivial and the differences must qualify as dissimilarities. Exclusion decisions can then occur when, for example, the differences at level 1 or level 2 are unambiguous thanks to a mark of excellent clarity.

In these cases, the expert may assign a probability of 0 to the first question ($Q1_c$). As soon as the mark lacks clarity, and distortion induces possible differences at all levels, the assessment is much more difficult and can no longer be clear-cut. In reality, there is a continuum in the assignment of that probability; it lies between 0 and 1. By explaining a difference—by qualifying it as a dissimilarity rather than a discrepancy—does not set the probability of the observations to 1, but simply sets it above 0. This is a critical concept that is often overlooked by examiners. When the examiner has resolved a difference as being a dissimilarity (as opposed to a discrepancy), there is a tendency to forget that the probability associated to the first question was not 1 and this should impact on the final assessment. The misattribution in the case of Mayfield (United States Department of Justice and Office of the Inspector General—Oversight and Review Division 2006) is a good example of the associated risks. When true discrepancies are erroneously justified by distortion and thereby dismissed, the error in source attribution can be the result. Potentially explained differences do not make them "expected observations"; they may still be true discrepancies!

In our case (referring back to Figure 2.21), our assignment of the probability in response to question $Q1_c$ is high. By high we mean 0.9. We had assigned low tolerances in the analysis phase—the mark shows a high-quality upper left area without signs of distortion—and the agreement with the features in the print is what was expected if that mark had been left by the same individual as the source of the print. Further evidence of this high reproducibility could be gained from the inspection of the plain impression (or other prints of that finger) on the fingerprint card(s). This probability will not be found in any structured or published statistical research or (for the time being) using any statistical model. It reflects our informed judgment based on our experience and the objective comparison process undertaken. The trust that the reader may give to our assignment derives from the strict separation between the analysis phase and the comparison phase. The value 0.9 translates our personal probability for these observations. As such, it is a *subjective* probability as we have defined before. In the section dealing with the analysis, we already touched upon the studies (albeit limited) that may assist the examiner in the above probabilistic assessment. In a specific case, though, an ideal way of gathering reliable experience for interpreting differences is through the setting up of controlled experiments where marks and prints from the putative donor are deposited and detected under the conditions set by the case circumstances. In the dispute regarding the identification of mark Y7 to the thumbprint of Shirley McKie, the crux of the matter was, as we have discussed before, in relation to the interpretation of differences. In our view, only empirical experiments can move the argument beyond a battle of expert opinions.

The above discussion has considered the main factors driving toward an exclusion (associated with question $Q1_c$); we should now move to the critical factor that will drive toward an identification, with this being the *specificity* of the corresponding features. To put the discussion into context, please refer again to the case shown in Figure 2.21 where a correspondence is illustrated between the mark and the print.

Considerable confusion exists among laymen, indeed also among fingerprint examiners, on the use of words such as *match, unique, identical, same,* and *identity.* Although the phrase "all fingerprints are unique" has been used to justify fingerprint identification opinions, it is no more than a statement of the obvious. Every entity is unique; no two entities can be "identical" to each other because an entity can only be identical to itself. Thus, to say that "this mark and this print are identical to each other" is to invoke a profound misconception; the two might be indistinguishable, but they cannot be identical. In turn, the notion of "indistinguishability" is intimately related to the quantity and quality of detail that has been observed. This leads to distinguishing between the source variability derived from good-quality prints and the expressed variability in the mark, which can be partial, distorted, or blurred (Stoney 1989). Hence, once the examiner is confident that they cannot exclude, the only question that needs to be addressed is simply:

$Q2_c$ What is the probability of observing the features in the mark (given their tolerances) if the mark originates from an unknown individual?

If the ratio is calculated between the two probabilities associated with $Q1_c$ and $Q2_c$, we obtain what is called a likelihood ratio (LR). $Q1_c$ becomes the *numerator* question and $Q2_c$ becomes the *denominator* question. Formally, it can be written as:

$$LR = \frac{Pr\left(x, y|H_p, K\right)}{Pr\left(x, y|H_d, K\right)} = \frac{Pr\left(E|H_p, K\right)}{Pr\left(E|H_d, K\right)}$$

where

x, y stands for the elements or features observed in the mark (y) and in the print (x), respectively, and shared between the mark and the print (in agreement and with, possibly, some dissimilarities). It is convenient for the rest of the book to use a single letter (E) to refer to (x, y). It is customary to view E, for evidence, as the observations made following the comparison between the mark and the print.

H_p is the proposition generally put forward by the prosecution that the mark has been left by the POI at the source of the print.

H_d is the proposition generally put forward by the defense that the mark has been left by an unknown individual (i.e., not the POI).

K is the background knowledge and information that will condition the probabilistic assignment. It can be, for example, knowledge regarding the anatomical area considered, the relevant population considered and it size, or the expert knowledge of the examiner.

In a nutshell, the numerator is the probability of the observed features if the mark is from the POI, while the denominator is the probability of the observed features if the mark is from a different source. When viewed as a ratio, the strength of the observations is conveyed not only by the response to one or the other of the key questions, but by a balanced assessment of both. The numerator of the ratio invites the examiner to consider the within-source variations, whereas the denominator of the ratio is more focused on between-source variations. Having equal attention on both sides of the problem is the key to a fair and balanced assessment. This echoes the early call from Bertillon (1912) that the examiner should, in fact, be as focused on dissimilarities as on concordances, and not be driven by the correspondences while ignoring or explaining away any differences. The LR is especially suitable for assessing the contribution of forensic findings. It applies regardless of the type of forensic evidence considered and has been put at the core of evaluative reporting in forensic science (Willis 2015). The range of values for the LR is between 0 and infinity. A value of 1 indicates that the forensic findings are equally likely under either proposition and they do not help the case in one direction or the other. A value of 10,000, as an example, means that the forensic finding provides very strong support for the prosecution proposition (same source) as opposed to its alternative (the defense proposition—different sources). A value below 1 will strengthen the case in favor of the view that the mark is from a different source than the POI. The special case of exclusion is when the numerator of the LR is equal to 0, making the LR also equal to 0. Hence, the value of forensic findings is essentially a relative and conditional measure that helps move a case in one direction or the other depending on the magnitude of the LR. The explicit formalization of the problem in the form of a LR is not new in the area of fingerprinting and can be traced back to Stoney (1985). The LR will set the generic framework for all subsequent discussion regarding the weight to be given to the observations. It also plays a critical role in the decision processes that will conclude the evaluation phase.

We now turn back to the assignment of the denominator of the LR (i.e., question $Q2_c$). It closely relates to the specificity of the features observed at the various levels, taking into account the tolerance initially set during the analysis of the mark. At this point, the print is irrelevant. Under the defense perspective, an unknown individual left the mark (and it is not the POI). Hence, the observations relate solely to those observations made on the mark. The specificity of the mark becomes the relevant question, not the specificity of the print. This distinction is essential in the identification process. Conceptually, the tolerances from the analysis phase will have set some sort of "match" window and the examiner sought an assignment for the probability that a print will fall within that window of correspondence. The size of this window is intrinsically linked to the clarity of the features.

In the literature, specificity was often treated by distinguishing "class" characteristics from "individual" characteristics. Level 1 features would normally be referred to as class characteristics, whereas levels 2 and 3 deal with "individual" characteristics. That classification had a direct correlation with the subsequent decisions: only comparisons involving "individual" characteristics could lead to an identification conclusion. Unfortunately, the problem of specificity is more complex than this simple dichotomy. This distinction between "class" and "individual" characteristics is just a convenient, oversimplified way of describing specificity. Specificity is a measure on a continuum (probabilities range from 0 to 1, without steps) that can hardly be reduced to two categories without more nuances. The term *individual characteristic* is particularly misleading, as a concordance of one minutia (leaving aside any consideration of level 3 features) would hardly be considered as enough to identify. The problem with this binary categorization is that it encourages the examiner to disregard the complete spectrum of feature specificity that ranges from low to high. It is proposed that specificity at each feature level be studied without any preconceived classification of its identification capability by itself. Indeed, nothing should prevent a specific general pattern—such as, for example, an arch with continuous ridges from one side to the other (without any minutiæ)—from being considered as extremely selective, since no such pattern has been observed to date.

More formally, if we decompose the observations using the three levels of detail, with $E = (e_1, e_2,$ and $e_3)$ representing, respectively, the elements observed in levels 1, 2, and 3 features, we are looking for the following joint probability:

$$Pr(E|H_d, K) = Pr(e_1, e_2, e_3|H_d, K)$$

What we mean here is the probability of jointly observing the three levels of features if an unknown person is at the source of the mark (H_d). Making such a combined assignment is always difficult. Hence, instead of attempting to assign the joint probability $Pr(e_1, e_2, e_3|H_d, K)$, it is efficient to focus on each level, one after the other, taking advantage of the law of conditional probabilities. This formally leads to

$$Pr(E|H_d, K) = Pr(e_1, e_2, e_3|H_d, K)$$
$$= Pr(e_1|H_d, K)Pr(e_2|e_1, H_d, K)Pr(e_3|e_1, e_2, H_d, K)$$

We hence need to assign the three probabilities as follows:

$Pr(e_1|H_d, K)$ The probability of observing the level 1 feature on the mark if H_d is true. In other words, to what extent do we expect to see these elements within a population (other than the POI)? That will be informed by data related to the specificity of level 1 features.

$Pr(e_2|e_1, H_d, K)$ The probability of observing the set of level 2 features (often minutiæ) if H_d is true, but conditional on the level 1 features observed. That will be informed by data related to the specificity of level 2 features, but keeping in mind the conditioning by e_1. This allows the capturing of effects such as pattern force or known dependencies between minutiæ and general pattern.

$Pr(e_3|e_1, e_2, H_d, K)$ The probability of observing the set of level 3 features if H_d is true, but conditional on the level 1 and level 2 features observed. That will be informed by data related to the specificity of level 3 features, but keeping in mind the conditioning by e_1 and e_2. It means that the strength of level 3 features has to be assessed in conjunction with level 1 and level 2 features.

Table 2.4 defines specificity for the three levels of friction ridge skin features and the sources of data accessible to an examiner to assist them in the assignment of probabilities. Even if the

TABLE 2.4

Specificity of the Three Levels of Friction Ridge Skin Features

Level	Specificity
Level 1	The contribution of the general pattern (and associated measures such as ridge counting or ridge tracing) as a means of differentiation is well known through widespread experience with fingerprint classification systems. Extensive statistical data can be obtained from these collections as shown previously in this chapter. The reader will benefit from the Bayesian network based on the NCIC data (Appendix A) to assign a probability to any combination of features associated with general patterns on fingers. Here, the inference will go from the causes to the effects, the reverse compared to the investigative use presented before. Data on palmar level 1 features have been published by Tietze and Witthuhn (2001) and Ray (2012). The authors provide extensive statistical data on the relative frequencies of defined general patterns.
Level 2	The specificity of level 2 features, especially the specificity of minutiae configurations, was the main argument in favor of the adoption of fingerprinting as a mean of personal identification (over Bertillon's anthropometry) at the turn of the nineteenth Century. Galton was probably the first to apply statistical analysis to minutiae (Galton 1892; Stigler 1995). Most past studies have been reviewed by Stoney (2001), Neumann (2012) and Abraham et al. (2013). Two other sources have covered previous work as well (Langenburg 2011; Expert Working Group on Human Factors in Latent Print Analysis 2012). We devote a specific section later in this chapter to the statistical models used to assign a probabilistic value to a configuration of minutiae (see Section 2.7). At this point of the discussion, we draw very selectively the attention of the reader to data that are readily available to examiners in the current mode of operation. One set of studies allows for an appreciation of the relative contribution of minutiae. As proposed by Kingston (1970), such studies provide valuable data to calibrate the subjective judgments of experts concerning the rarity of given fingerprint features. Osterburg and Bloomington (1964) explored the variations that can be observed between examiners in assessing the relative frequencies of various types of minutiae. Such variations have to be minimized, and statistical surveys provide an excellent baseline that help with examiner calibration. Many authors have studied the specificity of individual level 2 features. The most extensive studies are due to Champod and Margot (1996, 1997) (see Appendix B) and, more recently, to Gutiérrez-Redomero at al. (2007, 2011, 2012). However, these studies have limited applicability. They help to argue for the higher specificity of a given type of minutiae (e.g., a hook) compared to more basic types (e.g., a ridge ending). However, they are not adequate to assess the specificity of a configuration of minutiae, which requires the capturing of dependencies between minutiae. For configurations of minutiae (i.e., not considered individually but jointly), the best study to consult is the recent work by Neumann et al. (2012). Based on a very extensive dataset and using a model that limits the number of underlying assumptions, they computed LRs for a series of marks ranging from 3 to 12 minutiae. The graph reproduced in Figure 2.22 is helpful here.

(Continued)

TABLE 2.4 (Continued)
Specificity of the Three Levels of Friction Ridge Skin Features

Level	Specificity
Level 3	The extreme specificity of pore forms and pore relative positions was first postulated by Locard (1912a,b, 1913), who later received a very favorable echo in the United States (Wilder and Wentworth 1932). The possibility of using edge structures to discriminate between fingerprints was proposed by Chatterjee and Hague (1988) but was also mentioned by Locard. All related aspects were initially merged under the term *ridgeology* by Ashbaugh (1982b), but it is fair to say that ridgeology has a much wider mandate, covering all aspects of the identification process without being restricted to level 3 features. Experience is the first basis for support of the claimed specificity of these features. Additional knowledge comes from morphogenesis data (see Chapter 1) and a number of statistical studies. Ashbaugh (1982a) proposed a model to express pore variability, and this model has been refined by Stosz, Roddy, and coworkers (Stosz and Alyea 1994; Roddy and Stosz 1997, 1999). However, these models relied on questionable independence assumptions (Parsons et al. 2008); but, more importantly, they did not take into account the potential lack of reproducibility of these features from one impression to the next. The paper by Parsons et al. (2008) is an exception to this. The latest study on the contribution of pores (Anthonioz and Champod 2014) showed that they do bring some weight to a comparison when observed in concordance (in conjunction with level 2 features), but the magnitude of the LRs remains modest (a few hundreds when H_p is true). A descriptive analysis of pores based on the inked prints on glass slides of 115 females and 115 males is given by Nagesh et al. (2011). They showed that the number of pores per centimeter of friction ridge ranged from 5 to 16.3 (mean of 8.40 ± 2.01) in males and 5.3 to 16 (mean of 8.83 ± 2.09) in females. The closed type of pores is more frequent than pores that were open on the side of the ridges. The pores opening on both sides are the less frequent type (7%). Sizes range from 66 to 297 μm, with the largest pores being the less frequent (roughly 40% below 100 μm, 44% between 100 and 200 μm, and 16% only above 200 μm). The circular shape amounts to about 50% of the pores, 20% are oval, the rest taking other shape categories. These data are in line with other research (Bindra et al. 2000; Singh and Sachdeva 2012). To our knowledge, only one study looked at edges (as well as pores) on prints taken from 100 individuals on different types of papers (Khan 2011), but the study remains essentially qualitative and descriptive. Overall, we must recognize that, at present, the amount of structured data relative to pores and edge structures is limited. Even though some practitioners have relied heavily on these features in some cases [we refer to the anecdotal cases presented in (Barclay 1991, 1997; Jorgensen 1997; Clegg 1998; Reneau 2003)], we invite the reader to adopt a very cautious approach to giving value to these features except as a form of supportive information.

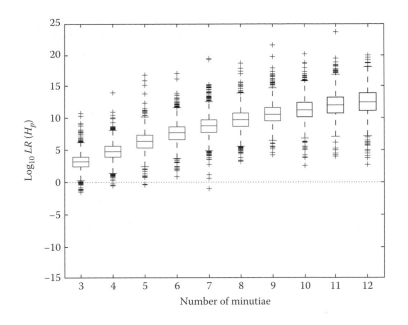

FIGURE 2.22 Magnitude of the likelihood ratios obtained as a function of an increasing number of matching minutiæ. (From Neumann, C. et al., *J. R. Stat. Soc.*, 175, 371, 2012 (with discussion). with permission.)

definition of data is broad and can incorporate the experience of the examiner, we tend to give precedence to published data (see e.g. Figure 2.22) as they help to calibrate and shape assignments by an examiner.

We can now return to the evaluation process with an awareness of the specificity of the features considered during a comparison. Referring to the case in question (Figure 2.21), we may assign our probability to the denominator of the LR in this case. The observations include seven corresponding minutiæ in the delta that are all pointing toward the delta. The general pattern cannot be ascertained, but we can readily exclude a left loop, arches, and tented arches. The additional three minutiæ marked in correspondence in yellow were seen only following comparison; hence, their weight will be reduced. There is no contribution of level 3 features apart from the wider furrows on the left of the delta. The denominator of the LR is in the order of 1/100,000. The data from Neumann et al. (2012) have been used here, but a lower value has been assigned given the influence of the pattern of the delta. Given our value of 0.9 for the numerator, a LR of 90,000 is our fair and reasonable assignment (even if, looking at the data of Neumann et al., the denominator may reasonably range from 1/70,000 to 1/130,000, the order of magnitude of the LR will remain well above 50,000 with very strong support for the proposition that the print from the POI and the mark are from the same source). If, based on the same set of features, another examiner had assigned a widely different order of magnitude (say 1/1000) to the denominator probability (compared to the value used here of 1/100,000), they will be required to explain the underpinning knowledge that would support such a different assignment. Subjective probabilities do not release the expert from the obligation of transparency and rationalization.

2.4.2 Decisions Reached Following Evaluation

The conclusions reached by fingerprint examiners came under renewed attention after the publication of the NRC report that, among other critical points, observed that experts testify in a language of absolute certainty (National Research Council 2009). The report, quoting Mnookin (2008), invites experts to adopt more modest claims about the meaning and significance of their findings. A review of the debate and positions since the release of the NRC report has been published by Champod (2015).

What is clear, though, coming from the scholarly literature, is that the days where invoking "uniqueness" as the main (if not the only) supporting argument for an individualization conclusion are over. This led the IAI to remove or modify rules that had seemed to be engraved in stone and to start considering fingerprint evidence in a more probabilistic way. It can be viewed as a return to the roots of fingerprint evidence as expressed by pioneers such as Locard (1914) and Heindl (1927).

The concept of a LR, as detailed earlier, can be integrated into the decision process of the expert. This will take advantage of the fundamental contribution of Biedermann et al. (2008, 2013) on the topic of decision theory in forensic science (Taroni et al. 2014) and, in particular, for identification issues. Decision theory is logical and the only way to understand and ultimately justify current practices. Decisions are made in the face of uncertainty.

2.4.2.1 Identification

In the fingerprint field, the term *identification* is often used synonymously with *individualization*. It represents a statement akin to certainty that a particular mark was made by the friction ridge skin of a particular person. This is the sense in which we will use the word *identification* throughout this book. Technically identification refers to the assignment of an entity to a specific group or label, whereas individualization represents the special case of identification when the group is of size 1. Individualization is what distinguishes forensic science from other scientific endeavors according to Kirk (1963). Tuthill and George (2002, p. 25) defined individualization as follows:

> The individualization of an impression is established by finding agreement of corresponding individual characteristics of such number and significance as to preclude the possibility (or probability) of their having occurred by mere coincidence, and establishing that there are no differences that cannot be accounted for.

We take two elements from this definition: (1) The whole process is described as probabilistic and (2) the reference population that the examiner invokes with individualization is the Earth's population. It has been called the Earth population paradigm (Champod 2009b). In that Earth population context, the word "individualization" is certainly appropriate. Kaye (2009) refers to "universal individualization" relative to the entire world. But identification could also be made without referring to the Earth's population, referring instead to a smaller subset, for example, the members of a country, a city, or a community. In that context, Kaye talks about "local individualization" (relative to a proper subset). This distinction between "local" and "global" was used in two cases [*State v. Hull*, (2008) No. 48-CR-07-2336 (Minn. D. Ct. Cty. of Mille Lacs), and *State v. Doe*, (2010) Case No 200924231 (Cir. Ct. Ore. Lane Cty)], where the examiners reserved the term "individualization" for the global case and the term "identification" for the local case. In these cases, the examiners did not testify to a global individualization (meaning to the exclusion of all others), but to a local identification where the mark and the print are considered in the context of a restricted pool of potential donors. Later in this chapter, we will show what is at stake in terms of evidential strength when an examiner is seeking global individualization and the difference it makes when a local individualization decision is made. It is intuitively obvious that more evidential power is required to reach global individualization. In fact, we will show that the required evidential power is so great that we would recommend avoiding using the term "individualization."

When a fingerprint expert concludes to an identification, he or she reaches a decision threshold. However, this threshold is highly subjective, whether the criterion is a minimum number of concordant minutiæ or, in addition to this quantitative element, qualitative factors are taken into account. As Ashbaugh (1999, p. 103) stated, "The opinion of individualization or identification is subjective." But, when it comes to the core issue of drawing inference from a comparison, the following is stated:

> Finding adequate friction ridge formation in sequence that one knows are specific details of the friction skin, and in the opinion of the friction ridge identification specialist that there is sufficient uniqueness within those details to eliminate all other possible donors in the world, is considered enough.

Here, we arrive at the crux of the matter. It is the expert who forms the opinion that there is "sufficient uniqueness … to eliminate all other possible donors in the world." Ashbaugh does not clarify how this inference is to be drawn. It has been argued that the decision process must be inductive as already rightly underlined by Kwan (1977), whose thesis is an essential contribution to forensic science. The expert is, however imprecisely, forming a view about the entire world when he cannot possibly have considered more than a subsample. The quotation from Ashbaugh, therefore, illustrates two points: (1) the opinion is based on inductive reasoning and must be probabilistic; and (2) the process by which the expert arrives at an opinion is ultimately obscure. The process relies undoubtedly on extensive and reliable experience, but this is not articulated. The point is that Ashbaugh evokes the need to eliminate all other possible donors in the world, but does not say how this can be done. Essentially, this is because it cannot be done. It cannot be done by scientific means but, even leaving science to one side, no one person can attain and retain comprehensive knowledge of the prints of every person in the world. The conclusion remains, as Stoney (1991) eloquently put it, "a leap of faith"; as such, it is ultimately obscure. Indeed, Stoney (1991, pp. 197–198) gave a very illustrative description of this process for fingerprint examination:

> Beginning with a reference point in one pattern, a corresponding point in a second pattern is sought. From this initial point the examiner then seeks neighboring details that correspond in their form, position and orientation. These features have an extreme variability, that is readily appreciated intuitively, and which becomes objectively obvious upon detailed study. When more and more corresponding features are found between two patterns, scientist and lay person alike become subjectively certain that the patterns could not possibly be duplicated by chance. What has happened here is somewhat analogous to a leap of faith. It is a jump, an extrapolation, based on the observation of highly variable traits among a few characteristics, and then considering the case of many characteristics. Duplication is inconceivable to the rational mind and we conclude that there is absolute identity. The leap, or extrapolation, occurs (in fingerprinting) without any statistical foundation, even for the initial process where the first few ridge details are compared.

The conclusion of certainty derives from the examiner's personal conviction that the chance of a correspondence within tolerances between the crime mark and an unknown person other than X is so small that it can be ignored. Effectively, the expert sets a personal threshold that rounds the probability assigned to the identification to 100%. This position appears, through custom and practice, to be acceptable to courts in all situations where statistical analyses are not possible: fingerprints, handwriting, toolmarks, footwear impressions, etc. The fingerprint expert's reasoning is based on the idea that the probability that another person would correspond the mark is so small that it can be discounted.

From 2002, through the crisis of the NRC report until today, the definition of individualization went from "excluding all others" to, now, a *decision* [a very detailed analysis is provided in Cole (2014)]. As we shall see, examiners have changed the wording of their conclusions to address voiced criticisms, but still believe that they can identify to the exclusion of all others and struggle to fully articulate their decision process.

Critical recommendations have also been instrumental to promote a rethinking of the meaning of the term individualization. Indeed, the conclusions had been historically draped with an aura of infallibility, describing a factual state of affairs. It is as if the probability component from Tuthill and George (2002) had vanished, with certainty being expressed by the examiner. We take the following two examples:

From the Expert Working Group on Human Factors in Latent Print Analysis: (2012):

> Recommendation 3.7: Because empirical evidence and statistical reasoning do not support a source attribution to the exclusion of all other individuals in the world, latent print examiners should not report or testify, directly or by implication, to a source attribution to the exclusion of all others in the world.

From the Fingerprint Inquiry report (Campbell 2011):

> Recommendation 1: Fingerprint evidence should be recognized as opinion evidence, not fact, and those involved in the criminal justice system need to assess it as such on its merits.

We also note an increasing tendency among courts, at least in the United States [case references are provided by Champod (2015)], to refrain from accepting fingerprint evidence as facts that can be expressed with 100% certainty or suggesting that the evidence alone is enabling the exclusion of all others in the world except the concerned individual. Legal scholars have echoed this call for more humble conclusions (Koehler and Saks 2010; Cole and Roberts 2012; Kaye 2013).

Two definitions taken from official bodies will set the scene for today's definition of individualization/identification:

1. SWGFAST (2013a) defines it as: Individualization is the decision by an examiner that there are sufficient features in agreement to conclude that two areas of friction ridge impressions originated from the same source. Individualization of an impression to one source is the decision that the likelihood the impression was made by another (different) source is so remote that it is considered as a practical impossibility.
2. The UK forensic science regulator (2015b, p. 16) defines it as: A practitioner term used to describe the mark as being attributed to a particular individual. There is sufficient quality and quantity of ridge flow, ridge characteristics, and/or detail in agreement with no unexplainable differences that in the opinion of the practitioner two areas of friction ridge detail were made by the same person.

SWGFAST (2013a) recently proposed the sufficiency graph that we have already discussed for analysis (Figure 2.7). It reflects the interplay between quality of the mark and quantity of minutiæ observed during the analysis of the mark, and its relation to the decision thresholds and levels of complexity based on a consensus of collective experience. The sufficiency graph is intended to illustrate the intellectual processes involved with the examination of friction ridge detail and the ensuing decisions. It illustrates thresholds wherein examiners should recognize the need for, and provide, enhanced documentation supporting their conclusions. Cases falling within the B and C areas of the graph will warrant identification with a certain degree of confidence given by the LR; however, for cases falling within A, no identification would be warranted.

Leaving the matter here would have two consequences. The first is that it leaves the decision process very obscure and ill-defined, hence offers no mechanism for scrutiny. As Sir Anthony Campbell indicated (2011 § 38.24): "What matters more than the choice of language (whether the witness says that he is "confident," "sure,' "certain" or "in no doubt") is the transparency of the opinion." The second is that it allows all conclusions to become just a matter of opinion. To cite Cole (2008, p. 110):

> To begin with, there is a sense in which "opinion" can become an all-encompassing shield that deflects all accountability.

The Expert Working Group on Human Factors in Latent Print Analysis (2012, p. 68) decomposed the steps taken by an examiner to reach a decision as follows: The examiner will (1) assign prior probabilities based on a perceived context and a perceived size of the relevant population of donors, (2) assign the weight to be assigned to the findings arising from the fingerprint examination, (3) update the probabilities to get the posterior probabilities and, finally, (4) make a decision considering the result of (3) and a weighted balance between benefits and costs associated with each decision. This is intimately linked with decision theory and we will delve deeper into it now. These four steps have been presented in a schematic diagram in Figure 2.23.

The purpose of Figure 2.23 is to highlight two main phases in the decision process by just reordering over time the four above-described steps. The first phase (*Phase A*) is concerned only with the assessment of the value to be assigned to the observations (E) made during the analysis of the mark and the following comparison with the print. It takes the form of the likelihood ratio after consideration of both reproducibility and specificity. The LR is not sufficient to decide whether

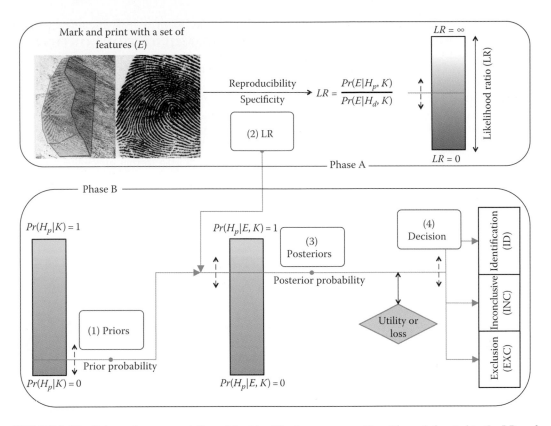

FIGURE 2.23 Schematic representation of the identification process with a *Phase A* devoted to the LR and a *Phase B* devoted to the decisions that follow.

or not the person of interest left the mark. Indeed, the LR just tells us how much more likely that proposition will be compared to its initial state but, without knowing how many individuals may be at the source, we cannot decide in the issue of source. In other words, the LR gives an informed magnitude of the value of the information, but the decision that follows (*Phase B*) is not independent from the case information. In that phase, the findings (and its associated weight) will be fitted into a framework pertaining to the case. It means two tasks: first to assign—and this is done completely implicitly—a *prior* probability to the proposition that the person of interest left the mark (H_p). That is indicated as $Pr(H_p|K)$ in the diagram. This probability is updated (in a proportional way) using the LR by the application of Bayes theorem (see Box 2.5). It gives the *posterior* probability of H_p, indicated by $Pr(H_p|E, K)$.

The value of $Pr(H_p|E, K)$ will generally not be 0 or 1 (otherwise, it would transform the decisions into simple deductions). So, there is a possibility of not having the right source. At that stage, the examiner needs to decide whether that probability $Pr(H_p|E, K)$ is high enough to make, for example, a decision of identification. Whether it will be considered high enough or not will not only depend on the posterior probability but also on the examiner's perception of the benefits or losses associated with the decision. We will call this generically the *utility* or *loss*. If the examiner decides on an identification, they will have reached that stage where they are happy to take the "leap of faith" as per Stoney (1991). The leap is taken because the probability of an error has reached a point where the benefits (utility) of a correct decision outweigh the losses associated with an error. This is, in broad terms, the basis of decision theory. The vertical double arrows in Figure 2.23 (<------->) illustrate the variability (either intra-examiner or inter-examiner) that can be expected in each of the steps in both phases. We have shown how examiners may vary in their

BOX 2.5   BAYES THEOREM APPLIED TO THE IDENTIFICATION CONTEXT

We aim here to show the mathematical relationship, through Bayes theorem, between the prior probability on H_p and the posterior probability on H_p given the knowledge of an additional finding (E) in the form of a correspondence between a fingermark and a fingerprint. Bayes theorem is an essential component of a logical approach to the interpretation of forensic evidence. A short introduction can be found in Champod and Evett (2009), with a much deeper coverage in the book by Aitken and Taroni (2004). Historically, the first application of Bayes theorem to the consideration of fingerprint evidence, in the format presented herein after, is due to Finkelstein and Fairley (1970).

Bayes theorem, in odds form, can be written as

$$\underbrace{\frac{Pr(H_p|E,K)}{Pr(H_d|E,K)}}_{posterior\ odds} = \underbrace{\frac{Pr(E|H_p,K)}{Pr(E|H_d,K)}}_{LR} \cdot \underbrace{\frac{Pr(H_p|K)}{Pr(H_d|K)}}_{prior\ odds}$$

$$posterior\ odds = LR \cdot prior\ odds$$

Note that, given H_p and H_d are here mutually exclusive and exhaustive, $Pr(H_d|K) = 1 - Pr(H_p|K)$.

Bayes theorem, in this form, simply states that the prior odds on an issue (H_p versus H_d) are increased or decreased by the likelihood ratio associated with the findings (E). What is called "prior" odds is the relative ratio of the probabilities on the propositions (H_p and H_d) as assigned by the decision-maker, meaning before the presentation of any scientific findings. These odds are assigned based on some prior knowledge (K) related to the case circumstances. For this reason, K appears in the formulæ after the conditioning bar (|). All indications on the right of the conditioning bar are known, whereas the probabilities refer to the uncertainties of the events shown before the conditioning bar. The "posterior" odds are the updated odds in favor of the propositions after hearing about the scientific findings (E); hence, its appearance now after the conditioning bar. The likelihood ratio (LR) follows the same definition as previously presented in the chapter. It represents the probabilities of the scientific findings assigned given H_p and H_d.

The key principle that we will explore further in this box is that there is a fundamental difference between the posterior odds and the LR. The LR refers to the probabilities associated with the findings (given the propositions), whereas the posterior odds refer to the probabilities associated with the propositions (given the findings). Confusing the two is a very easy logical error that is known as the prosecutor's fallacy (Thompson and Schumann 1987).

The decision-maker is dealing legitimately with the prior and posterior odds, whereas the forensic scientist provides guidance in the form of a LR. The tasks are associated thanks to Bayes theorem that specifies that the move from the prior odds to the posterior odds is by a simple multiplication by the LR.

An illustrative way to capture the process is to view the prior/posterior odds on an axis (from its minimum 0 to its maximum ∞), with progression along the axis being dictated by the magnitude of the LR. The stronger the LR in favor of one proposition, the more support it will provide for that proposition (by multiplication). But, without knowing the starting position on the axis, you cannot know where you will end up. The only information the LR is giving you is the distance that we will travel along that axis.

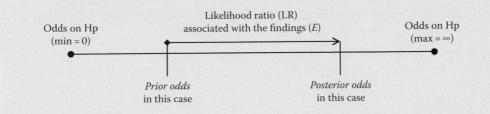

Example 1 (*low priors*): Assume that the LR associated with the fingerprint comparison amounts to a million (10^6) and the prior probability that the POI is at the source of the mark is low [$Pr(H_d|K) = 10^{-7}$] because the individual has been selected through an AFIS system holding 10 million individuals and nothing more suggests, at this stage, that the POI could be the donor. Then:

$$posterior\ odds = LR \cdot \frac{Pr(H_p|K)}{1 - Pr(H_d|K)} = 10^6 \cdot \frac{10^{-7}}{1 - 10^{-7}} = 1.000001$$

Hence, the posterior odds are almost odds of 1:1. It is counterintuitive at first, but keep in mind that we ask for the findings (*E*) to be able to compensate (to travel on our axis) from a very low prior probability (the starting point is very close to 0).

Prior odds are linked with probabilities using the following relationship:

$$Pr(H_p|K) = \frac{prior\ odds}{1 + prior\ odds}$$

$$Pr(H_p|K) = \frac{posterior\ odds}{1 + posterior\ odds}$$

Hence, in this example, the posterior probability $Pr(H_p|E, K)$ is then 0.50000025. Just above 50%. Here, the strength of the findings may not be enough to decide upon an identification.

Example 2 (*high priors*): Assume now that we are dealing with the context of a disaster victim identification case with a small plane holding 10 passengers. For one recovered body, a small fragment of friction ridge skin is compared against the fingerprints of one named individual who was on the list of passengers. A correspondence is found and a LR of a million (10^6) is associated with that comparison. In such a case, before considering the outcome of the fingerprint comparison, the prior probability that the person who gave the prints is also at the source of the fragment of friction ridge skin is much higher (say 1/10). Given the same evidence expressed by the LR, the odds that the person is really at the source of the fragment is now much different. Applying Bayes theorem, it gives:

$$posterior\ odds = LR \cdot \frac{Pr(H_p|K)}{1 - Pr(H_d|K)} = 10^6 \cdot \frac{1/10}{1 - 1/10} = 111111.11$$

This corresponds to a posterior probability $Pr(H_p|E, K)$ of 0.999991, which is a high probability of identity that may be enough for the trier of fact to decide on the identification. In this case, referring to our illustrative axis, we started very high in the odds; hence, the progression allowed by the LR results in a very high posterior probability.

Example 3 (Earth's population): Assume a total population of 7 billion (that amounts to about 70 billion fingers), If we accept that the posterior probability, $Pr(H_p|E, K)$ must be above a certain threshold value in order to declare an individualization, then it is possible to calculate the LR that must be considered to achieve such a preset value. If $Pr(H_p|E, K)$ is fixed at 0.9998—meaning "I want to be 99.98% sure of the individualization," then:

$$LR = \frac{posterior\ odds}{prior\ odds} = \frac{0.9998\,/\,(1-0.9998)}{\dfrac{1\,/\,70\cdot10^9}{1-\left(\dfrac{1}{70\cdot10^9}\right)}} = 3.499\cdot10^{14}$$

In other words, the strength of the findings to be able to compensate for a prior probability proportional to the size of the earth's population has to be enormous. Again, the principle is the same. If you start from extremely low prior odds, the strength that will be required from the findings to get close to certainty is very high.

assessment of the weight to be assigned to a mark during the analysis phase. In the comparison and evaluation phases, the same variability may occur. But the variability is not confined to the LR, but will also be expected for the prior probability and the utility or loss decision. It means that all decisions are personal and variations can be expected for a wide range of reasons, not all of them related to the mark and print under examination. Operationally speaking, it means that two examiners looking at the same mark and print may reach different conclusions because of potential differences in assessment of the mark and the print, and also other factors that may impact on the decision-making process. One way to reduce (but not eliminate) the variability between examiners would be to have them concentrate only on the LR and we will come to that recommendation and its impact on the reporting process later. For the time being, we will continue to explore the decision process.

A few examples are offered here to contextualize this decision process. On purpose, these are caricatures painted with a broad brush; however, we are sure that most examiners will have experienced these situations at one point or another in their careers.

A mark is collected at a scene and compared against a set of prints. All nine fingers of the tenprint card are excluded except for one of the prints. The mark and print are shown in Figure 2.24 without annotation.

Now a few scenarios, putting yourself in the mind of an examiner operating in a State agency in the United States. Some words of caution are essential here. The following examples are painted with a broad brush with the objective of having examiners realize the interplay between prior probabilities, utilities, and decisions. Some of the considerations that we make explicit may be completely subconscious. Examiners may not even realize that such factors interact and influence their decision-making. Our aim here is not to suggest that examiners should openly and consciously engage in considering these factors. In addition, at the end of this section, we will make very clear that contextual elements (not relevant to the actual examination of a mark and a print), such as the number of suspects or their credibility, have no place in fingerprint examination. We will define later a new division of labor where the experts concentrate solely on the strength of information that a comparison may bring and leave all other considerations to the fact finder. What we hope to show with these examples is that examiners have to take on an impossible role that is usurping the role of the fact finder.

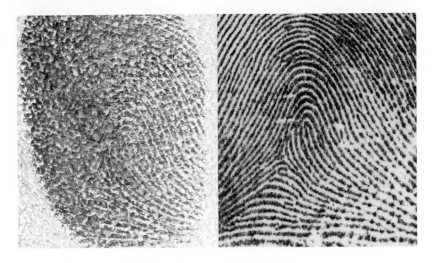

FIGURE 2.24 Case 13 taken from the study by Neumann et al. (2013).

1. You take the case on a Friday afternoon after a long week. You mark 8 minutiæ during the analysis phase that then fall in agreement within the tolerance with a print associated with a person of interest. Here, the weight of evidence is judged too low to warrant identification and so you concluded "inconclusive." Monday morning, your supervisor is asking you to have a fresh look on the case. Coming fresh to it, and following the ACE process, you end up with 12 minutiæ in agreement and conclude to an identification. A higher weight of evidence allowed you to reach this conclusion, because it is the best decision to make. In the implicit components of the first decision, you had not envisaged the entire earth's population as potential donors but a fairly large sized population (the size of the county, state or, at most, the country). The LR obtained led you to a high posterior probability but not high enough for you to take the risk of calling it an identification. You knew that if you miss the identification, the checker should detect it. If so, the consequence is fairly low unless it had occurred systematically over the last 6 months. On the other hand, you were cognizant of cases of close non-matches in these areas of friction ridge skin and know that a wrong identification would have detrimental consequences for your agency (and, perhaps, for your career). When you took that case again the following week, you not only had a tip from your supervisor that a checker may have a different view but, thanks to your new application of the ACE process, you obtained much more information in agreement. At this point, all things being equal, the LR is high enough to make the decision of identification.

2. Assume that the earlier 8 minutiæ in correspondence represent the total amount of information in agreement between the mark and the print. That mark is part of a series of marks found in association with a murder investigation. You already have attributed ten marks left on the same object to one individual whose prints have been submitted as the POI. You decide to individualize that mark. Here, the decision has been triggered because you implicitly assign a high prior probability (because of the other identified marks) to the proposition that the individual also left that mark. In addition, you know that your checker (who will know your conclusion) tends to agree with your conclusions.

3. The mark is the only mark you received in digital form in the context of a terrorist investigation in a distant country. The print has been obtained following a search in your IAFIS system (with about 110 million 10-print cards), and the same 12 minutiæ as in the first scenario are obtained. You know all the consequences of the erroneous identification that occurred in the case against Mayfield—you just read the latest report of the Office of the Inspector General on the subject (United States Department of Justice and Office of the

Inspector General—Oversight and Review Division 2011). The case is not involving US citizens. You decide not to identify. That decision is based on the same weight of evidence, but the IAFIS led you to adopt a very small prior probability, and the losses in the case of a wrong association are huge compared to the benefits as you perceive them.

4. The 10-print card of the person of interest is from the victim of a murder. He is a cab driver who has been killed in his taxi. All the marks have been collected within his car. You have already associated the suspect designated by the police on many other marks collected. The remaining mark shows 8 minutiæ in agreement (as before) with a print from the POI. You identify the victim as the source. Here, given the proximity of the victim to the mark and given that the suspect has been excluded, you took the decision to identify in order to avoid the investigation being misled by an additional mark that may be presented by the defense as the mark left a third party, the real killer (i.e., not their client). This is a typical scenario with what practitioners refer to as "elimination prints." However, this does not always proceed without difficulties as exemplified by the McKie case (Campbell 2011).

5. The print has been obtained from the body of a deceased boy who was recovered from a river. A family came forward to notify the disappearance of their child. The body is not in a state to allow it to be presented to the family for recognition, but the family recognized the garments as those worn by their child on the day of his disappearance. It is decided to attend the apartment of the family to collect items potentially touched by their son. A fingermark has been detected on a class book of the child. Without waiting for the other forensic results, you decide to identify the child and provide the information to the family. This decision has been driven by the strength of the association between the mark and the print (the same 8 minutiæ were seen in correspondence without discrepancy), the limited risk of making a wrong association given the context of the case, and the needs of the family.

The take home message is that the decision-making process is complex; it puts into action both the assessment of the mark and the print under consideration, but also implicit assessments regarding the mere possibility for the person of interest to leave the mark given the specific circumstances and the overall benefits and losses associated with the decision. Benefits and losses are personal to the examiner and span over societal, personal, and organizational values.

These decision mechanisms can be captured in a Bayesian network (Figure 2.25). For the sake of simplicity, it will be assumed here that the set of prints obtained from the person of interest are fully legible and represents all relevant areas of friction ridge skin. We shall discuss later, when we deal specifically with exclusion, what occurs when this assumption is relaxed.

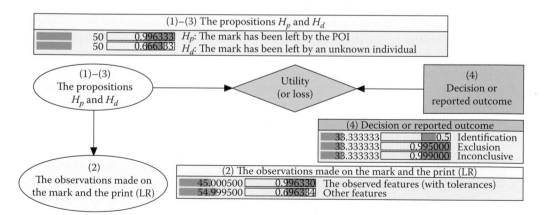

FIGURE 2.25 Bayesian network of the decision process as proposed by Biedermann et al. (2008). The values highlighted in green without boxes are the computed probabilities (expressed as percentages); the values highlighted in green within boxes are the computed utilities.

TABLE 2.5
Conditional Probability Table for Node (2) Related to the Observations

(2) The Observations Made on the Mark and the Print (LR)	(1)–(3) The Propositions H_p and H_d	
	H_p: The Mark Has Been Left by the POI	H_d: The Mark Has Been Left by an Unknown Individual
The observed features (with tolerances)	0.9	0.00001
Other features	0.1	0.99999

The first two nodes in yellow encapsulate through the arrow linking them the interplay between prior odds (1) and posterior odds (3) on the propositions when some findings are obtained. Indeed, the observations will bring some weight in favor of the propositions (H_p and H_d) in the form of a likelihood ratio (LR). It is through the application of Bayes theorem that the probabilities associated with the propositions will be updated in the light of the elements observed in the mark and in the print (we will use the letter E again for these). We will explore this interaction first with the LR of 90,000 as discussed before in relation to the case illustrated in Figure 2.21. Hence, the conditional probability table for node (2) will be as indicated in Table 2.5.

We start with a first case (*Case 1*) with a ratio of prior probabilities of 1:1, meaning that, before the examination of the mark, we set *a priori* that the POI has a probability of 0.5 to have left the mark. It is akin to a case where we have a closed set of two individuals that may be the source of the mark. When the evidence is entered (we declare that corresponding features within tolerances have been found), the BN will automatically compute the posterior probability on H_p by applying Bayes theorem (Figure 2.26). The mathematics involved is identical to what can be done analytically as indicated in Box 2.5. Given the observations (E), the probability on H_p has raised from 50% to 99.998889%. The prior odds have moved from 1:1 to 90,000:1 (in terms of odds, the progression from the prior odds to the posterior odds is a simple multiplication by the LR). Such a posterior probability may be viewed as high enough to decide that the mark has been identified (see later as to what is at stake when it comes to making such a decision).

In a second case (*Case 2*), the LR is the same, but the prior probability is different; say that, before the examination, the POI is considered as one among 100,000 potential sources, such as the population of a town or a limited geographical area, we simply adapt the probabilities associated with the node propositions (instead of 1:1, we put 1:99999). We then get, for the same observations, the updated results in Figure 2.27.

The probability of H_p being true is now rather low (47.37%). At first, this seems counterintuitive (the strength of the forensic evidence is very strong with a LR of 90,000), but it logically translates the fact that the strength of the observations needs to be put into the context of the case. When there is reasonable suspicion on the POI (the case with 1:1), the strength of the observation allows us to move up to a high probability for the POI being at the source of the mark. If the POI is less likely to be the source to start with (the case of 1 among 100,000 individuals), the findings will help to progress the prosecution case (with the same strength) but not to reach a very high posterior probability.

If we replace this into the context of the earth's population paradigm (when examiners attempts to conclude "to the exclusion of all others"), it would mean that the prior probability on the POI is very low (inversely proportional to the number of individuals on Earth, say 1: 7×10^9). If we want to individualize in that sense, we would need significant strength able to compensate for such a low prior probability and obtain a high posterior probability (say above 99.99%). We can arithmetically show (Champod 2009b) that the LR would need to be extremely high, above 7×10^{13}. That can be easily reproduced with the provided BN. If such posterior probabilities would be required

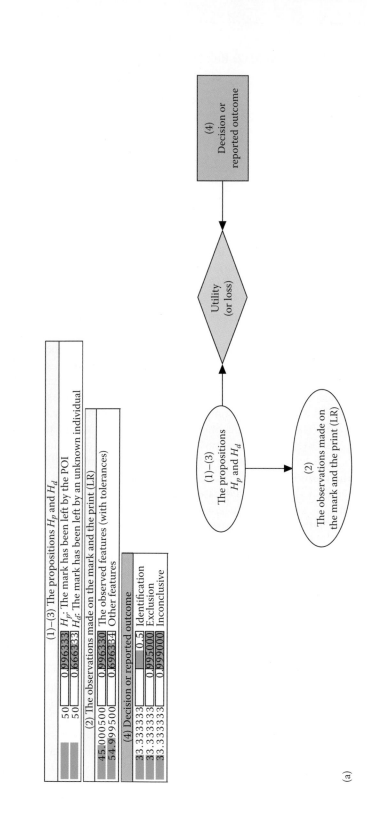

(a)

FIGURE 2.26 *Case 1* (a) Initial parameters of the BN with prior probabilities of 50%/50%.

(*Continued*)

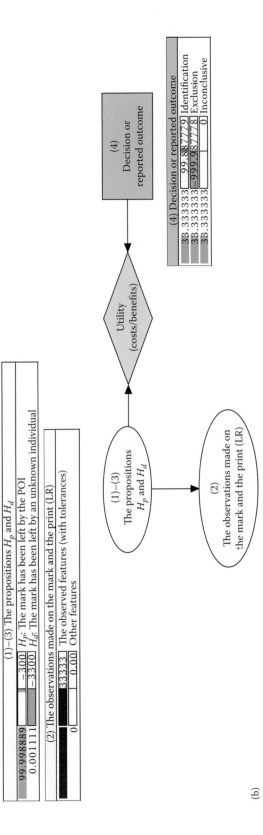

FIGURE 2.26 (Continued) *Case 1* (b) Updated probabilities once the corresponding features within tolerances (highlighted in red) have been observed. The posterior probability on H_p is 99.998889%. (Note that the values surrounded by a box are irrelevant at this point in the discussion.)

(b)

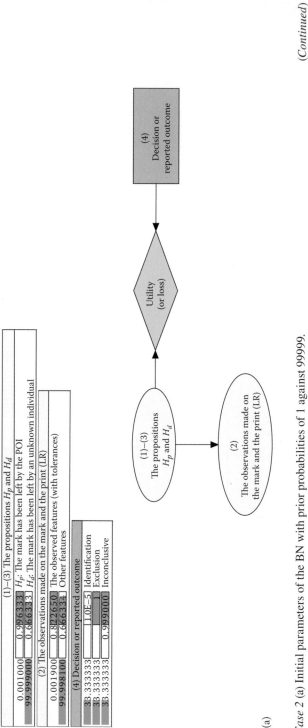

(a)

FIGURE 2.27 *Case 2* (a) Initial parameters of the BN with prior probabilities of 1 against 99999.

(Continued)

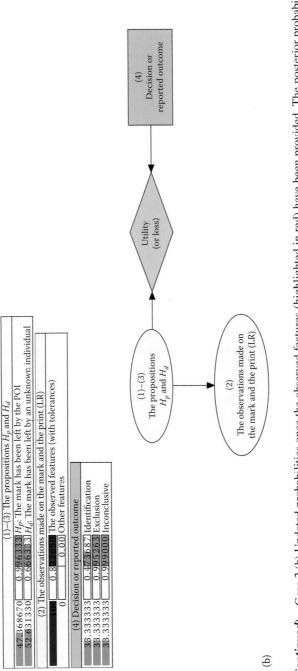

(b)

FIGURE 2.27 (Continued) *Case 2* (b) Updated probabilities once the observed features (highlighted in red) have been provided. The posterior probability on H_p is 47.37%. (Note that the values surrounded by a box are irrelevant at this point in the discussion.)

TABLE 2.6
List of Consequences Associated with Each Decision, Given the Propositions

	H_p: The Mark Has Been Left by the POI	H_d: The Mark Has Been Left by an Unknown Individual
d_1: Identification	Correct identification	False identification
d_2: Exclusion	False exclusion	Correct exclusion
d_2: Inconclusive	Neutral	Neutral

to individualize, then an examiner would be asked to assign a LR of that magnitude. We leave the reader to explore different options of prior odds and LR to become familiar with the interplay between propositions and LR.

The consequence of the aforementioned discussion is that the strength of the findings cannot be sufficient alone to clinch a case (apart from the extreme cases where the LR is 0 or infinite). The observations can progress toward a decision only through an update of the probabilities on H_p (and conversely on H_d). This posterior probability depends on the prior probability and on the LR. There is not just one component (the observations made on the mark and the print); two components are at play in the process.

The next stage is considering how do we make a decision once we know the posterior probability on H_p (or conversely on H_d). This is where the utility function comes into play. We apply here a theory of decision-making that was popularized by Lindley (1985) and directly implemented in Bayesian networks (Taroni et al. 2014).

In our BN (Figure 2.25), the square represents the available decisions and is linked to the propositions by a utility function (green diamond). Decisions will be made in the face of the remaining uncertainty on H_p but also accounting for the consequences of each possible decision d_i. The consequences for our case example according to the true state of H_p or H_d and the decisions that can be made are shown in Table 2.6 [adapted from Table 1 of Biedermann et al. (2008)].

Associated with each consequence is a degree of desirability also called the "utility". Utilities are expressed as numbers in order to quantify preferences (see Box 2.6).

We will adopt the set of utilities proposed by Taroni et al. (2010, Table 3.9, p. 97) who treated the same example. Both the utilities and the corresponding losses are presented in Table 2.7

The loss associated with a correct identification is zero, whereas the false identification leads to the highest possible loss. The unit itself is not critical, but what matters are the relative ratios between them. In the aforementioned scheme, we have imposed utilities to suggest that the gain for a correct identification is the same as for a correct exclusion, that the loss for concluding inconclusive is minimal regardless of the true state. And, finally, that the loss of a false exclusion is less than that for a false identification. The latter reflects that well-known societal maxim: "better leaving ten culprits outside than wrongly convicting an innocent." Utilities are an expression of preferences that belong to the decision-maker; here, they belong to Taroni and his colleagues. There are no right or wrong utilities as they reflect the personal values of the decision-maker.

What decision theory indicates is that if the decision-maker wants to maximize their overall satisfaction, then the most rational action is the one with the greatest expected utility (or the minimum expected loss). The expected utility for a given decision is the weighted average of the utilities of the consequences with respect to the probabilities of each consequence occurring as a result of choosing that decision. It will be automatically calculated by the BN informed with the above table of utilities.

Equipped with this decision model, what are the best decisions to make? The choice will depend on the posterior probability on H_p, and the utility function we have defined. For the first case (with a prior probability H_p of 0.5), when the findings are introduced and we focus on the decision box, it shows that the best decision to make (the one that maximizes the utility and

BOX 2.6   ASSIGNING UTILITIES

We follow here the method presented by Taroni et al. (2010) taken from Lindley (2014). Lindley gives a medical example in chapter 10 that can be very useful to readers who would like to explore further how utilities can be assigned.

For our fingerprint case, the utility of the best outcome (correct identification and correct exclusion) receives a utility of 1, the worst outcome (false identification) a utility of 0. The other consequences are ranked between these two and their utility values are assigned by a gambling experiment. Consider the following pair of gambles to assign the utility, for example, of excluding a suspect when he is the source of the mark:

Gamble 1: Obtain the consequence "excluding a person when he is at the source of the mark (false exclusion)";

Gamble 2: Obtain the best consequence (identification) with a probability u (utility) and the worst consequence (false identification) with a probability $1-u$.

If you must choose between gamble 1 and gamble 2, which one would you pick? The choice will depend on the value of the utility u. If you choose $u = 0.99$, then this means that you are indifferent between the sure consequence, that is wrongly excluding the suspect (gamble 1), and the option gamble 2, in which the best consequence (correctly identification) would be obtained with a probability of 0.99 and the worst consequence (false identification) with a probability of 0.01. So, stated otherwise, u is the value that would make gamble 2 acceptable to you in exchange to gamble 1, the sure consequence (i.e., a missed identification). This value u is the assignment for which gamble 2 would become acceptable for us compared to gamble 1. It is the decision-maker's utility for the consequence of interest (in our example the false exclusion). If the decision-maker is indifferent between the two gambles for a utility value of, say, 0.5, this means that he/she is indifferent between falsely excluding the POI for sure (gamble 1), that is a missed identification, and identifying when there is (only) a 0.5 probability of he being the donor of the mark (gamble 2).

The aforementioned example shows that assigning utilities is not a trivial task and they have to represent a coherent and rational behavior. For the sake of our argument here, we just need one set of utilities as we will argue that its consideration should not be one for the fingerprint examiner.

TABLE 2.7

Utilities and Losses for Each Decision Given the Propositions

| | Uncertain Propositions | | | |
| | Utilities | | Losses | |
Decisions	H_p	H_d	H_p	H_d
d_1: Identification	1	0	0	1
d_2: Exclusion	0.99	1	0.01	0
d_3: Inconclusive	0.999	0.999	0.001	0.001

---

minimizes the loss) is identification (expected utility of 0.999989); whereas, for the second case with much lower prior probabilities H_p, both the identification and the exclusion decision will lead to the lower benefit (expected utility of 0.473 and 0.995, respectively), the best option is to take the inconclusive decision (expected utility of 0.999). This expected utility for each outcome is visible in the pink decision box as shown later (Figure 2.28) with the numbers that

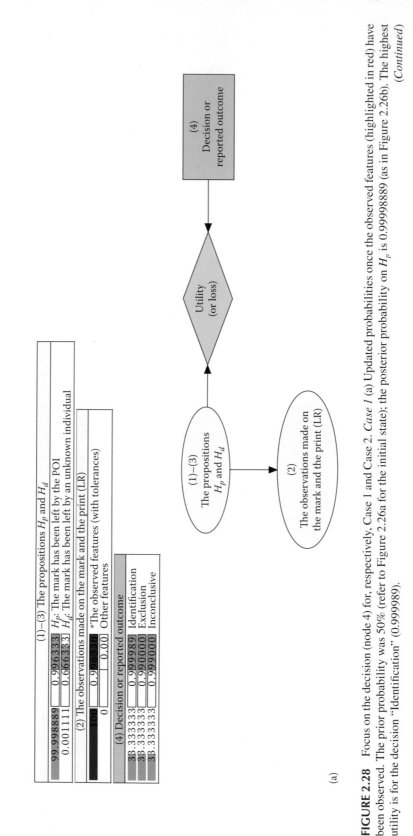

FIGURE 2.28 Focus on the decision (node 4) for, respectively, Case 1 and Case 2. *Case 1* (a) Updated probabilities once the observed features (highlighted in red) have been observed. The prior probability was 50% (refer to Figure 2.26a for the initial state); the posterior probability on H_p is 0.99998889 (as in Figure 2.26b). The highest utility is for the decision "Identification" (0.999989).

(Continued)

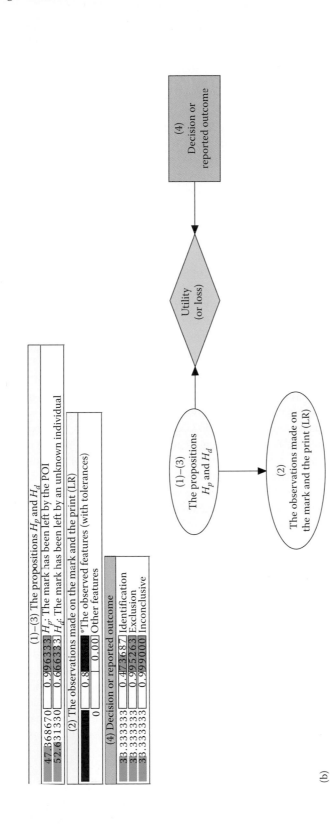

FIGURE 2.28 (Continued) Focus on the decision (node 4) for, respectively, Case 1 and Case 2. *Case 2* (b) Updated probabilities once the observed features (highlighted in red) have been observed. The prior probability was 1/10000 (refer to Figure 2.27a for the initial state); the posterior probability on H_p is 0.474 (as in Figure 2.27b). The highest utility is for the decision "Inconclusive" (0.999).

are within boxes. The unboxed numbers are the probabilities (expressed in % probabilities), and the numbers within boxes are the computed utilities.

There are important learning points from this full analysis using decision theory:

1. Rational decisions are driven by three factors that are linked by undisputed arithmetic: the prior probabilities, the LR, and a measure of the consequences (i.e., utilities and losses). It means that, when an expert is making a decision (of identification for example), they implicitly carry out three tasks—one concentrated on the mark and the print (the LR), but two others: one associated with an assignment of prior probability on H_p (and conversely H_d) and the application of a representation of their personal values through the utility function.
2. The LR alone is not sufficient to explain the decision reached by an examiner. The exception is when the LR is equal to 0; i.e., when an exclusion can be safely pronounced.
3. There is no need for a likelihood ratio to approach infinity to conclude identification. Given a utility function and reasonable priors, a decision of identification can be the most rational decision even if the strength of the findings is not extremely strong. In our first example, the identification can be declared with a LR of 90,000, given reasonable prior information about the person of interest.
4. There is no need for the posterior probability on H_d to be close to 0 before the identification is made (contrary to the definition of SWGFAST for individualization). Indeed, our previous case had a probability of H_d, given the forensic evidence, of 0.0011%. That probability is not a practical impossibility; it amounts to 1/90,000.

All decisions are then personal, and the aforementioned analysis aims at making this process transparent by identifying and reflecting on the steps taken by the decision-maker when arriving at a decision. To the question of whether or not it is appropriate for an expert to take responsibility for the whole decision process, our position is the following (Champod 2013b): The expert should only devote his or her testimony to the strength to be attached to the forensic findings and that value is best expressed using a likelihood ratio. Hence, the examiner should focus only on *Phase A* (refer back to Figure 2.7). The questions of the size of the relevant population (which impacts on prior probabilities) and decision thresholds (driven by the utilities and losses) are outside the expert's province but rightly belong to the fact finder. It means that *Phase B* should be left to the court. As stated already by Taroni and Margot (2000): "*Although it is not always clearly admitted, the burden of decision rests with the Court and not with the expert.*" A logical consequence of this division of labor, already expressed in 2008 (Champod 2008), is that experts should abandon the identification/individualization conclusion altogether. Cole (2009, 2014) followed with the same recommendation and other fingerprint experts have also started to come to the same conclusion (Swofford 2015). In practice, refusing to entertain *Phase B* of the identification process may require a detailed explanation to the judiciary, because courts have been accustomed to delegating this task to the fingerprint examiner. We are also aware of circumstances, such as in cases of disaster victim identification (DVI), where the decision is delegated to a committee of experts who will conduct both phases. We hope that the aforementioned section allows examiners to understand what is at stake here and provide them with some confidence and structure to explain to members of the judiciary that, if they accept that delegation, they will be performing tasks that ultimately and solely belong to the court. In Section 2.8, we will explore alternative ways to report fingerprint evidence that is just focused on the LR (hence *Phase A*) and leave to the court the duty of dealing with the decision (*Phase B*).

2.4.2.2 Exclusion

SWGFAST (2013a, p. 4) defines exclusion as follows:

> Exclusion is the decision by an examiner that there are sufficient features in disagreement to conclude that two areas of friction ridge impressions did not originate from the same source. Source refers to the area of friction skin. Exclusion of a subject can only be reached if all relevant comparable anatomical

areas are represented and legible in the known exemplars. Notes and reports shall clearly state if the exclusion refers only to the source or the subject.

Note that SWGFAST took care in distinguishing the exclusion of the area of friction ridge skin under examination from the exclusion of the individual from whom the prints have been taken. The reason for that distinction is the possibility for the 10-print form to be incomplete and not representing the whole surface of friction ridge skin. This consideration is linked with the concept of hierarchy of propositions that we will develop later.

This definition of exclusion states that this decision is reached after finding "sufficient features in disagreement." But the concept of sufficiency is never defined, nor is the decision process. To follow the probabilistic approach of this chapter, it all comes down to a likelihood ratio that is less than 1 and hence supporting the proposition that the mark and the print are from different sources.

Ray and Dechant (2013) set its standard for exclusion to be level 1 and level 2 details in disagreement. This is to mitigate the risk of a wrong exclusion due to a hasty examination (without a proper analysis phase) focused only on level 1 detail (e.g., Saviano [2003] or Hamm [2006]). Hence, a discrepancy is declared only when irreconcilable differences have been observed at these two levels of detail. For example, two or more target groups of minutiæ near an anchor point such as a delta or core must be in disagreement for exclusion to be concluded. It means that marks with a distinct pattern but lacking any legible minutiæ do not contain enough information for an exclusion to be possible. What Ray and Dechant are asking for is an increase in the amount of information (in disagreement) to reasonably assign a probability of 0 to the numerator of the LR.

Due to the popular belief that a wrong exclusion is more acceptable than a wrong identification, the exclusion process has received little attention. It is often heard that it is better to miss an identification (or to wrongly exclude) than to wrongly identify. The Bayesian network developed before captures this view in its utility function. This societal stand is reflected in the performances of fingerprint examiners as we shall see later in this section.

The overall decision theory framework that we presented in the context of identification applies to any of the decisions reached. Hence, the considerations made with regard to the identification decision hold true for exclusions. If the numerator of the LR is assigned a value of 0 by the examiner, then the exclusion is obvious and deductive, but there is no need to assign a probability of 0 to make exclusion the preferred decision. With the utility function that we previously defined, we leave it to the reader to observe, using the BN, that with a LR below 1/10,000, and even with prior odds of 1:1, that the weight of evidence in favor of H_d is enough to warrant a decision of exclusion.

2.4.2.3 Inconclusive

SWGFAST (2013a, p. 4) has defined the inconclusive conclusion, making a distinction between two approaches taken regarding suitability (approach #1 or approach #2). Both approaches have been presented thoroughly in Section 2.1.5. To recall these here, approach #1 refers to a decision scheme in the analysis stage where marks are judged of value for identification (VID) or of no value (NV). In approach #2, marks insufficient to be called VID may be used for exclusion purposes (value for exclusion only; VEO). The SWGFAST definitions under the heading of "inconclusive" read as follows:

An inconclusive conclusion resulting from a suitability decision as described in approach #1 occurs when an examiner is unable to individualize or exclude due to an absence of complete and legible known prints (e.g., poor quality fingerprints and lack of comparable areas). In such an instance, the inconclusive conclusion means that the impression needs to be reexamined using clearly and completely recorded known impressions.

An inconclusive conclusion resulting from a suitability decision as described in approach #2 can occur either as in approach #1 or when corresponding features are observed but not sufficient to individualize. Likewise, dissimilar features may be observed but not sufficient to exclude. In either case, the inconclusive conclusion means that the unknown impression was neither individualized nor excluded as originating from the same source.

In the present state of affairs, fingerprint experts have taken the position not to report opinions in terms of probabilities. The examination of a fingermark retained for comparison leads either to a decision of identification or exclusion, or the mark is judged as insufficient to reach any conclusion. Inconclusive means essentially that a *conclusive* decision (identification or exclusion) has not been reached. This approach has traditionally been termed the doctrine of "positivity." We have already covered in the previous edition (Champod et al. 2004, pp. 33–36) and elsewhere (Champod 1995, 2013a) the debate that led to this policy. We will concentrate here only on the more recent developments.

In a case where, perhaps because of the limited quality (or clarity) of a mark, the amount of information is not sufficient to convince the expert of a categorical decision, there may be corroborative evidence, of less weight, that may still provide useful guidance to the court. In our opinion, it would be preferable that the terminology used by the fingerprint expert renders explicit these contrasted values in a more effective way than "inconclusive." That weight is logically expressed in the form of the likelihood ratio in favor of either H_p or H_d as advocated fifteen years ago by Champod and Evett (2001). In this sense, Locard's third directive (see Section 2.6.1) is fundamental and places fingerprint evidence on the same footing as other types of transfer traces. This possibility is not taken on board by many agencies worldwide. We are aware of the provision of investigative information in some countries (according to a survey by Interpol [1995]). For example, in Belgium, when the comparison shows between 8 and 12 corresponding minutiæ, a "could be" conclusion is issued. Another example comes from some jurisdictions in Australia where, under certain circumstances and due to requirements for full disclosure, they provide "points consistent with" or "ridge detail consistent with" statements rather than "inconclusive." An example of such a statement is as follows: "Although there is friction ridge detail in the latent fingermark consistent with the right index fingerprint on the fingerprint form in the name of John Smith, there is insufficient detail to make a positive identification. However, the fingerprint of John Smith cannot be excluded in this matter."

Until 2010, fingerprint practitioners were discouraged [at the risk of being excluded from the International Association for Identification (IAI) according to its 1980 resolution (1980)] from initiating or volunteering, in a report or testimony, any probabilistic qualification of the strength of an association between a mark and a print. Following a three-year review, a committee of the IAI—named the Standardization II Committee—recommended rescinding the 1980 resolution (Polski et al. 2011). The new resolution (2010–2018) adopted by the IAI in 2010 specifies in its last points the following:

> 7. The use of mathematically based models to assess the associative value of the evidence may provide a scientifically sound basis for supporting the examiner's opinion. Examiners shall only use mathematically based models that have been accepted as valid by the IAI in partnership with the relevant scientific community and in which they have been trained to competency.

> 8. Mathematically based models may not be used as the sole determinant when concluding that friction ridge impressions share a common source. The use of mathematically based models does not relieve the examiner of responsibility for their expert opinion.

The resolution acknowledges recent progress in fingerprint statistics (see Section 2.7) and finally opens the possibility for fingerprint examiners to report strengths of opinions spanning over the whole spectrum of support in favor (or not) of an association that the observed features may bring. However, the meaning of "valid" (the word used in the resolution) has not been clarified by the IAI. Hence, at this time, the position is largely as follows: We do not currently have validated models; hence, we report "inconclusive" without any other qualifiers of the weight to be assigned to the comparison (when appropriate).

The resolution implicitly enforces the view, already expressed by Ashbaugh (1999), that probabilistic opinions should be avoided until validated tools for assessing cases are made available to the examiners. While a cautious approach is to be commended, it presents a peculiar state of affairs. An opinion of identification means for most examiners that the known individual is singularized with regard to almost the world's population. But, paradoxically, a fraction of a second earlier in the comparison process, when the information gathered is judged by the examiner as insufficient to identify, it is suggested that the examiner cannot give any opinion. In other words, the leap of faith is presented as a transition from a state of an absence of knowledge to a state of certainty. This approach is incompatible with the logic of the inference of identity of source that we developed throughout this chapter. If examiners are able to assign probability and make a decision regarding identification, they should also have an equal capacity to make assignments of probabilities in cases where the volume of information is judged as insufficient for an identification or exclusion. We are, therefore, back to a notion of subjective probabilities (Taroni et al. 2001) that we espoused and that are at play regardless of the decision reached (Biedermann et al. 2013).

Examiners could, at times, resort to terms such as "consistent with," "points consistent with," or "the investigated person cannot be excluded as the donor of the mark," but without offering any guidance as to the weight of evidence [see, for example, Maceo (2011a)]. In our view, these expressions are misleading. We object to information formulated in such broad terms that may be given more weight than is justified. These terms have been recently discouraged in the NRC report (National Research Council 2009) and by some courts (e.g., in England and Wales *R v. Puacca* [2005] EWCA Crim 3001). And this is not a new debate. As early as 1987, Brown and Cropp (1987) suggested to avoid using the expressions "match," "identical" and "consistent with."

There is a need to find appropriate ways to express the value of findings. The assignment of a likelihood ratio is appropriate. Resorting to the term "inconclusive" deprives the court of information that may be essential.

2.4.3 LEFT, TOUCHED OR HANDLED: THE HIERARCHY OF PROPOSITIONS

When dealing with the decision of exclusion, it was pointed out that concluding that a mark did not originate from a specified area of friction ridge skin does not mean *de facto* that the individual at the source of the prints is excluded from being the source of this mark. It indeed depends on the extensiveness of the inked impressions. So, to move from an exclusion of an area to an exclusion of an individual, there is a need to consider an ancillary question. The response to this question will be a probability assignment that is at times made to be 0 or 1. Zero (0) means that there are undisputed signs of incompleteness on the reference prints, 1 would mean that a fully legible and extensive set of prints—called major crime prints—are available. All other intermediate situations involve marks that do not show a lot of flow attributes to assist with their localization on the papillary surface, and leaving an element of uncertainty. The progression from the consideration of the area to the consideration of the individual is down to a probability assignment that may depend on the circumstances of the case. For example, a mark (double loop) is recovered on the side of a bathtub. Even though it could be excluded based on the general pattern from all the friction ridge skin areas of the hands of the person of interest, the examiner may not want to exclude that individual without having had the opportunity to verify the toe prints. If the mark had been recovered on a doorknob, such a supplementary verification will not be made in the first place (unless there is a change in the circumstances as understood initially by the examiner). Once again, we face here probability assignments and decisions conditioned by utility functions.

One can understand that different propositions or circumstances may change perspectives and the course of detection, analysis, comparison, and evaluation. A notion referred to as the "hierarchy of propositions," introduced in the United Kingdom by Cook et al. (1998b), can help explore these

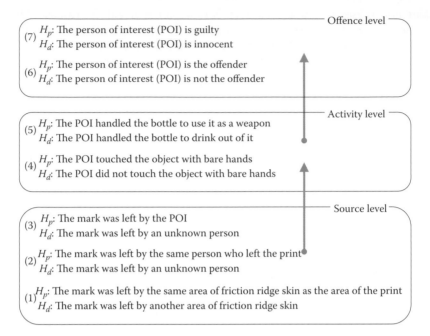

FIGURE 2.29   The hierarchy of propositions as applied to fingerprint considerations in the context of forensic cases.

ancillary questions. Such questions span over a range of issues that can be organized in the form of a hierarchy. We will explore the set of examples in Figure 2.29.

Our discussion regarding exclusion related to the progression from (1) to (2) in Figure 2.29. As we progress up within the hierarchy, the propositions considered by the parties (typically the prosecution and the defense) change. Indeed, these parties look at the results of the forensic examination from the perspective of the ultimate legal or moral issue (7). That progression requires the consideration of a series of ancillary questions. Some of these will be a matter for the court to decide; others will be in the domain of expertise of the forensic science examiner. For example, our first progression between (1) and (2) is clearly a matter of forensic science expertise.

The move between (2) and (3) is more down to the procedure and the chain of custody. Often the forensic science examiner is less informed than the court as to whether or not the name on the ten-print form is truly the individual in question. That can be tested if needed but, in any case, it will be a matter for the court to decide.

The issues exemplified by the set of propositions (1) to (3) are called *source level* issues. They have to be distinguished from the issues higher up on the hierarchy called *activity level* issues [(4) and (5)]. Indeed, the issues at this level relate to the mechanisms, whereby the mark had been left or the time at which the mark had been left. Generally, activity level issues are at the core of the dispute when the matter of source has been settled or accepted by the parties. It is typically following admission that the mark is linked with a person of interest that the court may be faced with the question as to how that mark was left. The example (4) suggests a dispute as to whether the receiving object had actually been touched or not. If a mark is present, allegations of forgery or mislabeling (of a fingermark lift, for example) may be raised. If no mark has been detected, then it may be suggested that the person never touched the object, otherwise marks should have been detected. Fingerprint examiners may be asked to provide guidance as to the probability of their findings given such a set of propositions. However, the nature of the expertise required is different from the expertise used to deal with source level issues. It is essential that the examiner is fully cognizant of that. In addition, the questions that need to be addressed to deal with activity level issues are probabilistic and cannot generally be answered by a simple yes or no. Take an example where no mark had been detected on an object. A typical case of *missing evidence* as defined by Lindley and Eggleston (1983). To the question: "does it mean that the suspect did not touch the object?" we hear very often: "NO, because you can touch an object without leaving marks." The answer is not wrong, but it is not qualified properly with the strength to be attached to the observations. No mark was detected and, even if it does not establish the absence of touch, it will provide some support for the contention that the person never touched the object. To act in all fairness, the examiner will have to deal with the problem using a probabilistic framework (i.e., expressing a LR). An example is shown in Box 2.7.

**BOX 2.7 LIKELIHOOD RATIO ASSOCIATED WITH
THE ABSENCE OF DETECTED MARKS**

Let us assume that a gun is submitted to the laboratory to search for potential fingermarks. The gun is subjected to cyanoacrylate fuming followed by dye staining. No mark of friction ridge skin is detected after this treatment. A POI is suspected of having manipulated the gun during the commission of a crime. The crime occurred 2 days ago and the gun had been discarded by the offender at the crime scene. Witnesses indicated that the offender was holding the gun with his bare hands. The defense is suggesting that the absence of detectable marks supports the view that the POI was not holding the gun during the offence as alleged, but another person was holding it.

A probabilistic approach to this problem requires us to specify the propositions at hand and clearly define the outcome of the examination. From the circumstances presented earlier, the prosecution proposition (H_p) is that the POI was holding the gun with his bare hands during the commission of the crime. The defense held the view (H_d) that an unknown individual was holding the gun (still with his bare hands). The examination findings (E) are that no mark has been detected. The likelihood ratio associated with these findings can be formally written as

$$LR = \frac{Pr(E|H_p, K)}{Pr(E|H_d, K)}$$

The numerator, $Pr(E|H_p, K)$, is asking for the probability of not detecting any mark if the POI actually touched the gun as alleged and the denominator, $Pr(E|H_d, K)$, is asking for the probability of the same absence of detection but if an unknown person (and not the POI) manipulated the gun. K stands for specific information that has a bearing on the assessment of the findings; here, this is the knowledge of the detection methods used, the protective measures taken regarding the gun, the time between the crime and the laboratory examination, the specific propensity of the POI or another individual to leave marks, the ability of that particular surface to retain deposited fingermarks, etc. If both probabilities are deemed to be equal, meaning essentially that the POI is no different in terms of depositing fingermark residue than an unknown person, then the LR will be 1. In such a case, the absence of a mark is not helping toward one side or the other. If, however, it can be shown that the POI is an excellent donor of marks (compared to the average person) then, under the alleged circumstances, we would have had higher expectations to find his fingermarks on the gun. The absence of detectable marks would then provide some support for the defense view. The magnitude of the support will be proportional to the relative difference between the POI and an unknown person in terms of donor capability (i.e., propensity to leave detectable fingermarks).

An individual may touch an object without leaving detectable marks. However, if that person has a different propensity than the average person to leave (or not) marks, then that will become relevant when considering the activities that may have occurred. There are, of course, other considerations such as the ability of the substrate to retain deposited marks and our ability to detect these marks.

The case of missing evidence can easily be constructed in the form of a Bayesian network as performed by Taroni et al. (2004). To conclude here, we invite examiners to be careful with the traditional saying "absence of evidence is not evidence of absence" used abundantly in the fingerprint literature (for example, Ray and Dechant [2013]) and often heard in court. The matter may appear to be trivial; however, making the court believe that it is trivial is not helping and generally only supports the prosecution case.

We turn now to a consideration of the issue raised by the set of propositions (5). Forensic science examiners are asked, at times, to consider the positioning of the marks and offer guidance as to whether these observations bring support for one type of handling versus another. We move from a previous discussion on touching to considerations on how the object was touched. We want to stress that the interpretation of such findings should conform with the principles of evidence interpretation (recalled by Willis [2015]). If the examiner can justify knowledge on the matter that goes beyond the general knowledge of the court, the examiner should assist the court. But this assistance should be offered within a highly defined type of answer. At no point should the examiner answer as to whether or not the person manipulated the object that way; they should only indicate the probability of making the observations if the object was handled according to a pair of propositions (usually the prosecution view or the probability of the observation if the object was handled according to the defense view). The findings will only indicate a support for propositions expressed by the parties; it will then be up to the court to decide on the issue. We advise examiners to limit their testimony to the LR when dealing with issues concerning the source (see Section 2.8); we reiterate that view when dealing with issues at activity level. The underpinning logic remains exactly the same.

Finally, referring back to Figure 2.29, to move from activity level to *offence level* questions clearly requires the resolution of ancillary questions that are in the domain of the court only. Forensic examiners generally refrain, quite rightly, from moving that high in the hierarchy.

Some may suggest avoiding at all cost moving from source to activity level issues; hence, to operate in the safe harbor of reproducibility and specificity without having to deal with why the mark was detected and how it got there. Our position is as follows: if the considerations associated with the mechanisms of deposition require expert knowledge and cannot be left to advocacy, then it is the duty of the forensic scientist to help the court as far as possible. It may be that the state of knowledge is so limited that the proposed LR will be 1 (meaning that the findings cannot help toward one or the other propositions). At least, it will highlight the complexity involved in the interpretation of the findings and may prevent others from giving them a meaning they do not deserve.

2.4.4 Reliability of the Evaluation Process

The reliability and reproducibility of fingerprint decisions after comparison have been tested in socalled "black box" studies (Ulery et al. 2011, 2012). For a corpus of experts (169), each conducting examinations on 100 cases, the percentage of decisions of identification and exclusion that correspond to the ground truth have been determined. A very low rate of false positives was observed (in four cases amounting to 0.1%). Among the marks determined to be of value for identification, examiners were unanimous on 48% of mated pairs and on 33% of non-mated pairs (on average, each pair was examined by 23 examiners), leaving 19% of cases with conflicting conclusions. This (lack of) reproducibility was then compared to the repeatability (intra-examiner variability). Here, 89.1% of individualization decisions and 90.1% of exclusion decisions remained unchanged when retested. Most changes of opinion were toward inconclusive decisions. However, none of the four false positive errors committed in this study were repeated (Ulery et al. 2012). As would be expected, the lack of repeatability and reproducibility increases with the difficulty or complexity of the marks as judged by the examiners.

A similar trend was observed in a more recent study where challenging cases were examined by more than 150 fingerprint practitioners (Neumann et al. 2013). In one case of a close non-match (a case selected through the use of an AFIS to maximize the chance of finding potential adventitious associations), 11 false identifications were reported from a total of 124 rendered conclusions, representing a false positive rate of 8.9% for that case.

It is important to keep in mind that false exclusions (false negatives) are more prevalent than false identifications (false positives). Ulery et al. (2011) reported a wrong exclusion rate of 7.5% compared to a wrong association rate of 0.1%. Tangen ct al. (2011) obtained, respectively, 7.88% false exclusions and 0.68% false positives. Finally, Neumann et al. (2013), on challenging cases, obtained overall 4.92% of false negatives and 0.67% of false positives. A typical example of the variation observed among experts on the examination of the same case is presented in Figure 2.30.

The Miami-Dade police department carried out the latest large-scale test with 109 US fingerprint practitioners (Pacheco et al. 2014). Marks were left by known donors under realistic conditions; marks and prints were then rated as a function of complexity on a scale between 0 and 21 based on the quality and quantity of the minutiæ and the overall clarity of the mark and print. From the submission of 80 cases, they obtained good reproducibility in the decisions reached following the whole ACE-V process (i.e., including verification), with no false positives and an overall false exclusion error rate of 2.9%. Before the verification process (see Section 2.5), 3% false positives (42 cases, most of them being clerical errors except for 3 cases), and 7.5% false negatives (235 cases)

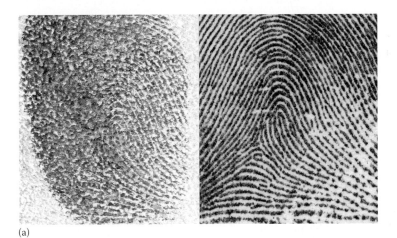

(a)

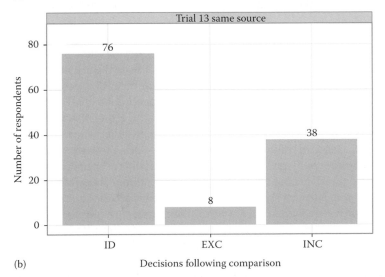

(b)

FIGURE 2.30 (a) Mark and print submitted to the consideration of 122 examiners. (b) The distribution of results between the three possible decisions (ID, EXC, and INC). *(Continued)*

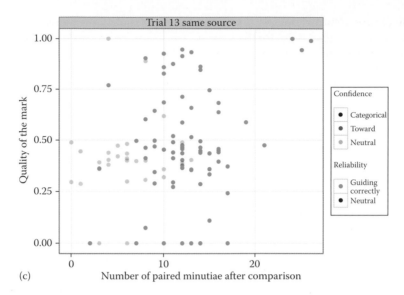

(c)

FIGURE 2.30 (*Continued*)   (c) Distribution of the number of annotated minutiæ following comparison. The dark green dots indicate the conclusions of ID and the grey dots the conclusions of INC. The light green dots are the conclusions of INC that were declared as guiding toward ID. The number of paired minutiæ for each ID decision ranged between 5 and 27 for the same images.

were reported. Examiners are more likely to miss an identification (false negative) than to report an incorrect identification (false positive). That relates to the utility function that we described previously. Examiners are more likely to commit a false negative error (an error that could possibly result in the guilty party going free) than a false positive error (an error that could possibly result in an innocent person being convicted). They tend to follow William Blackstone ratio: "for the law holds that it is better that ten guilty persons escape, than that one innocent suffers." We wonder again if it is the role of the scientist to make this choice.

All instances of false positives in the Pacheco et al. (2014) study were detected and corrected during the verification stage. This is the topic of the next section.

2.5   VERIFICATION

We have emphasized the subjective nature of the fingerprint evaluation stage. But this is not to say that fingerprint identification is not a reliable process. Nevertheless, such subjective judgments should be monitored in a structured and disciplined environment. There are various ways to achieve this, and each has been explored by the fingerprint profession; for example, the selection and training processes for fingerprint examiners, quality assurance programs, standard operating procedures, collaborative studies, proficiency tests, and internal/external audits. These initiatives allow forensic scientists to convince the court of their expertise, not by referring to years of service or thousands of comparisons completed, but by presenting a detailed portfolio recording their proficiency in a long series of independently conducted proficiency tests, for example. Reliability, therefore, stems from training standards, competency assessments, and proficiency testing.

In addition, a principal safeguard against error is obtained through independent verification procedures for each comparison by at least one experienced examiner. This form of peer review is a fundamental part of any scientific process. The procedure should be documented, and the processes to resolve any disagreement should be declared and applied where required. A practical difficulty is to ensure that this verification process is done blindly to avoid any confirmation bias.

The topic received more attention following the Mayfield case, where it has been agreed that verification decision of verifier was made knowing the previous decision reached by the other experts, up to the last court-appointed expert. As a result, research highlighted how vulnerable fingerprint examiners can be to contextual bias (Dror et al. 2005, 2006; Dror and Charlton 2006) and SWGFAST (2012) published a standard on blind verification.

Verification should be considered a dynamic process that can be based on the determination of mark and comparison complexity. For example, non-complex marks and comparisons might facilitate the use of a one-verification process, whereas complex marks and comparisons may require two or more independent verifications. Verification is termed "non-blind" when the verifier has previous knowledge of the conclusions reached by the first examiner. Verification is termed "blind" when the verifier is provided with no, or limited, contextual information, and has no expectation or knowledge of the determinations or conclusions of the original examiner. The situations and the process whereby blind verification will be conducted need to be explicitly defined, for example, blind verification may be advised in cases with strong risks of contextual influence, in time critical examinations (persons in custody), in cases involving complex marks or when non-consensual opinions had previously been reached in verification. Regardless of whether the verification is conducted in a "blind" or "non-blind" manner, the verification process should be conducted on unmarked copies of both mark and print. The verifier should not be presented with case documentation and annotations of the first practitioner. It is expected that the verifier will produce independent documentation in the same format and extent as the first examiner in cases where marks have been deemed "complex." Root cause analysis shall take place if the verifier(s) disagree(s) with the initial conclusion.

Empirical research has shown the merits of verification, although verification is not applied by the agencies to the same degree and for each reported conclusion (Black 2012). Verification is mainly used for identification conclusions. Verification is a good tool to detect wrong associations (Pacheco et al. 2014). Langenburg et al. (2009) showed that examiners were more resistant to bias suggestions toward individualization and less so to suggestions toward inconclusive and exclusion. The same observation was made by Ulery et al. (2011, 2012), where all wrong identifications were detected during the verification stage but only most of the wrong exclusions. Blind testing schemes may hence be more wisely employed where an initial examiner has reached a conclusion of exclusion. As stated by Langenburg (2012, p. 259): "present verification schemes are adequate for detecting some types of errors (e.g., false positives) but may be lacking for detecting others (e.g., false negatives)."

2.6 HOW MANY SIMILARITIES ARE REQUIRED FOR AN IDENTIFICATION?

The ultimate question has been traditionally expressed as follows (provided that no significant differences have been observed): "how many similarities are required to conclude to an identification?" Our previous sections have shown that this question is, by far, not the crux of the decision process; however, given that in some countries the practice is so focused on a minimum number of minutiæ (or points) to identify, we cannot avoid the discussion. The aims of this section are: (1) to explore this "magic number" by reviewing, in detail, the international views and practices; and (2) to update earlier reviews by Kingston and Kirk (1965) and the FBI (Anonymous 1972).

2.6.1 HISTORICAL MILESTONES

The first rules establishing the minimum number of minutiæ necessary for fingermark identification can be attributed to the famous Frenchman Edmond Locard as early as 1911. Locard suggested a tripartite rule, which followed from the discovery of poroscopy. It can be summarized as follows (Locard 1914):

1. If more than 12 concurring points are present and the fingermark is sharp, then the certainty of identity is beyond debate. (The imperative requirement for the absence of significant differences is implicit.)

   2. If 8 to 12 concurring points are involved, then the case is borderline, and the certainty of identity will depend on:

      a. The sharpness of the fingermark

      b. The rarity of its type (general pattern)

      c. The presence of the center of the figure (core) and the triangle (delta) in the exploitable part of the mark

      d. The presence of pores

      e. The perfect and obvious identity regarding the width of the papillary ridges and valleys, the direction of the lines, and the angular value of the bifurcations

     In these instances, certainty can only be established following discussion of the case by at least two competent and experienced specialists.

   3. If a limited number of characteristic points are present, the fingermark cannot provide certainty for an identification, but only a corroborative element of a strength proportional to the number of points available and their clarity.

Locard based his tripartite rule on various sources of information: the discovery of poroscopy, the limited (at that time) practical experience gathered by the identification bureaus around the world, and the statistical evaluation by Balthazard (1911), Galton (1892), and Ramos. (Galdino Ramos published statistical work in a book entitled *Da Identificação* [Rio de Janeiro 1906] that we were unable to locate.) This approach persists throughout the extensive writings of Locard (1931). His considerations (principally the first two) were largely taken up by the most eminent fingerprint researchers of the first half of the century, notably Wilder and Wentworth (1932), Cummins and Midlo (1961), Heindl (1927), and Bridges (1963). It is worth noting that the World population at the time of Locard was much less than today and the means of travels much more limited.

2.6.2 Current Views and Practices

On the fringe of this early view, the practice of fingerprint identification is nowadays confined to two distinct positions:

   1. The empirical criterion is based solely on a quantitative threshold expressed by the number of concordant minutiæ between the mark and the known print.

   2. The holistic criterion is a combined assessment of quantitative and qualitative aspects of the corresponding features.

In 1998, the Interpol European Expert Group on Fingerprint Identification (IEEGFI), created with the mandate to assess the feasibility of formulating a European fingerprint standard, came to the same conclusion (Interpol 2000). Although these two positions may appear to be drastically opposed, we believe that, as soon as the identification process is encapsulated within a strict regime of documented procedures and quality control measures, then the whole debate between these two schools (empirical vs. holistic) will disappear. Quality will be achieved by the publication and endorsement of transparent and detailed procedures describing the identification process and associated quality assurance measures. The driver toward quality is transparency.

2.6.2.1 Predetermined Minimum Number of Minutiæ: An Empirical Standard

The majority of European fingerprint experts favor a purely quantitative approach, ignoring the potential contribution of concordant qualitative aspects (such as level 3 features) in the decision process, by fixing a numerical standard—a minimum number of minutiæ necessary to establish identification. The numerical standard represents a lower limit; above this value, the identification is beyond doubt regardless of the type of minutiæ that are discerned. The interpretation of the concept of a numerical standard may vary from agency to agency (or even from examiner to examiner), as illustrated by a few examples (Table 2.8) based on a survey by the Interpol European Working Group on Fingerprint Standards (1995) and the

TABLE 2.8
Overview of Some Empirical Standards and Their Origins

Country	Points Criterion	Origin
Italy	16–17	The criterion is based on the questionable probabilistic calculation by Balthazard dating back to 1911 (Balthazard 1911). At the time, Balthazard adjusted the number of required minutiæ as a function of the size of the World population. If the inquiry restricted the pool of individuals to Europe or France, Balthazard suggested reducing that number from 16 to 11 or 12. The minimum standard is expressly mentioned from jurisprudence referring to Balthazard's work (Pirone 1976, 1991). The jurisprudence has been consistently applied (according to decisions from 1954 to 1989). This situation is quite paradoxical because Sorrentino, head of the School of Police Science in Rome in the 1950s, was advocating against the consideration of a predetermined minimum number of minutiæ (Sorrentino 1948, 1952, 1956).
England and Wales (before 2001), Scotland (before 2006), Australia (prior to 1941)	16	The origins of this standard (adopted by New Scotland Yard in 1924) date back to a misunderstanding of a paper published by Bertillon in 1912 (Bertillon 1912; Champod et al. 1993). Up to a recent date, the numerical standard was virtually impossible to circumvent and had been adopted nationally in 1953 and confirmed in 1984. If simultaneous impressions were available, the identification was allowed if there were at least 10 points in each mark. The purpose of the standard was to guarantee a high level of quality and faultlessness in the matter of fingerprint identifications (Lambourne 1984, 2008). The 16-point standard (for a review, refer to Evett and Williams [1996]), however, proved to be inadequate as an ultimate safeguard against error, as attested by the recent disclosure of erroneous identifications (Champod and Chamberlain 2009).
Albania, Australia (from 1942 to 1999), Belgium, England and Wales (before 1924), Finland, France, Hong Kong, Israel, Greece, Poland, Portugal, Romania, Serbia, Slovenia, Spain, The Netherlands, Turkey, USA (before 1973), South American countries	12	A number probably derived from Locard's first rule (although Locard's writing stated "more than 12"). Note that, in numerous countries, mechanisms to bypass the rigid threshold are in place. For example, in the Netherlands, a case of identification can be submitted with 10 minutiæ if a committee of three examiners unanimously agrees to that conclusion.
Czech Republic, Denmark	10	In the Czech Republic, the 10-point rule is based in part on a statistical model developed by Jozefek (1972) along with a survey of the relative occurrences of different types of minutiæ.
Germany, The Netherlands, Switzerland (before 2008)	8–12	This criterion is in agreement with Locard, even though sometimes, in practice, there is a clear tendency to respect a 12-point rule (Walder 1976). The practice in Germany is a generalization of Locard's first two points of his tripartite rule, asking the examiner to fully balance the quantity of minutiæ with qualitative aspects of the mark (visibility of pores, specificity of the minutiæ, etc.). Hence if, for example, the mark displays poor level 1 features, the examiner may reach an identification conclusion only after having noticed more than 12 concordant minutiæ without discrepancy (Steinwender 1958). The Netherlands is operating on an analogous regime between 10 and 12 points.

(Continued)

TABLE 2.8 (*Continued*)
Overview of Some Empirical Standards and Their Origins

Country	Points Criterion	Origin
Bulgaria	8	Following the statistical study presented by K. Mahacheb (1986) and considering a Bulgarian population of about 10 million individuals.
South Africa, Russia	7	According to Sherratt (1979) for South Africa. An interesting account of South African court cases is also provided by (Sherratt 1994) and (Verburg attorneys/Prokureurs 2015). The standard in Russia appears to be based on statistical considerations of the relative weights to be given to the various types of minutiæ (Edgubov 1996).

Note: The empirical standards may be different for the identification of simultaneous marks in anatomical sequences or for marks showing separate parts.

work of the Standardization II Committee (Polski et al. 2011). To the extent possible, we have traced the source of the empirical standard.

Despite the systematic use of a numerical standard, various countries (e.g., Finland, Greece, the Netherlands, Israel, and Portugal) have developed methods to bypass the rigid threshold when particularities (such as visibility of pores, ridge structures, or rare combinations of minutiæ) are observed during the comparison. The adoption of a range from 8 (or 10) to 12 points was found to be a way to relax an otherwise rigid threshold. In 1983, an addendum was even made to the "16-point standard" in England and Wales, stating that, in extremely serious cases such as acts of terrorism, an expert with long experience and high standing in the profession can offer an opinion on an identification that does not meet the nationally accepted standard.

2.6.2.2 No Predetermined Numerical Standard: A Holistic Approach

In 1970, a commission of experts from the International Association for Identification (IAI) was established to study the question of the relevancy of a fixed numerical standard for fingerprint identification (Anonymous 1970, 1971). The work of this committee led to a review of the state of empirical and scientific knowledge at that time (Santamaria Beltrán [1953, 1955]; Osterburg and Bloomington [1964]; Gupta [1968]). Hess (1971a–d) published excellent review papers as a result of this process, stressing the fact that some types of minutiæ were more selective than others (e.g., a double bifurcation in the periphery of the pattern is six times less frequent than two separate bifurcations). Qualitative features (such as level 3 features) may be added to minutiæ in the decision process. Finally, the absence of any minutiæ may be as decisive as their presence. It would be exceptional, for example, to observe a core area or a delta area where the ridges do not display any minutiæ. The observation of such a particularity would provide strong support for an identity of source. To conclude the work of this *ad hoc* committee, the following resolution was adopted by the IAI in 1973 (International Association for Identification 1973, p. 8):

> [The International Association for Identification], based upon a three-year study by its Standardization Committee, hereby, states that no valid basis exists for requiring a predetermined minimum number of friction ridge characteristics that must be present in two impressions in order to establish positive identification.

Another argument against any numerical standard stems from knowledge of the morphogenesis of the papillary lines (see Chapter 1). The various stresses involved in this process (regression of the volar pads, development of size, meeting of multiple development fronts) induce a variable formation of minutiæ (in terms of form and positioning). Around the 25th week of gestation, the development of papillary lines is finished on the dermis and has been projected onto the epidermal layer of the skin. From that moment, a final differentiation occurs on the papillæ pegs, which dictates the form of the gland ducts and ridge edges. The nature of this papillary variability prevents any justification for a predefined minimum number of ridge characteristics that must be in agreement (without significant differences) in order to conclude to an identification. Indeed, the extent of specific features is much broader than minutiæ alone.

In 1995, during a conference on fingerprint detection and identification techniques hosted by the Israel National Police in Ne'urim, Israel, 28 fingerprint experts and scientists (representing 11 countries) unanimously approved a slightly actualized variation of the IAI 1973 resolution (Margot and German 1996):

> No scientific basis exists for requiring that a pre-determined minimum number of friction ridge features must be present in two impressions in order to establish a positive identification.

That resolution has been reaffirmed following the work of the Standardization II Committee (Polski et al. 2011, p. 3) as follows:

> There currently exists no scientific basis for requiring a minimum amount of corresponding friction ridge detail information between two impressions to arrive at an opinion of single source attribution.

The process cannot, therefore, be reduced to counting minutiæ; each identification represents a unique set of circumstances and the judgment of the value of concurring features between a mark and a print depends on a variety of conditions that automatically exclude any minimum standard. It is not justifiable (or even scientific) to reduce the issue of fingerprint variability to numbers of minutiæ alone. The identification process involves a holistic assessment, balancing both quantitative (number of minutiæ), and qualitative aspects (general pattern, type of minutiæ, pores, edges) visible in the mark. This qualitative/quantitative approach is at the heart of Ashbaugh's view of the identification process (Ashbaugh 1999), which he previously placed under the term *ridgeology.*

Of course, when simultaneous marks are available (e.g., marks left by fingers in anatomical sequence), the full information can be used, provided that the analysis stage established the fact that the marks were associated. A good description of the process for dealing with simultaneous impressions is provided by Ostrowski (2001). One case heard by the US Supreme Judicial Court of Massachusetts is of interest here. In *Commonwealth v. Patterson* (840 N.E. 2d, 12, 33 [Mass., 2005]), the Court, in a Daubert hearing, rejected the testimony of a fingerprint examiner who concluded to the identification of an individual based on the aggregate consideration of a set of marks left, in his opinion, by a single hand. The Court held, in part, that the technique of jointly considering marks was not governed by appropriate standards and was lacking of any research in peer-reviewed journals to testify to the soundness and reliability of the technique. Since then, SWGFAST has issued a related standard SWGFAST (2008) and Black (2006) has demonstrated that examiners can successfully determine simultaneous depositions, or otherwise, the majority (88%) of the time. We are not aware of new court decisions on the admissibility of fingerprint evidence involving simultaneous impressions.

In practice, most fingerprint examiners recognize that the counting of matching points up to a number determined by policy does not precede the identification. On the contrary, it is usually the case that the expert reaches a state of personal conviction about the identification, based on a wide spectrum of features, before the point count is conducted. As indicated in Table 2.9, various countries have adopted the practice endorsed by the IAI/Ne'urim resolutions.

A review undertaken by a committee in England and Wales was a determining factor in the adoption of the IAI resolution by other countries. In 1989, Evett and Williams conducted a collaborative study among 130 fingerprint examiners in England and Wales. They sent to each participant ten mark/print comparisons (nine associations and one exclusion), asking each examiner to mark the number of concordant minutiæ and to express an opinion with respect to the identification. No misidentification was reported. But, when examining pairs of matching prints/marks, examiners varied widely in the number of points of comparison they found. In the case of one mark, the number varied from 11 to 40. In other words, some examiners would not have gone to court with this pair of impressions, although the most would have done so

TABLE 2.9
Overview of Some Holistic Approaches and Their Origins

Country	Comments
United States and Canada	Since 1973, following the IAI resolution.
Scandinavian countries (Finland, Sweden, Denmark, Iceland, and Norway)	To our knowledge, Norway was the first European country to move toward the abandonment of the 12-point numerical standard. The other Scandinavian countries followed.
United Kingdom (from 2001) and Scotland (from 2006)	In 1988, a committee was formed by the ACPO (Association of Chief Police Officers) and the Home Office to undertake a review of the origin and relevancy of the 16-point standard. Following this review (Evett and Williams 1996), the committee recommended abandonment of the numerical standard. Since 1996, a project group (ACPO National Fingerprint Evidence Standard Project Board) worked at implementing the change from the 16-point practice to no numerical standard. This was also in the light of new rules for disclosure, and the establishment of appropriate quality assurance mechanisms and procedures as well as training requirements. A 1999 appeal court decision *R v. Buckley* [1999] EWCA Crim 1191 paved the way toward the abandonment of the numerical standard by discussing and allowing a comparison with only eight minutiæ. The practice without a numerical standard was implemented beginning June 11, 2001. It took more time in Scotland due to the McKie case.
Australia (from 1999) and New Zealand	In Australia, the "12-point rule" was adopted in 1975. The move toward its abandonment started in some states and territories in 1992. The "12-point rule" was nationally abandoned in favor of the 1973 IAI resolution in 1999.
China	According to Shiquan Liu (personal communication, 2015), there is no numerical standard in China and the decision is left to the appreciation of the fingerprint experts. The practice tends to be within the range of 8–12 points as a minimum in the most cases. The 8–12 rule is explicit in some laboratory standard operating procedures.
Switzerland (from 1998)	Taking advantage of the debate in the United Kingdom and in Australia, and following the Ne'urim declaration, a committee undertook to manage the change toward a non-numerical practice. In 1997, after a survey analogous to the one undertaken in the United Kingdom, the heads of the fingerprint bureaus as a long-term objective adopted the abandonment of the 12-point numerical standard. Initially, the previous standard (12 points) had been kept as a quality assurance filter to distinguish between simple and complex cases. It has been abandoned by a new resolution adopted in 2014 that endorsed the SWGFAST approach to complexity (2013a). Current practice is, however, still largely focused on a 12-point rule.

(Evett and Williams 1996). A comparable survey was undertaken in Switzerland in 1997, leading to worrisome results, especially with regard to false exclusions. Evett and Williams' study led to the following main conclusions:

- The dogma adopted by numerous fingerprint examiners that fingerprint identification is an "exact" science is a misconception. The essence of science is inductive inference. Inference is a mental process that cannot be exact (or deductive). Fingerprint identification is scientific in that sense (Evett 1996).
- The precision implied by any number (12, 16, etc.) is also a lure. The determination of individual minutiæ or features is highly subjective. The use of any rigid numerical standard favors the process of gleaning sufficient points ("teasing the points") to reach the magic number (Tiller 1983). Is it worth recalling from Evett and Williams (1996) that 15 minutiæ in agreement was not reported by any of the tested examiners in their study (who were operating under a 16-point rule at the time). Clearly, if they reached 15 minutiæ, then they would make sure that they found 16!

- As a means of achieving quality, a numerical standard alone is poor. The way forward is to concentrate on professional standards rather than on rules about numbers of minutiæ. A quality management scheme is required that includes training, certification testing, performance testing, file audits, and blind trials.

We recommend three ways to move toward transparency. The first has been applied throughout this chapter already: It is clarifying the inference process. The second is to move away from considering experts as black boxes and provide them with assistance in their assignment of probability. That is the role of probability models. This does not mean that a statistical tool will replace fingerprint experts. The human will continue to outperform machines for a wide range of tasks such as assessing the features on a mark, judging its level of distortion, putting the elements into its context, communicating the findings and applying critical thinking. But statistical models will bring assistance in an assessment that is very prone to cognitive bias: probability assignment. An appropriate distribution of tasks between the human and the machine is the goal. The last required improvement is to put more weight on documentation, particularly during the analysis and comparison phases.

2.7 PROBABILITY MODELS APPLIED TO FINGERMARKS

One of the most frequent questions posed to statisticians regarding fingerprints is of the kind "if a comparison between a mark and a print shows a given set of features in agreement without discrepancies, could you demonstrate statistically the identity of the source?" The quick answer is no. As Stoney (1991) puts it, "you cannot achieve individualization through statistics." All that statistics can do are provide (1) a model for assigning a likelihood ratio in a given case and (2) guidance on setting that likelihood ratio in some kind of relevant population framework, the latter leading to an inference as to the probability of the mark and the print being from the same person. But statistics can do no more than provide a probabilistic answer when faced with alternative propositions.

Some may argue that the probability for an adventitious correspondence between fingerprints is so small that, whatever the framework, the probability of the identification will be so close to 100% that there is no need to disclose a specific number to the court. During the now-famous *Daubert* hearing in the *U.S. v. Mitchell* case in 1999, the FBI provided calculations based on experiments carried out on an AFIS system. The model has been described by Stoney (2001). For complete fingerprints, a random match probability of 10^{-97} was claimed. For partial marks, the match probability was given as 10^{-27}. Such figures, at first sight, appear to relegate the argument that we are presenting to the status of nit-picking. The figure of 10^{-97} transcends reality to the extent that it is amazing that it was admitted into evidence. This extraordinary number was obtained by a model-based formula that took the probability density of extreme points of a postulated probability distribution. Wayman (2000) has pointed out the weakness of this argument. We should not have unrealistic expectations of statistical studies, and the quoting of extravagantly extreme numbers is, ultimately, not productive. It follows that it is not possible to prove that a particular region of friction ridge skin must have left a given mark. The process being essentially inductive, a certainty is not logically and philosophically attainable through mathematical methods. Nevertheless, this limitation does not prevent statistics from offering a highly powerful tool for assessing the value of fingermark to fingerprint comparisons.

The previous edition of this book (Champod et al. 2004, pp. 37–39) included a critical analysis up to the studies carried out in the late 1990s. We relied heavily on the excellent review by Stoney (2001). A number of more recent studies have contributed to the body of knowledge since then. Reviews of the most recent efforts on statistical modeling have been published by Neumann (2012), followed by Abraham et al. (2013). There is a steady trend to invest in research that offers the potential to statistically qualify the weight to be assigned to a comparison. The purpose here is not to conduct this exhaustive review process again, but to focus on the main contributions that can have an operational impact.

Any research seeking to help assign the strength (LR) in the evaluation should follow strict rules with regard to:

1. Limiting the number of modeling assumptions (typically in relation to the independence of the variables)
2. Accounting for nonlinear distortion of the friction ridge skin
3. Testing the model on extensive data where the ground truth is known (the source has been established) and with a measurement of the rates of misleading evidence that may result

One model, published in the *Journal of the Royal Statistical Society*, represents the culmination of several years of research conducted by the Forensic Science Service in England and Wales. Neumann at al. (2012) presented a highly advanced model to compute likelihood ratios, integrating variations in annotations as well as distortion effects. Data concerning the validation of that model is also presented. To date, this work presents the most extensive validation exercise toward a probabilistic system that could be implemented in casework. The operational use of this model has also been studied (Neumann et al. 2011). The marks considered were those not recovered initially (due to low quality), recovered but considered of insufficient quality for identification in the analysis stage, or marks that were compared to a fingerprint and where the conclusion was inconclusive, all in the normal course of casework. A few additional associations were found by examining a large quantity of marks. While a generalized application of the model to all marks does not seem cost-efficient, some contexts are highlighted where the use of such marks together with a probability model may be viable.

The second group of models takes advantage of scores obtained from AFIS systems to assign a weight to a given comparison (Egli et al. 2007; Egli 2009; Alberink et al. 2014; Egli Anthonioz and Champod 2014). These models have been published and are moving toward operational validation and implementation.

We present later the LRs obtained for all the cases from the NIST SD27 database (Garris and McCabe 2000), using a statistical model adapted from Egli (2009). The model takes advantage of a background dataset of 963,710 fingerprints, none of them being associated with the NIST SD27 dataset. The NIST SD27 is made of 244 cases with marks and prints of known sources. For each comparison, the set of matching minutiæ between the mark and the print are provided. FBI fingerprint examiners have made these annotations. This facilitates calculation of the LRs for each case, knowing that the mark has been left by the print (same source), and also to compute the LR in situation where a random print is postulated as the source (hence, the mark is from a different source). Figure 2.31 presents a summary of all the LR values obtained. Such a graph is called a "Tippett plot": in red, the cumulative frequency of all the LRs computed for the cases from different sources; in blue, the cumulative frequency of all the LRs obtained for cases coming from the same source. The *x*-axis gives the $\log_{10}(LR)$, and the *y*-axis is the cumulative frequency from 0 (no observations) to 1 (100% of the observations). The plotted LRs have been calibrated according to the logistic regression method proposed by Brümmer and du Preez (2006) and Ramos-Castro (2007), and recently applied to fingerprint models (Morrison 2013; Haraksim et al. 2015). Two statistics are commonly used to characterize the performance for such a system. They are referred to as RMEP and RMED. In our case, they are as follows:

- The RMEP is the rate of misleading evidence in favor of the prosecution proposition (i.e., LRs above 1 when in fact the mark and the print are from different sources). For this system, the RMEP is 1.92%, meaning that the system will mislead in favor of the prosecution proposition with that rate. However, the highest LR obtained under such an adverse case is below 100.
- The RMED is the rate of misleading evidence in favor of the defense proposition (i.e., LRs below 1 when in fact the mark and the print are from the same source). For this system, this rate is 1.69%, with a minimum LR (in $\log_{10}$) of −2.

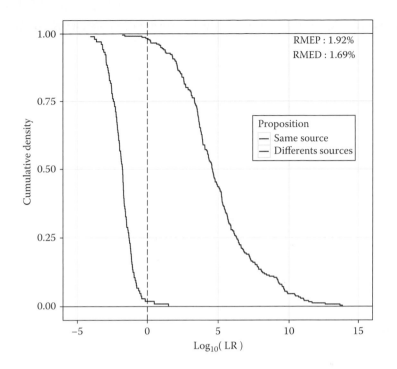

FIGURE 2.31 Tippett plot of the calibrated LRs obtained on the NIST SD27 database. (Courtesy of Marco de Donno University of Lausanne, Switzerland.)

We believe that such models—properly calibrated and characterized, with measured error rates (RMED and RMEP), on an adequate body of cases with known ground truth—will, in the future, help examiners in assigning the weight to be given to a comparison between a mark and a print. A worked example is provided later in Section 2.8.

The expected incorporation of an explicit statistical component in the daily work of the fingerprint examiner is not without challenges. The first relates to research. At present, no published models have gone through an extensive validation and implementation exercise from an operational perspective. It would mean deploying a model in operational practice, defining its scope of operation, monitoring rates of misleading evidence, and developing standard operating procedures. The second challenge relates to the training of experts and the development of mechanisms to resolve conflicting outcomes (i.e., an expert's opinion and the output of a model). The third challenge is one of the communications with the police, the courts, and all other stakeholders. The long tradition associated with fingerprint evidence makes any change difficult, and the beneficiaries of such findings would need to be fully informed and educated regarding the proposed changes outlined earlier.

To conclude this section, we emphasize that, at present, the whole identification process is mostly dominated by dogmatic positions rather than by a structured and documented approach. The (necessary) benefits brought by a statistical approach are not sufficient per se; procedures should also be fully documented to ensure transparency. The development of a corpus of standard operating procedures should include

- The identification process, from analysis to verification (with a clear descriptive model of the features used and an explicit inferential model)
- The process of note-taking from analysis to verification
- The procedures used to handle disputes and/or errors
- The processes for case file auditing and proficiency testing of fingerprint experts, and the potential associated actions

The fingerprint profession needs to operate with an ethical and unbiased culture in a free environment offering adequate reward mechanisms. Training, continuous education, and appraisal systems should all be in place. We will elaborate more on this in Chapter 5. And, finally, we call for the development of well-supported research programs directed at all aspects of fingerprint identification.

The higher level of scrutiny that the field has been subjected to, especially since the publication of the NRC report (National Research Council 2009), will not reduce. We believe this to be for the better. The NRC report has changed the attitude of the judiciary who are now, justifiably, much more inclined to ask for more detailed reports (e.g., a section in each report on methodological limits and current controversies) and to challenge the fingerprint findings put forward to them (Edmond et al. 2014). This means that practitioners will have to strengthen their communication skills, including their ability to articulate and justify—both in their reports and in oral testimony—what they do.

2.8 AN LR-BASED REPORTING SCHEME

We talked throughout this chapter about assigning likelihood ratios and potentially concentrating the reporting on the LR value without addressing the propositions themselves. An LR-based reporting scheme is at the basis of the guidelines for evaluative reporting from the European Network of Forensic Science Institutes (Willis 2015). Note that the guidelines themselves make it clear that categorical opinions are conclusions that go beyond the sole assessment of the findings. It is stated as follows (p. 18):

> The categorical conclusions of identification expressed by examiners in areas such as the comparative examination of fingerprints, handwriting, signatures, tool marks, firearms, footwear marks, go beyond the sole assessment of the forensic findings. These types of conclusions sit outside the scope of the document. However, even in these cases, the strict evaluation of the strength of forensic findings associated with the comparison remains a balance between (1) the degree of correspondence between features shared by the two specimens and (2) the probability that those features would be observed in another source, which amounts to an assignment of a likelihood ratio

In this section, we aim at presenting how fingerprint information can be reported using an LR format. A case recently published by Attias et al. (2015) will be used as an example (Figure 2.32).

From the case information reported in the paper, we understand that a group of young teenagers were involved in a violent fight with the use of knives and guns. One of them was badly injured by another man and all of them escaped before the arrival of the police on the scene. On a cigarette box found at the scene, three marks were detected using cyanoacrylate fuming. One of these marks

FIGURE 2.32 Mark and print with 6–7 matching minutiæ without discrepancy as published by Attias et al. (Reproduced from Attias, D. et al., *J. Forensic Sci. Criminol.*, 3, 302, 2015. With permission.)

is qualified as of value for comparison. Following a search in the national AFIS system, among the fifteen candidates returned by the system in the list, the print of one candidate (we will call him the POI) is retained as a potential source. The other 14 prints from the remaining candidates were excluded from being the source of the mark. The mark and print were submitted to independent examination by four examiners who all indicated that, although an identification decision could not be reached, the POI could not be excluded as being the source. As such, the information has some investigative value. We aim here to progress this case through an evaluative report. We would indicate this framework of circumstances in the report and state that, if this information changes, we would need to revise our assessment as new information may impact on the assessment of the strength of the forensic findings. This is to make transparent that all probabilities that will be assigned are conditional and are conditioned on some knowledge (K) as we have exposed previously.

We will assess the findings in the light of the following propositions: either the recovered mark has been left by the POI or it has been left by another unknown person. If the first proposition is true, it is our assessment that the probability of finding that level of agreement between the mark and the print is high (our probability assignment is 0.7 as an order of magnitude). Indeed, we observed corresponding features that have a reasonable level of reproducibility. It means that the features observed in the mark are what was expected if the corresponding print is provided. The value 0.7 is the assigned numerator in the likelihood ratio, and it directly answers the reproducibility question $Q1_c$.

Now, considering the alternative proposition that the POI has not left the mark, but the source is an unknown person, it is our assessment that finding such a level of agreement is very low. By very low, we mean that the probability of making these observations, with that level of agreement, on a print of another unknown person is below 1 in 9'260. That value addresses the specificity question $Q2_c$. Dividing $Q1_c$ by $Q2_c$ gives a LR of about 8333 (0.9/(1/9'260)).

This aforementioned assessment is based on the following two arguments:

1. The mark displays an area of friction ridge skin corresponding to a delta on the right of the core and probably left by a finger. The ridge count cannot be easily derived. The general pattern of the source is most probably a whorl or a left loop (including central pocket loops). That amounts to just over 60% of general patterns.
2. A limited number of minutiæ (6–7) have been annotated in correspondence and within the tolerances set during analysis. The probability of finding such an arrangement of minutiæ in another unknown print, below its delta, is low. Specialized literature, such as Neumann et al. (2012), indicates that such a configuration could be expected on average with a LR of 10^5 (see Figure 2.22). However, this is an average figure and the study showed that the LR for a given number of minutiæ can vary quite substantially as a function of the configuration and its position with regards to the core or delta. A more case-specific assignment can be obtained by running the case annotations through the AFIS-based model we discussed in Section 2.7 (Figure 2.31). The LR obtained in this manner is 4995. Considering the well-known pattern force effects in the delta area, the value of about 5000 reflects, in our opinion, a fair and reasonable assignment of the LR. Note that, when the above models are used to compute the LR, they automatically account for the numerator (using a distortion model). As such, the value of 0.9 discussed previously is no longer required.
3. The mark is not displaying any level 3 features that might otherwise make a contribution in addition to the observed level 1 and level 2 features.

Together, the combined LR of observing a delta of whorl or a left loop and these minutiæ with the level of agreement noted is 8333 ((1/0.6)*5000).

The observations on the mark in comparison with the print provide *moderately strong support* for the proposition that the mark was left by the POI rather than the proposition that the mark was left by an unknown person. By moderately strong support, we mean that the observations are at least 8000 times more likely if the mark was left by the POI rather than someone else. The verbal conversion from the likelihood ratio to the verbal equivalent is based on a convention giving the correspondence between orders of magnitude of the likelihood ratio and verbal terms. Here, the example verbal scale provided by Willis (2015) has been used.

It is important to stress that information should not be misconstrued as meaning that the mark has been associated with certainty to the POI or that the POI is very likely (or with a probability of 1−(1/8000)) to be at the source of the mark. If we do, we would be committing a logical fallacy known as the fallacy of transposing the conditional or Prosecutor's fallacy (Skorupski and Wainer 2015). The aforementioned information should not be read as meaning an "identification," but only provides strong support for an association. In order to put this information into the context of the case, it is necessary to relate the strength of the findings to the size of the relevant population of individuals who may have left the mark (if it was not the POI). For example, if, based on the other evidence available and before the forensic findings presented here, the court believes that the POI has a reasonable probability of being involved (more than 50%), then, based on the findings here, we could conclude with a probability above 99% that the mark was left by the POI. However, if the court has information to suggest initially that the POI was involved with a very low probability (1 in 10,000 corresponding to all young individuals in the city), our results will allow the court to conclude with a probability of less than 50% that the POI left the mark. The forensic information provided therefore has to be related to the initial assessment by the court of the probability that the POI has been at the source of the recovered mark. Both of the probabilistic arguments are derived via the application of Bayes theorem as previously described in Box 2.5.

To conclude, we hope that, overall, the reader will have realized that the notion of "uniqueness" does not have a place in the debate. In that sense, we deviate from other recent accounts of the identification process, where we can read:

> An example of a universal truth, a virtually unconditioned truth, a generalization, or a law within the forensic comparative science community of collaborating scientists is the law "Every natural pattern is unique." (Vanderkolk 2009)

> The rule of law in forensic comparative sciences is: pattern formations in friction ridge skin cannot be replicated, and their prints can be individualized. (Vanderkolk 2011)

There is no rule of law or universal truth in forensic comparative science; it is just a matter of inductive probabilistic inference and decision-making.

REFERENCES

Abraham, J., Champod, C., Lennard, C., and Roux, C. (2013), Modern statistical models for forensic fingerprint examinations: A critical review, *Forensic Sci. Int.*, 232, 131–150.

Acree, M. A. (1999), Is there a gender difference in fingerprint ridge density, *Forensic Sci. Int.*, 102, 35–44.

Aitken, C. G. G. and Taroni, F. (2004), *Statistics and the Evaluation of Evidence for Forensic Scientists*, 2nd ed., Chichester, U.K.: John Wiley & Sons Ltd.

Alberink, I., de Jongh, A., and Rodriguez, C. (2014), Fingermark evidence evaluation based on automated fingerprint identification system matching scores: The effect of different types of conditioning on likelihood ratios, *J. Forensic Sci.*, 59, 70–81.

Alexander, H. L. V. (1973), *Classifying Palmprints: A Complete System of Coding, Filing and Searching Palmprints*, Springfield, IL: Charles C. Thomas.

American National Standards Institute and National Institute of Standards and Technology. (2011), Data format for the interchange of fingerprint, facial & other biometric information, Technical ANSI/NIST-ITL 1-2011, Washington, DC: National Institute of Standards and Technology, http://fingerprint.nist.gov/standard/ (last accessed January 29, 2016).

Anonymous. (1970), Convention action, *Ident. News*, 20, 10–11.

Anonymous. (1971), Standards committee, *Ident. News*, 21, 14–15.

Anonymous. (1972), An analysis of standards in fingerprint identification, *FBI Law Enforcement Bull.*, 39, 7–11, 29–30.

Anthonioz, A. and Champod, C. (2014), Integration of pore features into the evaluation of fingerprint evidence, *J. Forensic Sci.*, 59, 82–93.

Anthonioz, A., Egli, N., Champod, C., Neumann, C., Puch-Solis, R., and Bromage-Griffiths, A. (2008), Level 3 details and their role in fingerprint identification: A survey among practitioners, *J. Forensic Ident.*, 58, 562–589.

Ashbaugh, D. R. (1982a), Poroscopy, *Fingerprint Whorld*, 19, 5–12.

Ashbaugh, D. R. (1982b), Edgeology/poroscopy /ridgeology—Our next evaluative step, *RCMP Gaz.*, 44(2)/45(2)/45(3), 4–6/12–17/10–14.

Ashbaugh, D. R. (1991a), Ridgeology, *J. Forensic Ident.*, 41, 16–64.

Ashbaugh, D. R. (1991b), Palmar flexion crease identification, *J. Forensic Ident.*, 41, 255–273.

Ashbaugh, D. R. (1992), Incipient ridges and the clarity spectrum, *J. Forensic Ident.*, 42, 106–114.

Ashbaugh, D. R. (1999), *Qualitative-Quantitative Friction Ridge Analysis—An Introduction to Basic and Advanced Ridgeology*, Boca Raton, FL: CRC Press.

Attias, D., Hefetz, I., and Ben-Shimon, E. (2015), Latent fingerprints of insufficient value can be used as an investigative lead, *J. Forensic Sci. Criminol.*, 3, 302.

Balthazard, V. (1911), De l'identification par les empreintes digitales, *Comptes rendus des séances de l'Académie des Sciences*, 152, 1862–1864.

Barclay, F. (1991), Identification des traces papillaires fondée sur la structure des pores: Une étude de cas, *La Gazette de la G.R.C.*, 53(10), 18–21.

Barclay, F. (1997), Friction ridge identification based on pore structure—A case study, *Fingerprint Whorld*, 23, 7–11.

Bazen, A. M. and Gerez, S. H. (2002), Thin-plate spline modelling of elastic deformations in fingerprints, in *Proceedings of Third IEEE Benelux Signal Processing Symposium (SPS-2002)*, Leuven, Belgium.

Bertillon, A. (1912), Notes et observations médico-légales—les empreintes digitales, *Archives d'anthropologie criminelle, de médecine légale et de psychologie normale et pathologique*, 27, 36–52.

Biedermann, A., Bozza, S., and Taroni, F. (2008), Decision theoretic properties of forensic identification: Underlying logic and argumentative implications, *Forensic Sci. Int.*, 177, 120–132.

Biedermann, A., Garbolino, P., and Taroni, F. (2013), The subjectivist interpretation of probability and the problem of individualisation in forensic science, *Sci. Justice*, 53, 192–200.

Bindra, B., Jasuja, O. P., and Singla, A.K. (2000), Poroscopy: A method of personal identification revisited, *Anil Aggrawal's Internet J. Forensic Med. Toxicol.*, http://www.anilaggrawal.com/ij/vol_001_no_001/paper003.html (last accessed January 29, 2016).

Black, J. P. (2006), Pilot study: The application of ACE-V to simultaneous (cluster) impressions, *J. Forensic Ident.*, 56, 933–971.

Black, J. P. (2012), Is there a need for 100% verification (review) of latent print examination conclusions? *J. Forensic Ident.*, 62, 80–100.

Brazelle, M. (2015), Whorl pattern analysis: Determining directional flow, *Ident. News*, 45, 9–11.

Brewer, S. B. (2014), *ACE-V Examination Method Training Manual*, Sacramento, CA: California State University.

Bridges, B. C. (1963), *Practical Fingerprinting*, New York: Funk & Wagnalls.

Brown, G. A. and Cropp, P. L. (1987), Standardised nomenclature in forensic science, *J. Forensic Sci. Soc.*, 27, 393–399.

Brümmer, N. and du Preez, J. (2006), Application-independent evaluation of speaker detection, *Comput. Speech Lang.*, 20, 230–275.

Budowle, B., Buscaglia, J., and Schwartz Perlman, R. (2006), Review of the scientific basis for friction ridge skin comparisons as a means of identification: Committee findings and recommendations, *Forensic Sci. Comm.*, 8, https://www2.fbi.gov/hq/lab/fsc/backissu/jan2006/research/2006_01_research02.htm (last accessed January 29, 2016)

Busey, T. A. and Dror, I. E. (2011), Chapter 15: Special abilities and vulnerabilities in forensic expertise, in *The Fingerprint Sourcebook*, ed. A. McRoberts, Washington, DC: National Institute of Justice, http://www.ncjrs.gov/pdffiles1/nij/225335.pdf (last accessed January 29, 2016).

Campbell, S. A. (2011), *The Fingerprint Inquiry Report*, Edinburgh, Scotland: APS Group Scotland.

Cappelli, R., Maio, D., and Maltoni, D. (2001), Modelling plastic distortion in fingerprint images, in *Advances in Pattern Recognition, ICAPR 2001* (Vol. LNCS 2013), eds. S. Singh, N. Murshed, and W. Kropatsch, Berlin, Germany: Springer Verlag, pp. 371–378.

Cassidy, M. J. (1980), *Footwear Identification*, Montreal, Québec, Canada: Canadian Government Printing Service.

Champod, C. (1995), Locard, numerical standards and "probable" identification, *J. Forensic Ident.*, 45, 132–159.

Champod, C. (1996), Reconnaissance automatique et analyse statistique des minuties sur les empreintes digitales, PhD thesis, Lausanne, Suisse: Université de Lausanne, Institut de Police Scientifique et de Criminologie.

Champod, C. (2008), Fingerprint examination: Towards more transparency, *Law Probab. Risk*, 7, 111–118.

Champod, C. (2009a), *Report to the Fingerprint Inquiry*, Edinburgh, Scotland: The Fingerprint Inquiry Scotland, http://www.webarchive.org.uk/wayback/archive/20150428163044/http://www.thefingerprintinquiryscotland.org.uk/inquiry/files/ED_0003.pdf (last accessed January 29, 2016).

Champod, C. (2009b), Identification and individualization, in *Wiley Encyclopedia of Forensic Science* (Vol. 3), eds. A. Moenssens and A. Jamieson, Chichester, U.K.: John Wiley & Sons, pp. 1508–1511.

Champod, C. (2013a), Friction ridge skin impression evidence—Standards of proof, in *Encyclopedia of Forensic Sciences*, eds. J. A. Siegel and P. J. Saukko, Waltham, MA: Academic Press, pp. 111–116.

Champod, C. (2013b), Overview and meaning of identification/individualization, in *Encyclopedia of Forensic Sciences*, eds. J. A. Siegel and P. J. Saukko, Waltham, MA: Academic Press, pp. 303–309.

Champod, C. (2015), Fingerprint identification: Advances since the 2009 National Research Council report, *Philos. Trans. R. Soc. Lond. B: Biol. Sci.*, 370 (1674). DOI: 10.1098/rstb.2014.0259.

Champod, C. and Chamberlain, P. (2009), Fingerprints, in *Handbook of Forensic Science*, eds. J. Fraser and R. Williams, Cullompton, U.K.: Willan Publishing, pp. 57–83.

Champod, C. and Evett, I. W. (2001), A probabilistic approach to fingerprint evidence, *J. Forensic Ident.*, 51, 101–122.

Champod, C. and Evett, I. W. (2009), Evidence interpretation: A logical approach, in *Wiley Encyclopedia of Forensic Science* (Vol. 2), eds. A. Moenssens and A. Jamieson, Chichester, U.K.: John Wiley & Sons, pp. 968–976.

Champod, C., Lennard, C., and Margot, P. A. (1993), Alphonse Bertillon and dactyloscopy, *J. Forensic Ident.*, 43, 604–625.

Champod, C., Lennard, C. J., Margot, P. A., and Stoilovic, M. (2004), *Fingerprints and Other Ridge Skin Impressions*, Boca Raton, FL: CRC Press.

Champod, C. and Margot, P. (1997), Analysis of minutiæ occurrences in fingerprints—The search for non-combined minutiæ, in *Current Topics in Forensic Science—Proceedings of the 14th Meeting of the International Association of Forensic Sciences* (Vol. 1), eds. T. Takatori and A. Takasu, Ottawa, Ontario, Canada: Shunderson Communications, pp. 55–58.

Champod, C. and Margot, P. A. (1996), Computer assisted analysis of minutiæ occurrences on fingerprints, in *Proceedings of the International Symposium on Fingerprint Detection and Identification*, eds. J. Almog and E. Springer, June 26–30, 1995, Ne'urim, Israel: Israel National Police, pp. 305–318.

Chapman, W., Hicklin, A., Kiebuzinski, G. I., Komarinski, P., Mayer-Splain, J., Taylor, M., and Wallner, R. (2013), *Markup Instructions for Extended Friction Ridge Features*, Technical NIST Special Publication 1151, Washington, DC: National Institute of Standards and Technology, http://nvlpubs.nist.gov/nistpubs/SpecialPublications/NIST.SP.1151.pdf.

Chatterjee, S. K. (1962), Edgeoscopy, *Fingerprint Ident. Mag.*, 44, 3–13.

Chatterjee, S. K. and Hague, R. V. (1988), *Fingerprint or Dactyloscopy and Ridgeoscopy*, Calcutta, India: M.K. Mukerjee Temple Press.

Clark, J. D. (2002), ACE-V: Is it scientifically reliable and accurate? *J. Forensic Ident.*, 52, 401–408.

Clegg, D. L. J. (1998), Poroscopy in practice, *Fingerprint Whorld*, 24, 102–105.

Cole, S. A. (2008), The 'opinionization' of fingerprint evidence, *BioSocieties*, 3, 105–113.

Cole, S. A. (2009), Forensics without uniqueness, conclusions without individualization: The new epistemology of forensic identification, *Law Probab. Risk*, 8, 233–255.

Cole, S. A. (2014), Individualization is dead, long live individualization! Reforms of reporting practices for fingerprint analysis in the United States, *Law Probab. Risk*, 13, 117–150.

Cole, S. A. and Roberts, A. (2012), Certainty, individualisation and the subjective nature of expert fingerprint evidence, *Crim. Law Rev.*, (issue 11), 824–849.

Comber, B. (2012), *Numerical Analysis and Comparison of Distorted Fingermarks from the Same Source*, Canberra, Australian Capital Territory, Australia: University of Canberra.

Cook, R., Evett, I. W., Jackson, G., Jones, P. J., and Lambert, J. A. (1998a), A model for case assessment and interpretation, *Sci. Justice*, 38, 151–156.

Cook, R., Evett, I. W., Jackson, G., Jones, P. J., and Lambert, J. A. (1998b), A hierarchy of propositions: Deciding which level to address in casework, *Sci. Justice*, 38, 231–240.

Coppock, C. A. (2007), *Contrast—An Investigator's Basis Reference Guide to Fingerprint Identification Concepts*, 2nd ed., Springfield, IL: Charles C. Thomas.

Cowger, J. F. (1983), *Friction Ridge Skin: Comparison and Identification of Fingerprints*, New York: Elsevier Science Publishing.

Cummins, H. H. and Midlo, C. (1961), *Fingerprints, Palms and Soles,* 2nd ed., New York: Dover Publications, Inc.

Deopa, D., Prakash, C., and Tayal, I. (2014), A study of fingerprint in relation to gender and blood group among medical students in Uttarakhand region, *J. Indian Acad. Forensic Med.*, 36, 23–27.

Doak, B. (2010), Checking the fingerprint impression, *Fingerprint Whorld*, 36, 184–188.

Doak, R. (2004), Dominant deltas—A concept, *Fingerprint Whorld*, 30, 118–123.

Dror, I. E., Champod, C., Langenburg, G., Charlton, D., Hunt, H., and Rosenthal, R. (2011), Cognitive issues in fingerprint analysis: Inter- and intra-expert consistency and the effect of a target' comparison, *Forensic Sci. Int.*, 208, 10–17.

Dror, I. E. and Charlton, D. (2006), Why experts make errors, *J. Forensic Ident.*, 56, 600–616.

Dror, I. E., Charlton, D., and Péron, A. E. (2006), Contextual information renders experts vulnerable to making erroneous identifications, *Forensic Sci. Int.*, 156, 74–78.

Dror, I. E., Péron, A., Hind, S.-L., and Charlton, D. (2005), When emotions get to the better of us: The effect of contextual top-down processing on matching fingerprints, *Appl. Cogn. Psychol.*, 19, 799–809.

Earwaker, H., Morgan, R. M., Harris, A. J. L., and Hall, L. J. (2015), Fingermark submission decision-making within a UK fingerprint laboratory: Do experts get the marks that they need? *Sci. Justice*, 55, 239–247.

Eboh, D. (2013), Fingerprint patterns in relation to gender and blood group among students of Delta State University, Abraka, Nigeria, *J. Exp. Clin. Anatomy*, 12, 82–86.

Edgubov, L. G. (1996), National standards of fingerprint identification, *Fingerprint Whorld*, 22, 153–160.

Edmond, G., Martire, K., Kemp, R., Hamer, D., Hibbert, B., Ligertwood, A., Porter, G. San Roque, M., Searston, R., Tangen, J., Thompson, M., White, D. (2014), How to cross-examine forensic scientists: A guide for lawyers, *Aust. Bar Rev.*, 39, 174–197.

Egli Anthonioz, N. M. (2009), *Interpretation of Partial Fingermarks Using an Automated Fingerprint Identification System*, Lausanne, Switzerland: University of Lausanne.

Egli Anthonioz, N. M. and Champod, C. (2014), Evidence evaluation in fingerprint comparison and automated fingerprint identification systems—Modeling between finger variability, *Forensic Sci. Int.*, 235, 86–101.

Egli Anthonioz, N. M., Champod, C., and Margot, P. (2007), Evidence evaluation in fingerprint comparison and automated fingerprint identification systems—Modelling within finger variability, *Forensic Sci. Int.*, 167, 189–195.

Ekanem, A. U., Abubakar, H., and Dibal, N. I. (2014), A study of fingerprints in relation to gender and blood group among residents of Maiduguri, Nigeria, *IOSR J. Dental Med. Sci.*, 13, 18–20.

Epstein, R. (2002), Fingerprints meet Daubert: The myth of fingerprint "science" is revealed, *South. Calif. Law Rev.*, 75, 605–658.

Evett, I. W. (1996), Expert evidence and forensic misconceptions of the nature of exact science, *Sci. Justice*, 36, 118–122.

Evett, I. W. and Williams, R. (1996), A review of the sixteen points fingerprint standard in England and Wales, *J. Forensic Ident.*, 46, 49–73. [Also published in 1995 in *Fingerprint Whorld*, 21, 125–143 and in 1996 in *Proceedings of the International Symposium on Fingerprint Detection and Identification*, Ne'urim, Israel, June 26–30, 1995: Israel National Police, pp. 287–304.]

Expert Working Group on Human Factors in Latent Print Analysis (2012), *Latent Print Examination and Human Factors: Improving the Practice through a Systems Approach*, Washington, DC: U.S. Department of Commerce, National Institute of Standards and Technology.

Faulds, H. (1913), Poroscopy, the scrutiny of sweat-pores for identification, *Nature*, 91, 635–636.

Fayrouz, I. N. E., Farida, N., and Irshad, A. H. (2012), Relation between fingerprints and different blood groups, *J. Forensic Leg. Med.*, 19, 18–21.

Ferguson, B. (1992), Minutiæ discrepancy in the delta area, *Fingerprint Whorld*, 18, 110.

Fieldhouse, S. J. (2015), An investigation into the effects of force applied during deposition on latent fingermarks and inked fingerprints using a variable force fingerprint sampler, *J. Forensic Sci.*, 60, 422–427.

Finkelstein, M. O. and Fairley, W. B. (1970), A Bayesian approach to identification evidence, *Harvard Law Rev.*, 83, 489–517.

Forensic Science Regulator. (2015a), *Information: Fingerprint Examination—Terminology, Definitions and Acronyms*, Birmingham, England: Forensic Science Regulator, https://http://www.gov.uk/government/uploads/system/uploads/attachment_data/file/415091/402_FSR_fingerprint_terminology_Issue1.pdf (last accessed January 29, 2016).

Forensic Science Regulator. (2015b), *Codes of Practice and Conduct: Fingerprint Comparison*, Birmingham, England: Forensic Science Regulator, https://http://www.gov.uk/government/uploads/system/uploads/attachment_data/file/415108/128_FSR_fingerprint_appendix__Issue1.pdf (last accessed January 29, 2016).

Galton, F. (1892), *Finger Prints*, London, U.K.: Macmillan and Co.

Garris, M. D. and McCabe, R. M. (2000), *Summary of NIST Latent Fingerprint Testing Workshop*, Washington, DC: U.S. Department of Commerce, National Institute of Standards and Technology, http://biometrics.nist.gov/cs_links/fingerprint/special_databases/ir_6534.pdf.

Gittelson, S., Bozza, S., Biedermann, A., and Taroni, F. (2013), Decision-theoretic reflections on processing a fingermark, *Forensic Sci. Int.*, 226, e42–e47.

Good, I. J. (1985), Weight of evidence: A brief survey, in *Bayesian Statistics 2*, eds. J. M. Bernardo, M. H. DeGroot, D. V. Lindley, and A. F. M. Smith, North Holland, the Netherlands: Elsevier Science Publishers B. V., pp. 249–270.

Grieve, D. L. (1988), The identification process: Attitude and approach, *J. Forensic Ident.*, 38, 211–224.

Grieve, D. L. (1990), The identification process: The quest for quality, *J. Forensic Ident.*, 40, 109–113.

Gupta, A., Buckley, K., and Sutton, R. (2007), The effect of substrate on the reproducibility of inked fingerprint pore dimensions examined using photomicrography, *Fingerprint Whorld*, 33, 156–163.

Gupta, A., Buckley, K., and Sutton, R. (2008), Latent fingermark pore area reproducibility, *Forensic Sci. Int.*, 179, 172–175.

Gupta, S. R. (1968), Statistical survey of ridge characteristics, *Int. Crim. Police Rev.*, 5(218), 130–134.

Gutiérrez-Redomero, E. and Alonso-Rodríguez, C. (2013), Sexual and topological differences in palmprint and ridge density in the Caucasian Spanish population, *Forensic Sci. Int.*, 229, 159.e151–159.e110.

Gutiérrez-Redomero, E., Alonso-Rodríguez, C., Hernández-Hurtado, L. E., and Rodríguez-Villalba, J. L. (2011), Distribution of the minutiae in the fingerprints of a sample of the Spanish population, *Forensic Sci. Int.*, 208, 79–90.

Gutiérrez-Redomero, E., Galera, V., Martínez, J. M., and Alonso, C. (2007), Biological variability of the minutiae in the fingerprints of a sample of the Spanish population, *Forensic Sci. Int.*, 172, 98–105.

Gutiérrez-Redomero, E., Quirós, J. A., Rivalderia, N., and Alonso, M. C. (2013a), Topological variability of fingerprint ridge density in a sub-Saharan population sample for application in personal identification, *J. Forensic Sci.*, 58, 592–600.

Gutiérrez-Redomero, E., Rivalderia, N., Alonso-Rodriguez, C., Martin, L. M., Dipierri, J. E., Fernàndez-Peire, M. A., and Morillo, R. (2012), Are there population differences in minutiae frequencies? A comparative study of two Argentinian population samples and one Spanish sample, *Forensic Sci. Int.*, 222, 266–276.

Gutiérrez-Redomero, E., Sanchez-Andrés, A., Rivalderia, N., Alonso-Rodriguez, C., Dipierri, J. E., and Martin, L. M. (2013b), A comparative study of topological and sex differences in fingerprint ridge density in Argentinian and Spanish population samples, *J. Forensic Leg. Med.*, 20, 419–429.

Haber, L. and Haber, R. N. (2008), Scientific validation of fingerprint evidence under Daubert, *Law Probab. Risk*, 7, 87–109.

Hamm, E. D. (2006), Friction ridge levels of details: Bane or boon? in *31st Annual Educational Conference of The Fingerprint Society*, Kingdom of Fife, Scotland: Scottish Police College, Tulliallan Castle.

Haraksim, R., Ramos, D., Meuwly, D., and Berger, C. E. H. (2015), Measuring coherence of computer-assisted likelihood ratio methods, *Forensic Sci. Int.*, 249, 123–132.

Heindl, R. (1927), *System und Praxis der Daktyloskopie,* 3rd ed., Berlin, Germany: Walter de Gruyter & Co., Vereinigung Wissenschaftlichen Verleger.

Henry, E. R. (1900), *Classification and Uses of Fingerprints,* 4th ed., London, U.K.: Georges Routledge.

Hess, J. (1971a), The reference shelf, *Finger Print Ident. Mag.*, 52(March), 12–14 & 17.

Hess, J. (1971b), The reference shelf, *Finger Print Ident. Mag.*, 52(April), 16–17 & 23.

Hess, J. (1971c), The reference shelf, *Finger Print Ident. Mag.*, 52(May), 11–13.

Hess, J. (1971d), The reference shelf, *Finger Print Ident. Mag.*, 52(June), 13.

Hicklin, R. A., Buscaglia, J., and Roberts, M. A. (2013), Assessing the clarity of friction ridge impressions, *Forensic Sci. Int.*, 226, 106–117.

Hicklin, R. A., Buscaglia, J., Roberts, M. A., Meagher, S. B., Fellner, W., Burge, M. J., Monaco, M. et al. (2011), Latent fingerprint quality: A survey of examiners, *J. Forensic Ident.*, 61, 385–418.

Huber, R. A. (1959), Expert witnesses, *Crim. Law Q.*, 2, 276–295.

Huber, R. A. (July–August, 1972), The philosophy of identification, *RCMP Gaz.*, 9–14.

Huber, R. A. and Headrick, A. M. (1999), *Handwriting Identification: Facts and Fundamentals*, Boca Raton, FL: CRC Press.

Hutchins, L. A. (2011), Chapter 5: Systems of friction ridge classification, in *The Fingerprint Sourcebook*, ed. A. McRoberts, Washington, DC: National Institute of Justice, http://www.ncjrs.gov/pdffiles1/nij/225325. pdf (last accessed January 29, 2016).

International Association for Identification. (1973), Standardization committee report, *FBI Law Enforcement Bull.*, 42, 7–8.

International Association for Identification. (1980), Resolution VII amended, *Ident. News*, 30, 3.

International Association for Identification. (2010), Resolution 2010-18, http://www.theiai.org/member/resolutions/2010/Resolution_2010-18.pdf (last accessed January 29, 2016).

Interpol (1995), European Working Group on Fingerprint Standards, European fingerprint standards, in *24th European Regional Conference*, Ljubljana, Slovenia.

Interpol. (2000), Interpol European expert group on fingerprint identification—IEEGFI, in *29th European Regional Conference*, Reykjavik, Iceland.

Interpol. (2004), Interpol European expert group on fingerprint identification II—IEEGFI II, *Part 2: Detailing the Method Using Common Terminology and Through the Definition and Application of Shared Principles*, Lyon, France.

Jackson, G. and Jones, P. J. (2009), Case assessment and interpretation, in *Wiley Encyclopedia of Forensic Science* (Vol. 2), eds. A. Moenssens and A. Jamieson, Chichester, U.K.: John Wiley & Sons, pp. 483–496.

Jorgensen, D. (1997), Practical ridgeology or a lesson in looking, *Fingerprint Whorld*, 23, 12–14.

Jozefek, A. (1972), Some problems of fingerprint identification [in Czech], *Ceskoslovenska Kriminalistika [Czechoslovak Criminalistics]*, 1–6.

Kalka, N. D. and Hicklin, R. A. (2014), On relative distortion in fingerprint comparison, *Forensic Sci. Int.*, 244, 78–84.

Kapoor, N. and Badiye, A. (2015b), An analysis of whorl patterns for determination of hand, *J. Forensic Leg. Med.*, 32, 42–46.

Kaye, D. (2009), Identification, individualization and uniqueness: What's the difference?, *Law Probab. Risk*, 8, 85–94.

Kaye, D. H. (2013), Beyond uniqueness: The birthday paradox, source attribution and individualization in forensic science testimony, *Law Probab. Risk*, 12, 3–11.

Kellman, P. J., Mnookin, J. L., Erlikhman, G., Garrigan, P., Ghose, T., Mettler, E., Charlton, D., and Dror, I. E. (2014), Forensic comparison and matching of fingerprints: Using quantitative image measures for estimating error rates through understanding and predicting difficulty, *PLoS ONE*, 9, e94617.

Khan, H. N. (2011), Identification from edgeoscopy and poroscopy in the examination of partial fingerprints and their significance in crime investigation, PhD thesis, Patiala, India: Punjabi University.

Kingston, C. R. (1970), The law of probabilities and the credibility of witness and evidence, *J. Forensic Sci.*, 15, 18–27.

Kingston, C. R. and Kirk, P. L. (1965), Historical development and evaluation of the twelve point rule in fingerprint identification, *Int. Crim. Police Rev.*, 20(186), 62–69.

Kirk, P. L. (1963), The ontogeny of criminalistics, *J. Crim. Law Criminol. Police Sci.*, 54, 235–238.

Koehler, J. J. and Saks, M. J. (2010), Individualization claims in forensic science: Still unwarranted, *Brook. Law Rev.*, 75, 1187–1208.

Kücken, M. U. (2004), On the formation of fingerprints, PhD thesis, Tucson, AZ: The University of Arizona, Graduate Interdisciplinary Program in Applied Mathematics.

Kwan, Q. Y. (1977), Inference of identity of source, D. Crim. Dissertation, Berkeley, CA: University of California.

Lambourne, G. T. C. (1984), Fingerprints standards, *Med. Sci. Law*, 24, 227–229.

Lambourne, G. T. C. (2008), Fingerprint standards, *Fingerprint Whorld*, 34, 118–121.

Langenburg, G. (2004), Pilot study: A statistical analysis of the ACE-V methodology—Analysis stage, *J. Forensic Ident.*, 54, 64–79.

Langenburg, G. (2008), Deposition of bloody friction ridge impressions, *J. Forensic Ident.*, 58, 355–389.

Langenburg, G. (2011), Chapter 14: Scientific research supporting the foundations of friction ridge examinations, in *The Fingerprint Sourcebook*, ed. A. McRoberts, Washington, DC: National Institute of Justice, http://www.ncjrs.gov/pdffiles1/nij/225334.pdf (last accessed January 29, 2016).

Langenburg, G. (2012), A critical analysis and study of the ACE-V process, PhD thesis, Lausanne, Switzerland: University of Lausanne, Institute of Forensic Science/School of Criminal Justice.

Langenburg, G. and Champod, C. (2011), The GYRO system—A recommended approach to more transparent documentation, *J. Forensic Ident.*, 61, 373–384.

Langenburg, G., Champod, C., and Wertheim, P. (2009), Testing for potential contextual bias effects during the verification stage of the ACE-V methodology when conducting fingerprint comparisons, *J. Forensic Sci.*, 54, 571–582.

Lawless, C., Shaw, I., and Mennell, J. (2009), *The Current Position of Fingerprint Evidence—A Literature Review*, Edinburgh, Scotland: The Fingerprint Inquiry Scotland, http://www.webarchive.org.uk/wayback/archive/20150428170245/http://www.thefingerprintinquiryscotland.org.uk/inquiry/files/EC_0001.pdf (last accessed January 29, 2016).

Leadbetter, M. (2009), Judicial enquiry—Fingerprint evidence—Shirley McKie (latent mark 'y7')—PowerPoint presentation, http://www.webarchive.org.uk/wayback/archive/20150428160609/http://www.thefingerprintinquiryscotland.org.uk/inquiry/files/TS_0005.ppt (last accessed January 29, 2016).

Lennard, C. J. (2013), Fingerprint identification: How far have we come? *Aust. J. Forensic Sci.*, 45, 356–367.

Leo, W. F. (1998), Distortion versus dissimilarity in friction skin identification, *J. Forensic Ident.*, 48, 125–129.

Liddle, D. (2001), *The Use of Poroscopy to Identify Points Consistent Fingerprint Identifications*, Canberra, Australian Capital Territory, Australia: Canberra Institute of Technology.

Lindley, D. V. (1985), *Making Decisions,* 2nd ed., Chichester, U.K.: John Wiley & Sons.

Lindley, D. V. (2014), *Understanding Uncertainty,* 2nd ed., Hoboken, NJ: John Wiley & Sons.

Lindley, D. V. and Eggleston, R. (1983), The problem of missing evidence, *Law Q. Rev.*, 99, 86–99.

Liu, S., Champod, C., Wu, J., and Luo, Y. (2015), Study on accuracy of judgments by Chinese fingerprint examiners, *J. Forensic Sci. Med.*, 1, 33–37.

Locard, E. (1911), Les laboratoires de police, *Archives internationales de médecine légale (Société de médecine légale de Belgique)*, 2, 105–117.

Locard, E. (1912a), L'identification des criminels par l'examen des glandes sudoripares, *La province médicale*, 23, 345–346.

Locard, E. (1912b), Les pores et l'identification des criminels, *Biologica—Journal scientifique du médecin*, 2, 357–365.

Locard, E. (1913), La poroscopie—identification par les orifices sudoripares, *Archives d'anthropologie criminelle, de médecine légale et de psychologie normale et pathologique*, 28, 528–546.

Locard, E. (1914), La preuve judiciaire par les empreintes digitales, *Archives d'anthropologie criminelle, de médecine légale et de psychologie normale et pathologique*, 29, 321–348.

Locard, E. (1931), *Traité de criminalistique vol.I à* VII, Lyon, France: Joannès Desvigne et fils Editeurs.

Maceo, A. V. (2009), Qualitative assessment of skin deformation: A pilot study, *J. Forensic Ident.*, 59, 390–440 [with a correction in 2009 *J. Forensic Ident.*, 59, 473–474].

Maceo, A. V. (2011a), Documenting and reporting inconclusive results, *J. Forensic Ident.*, 61, 226–231.

Maceo, A. V. (2011b), Chapter 10: Documentation of friction ridge impressions: From the scene to the conclusion, in *The Fingerprint Sourcebook*, ed. A. McRoberts, Washington, DC: National Institute of Justice, http://www.ncjrs.gov/pdffiles1/nij/225330.pdf (last accessed January 29, 2016).

Maceo, A. V., Carter, M., and Stromback, B. (2013), Palm prints, in *Encyclopedia of Forensic Sciences*, eds. J. A. Siegel and P. J. Saukko, Waltham, MA: Academic Press, pp. 29–36.

Mahacheb, K. (1986), *System for Identifying Persons from Traces of Hands with the Use of Computing Machine [in Bulgarian]*, Sofia, Bulgaria: Research Institute of Forensic Science and Criminology.

Mairs, G. T. (1933a), Finger prints indexed numerically "a finger print family tree", *Finger Print Ident. Mag.*, 15(4), 16–18 & 31.

Mairs, G. T. (1933b), Finger prints indexed numerically "a finger print family tree" (second and concluding installment), *Finger Print Ident. Mag.*, 15(5), 16–18 & 31.

Maltoni, D., Maio, D., Jain, A. K., and Prabhakar, S. (2009), Fingerprint classification and indexing, in *Handbook of Fingerprint Recognition,* 2nd ed., eds. D. Maltoni, D. Maio, A. K. Jain, and S. Prabhakar, London, U.K.: Springer-Verlag, pp. 235–269.

Margot, P. and German, E. (1996), Fingerprint identification breakout meeting, in *Proceedings of the International Symposium on Fingerprint Detection and Identification*, eds. J. Almog and E. Springer, Ne'urim, Israel: Israel National Police, p. 21.

McRoberts, A. (ed.) (2011), *The Fingerprint Sourcebook*, Washington, DC: U.S. Department of Justice, Office of Justice Programs, National Institute of Justice.

Mnookin, J. L. (2008), The validity of latent fingerprint identification: Confessions of a fingerprinting moderate, *Law Probab. Risk*, 7, 127–141.

Moenssens, A. A. (1971), *Fingerprint Techniques*, Radnor, PA: Chilton Book Company.

Morrison, G. S. (2013), Tutorial on logistic-regression calibration and fusion: Converting a score to a likelihood ratio, *Aust. J. Forensic Sci.*, 45, 173–197.

Nagesh, K. R., Bathwal, S., and Ashoka, B. (2011), A preliminary study of pores on epidermal ridges: Are there any sex differences and age related changes? *J. Forensic Leg. Med.*, 18, 302–305.

National Research Council (2009), *Strengthening Forensic Science in the United States: A Path Forward*, Washington, DC: The National Academies Press.

Neumann, C. (2012), Statistics and probabilities as a means to support fingerprint examination, in *Lee and Gaensslen's Advances in Fingerprint Technology,* 3rd ed., ed. R. S. Ramotowski, Boca Raton, FL: CRC Press, pp. 407–452.

Neumann, C., Champod, C., Yoo, M., Genessay, T., and Langenburg, G. (2013), *Improving the Understanding and the Reliability of the Concept of "sufficiency" in Friction Ridge Examination*, Washington, DC: National Institute of Justice, https://http://www.ncjrs.gov/pdffiles1/nij/grants/244231.pdf (last accessed January 29, 2016).

Neumann, C., Evett, I. W., and Skerrett, J. (2012), Quantifying the weight of evidence from a forensic fingerprint comparison: A new paradigm, *J. R. Stat. Soc. Ser. A. (Stat. Soc.)*, 175, 371–415 (with discussion).

Neumann, C., Mateos-Garcia, I., Langenburg, G., Kostroski, J., Skerrett, J. E., and Koolen, M. (2011), Operational benefits and challenges of the use of fingerprint statistical models: A field study, *Forensic Sci. Int.*, 212, 32–46.

Noblis Inc. (2013), Extended feature set training tool, Noblis, http://www.nist.gov/forensics/EFSTrainingTool/ResourcesTab/EFS_AllContent.pdf (last accessed January 29, 2016).

Nordby, J. J. (1992), Can we believe what we see, if we see what we believe?—Expert disagreement, *J. Forensic Sci.*, 37, 1115–1124.

O'Hagan, A., Buck, C. E., Daneshkhah, A., Eiser, J. R., Garthwaite, P. H., Jenkinson, D. J., Oakley, J. E., and Rakow, T. (2006), *Uncertain Judgements: Eliciting Experts' Probabilities*, Chichester, U.K.: John Wiley & Sons, Ltd.

Ohler, E. A. and Cummins, H. (1942), Sexual differences in breadths of epidermal ridges on finger tips and palms, *Am. J. Phys. Anthropol.*, 29, 341–362.

Olsen, R. D. (1981), Fiction ridge characteristics and points of identity: An unresolved dichotomy of terms, *J. Forensic Ident.*, 41, 195–197.

Olsen, R. D. and Lee, H. C. (2001), Identification of latent prints, in *Advances in Fingerprint Technology,* 2nd ed., eds. H. C. Lee and R. E. Gaensslen, Boca Raton, FL: CRC Press, pp. 41–61.

Osterburg, J. W. and Bloomington, S. A. (1964), An inquiry into the nature of proof "the identity of fingerprints", *J. Forensic Sci.*, 9, 413–427.

Ostrowski, S. H. (2001), Simultaneous impressions: Revisiting the controversy, *The Detail*, 13, http://www.clpex.com/Articles/TheDetail/1-99/TheDetail13.htm (last accessed January 29, 2016)

Pacheco, I., Cerchiai, B., and Stoiloff, S. (2014), *Miami-Dade Research Study for the Reliability of the ACE-V Process: Accuracy & Precision in Latent Fingerprint Examinations*, Washington, DC: National Institute of Justice, https://http://www.ncjrs.gov/pdffiles1/nij/grants/248534.pdf (last accessed January 29, 2016).

Parsons, N. R., Smith, J. Q., Thönnes, E., Wang, L., and Wilson, R. G. (2008), Rotationally invariant statistics for examining the evidence from the pores in fingerprints, *Law Probab. Risk*, 7, 1–14.

Pirone, G. (1976), Impronte digitali: Legge e tecnica, *La Giustizia Penale*, Parte Prima: I Presupposti 155–160.

Pirone, G. (1991), *La polizia scientifica—criminologia e indagini tecniche*, Rimini, Italy: Maggiolini.

Polski, J., Smith, R., Garrett, R., Ashbaugh, D. R., Babler, W. J., Chamberlain, P., Champod, C. et al. (2011), The report of the International Association for Identification, standardization II committee, National Institute of Justice, http://www.ncjrs.gov/pdffiles1/nij/grants/233980.pdf (last accessed January 29, 2016).

Praska, N. and Langenburg, G. (2013), Reactions of latent prints exposed to blood, *Forensic Sci. Int.*, 224, 51–58.

Pulsifer, D. P., Muhlberger, S. A., Williams, S. F., Shaler, R. C., and Lakhtakia, A. (2013), An objective fingerprint quality-grading system, *Forensic Sci. Int.*, 231, 204–207.

Puri, D. K. S. (1962), Réflexions dactyloscopiques, *Revue internationale de police criminelle*, 17(160), 225–227.

Puri, D. K. S. (1964), Complément à quelques réflexions dactyloscopiques, *Revue internationale de police criminelle*, 19(178), 130–134.

Puri, D. K. S. (1966), Est-il possible de déterminer à quelle main appartient une empreinte de pouce?, *Revue Internationale de Police Criminelle*, 21, 49–53.

Raloti, S. K., Shah, K. A., Patel, V. C., Menat, A. K., Mori, R. N., and Chaudhari, N. K. (2013), An effort to determine blood group and gender from pattern of finger prints, *Nat. J. Commun. Med.*, 4, 158–160.

Ramos-Castro, D. (2007), *Forensic Evaluation of the Evidence Using Automatic Recognition Systems*, Madrid, Spain: Universidad Autonoma de Madrid, Escuela Politecnica Superior.

Rastogi, P. and Pillai, K. R. (2010), A study of fingerprints in relation to gender and blood group, *J. Indian Acad. Forensic Med.*, 32, 12–13.

Ray, E. (2012), Frequency of patterns in palms, *J. Forensic Ident.*, 62, 568–587.

Ray, E. and Dechant, P. J. (2013), Sufficiency and standards for exclusion decisions, *J. Forensic Ident.*, 63, 675–697.

Reneau, R. D. (2003), Unusual latent print examinations, *J. Forensic Ident.*, 53, 531–537.

Reznicek, M., Ruth, R. M., and Schilens, D. M. (2010), ACE-V and the scientific method, *J. Forensic Ident.*, 60, 87–103.

Richmond, S. (2004), *Do Fingerprint Ridges and Characteristics within Ridges Change with Pressure?* Canberra, Australian Capital Territory, Australia: Australian Federal Police, Forensic Services, http://www.latent-prints.com/images/changes%20with%20pressure.pdf (last accessed January 29, 2016).

Roddy, A. R. and Stosz, J. D. (1997), Fingerprint features—Statistical analysis and system performance estimates, *Proc. IEEE*, 85, 1390–1421.

Roddy, A. R. and Stosz, J. D. (1999), Fingerprint feature processing techniques and poroscopy, in *Intelligent Biometric Techniques in Fingerprint and Face Recognition*, eds. L. C. Jain, U. Halici, I. Hayashi, S. B. Lee, and S. Tsutsui, Boca Raton, FL: CRC Press, pp. 35–105.

Ross, A., Dass, S. C., and Jain, A. K. (2004), Estimating fingerprint deformation, in *Proceedings of International Conference on Biometric Authentication (ICBA)*, Hong Kong: Lecture Notes in Computer Science, pp. 249–255.

Rudin, N. and Inman, K. (2004), Fingerprints in print: The apparent misidentification of a latent print in the Madrid bombing case, *CAC News*, 4th quarter 14–21.

Santamaria Beltrán, F. (June 24–29, 1953), Une nouvelle méthode d'évaluation des points caractéristiques des crêtes papillaires, in *Assemblée générale de la commission internationale de police criminelle*, Oslo, Norway.

Santamaria Beltrán, F. (1955), A new method of evaluating ridge characteristics, *Finger Print Ident. Mag.*, 36, 3–8 & 16–18.

Saviano, J. (2003), The significance of using level 1 detail in latent print examinations, *J. Forensic Ident.*, 53, 209–218.

Saviers, K. D. (July 7–10, 1987), Friction skin characteristics: A study and comparison of proposed standards, in *International Forensic Symposium on Latent Prints*, Quantico, VA: FBI Academy, pp. 157–163.

Saviers, K. D. (1989), Friction skin characteristics: A study and comparison of proposed standards, *J. Forensic Ident.*, 39, 157–163 [erratum in JFI 1989 39(5) 326–327].

Schiffer, B. and Champod, C. (2007), The potential (negative) influence of observational biases at the analysis stage of fingermark individualisation, *Forensic Sci. Int.*, 167, 116–120.

Schwarz, L. and Hermanowski, M.-L. (2012), The effect of humidity on long-term storage of evidence prior to using cyanoacrylate fuming for the detection of latent fingerprints, *J. Forensic Ident.*, 62, 227–233.

Scientific Working Group on Friction Ridge Analysis, Study and Technology (SWGFAST). (2008), Standard for simultaneous impression examination (latent), ver. 2.0, http://www.swgfast.org/documents/simultaneous/121124_Simultaneous_2.0.pdf (last accessed January 29, 2016).

Scientific Working Group on Friction Ridge Analysis, Study and Technology (SWGFAST). (2010), Standard for documentation of analysis, comparison, evaluation and verification (ACE-V) (latent), ver. 1.0, http://www.swgfast.org/documents/documentation/100310_Standard_Doumentation_ACE-V_1.0.pdf (last accessed January 29, 2016).

Scientific Working Group on Friction Ridge Analysis, Study and Technology (SWGFAST). (2012), Standard for the application of blind verification of friction ridge examinations (latent & tenprint), ver. 2.0. http://www.swgfast.org/documents/blind-verification/121124_Blind-Verification_2.0.pdf, (last accessed January 29, 2016)

Scientific Working Group on Friction Ridge Analysis, Study and Technology (SWGFAST). (2013a), Standards for examining friction ridge impressions and resulting conclusions, ver. 2.0, http://www.swgfast.org/documents/examinations-conclusions/130427_Examinations-Conclusions_2.0.pdf (last accessed January 29, 2016).

Scientific Working Group on Friction Ridge Analysis, Study and Technology (SWGFAST). (2013b), Standard terminology of friction ridge examination (latent/tenprint), ver. 4.1, http://www.swgfast.org/documents/terminology/121124_Standard-Terminology_4.0.pdf (last accessed January 29, 2016).

Sheets, H. D., Torres, A., Langenburg, G., Bush, P. J., and Bush, M. A. (2014), Distortion in fingerprints: A statistical investigation using shape measurement tools, *J. Forensic Sci.*, 59, 1113–1120.

Sherratt, J. M. P. (1979), UFOS (unfounded fingerprint opinions) as evidence in South Africa: When is a point not a point?, *S. Afr. Law J*, 96, 287–289.

Sherratt, J. M. P. (1994), Fingerprint identification evidence: Some observations, *South Afr. J. Crim. Justice (SACJ)*, 7, 228–234.

Singh, I., Chattopadhyay, P. K., and Garg, R. K. (2005), Determination of the hand from single digit fingerprint: A study of whorls, *Forensic Sci. Int.*, 152, 205–208.

Singh, P. (1963), Pressure distortions in finger printing, *Fingerprint Ident. Mag.*, 44 (9), 3–6.

Singh, R. K. and Sachdeva, M. P. (2012), Friction ridges pores: A reliable tool for personal identification, in *National Seminar on Relevance of Anthropology in Contemporary North-East India*, Imphal, India, pp. 1–8.

Skorupski, W. P. and Wainer, H. (2015), The Bayesian flip: Correcting the prosecutor's fallacy, *Significance*, 12, 16–20.

Smith, W. C., Kinney, R. W., and DePartee, D. G. (1993), Latent fingerprints—A forensic approach, *J. Forensic Ident.*, 43, 563–570.

Smrz, M. A., Burmeister, S. G., Einseln, A., Fisher, C. L., Fram, R., Stacey, R. B., Theisen, C. E., and Budowle, B. (2006), Review of FBI latent print unit processes and recommendations to improve practices and quality, *J. Forensic Ident.*, 56, 402–434.

Sorrentino, U. (1948), La preuve dactyloscopique devant les magistrats, *Revue internationale de criminologie et de police technique*, 2, 14–16.

Sorrentino, U. (1952), Empreintes digitales, *Revue internationale de police criminelle*, 7, 329–337.

Sorrentino, U. (1956), Identity of digital prints, *Fingerprint Ident. Mag.*, 37, 3–5.

Stacey, R. B. (2004), A report on the erroneous fingerprint individualization in the Madrid train bombing case, *J. Forensic Ident.*, 54, 706–718.

Steinwender, E. (1958), Der daktyloskopische Identitätsnachweis, *Kriminalistik*, 12, 186–194.

Stigler, S. M. (1995), Galton and identification by fingerprints, *Genetics*, 140, 857–860.

Stoney, D. A. (1985), Quantitative assessment of fingerprint individuality, D. Crim. Dissertation, Berkeley, CA: University of California, Graduate Division of the University of California.

Stoney, D. A. (1989), Letter to the editor—Source individuality versus expressed individuality—discussion of "probability analysis and the evidential value of bolt arrangements", *J. Forensic Sci.*, 34, 1295–1296.

Stoney, D. A. (1991), What made us ever think we could individualize using statistics, *J. Forensic Sci. Soc.*, 31, 197–199.

Stoney, D. A. (2001), Measurement of fingerprint individuality, in *Advances in Fingerprint Technology,* 2nd ed., eds. H. C. Lee and R. E. Gaensslen, Boca Raton, FL: CRC Press, pp. 327–387.

Stosz, J. D. and Alyea, L. A. (1994), Automatic system for fingerprint authentication using pores and ridge structures, in *Automatic Systems for the Identification and Inspections of Humans*, San Diego (California): SPIE-The International Society for Optical Engineering, pp. 210–223.

Swofford, H. J. (2005), Fingerprint patterns: A study on the finger and ethnicity prioritized order of occurrence, *J. Forensic Ident.*, 55, 480–488.

Swofford, H. (2015), The emerging paradigm shift in the epistemology of fingerprint conclusions, *J. Forensic Ident.*, 65, 201–213.

Swofford, H., Steffan, S. M., Warner, G., Bridge, C., and Salyards, J. (2013a), Impact of minutiae quantity on the behavior and performance of latent print examiners, *J. Forensic Ident.*, 63, 571–591.

Swofford, H., Steffan, S. M., Warner, G., Bridge, C., and Salyards, J. (2013b), Inter- and intra-examiner variation in the detection of friction ridge skin minutiae, *J. Forensic Ident.*, 63, 553–570.

Tangen, J. M., Thompson, M. B., and McCarthy, D. J. (2011), Identifying fingerprint expertise, *Psychol. Sci.*, 22, 995–997.

Taroni, F., Aitken, C. G. G., and Garbolino, P. (2001), De Finetti's subjectivism, the assessment of probabilities and the evaluation of evidence: A commentary for forensic scientists, *Sci. Justice*, 41, 145–150.

Taroni, F., Biedermann, A., Bozza, S., Garbolino, P., and Aitken, C. (2014), *Bayesian Networks for Probabilistic Inference and Decision Analysis in Forensic Science,* 2nd ed., ed. V. Barnett, Chichester, U.K.: John Wiley & Sons, Ltd.

Taroni, F., Biedermann, A., Garbolino, P., and Aitken, C. G. G. (2004), A general approach to Bayesian networks for the interpretation of evidence, *Forensic Sci. Int.*, 139, 5–16.

Taroni, F., Bozza, S., Biedermann, A., Garbolino, P., and Aitken, C. C. G. (2010), in *Data Analysis in Forensic Science: A Bayesian Decision Perspective*, eds. S. Senn and V. Barnett, Chichester, U.K.: John Wiley & Sons, Ltd.

Taroni, F. and Margot, P. A. (2000), Letter to the editor—Fingerprint evidence evaluation: Is it really so different to other evidence types? *Sci. Justice*, 40, 277–278.

Thompson, W. C. and Schumann, E. L. (1987), Interpretation of statistical evidence in criminal trials: The prosecutor's fallacy and the defence attorney's fallacy, *Law Hum. Behav.*, 11, 167–187.

Thornton, J. I. (1977), The one-dissimilarity doctrine in fingerprint identification, *Int. Crim. Police Rev.*, 32, 89–95.

Tietze, S. and Witthuhn, K. (2001), *Papillarleisten-struktur der menschlichen Handinnenfläche* (Vol. 9), Neuwied, Germany: Luchterhand.

Tiller, C. D. (1983), Fingerprint identification in united kingdom—Do they really need 16 points? *Can. Ident. Soc. Newslett.*, 6, 5–8.

Topper, A. R. J. (2011), Etude statistique des minuties sur les portions des phalanges, MSc thesis, Lausanne, Switzerland: Université de Lausanne, Ecole des Sciences Criminelles/Institut de Police Scientifique.

Triplett, M. and Cooney, L. (2006), The etiology of ACE-V and its proper use: An exploration of the relationship between ACE-V and the scientific method of hypothesis testing, *J. Forensic Ident.*, 56, 345–355.

Tuthill, H. H. (1994), *Individualization: Principles and Procedures in Criminalistics*, Salem, OR: Lightning Powder Co.

Tuthill, H. H. and George, G. (2002), *Individualization—Principles and Procedures in Criminalistics,* 2nd ed., Jacksonville, FL: Lightning Powder Company, Inc.

Ulery, B. T., Hicklin, R. A., Buscaglia, J., and Roberts, M. A. (2011), Accuracy and reliability of forensic latent fingerprint decisions, *Proc. Natl. Acad. Sci. USA*, 108, 7733–7738.

Ulery, B. T., Hicklin, R. A., Buscaglia, J., and Roberts, M. A. (2012), Repeatability and reproducibility of decisions by latent fingerprint examiners, *PLoS ONE*, 7, e32800.

Ulery, B. T., Hicklin, R. A., Kiebuzinski, G. I., Roberts, M. A., and Buscaglia, J. (2013), Understanding the sufficiency of information for latent fingerprint value determinations, *Forensic Sci. Int.*, 230, 99–106.

Ulery, B. T., Hicklin, R. A., Roberts, M. A., and Buscaglia, J. (2014), Measuring what latent fingerprint examiners consider sufficient information for individualization determinations, *PLoS ONE*, 9, e110179.

United States Department of Justice, and Federal Bureau of Investigation (1984), *The Science of Fingerprints*, Washington, DC: U.S. Government Printing Office.

United States Department of Justice, and Office of the Inspector General—Oversight and Review Division. (2006), *A Review of the FBI's Handling of the Brandon Mayfield Case* (unclassified and redacted), Washington, DC: U.S. Government Printing Office, https://oig.justice.gov/special/s0601/final.pdf (last accessed February 2, 2016).

United States Department of Justice, and Office of the Inspector General—Oversight and Review Division. (2011), *A Review of the FBI's Progress in Responding to the Recommendations in the Office of the Inspector General Report on the Fingerprint Misidentification in the Brandon Mayfield Case*, Washington, DC: U.S. Government Printing Office, https://oig.justice.gov/special/s1105.pdf (last accessed February 2, 2016).

Vanderkolk, J. R. (1999), Forensic individualization of images using quality and quantity of information, *J. Forensic Ident.*, 49, 246–256.

Vanderkolk, J. R. (2004), ACE+V: A model, *J. Forensic Ident.*, 54, 45–51.

Vanderkolk, J. R. (2009), *Forensic Comparative Science*, London, U.K.: Elsevier Academic Press.

Vanderkolk, J. R. (2011), Chapter 9: Examination process, in *The Fingerprint Sourcebook*, ed. A. McRoberts, Washington, DC: National Institute of Justice, http://www.ncjrs.gov/pdffiles1/nij/225329.pdf (last accessed January 29, 2016).

Verburg Attorneys/Prokureurs. (2015), Seven-point standard followed by the South African courts regarding fingerprint evidence, http://verburg.co.za/?p=262_ftn1 (last accessed January 29, 2016).

Vucetich, J. (1904), *Dactiloscopia comparada. El nuevo sistema argentino*, La Plata, Argentina: Jacobo Peuser.

Walder, H. (1976), Die Beweisführung in Strafsachen insbesondere des Indizienbeweis, *Kriminalistik*, 30, 178–182.

Wax, S. T. and Schatz, C. J. (2004), A multitude of errors: The Brandon Mayfield case, *The Champion*, September/October, 6–15.

Wayman, J. L. (2000), When bad science leads to good law: The disturbing irony of the Daubert hearing in the case of U.S. v. Byron C. Mitchell, http://www.nasams.org/forensics/for_lib/Documents/1048198555.79/publications_daubert.html.

Wertheim, P. A. (2000), Scientific comparison and identification of fingerprint evidence, *Fingerprint Whorld*, 26, 95–106.

Wilder, H. H. and Wentworth, B. (1932), *Personal Identification—Methods for the Identification of Individuals Living or Dead,* 2nd ed., ed. T. G. Cooke, Chicago, IL: The Fingerprint Publishing Association.

Willis, S M. et al. (2015), *ENFSI Guideline for Evaluative Reporting in Forensic Science*, Dublin, Ireland: European Network of Forensic Science Institutes, http://enfsi.eu/sites/default/files/documents/external_publications/m1_guideline.pdf (last accessed January 29, 2016).

Yoon, S., Cao, K., Liu, E., and Jain, A. K. (2013), LFIQ: Latent fingerprint image quality, in *2013 IEEE Sixth International Conference on Biometrics: Theory, Applications and Systems (BTAS)*, Washington DC, USA pp. 1–8.

Yoon, S., Liu, E., and Jain, A. K. (2012), On latent fingerprint image quality, in *Proceedings of the Fifth International Workshop on Computational Forensics*, Tsukuba, Japan.

3 Chemistry, Light, and Photography

For a complete understanding of fingermark detection techniques and their application, a good knowledge of chemical and physical phenomena (including a study of light and its interaction with matter) is required. The aim of this chapter is to give some general background theory that will assist the reader in comprehending the development methods described in this book. In addition to basic chemistry and light theory, the chapter also includes a discussion on forensic light sources (FLSs), general photography, and digital image enhancement. An understanding of these basic concepts can assist the examiner in achieving improved contrast and increased overall sensitivity with respect to the detection and recording of fingermarks.

3.1 STANDARD WEIGHTS AND MEASURES

The science of measurement is known as metrology. From three fundamental quantities—length, mass, and time—all other mechanical quantities (e.g., area, volume, acceleration, and power) can be derived. A comprehensive system of practical measurement should include at least three other bases, taking in the measurement of electromagnetic quantities, of temperature, and of intensity of radiation. Accordingly, the *11th General Conference of Weights and Measures*, held in Paris in 1960, adopted a number of quantities and units as the bases upon which the International System of Units (SI units) was established. The SI units constitute an international decimal system of weights and measures that extend the metric system of measurement. The system consists of seven basic units, from which other units are derived, as follows (with their respective symbols):

1. Length, the meter (m)
2. Mass, the kilogram (kg)
3. Time, the second (s)
4. Electric current, the ampere (A)
5. Luminous intensity, the candela (cd)
6. Amount of substance, the mole (mol)
7. Thermodynamic temperature, the kelvin (K)

A prefix is used to specify a multiplier for a measurement unit (Table 3.1). For example, a kilometer is equal to 1000 m (10^3 m), and a millimeter is equal to one-thousandth of a meter (10^{-3} m). Our eye can distinguish details down to about 250 μm (μm = 10^{-6} of a meter) (called visual acuity), while the light microscope can permit the visualization of biological structures smaller than 1 μm (such as the details on the surface of a grain of pollen; this is called the optical resolution). Modern electron microscopes can obtain images of structures up to even 100,000 times smaller, thus permitting us to distinguish nanometric particles (nm = 10^{-9} of a meter) and atoms whose diameter barely exceeds one ten-millionth of a meter (10^{-10} m, sometimes called 1 Å = 1 angström) (Figure 3.1). SI units are used throughout this book with the only practical exception being digital imaging where imperial units are still commonly employed (Section 3.6).

TABLE 3.1

Standard Prefixes for the Designation of Decimal Multiples or Fractions of Base Measurement Units

Multiplier		Prefix	Length		Weight		Volume	
1,000,000,000	10^9	Giga	Gigameter	(Gm)	Gigagram	(Gg)	Gigaliter	(GL)
1,000,000	10^6	Mega	Megameter	(Mm)	Megagram	(Mg)	Megaliter	(ML)
1,000	10^3	Kilo	Kilometer	(km)	Kilogram	(kg)	Kiloliter	(kL)
1	10^0	—	Meter	(m)	Gram	(g)	Liter	(L)
0.1	10^{-1}	Deci	Decimeter	(dm)	Decigram	(dg)	Deciliter	(dL)
0.01	10^{-2}	Centi	Centimeter	(cm)	Centigram	(cg)	Centiliter	(cL)
0.001	10^{-3}	Milli	Millimeter	(mm)	Milligram	(mg)	Milliliter	(mL)
0.000001	10^{-6}	Micro	Micrometer	(μm)	Microgram	(μg)	Microliter	(μL)
0.000000001	10^{-9}	Nano	Nanometer	(nm)	Nanogram	(ng)	Nanoliter	(nL)
0.0000000001	10^{-10}	—	Angstrom	(Å)	—		—	
0.000000000001	10^{-12}	Pico	Picometer	(pm)	Picogram	(pg)	Picoliter	(pL)

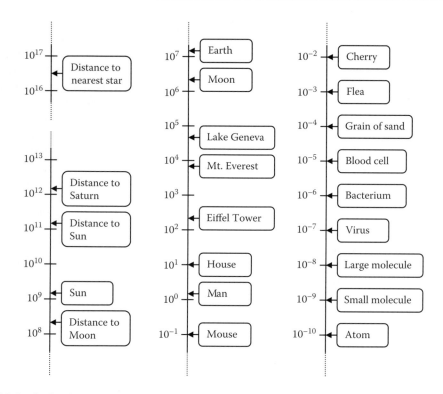

FIGURE 3.1 Scale of dimensions (in meters).

3.2 CHEMISTRY THEORY

All solid matter is composed of pure elements or combinations of elements called compounds. An element is a substance that cannot be decomposed into simpler substances by chemical or physical treatment. Examples of common elements are carbon, hydrogen, oxygen, and nitrogen. There are currently 118 known chemical elements; however, about 20% of these do not exist in nature (or are only present in trace amounts) and are known only because they have been

1	2	3	4	5	6	7	8	9	10	11	12	13	14	15	16	17	18
1 H 1.008																	2 He 4.003
3 Li 6.94	4 Be 9.01											5 B 10.81	6 C 12.01	7 N 14.01	8 O 16.00	9 F 19.00	10 Ne 20.18
11 Na 22.99	12 Mg 24.31	\<-----			TRANSITION ELEMENTS						----->	13 Al 26.98	14 Si 28.09	15 P 30.97	16 S 32.06	17 Cl 35.45	18 Ar 39.95
19 K 39.10	20 Ca 40.08	21 Sc 44.96	22 Ti 47.90	23 V 50.94	24 Cr 52.00	25 Mn 54.94	26 Fe 55.85	27 Co 58.93	28 Ni 58.71	29 Cu 63.55	30 Zn 65.38	31 Ga 69.72	32 Ge 72.59	33 As 74.92	34 Se 78.96	35 Br 79.90	36 Kr 83.80
37 Rb 85.47	38 Sr 87.62	39 Y 88.91	40 Zr 91.22	41 Nb 92.91	42 Mo 95.96	43 Tc (98)	44 Ru 101.07	45 Rh 102.91	46 Pd 106.42	47 Ag 107.87	48 Cd 112.41	49 In 114.82	50 Sn 118.71	51 Sb 121.76	52 Te 127.60	53 I 126.90	54 Xe 131.29
55 Cs 132.91	56 Ba 137.33	57 | 71	72 Hf 178.49	73 Ta 180.95	74 W 183.84	75 Re 186.21	76 Os 190.23	77 Ir 192.22	78 Pt 195.08	79 Au 196.97	80 Hg 200.59	81 Tl 204.38	82 Pb 207.20	83 Bi 208.98	84 Po (209)	85 At (210)	86 Rn (222)
87 Fr (223)	88 Ra (226)	89 | 103	104 Rf (267)	105 Db (268)	106 Sg (271)	107 Bh (272)	108 Hs (270)	109 Mt (276)	110 Ds (281)	111 Rg (280)	112 Cn (285)	113 Uut (284)	114 Fl (289)	115 Uup (288)	116 Lv (293)	117 Uus (294)	118 Uuo (294)

LANTHANIDES	57 La 138.91	58 Ce 140.12	59 Pr 140.91	60 Nd 144.24	61 Pm (145)	62 Sm 150.36	63 Eu 151.96	64 Gd 157.25	65 Tb 158.93	66 Dy 162.50	67 Ho 164.93	68 Er 167.26	69 Tm 168.93	70 Yb 173.05	71 Lu 174.97
ACTINIDES	89 Ac (227)	90 Th 232.04	91 Pa 231.04	92 U 238.03	93 Np (237)	94 Pu (244)	95 Am (243)	96 Cm (247)	97 Bk (247)	98 Cf (251)	99 Es (252)	100 Fm (257)	101 Md (258)	102 No (?59)	103 Lr (262)

FIGURE 3.2 Periodic table of the elements.

synthesized in the laboratory. The known chemical elements are typically displayed in the form of a table—the periodic table (Figure 3.2)—that arranges the elements according to similar structure and properties. The rows of the table are called periods and the columns are called groups. Elements with similar chemical properties generally fall into the same group in the periodic table.

All elements are composed of very small units called atoms. All the atoms of a single element are the same as each other in terms of their size, weight (with the exception of isotopes), and chemical properties but are different from those of every other element. Each element can be represented by a symbol that is short notation derived from the element's scientific name (e.g., S for sulfur, C for carbon, O for oxygen, and Si for silicon). Sometimes, the symbol is derived from the Latin name (e.g., Au for aurum, gold; Fe for ferrum, iron; and Na for natrium, sodium) or from other linguistic roots (e.g., W for wolfram, tungsten; from the German name "wolf rahm" or "wolf cream," and the Nordic word "tungsten" for heavy stone).

Every atom consists of a central core (or nucleus) of subatomic particles called protons (positively charged) and neutrons (neutral or uncharged) in various numbers, surrounded by a cloud of negatively charged electrons circulating around the nucleus-like planets around the sun (Figure 3.3). It is these electrons, and the ease with which they may be shared with (or donated to) other atoms, that determine the chemical reactivity of the element. The lightest of all atoms, hydrogen, has a diameter of approximately 1×10^{-10} m (0.1 nm; one angström [Å]) and weighs 1.7×10^{-24} g. The diameter of an atom is around 10,000 times larger than that of its nucleus.

Each element has a unique atomic number that indicates the number of protons present in the nucleus of each atom of that element. In their normal, uncharged state, each atom of an element has an equal number of protons and electrons. For example, carbon has the atomic number 6, indicating that there are six electrons and six protons in its atomic structure. Atoms with the same atomic number but different atomic masses differ in the number of neutrons contained in their nuclei, and these are called isotopes. Isotopes have identical chemical properties, yet they can have very different

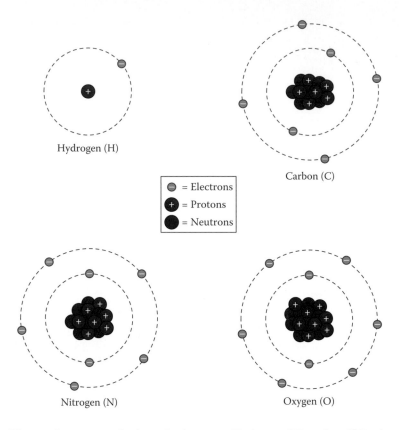

FIGURE 3.3 The atomic structures for the major isotopes of hydrogen (^{1}H), carbon (^{12}C), nitrogen (^{14}N), and oxygen (^{16}O).

nuclear properties. The nuclear properties of an atom include possible radioactivity, magnetic properties, and mass. The element potassium (K, kalium; atomic number 19), for example, has two natural isotopes, ^{39}K (its nucleus contains 19 protons and 20 neutrons) and ^{40}K (its nucleus contains 19 protons and 21 neutrons). They form exactly the same compounds, but ^{40}K is radioactive and decays into other elements. Because isotopes have the same number of protons, all of the isotopes of a given element occupy the same place in the periodic table of elements (Figure 3.2). Most elements have stable isotopes.

The term atomic weight, or atomic mass, refers to the mass of a fixed number of atoms of an element. The standard scientific unit for dealing with atoms in macroscopic quantities is the mole (mol), which is defined arbitrarily as the amount of a substance with as many atoms or other units as there are in 12 g of the carbon isotope ^{12}C (carbon-12). The number of atoms in a mole is called Avogadro's number, the value of which is approximately 6×10^{23}. The atomic mass of an element, commonly expressed as atomic mass units (amu), is the number of grams in one mole of the element. (Neutrons and protons have relative weights of approximately one amu, whereas an electron is only about 1/2000 as heavy.) The atomic mass of a given element, as indicated in the periodic table (Figure 3.2), is the weighted average of the different isotopes that naturally occur for that element. For example, chlorine has two common isotopes, ^{35}Cl and ^{37}Cl, and a weighted average atomic mass of 35.5 amu. Therefore, 35.5 g of chlorine will contain approximately 6×10^{23} individual chlorine atoms, being a mixture of the two common isotopes.

(Chlorine is a mixture of approximately three parts of chlorine-35 for every one part of the heavier chlorine-37 isotope.)

In their uncharged state, atoms have an equal number of protons and electrons. An imbalance between the number of protons and electrons in an atom results in the formation of an ion, which can be either positively charged (i.e., a cation; more protons than electrons) or negatively charged (i.e., an anion; more electrons than protons).

The atoms of nearly every element can combine with other atoms to form molecules by physical or chemical interaction. For example, a molecule of water (H_2O) is formed by the interaction of two atoms of hydrogen (H) with one atom of oxygen (O). A molecule of carbon dioxide (CO_2) is formed by the interaction of two atoms of oxygen (O) with one atom of carbon (C). A molecule can be defined as the smallest unit of a compound that retains the chemical characteristics of the original substance. The molecular weight of a pure compound such as water is calculated by taking the sum of atomic weights for the elements present. Thus, the molecular weight of water (H_2O)—one atom of oxygen (atomic weight of 16) plus two atoms of hydrogen (atomic weight of 1)—is 18. Similarly, the molecular weight of carbon dioxide (CO_2)—one atom of carbon (atomic weight of 12) plus two atoms of oxygen (atomic weight of 16)—is 44. Therefore, 18 g of water or 44 g of carbon dioxide will contain approximately 6×10^{23} individual molecules.

When two atoms come into contact and share electrons, a combined electron cloud enveloping both atoms results and a chemical covalent bond is said to have been formed. Depending on the number of electrons that have been shared, the covalent bond that is formed may be either single (one pair of electrons), double (two pairs of electrons), or triple (three pairs of electrons).

If an atom completely loses one or more electrons to another atom (i.e., the *bonding* electrons are no longer shared but are completely taken by one of the atoms), then an ionic bond results. Sodium chloride (NaCl), common table salt, is an example of an ionically bonded compound that can be represented as Na^+Cl^-. In the case of NaCl, each atom of chlorine has taken one electron from a sodium atom, resulting in a negatively charged chlorine atom and a positively charged sodium atom, with the atoms being held together in the final compound by the natural attraction between positively and negatively charged bodies.

Because of the specific number and arrangement of electrons around the nucleus of each atomic element, that element will prefer to combine with other atoms in particular ratios. For example, oxygen and carbon atoms may combine to give either carbon dioxide (CO_2), which constitutes about 0.03% of the air we breathe, or carbon monoxide (CO), the toxic gas emitted by imperfect combustion such as from a car's exhaust system. Gases such as hydrogen, oxygen, and nitrogen do not exist for very long as single or free atoms and prefer to be in combination with other atoms. For example, two atoms of hydrogen (H) will combine with each other to form a relatively stable diatomic molecule (i.e., having two atoms) of hydrogen gas, represented by the chemical formula H_2. When hydrogen is oxidized, two diatomic molecules of hydrogen combine with one diatomic molecule of oxygen to form two molecules of water. The chemical reaction can be written as follows:

$$2H_2 + O_2 \rightarrow 2H_2O$$

Compounds can be represented by their numerical or empirical formulas—such as H_2O, CO_2, and O_2—or by structural formulas in which lines are used to represent the sharing of electrons by the atoms of a molecule (Table 3.2). The lines represent the forces or bonds between the atoms of elements making up the molecule. A single line indicates that one pair of electrons is shared (i.e., a single bond), two lines indicate two shared pairs (i.e., a double bond), and three lines mean three pairs (i.e., a triple bond). In this way, the structural formula shows not only how many atoms are in

TABLE 3.2
Some Empirical and Structural Formulas

Chemical Name	Empirical Formula	Structural Formula
Hydrogen	H_2	H——H
Oxygen	O_2	O=O
Nitrogen	N_2	N≡N
Carbon dioxide	CO_2	O=C=O
Water	H_2O	
Ammonia	NH_3	
Methane	CH_4	
Ethane	C_2H_6 (CH_3CH_3)	
Ethanol	C_2H_6O (CH_3CH_2OH)	
Ethylene	C_2H_4 (CH_2CH_2)	
Acetylene	C_2H_2 $(CHCH)$	H——C≡C——H

a molecule, but in what order they are arranged and the nature of the chemical bonds between them, thus providing a great deal of information in a small space. Rings of carbon atoms containing $2n + 2$ carbons (i.e., 4, 6, 8, 10) and having alternating single and double bonds (also called π-bonds) are termed aromatic rings. An example of an aromatic ring is benzene (C_6H_6), which forms the basis of many organic compounds and can be represented by any of the structures depicted in Figure 3.4.

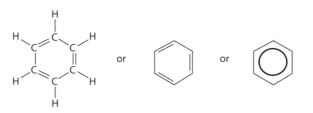

FIGURE 3.4   Different graphical representations for a benzene ring (C_6H_6).

Matter can exist in one of four states:

1. *Solid*: The position and distance between the particles (atoms or molecules) are fixed.
2. *Liquid*: The particles interact with each other and the distance between them is more or less stable (limited movement).
3. *Gas*: The particles move freely, changing distance and position among themselves.
4. *Plasma*: Where, at high temperature, the substance is entirely ionized to form "naked" atomic nuclei and free electrons that are in thermal motion.

Within a solid, very strong bonding forces keep the atoms in a lattice structure; individual atoms are unable to move but can vibrate around a fixed position. The degree of atomic vibration increases with increasing temperature. Within a liquid, the bonding forces between the molecules are weaker, with no lattice structure in place, but sufficient to keep the molecules together. The limited movement of molecules results in elastic collisions where there is an exchange of kinetic energy, the energy being directly proportional to the temperature (i.e., increasing kinetic energy with increasing temperature). Within a gas, the bonding force between individual molecules is weak and insufficient to keep the molecules together. Gas molecules tend to disperse and occupy all the available space, with free movement of molecules within this space. Elastic collisions, with an exchange of kinetic energy, occur as for liquids (energy proportional to temperature).

The compounds that are based on carbon are so numerous and so vital to life processes that they are considered a chemistry in themselves. The study of carbon-containing compounds (with the exception of carbonates and cyanides) is called organic chemistry. All other compounds, based on combinations of elements except carbon and generally having a mineral origin, fall into the general category of inorganic chemistry.

3.3 LIGHT THEORY

3.3.1 INTRODUCTION

All living organisms on Earth obtain their energy needs directly or indirectly from sunlight. Light plays such an important role in human existence that optical phenomena have been studied since the earliest times. Cavemen, watching the flickering flames of a fire, thought that the yellowish light was a magical, mysterious spirit. The ancient Greeks knew that when a ray of light is reflected from a mirror, the angle of incidence is equal to the angle of reflection. Various theories of light have been formulated throughout the centuries. Today, it is known that light is a form of energy that is dualistic in nature, having both wave and particle properties. When light interacts with macroscopic objects (bulk matter), it is regarded as a beam of electromagnetic waves. When light interacts with microscopic objects (e.g., atoms or molecules), it is regarded as a beam of pure energy particles known as photons.

The perception of color and of photoluminescence emission represents the observation of physical phenomena due to the interaction of light with matter. To explain and to efficiently employ the observed phenomena, it is essential that some fundamental properties of light be understood. Light is a form of electromagnetic energy, part of a group that includes x-rays, microwaves, and radio waves. Visible radiation, which makes up white light, forms only a small part of the electromagnetic spectrum (Figure 3.5).

3.3.2 WAVE THEORY

In the early nineteenth century, Thomas Young found strong evidence to support the wave theory of light. The electromagnetic wave model was subsequently established. Electromagnetic energy propagates in the form of waves that can be described by their wavelength λ (measured in units of nanometers [nm], 10^{-9} m) or their frequency ν (oscillations per unit time, measured in units of

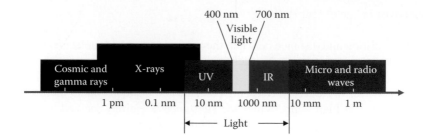

FIGURE 3.5 The electromagnetic spectrum. Light consists of three parts: UV, visible, and infrared. Visible light is a very small portion in this region.

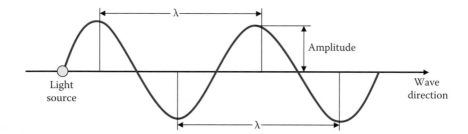

FIGURE 3.6 Wave theory; schematic representation of a light wave. The distance between the two nearest points in the same phase is known as the wavelength (λ).

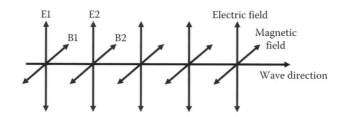

FIGURE 3.7 Depiction of an electromagnetic wave showing the separate electric (E) and magnetic (B) components.

hertz [Hz]) (Figure 3.6). The frequency ν can be calculated from the wavelength λ using the formula $\nu = c/\lambda$, where c, the speed of light, is a constant (c is approximately 300 million m/s).

The term electromagnetic refers to the fact that light energy has both electric and magnetic components. An electromagnetic wave exists and travels in the form of alternate electric and magnetic fields. An electric field E1 vibrates creating a vibrating magnetic field B1 (Figure 3.7). The vibrating magnetic field B1 creates a new vibrating electric field E2. The newly created electric field E2 in turn creates a new vibrating magnetic field B2, and so on. The chain of electric and magnetic fields represents an electromagnetic wave, which carries energy and does not require a material medium to propagate. The electric and magnetic fields are perpendicular to each other. If, for example, the electric field lies in the vertical plane, the magnetic field lies in the horizontal plane and both fields are perpendicular to the direction of propagation (Figure 3.7).

3.3.3 PARTICLE THEORY

Max Planck and Albert Einstein, Nobel Prize winners in physics, proposed that light, which usually travels in waves, sometimes behaves as if it were made up of a stream of small energy particles or photons traveling at the speed of light (Figure 3.8). Light is always emitted or

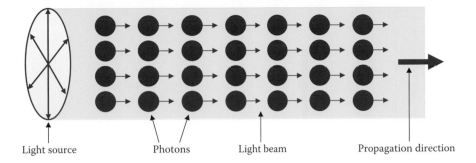

Light source   Photons   Light beam   Propagation direction

FIGURE 3.8   Particle theory; a beam of pure energy particles, called photons, traveling at the speed of light.

absorbed as a number of whole photons. The intensity of a light source is equal to the number of emitted photons per second.

During light interaction with matter, a photon may be totally absorbed by an atom or molecule of that matter. The atom (or molecule) gets excited to the extent of energy equal to the energy of the absorbed photon. The energy, ε, of a photon can be calculated using the following equation, where h is a universal constant (Planck's constant), ν is the light frequency, λ is the wavelength, and c is the speed of light:

$$\varepsilon = h\nu = \frac{hc}{\lambda}$$

As can be seen from this equation, the energy of a photon (ε) is inversely proportional to the wavelength (λ) of the corresponding light wave. Therefore, the shorter the wavelength, the higher is the energy of the corresponding photon. The longer the wavelength, the lower is the energy of the photon.

3.3.4   WHITE LIGHT AND COLORED LIGHT

Newton carried out a series of experiments in which a beam of white light was passed through a prism. He observed that the prism separated white light into a band representing all the colors of the rainbow, from violet to red, and he concluded that white light consists of a mixture of various colors. The colors—identified as violet, indigo, blue, green, yellow, orange, and red—represent the visible spectrum. The human eye only sees *visible* light, which is any electromagnetic radiation falling within the wavelength range of approximately 400–700 nm. Color perception is related to wavelength; for example, radiation at 450 nm is observed as blue light, at 550 nm as green, and at 650 nm as red. When each color (wavelength) of the visible spectrum is present with the same relative intensity, it is perceived by the human eye as white light (Figure 3.9). If some colors are missing,

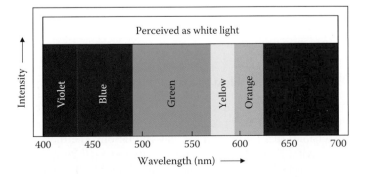

FIGURE 3.9   When each color (wavelength) of the visible spectrum is present with the same relative intensity, it is perceived as "white light."

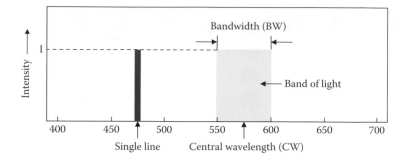

FIGURE 3.10   When a narrow range of colors (visible wavelengths) is present, we have a monochromatic band of light.

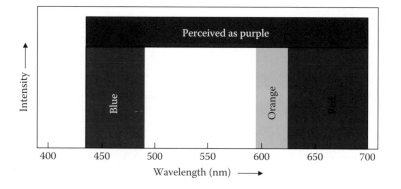

FIGURE 3.11   A blue band combined with an orange/red band will produce polychromatic light that will be perceived by the human eye as being purple in color.

then the mixture of remaining colors is perceived as colored light. (Black is the *color* perceived by the brain when no visible light is present, but this does not preclude the presence of nonvisible radiation such as x-rays, ultraviolet [UV], or infrared [IR].)

Colored light can be polychromatic (many colored) or monochromatic (single colored). When only one single wavelength is present, we have pure monochromatic light. When a narrow range of colors (visible wavelengths) is present, we have a monochromatic band of light (Figure 3.10). It is obvious that the narrower the band, the purer the color will be (i.e., more monochromatic). A band of light is defined by its central wavelength (CW) and its bandwidth (BW).

Light that is composed of two or more monochromatic bands is referred to as polychromatic. For example, a blue band combined with an orange/red band will produce polychromatic light that will be perceived by the human eye as being purple in color (Figure 3.11). Incidentally, this is the color of fingermarks developed with ninhydrin.

3.3.5   Spectral Sensitivity of the Human Eye

The search for forensic traces can sometimes require examination through the entire visible region (i.e., from 400 to 700 nm) as well as, in some cases, nonvisible regions such as the UV and IR. It is important to understand that the human eye has limitations, the most important of which is restricted spectral sensitivity. From the spectral sensitivity curve (Figure 3.12), it can be seen that the human eye has the highest sensitivity at around 550 nm (green/yellow region). Sensitivity is very low in the violet region, below 450 nm, and in the red region, above 650 nm. This should be taken into account when working at these wavelengths. Similarly, when recording marks, the specialist

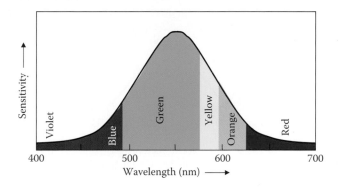

FIGURE 3.12   The spectral sensitivity of an average human eye.

needs to be aware of the spectral sensitivity of the imaging system being used, which may differ considerably from that of the eyes.

Sometimes, quite useful marks are rejected by the examiner as they do not "look good" when observed with the naked eye. A typical example is a weak fingermark in blood on a lightly colored surface. Violet light can be used to enhance the mark, as blood has an absorption peak in this wavelength range. The human eye has a very low sensitivity in the violet region, and a fingermark in blood may not show any significant enhancement to the unaided eye under these conditions. When photographed, however, an excellent image may be produced, as digital cameras exhibit good sensitivity in this region. The camera sensor "sees" the fingermark very well under violet light, much better than the human eye.

3.3.6   ABSORPTION AND REFLECTION OF LIGHT

At a macroscopic level, a light beam directed onto a surface will be reflected, absorbed, and/or transmitted. For example, if the material is transparent, most of the light is transmitted, some is absorbed, and the rest is reflected. The total energy of the system is conserved so that the initial irradiating intensity I_0 is equal to the sum of the reflected intensity I_R, the absorbed intensity I_A, and the transmitted intensity I_T (Figure 3.13).

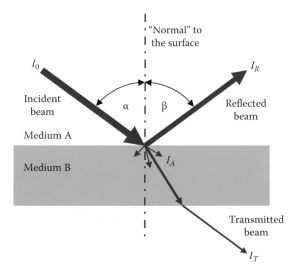

FIGURE 3.13   Transformation of incident light after irradiation of an object. (Note that the "normal" is defined as being perpendicular to the surface.)

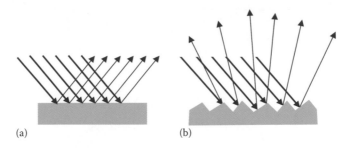

(a)   (b)

FIGURE 3.14   (a) Specular reflection from a flat surface. (b) Diffused reflection from a rough surface.

For a nontransparent surface, $I_T = 0$ and all light is absorbed or reflected. The reflected light is the light seen by our eyes (or camera or photosensitive detector), which gives us a colored image of the object observed. If the object appears white under white light, then the surface reflects all of the wavelengths of the visible spectrum to an equal extent; there is no selective absorption and the surface will appear to be the same color as the incident light.

When the incident light is white but the reflected light is colored, we have the phenomenon of selective absorption: certain wavelengths are absorbed or transmitted while others are reflected—our eyes only perceive the latter. For example, if an object appears red under white light, all wavelengths have been absorbed or transmitted except for the red, which is reflected and perceived. Under a green or blue light, the same object will appear black (all incident light is absorbed), while under a red light it will appear red (all incident light is reflected). It must be noted that in this latter case (red incident light), a white object will also appear red, since most of the incident light is reflected. As a result, a red object cannot be distinguished from an identical, but white, object under red lighting. This phenomenon is recognized in police circles when it comes to describing the color of an object under different lighting conditions. For example, a yellow car seen at night under artificial light will be difficult to distinguish from a similar white car observed under the same conditions.

One of the fundamental laws of reflection is that the angle of incidence of the light beam (α in Figure 3.13) is equal to the angle of the reflected light (β). This angle is measured with respect to a line perpendicular to the surface (normal to the surface) at the point of incidence. For a perfectly flat, shiny surface (e.g., a mirror), all rays will be reflected in the same direction. This is termed specular reflection (Figure 3.14a). A rough surface gives randomly oriented reflected rays (due to the random orientation of the normals to the surface), producing what is termed diffused reflection (Figure 3.14b).

3.3.7   POLARIZATION OF LIGHT

An ordinary light beam consists of many electromagnetic waves, each being created by the energy decay of an electron at a certain point in space and time. As orbiting electrons are randomly positioned at the moment of energy decay, electromagnetic waves produced by energy decay have randomly oriented electric (magnetic) fields. As a result, an ordinary light beam consists of many electromagnetic waves, each one having an electric field oriented at a different angle in space. Therefore, light emitted by ordinary light sources is unpolarized in that the light waves are vibrating in more than one plane. Polarized light has light waves in which the vibrations occur in a single plane. Light can be partially polarized by reflection off nonmetallic surfaces or via scattering by ultramicroscopic particles suspended in air or water. Polarized light can also be produced by selective absorption where all waves except those oriented in one particular direction are absorbed. Polarizing filters are made of a material that exploits this phenomenon (Figure 3.15). Such filters are commonly employed in sunglasses to help reduce glare. A polarizing filter for photographic purposes is typically mounted in a special ring that can be rotated around its base so that the user can choose the direction of polarization of the light transmitted by the filter. The unaided human eye cannot discern polarized from unpolarized light but certain animals, including insects, have this capability.

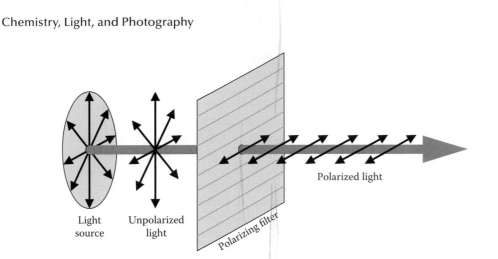

FIGURE 3.15 Use of a polarizing filter in front of a light source to produce polarized light.

3.3.8 PHOTOLUMINESCENCE

Luminescence is a general term that incorporates phenomena such as thermoluminescence (light emission that results from the absorption of heat energy), bioluminescence (light emission from a biological process, such as with a glowworm or firefly), chemiluminescence (light emission from a chemical process, such as the glow of luminol in the presence of blood), as well as photoluminescence (light emission that results from the absorption of light energy). The correct term in the context of this book is therefore photoluminescence.

When light interacts with matter, a photon of light may be absorbed by a molecule (or atom) of that matter (Figure 3.16). After absorption of the photon, the molecule has an excess of energy, equal to the energy of the absorbed photon, and is no longer in its normal (ground) state. The molecule (or atom) is promoted to a higher energy (excited) state. The molecule tends to rapidly

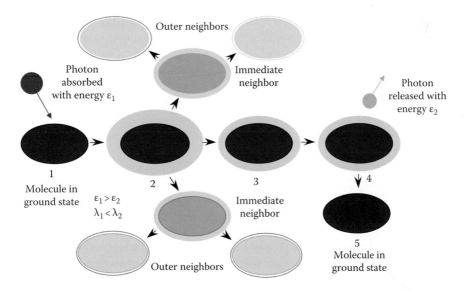

FIGURE 3.16 Absorption and emission of a photon—photoluminescence. (1) A molecule in its normal (ground) state just before absorption of a photon. (2) The molecule becomes excited by the amount of absorbed energy. It immediately shares some of its extra energy with its nearest neighbors. Shared energy spreads out to other molecules. (3) The molecule is less excited by the amount of the shared energy. (4) The molecule releases (emits) its remaining extra energy in the form of a photon. (5) The molecule returns to its ground state.

return to its ground state (the state before absorption of the photon) by releasing the excess energy in some form. This process is complex, and some simplification is required to highlight parts of the phenomena that are useful in fingermark detection. To release the excess energy, the molecule may undergo a chemical change, may transfer the energy to other molecules through collision or vibration (producing heat), or may emit the energy as another photon (Figure 3.16).

All these processes compete with each other, and a return to the ground state seldom occurs through a single pathway. Our particular interest is the process of emission of another photon. Before emission of another photon takes place, some faster processes, in which the molecule loses part of its extra energy, are occurring. The molecule shares a part of its extra energy with immediate neighbors. Shared energy spreads out to other molecules in the form of increased vibration (increased heat). The molecule then emits the remainder of its extra energy in the form of a secondary photon (Figure 3.16). The energy of the emitted photon is smaller than the energy of the absorbed photon by the amount of shared energy. This means that the photoluminescence emission has a longer wavelength (lower energy) compared with the absorbed light that was used to excite the molecule (the *excitation* light). It is said that the photoluminescence emission is *red shifted* (i.e., shifted toward the red end of the visible spectrum) in comparison to the excitation light.

The direct emission of light by a photoluminescent material is referred to as fluorescence. If there is a delayed emission (due to a process that involves an intermediate, metastable state), then it is referred to as phosphorescence. Because it is the result of a direct transition, the fluorescence process is fast, and fluorescence emission occurs only during exposure of the matter to the excitation beam. When the excitation source is removed, fluorescent emission ceases. Where photoluminescence methods are used for fingermark detection and enhancement, it is typically fluorescence that is being observed, not phosphorescence. While fingermark detection techniques are available that exploit phosphorescence—for example, time-resolved luminescence imaging (Murdock and Menzel 1993)—these tend to be highly specialized and not practical for routine casework.

In summary, a photoluminescent material absorbs light at a particular wavelength and then reemits the absorbed energy as light at a longer wavelength (due to energy losses that are inherent in the process). Photoluminescence can occur as either fluorescence (light emission only occurs during excitation, which is typically the case for fingermark applications) or phosphorescence (light emission continues to occur for a short period after excitation). Elsewhere in this book, where the general term luminescence is employed, this should be taken to mean "photoluminescence."

3.3.9   OPTICAL FILTERS

There are three principal modes of acquiring information from a surface or object using light:

1. Absorption mode
2. Diffused reflection mode
3. Photoluminescence mode (based on the detection of a photoluminescent material)

The majority of illumination techniques used for forensic examinations employs one of these three modes. The aim is to increase both selectivity, with the trace of interest being clearly seen against its background (contrast), and sensitivity, whereby smaller and smaller quantities of material can be detected (such as weak fingermarks). The implementation of these optical enhancement methods is heavily dependent on the use of optical filters. An optical filter is a device designed to select specific colors (wavelengths) of light from the range of colors (wavelengths) available.

Filters can be classified, according to their transmission characteristics, as either short pass, long pass, or bandpass. A short-pass filter is designed to transmit shorter wavelengths while rejecting longer wavelengths (Figure 3.17). The midpoint between transmitted and rejected regions is called the edge wavelength (EW). The EW (in nanometers) is labeled on each filter as the characteristic of that filter. The transmission is limited on the left side (shorter wavelengths) by the substrate of

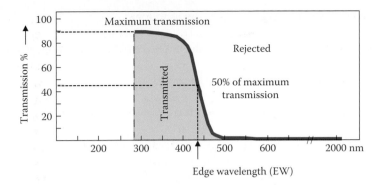

FIGURE 3.17 Typical transmission characteristics of a short-pass filter.

which the filter is made. For example, if a glass substrate is used, the transmission falls sharply below 380 nm. A long-pass filter is designed to transmit longer wavelengths while rejecting shorter wavelengths (Figure 3.18).

A bandpass filter is designed to transmit over a discrete wavelength range while rejecting all other wavelengths (Figure 3.19). In this way, the bandpass filter creates a monochromatic band of light. The combination of a long-pass filter and a short-pass filter with overlapping transmission bands will result in a bandpass filter.

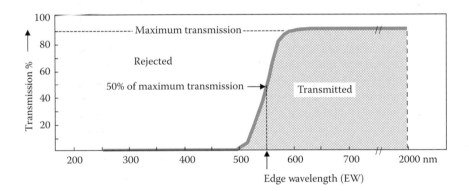

FIGURE 3.18 Typical transmission characteristics of a long-pass filter.

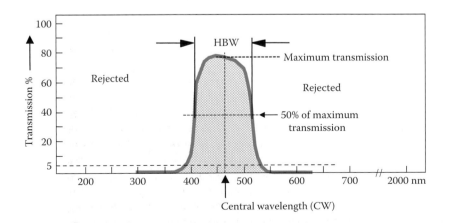

FIGURE 3.19 Typical transmission characteristics of a bandpass filter.

The basic characteristics of a bandpass filter are as follows:

- *CW*: The wavelength that corresponds to the midpoint of the band as measured at 50% of the maximum transmission.
- *Half-bandwidth* (*HBW*): The width of the transmission band measured at 50% of the maximum transmission.
- *Passband*: The width of the transmission band measured between the 5% transmission points on each side of the band.
- *Blocking region*: The attenuation of transmitted radiation in specified spectral regions outside the passband. Blocking is specified by the percentage of transmitted light. For a good filter, transmission should not be higher than 0.0001% (10^{-4} %) in this region.

When the transmission band of a long-pass filter is compared with that of a relevant bandpass filter, it can be seen that the long-pass filter transmits significantly more light (energy) but is less selective (Figure 3.20). This should be taken into account when selecting an observation filter (barrier filter) for a particular application, especially in cases where a colored or photoluminescent background prevents the recording of satisfactory results.

With regard to the process of wavelength rejection, there are two different types of optical filters: energy absorbing and energy reflecting. Energy-absorbing filters are based on the absorption of some wavelengths by colored matter present in the filter. When a light beam passes through a colored substance, certain wavelengths are absorbed and the rest are transmitted (Figure 3.21). Since light is pure energy, and the energy conservation law applies, the absorbed light is converted into heat. The filter must dissipate this absorbed energy at the same rate as it receives it; otherwise, the temperature of the filter increases. Increased temperature can cause destruction of the filter. The manufacturing of energy-absorbing filters is relatively simple and inexpensive; a suitable colored matter is embedded into glass, gelatin, or plastic, for example, or dissolved in a liquid. The two major disadvantages of these filters are as follows: (1) often it is difficult or impossible to find a colored matter to suit particular wavelength requirements; and (2) due to heat buildup, they cannot be used with high-intensity light. Energy-absorbing filters can be successfully employed as barrier filters in front of the eyes or a camera but may be damaged if placed in front of a high-intensity light source.

A typical example of an energy-reflecting filter is the interference filter. Interference filters are made by deposition, under high vacuum, of alternating thin layers of material with high and low refractive indices. There are several types of interference filters with regard to the materials that are used in the manufacturing process, e.g., metal–dielectric–metal, metal–dielectric, and all dielectric.

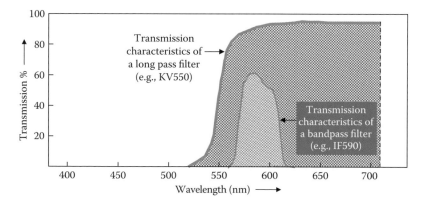

FIGURE 3.20 Transmission characteristics of a long-pass filter (KV550) compared with transmission characteristics of a bandpass filter (IF590/40).

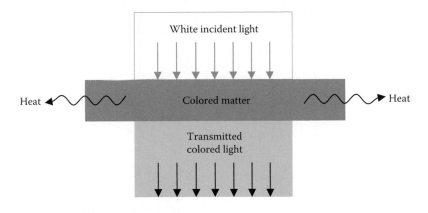

FIGURE 3.21   White light filtered through an energy-absorbing filter.

The two types of all-dielectric filters, known as "soft coated" and "hard coated," are the most commonly used filters. Hard-coated filters are manufactured by using metal oxides; they are insensitive to moisture, are hard wearing, and are very long lasting. Soft-coated filters are manufactured using zinc sulfide (refractive index = 2.35) and cryolite (refractive index = 1.35). To obtain good "square" transmission characteristics, with an acceptable rejection ratio away from the transmission band, it is necessary to deposit many alternate thin layers of zinc sulfide and cryolite on a glass substrate under high vacuum (Figure 3.22). Both zinc sulfide and cryolite are colorless, and therefore the absorption of light within the filter is minimal. The required wavelength band is obtained by the interference of transmitted light through the filter. Positive interference enhances the desired signal while negative interference cancels out the unwanted signal. Rejected wavelengths are reflected back toward the light source. The range of transmitted wavelengths depends only on the thickness of the filter layers. By varying the layer thickness, an interference filter can be designed and manufactured to give specific filter characteristics. The number of layers influences the shape of the transmission curve. Better quality interference filters, with a multilayered construction, have transmission curves that display a better defined passband (much sharper cutoff/cut-on edges).

   An interference filter transmits or reflects light, while absorption is negligible. This property of interference filters allows them to be used with high-intensity light without significant risk of overheating and filter damage. All three types of filters mentioned in the previous section (bandpass, short pass, and long pass) can be made in the form of interference filters. However, due to the complex manufacturing process required, interference filters are very expensive.

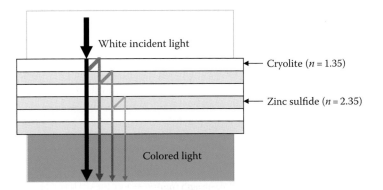

FIGURE 3.22   An interference filter can be made from many alternate layers of zinc sulfide and cryolite. Beams with different light paths through the filter interfere with each other, which leads to only certain wavelengths appearing in the transmitted light.

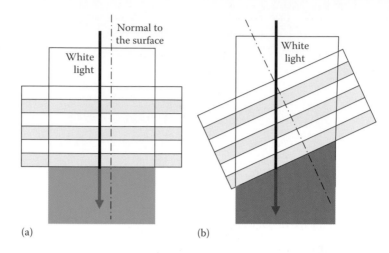

FIGURE 3.23 (a) Conventional use of an interference filter compared with (b) down-tuning, where the filter is tilted with respect to the incident beam. The light path through the filter layers becomes longer, resulting in a shift of the band toward shorter wavelengths.

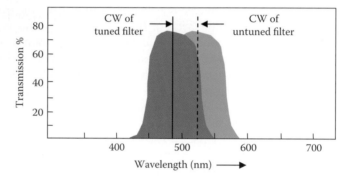

FIGURE 3.24 Tilting of an interference filter results in the shifting of its passband toward shorter wavelengths (wavelength down-tuning).

The standard transmission characteristics of an interference filter refer to the case where the incident light beam is perpendicular to the filter's surface (Figure 3.23a). In this case, the normal to the filter's surface and the incident light beam are parallel and it is said that the angle of incidence is 0°. When the incident angle increases (i.e., when the filter is tilted with respect to the light beam), the CW is shifted toward shorter wavelengths due to a longer light path through the filter layers (Figure 3.23b). The shift depends on the transmitted wavelength and is proportional to the incident angle. The shape of the transmission curve and the transmission intensity do not change significantly during the "down-tuning" process. A maximum wavelength shift of about 30 nm (visible region) can be achieved for an incident angle of 45° (Figure 3.24). This fine-tuning property of interference filters can be of significant benefit in some forensic applications (e.g., for attenuating background interference when recording weakly luminescent fingermarks).

3.3.10 ABSORPTION MODE

The method of acquiring information from a surface based on color difference (or selective absorption) is known as the absorption mode. Selective absorption can be demonstrated by considering how colored spots—blue, yellow, and red—on a white background will appear under different bands of colored light or when visualized through different bandpass filters (Table 3.3).

TABLE 3.3

Absorption Mode Demonstrated Using Three Colored Spots (Blue, Yellow, and Red) on a White Substrate

Observation Conditions	Appearance	Effect
White incident light (no observation filter)	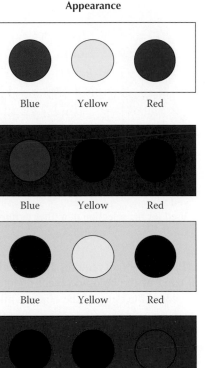 Blue Yellow Red	White substrate will appear white (reflects all colors). Blue spot will appear blue (reflects blue, absorbs all other colors). Yellow spot will appear yellow (reflects yellow, absorbs all other colors). Red spot will appear red (reflects red, absorbs all other colors).
Blue incident light (no observation filter) *or* white incident light with observation through a blue bandpass filter	Blue Yellow Red	White substrate will appear blue. Blue spot will appear blue. Yellow spot will appear black (absorbs blue, no reflected light). Red spot will appear black (absorbs blue, no reflected light).
Yellow incident light (no observation filter) *or* white incident light with observation through a yellow bandpass filter	Blue Yellow Red	White substrate will appear yellow. Blue spot will appear black (absorbs yellow, no reflected light). Yellow spot will appear yellow. Red spot will appear black (absorbs yellow, no reflected light).
Red incident light (no observation filter) *or* white incident light with observation through a red bandpass filter	Blue Yellow Red	White substrate will appear red. Blue spot will appear black (absorbs red, no reflected light). Yellow spot will appear black (absorbs red, no reflected light). Red spot will appear red.

A colored object or stain can be readily visualized by enhancing the color difference against the background substrate. A colored band of light is chosen that is opposite to the color of the object (or stain) in question. Enhancement is achieved because the object is "darkened" due to selective absorption properties. For example, illuminating an orange stain on a blue surface with a blue band of light can enhance the orange stain. The stain will appear dark against a light background because the blue light is absorbed by the stain but reflected by the surface. Alternatively, the surface can be illuminated with white light but visualized through a blue filter (the orange stain is not reflecting any blue light so it will appear dark through a blue filter). The only requirement for enhancement is that the background and the object do not absorb at the same wavelength (even if the color is similar), thus introducing some degree of contrast that can be further improved through the judicious use of filters. The use of absorption and reflection properties of matter is the basis of colorimetric techniques (i.e., techniques based on the measurement of color). Such techniques are among the most practical, but they are less sensitive than methods based on photoluminescence, which are described later. For a fingermark, approximately 100 ng of reactant product is generally necessary to obtain a significant colorimetric signal.

As a general rule, the selection of a filter, or a colored incident light, to improve contrast can be made with the aid of a color wheel (Figure 3.25). Opposite (complementary) colors on this wheel will darken the color observed (i.e., increase the contrast), while adjacent colors will tend to lighten the observed color (i.e., reduce the contrast). The absorption mode improves photographic contrast

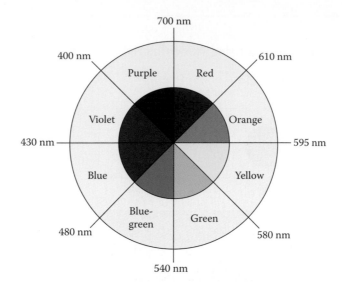

FIGURE 3.25 The color wheel can be used for the selection of a filter to improve contrast. Colors that are opposite on the wheel are complementary.

and is relatively simple to implement (Barker 1999). It requires any white light source and a bandpass filter compatible with an absorption band of the colored object of interest. In simple terms, the bandpass filter should be opposite in color to the color of the object while being as close in color to the background substrate as possible.

To illustrate the implementation of the absorption mode, consider a red fingermark on a white surface. The simplest way to photographically enhance the mark is to use the absorption mode. The absorption mode can be implemented in two ways: (1) with an appropriate filter (a blue–green filter in this case) in front of the camera; and (2) with the same filter in front of the light source. The filter used in front of the camera is known as the barrier filter. The method with a filter in front of the camera (Figure 3.26) can be used in all situations even if daylight or artificial light is present. If an appropriate barrier filter is not available but is incorporated into the light source, the absorption mode can be implemented by using this band of light (Figure 3.27). In the latter case, the room must be darkened for optimum results.

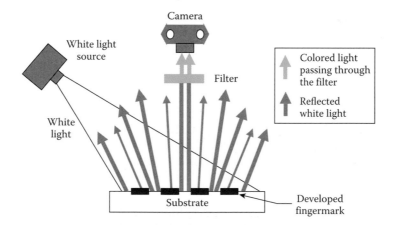

FIGURE 3.26 Schematic representation of the absorption mode with the appropriate filter used in front of the camera. This method can be used in all situations in the presence or absence of daylight or artificial light.

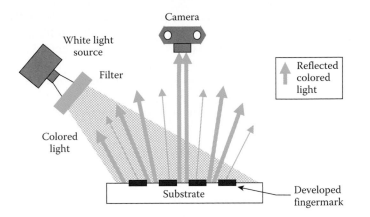

FIGURE 3.27 A schematic representation of the absorption mode with the appropriate filter in front of a white light source. This method can be used only in dark or semidark situations.

Enhancement using the absorption mode may be unsuccessful if the surface is similar in color to the object of interest. Changing the wavelength of the band of light can sometimes produce better results. (A light source with fine-tuning capabilities will be an advantage in such cases.) If the color of the object is pale, or if the object appears transparent, the absorption mode may not offer satisfactory enhancement, and other modes (or chemical treatment to modify the colorimetric properties of the object) should be exploited to achieve possible enhancement.

A ninhydrin-developed fingermark, when viewed under white light, will appear purple in color. Some wavelengths will be absorbed by the mark, while others are reflected. The combination of reflected wavelengths (principally in the blue and red regions) is perceived by the human eye as being purple in color. The purple color is due to a compound known as Ruhemann's purple, which is the product formed when ninhydrin reacts with the amino acids in a latent fingermark. The absorption characteristics of Ruhemann's purple need to be taken into consideration if the best contrast is to be obtained using the absorption mode.

A typical absorption spectrum for a ninhydrin-developed fingermark is depicted in Figure 3.28. It can be seen that there are two absorption bands: a narrow band with a maximum at around 415 nm

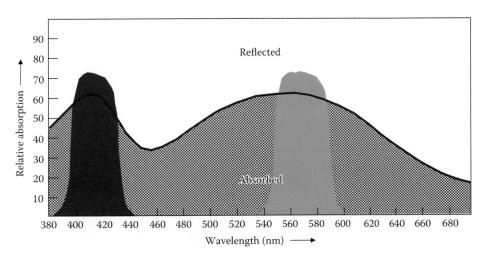

FIGURE 3.28 A typical absorption spectrum for a ninhydrin-developed fingermark, with the shaded area under the curve representing the light absorbed. There are two absorption bands: a narrow band with a maximum at around 415 nm (violet region) and a broad major band with a maximum at around 550–570 nm (green–yellow region). Possible bandpass filters, for use in front of the light source or in front of the camera, are indicated as colored bands.

(violet region) and a broad major band with a maximum in the region of 550–570 nm (green–yellow region). The best contrast can be obtained by using a bandpass filter in front of the camera, or in front of the light source, that suits one maxima (550–570 nm) or the other (415 nm) in the absorption spectrum.

When working in the violet or red regions of the spectrum, it must be remembered that the human eye has low sensitivity at these wavelengths. Enhancement under such conditions may appear poor to the unaided eye but will generally be significantly improved in any photographic images.

3.3.11 DIFFUSED REFLECTION MODE

This method of acquiring information is based on diffused reflection from a rough object on a surface that is dark or that is flat and shiny (Figure 3.29). In such a case, more diffusely reflected light from the object will reach the camera than reflected light from the surface. The object will, therefore, appear light against a dark background. This method can be used for the observation and photography of an object that is on top of, or indented into, a surface. Classical examples include a finger or footwear mark in blood on a dark or a flat and shiny surface, a footwear impression in dust, or a greasy fingermark on a smooth shiny surface. With the work area darkened, the light beam used for illumination should be directed at an angle to the surface, starting at 45° then varying the angle as required until the best contrast between the object of interest and the substrate is achieved. The goal is to maximize light reflection from the object while minimizing light reflection from the surface.

In the case of a colored object, a monochromatic light band of similar color to the object should be used to enhance the diffused reflection. In the case of a colored surface, a monochromatic light band with a color opposite to the color of the surface should be used to darken the surface (i.e., increase the contrast between the object and the surface). Oblique lighting (i.e., light beam almost parallel to the surface) is required in some cases (e.g., footwear impressions in dust or cyanoacrylate-developed fingermarks).

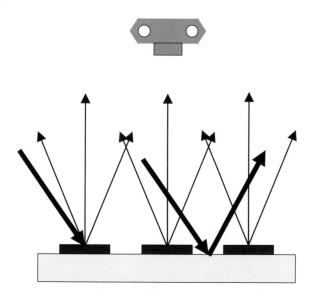

FIGURE 3.29   A schematic representation of the diffused reflection mode applied to a flat shiny surface. The incident light is specularly reflected by the surface but diffusely reflected by the fingermark.

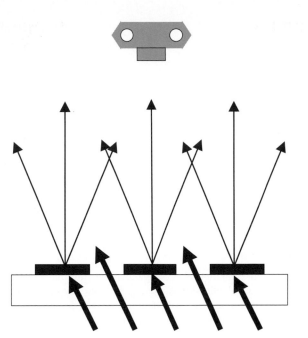

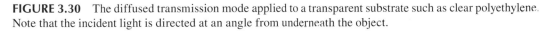

FIGURE 3.30 The diffused transmission mode applied to a transparent substrate such as clear polyethylene. Note that the incident light is directed at an angle from underneath the object.

Used in the transmission mode, this technique is the basis of dark-field illumination in light microscopy. The phenomenon is observed when the incident light rays are diffused and refracted differently by a sample on a transparent surface such as glass. A fingermark on glass, with transmitted oblique lighting, will be observed as light ridges against a dark background (Figure 3.30).

This method, already documented in forensic science more than 100 years ago (Reiss 1903), can be used to efficiently image marks on glass surfaces. Diffused transmission techniques can also be utilized for the fast screening of cyanoacrylate-developed marks on clear plastic bags. The light beam from a FLS is directed onto one side of the bag, with examination done from the other side. Extreme care should be exercised, however, to ensure that the eyes are not exposed to the direct beam from the light source!

3.3.12 Episcopic Coaxial Illumination

Episcopic coaxial illumination is a special implementation of the diffused reflection mode for use on flat, shiny surfaces. The incident light is directed along the camera lens axis (i.e., perpendicular to the surface). This effect can be achieved by mounting a semitransparent mirror (or flat piece of glass) in front of the camera at an angle of 45° toward the lens axis/light path (Figure 3.31). The incident light beam is directed onto the mirror at an angle of 45° toward the mirror. To avoid "hot" spots, a diffuser is recommended in front of the light source. Part of the incident beam is reflected from the semitransparent mirror and travels along the lens axis toward the exhibit. The other part of the incident beam passes through the mirror and is trapped by a black surface. The incident light is reflected more from the flat surface (specular reflection) than from the ridges (diffused reflection), producing the opposite result to the conventional diffused reflection mode (i.e., it results in a dark image against a light background). Episcopic coaxial illumination can be successfully used for photographing latent fingermarks, fingermarks in blood, or cyanoacrylate-developed fingermarks on smooth shiny surfaces (e.g., glass, metal, plastic) (Pfister 1985; Ziv and Springer 1993). The surface must be as flat as possible to obtain optimum results.

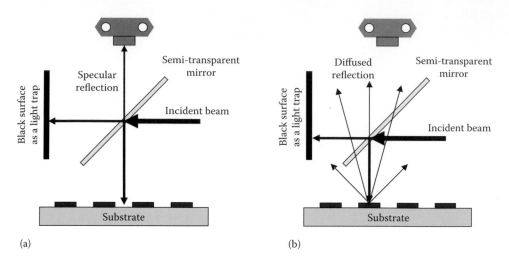

(a)   (b)

FIGURE 3.31   A schematic representation of episcopic coaxial illumination. (a) When the reflected light beam hits the shiny surface, specular reflection is back in the same direction, toward the camera. (b) Light that hits the fingermark is diffusely reflected. More light reaches the camera from the surface than from the fingermark, so the ridges will be dark against a light background.

3.3.13 PHOTOLUMINESCENCE MODE

Photoluminescence emission is always very weak compared with the excitation light and it is shifted toward the red end of the spectrum (Figure 3.32). If white light is used for excitation, weak photoluminescence emission cannot be seen as it is swamped by the high intensity of the incident light.

The chemical compounds of interest to us usually have one main excitation band and will absorb only those wavelengths (colors) that match this band. White light can be reduced to the wavelengths of interest by placing a bandpass filter in front of the light source. Where possible, the transmission characteristics of the bandpass filter should match the excitation band (Figure 3.33).

A barrier filter is then required in front of the eyes (or camera) that will reject the very strong excitation light reflected from the surface while transmitting the weak photoluminescence emission.

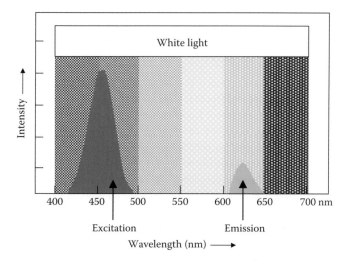

FIGURE 3.32   Excitation and emission curves for a theoretical photoluminescent material with white incident light.

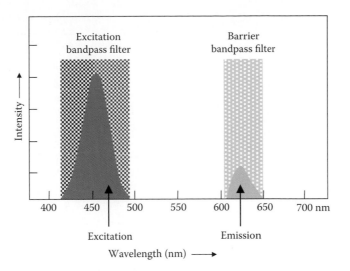

FIGURE 3.33 Excitation and emission curves for a theoretical photoluminescent material with choice of appropriate excitation and barrier filters.

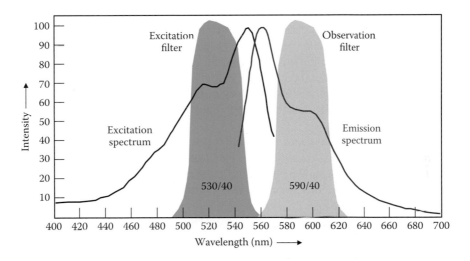

FIGURE 3.34 Excitation and emission spectra for a fingermark developed with indanedione–zinc (as an example) with an indication of possible filters for excitation and observation. It is important to ensure that the excitation band from the light source does not overlap with the transmission band of the barrier filter.

The transmission characteristics of the barrier filter should therefore match the emission band without overlapping with the excitation band. This method of gathering information based on the photoluminescence emission of a material is known as the photoluminescence mode.

In practice, the choice of appropriate filters is made according to excitation and emission spectra of the photoluminescent compound of interest (Figure 3.34). An excitation spectrum shows the change in emission intensity vs. excitation wavelengths for a fixed emission wavelength. In general, this spectrum corresponds to the absorption spectrum of the compound. The emission spectrum shows the change in emission intensity vs. emission wavelength for a fixed excitation wavelength. Excitation and emission spectra for a given material are often displayed on the same graph (and are generally referred to as luminescence spectra).

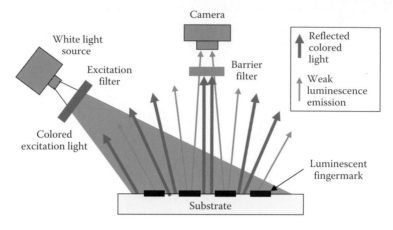

FIGURE 3.35 Arrangement for photoluminescence observations.

To implement the photoluminescence mode, two filters are necessary: one in front of the light source and another in front of the eyes (or camera) (Figure 3.35). The only exception to this is when a monochromatic light source (e.g., laser or monochromatic band from a nonlaser FLS) is employed. In this case, only a barrier filter is required. Due to the weak light emission that results, all observation and recording in this mode must be done under darkened conditions (as dark as possible). In addition, the excitation source should be powerful, and the barrier and excitation filters must be compatible (i.e., the barrier filter should not transmit any of the excitation light). Under ideal conditions, a photoluminescent object will produce a light image (luminescent) against a dark background (nonluminescent). In reality, a substrate always shows some photoluminescence, and the background may be more or less dark, but rarely black. The photoluminescence of the substrate has to be taken into account during recording, and conditions must be optimized to obtain the best possible contrast.

The intensity of photoluminescence emission depends on temperature. As the temperature decreases, some of the competing processes mentioned earlier (e.g., energy loss by molecular vibration) are attenuated, thus enhancing the photoluminescence pathway. Sometimes, this enhancement is dramatic, as is the case for Ruhemann's purple–metal complexes (e.g., produced by treating ninhydrin-developed fingermarks with zinc or cadmium metal salts). At room temperature, the photoluminescence of these complexes is negligible, while at the temperature of liquid nitrogen (77 K or −196°C), the photoluminescence is very strong and can be used for the enhancement of weak ninhydrin-developed latent fingermarks.

The main advantage of the photoluminescence mode is its sensitivity. When used under optimum conditions, sub-nanogram (ng = 10^{-9} g) quantities of a substance can be detected, while in the absorption mode (colorimetric techniques), detection limits are typically around 100 nanograms (100 ng = 10^{-7} g). It is for this reason that significant research has been conducted over the last 30 years directed at the development of luminescence techniques for the detection of latent fingermarks.

3.3.14 POLARIZED LIGHT EXAMINATIONS

Polarized light can be useful for removing glare ("hot spots") from shiny surfaces to improve contrast. A typical setup for enhancement using this method is shown in Figure 3.36. Two polarizers (polarizing filters) are required: one polarizer is placed in front of the light source while another is placed in front of the camera. The polarizer in front of the camera is then rotated till the best contrast is achieved. This arrangement is only useful for shiny surfaces with a diffusely reflecting subject (such as a latent fingermark, a fingermark in blood, or a fingermark developed by cyanoacrylate fuming). The subject depolarizes the light allowing it to pass through the camera polarizer

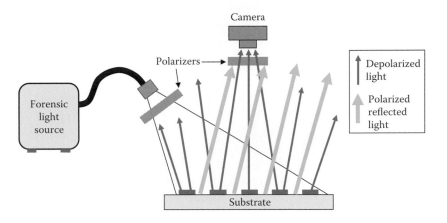

FIGURE 3.36 Setup required for enhancement using polarized light.

while the shiny surface reflects the polarized light. This reflected polarized light can be blocked by rotating the camera polarizer to the correct position.

Care should be exercised with the polarizer in front of the light source. When white light is employed, the light intensity from the light source should be reduced to a minimum and the polarizer should not be kept too long in front of the beam. Most FLSs have very strong white light that can damage the polarizer in a matter of seconds due to the heat generated.

3.3.15 ULTRAVIOLET ILLUMINATION TECHNIQUES

A range of UV illumination techniques are available that can be generally classified as follows:

- *UV–VIS photoluminescence*: Illuminating the surface with UV light (short- or long-wavelength UV) while observing luminescence emission in the visible (VIS)
- *UV–UV photoluminescence*: Illuminating the surface with short-wavelength UV light (200–300 nm; UV B) while observing luminescence emission in the long-wavelength UV region (300–400 nm; UV A)
- *UV reflection*: Illuminating the surface with UV light (short- or long-wavelength UV) while observing light reflected in the same wavelength region

Working with any UV illumination technique poses a number of hazards to the operator, in addition to technical difficulties, when recording results. The human eye and general-purpose digital cameras are insensitive to UV light, so any observation in the UV region cannot be achieved directly (specialized digital imaging equipment is required). Due to its high energy, UV light can cause significant eye and skin damage, so personal protection is required. Short-wavelength UV lamps generate ozone that can be hazardous to the operator. In addition, short-wavelength UV is damaging to DNA so caution must be exercised when examining items that may require subsequent biological testing.

Glass absorbs short-wavelength UV light, so observations in this region cannot be achieved using conventional glass lenses, thus requiring the use of very expensive optical components (quartz, fluorite, etc.). Glass also absorbs a large proportion of long-wavelength UV light, so quartz optical components are also recommended in this instance. In addition, general-purpose digital cameras are not sensitive in the UV range due to how the sensors are manufactured. Specialized UV-sensitive digital imaging systems are therefore required when working at these wavelengths. While these difficulties can be largely overcome, particularly with respect to recent technological advances, they have limited the widespread use of UV illumination techniques at the crime scene.

UV–VIS photoluminescence is the simplest mode to apply, in that the observation of results is conducted in the visible region and therefore can be achieved with the naked eye. The technique can

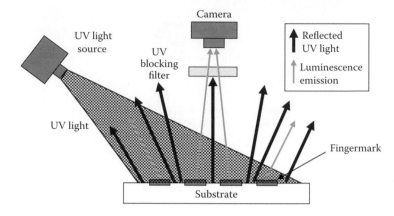

FIGURE 3.37 Typical setup for the photoluminescence mode with ultraviolet excitation and observation in the visible region.

be used to locate items that are luminescent in the visible spectrum when illuminated with UV light. Optical brighteners used in textile fibers, paper, and paint typically show strong photoluminescence emission under such conditions. Alternatively, the technique can be used to locate UV-absorbing materials (e.g., blood) on highly luminescent surfaces. Photography (or video capture) should be conducted with a filter on the camera that transmits in the visible but blocks any reflected UV light (Figure 3.37).

UV–UV photoluminescence requires illumination of a surface with short-wavelength UV light. A UV-sensitive camera, fitted with a quartz lens and a barrier filter that only transmits long-wavelength UV light, is required for image capture. It has been determined that a range of biological fluids (including latent fingermark deposits) can photoluminesce under such conditions (Bramble et al. 1993; Springer et al. 1994). In general, photoluminescence emission in the UV is very weak, and it is difficult to capture an image using a conventional charge-coupled device (CCD) camera. The problem can be overcome by either (1) using a CCD camera with image integration capabilities or (2) using a light-intensifier device, in which case information is not acquired directly from the object but from the phosphor screen of the image intensifier.

UV reflection requires the use of either a short- or long-wavelength UV lamp and an imaging system fitted with a barrier filter that only transmits in this region (i.e., either short- or long-wavelength UV) (Figure 3.38). It is important that only reflected light is recorded, not light reemitted at longer wavelengths (i.e., photoluminescence emission). If light reflected in the short-wavelength region is being recorded, quartz objectives must be employed. Reflected UV techniques have been demonstrated to be effective for the visualization of untreated fingermarks and footwear impressions, in addition to the recording of wounds or bruising on human skin (West et al. 1990; Sanfilippo et al. 2010).

Over recent years, a number of manufacturers have developed specialized image intensifiers for capturing and recording images in the short-wavelength UV region. Generally referred to as a reflected UV imaging system (RUVIS), the imager is used in conjunction with a low-power short-wavelength UV lamp. By varying the angle of the light source with respect to the surface under investigation, untreated latent fingermarks may be revealed. Depending on the substrate and the nature of any fingermarks that are present, there are three possible outcomes:

1. The surface reflects less UV than the fingermarks, so the ridges will be light against a dark background.
2. The surface and the fingermarks reflect the same amount of UV so no result is obtained (ridges cannot be discerned).
3. The surface reflects more UV than the fingermarks, so the ridges will be dark against a light background.

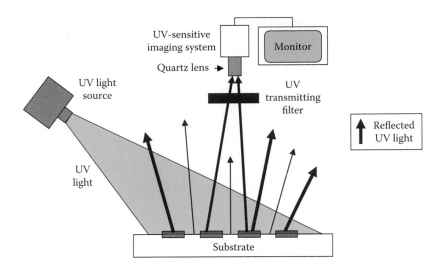

FIGURE 3.38   Implementation of the ultraviolet reflection mode.

3.4   FORENSIC LIGHT SOURCES

3.4.1   CONVENTIONAL LIGHT SOURCES

Specialized light sources, including lasers and high-intensity filtered lamps, have been employed for many years as an aid to fingermark enhancement and crime scene examination in general. The term "forensic light source" is commonly used to refer to an illumination system adapted for such use. Numerous FLSs, from a number of manufacturers, are available on the market. When used correctly, an FLS can facilitate the search for a range of forensic traces including footwear impressions, hairs and fibers, firearm discharge residues, lubricant stains, biological material (e.g., blood, semen, urine, and saliva), and latent fingermarks (both pre- and posttreatment).

An interest in the forensic application of lasers was initiated in 1977 when Dalrymple and coworkers (1977) reported on the detection of untreated latent fingermarks using photoluminescence techniques. The development of high-intensity filtered lamps as more versatile, less expensive alternatives to the laser was subsequently pursued in the early 1980s in Australia, Great Britain, and Canada (Stoilovic et al. 1987; Watkin 1987; Haylock 1989). A nonlaser FLS is sometimes referred to as an alternate light source.

The laser (light amplification by stimulated emission of radiation) offers high light intensity and precisely delimited operating wavelengths (monochromatic laser lines). Compared to nonlaser light sources, lasers tend to suffer from a lack of flexibility (as, for a given type of laser, only a limited number of wavelengths are available) and a relatively high cost (Watkin and Misner 1990). However, while lasers were traditionally large, fixed laboratory instruments, they are now available as portable units that are more cost-effective.

The nonlaser FLSs currently on the market are typically designed around a strong white light source (e.g., xenon arc lamp) fitted with a range of filters that allow for the selection of a particular monochromatic band of light. The power of the light source and the characteristics of the filters (e.g., BW and transmission at the center wavelength) determine the light intensity of each band. The quality of the filters (e.g., light rejection outside the bandpass region) is critical if optimum results are to be achieved. The use of high-quality interference filters has the advantage that such filters can be tilted in the light path to shift the transmission band to shorter wavelengths. (This fine-tuning capability can be particularly important in cases where background luminescence creates a

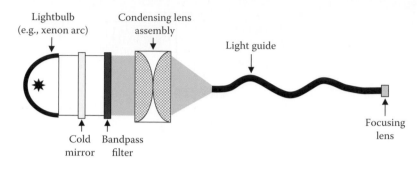

FIGURE 3.39 A schematic representation of a typical nonlaser forensic light source.

contrast problem.) A schematic diagram of a typical filtered light source is provided in Figure 3.39. The essential components are as follows:

- *Lamp*: The lamp (lightbulb) determines the initial power available and should be of a long-lasting type (e.g., arc lamp). The lamp output should adequately cover the UV and the entire visible spectrum. The minimum recommended power is 300 W.
- *Cold mirror*: A cold mirror is used to reject IR radiation (heat) by reflection and transmit UV and visible light. The mirror should have a high transmittance in the UV and visible regions. If IR output is required, then the cold mirror needs to be bypassed. A cold mirror may not be necessary if hard-coated filters are employed.
- *Bandpass filters*: Bandpass filters determine the monochromatic bands of light that can be selected. The filters have to be of high quality, preferably hard-coated multilayer interference filters with an antireflective coating. The color of a band is determined by the filter's CW, while the HBW and maximum transmission determine the purity and power. Requirements for higher purity of a band result in the lowering of the transmitted power. Therefore, a compromise has to be made for each band.
- *Collimating lens assembly*: The collimating lens assembly should focus the colored light beam onto a small spot at the entrance of the light guide. The lens should be highly efficient, with an antireflective coating.
- *Light guide*: The light output should be delivered through a light guide so that the beam can be readily directed at an area of interest. Single-core liquid light guides (7–10 mm diameter) are favored, as they have a much higher transmission efficiency compared with fiber-optic bundles. High transmittance is required from the UV through the entire visible region.
- *Focusing lens*: A focusing lens at the end of the light guide should be able to focus the light spot with sharp edges in order to achieve a uniform light field. Uniformity of the light spot is of utmost importance for successful photography. It should be possible to focus the beam over a large area for rapid screening or over a small area (several square centimeters) for the photography of a small subject such as a single luminescent fingermark.

Before the recording of an object using illumination from an FLS of this type, the light spot needs to be focused and its size correctly adjusted. The spot size is adjusted by varying the distance between the light guide and the object. The focusing can then be done with the lens attached to the end of the light guide. When photographing an object (e.g., fingermark), it is important that the light spot covers the entire field of view of the camera; otherwise, the automatic exposure as calculated by the camera's microprocessor will not be correct.

3.4.2 LED-BASED LIGHT SOURCES

Light sources based on light-emitting diodes (LEDs) are portable, solid-state devices capable of producing light of relatively high intensity. The first LEDs appeared in the early 1960s and

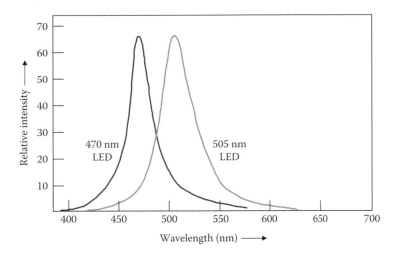

FIGURE 3.40 Typical emission curves for 470 and 505 nm light-emitting diodes.

they were initially employed in numerical displays for watches and calculators. Through ongoing research, LEDs have become more powerful, making them suitable as general-purpose light sources. However, at this point in time, only certain wavelengths suitable for forensic applications can be provided by LEDs (e.g., 360, 395, 415, 450, 470, 505, and 530 nm). As for portable lasers, LED-based light sources are not tunable (i.e., they are fixed wavelength).

The typical emission band of a LED is very narrow at the point of maximum emission, but is relatively broad at the base of the emission curve, resulting in long "tails" on both sides of the maximum emission. The emission curves for 470 and 505 nm LEDs are shown in Figure 3.40. The long tail to the left may produce an unwanted luminescent background (due to short-wavelength excitation), while the long tail to the right may overlap with the transmission of the barrier filter, which can interfere with the capture of weak luminescence emissions. In order to remove the long tails, an interference bandpass filter centered at the maximum LED emission wavelength is necessary (Figure 3.41). An unfiltered LED has very limited applications because of its broad emission characteristics. This has to be taken into account if a LED-based system is to be used as an FLS.

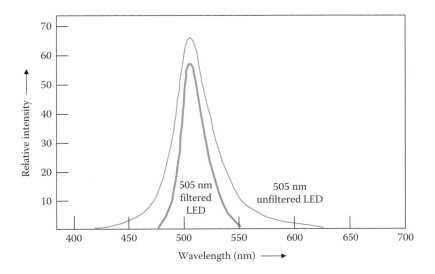

FIGURE 3.41 Use of an interference filter to improve the emission characteristics of a light-emitting diode light source.

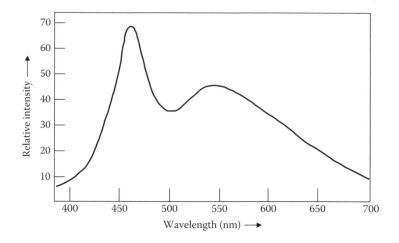

FIGURE 3.42   Typical emission curve for a white light-emitting diode.

There are several different *white* LED systems on the market. One of the common systems produces two broad emission bands as depicted in Figure 3.42. The blue component of the emission (around 460 nm) is very strong, which makes the light from this type of white LED look "whiter."

LED-based FLSs became available in the late 1990s and, through ongoing improvements, their emission is now comparable in both intensity and spectral output to some of the filtered light sources on the market. LED-based systems have become viable options for a number of forensic science applications, particularly given their increased portability and an ability to operate for long periods on battery power. However, it must be appreciated that the sensitivity of photoluminescence detection relies heavily on the output power and spectral quality provided by the light source. For example, the detection of a weakly-luminescent fingermark will generally be more efficient with a laser, followed by a high-intensity non-laser FLS, followed by a LED-based system (assuming that a similar excitation range is being considered).

3.4.3   FLS REQUIREMENTS

A multipurpose FLS needs to be portable yet powerful enough for use under a range of conditions. To cover all potential forensic applications, the light source must be versatile, offering a range of different light bands from the UV through to the red end of the visible spectrum. Ideally, these bands should be as narrow as possible (typically less than 50 nm in width) while maintaining sufficient light intensity. This is particularly important if the luminescence mode is to be employed.

A dedicated FLS for crime scene applications should be able to provide a narrow band of intense light at any wavelength of interest to the investigator. The essential bands for an FLS are represented in Table 3.4. Depending on the equipment available, a number of different light sources may be necessary to satisfy these requirements.

Other bands may be beneficial under particular circumstances. A list of recommended barrier filters and goggles is provided in Table 3.5. Given the high intensity of light produced by modern light sources, suitable eye protection must be worn and precautions taken to ensure that the eyes are never directly exposed to the full intensity of the beam. For example, care must be exercised when examining highly reflective surfaces using an FLS. Manufacturers' recommendations should be followed to avoid potential eye damage.

The relative performance of different light sources has been compared by a number of authors (Warrener et al. 1983; Auvdel 1988; Wilkinson and Watkin 1994; Lam and Wilkinson 2011; Dalrymple and Almog 2012). In addition, some light source evaluations have been conducted by the

TABLE 3.4
Recommended Output Bands for a Forensic Light Source

CW (nm)	HBW (nm)	Typical Applications
White light	—	Visible fingermarks or stains, impressions in dust (oblique lighting), trace evidence on smooth surfaces (oblique lighting), general searching
350	50–80	Latent fingermarks on UV-luminescent surfaces, marks dusted with UV-luminescent powder, semen stains, firearm discharge residues, textile fibers, paint flakes, and lubricants
415	30–40	Dried bloodstains, fingermarks in blood, semen stains, firearm discharge residues, textile fibers, and lubricants
450	60–100	Inherent fingermark luminescence, general searching in the luminescence mode, semen stains, firearm discharge residues, textile fibers, and lubricants
500	30–50	Semen stains, firearm discharge residues, and enhancement of metal-salt-treated ninhydrin marks (absorption mode)
550	30–50	Semen stains and enhancement of ninhydrin-developed marks (absorption mode)
600	30–50	Enhancement of blood marks stained with amido black or fingermarks developed with iodine/benzoflavone (absorption mode)

TABLE 3.5
Recommended Barrier Filters and Goggles
for Use with a Forensic Light Source

Bandpass Filters

CW (nm)	HBW (nm)
410–420	30–40
550–570	30–50
580–600	30–50

Long-Pass (Cutoff) Filters

EW (nm)	Color
400–420	Clear
460–480	Yellow
490–520	Yellow
530–570	Orange
580–600	Red
620–650	Red

Goggles

EW (nm)	Color
400–420	Clear
480–520	Yellow
560–580	Orange
600–650	Red

U.S. National Forensic Science Technology Center (www.nfstc.org) and the associated assessment reports can be downloaded from their website.

3.5   PHOTOGRAPHY

3.5.1   INTRODUCTION

The word photography comes from two ancient Greek words: phôtos, for "light," and graphein, for "writing." Photography can therefore be described as "writing with light." When a photograph is taken, light or some other form of radiant energy, such as x-rays, is used to record a picture of an object or scene on a light-sensitive surface. The two types of light-sensitive surfaces typically employed are based on (1) the photochemical reaction of a light-sensitive material (classical film photography) and (2) the photoelectrical effect on a light-sensitive chip (digital photography). Light is the essential ingredient in all forms of photography, and therefore the physical principles of the technique are governed by the physics of light. A number of good textbooks exist (e.g., Jacobson et al. 2000; Allen and Triantaphillidou 2011; London et al. 2013) that give a thorough treatment of the material outlined in this section. Only the more critical parameters are summarized here, with an emphasis on digital imaging (which has largely replaced film photography), for the benefit of fingermark detection specialists.

3.5.2   BASIC IMAGE FORMATION AND CAPTURE

An image can be formed on a flat surface using either a pinhole (Figure 3.43) or a lens (Figure 3.44). A pinhole forms an image using a single ray from each object point. The number of rays coming from the object is therefore drastically reduced, resulting in a very faint and somewhat blurred image due to diffraction effects. Very sensitive photographic media and/or long exposure times are needed to record such an image. Much better images can be obtained using a lens. Lenses can focus light rays, producing much sharper images. Due to a much larger aperture (lens opening equal to

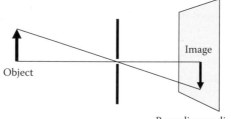

FIGURE 3.43   Formation of an image using a pinhole.

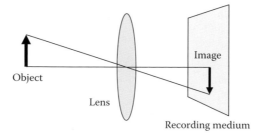

FIGURE 3.44   Formation of an image using a lens.

the approximate diameter of the lens), light throughput through the lens is several thousand times higher than that of a pinhole.

A simple lens suffers from a number of limitations, called "aberrations," that prevent the formation of a perfectly focused image. Two of the most important limitations are spherical and chromatic aberrations. Spherical aberration is the phenomenon whereby perimeter rays bend more (i.e., focus at shorter distances) than axial rays (Figure 3.45). The spherical aberration effect can be reduced by masking the perimeter rays through the introduction of a diaphragm in front of the lens (Figure 3.46). Chromatic aberration is the phenomenon whereby shorter wavelengths bend more (i.e., focus at shorter distances) than longer wavelengths (Figure 3.47).

Although modern camera lenses are made of many sophisticated components, aberrations can only be reduced (not eliminated), and the effects may still be apparent in some situations. It is important to be aware of the limitations imposed by these aberrations and to take precautions, where possible, to limit their effects.

Once an image has been formed by the camera lens and projected toward the back of the camera, this needs to be captured. Historically, this was achieved using photosensitive film. Digital images, however, are created by light falling on an electronic receptor, generally a CCD or complementary metal-oxide

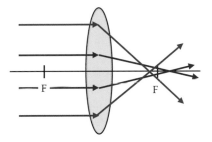

FIGURE 3.45   A schematic representation of spherical aberration.

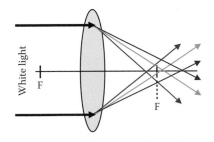

FIGURE 3.46   A diaphragm in front of the lens reduces the lens aperture, thus reducing the spherical aberration effect.

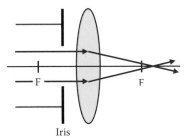

FIGURE 3.47   A schematic representation of chromatic aberration.

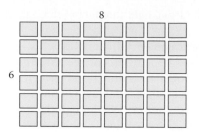

FIGURE 3.48 Example of a 2D array of photosensitive picture elements (pixels) as found in digital imaging sensors, with the most common aspect ratio being 4:3.

semiconductor (CMOS) sensor chip, that converts light into an electrical signal that is then processed by a computer (in-camera microprocessor) to form an image. Image sensors such as CCDs are made up of individual picture elements (pixels) that generally present a square or rectangular shape of uniform size and light sensitivity to the incoming light. These pixels are arranged in a 2D array (Figure 3.48). The resulting image is a mosaic of minute blocks representing colors and light intensities. Sensor chips with large numbers of pixels generally produce higher-resolution images than those with lower pixel counts. The size of each pixel determines the sensitivity of the chip; chips with large pixels can gather more light per pixel and therefore have a higher light sensitivity than chips with smaller pixels. Chips with larger pixels also have a greater dynamic range (exposure latitude) than those with small pixels. Overall image quality is therefore determined by both the total pixel count of the sensor and the size of the individual pixels. Professional digital cameras employ large image sensors with large pixels, while consumer digital cameras typically have very small chips with small pixels.

The total number of pixels can be calculated by multiplying the number of horizontal pixels by the number of vertical pixels. The majority of compact and digital single-lens reflex (DSLR) cameras use an aspect ratio of 4:3 (width/height; $W:H$) (Figure 3.48). For example, a 1.92 megapixel (MP) sensor has dimensions of $W = 1600$ pixels and $H = 1200$ pixels ($1600 \times 1200 = 1,920,000$ pixels).

The electronic responses from each sensor pixel are converted by a microprocessor into numbers via a binary code (made up of zeros and ones) that represent the amount of light detected at each pixel location. The binary digits (*bits*) for each pixel are then stored in the camera's memory as a sequence, often in a compressed form. The recorded sequence of bits can be later read and interpreted to produce an analog version of the image for display or printing. One of the biggest advantages afforded by digital imaging technologies is the ability to quickly and easily apply a range of image processing tools as will be discussed later in this chapter.

3.5.3 Digital Cameras

3.5.3.1 Image Sensors

As indicated earlier, two types of sensors are commonly used in modern digital cameras: the CCD and the CMOS. With the CCD sensor, a charge produced by light is held at each pixel and then transferred from one pixel to another along the array, until it arrives at the last pixel where it is captured and amplified as a voltage. The CMOS sensor, on the other hand, is an *active* pixel sensor, with each pixel containing a photo detector and an amplifier. The charge produced by light is amplified at each pixel, then converted to a voltage, and captured as a signal. In comparison of the two technologies, the CMOS sensor is faster, consumes less energy, has less image lag, and has a higher sensitivity. However, the CMOS has increased design complexity, lower pixel uniformity, and a reduced area for light capture. Neither technology has a clear advantage in terms of overall image quality.

Each pixel in the image sensor converts light into a voltage that is proportional to the light intensity (brightness), which is passed to an analog-to-digital converter (ADC). The ADC translates the signal fluctuations into a discrete binary code. This digital output is then sent to a digital signal processor (DSP). The DSP adjusts contrast and image detail, and then compresses the image before sending it to the storage medium (e.g., flash card or memory stick). The brighter the light striking a sensor pixel, the higher the voltage and the brighter the resulting computer pixel when the image is displayed on a screen. The more pixels, the higher the resolution and the greater the detail that can be captured (and the more computer memory required to store the resulting image).

Silicon-based imaging chips are sensitive over a wide wavelength range, from UV to IR. Note, however, that most digital cameras have a filter mounted in front of the sensor to block IR radiation (while short-wavelength UV and a significant amount of long-wavelength UV is blocked by the glass used in the camera optics). The IR blocking filter is required to ensure that only visible light is captured. In digital cameras adapted for IR imaging purposes, this filter has been removed.

Monochrome (black-and-white) digital cameras use unmodified sensors to record light intensity only at each pixel, not color. To record color images, color filters are introduced above every sensor pixel. A microlens is also added on top to collect and focus more light on the pixel (Figure 3.49). While several approaches are available to create a color sensor, most camera manufacturers use a Bayer array of red, green, and blue (RGB) filters (Figure 3.50a). The Bayer array consists of alternating rows of red–green and green–blue filters over the pixels that make up the imaging sensor. A Bayer *cell* consists of two green, one red, and one blue pixel, arranged as indicated in Figure 3.50b; the sensor will therefore contain twice as many green pixels compared to red or blue. This is done deliberately to mimic the human eye, which has the greatest sensitivity

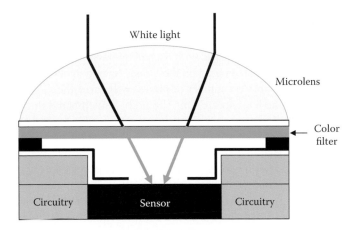

FIGURE 3.49 To improve sensitivity and obtain color information, a microlens and a color filter (red, green, and blue) are added to each sensor pixel.

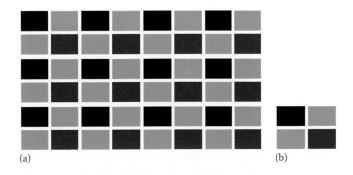

FIGURE 3.50 (a) A Bayer pattern of red, green, and blue pixels in a sensor array. (b) A Bayer *cell* consists of two green, one red, and one blue pixel.

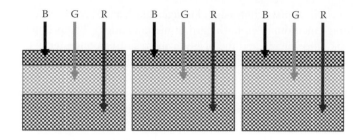

FIGURE 3.51   The Foveon X3 chip records data for all three primary colors at every pixel, with each color at a different layer in the chip.

in the green region of the visible light spectrum. Each pixel can record the intensity of only one color according to the filter above it. The camera's microprocessor has to calculate the final color (RGB) value for each pixel by taking into consideration the values measured across neighboring pixels using a process known as interpolation. This is a complex calculation and requires a powerful and rapid inbuilt microprocessor, which adds to the overall cost of the camera. No interpolation is required with monochrome cameras (used for specialized laboratory applications, for example) as each sensor pixel directly contributes to the grayscale value for each corresponding pixel in the recorded image.

Consider a 4 MP color camera as an example. According to the Bayer pattern (Figure 3.50), the camera's sensor will have 2 MP of green pixels, 1 MP of red pixels, and 1MP of blue pixels. The resulting images, however, will still be 4 MP in size, with each pixel having its own RGB value. The "missing" values for each pixel are calculated based on the values from neighboring pixels. It can be seen that the green channel, with the greatest number of pixels, will carry the most information and will have the strongest signal (i.e., the least noise). This should be remembered in cases where there is a weak color image. By using the green channel only, it may be possible to extract more information.

It is worth noting that there are other image sensors on the market such as the Foveon X3 chip. This chip, based on CMOS technology and developed by the company Foveon, Inc. (now part of Sigma Corporation), is named after the fovea of the human eye, which enables sharp imaging while reading or watching television. Instead of having a single filtered photodetector at each pixel location, it has a multilayered design with three vertically stacked photodiodes—one red, one green, and one blue—at each pixel (Figure 3.51). There is no need for interpolation in this case as the X3 sensor simultaneously captures RGB intensities at each pixel. This type of sensor can produce ultrasharp detailed images, with full-color single-pixel resolution. Sigma was the first camera manufacturer to employ the Foveon X3 chip in their cameras.

3.5.3.2   Digital Single-Lens Reflex Camera

DSLR cameras evolved from film-based SLR cameras, with the film being replaced with an image sensor chip and a microprocessor added for reading and amplifying the signal from the sensor pixels, creating and storing images, and controlling all camera operations. A removable storage device in the form of a memory card is also typically employed. A schematic diagram of a DSLR camera is shown in Figure 3.52. In the "reflex" design, light travels through the camera lens to a mirror that alternates between sending the image to the viewfinder or to the image sensor. This system uses a *single lens*. The alternative, commonly employed in compact camera, is to have a viewfinder with its own lens (meaning that the viewfinder uses a different light path and, therefore, the viewfinder image may differ from that captured by the camera's sensor). DSLRs typically use interchangeable lenses with a proprietary lens mount, while compact cameras generally have fixed, multipurpose lenses. More recently, mirrorless interchangeable-lens cameras have appeared on the market.

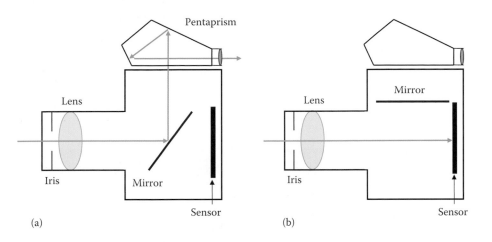

FIGURE 3.52 Basic design of a digital single-lens reflex camera: (a) mirror position for scene selection via the viewfinder (mirror blocks sensor, sending the image to the viewfinder via a pentaprism) and (b) mirror position for image recording (sensor exposed to the image produced by the lens).

3.5.3.3 Camera Lenses

Camera lenses are often referred to in generic terms such as wide angle, normal, and telephoto. These terms refer to the *focal length* of the lens, which is typically measured in millimeters. Focal length is defined as the distance from the center of the lens to the image it forms when the image source is at infinity. In practice, focal length affects the field of view, magnification, and depth of field of a lens. Extreme wide-angle, or fish-eye, lenses provide fields of view of 180° or more. Lenses with focal lengths from 20 to 35 mm are generally considered wide-angle lenses. They provide greater depth of field and encompass a larger field (or angle) of view but provide relatively low magnification. Lenses with focal lengths from 45 to 55 mm are referred to as normal lenses because they produce an image that approximates the field of view of the human eye. Lenses with longer focal lengths, called telephoto lenses, constrict the field of view and decrease the depth of field while greatly magnifying the image. Lenses with focal lengths of 85 mm or more are considered telephoto. A fourth generic lens type, the zoom lens, is designed to have a variable focal length, which can be adjusted continuously between two fixed limits. These lenses allow continuous control of image scale between the two limits. With most lenses, focusing can be manual or automatic.

In fingerprint work, a further lens type should be used in most cases—the close-up macrolens, which usually has a focal length of approximately 50 mm. This permits close-up photography. It is standard practice to use extension rings to come even closer to the mark that is being documented. This allows full-size reproduction using the whole image field (for single fingermark photography), permits more concentrated fingermark illumination (more effective use of the light source), guarantees maximum resolution and, particularly for luminescent marks, limits light dispersion, thus resulting in a sharper image.

3.5.3.4 Camera Settings

The shutter is a mechanical or electronic device in the camera that, on command, opens the light path toward the sensor and/or turns on the sensor for a preselected time (shutter speed) so that an image can be captured at a particular exposure. The shutter speed is given in numbers that represent the reciprocal value of the exposure time in seconds. Common camera shutter speeds are given in Table 3.6.

When the shutter is open, the light flux through the lens and onto the image sensor is controlled by a diaphragm consisting of several overlapping metal or plastic leaves that control the lens aperture (opening). The diaphragm is usually mounted within the lens itself. The relative aperture,

TABLE 3.6

Camera Shutter Speeds

Shutter speed	1	2	4	8	15	30	60	125	250	500
Exposure time (s)	1	1/2	1/4	1/8	1/15	1/30	1/60	1/125	1/250	1/500

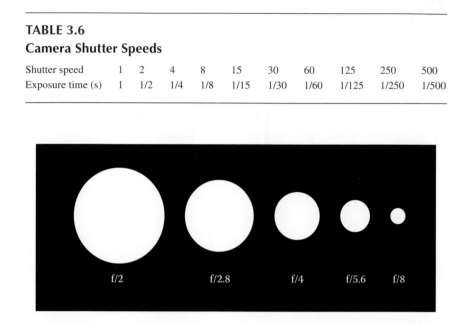

FIGURE 3.53 Lens aperture is specified by the f-stop (f-number), where each f-stop value represents a halving of the light intensity from the previous value.

defined as the ratio between the focal length of the lens and the aperture diameter, is used to represent the amount of light reaching the sensor. The relative aperture is known as the "f-number" or "f-stop" (for "stopping down," reducing the amount of light), and a series of consecutive f-numbers (f-stops) may be represented on a knurled ring on the lens or be accessible via the camera's electronics. Each consecutive number in this series represents half the amount of light as the previous one (i.e., increasing the f-number decreases the diaphragm opening) (Figure 3.53). Modern lenses use a standard f-stop scale—f/1, f/1.4, f/2, f/2.8, f/4, f/5.6, f/8, f/11, f/16, f/22, etc.—with each f-stop value representing half the light intensity from the previous value. The maximum relative aperture (the first number in the series) depends on the lens characteristics, maximum aperture diameter, and focal length; therefore, each type of lens has its own series.

A proper exposure is obtained by adjusting the shutter speed and the diaphragm aperture. These settings are directly proportional; a one-increment change in shutter speed is equal to a change of one f-stop. A one-stop adjustment in exposure can refer to a change in either shutter speed or aperture setting; the resulting change in the amount of light reaching the film will be the same. Thus, if the shutter speed is increased, a compensatory increase must be made in aperture size to allow the same amount of light to reach the film. For example, an image recorded at f-stop f/8 and shutter speed 125 will have the same exposure as an image recorded at f-stop f/5.6 and shutter speed 250.

The depth of field (or "zone of focus") refers to the area from near to far in the picture in which objects will be sharply focused. The depth of field is inversely proportional to both the camera–object distance and the lens aperture (i.e., the closer the object, the smaller the depth of field; and the smaller the aperture, the larger the depth of field). This aspect is of utmost importance in close-up photography, such as the recording of fingermarks, when the camera–object distance is typically less than 20 cm. The depth of field is so shallow that any unevenness in the object surface can result in part of the fingermark being out of focus at larger apertures (e.g., f-stop 4). To increase the depth of field in such close-up photography, it is recommended to use f-stop 8 or higher. On most DSLR cameras, the lens ring contains a depth-of-field scale that shows the approximate sharp-focus zone for the different aperture settings. However, this scale is not valid if an extension ring is employed.

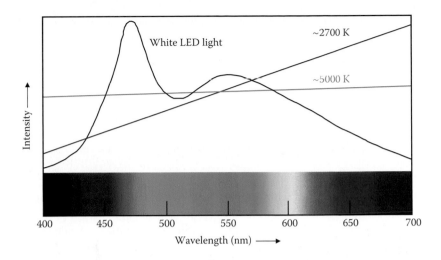

FIGURE 3.54 White light spectra from different white light sources can differ significantly, emphasizing the importance of performing a white balance adjustment on the camera if accurate color representation is required.

Digital cameras generally offer a range of exposure modes, including manual, automatic (auto), shutter priority, and aperture priority. The easiest of all is auto mode where the camera determines optimum aperture and shutter speed according to the intensity of the light reaching the image sensor. The manual setting requires the user to specify both the aperture (f-stop) and shutter speed. When photographing a moving object, shutter priority mode should be employed with a high shutter speed (e.g., 250 or 500), with the camera left to determine the correct aperture according to available light. When a particular depth of field is required, then aperture priority should be selected (in this case, the camera selects the appropriate shutter speed). An example of this is close-up photography of stationary objects, such as fingermarks or footwear impressions. To improve the depth of field, a small aperture (high f-number) should be selected. As this may result in a relatively long exposure time, a tripod or stand is recommended to keep the camera steady.

Sunlight and various forms of artificial light (depending on the types of lamps employed) have different white light spectra that can affect the colors obtained in recorded images (Figure 3.54). As a result, if "true" color representation is required in the image then the camera's white balance should be adjusted in accordance with the manufacturer's recommendations.

3.5.3.5 Sensitivity and Noise

Early digital cameras were lacking in sensitivity and thermal electronic noise (random background interference generated within the sensor) was significant. To increase the sensitivity of image sensors, microlenses were added on top of each sensor pixel during manufacture. This resulted in an improved signal-to-noise (S/N) ratio. Thermal noise can be further reduced by improving the microlens design, increasing the sensor size, and cooling the sensor. Peltier cooling, for example, is commonly employed in specialized laboratory-based digital cameras for low light level imaging (where long exposure times may be required).

Film speed is the measure of a photographic film's sensitivity to light and is designated by an International Organization for Standardization (ISO) number. In the ISO scale, corresponding to the American Standards Association system, a doubling of the sensitivity of a film results in the doubling of the numerical speed value (doubling of the ISO number). Since digital cameras do not use film but an image sensor, the ISO equivalent is usually provided to denote how sensitive the sensor is to the amount of light present. The higher the ISO value, the more sensitive the image sensor, and therefore the greater the possibility of taking images under low-light-level situations.

An image sensor is usually calibrated so that it gives the best image quality (greatest S/N ratio) at its lowest possible ISO speed (default ISO). For most consumer digital cameras, this value will generally be ISO 50, ISO 64, or ISO 100. More expensive digital cameras may have ISO 200 as their lowest setting.

The sensitivity of a digital camera can be boosted by amplification of the signal coming from the image sensor (i.e., by selecting a higher ISO). An image sensor is an analog device and it creates its own thermal electronic noise. Amplification of the signal will also amplify the thermal noise, so the S/N ratio will degrade. Quite often, thermal noise will become obvious when using a higher ISO setting. This has to be taken into account, for example, during the photography of weakly luminescent objects. It is far better to use longer exposure times than higher ISO settings.

3.5.3.6   Choosing a Digital Camera

Modern digital cameras, combined with computer equipment and image processing software, can provide significant operational advantages for the capture and enhancement of potential fingermark evidence. When choosing a digital camera for the recording of such marks, some important considerations are as follows:

- Field-based image recording requires portability and flexibility, which leads inevitably to the use of handheld DSLR cameras.
- In the laboratory, specialized high-sensitivity and high-speed imaging cameras offer extra capabilities beyond SLRs in terms of cooled image sensors, extended exposures, or multiple averaged images (to reduce image noise and therefore improve the overall S/N ratio).
- An ability to capture images in a proprietary camera format (*RAW*, unprocessed) has advantages from an evidential point of view as these can be safeguarded as *primary* (original) images.
- The camera must be *fit for purpose* in terms of resolution, light sensitivity (dynamic range), available lenses, etc., and this must be demonstrated through an appropriate validation process.

Note that the Scientific Working Group on Friction Ridge Analysis, Study and Technology (SWGFAST) has published standards for the digital recording of friction ridge impressions for examination purposes (SWGFAST 2013). Such impressions should be captured (color or grayscale) at a resolution no less than 1000 ppi when the images are sized 1:1 for comparison purposes.

3.5.3.7   Photography in the Luminescence Mode

Close-up photography and the recording of weak luminescence emissions both require different skills and different camera settings compared to normal daylight photography. Some general guidelines, based on the use of DSLR cameras, are provided in this section to assist in achieving optimum results.

Modern DSLR cameras provide an ability to review images immediately after capture (via the LCD screen on the back of the camera). Typically, image histograms can also be displayed. Combined with appropriate training, such functionalities assist in ensuring that images are exposed correctly, minimizing the need for exposure bracketing. Nevertheless, exposure bracketing (as described as follows) is recommended under certain circumstances such as when weak luminescence emission needs to be recorded. Recommended camera settings are as follows:

- *ISO setting*: Select the lowest ISO setting for the camera in use. For very weak luminescence, the next two higher ISO settings may be used.
- *Mode*: Aperture priority mode.
- *Aperture*: A good starting point is to select an aperture that is midrange for the camera (e.g., f/8) and check that it is appropriate for the subject being photographed. A smaller f-number (larger aperture) can be used for flat surfaces not requiring a large depth of field. A larger f-number (smaller aperture) may be necessary for subjects requiring a greater depth of field.
- *Exposure bracketing*: Take one shot without bracketing (i.e., normal auto exposure) and then additional shots with at least one stop up and one stop down from the normal exposure setting.

Exposure bracketing is a simple technique that can be used to ensure that an object is properly exposed during photography, especially under challenging lighting situations. Exposure bracketing means that more shots of the same object are taken at different exposure settings but without change to the lighting conditions. The reason for doing this is that the camera may be "deceived" by the actual light level that is passing through the lens (i.e., under- or overestimating the light intensity), and the object may be under- or overexposed using the normal exposure setting.

Most DSLR cameras have a bracketing capability in both auto and manual modes as a standard feature. With bracketing, the camera is "fooled" with regard to the ISO setting, and the camera responds accordingly by changing the exposure time. Bracketing is usually available as a range of exposure values (EVs) from −3 to +3 stops (e.g., −3, −2, −1, 0, +1, +2, and +3, where 0 is the normal exposure setting). Some cameras have 1/3 and 2/3 stops in between these settings. It should be noted that negative (−) settings produce underexposed images, while positive (+) settings produce overexposed images. An EV of +1 corresponds to a doubling of the normal exposure time. An EV of −1 corresponds to the halving of the normal exposure time. Rather than recording just one image under a particular set of conditions that may not produce the best result, three images could be recorded: one at EV 0, one at EV +1, and one at EV −1. A broader exposure range may be required for difficult cases (e.g., extremely weak luminescence emission).

3.6 DIGITAL IMAGING

3.6.1 INTRODUCTION

Digital imaging technology has essentially replaced traditional film-based photography for the recording of potential forensic evidence such as fingermarks. The ability to enhance digital images will continue to advance as hardware costs fall while resolution, processing speeds, and software technologies improve.

Detail present in an image may not be discernible to the human eye, but it can be extracted using digital enhancement procedures. Digital recording systems and advancements in information technology also permit the remote capturing of images, with subsequent transmission of such data to any destination in the world. With such technology, when applied in the forensic arena, comes the responsibility of ensuring that the original image is protected from alteration. Any enhancement must be confined to a copy of the original image, with each step in the enhancement process being documented and repeatable. Procedures must be adopted that safeguard the original data and maintain an unbroken "digital image chain of custody" that demonstrates the production of an enhanced image (Berg 2000). In this respect, modern digital cameras automatically incorporate metadata into the image, which are like tags giving information that documents the resources used when taking the image. Exchangeable image file (EXIF) is a standard developed by Japan Electronic Industries Development Association (JEIDA) for storing interchange information in image files. The file format incorporates technical information related to the image recording process at the time of image capture (date, time, geographical location [GPS data], lens, exposure time, diaphragm, resolution, size, etc.). Under some conditions, these *tags* may stay with each image through the various treatments that are applied. This follows standards that have been proposed through international agreement (e.g., Dublin Core Metadata Initiative; see http://www.dublincore.org).

The term resolution refers to the amount of discernible detail in a digital image. As previously discussed, a digital image is composed of an array of discrete picture elements known as pixels. Spatial resolution, also referred to as spatial density, is a measure of the number of pixels in a digital image. The term samples per inch (spi) is used to describe image capture resolution, pixels per inch (ppi) to describe display resolution, and dots per inch (dpi) to describe hardcopy output resolution. Higher-resolution images contain more information and therefore require more storage space and more image processing power than lower-resolution images.

Once a digital image has been captured, it needs to be saved in an appropriate digital image file format. An image file format defines a particular data storage protocol. There are probably over 100 different file formats for digital images. Some of these file formats are unique to specific programs, while others are general formats that extend over several platforms. Standard file formats allow for the exchange and manipulation of digital images by image processing systems from different manufacturers. The two things to consider when discussing file formats are the representation scheme (how the computer interprets data to reproduce it) and the compression scheme (how the computer utilizes memory to store the image). The simplest bitmap image files will have two or three parts: the header, bitmap data, and—optionally—the footer. The header contains important information to prepare the computer for the data that follow. Bitmap data make up the bulk of the file and consist of values for each pixel in the image. The computer reads these values and, using the information from the header, reproduces them in the proper place in the image. The footer is an optional addition to the format.

Off-the-shelf personal computers, image capture devices, and affordable software packages can be combined to form a digital enhancement system that can be used to significantly improve weak or otherwise obscure traces. This can be achieved because the digitization of an image affords the operator much greater control over each individual picture element (pixel) than is possible with a conventional photographic (analog) image. The computer is able to differentiate between 256 separate values of gray in a grayscale image (8-bit images have pixel values from black [0] to white [255]). In addition, it is possible to separate images into different color ranges (RGB) and treat the tonal range for each color individually before combining the various signals together. By comparison, the human eye can only differentiate approximately 32 separate gray values.

3.6.2 DATA COMPRESSION AND FILE FORMATS

Compression manages the image data so that less space is required to store the image. Most compression schemes fall into one of two categories: lossless and lossy. Lossless compression means that no data are irreparably altered in the process of shrinking and expanding a file. Lossy compression, on the other hand, does change the original data. In most cases, the changes are insignificant, and rarely can the naked eye make them out even when magnified to several times normal size. However, lossy compression can result in degradation of image quality and, in some cases, the introduction of artifacts. The advantage of lossy over lossless is that lossy schemes usually offer much better compression ratios.

Some of the more common cross-platform file formats for the storage and manipulation of digital images include the following:

- *Bitmap* (*BMP*): This is a widely recognized format made popular by the Microsoft Windows operating system. It supports several data types ranging from black and white all the way up to 24-bit true color. Although the BMP format supports compression, most programs do not take advantage of it.
- *Graphics interchange format* (*GIF*): A format commonly used to display graphics and images on the Internet. It is a compressed format that is only capable of reproducing 256 colors.
- *Tagged image file format* (*TIF or TIFF*): This file format was released in 1986 from a joint venture between Aldus Corporation (now merged with Adobe) and Microsoft. TIF is a standard file format for most imaging programs, supporting all data types from monochrome up to 24-bit true color, as well as many color models and compression schemes. An even more powerful aspect of TIF is that its files can move easily between platforms (e.g., Windows, UNIX, and Apple), making it an ideal format for storing image data. The lossless TIF format is recommended for forensic applications including the recording of potential fingermark evidence.

- *JPEG file interchange format (JPG)*: The Joint Photographic Experts Group (JPEG) format was developed to create a standard for sending images over digital communication lines. Although it is a lossy compression method, moderate compression levels result in little to no obvious image degradation. As a result, it has become the most popular format in use today. The JPEG format is suitable for digital photographs and other natural-looking images. It is not as good for precise artwork such as line art. This is because some averaging takes place during compression and edges may become blurred. In photographs, this is not particularly noticeable because such sharp edges are rare. JPEG can achieve compression ratios of up to 100 to 1, which is far better than the 10 to 1 generally possible with other compression methods. The format supports grayscale and true color data types, while black-and-white data types do not reproduce well and are not supported. One interesting feature of this format is that you can vary the degree of compression. This makes it possible to select a level of data retention versus space saving that is best for a particular application. High compression levels, however, can lead to reduced image quality and noticeable compression artifacts. JPEG 2000 (JP2) is similar to JPEG but uses a different mathematical function. Compared to standard JPEG, JPEG 2000 can achieve a greater compression of image files while maintaining the same image quality.

Most digital cameras provide the option of recording images in one of at least two cross-platform file formats (e.g., TIF and JPG). In addition, there may be the option of saving the data in a proprietary camera format (RAW), which records a raw image to the camera's media card. The data block of a RAW file contains the unprocessed pixel readings from the sensor chip plus camera metadata. Software capable of reading this format is required, although popular image processing packages such as Adobe Photoshop have utilities or plug-ins that can read most RAW formats.

When considering file formats and compression, agencies have to balance cost, workflow, time, and image quality. An important implication of compression is the possibility of data loss and the generation of compression artifacts. For this reason, the compression of data using lossless processes is generally preferred for evidentiary images. With improvements in compression methods and the increasing sizes of digital images (i.e., number of pixels), however, detrimental compression effects are becoming less significant. Regardless, when different file formats and compression methods are being considered for a particular application, performance checks should be undertaken to ensure suitability.

3.6.3 IMAGE PROCESSING TECHNIQUES

Image processing can be defined as any activity that transforms an input image into an output image. Of the processes that can be applied, image enhancement is intended to improve the visual appearance of an image or enhance specific features within the image. The following are examples (Scientific Working Group on Imaging Technology 2010; https://www.swgit.org/):

- *Brightness adjustment*: Used when the image is too bright or too dark
- *Contrast adjustment*: Used when the image lacks sufficient contrast
- *Cropping*: Used to remove that portion of the image that is outside the area of interest
- *Color processing*: Used to modify the color characteristics of objects within an image
- *Linear filtering (such as sharpening, deblurring, edge enhancement, and deconvolution)*: Used to increase the contrast of small detail in an image
- *Nonlinear contrast adjustments (such as gamma correction, grayscale transformation, and the use of curves)*: Used to adjust the contrast in selected brightness ranges within the image

- *Pattern noise reduction filters*: Used to identify and remove repeating patterns in an image (such as fabric weaves, window screens, and security patterns)
- *Random noise reduction* (*such as low-pass filtering, Gaussian blurring, median filtering, and despeckling*): Used to reduce the contrast of small detail in the image in order to suppress random noise

Image restoration is any process that is applied to an image that has been degraded by a known cause (e.g., defocus or motion blur) with the intention of partially or totally removing the effects of that degradation. Examples include (Scientific Working Group on Imaging Technology 2010):

- *Blur removal*: Designed to partially or completely remove an image blur
- *Warping*: Changes the spatial relationships among the objects in an image to, for example, remove perspective from an image
- *Geometric restoration*: Removal of specific geometric distortion from an image to restore the proper spatial relationships among the objects in the scene (e.g., to remove geometric distortion introduced by a curved mirror or a fish-eye lens)

Image processing techniques generally operate either in the *spatial domain* or the *frequency domain*. The spatial domain operates directly on the pixels in the image and the output of these functions is a change to the pixel values that will depend on the initial pixel values and the particular mathematical function applied. The frequency domain image (power spectrum) displays the spatial domain image data in an alternative but mathematically equivalent format, in which frequency, regularity, and direction of features in the image detail can be interpreted. An image can be transformed from the spatial domain to the frequency domain by the fast Fourier transform (FFT) function. Once in this domain, relevant frequency elements can be amplified, isolated, suppressed, or otherwise filtered with an intention to enhance, isolate, or remove specific detail in the corresponding spatial image. After editing the image in the frequency domain, the inverse transform (inverse FFT) is performed to return the image to the spatial domain with the changes incorporated. Sometimes valuable forensic information in an image (such as a fingermark) is obscured by background interference. When the image is represented as a power spectrum, it is relatively easy to recognize and eliminate periodic background noise (such as a weave pattern or printed background pattern). As FFT methods involve sophisticated mathematical transformations, they should be used with great care and appropriate expertise.

Two or more images can be combined, and each image may include changes of lighting. When the direction of the incident light is changed, the shadows cast by the subject and the reflection of that light from the subject also changes. By keeping the subject and the camera still, and keeping the same lens and filters, multiple images of the subject will be in perfect registration (i.e., they will line up with each other). By averaging multiple images that were captured while the incident light is moved, shadows and flares can be reduced or eliminated.

One image can also be subtracted from another, which can be achieved using the subtraction function in the image processing software or by inverting one image before adding it to the other. Where the application of light can cause fingermark detail to become more or less visible against an interfering background, two images can be captured: (1) one image where the fingermark visibility is maximized; and (2) a second image where the ridge detail is minimized but the background is still visible. An appropriate proportion of the second image is then subtracted from the first to enhance the visibility of the fingermark while suppressing the contributions from the background.

There is a large range of software that can be used to process digital images. The choice of software should be governed by the intended application and the level of expertise of the operator.

It is beyond the scope of this chapter to provide a comprehensive list of available software packages. Some representative examples include the following:

- *Adobe Photoshop* (www.adobe.com): One of the most widely accepted and employed programs in the imaging industry. Photoshop has a wide selection of imaging functions and has a facility for *plug-ins* from third parties. Batch processing of images can also be performed.
- *V++* (www.digitaloptics.co.nz): An image analysis program that has a wide range of menu-selectable functions, including a scripting facility based on Pascal. Forensic documentation requirements are easily met with the use of scripts, with an ability for these to be recorded and used at a later time to demonstrate process repeatability.
- *ImageJ* (imagej.nih.gov/ij/): Similar to V++ in function, but written and scripted in Java. The program and plug-ins are available at no cost from the National Institutes of Health website. There are many plug-ins available from an active online community.
- *Thumbs Plus* (www.cerious.com): An image handling facility with a range of simple image enhancement and editing functions. The program is a useful tool when the power of Photoshop is not required.

The conditions employed for the capturing of a digital image and for any subsequent image processing should be fit for purpose. Such conditions need to be appropriate for the intended purpose, including any subsequent examination of the image that may be required. The capturing of substandard images with a heavy reliance on subsequent image processing often results in the loss of valuable information and the introduction of unwanted artifacts or *noise*.

Image processing cannot make up for inadequate data!

3.6.4 LEGAL REQUIREMENTS

The widespread availability of image processing technologies has raised questions as to the validity and acceptability of "photographic" evidence presented in court. There are generally two types of images used in evidence, those that are visually verifiable and those that are analyzed and treated (enhanced). The first category is usually without problem; whatever the technology used, these are images that document a state, such as crime scene photographs, and are used for descriptive or illustrative purposes. While this does not mean that manipulation cannot occur, it is mostly independent of the technology employed. On the other hand, images that are analyzed and transformed in some way may generate questions as to the validity of the information highlighted by this treatment. Is the evidential image a transformation that has been fabricated to support a speculative position, or is it highlighting otherwise latent data that constitute factual information? Image processing can yield information that was not readily apparent in the original image, which could result in an examiner drawing a conclusion that might not otherwise have been reached.

Standard operating procedures are required for quality assurance purposes and to satisfy legal requirements by offering the opportunity to track (and reproduce) the whole image analysis and transformation process. It is a legal prerequisite for the admissibility of evidence that the evidence being presented before the court can be adequately authenticated. For physical evidence, this requires that there is sufficient information available to demonstrate that the exhibit is what the proponent claims it to be. With respect to a photographic image, authenticity needs to be demonstrated via an audit trail—written and/or electronic—demonstrating that it originated from a primary image captured and recorded on a particular camera at a specific point in time and under a specific set of circumstances. Where image processing has been applied and authenticity is challenged, qualified witnesses may need to provide testimony as to the nature of the transformations involved, particularly where advanced enhancement methods have been employed.

A number of organizations have published guidelines addressing the capture, processing, and storage of digital images for evidential purposes. Examples include documents produced by:

- The U.S. Scientific Working Group on Imaging Technology (SWGIT)
- The UK Home Office Centre for Applied Science and Technology (CAST)
- The Australian Electronic Evidence Specialist Advisory Group (EESAG), Senior Managers Australian, and New Zealand Forensic Laboratories (SMANZFL)

The guidelines formulated by these three groups are available from the SWGIT website (https://www.swgit.org/documents). The general concepts contained within these guidelines are summarized as follows.

A complicating factor with digital images is that they exist in a binary, electronic form that can be readily copied, saved in different formats, and modified in various ways (some obvious and others difficult to detect). The first recorded instance of an image, such as that captured by a digital camera and saved on the camera's removable flash card, is generally referred to as the primary image. Any exact binary (bit-for-bit) copy of the primary image is then termed an original (or master) image, irrespective of the recording media. There can be any number of original images, with each copy being identical in every respect to the primary image. By default, the original image files will be in the same format as the primary image. At least one original image must be retained in its original, unaltered state as an exhibit, with all associated continuity and secure storage requirements satisfied. Where any type of image processing is to be employed, this should only be performed on a working copy. The working image is a copy of the primary or original image that may be subjected to a change in file format and/or data alteration due to enhancement, compression, filtering, cropping, etc. No primary or original images should be deleted without authority and any intentional or accidental deletion must be recorded in the audit trail.

When images are captured onto any form of reusable media, such as removable camera flash cards, they should be transferred onto secure media (e.g., CDs, DVDs, or secure network storage) as soon as practical. The purpose here is to limit the time and opportunity for accidental or alleged malicious alteration to the images. Once the images have been transferred onto secure media, the reusable media should be reformatted. It is important to recognize that optical storage media such as CDs and DVDs are designed for short-to-medium term storage periods only. To ensure the integrity of recorded data, the files need to be transferred to new media regularly—possibly as often as every 5 years—or transferred to an appropriate long-term data archiving system.

An audit trail, documented contemporaneously, should include the following:

- Details of the case
- Information on the capture equipment employed
- Description of each primary image recorded and the media used
- The creation and defining of the original image
- The creation and defining of additional original images or working copies
- Chain of custody and storage/archiving details for the original image
- Any significant use, processing, and distribution of working copies (particularly for working copies that are produced as evidence)
- Each software package employed for data treatment (with version numbers)
- The date and time of each significant action

Any image processing applied for forensic purposes needs to be approached in a methodical and structured manner. Each processing step should be documented in sufficient detail to permit independent repeatability of the whole process, starting from the original image and progressing through

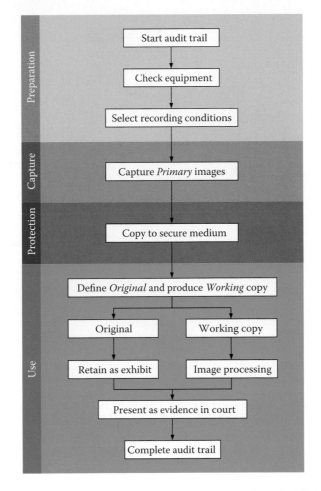

FIGURE 3.55 Recommended workflow for the capture and preservation of digital images for evidential purposes.

to the final, processed working copy presented as evidence. The development and use of software scripts, where possible, is highly recommended. Such script can promote the consistent application of standard protocols and ensure reproducibility.

A suggested digital imaging workflow is summarized in Figure 3.55.

3.7 HYPERSPECTRAL IMAGING

One special application of digital imaging is the combination of this technology with molecular spectroscopy to result in a technique known as hyperspectral imaging (HSI; otherwise known as spectral imaging, imaging spectroscopy, multispectral imaging, or chemical imaging). With HSI, images are collected and processed across a particular range of the electromagnetic spectrum, with the purpose of obtaining a spectrum for each pixel in the image. The information generated is typically represented in the form of an image cube. The X and Y coordinates represent images, with the Z coordinate corresponding to wavelength (Figure 3.56). Each cell in the cube has an intensity value. The data can be processed with a view to identifying materials in the sample (depending on the wavelength range), finding particular objects, or differentiating an object of interest (e.g., a fingermark) from its background, for example.

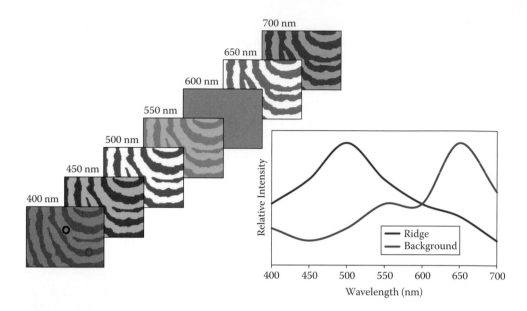

FIGURE 3.56 Hyperspectral imaging data can be viewed as images (recorded at each wavelength) or spectra (recorded at each pixel). From the image cube, a region of interest can be selected and an average spectrum generated. In this example, the area within the blue circle represents a fingermark ridge and the area within the red circle represents the background, with the resulting spectra displayed.

The combination of molecular spectroscopy and digital imaging into a single method allows for spatial (imaging) and spectral (chemical) information to be collected simultaneously. The dataset generated from an item contains a full image at each individual wavelength and a full spectrum at each individual pixel. The spectra of individual pixels can be examined, or multiple pixels selected to produce an average spectrum for a particular region of interest (ROI; Figure 3.56).

Various HSI methods are available that differ depending on the area of the electromagnetic spectrum that is examined, the scanning method, and componentry (such as the spectrometer and detector). A variety of spectroscopic techniques can be encompassed, such as visible spectroscopy (absorption and luminescence), near-IR and mid-IR spectroscopy, and Raman spectroscopy. HSI datasets can be generated by a number of methods, including point-by-point analysis, line scanning, and wide-field spectral imaging. Of these, wide-field imaging is the most rapid, making it the favored technique for applications in forensic science. Depending on the instrumentation, spectral selection may be achieved using prisms, gratings, interferometers, or tunable filters, for example. Tunable filters are devices that have a range of spectral transmissions that can be controlled electronically, which has the advantage that there are no moving parts and desired wavelength bands can be rapidly selected.

The most prevalent form of HSI for forensic science applications, including fingermark analysis, has been with respect to absorption and luminescence emission in the visible and near-IR regions of the electromagnetic spectrum (Payne et al. 2005). A particular advantage of HSI over conventional imaging is that images can be captured over a wide spectral range, which is particularly useful when the spectral characteristics of a particular specimen are unknown. In addition, chemometric processes such as principal components analysis (PCA) can be applied to exploit small variations in the data, such as minor spectral differences between a fingermark and the substrate on which it was deposited.

The application of HSI for evidential purposes, such as the enhancement of weak fingermarks, needs to satisfy the same legal requirements as those discussed in Section 3.6.4.

REFERENCES

Allen, E. and Triantaphillidou, S. (2011), *The Manual of Photography*, 10th ed., Oxford, U.K.: Focal Press.

Auvdel, M. J. (1988), Comparison of laser and high-intensity quartz arc tubes in the detection of body secretions, *J. Forensic Sci.*, 33, 929–945.

Barker, D. A. (1999), Contrast from the past, *J. Forensic Ident.*, 49, 589–593.

Berg, E. C. (2000), Legal ramifications of digital imaging in law enforcement, *Forensic Sci. Commun.*, 2(4), http://www.fbi.gov/about-us/lab/forensic-science-communications/fsc/oct2000/berg.htm (accessed February 20, 2015).

Bramble, S. K., Creer, K. E., Gui Qiang, W., and Sheard, B. (1993), Ultraviolet luminescence from latent fingerprints, *Forensic Sci. Int.*, 59, 3–14.

Dalrymple, B. and Almog, J. (2012), Comparison of latent print detection using semiconductor laser and LED light sources with three chemical reagents, *J. Forensic Ident.*, 62, 14–27.

Dalrymple, B. E., Duff, J. M., and Menzel, E. R. (1977), Inherent fingerprint luminescence—Detection by laser, *J. Forensic Sci.*, 2, 106–115.

Haylock, S. E. (1989), The light fantastic, *Fingerprint Whorld*, 14(56), 113–115.

Jacobson, R. E., Ray, S. F., Attridge, G. G., and Axford, N. R. (2000), *The Manual of Photography: Photographic and Digital Imaging*, 9th ed., Oxford, U.K.: Focal Press.

Lam, R. and Wilkinson, D. (2011), Forensic light source and environmental effects on the performance of 1,2-indanedione-zinc chloride and 1,8-diazafluoren-9-one for the recovery of latent prints on porous substrates, *J. Forensic Ident.*, 61, 607–620.

London, B., Upton, J., and Stone, J. (2013), *Photography*, 11th ed., Upper Saddle River, NJ: Pearson.

Murdock, R. H. and Menzel, E.R. (1993), A computer interfaced time-resolved luminescence imaging system, *J. Forensic Sci.*, 38, 521–529.

Payne, G., Wallace, C., Reedy, B., Lennard, C., Schuler, R., Exline, D., and Roux, C. (2005), Visible and near-infrared chemical imaging methods for the analysis of selected forensic samples, *Talanta*, 67, 334–344.

Pfister, R. (1985), The optical revelation of latent fingerprints, *Fingerprint Whorld*, 10(39), 64–70.

Reiss, R.-A., 1903, *La photographie judiciaire*, Paris, France: Mendel.

Sanfilippo, P., Richards, A., and Nichols, H. (2010), Reflected ultraviolet digital photography: The part someone forgot to mention, *J. Forensic Ident.*, 60, 181–198.

Scientific Working Group on Friction Ridge Analysis, Study and Technology (SWGFAST). (2013), Standard for friction ridge impression digital imaging (latent/tenprint), version 2.0, http://www.swgfast.org/documents/imaging/130427_Standard_Imaging_Final_2.0.pdf (accessed February 10, 2016).

Scientific Working Group on Imaging Technology (SWGIT). (2010), Section 5 Guidelines for Image Processing, version 2.1, https://www.swgit.org/pdf/Section%205%20Guidelines%20for%20Image%20Processing?docID=49 (accessed February 20, 2015).

Springer, E., Almog, J., Frank, A., Ziv, Z, Bergman, P., and Gui Qiang, W. (1994), Detection of dry body fluids by inherent short wavelength UV luminescence: Preliminary results, *Forensic Sci. Int.*, 66, 89–94.

Stoilovic, M., Warrener, R.N., Margot, P., and Lennard, C.J. (1987), Design of a versatile light source for fingerprint detection and enhancement, in *Proceedings of the International Forensic Symposium on Latent Prints*, FBI Academy, Quantico, VA, pp. 153–154.

Warrener, R. N., Kobus, H. J., and Stoilovic, M. (1983), An evaluation of the reagent NBD chloride for the production of luminescent fingerprints on paper: I. support for a xenon arc lamp being a cheaper alternative to an argon ion laser as an excitation source, *Forensic Sci. Int.*, 23, 179–188.

Watkin, J. E. (1987), Alternative lighting methods of detecting latent prints, in *Proceedings of the International Forensic Symposium on Latent Prints*, FBI Academy, Quantico, VA, pp. 39–44.

Watkin, J. E. and Misner, A. H. (1990), Fluorescence and crime scenes in the 90s, *RCMP Gaz.*, 52(9), 1–5.

West, M. H., Barsley, R. E., Frair, J., and Hall, F. (1990), Reflective ultraviolet imaging system (RUVIS) and the detection of trace evidence and wounds on human skin, *J. Forensic Ident.*, 40, 249–255.

Wilkinson, D. A. and Watkin, J. E. (1994), A comparison of the forensic light sources: Polilight, Luma-Lite, and Spectrum 9000, *J. Forensic Ident.*, 44, 632–651.

Ziv, Z. and Springer, E. (1993), More applications of coaxial illumination in fingerprint detecting and photography, *J. Forensic Ident.*, 43, 362–367.

4 Fingermark Detection and Enhancement

4.1 TYPES OF FINGERMARKS

There are two general categories to describe the potential fingermark* evidence that may be found at a crime scene or on an item related to a criminal matter: *visible* (or patent) fingermarks and *latent* fingermarks. These categories are not mutually exclusive, since an item or surface can carry both visible and latent marks. Any search for fingermarks must take into consideration the possible presence of both types of impressions. For example, a visible fingermark (e.g., a blood mark) should not be enhanced to the exclusion of any latent fingermarks that may also be present on the item or surface under examination.

4.1.1 VISIBLE FINGERMARKS

Visible fingermarks, as the term suggests, are visible without any particular treatment. Such marks may be

- *Positive*, where skin ridges form an image contaminated with a colored substance such as blood, ink, and paint
- *Negative*, where the fingerprint ridges remove surface material such as dust and soot (Figure 4.1)
- *Indented* (molded/plastic), caused by the contact of the finger with a malleable substance (putty, candle wax, wet paint, etc.) that subsequently retains a three-dimensional image of the ridges

The fingermark is visible as long as there is sufficient contrast between the mark and its support; it may be necessary to use colored or oblique lighting to observe weakly visible marks. Fingermarks in blood are a common example, and these can be enhanced using specific optical techniques or by the application of an appropriate staining procedure or chemical treatment. On some metal surfaces such as aluminum and brass (e.g., firearm cartridge cases), corrosion processes may take place between the metal and certain salts and acids in the fingermark residue to produce a visible fingermark (Bobev 1995; Wightman et al. 2015).

Indented fingermarks may be difficult to visualize or record photographically, and good lighting techniques are usually required (oblique lighting, for example); powdering (to improve contrast) or casting may sometimes be advantageous. Silicone casting material, as used for recording toolmarks, can be successfully employed in some cases.

4.1.2 LATENT FINGERMARKS

The term *latent* literally means "present and capable of emerging or developing but not now visible, obvious, active, or symptomatic" (from Latin *latent-*, *latens*, from present participle of *latēre*, to lie hidden; Merriam-Webster online dictionary, http://www.merriam-webster.com, 2013). The latent fingermark is the most common type of ridge impression and also the one that is the most challenging: it is present but invisible. The application of an optical (e.g., ultraviolet [UV] imaging), physical

---

* Note that the general term "fingermark" has been used throughout this chapter but the information is also relevant to marks left by other areas of friction ridge skin (such as palmar impressions).

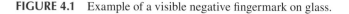

FIGURE 4.1   Example of a visible negative fingermark on glass.

(e.g., powdering), or chemical treatment (e.g., ninhydrin) is required in order to visualize a latent fingermark. This is where a detailed knowledge of the human secretions, and of the environment in which the substrates have been stored, are essential in order to choose the optimum techniques for fingermark development—the techniques that will give the best chance of fingermark detection. It is interesting to note that certain detection techniques, still valid today, were originally proposed for the study of perspiration fluids and secretions before fingerprints became used for personal identification. In 1863, Coulier detected ridge detail on forged documents using iodine vapor and suggested that such detail could be used to identify the source of the marks (Quinche and Margot 2010). In 1878, Aubert reported on the absorption of iodine vapor by sebaceous secretions and the reaction between alkaline salts in the sweat and silver nitrate (Aubert 1878).

The latent fingermark, deposited by the ridges of the finger or palm, is a complex mixture of (1) natural secretions, (2) compounds from the epidermis (outermost layer of skin), and (3) contaminants from the environment. Three types of glands are responsible for the natural secretions of the skin: the sudoriferous eccrine and apocrine glands, and the sebaceous glands. These three types of glands have well-defined functions, and the composition of their secretions varies in consequence. The sudoriferous glands are distributed all over the body and produce the sweat that is generally considered to be more than 98% water. The secretory body of each gland is in the form of a long coiled tube situated in the subcutaneous layers of the skin. The glands traverse the epidermal layers to open at the summits of the papillary ridges to form *sweat* or sudoriferous pores. The sweat is produced by the cells of the secretory body, without loss of cell cytoplasm in the case of the eccrine glands, in contrast to apocrine glands. This explains the differences in chemical composition between these two types of secretions.

The palms of the hands and the soles of the feet produce only eccrine gland secretions, whereas the apocrine glands are located in the groin, in the armpits, in the perianal regions (where they generally open at the hair follicles), the lips of the vagina, the glands of the penis, and the mammary areolae. These belong to the apocrine glands. The sebaceous glands are found on the chest and the back (where they are associated with hair roots), and on the forehead. These glands secrete an oil (the sebum) that serves to protect the skin and hair against water, to act as a lubricant, and also to help absorb fat (lipid) soluble substances.

As the ridges of the hands are covered exclusively by eccrine glands, eccrine gland secretions are present to some degree in every fingermark at the moment of deposition. Contamination by sebaceous gland secretions is also very common, due to activities such as combing the hair and touching the face, whereas that from the apocrine glands is infrequent but may be important in certain crimes (e.g., crimes of a sexual nature).

TABLE 4.1
Main Chemical Constituents of the Glandular Secretions

Source	Location	Constituents	
		Inorganic	Organic
Eccrine glands	All over the body, but the only type of glands on the friction ridge skin (fingers and palms of the hands, and the soles of the feet)	Chloride Metal ions (Na^+, K^+, Ca^{2+}) Sulfate Phosphate Bicarbonate Ammonia Water (>98%)	Amino acids Urea Uric acid Lactic acid Sugars Creatinine Choline Proteins Polypeptides Vitamins
Apocrine glands	In the groin and the armpits; associated with hair follicles around the genitals and mammary glands	Iron Water (>98%)	Proteins Carbohydrates Sterols
Sebaceous glands	All over the body, except on the areas of friction ridge skin; the highest concentration is on the forehead and on the back; associated with hair roots	—	Fatty acids (30%–40%) Wax esters (20%–30%) Glycerides (20%–25%) Squalene (10%–15%) Sterols (3%–4%) Sterol esters (2%–3%)

Sources: Adapted from Knowles, A.M., *J. Phys. Ser. E: Sci. Instrum.*, 11, 713, 1978; Ramotowski, R.S., Composition of latent print residue, in *Advances in Fingerprint Technology*, 2nd edn., H.C. Lee and R.E. Gaensslen, Eds., CRC Press, Boca Raton, FL, 2001, pp. 63–104; Girod, A. et al., *Forensic Sci. Int.*, 223, 10, 2012.

The major chemical constituents of the natural secretions are given in Table 4.1 (Knowles 1978; Ramotowski 2001; Girod et al. 2012). Secretions from eccrine and apocrine glands are mixtures of inorganic salts and water-soluble organic components that result in a water-soluble deposit (WSD). Secretions from sebaceous glands consist of a semisolid mixture of fatty acids, wax esters, glycerides, and long-chain hydrocarbons that result in a non-water-soluble deposit (NWSD). The chemical composition of these natural secretions has been extensively reviewed by Ramotowski (2001), Girod et al. (2012), and Cadd et al. (2015).

Latent fingermarks deposited by children have been found to have a different chemical composition than deposits from adults (Buchanan et al. 1997; Bohanan 1998; Mong et al. 2001; Antoine et al. 2010). Children leave considerably less residue on a surface—as little as 1/20 that of adults—and the lipid portion of their latent marks is more volatile in nature (Mong et al. 2001). As a result, latent fingermarks from children tend to degrade more rapidly than marks left by adults (Bohanan 1998; Blasdell 2001).

It is unclear to what extent gender may influence fingermark composition as contradictory results have been reported. While Asano et al. (2002) concluded that no significant differences could be observed in fingermark residue composition between male and female donors, other studies have highlighted that variations can occur that may be the result of different metabolic processes related to hormones and secretory glands (Buchanan et al. 1997; Hartzell-Baguley et al. 2007; Ferguson et al. 2012).

In addition to compounds from the secretory glands, fingermarks may also contain proteins (such as keratins and cathepsins) that are naturally expressed by the epidermis during desquamation, which is the shedding of dead skin cells required for skin renewal (Girod et al. 2012). Fingermark deposits will also contain contaminants (exogenous substances) that may include dust, food residue, cosmetics, and other materials related to recent activity.

There are many factors that can influence the initial chemical composition of a latent fingermark. Such factors include donor characteristics (age, gender, ethnic origin, diet, medication, health, etc.), contact with foreign substances (food, drugs, cosmetics, etc.), recent activities (e.g., exercise, hand washing), deposition conditions (e.g., pressure and contact duration), and the nature of the substrate receiving the fingermark (porosity, temperature, electrostatic forces, pH, etc.). In addition, once deposited, a latent fingermark will change in composition over time due to the influence of the substrate and environmental conditions. The environmental factors that can play a role include humidity, light exposure, temperature, air circulation, exposure to dust and pollution, and bacterial attack (Girod et al. 2012; Cadd et al. 2015) (see Section 5.4).

4.2   SURFACE CHARACTERISTICS

Few studies have considered the interaction between the friction ridge skin, the secretions, and the surface at the moment of deposition, or the later interaction between the deposited material and the substrate. Thomas (1978) reviewed fingerprint physics, with an emphasis on the mechanics of latent mark formation, and the results of microscopic observations that shed some light on the interaction of fingermarks with flat surfaces. Bobev (1995) considered latent fingermark formation as a physicochemical process on the border or contact area between the ridged skin and the mark-receptive surface. Such interactions have also been reviewed by Voss-De Haan (2006). When the fingers touch a solid surface, secretions are transferred, depending on a number of factors, including

- Temperature of the surface (sebaceous material adheres better to a surface that is cooler than the human body)
- Surface structure (the rougher the surface, the greater are the adhesive forces)
- Electrostatic forces on the mark-receptive surface

Surface phenomena play an important role, and Bobev (1995) presented a number of observations regarding the behavior of fingermark deposits on different surfaces under different environmental conditions.

The *porosity* of the substrate and its capacity to retain transferred fingermark components are important characteristics; the higher the porosity, the greater the adhesion forces and the greater the migration of fingermark compounds into the substrate (Bobev 1995). Almog et al. (2004) confirmed in a study of different paper types that the depth of penetration of the residue into the substrate was proportional to substrate porosity. In addition, an inverse relationship was observed between the smoothness of the paper and the penetration depth; higher smoothness values result in lower depths of penetration.

Most common surfaces submitted for fingermark examination can be divided into three general categories: porous, semiporous, and nonporous (Table 4.2). This is an important consideration when selecting a technique, or sequence of techniques, for fingermark detection. Properties of an unknown surface have to be considered before any attempt is made to develop latent fingermarks. This may mean evaluating a proposed detection sequence on test samples of the same type of surface before proceeding with the treatment of evidential items.

A number of studies have looked at other surface characteristics and how these can impact on fingermark development. For example, Jones et al. (2001a) determined that different polymer types, used to manufacture common plastic substrates, influenced the nature of the fingermark development achieved using vacuum metal deposition (VMD). Jones et al. (2010a) employed atomic force microscopy to the study of surface topography for a number of plastic substrates. They investigated how surface structures can affect fingermark development using a powder suspension.

TABLE 4.2

Types of Surfaces and Their Interactions with the Latent Fingermark Deposit

Types of Surfaces		
Porous	**Semiporous**	**Nonporous**
Porous surfaces absorb the WSD very quickly (within seconds) after deposition.	Semiporous surfaces absorb the WSD slowly after deposition (minutes to hours).	Nonporous surfaces do not absorb any part of the latent fingermark deposit.
The NWSD stays on top of the surface for a longer period (hours to days).	The NWSD stays on top of the surface much longer (days to weeks).	The WSD and NWSD, as an emulsion, remain on top of the surface for a very long time (until degraded).
A small amount of the NWSD stays on the surface for a significant period (months to years).	A small amount of the NWSD stays on the surface for a significant period (months to years).	Latent deposits on such surfaces are very fragile (marks are easily damaged by friction).
Typical examples	**Typical examples**	**Typical examples**
Paper	Certain types of plastic	Certain types of plastic
Cardboard	Waxed surfaces	Glass
Some fabrics (e.g., fine-weave cotton)	Certain types of wall paints and wallpapers	Metal surfaces
Untreated wood	Varnished wood	Glazed ceramics
		Glossy paints

Note: WSD, water-soluble deposit; NWSD, non-water-soluble deposit.

4.2.1 PoroUS SURFACES

Any surface that tends to absorb the latent fingermark deposit very quickly can be classified as a porous surface (e.g., paper, cardboard, or untreated wood). The WSD is taken into the first few layers of the surface within seconds of deposition (Figure 4.2). During absorption, water evaporates, leaving a mixture of residues behind, including amino acids, urea, and chlorides (sodium chloride—common salt—in particular). An image of the latent fingermark is produced in the form of residual, water-soluble components. How deeply the latent fingermark deposit penetrates into the surface depends very much on the environmental conditions, in particular the relative humidity (RH—defined as the amount of water vapor present in the air expressed as a percentage of the amount that the air could hold at a given temperature), and the degree of porosity of the surface. Once absorbed into the surface, the latent image based on the WSD will be relatively well preserved under normal conditions, cannot be rubbed away, but can be easily destroyed (washed away or diffused) with water.

As the fingermark ages, the amino acids will remain relatively stable provided that the porous substrate is stored under normal environmental conditions (RH <80%). Other components such as urea and sodium chloride, however, will tend to migrate continuously, depending on the environmental conditions (RH in the first instance). The higher the RH, the faster is the migration. Under normal conditions (RH < 80%), minimal diffusion will be evident over the first week after deposition. Older marks will tend to show significant diffusion of urea and chlorides, thus producing blurred images for any detection method targeting these components.

The NWSD, a semisolid complex mixture of fats, waxes, and long-chain hydrocarbons, remains longer on the surface of the substrate (Figure 4.1). Mobility of the NWSD depends primarily on the ambient temperature. At around 20°C, mobility is relatively slow and the NWSD can stay on top of the surface for several days. Above 35°C, however, mobility increases significantly and the NWSD is quickly diffused. Under normal conditions, a small amount of the NWSD will remain on top of the surface for a significant period (years). This small amount will not attract fingerprint powders, but it can be detected using more sensitive techniques such as physical developer (PD).

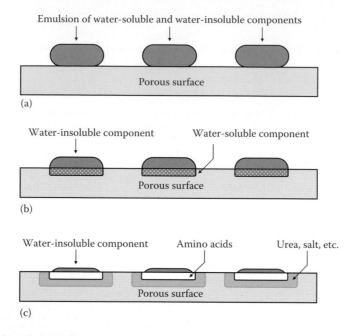

FIGURE 4.2 Aging of a latent fingermark on a porous substrate (e.g., paper). (a) Cross section of latent deposit immediately after deposition, (b) seconds/minutes after deposition, and (c) days/weeks after deposition.

4.2.2 NONPOROUS SURFACES

Any surface that does not absorb any component of the latent fingermark deposits is classified as a nonporous surface. Classical examples of nonporous surfaces include polyethylene (polythene) plastic bags, glass, and shiny metal surfaces. An emulsion consisting of water-soluble and non-water-soluble components of the latent fingermark deposit remains on top of the surface for a significant period of time (Figure 4.3) unless it is removed (rubbed off) from the surface or has degraded through age or environmental effects. As all of the deposit remains on the surface of a nonporous substrate, the latent marks are very fragile, and care must be taken when handling or packaging such items. In addition, such marks are readily removed by the action of organic solvents. While water will tend to remove any water-soluble material, the water-insoluble component will be unaffected if the surface gets wet. As the fingermark ages, components of the deposit will be lost through physical, chemical, or biological degradation.

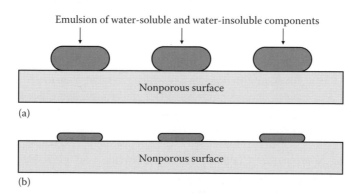

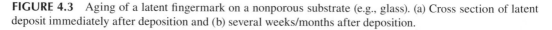

FIGURE 4.3 Aging of a latent fingermark on a nonporous substrate (e.g., glass). (a) Cross section of latent deposit immediately after deposition and (b) several weeks/months after deposition.

4.2.3 SEMIPOROUS SURFACES

Any surface with intermediate characteristics that does not fit well into the porous or nonporous groups is generally classified as semiporous. Typical examples of this type of substrate are some painted surfaces (e.g., matt painted or varnished surfaces), polymer banknotes, and glossy or waxed paper. The surface absorbs the water-soluble component, but more slowly than for porous surfaces. The non-water-soluble component remains on top of the surface much longer than it does on a porous surface, but some diffusion into the substrate will occur over time (which is not the case for a nonporous surface).

4.3 OPTICAL DETECTION TECHNIQUES

Optical detection methods have the advantage of being nondestructive with respect to the latent fingermark deposit (provided, of course, that fingermarks are not exposed to extremely high light intensities as may occur, for example, with high-powered lasers). As a result, these techniques do not preclude the later application of conventional fingermark development procedures. The simple observation of an object under white light may disclose a visible fingermark that can be photographed without any further treatment. The contrast in marks contaminated with a colored material such as blood can be significantly enhanced using selective absorption techniques. On the other hand, more complex optical detection methods can sometimes reveal otherwise invisible marks that may not be developed by other techniques. A fingermark detection sequence should therefore always commence with an optical examination using different illumination techniques as dictated by the surface type and any likely fingermark contamination.

4.3.1 ABSORPTION

The absorption mode can be useful for the enhancement of visible fingermarks. If the fingers are contaminated with a colored material, deposited fingermarks may have characteristic absorption properties that can be exploited to improve contrast. For example, dry blood has a strong absorption peak at 415 nm (Stoilovic 1991). This characteristic absorption can be used to optically enhance fingermarks in blood. Similarly, a colored fingermark that is the result of a particular detection technique (e.g., ninhydrin treatment to produce a purple mark) can be optically enhanced using selective absorption.

When enhancing colored marks, consideration must be given not only to the color of the fingermark but also the color of the surface. The color wheel (Figure 3.25; see Section 3.3.10) should be used to select an illumination wavelength range that will darken the mark (favor absorption) and lighten the surface (favor reflection). As an example, a blue fingermark on a red surface can be significantly enhanced if viewed under orange–red illumination (e.g., around 600 nm), as this color will be strongly absorbed by the mark but totally reflected by the surface. Alternatively, white light illumination can be used and the fingermark viewed through an orange–red filter. Only the light reflected by the surface will be transmitted through the filter, thus giving the impression of a light background (while the fingermark will be dark).

4.3.2 LUMINESCENCE

Untreated latent fingermarks may exhibit weak luminescence that can sometimes be observed and captured on nonluminescent surfaces, particularly when high-powered excitation sources such as lasers are employed (Dalrymple et al. 1977; Menzel 1980, 1985, 1999; Dalrymple and Almog 2012). It is unlikely that this luminescence is due to naturally secreted compounds alone and, when observed, it is more likely to be due to the presence of a luminescent contaminant picked up from the environment (Salares et al. 1979; Creer 1996).

Despite the relatively low success rate of the technique in actual casework, a search for inherently luminescent fingermarks should always precede the application of a destructive

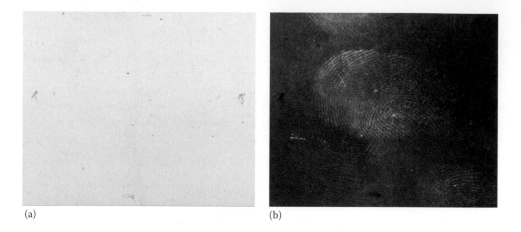

(a)   (b)

FIGURE 4.4 Example of a luminescent latent fingermark that was discovered on the white glossy cover of a book: (a) under white light and (b) in the luminescence mode, with excitation under a forensic light source at 530 nm and observation using a 590 nm bandpass barrier filter.

detection method. The evidential object should be illuminated at different wavelengths using a suitable high-intensity light source (not necessarily a laser) while observing through appropriately filtered goggles. A good starting point is to use high-intensity blue light (e.g., a filtered light source operating at 450 nm) while wearing yellow/orange goggles, which act as a long-pass barrier filter. Such an examination must be conducted under darkened conditions (total darkness if possible); otherwise, weakly luminescent marks will not be detected. If a luminescent mark is detected, different excitation/observation wavelengths should then be evaluated to find the optimal conditions for recording purposes. An example of a luminescent latent fingermark is provided in Figure 4.4.

4.3.3 DIFFUSED REFLECTION

Light tends to be diffusely reflected from a latent fingermark deposit. This property can be used for the detection of latent marks on smooth, shiny surfaces such as glass, plastic (e.g., credit cards), and polished metal; i.e., on surfaces that exhibit specular reflection. Oblique lighting on shiny surfaces can sometimes reveal latent fingermarks, fingermarks contaminated with material such as dust or blood, or fingermarks already developed by other techniques (such as powdering or cyanoacrylate [CA] fuming). Under these conditions, marks will be visible as light images against a dark background due to the light diffusely reflected by the ridge deposits.

For transparent substrates such as clear plastic or glass, a dark-field illumination technique using transmitted light may provide enhancement due to light rays being diffused and refracted by fingermark deposits. Using transmitted oblique lighting, a fingermark on glass, for example, will be observed as light ridges against a dark background (Figure 4.5a).

Episcopic coaxial illumination is a specific optical setup that is particularly effective for exploiting diffused reflection (Pfister 1985). The technique involves the use of a semitransparent mirror to observe the reflection of light perpendicular to the surface (see Section 3.3.11), with illumination, reflection, and observation being along the same coaxial path. The light is diffused by the fingermark deposit but specularly reflected by the surface; therefore, the fingermark is visible as dark ridges against a light background (Figure 4.5b). As well as detecting untreated latent marks, the technique can also give excellent results for the enhancement of blood marks and marks developed by techniques such as CA fuming and VMD (Lennard and Margot 1988; Ziv and Springer 1993; Bullock et al. 1994). Commercial accessories are available for the application of this method; for example, the "Coaxial Light Guide and Illuminator" from Arrowhead Forensics.

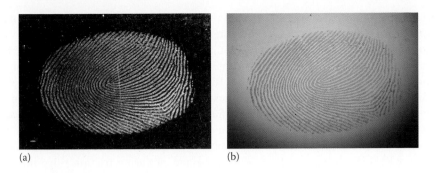

(a)   (b)

FIGURE 4.5   Example of a latent fingermark on clear glass imaged using (a) transmitted oblique lighting and (b) episcopic coaxial illumination. (Images courtesy of S. Moret.)

4.3.4   ULTRAVIOLET IMAGING

Japanese workers (cited by German [1987]) were the first to propose the optical detection of latent fingermarks by shortwave UV reflection. The technique requires the use of a UV-sensitive digital camera (equipped with a quartz lens) and a source of UV light (West et al. 1990). The Hamamatsu company marketed, for several years, a complete Reflected UV Imaging System (RUVIS) for the detection of traces, including fingermarks, footwear impressions, and bite marks on skin. Advances in digital imaging technology have since revolutionized this technique, making it much more practical. Units based on image intensifiers are now available; examples include the KrimeSite™ Imager (Sirchie), the SceneScope™ (SPEX Forensics), and the 16MP Digital RUVIS (Syntronics). The technique is based on generating contrast between the surface, which may absorb or reflect UV light, and the fingermark deposit that absorbs some UV radiation and diffusely reflects the remainder. The technique may therefore give either light ridges on a dark background or dark ridges on a light background, depending on the nature of the surface and the composition of the fingermark deposit (Wang 1996) (Figure 4.6). The type of UV lamp employed and the angle of incidence of the UV illumination are both critical factors for obtaining

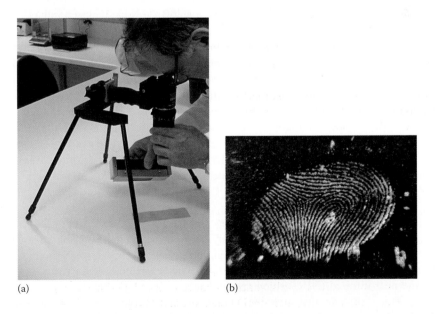

(a)   (b)

FIGURE 4.6   Example of (a) a Reflected UV Imaging System being used to examine the adhesive side of packaging tape and (b) a fingermark image obtained.

satisfactory results. Cantú (2014) has reviewed the key principles of physics that explain how a RUVIS can detect latent fingermarks on smooth, nonporous surfaces.

Keith and Runion (1998) found that the routine casework application of real-time shortwave UV imaging was a valuable supplement to conventional white light and forensic light source examinations. The authors also indicated that RUVIS can be extremely helpful when working with CA-fumed, dye-stained surfaces that luminesce excessively when excited with a forensic light source at wavelengths between 400 and 580 nm. Saferstein and Graf (2001) evaluated a commercial imaging system and confirmed that the detection of latent fingermarks by RUVIS was a practical and worthwhile undertaking, particularly on smooth, nonporous surfaces. Gardner (2010) demonstrated that a RUVIS can be effective for locating and capturing friction ridge impressions on postblast debris, despite the extreme thermal conditions that the substrate may have been exposed to due to the blast itself. More recently, Gibson et al. (2012) compared the effectiveness of three UV-sensitive imaging systems, used in conjunction with illumination at 254 nm, for the detection of latent fingermarks on both paper and glass substrates.

The London Metropolitan Police reported the use of reflection techniques in both the long- and shortwave UV region on a range of surfaces (Creer 1993, 1996). In addition, they reported that the illumination of latent marks on paper using the 266 nm radiation from a frequency-quadrupled Nd:YAG laser, with photographic detection of luminescence emission in the long-wave UV region (300–400 nm), can produce images with good ridge detail (Bramble et al. 1993). However, the method was reported to be impractical, with approximately 2 hours needed to search for fingermarks on an A4 sheet of paper using the procedure described (Creer 1993). Furthermore, almost all of the fingermarks detected by UV luminescence could be enhanced by conventional chemical treatment. Springer et al. (1994) confirmed that a range of different body fluids, including blood, semen, and saliva, can be readily detected by shortwave UV luminescence.

The design of an illumination–imaging system for the observation of shortwave UV luminescence, based on a portable mercury–xenon lamp and a cooled CCD camera, has been described (Ben-Yosef et al. 1998). The system was evaluated for the detection of latent fingermarks and various body fluid stains. Of the eccrine-rich latent marks examined in the study, only a small number (around 10%) exhibited significant luminescence. Akiba et al. (2007) studied the luminescence generated in sebum-rich latent fingermarks when excited with a tunable laser operating in the UV region. Li and coworkers (2013) reported on the use of a 266 nm Nd:YAG laser and a UV-intensified CCD imaging system for the noninvasive detection of fingermarks on a range of surfaces.

Some surfaces, such as white glossy paper, absorb UV light and produce a strong luminescence emission in the visible spectrum due to the presence of optical brighteners. The illumination of such surfaces with UV light can sometimes reveal latent marks, particularly if such marks are contaminated with UV-absorbing material. Marks of this type will be seen as dark images against a bright luminescent background (Creer 1996). No special equipment other than a UV lamp is required.

Any examination method that requires illumination with shortwave UV should be applied with caution. First, UV radiation is damaging to the skin and eyes so skin and eye protection is required. Second, shortwave UV irradiation of an item under examination may compromise subsequent DNA analysis (as DNA can be damaged) if a high-intensity lamp is employed or if exposure is prolonged.

4.3.5 Near-Infrared Imaging

The imaging of fingermarks has almost exclusively been conducted in the visible region of the electromagnetic spectrum. However, as demonstrated earlier with respect to UV imaging, improved visualization can sometimes be achieved by working outside of this region (Bandey et al. 2006). Imaging in the near-infrared (NIR) region from 700 to 1100 nm, for example, can offer a number of advantages. This is a region that is well known to questioned document examiners as writing and printing inks can often be discriminated based on NIR reflection or NIR luminescence emission (under visible light excitation). While these observation modes will not generally reveal latent fingermarks, they can aid in the visualization of fingermarks developed by various processes. The conventional sensors used in most digital cameras are sensitive to wavelengths up to around 1100 nm. However, most consumer cameras incorporate an IR-blocking filter that is bonded directly to the image sensor chip to ensure that only visible light is captured. Therefore, to record images in the NIR, this blocking filter must be removed, which is already the case for a number of special-purpose SLR cameras and scientific imaging systems (such as the cameras typically employed for questioned document examination).

Imaging fingermarks using NIR reflection requires illumination with a light source that emits in this wavelength range, such as conventional tungsten lamps or NIR LEDs. In addition, a NIR bandpass or long-pass filter (e.g., a filter with a cut-on wavelength of 700 nm) is required in front of the camera to block any reflected visible light while transmitting the NIR radiation. To observed luminescence emission in the NIR, a monochromatic visible band is required for excitation (e.g., a suitable visible laser line or a visible light band from a filtered lamp or LED-based light source) while viewing with a NIR-sensitive camera fitted with a NIR bandpass or long-pass filter as for the NIR reflection mode.

Bramble and coworkers (2000) reported that fingermarks treated with gentian violet display a luminescence emission in the red/NIR region (>620 nm) when excited at shorter wavelengths (approximately 400–600 nm). Imaging in the luminescence mode under these conditions proved effective for the enhancement of developed marks on dark surfaces as well as weak marks on light surfaces.

Bleay and Kent (2005) conducted a study on the use of infrared filters in conjunction with a digital camera sensitive in the NIR region for the removal of colored background patterns from fingermark images. In the NIR reflection mode, many of the pigments used in printing inks are transparent while the fingermarks produced via some detection methods remain visible under these conditions. They demonstrated that NIR reflection can remove multicolored backgrounds from marks developed using PD, VMD, aluminum powder, black powder suspension (BPS), and small particle reagent (SPR).

Maynard et al. (2009) employed a hyperspectral imaging (HSI) system to enhance fingermarks in the NIR region. A variety of porous, nonporous, and semiporous surfaces were tested using a range of chemical and physical enhancement techniques. Both the absorption and luminescence properties of the treated marks were examined over the spectral range 650–1100 nm. Significant NIR absorption was observed for marks developed using ninhydrin, iodine–benzoflavone, PD, and fingerprint powder. NIR luminescence emission was recorded for marks treated with diazafluorenone (DFO), ninhydrin plus zinc(II) post-treatment, 1,2-indanedione (IND), and genipin. Significant NIR luminescence emission resulted when CA-developed marks were stained using a methanolic solution of NIR laser dye. In addition, it was found that fingermarks on patterned and highly luminescent surfaces could be readily enhanced in the NIR region using metal oxide powders coated with NIR dyes. Further studies on the use of NIR laser dyes for the luminescence enhancement of fingermarks in the NIR region have been reported by this research group (Chadwick et al. 2011; Chadwick 2013).

4.3.6 Visible Hyperspectral Imaging

Visible HSI—also referred to as chemical imaging—was first proposed for latent fingermark detection by Exline and coworkers in 2003. Luminescence chemical imaging and visible absorbance chemical imaging were successfully applied to the enhancement of fingermarks treated with ninhydrin, DFO, CA, and luminescent stains. In addition, absorption mode analysis was able to visualize untreated latent fingermarks on paper in some cases. The HSI system employed produced results that were at least as good as, and in many cases better than, those obtained using a conventional image capturing system. Visible HSI can provide improved sensitivity for the enhancement of weaker fingermark deposits. Further optimization of the technique was reported by Payne et al. (2005), with confirmation that chemical imaging offers advantages for the enhancement of weak or borderline marks developed by conventional methods, particularly for fingermarks on surfaces that produce highly luminescent backgrounds. More recently, Plese and coworkers (2010) demonstrated that improvements in HSI data collection and processing enhanced the visualization of latent fingermarks on both porous and nonporous substrates. This may be of benefit in cases where fingermarks need to be detected and recorded without the application of physical or chemical detection methods. HSI in the NIR region has also been demonstrated (Maynard et al. 2009), with imaging over the spectral range 650–1100 nm being shown to have advantages for fingermark detection on some substrates, particularly in difficult cases involving patterned or highly luminescent surfaces.

Nakamura and coworkers (2015) evaluated a portable HSI system used in combination with a continuous wave green laser operating at 577 nm. They found that untreated latent fingermarks could be readily detected in the luminescence mode on steel-based and plaster walls. In addition, further processing of the hyperspectral data can, under certain circumstances, permit the spectral separation of overlapping ridge impressions.

Commercial equipment is available for the application of visible and NIR HSI techniques to fingermark detection. An example is the HSI Examiner™ series of HSI systems from ChemImage Corporation (www.chemimage.com, last accessed February 7, 2016).

While the visualization of fingermarks using HSI in the mid-infrared region—from approximately 2,500 to 25,000 nm—has been shown to offer improved sensitivity and specificity (Tahtouh et al. 2005; Crane et al. 2007; Tahtouh et al. 2007), high instrument cost and long data acquisition times are significant limitations. With improvements in technology, however, imaging in this region of the electromagnetic spectrum may become a viable option in the future.

4.4 DETECTION TECHNIQUES FOR POROUS SURFACES

4.4.1 Ninhydrin

4.4.1.1 General

Ninhydrin reacts with primary and secondary amines (including amino acids, proteins, and peptides) to give a dark purple product known as Ruhemann's purple (RP) (Figure 4.7)—named after the chemist who first described this reaction. As the eccrine component of a latent mark deposit contains amino acids, this reaction can be exploited as a means of developing fingermarks on porous surfaces such as paper and cardboard. The use of ninhydrin as a fingermark detection reagent was first proposed in 1954 by Odén and von Hofsten (1954). Since then, ninhydrin has become a popular technique for fingermark detection on porous substrates.

Eccrine glands secrete a range of different amino acids that may ultimately be present in a latent fingermark deposit (Hamilton 1965; Ramotowski 2001; Girod et al. 2012) (see Table 4.3 and Figure 4.8). Ninhydrin is a nonspecific amino acid reagent in that it reacts in the same manner with different amino acids. In this way, each amino acid present in the latent fingermark deposit will contribute to the developed fingermark image. Amino acids are stable compounds that, due to an affinity for cellulose, do not migrate to any significant extent through dry paper substrates. As a result, very old latent marks can be developed with amino acid reagents such as ninhydrin (for example, the development of 40-year-old marks has been recorded). In addition, the amino acid

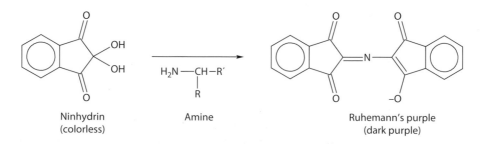

FIGURE 4.7 Chemical reaction between ninhydrin and a primary or secondary amine, resulting in the formation of a dark purple product known as Ruhemann's purple.

TABLE 4.3

Quantities of Major Amino Acids Found in a Single Wet Thumb Mark

Amino Acid	Amount (μmol)	Serine Ratio
Serine	0.106	100
Glycine	0.071	67
Ornithine	0.034	32
Alanine	0.029	27
Aspartic acid	0.023	22
Threonine	0.018	17
Histidine	0.018	17
Valine	0.013	12
Proline	0.011	10
Leucine	0.011	10
Lysine	0.011	10

Sources: Hamilton, P.B., *Nature*, 205, 284, 1965; Ramotowski, R.S., Composition of latent print residue, in *Advances in Fingerprint Technology*, 2nd edn., H.C. Lee and R.E. Gaensslen, Eds., CRC Press, Boca Raton, FL, 2001, pp. 63–104.

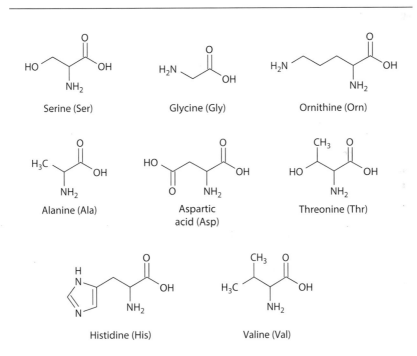

FIGURE 4.8 Structures of the major amino acids found in a typical latent fingermark deposit.

composition of the eccrine secretion appears to remain relatively constant. Due to these qualities, the use of amino acid reagents (ninhydrin and ninhydrin analogs, including 1,8-diazafluoren-9-one [DFO] and IND) constitutes an effective chemical technique for the development of latent fingermarks on paper surfaces.

The ninhydrin reaction is much more complex than the simplified process depicted in Figure 4.7. The generally accepted mechanism for the reaction with amino acids is given in Figure 4.9 (Grigg et al. 1986; Hansen and Joullié 2005; Jelly et al. 2009). The reaction commences with a Schiff's base condensation involving attack of the amine group on the central carbonyl of the triketone form of

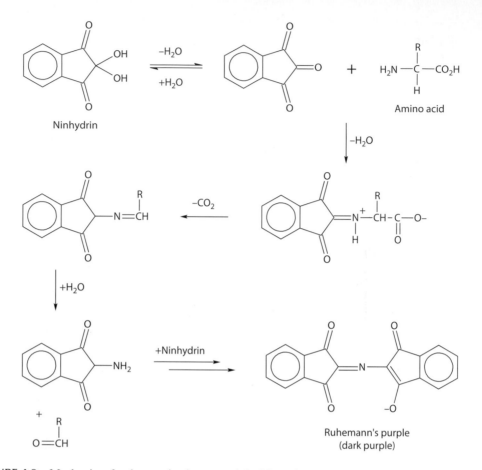

FIGURE 4.9 Mechanism for the reaction between ninhydrin and an amino acid.

ninhydrin (which is in constant equilibrium with its hydrated form). The resulting Schiff's base then undergoes decarboxylation to yield an intermediate aldimine that is hydrolyzed to the aldehyde and 2-amino-1,3-indanedione. This 2-amino intermediate then condenses with a second molecule of ninhydrin to produce RP. Due to this complex mechanism, and the possibility of side reactions that can lead to other products being formed, reaction conditions must be tightly controlled if the optimum yield of RP is to be obtained. The reaction rate will depend on temperature, RH, and pH (acidity). It has been shown that an optimum reaction rate will be obtained under slightly acidic conditions, around pH 5 (Lamothe and McCormick 1972).

Paper items are generally treated with ninhydrin by briefly dipping in a solution of the reagent (typical concentration 0.5% w/v in a mixture of organic solvents). As an alternative to dipping, the reagent can be applied with a brush or spray. The items are then air-dried and the development allowed to proceed at room temperature over 24–48 hours. The reaction is the most efficient when the RH is between 50% and 80%. If rapid results are required for operational reasons, special-purpose ninhydrin development cabinets can be employed where the temperature and humidity are precisely controlled (80°C with 65% RH; development time approximately 5 minutes [Home Office 1998]). While the ninhydrin technique can develop latent fingermarks on a wide range of porous substrates, some paper surfaces (e.g., certain types of banknote paper) react strongly with the reagent, and its use is limited in such cases.

A ninhydrin-developed fingermark is dark purple in color due to the formation of RP along the ridge impressions. The absorption spectrum of RP on paper (Figure 4.10a) shows two absorption maxima: a narrow band centered at 415 nm (violet region) and a broad, main band centered

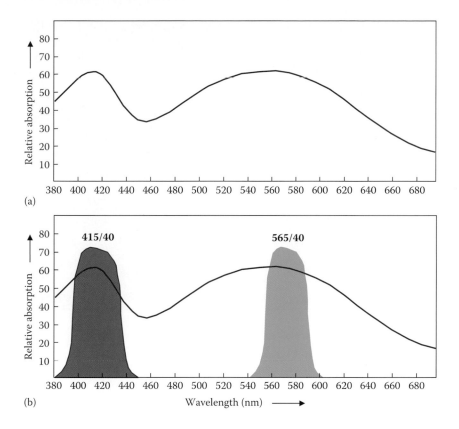

FIGURE 4.10 (a) Typical absorption spectrum of a ninhydrin-developed fingermark on paper and (b) recommended bandpass filters for observation in the absorption mode.

around 550–570 nm (green–yellow region). Photography of ninhydrin-developed latent marks is best achieved using the absorption mode. To achieve the best contrast when photographing ninhydrin-developed marks, the main absorption band of RP (i.e., 550–570 nm) should be exploited. This is achieved using white light illumination and a green–yellow bandpass barrier filter in front of the camera (e.g., central wavelength [CW] = 550–570 nm; half bandwidth [HBW] = 40–50 nm; Figure 4.10b). In cases where a colored background prevents good contrast from being obtained under these conditions, it is possible to utilize the 415 nm RP absorption band (Figure 4.10b). Some forensic light sources are fitted with a violet filter (e.g., CW = 415 nm; HBW = 40 nm) that can be used for this purpose. Photography should be conducted in a darkened room with the marks illuminated with the violet band from the light source. No barrier filter is required on the camera in this case. An example of a ninhydrin-developed fingermark photographed under white light and through a green filter is provided in Figure 4.11.

4.4.1.2 Ninhydrin Formulations
Amino acid reagents such as ninhydrin are generally made up in a solution that contains the reagent itself, a small amount of polar solvent (generally ethanol or methanol) to keep the reagent in solution, acetic acid (to ensure that the reaction takes place under slightly acidic conditions), and a carrier solvent that makes up the bulk of the solution. Other solvents may be added to increase the stability of the working solution. Ideally, the carrier solvent should be volatile (low boiling point, to quickly evaporate from treated surfaces), nontoxic, nonflammable, nonpolar (to minimize ink running on treated documents), and cost-effective. It is recommended that the total concentration of polar solvents in the final working solution does not exceed 10% v/v.

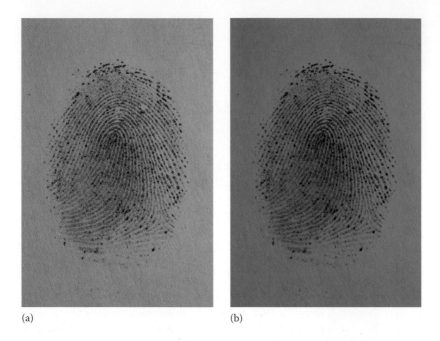

(a)   (b)

FIGURE 4.11 Example of a ninhydrin-developed fingermark on white paper imaged under white light (a) without a barrier filter on the camera and (b) with a green barrier filter on the camera. (Images courtesy of S. Moret.)

The solvent 1,1,2-trichlorotrifluoroethane (sold under various names such as Arklone P, Fluorisol, Freon 113, and CFC-113) was generally favored as the ideal carrier solvent for fingermark reagents. The first such formulation was nonflammable ninhydrin, proposed by Morris and Goode in 1974 and widely used since that time (Morris and Goode 1974). Unfortunately, due to its harmful effects on the Earth's ozone layer, CFC-113 is no longer manufactured, and its use is now prohibited in most countries. This is a direct result of the 1987 Montreal Protocol that placed restrictions on substances that deplete the ozone layer.

Alternative carrier solvents for ninhydrin and other amino acid reagents have been proposed by a number of research groups. Jungbluth (1992, 1993) reported good results with the solvents Genesolv 2020 (a mixture of dichlorofluoroethane and dichlorotrifluoroethane) and Genesolv 2000 (dichlorofluoroethane; HCFC 141b). However, both of these solvents are based on hydrochlorofluorocarbons (HCFCs; considered as transitional CFC replacements) that are also being phased out due to their ozone-depleting potential (albeit lower than that of CFC-113). A number of authors have reported success with formulations based on hexane, heptane, or petroleum ether as carrier solvents (Watling and Smith 1993; Hewlett and Sears 1997). The flammability of such solvents, however, means that they are not a safe alternative for most operational laboratories. Formulations based on these solvents should only be used if laboratory facilities are adequate (e.g., availability of fume cupboards certified for flammable liquid use).

The carrier solvents currently recommended for use with ninhydrin and other amino acid reagents are the hydrofluoroether (HFE) methoxynonafluorobutane (HFE-7100; Novec™ 7100) from 3M and the hydrofluorocarbon (HFC) decafluoropentane (HFC-4310mee; Vertrel® XF) from DuPont (Kent 1996). These solvents are nonflammable and are reported to have a zero ozone depletion potential. Operational trials have indicated that ninhydrin formulations based on either of these two carrier solvents perform at least as well as, if not better than, CFC-113-based formulations (Hewlett et al. 1997; Hewlett and Sears 1999; Petruncio 2000; Rajtar 2000). However, the relatively high cost of these solvents may be problematic for some laboratories.

It must also be appreciated that our knowledge of environmental effects from the use of such solvents is still incomplete and, as associated legislation evolves, other carrier solvents may need to be considered in the future.

4.4.1.3   Secondary Metal Salt Treatment

Fingermarks developed with ninhydrin can be further enhanced by treatment with a zinc (Zn) or cadmium (Cd) metal salt solution. This treatment results in a color change, orange for zinc(II) and red for cadmium(II), which is due to the formation of a coordination complex between the RP (the product from the ninhydrin reaction) and the metal salt (Lennard 1986; Lennard et al. 1987). While it has been shown that zinc(II) and cadmium(II) will form complexes with RP in both a 1:1 and 1:2 metal–ligand ratio depending on the reaction conditions, the 1:1 complex (Figure 4.12) is likely to be dominant in fingermark enhancement work (Davies et al. 1995).

RP-Zn and RP-Cd complexes show stronger absorption properties than RP itself, and this may be useful in the absorption mode when the background color leads to poor contrast after initial ninhydrin development. Absorption spectra for these complexes are shown in Figure 4.13a. Posttreatment with zinc nitrate changes the purple color of ninhydrin-developed marks to orange, with the maximum absorption shifted to around 490 nm. Enhancement photography of zinc posttreated marks can therefore be achieved in the absorption mode with a 490 nm bandpass barrier filter in front of the camera (or using illumination from a forensic light source operating at this wavelength) (Figures 4.13b and 4.14). Posttreatment with cadmium nitrate changes the purple color of ninhydrin-developed marks to red, with the maximum absorption shifted to around 505 nm. Enhancement photography of cadmium posttreated marks can therefore be achieved in the absorption mode with a 505 nm bandpass barrier filter in front of the camera (or using equivalent illumination from a forensic light source) (Figure 4.13c). Given the high toxicity associated with cadmium salts, their use for enhancement work is not recommended and, therefore, zinc(II) posttreatment is preferred.

As well as the observed color change, ninhydrin-developed marks that have been posttreated with zinc(II) or cadmium(II) are also luminescent under certain conditions. The luminescence emission, which is very weak at room temperature, can be significantly enhanced by cooling the marks with liquid nitrogen ($-196°C = 77$ K; Kobus et al. 1983; Almog et al. 2007). Typical luminescence spectra for a ninhydrin-developed fingermark posttreated with zinc nitrate are shown in Figure 4.15 together with the recommended filters for excitation and observation. Considerable enhancement of ninhydrin-developed fingermarks can be obtained by exploiting these luminescence properties (Herod and Menzel 1982; Kobus et al. 1983; Stoilovic et al. 1986) (Figure 4.16). Early research promoted the use of cadmium(II) salts for this enhancement (Stoilovic et al. 1986); however, as indicated earlier, cadmium(II) posttreatment should be avoided due to toxicity concerns.

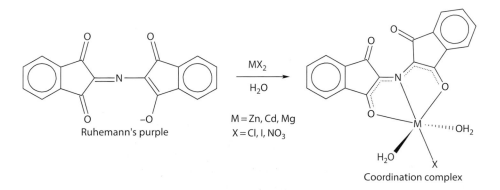

FIGURE 4.12   Treatment of Ruhemann's purple with certain metal salts results in the formation of a coordination complex. (From Lennard, C.J. et al., *J. Forensic Sci.*, 32, 597, 1987.)

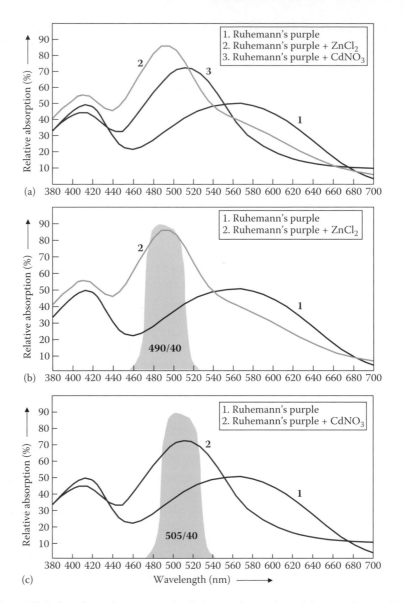

FIGURE 4.13 (a) Relative absorption spectra for Ruhemann's purple and its complexes with zinc(II) and cadmium(II), (b) recommended bandpass filter for observation in the absorption mode after zinc(II) treatment, and (c) recommended bandpass filter for observation in the absorption mode in the case of the cadmium(II) treatment.

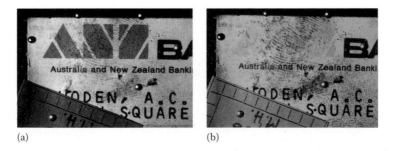

FIGURE 4.14 Casework example of a ninhydrin-developed fingermark (a) photographed under white light and (b) treated with zinc nitrate and photographed in the absorption mode under a forensic light source at 490 nm.

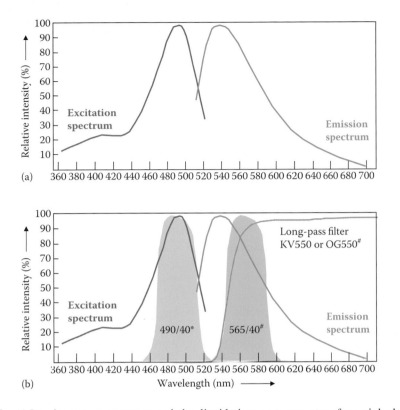

FIGURE 4.15 (a) Luminescence spectra recorded at liquid nitrogen temperature for a ninhydrin-developed mark posttreated with zinc nitrate and (b) recommended filters for excitation (*) and observation (#) in the luminescence mode.

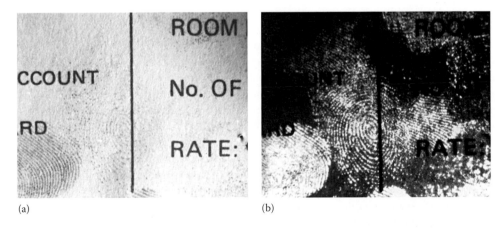

FIGURE 4.16 Casework example of a weak ninhydrin-developed fingermark (a) under white light and (b) treated with zinc nitrate, cooled to liquid nitrogen temperature, and photographed in the luminescence mode under a forensic light source at 490 nm and with a 565 nm bandpass filter on the camera.

Almog and coworkers (2007) evaluated ninhydrin formulations that contained zinc or cadmium salts. In this manner, the RP-zinc(II) or RP-cadmium(II) complexes can be formed in a single reaction. They found that the application of these premixed solutions to latent fingermarks on paper was as efficient, for visualization in both the absorption and luminescence modes, as the two-stage process beginning with ninhydrin and then following this with separate metal salt treatment.

After metal salt treatment (or using the one-step process described earlier), the item is inspected under a forensic light source operating at a suitable wavelength. To favor the luminescence, the sample is cooled to liquid nitrogen temperature ($-196°C$), which is achieved by placing the sample in an insulated container (such as a polystyrene foam tray) and covering it with a thin layer of liquid nitrogen. A suitable barrier filter is then required to observe the luminescence emission. As the fingermark luminescence is often weak, photographic recording generally requires long exposure times (from a few seconds to several minutes).

It should be noted that the enhancement of ninhydrin-developed fingermarks in the luminescence mode at liquid nitrogen temperature, following posttreatment with a suitable metal salt solution or using a one-step process, is now considered to be redundant due to the availability of more sensitive amino acid reagents. Such alternatives, now used routinely, include DFO and IND as presented later in this chapter. These reagents produce strong room-temperature luminescence, without the need for secondary metal salt treatment or cooling with liquid nitrogen. While not replacing ninhydrin, such reagents can be used prior to ninhydrin in the detection sequence and their use will generally result in more fingermarks being detected than with ninhydrin alone.

4.4.2 Ninhydrin Analogs

Ninhydrin analogs are amino acid–specific reagents that are structurally similar to ninhydrin itself (so a similar reaction with amino acids is assumed), but where different functional groups have been introduced with the purpose of improving fingermark detection capabilities (Figure 4.17). The requirements for an ideal replacement for ninhydrin are good initial color, superior luminescence properties (preferably without the need for metal salt treatment or cooling with liquid nitrogen), low cost, good solubility in a range of solvents (preferably nonpolar), and low toxicity (Ramotowski et al. 1997). Excellent reviews on the synthesis and applications of ninhydrin and its analogs have been published by Joullié et al. (1991), Almog (2001, 2012), Hansen and Joullié (2005), Jelly et al. (2009), and Ramotowski (2012).

Almog and colleagues, in Israel in the early 1980s, were the first to explore the potential of ninhydrin analogs and thereby inspire other research groups around the world (Almog et al. 1982). Some of the more promising compounds that were synthesized at that time included benzo[f]ninhydrin (Almog et al. 1982) and 5-methoxyninhydrin (Lennard et al. 1986, 1988; Almog and Hirshfeld 1988) (Figure 4.17). These reagents develop latent fingermarks on paper with a sensitivity similar to that of ninhydrin but, after metal salt treatment, offer considerably stronger luminescence emission, even at ambient temperature. In addition, the red-shifted absorption and emission from benzo[f]ninhydrin-developed marks was found to be particularly useful on certain luminescent substrates, such as cardboard and yellow paper. While benzo[f]ninhydrin and 5-methoxyninhydrin became commercially available, they remained very expensive alternatives to ninhydrin itself and the advantages displayed were insufficient to justify routine use (Almog et al. 2000).

The synthesis of a number of amino-substituted ninhydrin analogs has also been reported (Almog et al. 1991). Of these, the compound 5-aminoninhydrin (Figure 4.17) showed some promise as a fingermark reagent, producing strong room-temperature luminescence in developed marks, even without secondary metal salt treatment. However, Pounds and Allman (1992) found that the reagent produced a highly luminescent background that tended to obscure developed marks. Sulfur-containing groups at position 5 were subsequently investigated and were found to exhibit excellent properties as fluorogenic reagents (Heffner and Joullié 1991b; Almog et al. 1992). Preliminary experiments indicated that 5-methylthioninhydrin (Figure 4.17) showed a sensitivity that markedly exceeded that of both ninhydrin and 5-methoxyninhydrin.

A number of ninhydrin analogs composed of extended aromatic rings, bis-ninhydrins, and sulfur-containing compounds were synthesized by Joullié's group at the University of Pennsylvania (Heffner and Joullié 1991a,b; Cantú et al. 1993; Hark et al. 1994; Hark 1996). The sulfur-containing analogs 5-methylthioninhydrin, thieno[f]ninhydrin, and 5-(2-thienyl)-ninhydrin (Figure 4.17) were

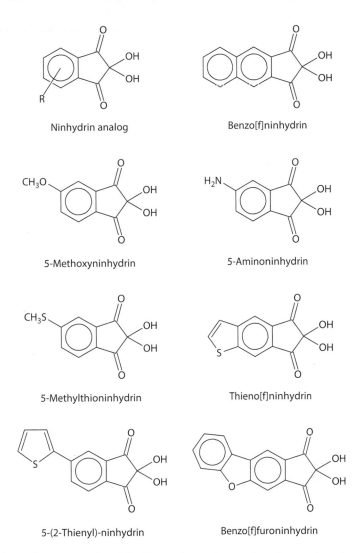

FIGURE 4.17 General structure of a ninhydrin analog and a number of examples of synthesized analogs from published studies.

found to be very sensitive reagents for latent fingermark detection, particularly after metal salt treatment. It was suggested that these analogs were at least as sensitive as the amino acid reagent 1,8-diazafluoren-8-one (DFO; see Section 4.4.3) for the detection of fingermarks on paper. Similar results were independently reported by Pounds and Allman (1992). However, Hark and coworkers (1994) indicated that the estimated cost of manufacturing analogs such as 5-(2-thienyl)-ninhydrin would likely limit their widespread distribution and use.

Cantú and coworkers (1993) compared ten amino acid reagents (ninhydrin, eight ninhydrin analogs, and DFO) in their ability to visualize spots of the amino acid glycine on paper. The evaluation considered parameters such as color development, luminescence, luminescence after zinc(II) treatment, and background interference. The role of acetic acid in the reagent formulations was also evaluated. Of the reagents tested, the analog thieno[f]ninhydrin was found to be the most sensitive visualizing reagent when zinc(II) treatment was employed. The study also confirmed that RP combines with zinc(II) in a 1:1 ratio under normal circumstances.

Nitrophenylninhydrin, benzo[f]furoninhydrin, and six ninhydrin analogs containing oxygen, sulfur, and selenium substituents at position 5 were evaluated as fingermark development reagents by Kobus and coworkers (2002). The analogs all showed good color development, but this was not superior to that obtained with ninhydrin itself. The reaction product obtained with benzo[f] furoninhydrin showed strong room-temperature luminescence following zinc complexation. Of the compounds evaluated by this group, the benzo[f]furo analog (Figure 4.17) showed the greatest potential as a fingermark reagent, with results comparing favorably with those obtained with DFO.

Almog and colleagues (2008) investigated premixed solutions of 5-methoxyninhydrin and 5-methylthioninhydrin (5MTN) with zinc and cadmium salts as dual fingermark reagents, capable of producing both colored and luminescent impressions in a single step. They found that the 5MTN-zinc(II) reagent was as sensitive as DFO in the luminescence mode and considerably more sensitive in the absorption mode (color development). An additional evaluation of this "dual action" reagent, on six paper types and under UK conditions, was reported by Porpiglia et al. (2012). While 5MTN-zinc(II) was found to be an effective fingermark reagent, comparative tests indicated that it did not exceed the performance of other recommended processes (including DFO).

4.4.3 DIAZAFLUORENONE

The compound DFO (Figure 4.18) is an amino acid–sensitive reagent that gives a reaction product that is pale purple in color (lighter than the color obtained with ninhydrin). The advantage of the reagent is that, without any secondary treatment, developed marks show a strong room-temperature luminescence (Grigg et al. 1990; Pounds et al. 1990). Heat is required for the reaction to proceed, but results are obtained within a very short period of time (less than 30 minutes). The chemical reaction involved is believed to be similar to the reaction between ninhydrin and the amino acids present in the fingermark deposit. Grigg and coworkers (1990) trapped and characterized a number of reaction intermediates and were able to detail a possible reaction scheme (Figure 4.18). The final reaction product proposed by this group has since been identified by x-ray crystallography (Wilkinson 2000b).

The development process is simple and rapid: the document is dipped in a solution of DFO, dried, and then heated at 100°C for 20 minutes. As an alternative, Stoilovic (1993) has shown that 20–30 seconds at 160°C or 10 seconds at 180°C (e.g., using an ironing press) produces superior development, with at least twice the fingermark luminescence and less background development. The color of DFO-developed latent fingermarks is faint, and only strong latent fingermarks will develop a good color sufficient for photography in the absorption mode. The absorption maximum is at approximately 560 nm. Detection of DFO-treated marks is much more sensitive in the luminescence mode. Weak marks can often be further enhanced by repeating the DFO process (i.e., retreatment with DFO solution and reheating).

DFO-developed latent marks produce excellent photoluminescence without any posttreatment or cooling. The excitation spectrum is very broad and covers the region from 430 to 580 nm, with maxima at 460, 530, and 560 nm (Figure 4.19a). The best luminescence can be produced

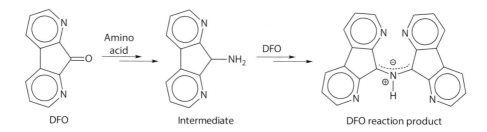

FIGURE 4.18 Reaction between diazafluorenone and an amino acid to produce a luminescent product. (From Grigg, R. et al., *Tetrahedron Lett.*, 31, 7215, 1990; Wilkinson, D., *Forensic Sci. Int.*, 109, 87, 2000b.)

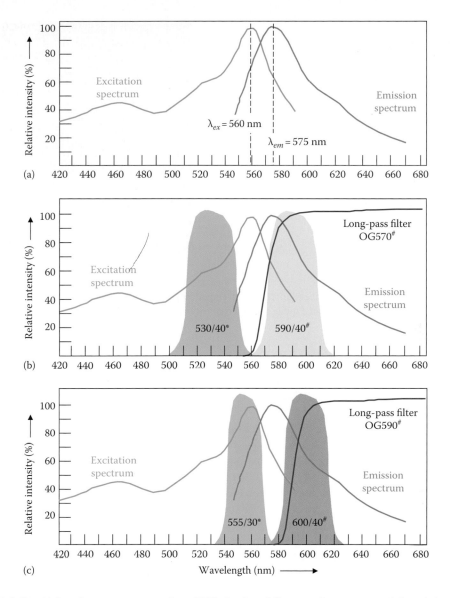

FIGURE 4.19 (a) Luminescence spectra for a DFO-developed fingermark on paper and (b and c) suggested filters for excitation (*) and observation (#) in the luminescence mode.

by excitation between 540 and 570 nm (i.e., the main excitation region). If excitation at the main maximum produces a highly luminescent background, one of the other two excitation bands (530 or 460 nm) can also be used for excitation. The emission band is quite broad and covers the region between 560 and 620 nm (Figure 4.19a). It must be noted that the luminescence is at its maximum immediately after the heating process and then decreases slightly with time due to the absorption of ambient humidity. The luminescence can be restored to its original intensity by reheating the marks. Secondary metal salt treatment has only a minimal effect on the luminescence of DFO-treated marks, although it has been shown that metal complexes are formed (Conn et al. 2001).

Operational trials on casework material have shown that DFO reveals approximately two to three times more latent fingermarks than ninhydrin (McComiskey 1990; Pounds and Allman 1991). However, the effective visualization of developed marks requires use of the luminescence mode

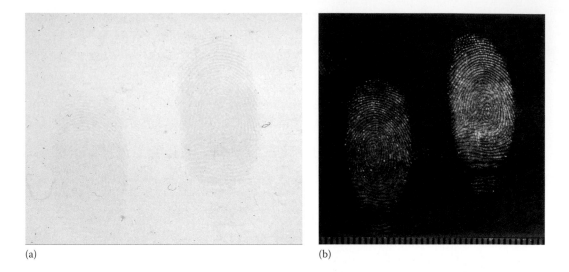

(a)   (b)

FIGURE 4.20   Example of weak diazafluorenone-developed fingermarks on white paper visualized (a) under white light and (b) in the luminescence mode under a forensic light source at 530 nm with a 590 nm bandpass filter on the camera.

with a suitable high-powered light source and an appropriate barrier filter (Figure 4.20). If such conditions cannot be achieved, the advantages of using DFO over ninhydrin may be lost as weak fingermarks will not be detected (Hardwick et al. 1993). Fingermarks developed with DFO can be further treated with ninhydrin.

Hardwick and coworkers (1993) modified the original DFO formulation (Pounds et al. 1990) to obtain a solution that is easier to produce and stable for several months. Their suggested formulation, however, is based on the ozone-depleting solvent CFC-113. Masters and coworkers (1991) proposed the use of a petroleum ether/xylene formulation. Didierjean and colleagues (1998) evaluated a DFO formulation based on HFE-7100 as the carrier solvent to replace CFC-113. Their proposed formulation is reported to be stable at room temperature for several weeks after preparation, with fingermark detection results at least as good as those obtained using a CFC-based solution. A similar formulation was proposed by the UK Police Scientific Research Branch (Home Office 1998). Wilkinson (2000b) confirmed that methanol is an important component of the DFO formulation, as this appears to result in the formation of an unstable hemiketal that is the reactive species. More recently, Merrick and colleagues (2002) evaluated a DFO formulation based on a mixture of HFE-7100 and *trans*-1,2-dichloroethylene. This formulation was found to be a suitable replacement for the previously recommended formulation based on CFC-113. The same research group subsequently reported that, in their view, it is essential that *trans*-1,2-dichloroethylene is used as a cosolvent in the DFO formulation and, if omitted, developed fingermarks will exhibit significantly weaker luminescence (Sears and Hewlett 2003; Sears et al. 2009).

Bratton and Juhala (1995) reported the application of DFO in the dry state for the development of latent marks on papers. The technique does not use any petroleum ether, heptane, or Freon in the working solution. The technique involves the application of DFO from DFO-soaked filter papers and processing with a steam iron filled with a 5% acetic acid solution before heating in a mounting press at 100°C for 10 minutes. The authors reported that the "DFO-dry" procedure provides the same luminescence intensity as conventionally applied DFO, without ink running, damage to documents, or background-induced luminescence due to the DFO solution.

DFO is clearly a more sensitive reagent than ninhydrin for the detection of latent fingermarks on paper. However, there is evidence to suggest that the reaction between DFO and the available amino acids in the fingermark deposit does not go to completion under the conditions typically employed (Wiesner et al. 2001; Mink et al. 2013). For this reason, further development with ninhydrin is still possible after DFO treatment and additional fingermarks may be revealed. This justifies the continued use of ninhydrin in sequence after DFO development.

4.4.4 INDANEDIONE

In 1997, Ramotowski and colleagues from the U.S. Secret Service and the University of Pennsylvania introduced INDs as a new class of amino acid visualizing compounds (Ramotowski et al. 1997; Hauze et al. 1998). Several substituted INDs as well as the unsubstituted IND parent compound (Figure 4.21b) were evaluated for their ability to detect latent fingermarks and glycine spots of varying concentration on paper. Using a steam iron to assist development, most of the INDs evaluated produced a light pink initial color as well as a strongly luminescent reaction product (at room temperature), with zinc salt posttreatment further increasing the luminescence intensity. The observed luminescence was found, in many cases, to be superior to that obtained using DFO. Considerable enhancement of both color and luminescence resulted from the incorporation of zinc salts in the IND formulation, with the only drawback being a reduced shelf life for the formulation employed.

Following from the U.S. study, Almog and coworkers (1999) synthesized and evaluated unsubstituted IND and a number of mono- and dimethoxy-derivatives as fluorogenic reagents for fingermark detection on paper. The authors found that the IND parent compound, with its ease of preparation, good solubility in nonpolar solvents, and high sensitivity relative to DFO, made it a good candidate for use as a routine fingermark reagent. In contrast to the U.S. study, they found that zinc(II) treatment did not consistently enhance the luminescence.

Roux and colleagues (2000) confirmed the significant potential displayed by IND in comparison with DFO and found that the luminescence can be improved by using a heat press for development, rather than an oven, and with the application of a secondary zinc salt treatment. Wiesner and colleagues (2001) processed a large number of actual exhibits (used bank checks) and found that IND developed 46% more identifiable marks than the sequence DFO followed by ninhydrin. However, they observed that no new fingermarks were developed when ninhydrin was applied after IND. In their study, optimal development conditions were found to be 100°C for 20 minutes with 60% RH.

Wilkinson (2000a) conducted spectroscopic studies on IND using nuclear magnetic resonance spectroscopy and mass spectrometry (MS). These studies indicated that when IND is dissolved in methanol, a stable hemiketal is formed similar to that proposed for DFO when it is dissolved in methanol. In contrast to DFO, where reactivity to amino acids appears to be enhanced by hemiketal formation, the reactivity of IND toward amino acids is diminished. Alcohols, particularly methanol, should therefore be avoided when formulating IND as a fingermark reagent (Wilkinson 2000a; Wiesner et al. 2001).

A general pathway for the reaction between IND and amino acids was proposed by Petrovskaia et al. (2001). The suggested mechanism is analogous to that of the ninhydrin reaction, with 2-amino-1-indanone formed as an intermediate that reacts further with excess IND to form a RP-like reaction

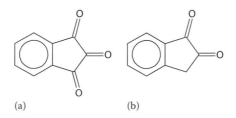

(a)   (b)

FIGURE 4.21 Chemical structures for (a) ninhydrin in its anhydrous form (1,2,3-indanetrione) and (b) 1,2-indanedione.

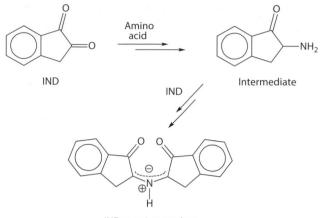

FIGURE 4.22 Reaction between 1,2-indanedione and an amino acid to produce a luminescent product. (From Petrovskaia, O. et al., *J. Org. Chem.*, 66, 7666, 2001; Spindler, X. et al., *Forensic Sci. Int.*, 212, 150, 2011b.)

product (Figure 4.22). While the proposed reaction product was not isolated and characterized, trapping experiments provided indirect evidence for the presumed reaction mechanism. Further support for this pathway, including the structure of the reaction product, has since been provided by Spindler and coworkers (Spindler et al. 2011b).

Merrick and coworkers (2002) reported that, under UK conditions, IND was the least-effective reagent in a comparison with ozone-friendly DFO formulations based on HFC-4310mee and HFE-7100. Gardner and Hewlett (2003) presented an optimized IND formulation in HFE-7100-containing acetic acid and ethyl acetate, with treated articles heated at 100°C for 10 minutes at ambient humidity and stored in the dark before recording in the luminescence mode. Comparisons of the performance of their IND formulation with that of DFO (in CFC-113), on a limited range of paper substrates, confirmed the potential of IND as a fingermark detection reagent. However, they noted that their IND-developed marks exhibited less intense luminescence than those developed using DFO. Conflicting results were reported in an Australian study (Wallace-Kunkel et al. 2007) where a pseudo-operational trial resulted in more fingermarks being developed by IND than with either DFO or ninhydrin, or with the sequence DFO followed by ninhydrin. IND development with a heat press set at 165°C for 10 seconds proved to give the best initial color and the most intense luminescence, with secondary metal salt treatment improving both initial color and luminescence with weak fingermarks.

Further research in Australia demonstrated that the IND reaction with latent fingermarks on porous surfaces is dependent on the RH that the exhibit has been exposed to prior to treatment (Stoilovic et al. 2007). If the RH is above 70%, the IND reaction appears to be relatively good; however, in situations when the RH is below about 50%, the IND reaction is poor, making the reagent far less effective. The influence of zinc(II) on the reaction was investigated via a new combined indanedione–zinc (IND-Zn) reagent prepared by the addition of a small amount of zinc chloride solution to an optimized HFE-based IND formulation. The application of this one-step IND-Zn process developed latent fingermarks that were generally more intense in color and in luminescence compared to the conventional IND reagent (Figure 4.23), and results appeared to be less dependent on RH. In a limited laboratory-based study, IND-Zn significantly outperformed routine DFO processing. This represented a substantial increase in sensitivity to the extent that the optimized IND-Zn reagent was subsequently introduced for routine use within the Australian Federal Police as a replacement for DFO.

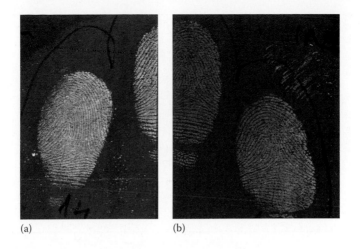

(a)   (b)

FIGURE 4.23 Fingermarks on paper developed with (a) 1,2-indanedione (IND)-Zn and (b) conventional IND, with visualization in the luminescence mode under a forensic light source at 505 nm and with a 550 nm long-pass filter on the camera.

Excellent results can be obtained with IND-Zn-developed marks in the luminescence mode provided that the substrate does not exhibit strong background luminescence under the same observation conditions. The excitation spectrum of treated marks is very broad, covering a region from 490 to 560 nm and with two maxima: one at approximately 515 nm and a main excitation peak at 550 nm (Figure 4.24a; Stoilovic et al. 2007). The emission band is also quite broad, and covers a region from 550 to 620 nm, with a maximum emission at 560 nm and a second peak at around 590–600 nm. Examples of filter combinations that can be used for the luminescence visualization of marks developed with IND-Zn are provided in Figure 4.24. If the substrate exhibits high background luminescence and this interferes with fingermark detection after IND-Zn treatment, then conventional ninhydrin processing can still be applied and this is recommended in such cases.

Spindler and coworkers (2009) undertook spectroscopic studies on the reaction between amino acids and IND, IND-Zn, DFO, and ninhydrin on three types of cellulose-based media: filter paper, copy paper, and cellulose-coated chromatographic plates. The results suggested that incomplete reactions were occurring when amino acid spots were treated using an IND formulation and development conditions typically employed in casework. In contrast, IND-Zn produced remarkably consistent absorption and luminescence spectra, regardless of the amino acid tested. Given that the IND-Zn formulation contains a relatively low concentration of zinc chloride, this suggested that the zinc(II) present in the solution was having a catalytic effect and was directing the formation of the desired reaction product. This was confirmed in a subsequent study where it was determined that zinc(II) ions added to the IND working solution act as a Lewis acid catalyst, stabilizing a key intermediate (Spindler et al. 2011b). Furthermore, studying the reaction on chromatography-grade cellulose indicated that the cellulose in paper substrates plays a major role in facilitating the IND–amino acid reaction by acting as a surface catalyst in the early stages of the reaction and by directing the formation of the luminescent product—a compound referred to as Joullié's Pink, after the pioneering work done by Professor Madeleine Joullié and her research group at the University of Pennsylvania.

Bicknell and Ramotowski (2008) evaluated an IND-Zn formulation based on petroleum ether as a carrier solvent and found that it performed better, both in initial color development and luminescence, than did DFO for both fresh and aged fingermarks on a number of paper substrates. In contrast, a UK laboratory trial compared the performance of a modified IND-Zn formulation with that of DFO and found that DFO developed more high-quality fingermarks overall, across a range of paper types (Sears et al. 2009). However, they reported that IND-Zn may give better results on brown and lower-grade papers, such as newspaper and magazines, where substrate luminescence

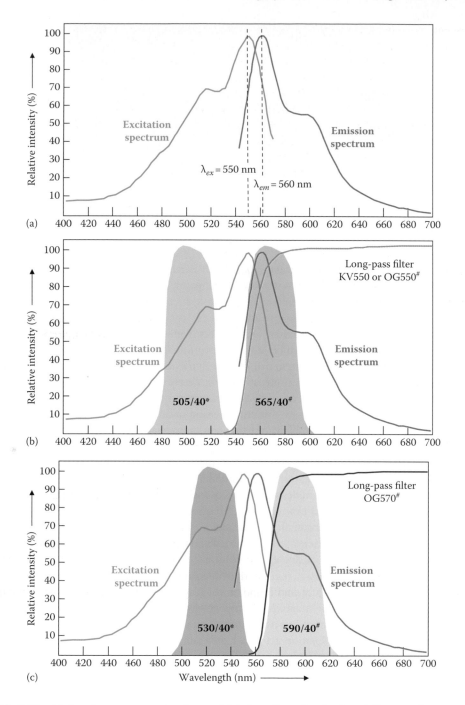

FIGURE 4.24   (a) Luminescence spectra for an 1,2-indanedione-Zn developed fingermark on paper and (b and c) suggested filters for excitation (*) and observation (#) in the luminescence mode.

can interfere with that of DFO-developed fingermarks, resulting in reduced contrast when DFO is employed. A Canadian study published by Lam and Wilkinson (2011) compared split fingermarks, from multiple donors and aged up to 12 weeks, on a variety of substrates to determine whether DFO could be replaced with IND-Zn as a standard development method for porous substrates. It was found that IND-Zn developed more latent fingermarks, which also appeared to be more intensely luminescent than those treated with DFO. In addition, the performance of DFO was reduced in high RH (above 70%), whereas IND-Zn did not appear to be affected by variations in humidity. Because of the superior results achieved with IND-Zn, the Royal Canadian Mounted Police (RCMP) initiated a nationwide field trial with a view to casework implementation of the method.

Patton et al. (2010) proposed a solventless "dry contact" method for the application of IND-Zn. The method is based on contact between the paper sample and reagent-impregnated treatment sheets. For heat-sensitive exhibits (e.g., thermal paper), development can be allowed to proceed at room temperature for over 24–48 hours. For normal paper, accelerated development can be achieved using a heat press at 160°C for 10 seconds. However, compared to the normal solvent-based application of IND-Zn, the dry contact method was found to be less sensitive, developing marks that were less intense in both color and luminescence (Patton et al. 2010; Frick et al. 2013).

4.4.5 OTHER AMINO ACID REAGENTS

Over the last 30 years, the significant research into amino acid reagents for latent fingermark detection has focused mainly on ninhydrin and related compounds (including DFO and IND). More recently, however, novel reagents based on natural products have been investigated. Almog and coworkers (2004) found that genipin (Figure 4.25a), the hydrolytic product of geniposide, which is extracted from gardenia fruit (*Gardenia jasminoides*), showed good potential as a fingermark reagent. Fingermarks developed with genipin exhibited a dark blue coloration and good room-temperature luminescence when illuminated at 590 nm (with maximum emission around 610 nm). The authors proposed that, because the gardenia blue pigment is used as a traditional medication, a food additive, and a natural food and fabric colorant, genipin-based formulations showed potential as safe and less hazardous alternatives to ninhydrin. Further work reported by this research group was directed at determining optimal conditions for fingermark developed (Levinton-Shamuilov et al. 2005). They found that, on brown wrapping paper and on papers with highly luminescent backgrounds, genipin developed more visible and clearer prints than did classical reagents such as ninhydrin or DFO. The strong color and red-shifted luminescence properties of the reaction product were seen as particular advantages. In a subsequent study, genipin was confirmed as a useful *dual fingerprint reagent* (developing fingermarks in a single step that are both colored and luminescent) and a reagent of choice for fingermarks on brown wrapping paper (Almog et al. 2008). While a reaction with amino acids has been demonstrated, the exact mechanism is still unknown.

Lawsone (2-hydroxy-1,4-naphthoquinone; Figure 4.25b), present in the leaves of the henna plant (*Lawsonia inermis*), is presumed to be the compound responsible for the staining properties of henna, which has been used as a hair and skin dye for millennia. Jelly et al. (2008) investigated its use as a potential fingermark reagent and found that it reacts with fingermark deposits on paper to yield purple–brown impressions that are also luminescent under 590 nm excitation (with maximum emission around 640–650 nm). A pathway for the reaction between lawsone and primary amino acids was proposed. The authors subsequently reported the evaluation of a number of substituted

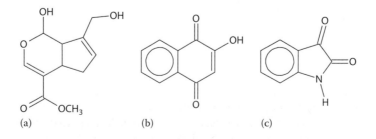

(a)   (b)   (c)

FIGURE 4.25 Chemical structures for (a) genipin, (b) lawsone, and (c) isatin.

naphthoquinones as potential amino acid reagents for developing fingermarks on paper (Jelly et al. 2010). All of the tested compounds yielded purple–brown visible fingermarks, which also exhibited luminescence when illuminated over the range 530–590 nm.

Berdejo et al. (2012) compared the effectiveness of 5MTN, IND, and lawsone with that of ninhydrin and DFO for fingermark development on a range of porous substrates. They reported that only weak luminescence was observed with lawsone-developed fingermarks, much less intense than that achieved using DFO, and only on the white substrates tested. It was concluded that more research was required to investigate the potential of lawsone for this application. Thomas and Farrugia (2013) investigated the ability of genipin and lawsone to enhance blood-contaminated fingermarks on paper. The results indicated that, while genipin showed some potential as a reagent for the enhancement of latent fingermarks, it was not suitable for the enhancement of fingermarks in blood. Lawsone failed to successfully enhance either type of fingermark.

Isatin (1H-indole-2,3-dione; Figure 4.25c) is found in many plants, such as *Isatis tinctoria* (woad), *Calanthe discolor* (a species of orchid), and *Couroupita guianensis* (cannonball tree). The compound is structurally similar to ninhydrin and IND, and it is commercially available. Its potential as a reagent for fingermark detection of paper was investigated by Chan et al. (2010). Fingermarks developed with isatin and posttreated with a zinc chloride solution did not exhibit any coloration but were found to be luminescent using excitation at 505 nm and observation with a 555 nm long-pass barrier filter. However, the results were found to be inferior to those obtained using DFO and IND-Zn.

4.4.6 Physical Developer

PD is a fingermark processing technique for porous surfaces that was developed in the 1970s by the Atomic Weapons Research Establishment (AWRE) under contract to the Police Scientific Development Branch (PSDB), United Kingdom (Hardwick 1981; Goode and Morris 1983). The technique is sensitive to water-insoluble components of the latent fingermark deposit, and therefore PD can be effective even if the surface has been wet. Fingermarks developed by this procedure are visible as dark gray to black images due to the deposition of silver metal along the fingermark ridges (Figure 4.26).

PD, based on a photographic PD, is an aqueous solution containing silver ions, a ferrous/ferric redox (reduction/oxidation) system, citric acid, a cationic surfactant (generally *n*-dodecylamine acetate), and a nonionic surfactant (generally either Synperonic N or Tween 20). The ferrous (Fe^{2+})

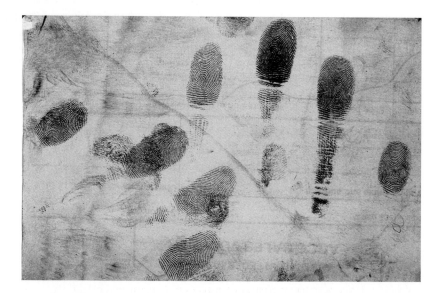

FIGURE 4.26 Fingermarks on white paper developed with physical developer.

ions in solution reduce the silver (Ag⁺) ions to silver metal (Ag⁰), with ferric (Fe³⁺) ions being present to retard the reaction (Figure 4.27). Citric acid is required as a complexing agent and to maintain a low pH.

The action of the cationic surfactant is to inhibit the premature deposition of silver metal by trapping randomly generated silver particles, as they are formed, within positively charged spheres of surfactant molecules known as micelles (Figure 4.28). The micelles repel the positive silver ions in solution (and other micelles), thereby blocking further silver formation (Jonker et al. 1969; Cantú 2001; Cantú and Johnson 2001). The nonionic surfactant serves to further stabilize the developer. The PD solution is therefore a delicate balance of ferrous, ferric, and silver ions stabilized by the presence of citric acid and surfactants.

When a document is placed in the PD reagent, silver slowly deposits from solution. This deposition is generally heavier on areas of surface contamination such as fingermark residue. The process is autocatalytic in that the deposited silver serves as catalytic sites for further silver deposition. Developed marks appear as dark gray images against a light gray background. A conclusive explanation as to why the stabilized PD reagent can selectively develop latent marks on paper has yet to be found, although several theories have been expressed (Cantú 2001; Cantú and Johnson 2001). While a water-insoluble fraction is clearly being targeted, the mechanism is likely to involve a range of compounds rather that one specific class. For example, the proteins present in the eccrine secretions and trapped in an emulsion with sebaceous material at the time of fingermark deposition may play a role. One suggested mechanism is that the negatively charged silver colloids (silver nanoparticles capped with citrate ions) are electrostatically attracted to the proteins in the latent

$$Fe^{2+}_{(aq)} \; + \; Ag^+_{(aq)} \; \rightleftharpoons \; Fe^{3+}_{(aq)} \; + \; Ag^0_{(s)}$$

FIGURE 4.27   The redox (reduction/oxidation) reaction that is the chemical basis of the physical developer process.

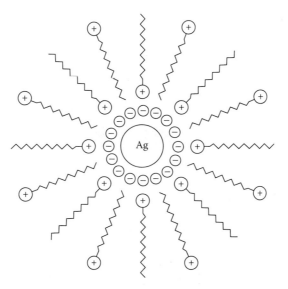

FIGURE 4.28   In the physical developer reagent, cationic surfactant molecules form positively charged micelles, each encapsulating a negatively charged silver colloid (metallic silver nanoparticles surrounded by negatively charged citrate ions). These positively charged micelles stabilize the reagent by repelling nearby silver ions and other micelles. (From Cantú, A.A., *Forensic Sci. Rev.*, 13, 29, 2001; Cantú, A.A. and Johnson, J.L., Silver physical development of latent prints, in *Advances in Fingerprint Technology*, 2nd ed., H. C. Lee and R. E. Gaensslen, Eds., CRC Press, Boca Raton, FL, 2001, pp. 241–274.)

fingermarks, which will be positively charged at low pH (Bécue and Cantú 2012). Once on the fingermark deposit, these silver colloids will be neutralized and will serve as nucleating sites for further silver deposition.

Development time can be anywhere from 10 to 60 minutes, and items must be removed from the solution when good contrast is obtained as overdevelopment cannot be reversed. Some paper substrates that have alkaline binders and fillers such as calcium carbonate react strongly with PD. An acid prewash, typically using a solution of maleic acid, can be used to neutralize alkaline papers and thus improve the PD development of marks (Ramotowski 1996b, 2000; Cantú 2001; Cantú and Johnson 2001).

Contrary to amino acid reagents such as ninhydrin and IND-Zn, the PD reagent is sensitive to components in the latent mark that are not lost if the substrate has been wet (i.e., sebaceous secretions and water-soluble materials trapped within a water-insoluble emulsion). On wet paper or paper that has been wet, PD is one of the only techniques that can permit the satisfactory development of latent fingermarks. The PD process can also be used in sequence after the application of reagents such as DFO, IND-Zn, and ninhydrin if these techniques fail to reveal useful marks on paper surfaces that have not been wet. PD is complementary to amino acid reagents and it can therefore reveal ridge detail not detected by such techniques. In one study, DFO and ninhydrin failed to reveal useful fingermark detail on a range of 55-year-old documents while PD, used in sequence, resulted in the development of a number of useable marks (Home Office 2003). The ability of PD to develop aged fingermarks indicates that the components of the fingermark targeted by this reagent are relatively stable over time. Bradshaw et al. (2008) demonstrated that PD can develop fingermarks on paper substrates that have been subjected to high temperatures (up to 200°C for several hours) and simulated fire conditions. This again demonstrates the stability of the fingermark components targeted by PD.

De Puit and coworkers (2011) recently evaluated the performance of PD when used in sequence after DFO and ninhydrin. The treatment of 62 items of evidence with DFO–ninhydrin resulted in the development of 64 fingermarks. Subsequent processing with PD improved the quality of more than 50% of these marks and five additional fingermarks were developed. In a recent Australian study (Marriott et al. 2014), the sequential processing of 5-year-old university examination papers confirmed that PD could developed fingermarks not detected by the amino acid reagents DFO, IND-Zn, and ninhydrin.

PD-developed marks can, in some cases, be further enhanced by retreatment with the PD reagent and/or treatment with a sodium hypochlorite solution (dilute household bleach). Treatment with bleach solution lightens the background and darkens the mark due to the formation of black silver oxide (Phillips et al. 1990; Cantú 2001; Cantú and Johnson 2001). This can be particularly effective for improving contrast on dark surfaces such as brown paper. The application of radioactive ^{35}S toning has also been explored for the elimination of complex background patterns such as those encountered on paper banknotes (Goode and Morris 1983). This process involves the conversion of the silver metal deposited by the PD reagent into radioactive silver sulfide. Autoradiography is then used to image the radioactive marks. While this toning process can be particularly effective, its use is restricted to specialized laboratories that are authorized to handle radioactive materials. A scanning electron microscope (SEM) can also be used to improve the contrast in PD-developed marks using the backscatter electron image mode (Nolan et al. 1984). This method is, however, limited to small items that can be placed in the SEM sample chamber.

The PD technique presents some major inconveniences: it is delicate and time consuming to prepare (good-quality reagents and clean glassware must be employed), it is relatively expensive, the working solution has a short shelf life (generally less than 2 weeks), and the process is destructive (documents are permanently stained and no further fingermark treatment is generally possible). Despite these reservations, PD is a sensitive technique that can give results where other methods fail or improve the quality of fingermarks already developed.

Commercial PD kits are available and a number of these have been evaluated by Ramotowski (2000). In addition, various modifications to the original PD process have been proposed and evaluated. Wilson and coworkers (2007) studied the acid prewash step, comparing the performance of malic acid and nitric acid solutions for the neutralization of paper substrates prior to PD treatment. Malic acid washes were shown to result in better PD development than nitric acid washes for nearly all the paper types examined. Houlgrave et al. (2011) reported that PD working solutions incorporating Synperonic N had a shelf life ranging from 10 to 15 days, whereas PD working solutions incorporating Tween 20 as the nonionic surfactant had a shelf life of approximately 2½ months. However, it was found that PD working solutions incorporating Tween 20 should be allowed to age for approximately 24–48 hours in order to achieve optimal development of latent fingermarks. Sauzier et al. (2013) confirmed that the substitution of Tween 20 for Synperonic N in the PD working solution gave at least equivalent performance in terms of fingermark development but that the Tween 20–based reagent appeared to be more stable. For the acid prewash step, they found that malic acid gave equivalent fingerprint development but a higher background in comparison to maleic acid.

Application of the PD technique can be problematic in that the performance of the reagent can be unpredictable. To help overcome this difficulty, Kupferschmid and coworkers (2010) proposed the use of a test strip as a quality control check prior to the application of a freshly prepared or stored PD solution. The strips, produced using a modified inkjet printer, contain fields of ascorbic acid at four different loadings and one field of oleic acid. The authors demonstrated good correlation between the quality of fingermark development and the number of fields made visible by the PD reagent on the test strips. An alternative approach reported by Houlgrave and Ramotowski (2011) involved the use of EDTA tetra sodium salt spot tests to validate PD working solutions prior to use.

4.4.7 Lipid Stains

4.4.7.1 Oil Red O

Oil Red O (ORO; Figure 4.29a) is a lipophilic stain that was first proposed by Beaudoin in 2004 as an alternative method for revealing latent fingermarks on porous surfaces that have been wet (Beaudoin 2004). Compared to PD, ORO treatment is simple to apply as a three-step process involving coloration, neutralization, and drying. Developed fingermarks are visible as

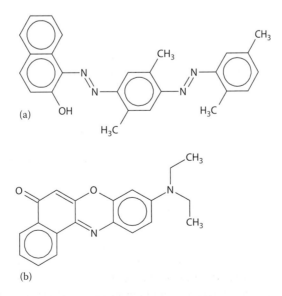

FIGURE 4.29 Chemical structures for the lipophilic stains (a) Oil Red O and (b) nile red.

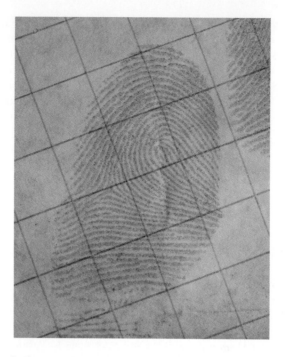

FIGURE 4.30   Example of a fingermark on paper developed with Oil Red O. (Image courtesy of S. Moret.)

red ridges against a pink background (Figure 4.30). In a subsequent study, Rawji and Beaudoin (2006) compared the performance of ORO with that of PD on three types of paper substrates. They reported superior results with ORO that supported the use of this stain for the treatment of porous surfaces that have been wet. The use of ORO in sequence with other detection methods was investigated by Guigui and Beaudoin (2007). For dry paper substrates, they reported successful results with the sequence DFO→ninhydrin→ORO→PD, whereas the sequential use of ORO and PD was recommended for surfaces that had been wet. They concluded that it was not detrimental to include ORO in such sequences and that this may improve overall results. A more detailed study was reported by McMullen and Beaudoin (2013), who assessed the DFO→ninhydrin→ORO sequence on a broader range of paper types. While the performance of the ORO sequential treatment was variable depending on the paper type, with lower contrast observed than with ORO alone, the usefulness of the overall sequence was confirmed, with ORO enhancing some fingermarks already developed by the amino acid reagents and with additional marks being revealed in cases.

Salama and coworkers (2008) tested ORO on a wide range of porous and nonporous substrates, with latent fingermarks aged up to 8 weeks. For the porous substrates, the stain was also tested in sequence with DFO, IND-Zn, ninhydrin, and PD to determine the most appropriate position for ORO in routine fingermark detection sequences. While good results were obtained on nonporous surfaces such as glass and plastic, the long staining times required made the technique impractical. A direct comparison between ORO and PD indicated that ORO tended to outperform PD on relatively fresh fingermarks but that, for marks older than approximately 4 weeks, PD gave superior results. In addition, ORO performance decreased with increased fingermark immersion time in water, whereas water treatment had little effect on PD fingermark quality. The ability to use ORO in sequence after amino acid reagents was confirmed, although hydrocarbon carrier solvents such as pentane, hexane, or petroleum ether need to be avoided as these may dissolve the lipids targeted by the stain. Some alternative ORO formulations tested did not perform as well as the original formulation proposed by Beaudoin (2004). The authors concluded that ORO was not a replacement for PD but that it could be considered for use, prior to PD treatment in the sequence, for latent fingermarks likely to be less than 4 weeks old. Contrasting with this view, Beaudoin (2011) subsequently described the use of ORO on paper exhibits from a 21-year-old cold case. Initial DFO treatment failed to develop any fingermarks, whereas the subsequent application of ORO revealed two useable marks.

Wood and James (2009) investigated a range of fingermark detection methods on surfaces that had been submerged in water for up to 1 week. For the porous surface tested (plain white paper), ORO proved to be an effective detection technique, with results that were superior to those obtained using PD. However, only charged fingermarks with a high sebaceous content were considered in the study.

Frick et al. (2012) proposed a simplified ORO treatment that did not require a neutralization step. They found that the revised ORO formulation produced comparable results to those achieved using the original method. Additionally, both ORO approaches performed similarly to, or better than, PD on charged (highly sebaceous) fingermarks aged for less than 1 week. However, superior results were achieved with PD for both older and uncharged latent fingermarks. The simplified ORO method was subsequently tested in the sequence IND-Zn→ORO→PD and it was confirmed that the inclusion of ORO increased the number of latent marks detected compared to the sequence IND-Zn→PD (Frick et al. 2013). The authors commented that ORO appears to target relatively short-lived "fragile lipids", while PD was sensitive to a more stable and long-lived "robust fraction" made up of water-insoluble substances.

Both PD and ORO are problematic on dark surfaces as successful results rely on a contrast difference, in the absorption mode, between the developed ridges and the background. As discussed previously, the application of a bleach solution after PD treatment can sometimes lighten the surface while darkening the ridges. Another technique that can be considered is to induce luminescence in the background via the application of a luminescent stain such as rhodamine 6G. This has been demonstrated by Beaudoin (2012a) to be effective after ORO treatment. The end result, when viewed in the luminescence mode, is dark ridges against a luminescent background. A similar approach can be employed to enhance PD-developed fingermarks.

4.4.7.2 Nile Red

Nile red (NR; Figure 4.29b) is a lipophilic stain that is strongly luminescent when in a lipid-rich environment. It was first proposed for use as a fingermark detection reagent by Saunders (1993), with the potential that it could serve as a luminescent alternative to PD. An initial evaluation undertaken by researchers at the University of Technology Sydney confirmed that NR could develop latent fingermarks on paper surfaces that have been wet (Deppe et al. 2010). Developed fingermarks were luminescent when excited using a 505 nm excitation band and visualized using a 555 nm bandpass barrier filter.

Further research was directed at optimizing the NR working solution, evaluating its use in sequence after amino acid reagents, and comparing its performance with that of PD on a variety of common paper substrates with both fresh and aged fingermark samples (Braasch et al. 2013). NR was found to produce excellent results on fresh, heavily sebaceous fingermarks, with PD being the better detection method for natural (uncharged) and aged marks. When NR was applied in a sequence before PD, the PD treatment resulted in high background development. When NR was applied after PD, some enhancement of the PD development was observed in some cases. As a result, it was concluded that NR should be applied as the final technique in the detection sequence. In a pseudo-operational trial undertaken on 5-year-old examination booklets, NR applied after PD treatment was able to reveal additional fingermarks. As such, NR appeared to be targeting a different water-insoluble component of the latent fingermarks, which is consistent with observations made regarding the lipid stain ORO. The authors concluded that PD remains the most reliable and sensitive technique for targeting the water-insoluble fraction of latent fingermarks and, therefore, NR cannot be considered as a replacement for this technique. However, the use of NR in sequence after PD may enhance fingermarks that were partially developed or remained undeveloped with PD.

While Braasch and coworkers (2013) demonstrated that NR could be used in sequence after HFE-based IND-Zn and ninhydrin, a subsequent pseudo-operational trial using the full sequence IND-Zn→ninhydrin→PD→NR gave conflicting results (Marriott et al. 2014). NR failed to produce any ridge detail when used at the end of this sequence. While not verified, this may have been the result of a cumulative effect of the solvents and/or heat treatment used earlier in the sequence with the amino acid reagents. The use of NR at the end of a full sequence is, therefore, not currently justified; however, NR may still be useful in sequence after PD for samples that have previously been wet (i.e., where amino acid reagents are not employed). Additional research is required to determine which fraction of the sebaceous deposit is being targeted by lipid stains such as NR compared to the components of the latent fingermark deposit being targeted by PD.

Frick et al. (2014) proposed the use of an aqueous solution of nile blue as a simple and cost-effective method for the detection of fingermarks on a range of porous and nonporous surfaces. On paper, fingermarks treated with the nile blue solution appeared as very pale blue-purple impressions on a blue background when viewed under white light. However, treated marks exhibited strong luminescence that was attributed to residual NR that is present as an impurity, together with NR that may be formed due to the hydrolysis of nile blue. The nile blue solution was also found to develop latent fingermarks deposited on glossy, nonporous surfaces and on the adhesive side of electrical tapes.

Further work by de la Hunty and colleagues (2014) led to a revised NR formulation with the luminescent dye contained in an aqueous microemulsion. The performance of the microemulsion for fingermark detection on porous surfaces was found to be similar to that of the previously published methanolic NR formulation (Braasch et al. 2013) but at a much lower cost and with an extended shelf life. In addition, the microemulsion was found to outperform the aqueous nile blue method for the development of both charged and natural fresh fingermarks, requiring lower exposure times for image recording.

4.4.8 Recommended Detection Sequence

The recommended sequence of techniques for fingermark detection and enhancement on porous surfaces such as paper is displayed in Figure 4.31. This and the other detection sequences in this book should be considered as only a general guide that will give satisfactory results in at least 70% of cases. Different situations and surfaces will necessitate the consideration of modified sequences or the application of other detection methods.

All detection sequences should start with an optical detection step that involves an examination of the surface under different lighting conditions. For example, white light examination may reveal visible fingermarks, while an examination in the luminescence mode may reveal inherently luminescent marks that might go undetected by other techniques (Dalrymple and Almog 2012). HSI methods, if available, can also be applied. Potentially identifiable marks detected at any point in a sequence of examinations should be recorded photographically before proceeding with the next treatment.

If the porous surface (paper, cardboard, etc.) is or *has been* wet, then the water-soluble component of the latent deposit will no longer be available for fingermark detection. For example, any free amino acids will have been washed away or diffused, hence the application of an amino acid reagent such as IND-Zn, DFO, or ninhydrin would serve no purpose. In this case, the preferred treatment, after optical examination, is with PD. An alternative, which might be a consideration for problematic paper substrates that react with PD itself, is single-metal deposition (SMD) as discussed in Section 4.6.3.

Apart from the PD enhancement methods discussed previously, there are few techniques that can be effective after PD treatment. One technique that may be considered at the end of the sequence

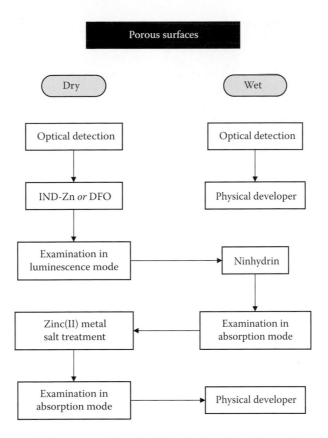

FIGURE 4.31 Recommended sequence of methods for the detection of latent fingermarks on wet and dry porous surfaces (e.g., paper, cardboard). A porous surface that has been wet, even if received dry, should be treated as a wet surface. Depending on the substrate, single-metal deposition may be used as an alternative to physical developer.

is the use of a lipid stain such as NR, which has been shown to be capable of providing additional fingermark detail in some instances (Braasch et al. 2013).

For porous surfaces that have not been wet, optical examination should be followed by the application of amino acid–sensitive reagents, such as DFO followed by ninhydrin or IND-Zn followed by ninhydrin. While both DFO and IND-Zn produce luminescent fingermarks and are generally more sensitive reagents than ninhydrin, ninhydrin may still produce additional ridge detail in some cases. This is particularly so on surfaces where high background luminescence interferes with the visualization of luminescent marks. Various studies have confirmed that ninhydrin should be retained in the sequence as additional fingermarks may be revealed. For example, Pounds and Allman (1991) reported that conventional ninhydrin processing can result in up to 10% more fingermarks than those already detected by DFO treatment. However, the performance of ninhydrin has been shown to be better when used in sequence after DFO than when used after IND-Zn (Sears et al. 2009; Marriott et al. 2014).

While IND-Zn is currently considered to be the single best fingermark detection method for paper substrates, it has been suggested that the sequence DFO→ninhydrin may actually develop more fingermarks than the sequence IND-Zn→ninhydrin. Under UK conditions and on paper substrates sourced in the United Kingdom, Porpiglia and coworkers (2012) found that IND-Zn was the most effective reagent of those studied if a single treatment is employed. However, while the sequence DFO→ninhydrin developed 87% of the test fingermarks in their trials, the sequence IND-Zn→ninhydrin only developed 78%. The authors concluded that the DFO→ninhydrin

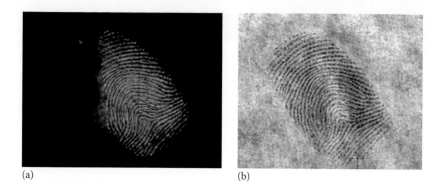

(a)   (b)

FIGURE 4.32 A fingermark on paper that was partially immersed in water, dried, and then developed with 1,2-indanedione (IND)-Zn. (a) The image on the left is in the luminescence mode after IND-Zn treatment (excitation at 505 nm; observation with a 550 nm long-pass filter). (b) The image on the right is after subsequent physical developer (PD) treatment. Note that the area where amino acids have been removed by immersion in water has been fully developed by PD.

sequence was more effective than the alternative sequences investigated. In an Australian study, Marriott and colleagues (2014) conducted a pseudo-operational trial on pages taken from 5-year-old university examination booklets. The sequence IND-Zn→ninhydrin was found to develop 23% more fingermarks than the sequence DFO→ninhydrin. The authors concluded that IND-Zn followed by ninhydrin was the preferred sequence for use on common paper substrates under Australian conditions. Clearly, the choice between IND-Zn and DFO, and between sequences containing these reagents, comes down to studies undertaken under local conditions. Operational laboratories need to perform their own validation studies to determine what individual methods, and what sequences of methods, give the best results on typical casework items. It should be noted, however, that DFO is becoming more expensive and more difficult to source.

With the introduction of DFO and IND-Zn, the secondary metal salt treatment of ninhydrin-developed marks has become of less value as a luminescence enhancement process. The reason for this is that, if DFO or IND-Zn is ineffective on a particular surface due to background luminescence, then luminescence enhancement through metal salt treatment after ninhydrin processing will be equally ineffective. Despite this, the metal salt treatment of ninhydrin-developed marks, such as the application of a zinc(II) solution, may provide additional ridge detail when absorption mode enhancement is required (e.g., when substrate properties interfere with luminescence mode observations).

A full detection sequence for porous surfaces that have not been wet should include PD (or SMD) as the last technique. PD is sensitive to water-insoluble components of latent marks, while reagents such as IND-Zn, DFO, and ninhydrin are sensitive to the amino acid (eccrine, water-soluble) component (Figure 4.32). Since the proportions of these two components in the latent mark are not correlated and vary widely for different donors, PD is an effective complementary reagent that can often develop additional fingermarks or enhance marks already detected using amino acid reagents.

4.5 DETECTION TECHNIQUES FOR NONPOROUS SURFACES

4.5.1 FINGERPRINT POWDERS

The traditional fingermark detection technique for treating smooth nonporous surfaces is the application of a fine powder using a soft brush. The process is a physical one, with powder particles adhering to the moist, sticky, or greasy substances in the latent fingermark deposit. The application of powder is relatively simple and inexpensive, and little experience is necessary to obtain satisfactory results. Marks developed by powdering can also be conveniently lifted using adhesive tape, gel lifters, or even silicone casting material (McGraw 1984). Despite these advantages, powdering is an insensitive detection method and only relatively fresh fingermarks will normally be developed. The reason for this is that, over time, the fingermark deposit dries out and loses its stickiness. Difficulties also arise with certain surfaces that give high backgrounds when treated with a fingerprint powder. Powdering is not recommended for porous surfaces as, generally, only recently deposited marks will be revealed due to the fingermark deposit being quickly absorbed into the substrate. The powder technique for latent fingermark detection has been reviewed by Sodhi and Kaur (2001) and, more recently, by Bandey and coworkers (2012).

Fingerprint powders are generally reserved for crime scene use on fixed surfaces or on objects that cannot be readily transported back to the laboratory. Among the multitude of powders and brushes available, the choice is often made according to experience or personal preference. When the choice of a powder is not clear, it is recommended that different powders be tested on an identical surface before proceeding with the evidential object. Another consideration is the risk of DNA contamination from the reuse of fingerprint powders and brushes, as discussed in Section 4.17.2. For example, a brush contaminated with DNA from one scene could potentially transfer DNA to a surface at a different scene. Consideration should be given to the frequent cleaning of fingerprint brushes or the use of disposable brushes, for example.

Fingerprint powdering has been used as a detection technique since the early 1900s. Over this period, many fingerprint powder formulations have been in use, with each formula generally consisting of a colorant for contrast and a resinous material for good adhesion (Lee and Gaensslen 2001). Metallic oxides, sulfides, and carbonates have commonly been used as colorants, offering a wide range of possible colors for different applications. Lead- and mercury-based formulations were once quite common but are now rarely employed because of their toxicity. In addition to the numerous powder formulations that are available, fingerprint brushes come in various styles that are generally distinguished by the types of fibers used to make them (e.g., synthetic fibers, natural fibers, and glass fibers) (Bandey et al. 2012). Powder application via an aerosol spray has also been investigated (Swofford and Kovalchick 2012).

A commonly employed fingerprint powder, recommended by Thomas (1973, 1975, 1978), is metallic aluminum powder (also known as "argentoratum"). James and coworkers (1991a) confirmed that this is indeed the most effective powder for fingermark detection. Aluminum flake, employed as a metallic paint pigment, is manufactured by passing aluminum grit through a ball mill, where stearic acid is added as a milling agent. The final product is composed of flat, platelike particles of aluminum (5–10 µm long and about 0.5 µm thick) containing from 3% to 5% w/w stearic acid. The research group was able to produce an even more efficient fingerprint powder by increasing the stearic acid content to about 10% w/w. It was found that this modified aluminum powder gave a lower background and thus better contrast in developed fingermarks.

The use of fluorescent powders (which are typically luminescent under UV illumination) has advantages on reflective or multicolored surfaces where contrast may be a problem with conventional powders. A wide range of fluorescent powders is available on the market and, again, the choice generally comes down to experience and personal preference. Background colors and substrate luminescence should be taken into consideration when selecting an appropriate fluorescent powder. Developed marks need to be examined and recorded in the luminescence mode (so, under darkened conditions), using an appropriate light source and barrier filter, prior to lifting as for conventional powders.

Magnetic powders, generally made by mixing coarse iron grit with either aluminum or copper flake powder, are applied using a magnetic wand rather than a conventional brush. The coarse magnetic particles form the "brush," while the fine powder develops the marks. The use of magnetic powders avoids the brushing, and hence potential destruction, of fragile latent fingermarks (James et al. 1991c). However, the technique is difficult to apply on vertical surfaces. James and coworkers (1991b) found that an improved magnetic powder could be produced by passing the iron grit through a ball mill to give iron flakes with diameters in the range 10–25 μm and stearic acid contents of 3% to 5% w/w. These flat, platelike iron particles are more efficient for fingermark development than the iron grit normally employed in commercial magnetic powders (James et al. 1993). Improved magnetic applicators were also produced that incorporate powerful rare-earth magnets rather than conventional permanently magnetized steel rods (James et al. 1992). These applicators, used in association with magnetic flake powders, provide a rapid and efficient means of developing marks over large surface areas. In addition, the magnetic flake attached to the fingermark residue, and in some cases the powder adhering to the support itself, can be completely removed by touching the surface with a clean rare-earth magnetic applicator. In this manner, relatively smooth surfaces can be cleared of virtually all traces of powder after fingermark development. Optimized magnetic flake powders and applicators are now commercially available, with field trials indicating that this new powdering technology can develop marks in some cases where conventional fingerprint powders do not work (Milne 1996; Moorcroft 1996). The production and evaluation of a dark iron magnetic flake powder, for improved contrast on light backgrounds, has also been reported (Nag et al. 2010).

4.5.2 Powder Suspensions

4.5.2.1 Small Particle Reagent

Latent fingermarks on nonporous surfaces may be made visible by treatment with a suspension of an insoluble powder in a weak detergent solution. The powder suspension is commonly referred to as SPR, and the technique is essentially a wet powdering method. SPR is sensitive to the sebaceous (water-insoluble) components of the latent fingermark and it is effective on surfaces that are wet, a condition that excludes the use of conventional powders or reagents sensitive to the eccrine (water-soluble) material in the deposit. Treatment with the suspension is by immersion or spray application (using a handheld garden spray, for example); the sample is then rinsed with water to remove excess powder from the substrate (Figure 4.33).

Conventional SPR is a suspension of dark gray molybdenum disulfide particles (Goode and Morris 1983), the fine crystalline structure of which is critical for effective fingermark development. In 1989, Haque and coworkers (1989) proposed the use of a suspension of iron oxide powder in place of molybdenum disulfide. Franck and Almog (1993) proposed a white SPR formulation based on zinc carbonate powder. This formulation is designed for use on dark surfaces. As with molybdenum disulfide, it was found that the dimensions of the zinc carbonate particles had a significant influence on the quality of the fingermark development. White SPR formulations based on the use of white titanium dioxide powder have also been reported (Wade 2002;

FIGURE 4.33 A fingermark on wet glass developed using small particle reagent.

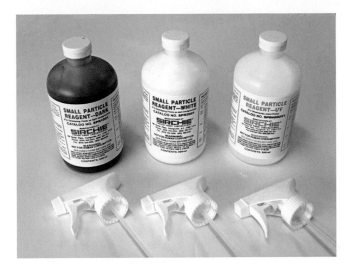

FIGURE 4.34 Commercially available dark, white, and fluorescent small particle reagents.

Williams and Elliott 2005). Springer and Bergman (1995) described the preparation of a fluorescent SPR via the addition of an ethanol solution of Basic Yellow 40 (BY40) to the standard SPR stock suspension. Marks developed with BY40 SPR can be visualized in the luminescence mode with excitation at 450 nm and observation using a 550 nm cutoff barrier filter. A number of fluorescent SPR formulations, based on mixtures of zinc carbonate powder and luminescent dyes such as rhodamine 6G and eosin Y, have been proposed by Indian researchers (Jasuja et al. 2008; Sodhi and Kaur 2010). While powder suspensions are relatively easy to prepare, commercial SPR kits are available that offer preprepared dark, white, and fluorescent SPR suspensions that can be readily applied using hand sprays (Figure 4.34).

The effectiveness of SPR for the detection of fingermarks on wet nonporous surfaces has been well documented. Kerr et al. (2008) evaluated a number of methods for the detection of fingermarks on glass after exposure to water, with the best results achieved using powder-based techniques such as SPR. Studies undertaken in Israel have confirmed that SPR can even be effective for the development of latent marks on glass surfaces that have been washed with flammable liquids, such as those employed in incendiary bottles (Elkayam et al. 1996; Shelef et al. 1996).

4.5.2.2 Thick Powder Suspensions

The application of thick powder suspensions as a fingermark detection method was first proposed in Japan in the early 1990s for use on the sticky side of adhesive tape (Yamashita et al. 1993; Burns 1994). Referred to as "sticky-side powder," the original formulation was a thick suspension of black fingerprint powder in a detergent solution, having a consistency of thin paint. Such suspensions need to be applied with a brush as they are typically too viscous for spray application (unlike SPR, which is a much more dilute powder suspension). After the suspension is "painted" onto the surface, it is left in place for a short period of time (typically 10–30 seconds) then rinsed off with water. If development is inadequate, the treatment can be repeated. It was found to be an extremely simple but effective technique for the detection of latent fingermarks on adhesive surfaces (Figure 4.35). It was subsequently determined that such suspensions can be effective for fingermark development on a range of nonadhesive nonporous surfaces (Figure 4.36).

Wade (2002) experimented with white powder suspensions (WPSs) based on titanium dioxide (TiO_2) and found that they were able to develop latent marks on both sides of dark adhesive tape. In 2005, the Home Office indicated that several UK forces had reported success with wet powder suspensions and that this technique could be considered for use as a final treatment if all

FIGURE 4.35   Fingermarks on the adhesive side of packaging tape developed with black "sticky-side powder" (thick powder suspension).

FIGURE 4.36   One-year-old fingermarks on black plastic developed using a commercial white powder suspension.

other recognized techniques had failed (Home Office 2005b). Nic Daéid and coworkers (2008a) tested three WPSs on fingermarks that had been deposited on several nonporous surfaces that were subsequently submerged in water and then dried. All three powder suspensions were successful in developing the test impressions. In subsequent work, Nic Daéid et al. (2008b) compared the performance of VMD (see Section 4.5.4) with that of a commercial WPS for the recovery of fingermarks from dark nonporous substrates that had been wet. The powder suspension method proved to be rapid, effective, simple to use, and inexpensive, with similar performance to that of VMD across the nonporous surfaces tested. Wetwop, a commercial powder suspension, was reported by Pleckaitis (2007) to be effective for the development of ridge detail on the interior of latex and nitrile gloves.

The UK Centre for Applied Science and Technology (CAST) undertook a pseudo-operational trial in 2009 to investigate the development of latent fingermarks on flexible plastic packaging films using VMD, CA fuming followed by staining with BY40, and two powder suspensions—a commercial titanium dioxide–based WPS and an iron oxide–based BPS (Downham et al. 2012). In contrast to results from a similar trial conducted in 1986, it was determined that the effectiveness of VMD had diminished relative to that of CA fuming plus BY40 treatment. In addition, the effectiveness of the powder suspensions was found to be similar to that of the CA method. The diminished performance of VMD was thought to be due to changes in the chemistry of the plastic materials on the market since the 1986 trial.

Bleay et al. (2006) reported on the work carried out by the UK Home Office Scientific Development Branch (HOSDB; now CAST) to identify best practice for the development of latent fingermarks on articles retrieved from fire scenes. It was determined that the most effective development process for general use on nonporous surfaces at such a scene is powder suspension (both black and white variants), which can be applied both at the scene and in the laboratory. Bradshaw and coworkers (2008) assessed a number of fingermark detection methods on substrates exposed to high temperatures and articles subjected to simulated fire environments. Under the test conditions reported, BPS was found to be particularly effective for the development of marks on nonporous surfaces. The ability of powder suspensions to recover fingermarks on nonporous surfaces exposed to elevated temperatures up to 200°C was further demonstrated in a study reported by Dominick et al. (2011). An advantage of the powder suspension method was found to be that the detergent within the formulation can assist in the removal of soot from fire-exposed articles.

Gaskell et al. (2013b) investigated fingermark enhancement methods on grease-contaminated, nonporous substrates. It was determined that powder suspensions (BPS and WPS) were particularly effective when latent marks and contaminants were present in combination on a surface. The recommended detection sequence was to use BPS or WPS (depending on the color of the substrate) after initial optical examination. Powder suspensions target latent marks, leaving greasy contaminants largely unaffected. Stains that target the contaminant itself can then be applied at the end of the sequence. The good results achieved with powder suspensions were in agreement with a previous study of fingermarks on vehicles that had been oversprayed with WD-40®, which concluded that BPS was the most effective detection method of those assessed (Home Office 2006b).

4.5.3 CYANOACRYLATE FUMING

4.5.3.1 Conventional Cyanoacrylate Fuming

CA esters (generally the ethyl ester) are colorless, monomeric liquids sold commercially as rapid, high-strength glues (e.g., Superglue). CA liquid forms a vapor that reacts with certain eccrine and sebaceous components in a latent fingermark. The vapor selectively polymerizes on the fingermark ridges to form a hard, white polymer known as polycyanoacrylate (Figure 4.37). The discovery of CA fuming as a development method for latent fingermarks apparently occurred almost simultaneously in Japan, the United Kingdom, and North America in the late 1970s (Lee and Gaensslen 1984; Wood 1991). Since then, CA fuming has become the most widely used process for the laboratory development of fingermarks on nonporous surfaces such as glass, plastic, and metal (Figure 4.38).

The polymerization of CA monomers is considered to proceed via an anionic polymerization mechanism with an anionic initiator such as OH^-. However, neutral nucleophiles such as water or amines can also initiate polymerization (Czekanski et al. 2006). Why the polycyanoacrylate selectively forms along the ridge pattern rather than on the substrate material is not well understood. Clearly, there are components of the fingermark deposit that are responsible for initiating polymerization. The accumulation of CA monomer in the sebaceous component of the fingermark deposit, combined with the presence of moisture, may be an important factor. Wargacki and colleagues (2007) proposed that the primary initiator was most likely a carboxylate group, while Velthuis and de Puit (2011) found that amines in amino acids and the alcohol moiety in lactic acid have greater initiating properties for the polymerization of CA than the acid functionality. Czekanski et al. (2006) reported that neither inorganic salts nor amino acids alone could lead to

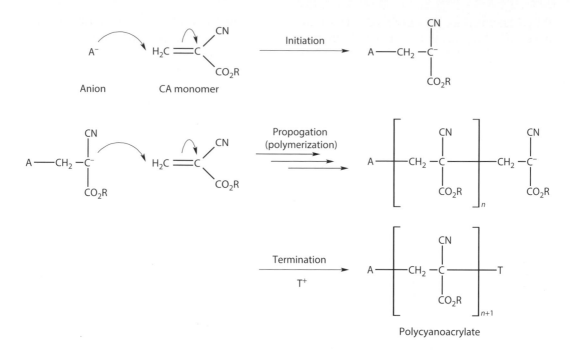

FIGURE 4.37   Cyanoacrylate polymerization reaction that results in the formation of a hard white polymer known as polycyanoacrylate.

FIGURE 4.38   Fingermarks on black plastic developed by cyanoacrylate fuming.

selective polymerization. Other studies on CA esters have indicated that polymerization is possible via a classic anionic mechanism—initiated by simple anions (Figure 4.37)—or by covalent organic bases, in which case the growing species are zwitterions (Donnelly et al. 1977). There is a general view that traces of moisture in the latent fingermark play a major role in the selective polymerization of CA along the fingermark ridges (Burns et al. 1998; Edwards and Day 2006). In a photoelectron spectroscopic study reported by Zhang and coworkers (Zhang et al. 2013), it was suggested that the relatively high electron affinity of the ethyl CA monomer was responsible for the fact that its anionic polymerization mechanism can proceed even with weak nucleophiles such as water.

Lewis et al. (2001) found that latent fingermarks stored under low-humidity conditions (~7% RH) for four hours or more did not develop when exposed to CA vapor. The authors proposed that the initiators of CA polymerization are water-soluble components, which are less effective when moisture is lost from the deposit. It has been suggested that, at a RH of around 80%, sodium chloride crystals in the latent fingermark—originating from the dehydration of eccrine material—will absorb atmospheric moisture to initiate the CA polymerization process (Kent and Winfield 1996; Bandey and Kent 2003). There are several possible mechanisms to explain the observed polymer growth, and there are many nucleophilic substances in the deposit, including water, which may play a role in the reaction.

Numerous methods for CA treatment have been proposed, and many commercial units are now available on the market. Simple homemade systems can be constructed at minimal cost. These generally consist of a chamber, such as a glass aquarium, that can be sealed up to contain the CA vapor generated by means of a suitable heat source (e.g., temperature-controlled hot plate). Items to be treated are suspended or placed in the chamber, and a small quantity of liquid CA is heated to produce sufficient vapor. A container of water may also be placed in the tank to ensure sufficient humidity for the development process, as low humidity tends to produce weakly developed marks that show poor contrast. Excess heat should be avoided and fingermark development regularly inspected to avoid overdevelopment.

Commercial CA fuming chambers, while more expensive than homemade systems, have a number of advantages and are recommended for routine application of the technique. Such advantages include better temperature control, more efficient vapor circulation leading to more even fingermark development, accurate control of fuming times, and automated removal of the CA vapor when the process is finished, which is important from a health and safety perspective (Figure 4.39). Some systems also have automatic humidity control (e.g., set at 80% RH) to optimize development, which is particularly important when the ambient humidity is low. Regardless of the fuming system employed, it is good practice to place a control fingermark, on a glass microscope slide for example,

FIGURE 4.39   One of the authors (MS) using a commercial cyanoacrylate fuming chamber.

next to the objects to be treated. When the control mark is sufficiently developed, the objects should be removed from the chamber and checked for ridge detail. The treatment can be repeated if insufficient fingermark development is observed.

In a UK study, Paine and coworkers (2011) investigated the influence of RH on the effectiveness of the CA fuming process and on the polymer morphology in developed marks. It was found that, for optimum fingermark development, an RH of approximately 80% was required in the CA chamber. At these humidity levels, the CA fuming of natural fingermarks results in a characteristic noodle-like polymer structure. This structure is thought to scatter more light—giving whiter, more visible development—and retain colored or luminescent stains better than the structures formed at other humidity levels. At low humidity levels (e.g., 60%), a flat, film-like structure is observed. Highly sebaceous marks, on the other hand, are less affected by changes in RH and tend to produce a different polymer morphology, resembling a flat film containing fine nodular structures. Clearly, then, the nature of the polymer formed along the fingermark ridges depends on both RH during the fuming process and the chemical composition of the deposit. Excessive humidity needs to be avoided as there is a risk of overdevelopment and polymer deposition on the background, reducing overall contrast between the fingermark ridges and the substrate.

Given the likely role that moisture plays in the polymerization of CA, the inability to develop some fingermarks by CA fuming can be attributed to dehydration of the deposit, which occurs naturally as a fingermark ages over time. Wargacki and coworkers (2007, 2008) reported that water itself was not the primary initiator of the CA polymerization process but that CA development was hindered when moisture was lost from the deposit. Various pretreatment strategies have been proposed for the rejuvenation of aged latent fingermarks so that they are more responsive to CA treatment. Examples include exposing the fingermarks to water, acetic acid, ammonia, or methylamine vapor prior to the application of the CA fuming method (see, for example, Montgomery et al. 2012). Such strategies are designed to rehumidify the latent marks and, in the case of acetic acid, ammonia, and methylamine, increase the concentration of initiators available to promote polymer deposition.

Steele and coworkers (2012) reported that increased polymer formation and improved overall fingermark development could be achieved by precooling items prior to CA treatment. Similarly, Dadmun (2014) found that lowering the temperature of the object carrying the latent fingermarks to ~8°C–10°C increases the amount of polycyanoacrylate that is formed on the deposit during the fuming process and that this was particularly effective for aged impressions. The author argued that the lower temperature improved the efficiency of the CA polymerization initiators that remain in the fingermark residue after aging. Further research is clearly required to explore the combined impact of humidity and temperature on the molecular interactions that are occurring during the CA development process.

CA vapor is classified as an eye and respiratory tract irritant, therefore exposure to the vapor should be minimized (Hughes 1993). Mock (1985) indicated that, if the glue is heated to temperatures above approximately 220°C, toxic hydrogen cyanide (HCN) gas may be formed. Therefore, whenever heat is used to generate CA vapor, care must be taken to ensure that elevated temperatures of this magnitude are avoided. CAs are also reported to have a flashpoint just over 90°C, which means that CA vapors could ignite under certain circumstances (Mock 1985). Masters (2002) indicated that cyanide gas is formed when cured (polymerized or hardened) CA is heated above 205°C. A recent Australian study (Fung et al. 2011) confirmed that detectable and quantifiable amounts of HCN were generated from the thermal decomposition of CA monomer and polymer at temperatures as low as 200°C. Despite the concerns raised by these results, it was determined that the HCN concentration likely to be generated within a commercial CA fuming cabinet, when operated according to manufacturer's instructions, will be well below occupational safety exposure limits. This may not necessarily be the case for "improvised" CA fuming systems and it is recommended that the heating of CA monomer or polymer is limited to temperatures below 240°C to minimize the risk of significant quantities of HCN being generated.

4.5.3.2 Portable Fuming Systems

Portable CA fuming wands, first proposed by Weaver and Clary (1993), have been investigated for field use and a number of commercial systems are now available. The fuming wand is based on a butane torch on which is placed a commercially manufactured cartridge containing CA polymer. When ignited, the torch heats the cartridge and CA vapor is rapidly released via a thermal depolymerization mechanism. The fumes are directed onto the item to be processed until developed marks become visible to the naked eye. A comparison of this system with conventional chamber development indicated that the portable wand gives inferior results and is generally not recommended (Froude 1996). Fingermark development with a portable wand can be difficult to control, typically leading to uneven development or overdeveloped marks. In addition, the butane torch generates high temperatures in the CA cartridges (measured in our experiments to be up to 350°C), which would be expected to result in the production of HCN as indicated earlier.

Another portable fuming device known as a Handy Fumer™ was evaluated by Geller and coworkers (1998) and was found to give results comparable with those obtained using a conventional fuming cabinet. Tissier et al. (1999) described a portable case that can be used to generate CA vapor that, in turn, is fed through a hose into a motor vehicle that requires fingermark processing. The vapor generator can also be used to provide CA fumes for plastic tents built around items requiring treatment. More recently, commercial CA generators have become available that can provide a safer, more reliable means of applying the CA fuming process in the field. An example is the SUPERfume® portable CA fuming kit marketed by the UK company Foster and Freeman (www.fosterfreeman.com, last accessed February 7, 2016).

Bandey and Kent (2003) reported on a comparative study of CA fuming at the crime scene using the SUPERfume®, CA fuming under controlled laboratory conditions, and aluminum fingerprint powder. The trial involved the treatment of approximately 2000 fingermarks deposited on a variety of surfaces using different fingermark donors and ages of fingermarks. The results indicated that the fingerprint powder was at least as effective as the SUPERfume® on all but textured surfaces. On surfaces where CA fuming was effective, the fuming of items in a laboratory chamber gave better development than treatment at the scene using the SUPERfume®. It was therefore recommended that portable items are removed from the scene and subjected to laboratory examination for optimum results. However, for fixed textured plastic or rubber surfaces, CA fuming at the scene may be the only option that will yield results. A similar study reported by Fieldhouse (2011) suggested that CA fuming with the SUPERfume® was more effective than aluminum powder for the development of fingermarks on textured and smooth plastic surfaces and for marks stored at 37°C. However, aluminum powder was more effective on glass, enamel paint, and varnished wood, and for storage temperatures below 20°C.

4.5.3.3 Vacuum Cyanoacrylate Fuming

A vacuum cyanoacrylate (VCA) fuming technique was first developed by Watkin for the National Research Council of Canada (Watkin and Misner 1990; Campbell 1991b). Development is achieved by placing the evidential objects in a large metal chamber, together with a small quantity of liquid CA glue; then the pressure is reduced to approximately 200 mtorr (i.e., 0.2 torr, compared with standard atmospheric pressure of 760 torr) using a rotary pump. At this pressure, the evaporation of the CA is accelerated and the development time subsequently reduced. The contents of the chamber are kept under reduced pressure, in the presence of CA, for about 20 minutes; then air is admitted and the objects checked for fingermark development.

The VCA method is claimed to give more uniform fingermark development than the traditional CA procedure. In addition, fingermarks developed by the vacuum process tend to show sharper ridge and pore detail (LeRoy 1993; Bentsen et al. 1996). There is also less risk of fingermark overdevelopment, and the operator is not exposed to CA vapor. Under vacuum, CA vapor spreads quickly to all parts of the chamber, hence fingermarks can be developed on surfaces that are not exposed directly to the fumes, such as the inside of sealed plastic bags, making it unnecessary to open and suspend such items. This can be of significant practical benefit when large quantities of plastic wraps (e.g., from drug seizures) require processing. Certain items, such as cans and bottles of soft drink, cannot be treated by vacuum CA fuming, as they may explode when placed under reduced pressure. Also, any object that is wet must be thoroughly dried before being placed in the VCA chamber.

Marks developed by VCA tend to be translucent and only weakly visible to the naked eye. Care must therefore be taken to avoid overlooking weak marks. To obtain good contrast, enhancement of VCA-developed marks with a luminescent stain is generally required. Scanning electron micrographs of marks developed in a conventional heat/humidity CA chamber indicate that the CA polymer formed under these conditions is fibrous in appearance. On the other hand, the polymer formed under vacuum has a smooth, more continuous appearance (Watkin et al. 1994). These observations explain why marks developed by VCA fuming do not appear as white as marks fumed in a conventional CA chamber. Lewis and coworkers (2001) have reported that the formation of a translucent polymer can be attributed to the dehydration of the fingermark deposit under vacuum during processing.

The VCA fuming process does not generally require the heating of the CA glue to achieve adequate fingermark development. However, Grady (1999) reported that CA fuming using heat and vacuum can produce more uniform results, particularly on highly irregular surfaces, with no danger of overdevelopment or background interference. This modification to the VCA procedure also reduces fuming times without compromising the excellent ridge detail that is a characteristic of vacuum development. While early work was undertaken on homemade systems, a range of commercial VCA units is now available from several manufacturers.

There is some debate concerning the perceived benefits of vacuum CA fuming, with some authors claiming that the technique offers no obvious advantage over a humidity-controlled system operating at atmospheric pressure (Kent and Winfield 1996; Kent 2005). Bessman et al. (2005) described the construction of both a humidity-controlled atmospheric-pressure fuming cabinet and a vacuum CA unit. The most common problem observed with the vacuum system was the faintness or translucent quality of the developed marks; however, one of the biggest advantages of vacuum treatment was the lack of background development, which can improve overall contrast after treatment with a luminescent stain. Compared to a normal CA cabinet (i.e., without humidity control), both the humidity and vacuum systems displayed superior performance on most of the substrates tested. For some substrates, the vacuum system gave the best results while, on other substrates, the humidity-controlled cabinet gave better fingermark development. The choice comes down to equipment availability and method validation under local conditions.

4.5.3.4 Enhancement of CA-Developed Marks

Solid CA polymer does not have any significant absorption band from the near UV through the visible to the infrared, but diffusely reflects most wavelengths over this range. The choice of illumination therefore depends on the color of the particular exhibit, i.e., the illumination band should be opposite to the color of the exhibit's surface. This results in light ridges against a dark background. White light and/or the 450 nm band from a forensic light source are recommended for the initial examination of CA-developed fingermarks. No barrier filter or goggles are required for this examination, and quite often it is necessary to use oblique light for the detection of developed marks. On white or multicolored surfaces, the coaxial illumination method can be very effective for searching and photography. In the case of plastic bags, an embroidery hoop can be used to produce a flat surface as required for the application of this technique.

The enhancement of CA-developed marks can also be achieved using a RUVIS. Mid-infrared chemical imaging has also been proposed for the visualization of CA-treated marks, particularly on highly patterned surfaces that are otherwise problematic (Tahtouh et al. 2005, 2007); however, high instrument costs and long analysis times preclude the use of such techniques in routine casework.

After the application of optical methods, the contrast produced by fingermarks developed with CA can be enhanced by the application of a colored or luminescent stain. To obtain the

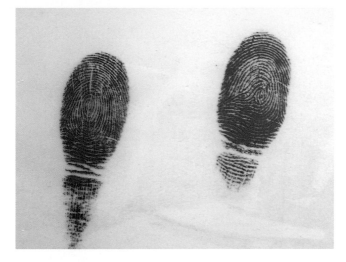

FIGURE 4.40 Fingermarks on white plastic fumed with cyanoacrylate and stained with gentian violet.

best results with these stains, the CA development must be precisely controlled and overexposure rigorously avoided. In addition, to limit the risk of washing CA-developed marks off the surface with the staining solution, the marks should be left overnight to allow the white polymer to harden on the fingermark ridges before application of the stain. The choice of a particular staining technique will depend on the color and luminescence properties of the surface to be treated. If in doubt, tests should be conducted on a similar surface before treatment of the evidential article.

Staining involves treating the CA-developed marks with a stain formulation that contains a colored or luminescent material dissolved in a solvent mixture. The solvents used in the stain solution are critical in that they must soften the CA polymer to allow penetration of the stain itself without damaging the fingermark image. In most cases, the article needs to be rinsed with water after stain application in order to remove excess stain (i.e., destain the background). Colored stains such as gentian violet can be used to enhance CA-developed marks, but their use is generally restricted to lightly colored surfaces (Figure 4.40). The use of luminescent stains is preferred for all but highly luminescent surfaces as the process is more sensitive and can produce results on dark or multi-colored surfaces. However, the use of a luminescent stain requires the use of an appropriate light source for luminescence visualization. The most popular luminescent stains for this application include rhodamine 6G, Ardrox®, and BY40.

Rhodamine 6G is a multipurpose luminescent compound that has a particularly high quantum yield (luminescence efficiency). Luminescence spectra for CA-developed marks stained with rhodamine 6G are represented in Figure 4.41a. The excitation spectrum is relatively broad, with excitation maxima at 490 and 530 nm. The emission spectrum comprises a single band with a maximum at 565 nm. Treated marks can generally be visualized using an excitation in the 450–550 nm range (Figure 4.41b and c), with observation in the 550–600 nm region. Two filter combinations are suggested in Figure 4.41 and, in general, either will produce an excellent result (Figure 4.42). There may be special circumstances where one particular filter combination works better than another (e.g., if there is interference from background luminescence). Marks treated with rhodamine 6G are only weakly luminescent under UV light. Early reports suggesting that rhodamine 6G is carcinogenic have proven to be largely unfounded according to information provided by Masters (1990, 1992). Rhodamine 6G is not a human carcinogen, although it is toxic.

Ardrox®, originally marketed by the Canadian company Ardrox Limited as a fluorescent penetrant, is a highly luminescent oily liquid that can be diluted to give an efficient staining solution

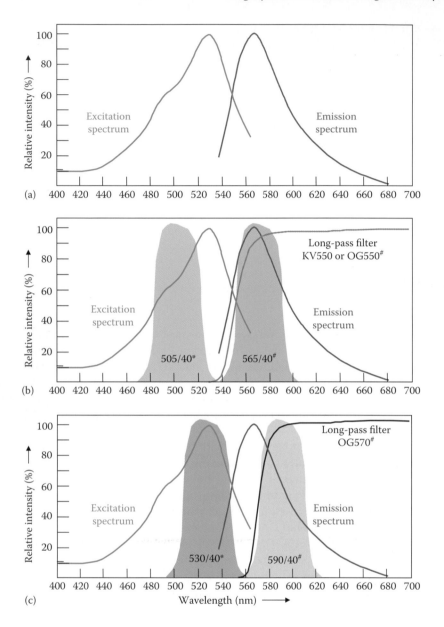

FIGURE 4.41 (a) Luminescence spectra for a cyanoacrylate-developed fingermark stained with rhodamine 6G and (b and c) recommended filter combinations for excitation (*) and observation (#) in the luminescence mode.

for CA-developed marks (Lennard and Margot 1988; McCarthy 1990; Olenik 1992; Gamboe and O'Daniel 1999). Ardrox®-treated marks can be visualized using an excitation in the 250 (UV) to 500 nm range, with observation in the 450–650 nm region. An advantage with Ardrox® is that a simple UV lamp (short or long wavelength) can be used for the detection of treated marks. The UV-excited luminescence is stronger than that observed with rhodamine 6G or BY40.

BY40 is a luminescent dye that has been used as a CA stain in a number of countries including the United Kingdom and Australia (Hardwick et al. 1990; Home Office 1998; Jones et al. 2003a). Luminescence spectra and a recommended filter combination for CA-developed fingermarks stained with BY40 are represented in Figure 4.43. The excitation spectrum is broad, with a maximum at 445 nm. The emission spectrum is relatively narrow, with a maximum at 495 nm.

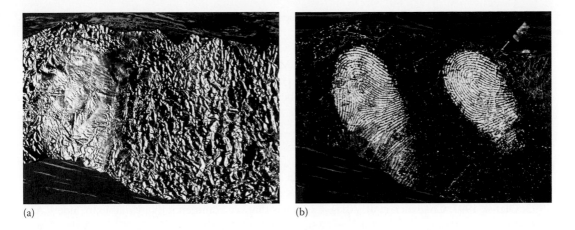

(a)   (b)

FIGURE 4.42 Fingermarks on aluminum foil fumed with cyanoacrylate and visualized (a) under white light and (b) in the luminescence mode after staining with rhodamine 6G (excitation at 505 nm with a 550 nm long-pass filter on the camera).

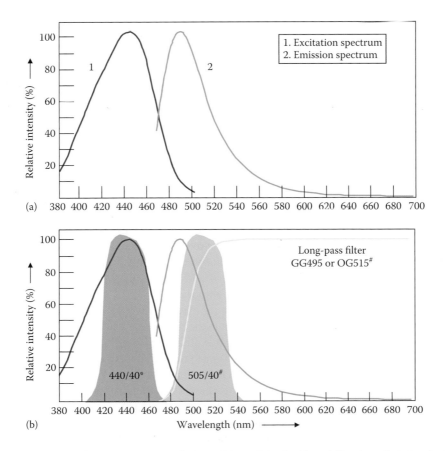

FIGURE 4.43 (a) Luminescence spectra for a cyanoacrylate-developed fingermark stained with Basic Yellow 40 and (b) recommended filter combination for excitation (*) and observation (#) in the luminescence mode.

Many other luminescent compounds have been evaluated as stains for the enhancement of CA-developed marks. Examples include

- Basic red 28 (λ_{ex} = 495 nm, λ_{em} = 585 nm; Mazzella and Lennard 1995)
- Safranine O (λ_{ex} = 520 nm, λ_{em} = 560 nm; Hardwick et al. 1990)
- MBD [7-(p-methoxybenzylamino)-4-nitrobenz-2-oxa-1,3-diazole] (Cummings et al. 1990)
- NR (Day and Bowker 1996)
- Thenoyl europium chelate (λ_{ex} = 350 nm, λ_{em} = 614 nm) (Misner et al. 1993; Wilkinson and Watkin 1993; Lock et al. 1995)

In addition to single-dye formulations, a number of authors have proposed the use of mixed-dye solutions that may have advantages on some surfaces (Cummings et al. 1993; Mazzella and Lennard 1995; Olenik 1997; Chadwick et al. 2011). Examples that are commercially available include RAM (a mixture of rhodamine 6G, Ardrox®, and MBD) and RAY (a mixture of basic red 28, Ardrox®, and BY40). Dye mixtures of this type can generate luminescent marks that have very broad excitation and emission spectra. Other novel approaches for the staining of CA-developed fingermarks have included the use of laser dyes such as Styryl 11 that emit in the NIR (Chadwick et al. 2011) and upconverters (Ma et al. 2011), which are luminescent compounds that are excited at long wavelengths and emit at shorter wavelengths (also referred to as anti-Stokes luminescence). Such approaches can be beneficial on substrates that exhibit high background interference with conventional CA stains.

Stain solutions cannot be applied to some surfaces (e.g., certain semiporous surfaces such as varnished wood) as the substrate itself strongly absorbs the stain and destaining with water is ineffective. In addition, no enhancement is achieved with luminescent stains if the surface itself is highly luminescent. In such cases, the application of a fingermark powders may improve the contrast in CA-developed marks. Black magnetic powder is recommended due to its easy application and the excellent ridge clarity that can be obtained. After powdering, the enhanced marks can be photographed and then lifted, which is an advantage on multicolored or curved surfaces. For dark substrates, the reflection mode at 415 nm may be effective for the recording of marks treated with black magnetic powder. Luminescent powders can be used as an alternative to conventional powders, offering potentially greater sensitivity on some surfaces, as long as the surface itself is not strongly luminescent, but requiring the use of an appropriate light source and barrier filter.

Recent studies have been directed at the development and evaluation of a one-step luminescent CA fuming process to circumvent the separate application of a staining solution. As a first step toward this goal, Takatsu and coworkers (2012) proposed the vapor-phase staining of CA-fumed fingermarks using p-dimethylaminobenzaldehyde. The logical extension to this is to combine the vapor-phase staining with the CA fuming process itself. Commercial CA–dye mixtures are now available that operate in this fashion. Examples include PolyCyano UV (Foster and Freeman; www.fosterfreeman.com, last accessed 7 February 2016) and Lumicyano™ (Crime Scene Technology; www.crimescenetechnology.com, last accessed 7 February 2016). PolyCyano UV is a solid CA polymer/dye mixture that requires heating at 230°C in the fuming chamber to liberate the luminescent dye and CA monomer. Developed fingermarks emit in the blue region when viewed under a UV lamp. On the other hand, Lumicyano™ is a CA monomer/dye mixture that can be used under standard fuming conditions (120°C and 80% RH recommended), with treated marks exhibiting a yellow emission under UV (Figure 4.44). Hahn and Ramotowski (2012) evaluated the PolyCyano UV process and found that it was capable of producing quality fingermarks on a range of nonporous substrates, with results that were comparable to those obtained using the two-step CA fuming/dye staining method. Prete et al. (2013) reported that Lumicyano™ development resulted in equal or better sensitivity and ridge detail than conventional CA fuming across a range of nonporous and semiporous substrates. In the luminescence mode, while good ridge clarity and contrast were observed, Lumicyano™ treatment sometimes resulted in less intense luminescence than that achieved using the two-step process. However, if required, conventional enhancement with a luminescent stain solution can still be carried

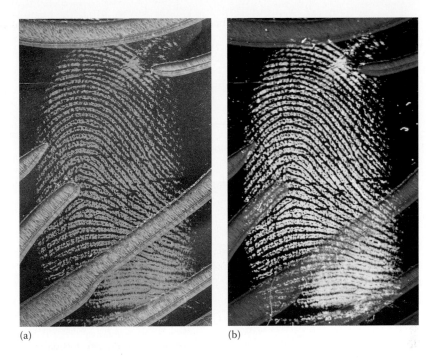

(a)   (b)

FIGURE 4.44 Fingermark on a plastic shopping bag developed with Lumicyano™ (cyanoacrylate-monomer/dye mixture) and visualized (a) under white light and (b) in the luminescence mode under long-wave ultraviolet excitation (300–400 nm). (Images courtesy of S. Moret.)

out after Lumicyano™ fuming. The one-step process is an advantage on certain semiporous or solvent-sensitive substrates where the application of normal CA stains may be problematic.

More recently, Farrugia and coworkers (2014) undertook a pseudo-operational trial on plastic carry bags to compare the performance of Lumicyano™ with the results achieved using conventional CA fuming followed by BY40 staining and using powder suspensions. It was found that a comparable number of fingermarks were detected by each technique; however, additional fingermarks resulted when items treated with Lumicyano™ were sequentially processed with BY40.

Another approach to a one-step luminescent CA fuming process is to synthesize CA derivatives that can be used as fuming agents to generate a luminescent polymer on the fingermark ridges. This avenue has proven to be problematic as the functional groups that promote luminescence are generally quite bulky. Adding such groups to the CA monomer therefore tends to result in reduced volatility, making vapor generation difficult, and reduced reactivity toward the fingermark deposit. In recent studies, this approach has had only limited success (Bentolila et al. 2013; Groeneveld et al. 2014).

4.5.4 Vacuum Metal Deposition

Fingermark contamination on a surface can hinder the deposition of metallic films following metal evaporation under vacuum. This phenomenon has been known for a long time, but it was only in the late 1960s and early 1970s that it was applied to the detection of latent fingermarks (Theys et al. 1968; Kent et al. 1976; Thomas 1978). It is now accepted that VMD is an extremely sensitive and useful technique for fingermark detection on a variety of surfaces, and it can be employed in conjunction with other development methods such as CA fuming.

With the conventional VMD process, gold is evaporated under vacuum to form a very thin layer of metal on the surface under examination (this layer is invisible to the naked eye). A second layer

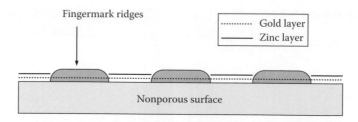

FIGURE 4.45   General principle of fingermark development by vacuum metal deposition.

FIGURE 4.46   Three-year-old fingermarks on a glass microscope slide developed by vacuum metal deposition.

of zinc or cadmium (the latter is rarely used because of its toxicity) is deposited in the same manner. The gold film is uniformly deposited across the surface of the item and penetrates the fingermark deposit. The zinc is deposited preferentially on the exposed gold but does not penetrate the fingermark deposit. The ridges are therefore left transparent, while the background becomes plated with a layer of zinc (Figure 4.45). Excellent fingermark detail can be obtained in this way, with best results generally being obtained on nonporous surfaces such as plastic and glass (Figure 4.46).

Under normal circumstances, VMD treatment produces negative marks, as zinc deposits on the background substrate and not the fingermark ridges themselves. A phenomenon of reverse development, when zinc deposits onto the fingermark ridges and not the background, has been reported by many authors but, until recently, its cause had not been conclusively identified (Kent et al. 1976; Grant et al. 1996; Masters and DeHaan 1996). Jones and coworkers extensively studied the VMD development of latent marks on a range of different polymer substrates (Jones et al. 2001a,b,c; Jones 2002). It was determined that reverse development would only occur on certain polymer types, such as low-density polyethylene (LDPE), and then only under specific VMD conditions. The quality of VMD development was found to depend to a significant extent on both the polymer type and the amount of gold deposited in the first step. The amount of deposited gold therefore needs to be accurately controlled. No one set of VMD conditions will result in good fingermark development in all situations. Pretreatment of items by CA fuming will also affect the quality of VMD development, with CA pretreatment being particularly beneficial for certain polymer types (such as polyethylene terephthalate [PET] and polyvinyl chloride [PVC]). Guidelines have been developed for optimizing the VMD development of latent marks on various polymer substrates (Jones et al. 2001a).

VMD can sometimes reveal fingermark detail when all other techniques have failed. Excellent results have also been obtained using VMD after CA development followed by luminescent staining (Yong 1986; Yong et al. 1986; Taroni et al. 1990; Murphy 1991). Misner (1992), working for the RCMP, compared the relative performance of VMD and VCA fuming for the detection of latent fingermarks on LDPE. Although only a relatively small sample size was employed, the study suggested that VMD is a more sensitive fingermark detection technique, particularly with older marks

(79% success rate for VMD, compared with 62% for VCA treatment). According to Misner, the high capital costs associated with VMD negates its widespread use. CA combined with the use of a luminescent stain is therefore recommended for routine casework, with VMD being reserved for major cases and particular problematic substrates. Batey and coworkers (1988) summarized the VMD technique and provided a number of examples to illustrate how VMD has been extremely useful in several high-profile cases.

Masters and DeHaan (1996) compared VMD and CA fuming for the detection of aged latent marks that had been deposited on glass slides. VMD was found to be more sensitive for the detection of older marks (>24 months old) than CA fuming alone. For relatively fresh latent marks (<2 months old), VMD and CA fuming showed similar sensitivity. The authors reported that CA fuming followed by VMD treatment may yield more identifiable detail than either technique alone, but care must be taken to avoid losing ridge detail already developed. Jones and coworkers (2012) utilized SEM to explore the interaction between the two techniques when VMD is used to enhance CA-developed fingermarks on polyethylene. They observed that CA tended to act principally on the eccrine deposits around the sweat pores. While the subsequent deposition of zinc tended to be by interaction with the CA polymer, areas with limited polymer coating may be enhanced by VMD treatment, resulting in additional ridge detail being revealed.

In a preliminary study, Flynn and coworkers (1999) determined that VMD was one of the few techniques that could reliably detect aged latent marks on Australian polymer banknotes. A more extensive study completed in 2002 confirmed these results, with an optimized fingermark detection sequence being established (Jones 2002; Jones et al. 2003a). Polymer banknotes represent a semiporous surface that does not respond well to conventional fingermark detection techniques. Fingerprint powders or CA fuming alone will generally only detect latent marks on this surface that are less than 1 week old. On the other hand, VMD treatment, applied after CA treatment and before the application of a luminescent stain, has been demonstrated to be capable of developing latent marks that are more than 18 months of age (Figure 4.47).

From 2011, polymer banknotes were introduced in Canada. Canadian researchers subsequently evaluated the relative performance of CA, VMD, and the sequence CA→VMD to develop fingermarks on this substrate (Lam et al. 2014). It was determined that the combination of CA fuming, VMD, and dye staining revealed the most fingermarks with visible ridge detail. In a related study,

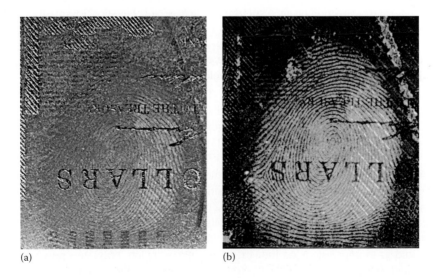

(a)   (b)

FIGURE 4.47 Fingermark on an Australian polymer banknote after cyanoacrylate fuming and vacuum metal deposition treatment: (a) photographed under white light and (b) recorded in the luminescence mode after treatment with Basic Yellow 40.

lighting, photographic and digital enhancement techniques were optimized for the capture of fingermarks on Canadian polymer banknotes developed using the CA → VMD → luminescent stain sequence (Lam 2014).

Suzuki and coworkers (2002) reported that VMD was more sensitive than routine techniques for the development of latent fingermarks on ferromagnetic-coated surfaces (used for train tickets in Japan). They also found that VMD was superior to routine techniques on Styrofoam substrates, while other research found that Multimetal Deposition II (MMD II) was superior to VMD on the same surface type (Jones et al. 2003b). Nic Daéid et al. (2008b) compared VMD and a WPS for the development of latent fingermarks on wetted nonporous dark substrates. The performance of the powder suspension was found to be comparable with VMD across the nonporous surfaces tested. The authors concluded that powder suspension was an effective, straightforward, cost-effective, and rapid method for fingermark detection under these circumstances. If VMD development fails on a particular nonporous surface, then a powder suspension can be used in an attempt to develop any latent fingermarks that may be present.

It has been observed that, in recent years, conventional Au/Zn VMD processing has shown a reduction in performance with respect to fingermark detection on plastic substrates (Gunaratne et al. 2007; Downham et al. 2012). This may be due to the changing nature of the polymer substrates being encountered in operational casework. Manufacturers are now using a wider range of base polymers, in addition to recycled materials and various additives such as antimicrobial treatments and plasticizers (which tend to congregate at the surface of the polymer). In terms of fingermark development, the resulting changes in surface characteristics may have resulted in a drop in sensitivity of the traditional VMD process. Downham and coworkers (2012) found that the effectiveness of VMD development on plastic substrates has diminished relative to that of CA fuming plus luminescent staining, but that VMD may still find additional fingermarks when used in sequence after CA treatment.

Gunaratne and coworkers (2007) compared conventional gold/zinc vacuum metal deposition (Au/Zn VMD) with a new one-step aluminum process (Al VMD). The sensitivity was compared for latent fingermark detection on a variety of common plastic substrates. The results indicated that Al VMD could produce significantly more usable marks than Au/Zn VMD for fresh samples (<48 hours), but not for aged samples (>90 days) where a drop in efficiency was noted for both processes. The authors concluded that Al VMD is an effective alternative to the conventional VMD method for fingermark detection on such surfaces. However, subsequent assessment of Al VMD by the UK CAST suggested that there was no benefit over existing processes (Bleay et al. 2013).

Philipson and Bleay (2007) investigated the deposition of single metals as an alternative to the standard gold and zinc combination. Trials were conducted with copper, silver, gold, indium, and tin. Silver was found to be the most suitable metal, with silver deposition developing extra detail compared to standard gold and zinc deposition. This was particularly the case where gold and zinc deposition resulted in "empty" or "halo" prints, which is where metal deposition has occurred around the fingermark area but with no visible ridge detail. In these situations, the application of silver deposition (Ag VMD) produced ridge detail in the fingermarks.

Yu et al. (2011) reported that direct zinc oxide (ZnO) deposition under vacuum was effective for the development of fresh fingermarks on PET. While the technique was found to be less effective on aged samples, the authors claimed that ZnO deposition produced better results on the PET substrate tested than those obtained using conventional Au/Zn VMD. These claims needs to be further investigated as the study involved only heavily sebaceous fingermarks from one donor.

Fraser and coworkers (2011) investigated the application of Au/Zn VMD to the visualization of fingermarks and grab impressions on four different fabrics: nylon, polyester, polycotton, and cotton. It was found that greater ridge detail could be developed on the smoother, nonporous fabrics such as nylon, whereas, on rougher, porous fabrics such as cotton, only empty impressions, rather than ridge detail, were obtained. Regardless, the technique can reveal touch marks that can then be targeted for DNA recovery, which may be important when examining items of clothing from cases involving assault. In subsequent work, the research group evaluated Ag VMD for the same application (Knighting et al. 2013). They concluded that Ag VMD was a viable process for visualizing fingermarks on certain dark fabrics, such as satin and polyester, with the advantage over Au/Zn VMD being that developed marks are light in color, providing good contrast on dark substrates.

4.5.5 RECOMMENDED DETECTION SEQUENCE

The recommended sequence of techniques for fingermark detection and enhancement on nonporous surfaces is given in Figure 4.48. Where possible, a wet nonporous surface should be allowed to dry at room temperature and then treated as a dry surface. If fingermark detection is required while the surface is still wet, then—after a general examination—SPR or a thick powder suspension should be employed, depending on the nature of the substrate.

A dry nonporous surface can undergo a detailed examination using different optical techniques. A complete range of such methods should be applied, including UV and HSI if available. This is generally followed by CA fuming as the routine laboratory technique for processing nonporous surfaces such as metal, plastic, and glass. However, conventional fingerprint powder may be preferred under some circumstances and powder suspensions may be considered for certain substrates where CA fuming is problematic. If fingerprint powder is employed, then developed marks can be lifted after they have been recorded photographically.

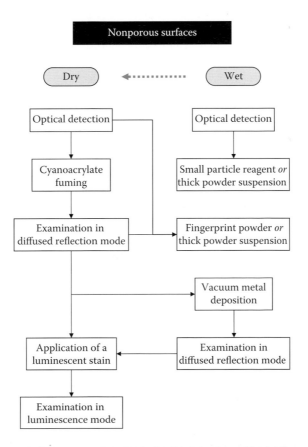

FIGURE 4.48 Recommended sequence of methods for the detection of latent fingermarks on wet and dry nonporous substrates (e.g., plastic, glass, gloss-painted surfaces). Where possible, wet surfaces should be allowed to dry at room temperature before being processed. Note that cyanoacrylate fuming may be less effective if the item has been wet.

The diffused reflection mode (e.g., using episcopic coaxial illumination) can be very effective for the visualization of CA-developed marks. Further enhancement can be achieved using a luminescent stain followed by observation and recording in the luminescence mode. The enhancement of CA-developed marks with a luminescent stain is unsuccessful on some surfaces due to either background luminescence or luminescence quenching. If this is the case, then application of a fingerprint powder may be considered as an alternative. If VMD is available and can be applied to the item under examination, then this can be employed after the CA treatment and before the application of the luminescent stain to eliminate background effects and provide additional fingermark detail.

There are operational advantages to using VMD as an enhancement process for CA-treated items (Jones 2002). Not all laboratories have access to VMD, while CA fuming is a widespread technique. With the sequence proposed in Figure 4.48, all labs can conduct routine CA processing with only certain items being submitted to a laboratory equipped for VMD enhancement. Provided that items are not overdeveloped with CA, VMD processing is not precluded and is, in fact, enhanced in most cases. Jones and coworkers, for example, have demonstrated that the CA preprocessing of some polymer surfaces results in better VMD development (Jones et al. 2001a; Jones 2002). The ability of VMD to develop additional ridge detail when used after CA fuming was confirmed by Jones and coworkers (2012).

4.6 NANOPARTICLE-BASED DETECTION METHODS

Nanotechnology is generally defined as the manipulation of matter that has at least one dimension from 1 to 100 nm, with this matter also referred to as nanoscale materials or nanomaterials. Interest in these materials is primary because they exhibit novel physical, chemical, and electronic properties. There is significant ongoing research into the application of nanomaterials for fingermark detection as a novel approach that promises increased sensitivity and selectivity. This has included the development of nanopowders as an alternative to conventional fingerprint powders, gold nanoparticles that target proteins in the fingermark deposit, functionalized luminescent and nonluminescent nanoparticles, and intrinsically luminescent nanocrystals (quantum dots [QDs]) (Choi et al. 2008; Dilag et al. 2011; Bécue et al. 2012; Hazarika and Russell 2012; Bécue and Cantú 2012).

4.6.1 NANOPOWDERS

Conventional fingerprint powders typically have particles in the range of 1–20 μm in diameter. Nanoparticles, on the other hand, have nanometer-scale dimensions, generally 1–100 nm. Such particles have a far greater surface area-to-volume ratio and, when used as fingerprint powders, can potentially reveal much finer ridge detail. Small, fine particles would be expected to adhere more readily to fingermark deposits than large, course ones.

Choi and coworkers (2006) prepared gold and silver nanopowders using oleylamine as a stabilizer. As the gold nanopowder produced better contrast and was easier to prepare than the silver nanopowder, it was evaluated for fingermark detection on nonporous surfaces in comparison with conventional fingerprint powders (black powder, magnetic powder, aluminum powder, and white powder). The gold nanopowder was found to provide sharp and clear ridge development without background staining. The long alkyl chain stabilizing group was thought to be responsible for the high selectivity observed, as this imparts a lipophilic character to the gold nanoparticles for preferential binding to the sebaceous component of the latent fingermark deposit. In subsequent work, Choi et al. prepared luminescent nanopowders using titanium dioxide nanoparticles and a new perylene diimide dye (Choi et al. 2007), and using nanostructured zinc oxide (Choi et al. 2008). Again, these nanopowders were shown to produce sharp and clear fingermark development, with tertiary-level ridge detail and almost no background development.

Chadwick and coworkers (2012) produced a NIR-luminescent fingerprint powder by coating aluminum oxide nanopowder with a mixture of rhodamine 6G and the NIR laser dye Styryl 11 (referred to as "STaR 11") and mixing this with conventional silver magnetic powder. Compared to the commercial luminescent magnetic powder Blitz Green®, the STaR 11 magnetic powder was found to show advantages on textured surfaces and for older fingermarks. The STaR 11 powder also had the advantage that the luminescence emission could be observed in both the visible and NIR regions, which can be an advantage on certain substrates.

4.6.2 MULTIMETAL DEPOSITION

Multimetal deposition (MMD), developed by Saunders (1989), involves a two-step process, the first being immersion of the item in a colloidal gold solution (pH approximately 2.7). Colloidal gold, consisting of negatively charged gold nanoparticles due to the adsorption of citrate ions, is prepared by treating a solution of tetrachloroauric acid (gold chloride) with sodium citrate and a detergent. The use of colloidal gold is an established technique in biochemistry for the detection of proteins and peptides. The widely accepted theory is that, at low pH, the negatively charged gold nanoparticles are attracted to organic residues that will be positively charged (Bécue and Cantú 2012). Gold subsequently deposits on any fingermark residue on the item being treated. Weak marks will be barely visible at this stage, while stronger marks may be pale salmon pink in color. The second step involves the treatment of fingermarks developed by the colloidal gold process with a modified PD (MPD) solution. The bound colloidal gold provides nucleation sites around which silver precipitates from the MPD solution. This step greatly amplifies the visibility of treated marks that, after this second treatment, can vary in color from light gray to almost black (Figure 4.49).

Many types of surfaces—porous or nonporous, wet or dry—can be treated by this technique (e.g., wet and dry paper, plastic, glass, expanded polystyrene, and both sides of adhesive tape). Fingermarks in blood can also be enhanced by the treatment. Allman and coworkers (1992) found that MMD showed promise in developing marks on nonporous substrates that in the past have proven difficult; for example, masking tape, beer bottle labels, and plastic gloves.

The MMD process was further optimized by Schnetz and Margot to improve its sensitivity and specificity (Schnetz 1999; Schnetz and Margot 2001). The optimized process, known as MMD II, requires the use of silanized glassware and 14 nm colloidal gold particles, whereas the original formulation resulted in 30 nm particles. In addition, a PD based on silver acetate and hydroquinone is preferred over the original formulation based on silver nitrate and a ferrous/ferric redox system. Jones et al. (2003b) confirmed that MMD II produces superior fingermark detail compared to the original MMD formulation and found that it was particularly effective on a number of semiporous

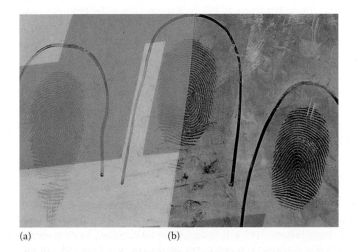

(a)   (b)

FIGURE 4.49 Multimetal deposition development on a plastic bag: (a) after initial colloidal gold treatment and (b) after subsequent enhancement with modified physical developer.

surfaces including latex and nitrile gloves, expanded polystyrene (Styrofoam), and waxed paper. MMD (and MMD II) can therefore produce results on surfaces where more conventional techniques are ineffective. However, MMD suffers from some of the disadvantages of conventional PD: the reagent is delicate and time consuming to prepare and apply, the chemicals required are expensive, and the process can only be used at the end of a detection sequence.

Choi and coworkers (2006) used scanning electron microscopy to investigate the binding of gold nanoparticles to fingermark deposits. They confirmed that, under standard MMD II conditions, the gold nanoparticles preferentially target the fingermark ridges. Variations in surfactant concentration were found to influence background development while pH variations influenced the binding of the gold nanoparticles to the ridges.

Further changes to the MMD method were proposed by Bécue and coworkers (2007) with a reduction in the number of immersion baths and a modification of the surface of the gold nanoparticles using thiolated cyclodextrins. This modification allows for the trapping of dyes to improve contrast, thus negating the need to enhance the gold deposition results using a MPD. In subsequent work, Bécue et al. (2008) investigated the formation of a zinc oxide layer on deposited gold nanoparticles to produce luminescent fingermarks. This two-step process can be an advantage on substrates where background coloration is problematic with conventional MMD.

Fairley and coworkers (2012) compared the performance of different MMD processes for the development of fingermarks on "low-yield" surfaces such as cling film, leatherette (simulated leather), and vinyl shower curtains. Of the formulations tested, MMD II proved to be the most effective. However, it was found that the original MMD method could be improved by reducing the pH of the colloidal gold used in the first step and that this modified MMD was a better overall compromise between practicality and effectiveness. MMD produced encouraging results on the cling film and vinyl polymer-based surfaces while conventional techniques such as VMD and CA fuming gave inferior and inconsistent results. Charlton et al. (2013) explored whether MMD was effective on cling film surfaces that had been exposed to simulated operational conditions including contamination with drugs, immersion in water, and physical distortion. The results indicated that MMD continues to develop fingermarks under such conditions and there are potential benefits in implementing the process more widely.

A novel MMD approach for fingermark detection on paper, proposed by researchers at the Hebrew University of Jerusalem (Jaber et al. 2012; Shenawai et al. 2013), involves functionalizing the gold nanoparticles so that they target the cellulose in the substrate rather than the latent mark itself. Subsequent silver deposition results in high-quality "negative" impressions, with the fingermark acting as a mask. The advantage of this approach is that the results are less dependent on the composition of the fingermark deposit.

The electrostatic mechanism typically used to explain the interaction between colloidal gold and the fingermark deposit has recently been questioned by Moret (2013). Using functionalized silica-based nanoparticles, it was determined that neither the charge of the particles nor the pH of the solution played a major role. Rather, a chemical interaction involving the creation of amide linkages was apparent. The results suggest that covalent bonds of this type are formed between carboxyl groups on the surface of the nanoparticles and amino groups (e.g., protein-based amino groups) present in the fingermark deposit.

4.6.3 SINGLE-METAL DEPOSITION

While MMD can offer good sensitivity for fingermark detection on a range of substrates, it is a relatively complex and time-consuming process to apply. A simpler alternative that offers similar results was proposed by Stauffer and coworkers (2007). Referred to as SMD, the silver enhancement of the deposited gold nanoparticles is replaced by a gold enhancement procedure. This reduces the number of reagents and the number of immersion baths required. Another alternative to MMD, involving a one-step SMD method using glucose-stabilized gold nanoparticles, has been reported by Gao et al. (2009).

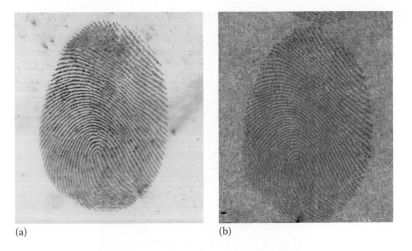

(a)   (b)

FIGURE 4.50   Fingermarks developed using single-metal deposition II: (a) on polypropylene film and (b) on recycled paper. (Images courtesy of S. Moret.)

The original SMD process was further optimized by Durussel and colleagues (2009), who reported the resilience of the method to changes in application parameters. The optimized SMD performed well in comparison with MMD on a range of porous and nonporous surfaces, although both methods can exhibit difficulties on substrates that have a basic pH.

Ongoing research at the University of Lausanne has been directed at improving both MMD and SMD, to make them more robust, more user friendly, and less labor intensive (Bécue et al. 2012, Moret and Bécue 2015). The protocol for reagent preparation has been simplified and efficiency improved by adding aspartic acid, conjointly with sodium citrate, during the colloidal gold synthesis. This modification extends the operational pH range for the colloidal gold treatment, which may improve the ability of both SMD and MMD to achieve results on substrates that tend to increase the pH of the reagent after their immersion. The latest optimization of SMD—referred to as SMD II—is reported to be more efficient than the previous version (SMD I), detecting at least 50% more marks, and more robust with respect to processing porous surfaces (Moret and Bécue 2015) (Figure 4.50). The use of SMD II should be considered on a case-by-case basis, particularly for problematic porous or nonporous substrates where standard techniques are inefficient.

4.6.4   QUANTUM DOTS

QDs are highly luminescent semiconductor nanocrystals with unique optical and electronic properties that are size dependent; excitation and emission characteristics can be tailored by adjustment of the nanocrystal size. The application of QDs for fingermark detection was first proposed by Menzel and coworkers in 2000 (Menzel et al. 2000; Menzel 2001). Since then, several research groups have investigated the potential advantages offered by this approach.

Sametband and coworkers (2007) demonstrated that CdSe/ZnS QDs stabilized with n-alkaneamines in organic solution can be used for the direct visualization of latent fingermarks on wet nonporous surfaces. Wang et al. (2009) prepared CdSe nanoparticles in an aqueous solution, using TGA (mercaptoacetic acid) as a stabilizer, and proposed their use for the development on latent fingermarks on the sticky side of adhesive tape.

CdS/dendrimer nanocomposites have been prepared and used in organic solution for the enhancement of CA-fumed fingermarks (Jin et al. 2008). Dilag et al. (2009) prepared a freeze-dried QD surfactant powder made of CdS/chitosan nanocomposites and demonstrated that this was effective for the development of fresh fingermarks on aluminum foil. In subsequent work, CdS/polymer

FIGURE 4.51 Fingermark in blood on aluminum foil treated with a solution of copper-doped zinc sulfide (ZnS:Cu) quantum dots and visualized in the luminescence mode under ultraviolet excitation (300–400 nm). (Image courtesy of S. Moret.)

nanocomposites were synthesized and evaluated for both the solution-based and powder-based development of latent fingermarks on glass and aluminum foil (Dilag et al. 2013).

Bécue and coworkers (2009) proposed the use of CdTe QDs in aqueous solution for the detection of weak fingermarks in blood on nonporous surfaces. In comparisons with the protein stain acid yellow 7 (AY7), the QD method was equally efficient for enhancing blood marks on glass, polyethylene, and polypropylene surfaces, and it was superior to AY7 on aluminum. The use of CdTe QDs for fingermark detection has also been investigated by a number of other researchers (Cheng et al. 2008; Gao et al. 2011; Yu et al. 2013; Cai et al. 2013).

Given the health and safety concerns related to the use of cadmium-based reagents, Bécue et al. subsequently prepared and evaluated cadmium-free QDs in aqueous solution (Moret et al. 2013). Copper-doped zinc sulfide (ZnS:Cu) QDs were successfully synthesized, characterized in terms of size and optical properties, and optimized for the detection of fingermarks in blood. The ZnS:Cu QDs proved to be better than AY7 and at least as efficient as CdTe QDs on most of the substrates tested, thus offering an effective and safer alternative for routine use (Figure 4.51).

4.6.5 SILICA-BASED NANOCOMPOSITES

Liu and coworkers (2008) explored the use of novel SiO_2 nanocomposites doped with a highly luminescent europium/sensitizer complex. The nanocomposites were used to prepare luminescent magnetic powders that were capable of developing fingermarks on various surfaces, including aluminum foil, glass, and plastic.

A more extensive evaluation of silica-based nanoparticles, rendered luminescent by the addition of rhodamine 6G, was undertaken by Moret (2013). The surface properties of these nanoparticles can be readily modified and this was exploited to study the influence of certain parameters including surface charge, surface functionalization, and pH. It was determined that chemical rather than electrostatic interactions play a major role in the solution-based detection of fingermarks using nanoparticles. As well as being a useful research tool to investigate these interactions, the SiO_2 nanoparticles proved to be effective for fingermark detection on a range of nonporous substrates.

4.6.6 HEALTH AND SAFETY CONCERNS

The commercial application of nanoparticles has increased significantly over recent years, and there are growing concerns regarding possible health hazards associated with their use (Bécue and Cantú 2012). Nanosized materials may interact adversely with biological systems and questions have been raised in relation to potential toxicity, long-term secondary effects, and biodegradability. While there are no conclusive data to indicate that there are significant toxic effects related to nanomaterials, potential health risks cannot be ignored. As for all fingermark detection methods, proper protective equipment is required to reduce any risk associated with both short- and long-term exposure to these materials.

The proposed use of cadmium-based nanoparticles, such as CdSe, CdS, and CdTe QDs, raises significant health and safety concerns given the high toxicity of cadmium. Bécue et al. (2009) suggested that the risks are greatly lowered if such reagents are synthesized and applied in aqueous solution rather than drying them and using them as dusting powders. The use of core/shell QDs, where a ZnS or ZnTe shell surrounds the cadmium-based core, could greatly reduce the toxicity of the resulting QDs. Cadmium-free alternatives are also being explored (Moret et al. 2013). Safer options will need to be developed and evaluated if such approaches are to be adopted for routine use.

4.7 MISCELLANEOUS TECHNIQUES

4.7.1 IODINE–BENZOFLAVONE

Reported by Coulier in 1863, iodine treatment is the oldest suggested method for the development of latent fingermarks (Quinche and Margot 2010). Iodine vapor is absorbed by the lipids (sebaceous material) present in the latent fingermark deposit to produce a brownish image of the mark. It is a reversible physical process rather than a chemical reaction that, in principle, does not exclude the later application of other techniques. While the technique is simple, rapid, and economic, fingermarks developed with iodine are difficult to record because the contrast is generally poor and transitory (due to the reevaporation of iodine) unless the marks are chemically fixed. The technique can be applied to a wide range of porous and nonporous surfaces (such as paper, wood, plastic, and glass), but, due to its limited sensitivity, marks older than 3–5 days are unlikely to be detected. In addition, iodine vapor is toxic and corrosive; prolonged exposure to iodine fumes must be avoided. Because of these limitations, iodine vapor treatment is now rarely used as a routine fingermark detection technique.

Two simple systems can be used for the development of fingermarks using iodine vapor:

1. Small items can be exposed to iodine vapor in an enclosed glass chamber (or similar transparent container). The vapor is provided by a few crystals of iodine placed at the bottom of the chamber (iodine readily sublimes at room temperature), and the exposure time is determined by visual assessment of the fingermark development.
2. To treat specific areas or large immovable surfaces, portable iodine fuming pipes are commercially available or can be easily constructed using standard laboratory equipment. Iodine vapor is generated by gently passing air through a hand-warmed glass pipe containing iodine crystals. The continuous supply of iodine vapor using this system allows rapid fingermark development over relatively large surfaces.

The application of iodine followed by transfer to a silver plate has had limited success for the detection of fresh latent fingermarks on skin and leather, but the results are difficult to reproduce and depend on factors difficult to control (Adcock 1977; Gray 1978; Arndt 1985). To apply the

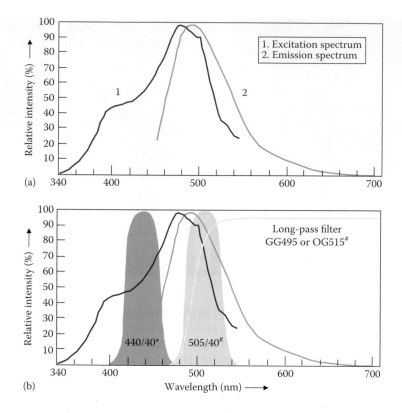

FIGURE 4.54 (a) Luminescence spectra for a dimethylaminocinnamaldehyde-developed fingermark and (b) recommended filter combination for excitation (*) and observation (#).

and humidity. Developed marks are initially visualized under white light and then in the luminescence mode with excitation in the 450–530 nm range and observation using a 550 nm cutoff filter. Fingermarks more than 4 months old have been developed using this procedure. In addition, tests have indicated that DMAC fuming can be effectively employed in sequence with DFO, ninhydrin, and PD. A DMAC dry-transfer process has also been reported as an alternative to the fuming method (Ramotowski 1996a). In a study conducted by Francis (2002), dry-transfer sheets were prepared by treating sheets of clean copy paper in 0.25% w/v DMAC in methanol. The sheets are allowed to air dry and are then sealed in a plastic bag and stored in a refrigerator. Exhibits are treated by placing them between dry-transfer sheets in a cold press for up to 1 hour. Developed marks are left overnight and are then examined in the luminescence mode (Figure 4.54). Excellent casework results have been achieved using this technique on thermal paper (Figure 4.55).

Lee and coworkers (2009) evaluated the DMAC dry-transfer technique and compared its effectiveness to that of other techniques proposed for thermal paper. The study concluded that the DMAC dry-transfer process primarily targets certain amino acids in the fingermark deposit but that these may be less persistent than the constituents normally targeted by reagents such as ninhydrin and DFO; consequently, the effectiveness decreases more rapidly as the fingermarks age.

In more recent research reported by Fritz et al. (2015), a new DMAC formulation is proposed for the luminescence detection of fingermarks on paper. After treatment with the solution, impressions are developed by heating in a heat press or by allowing the reaction to proceed at room temperature for over 2–3 hours. Results were found to be similar to those achieved using IND-Zn, although the latter was found to be more sensitive overall. Spot tests confirmed that the reagent was reacting with amino acids in the fingermark deposit rather than urea.

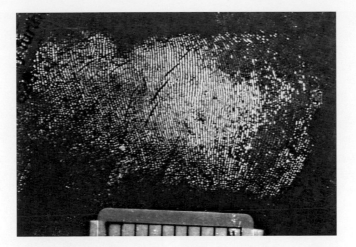

FIGURE 4.55 Casework example showing a palm impression on thermal paper developed using the dimethylaminocinnamaldehyde dry-transfer process and recorded in the luminescence mode (excitation at 440 nm; 495 nm long-pass barrier filter).

4.7.3 RUTHENIUM TETROXIDE

Latent fingermarks exposed to ruthenium tetroxide (RuO_4; RTX) vapor develop as dark gray images due to a reaction with the double bonds present in the unsaturated organic components of the deposit (sebaceous gland secretion). Previous fuming methods called for the potentially hazardous application of heat in order to volatilize the reagent (RuO_4 decomposes explosively at 108°C) (Olsen 1978). More recently, Japanese workers proposed a safe procedure for the generation of RTX vapor (Mashiko et al. 1991). Equal volumes of 0.1% ruthenium(III) chloride hydrate solution and 11.3% ceric ammonium nitrate solution are mixed together at room temperature in a closed container; RTX fumes are generated chemically by the oxidation of ruthenium chloride. Any latent marks that come into contact with these fumes are developed over about 10–20 minutes, depending on the substrate. RTX works well when sebaceous material is present in the latent fingermark, but it is generally ineffective on eccrine secretions. A 4% sodium hypochlorite solution can be used to clear RTX-developed marks.

Small objects can be enclosed in a glass or plastic container and treated with the RTX fumes generated by the mixing of the two solutions. Relatively large surfaces, such as doors, can be fumed using several milliliters of each solution added to a plastic wash bottle. By gently squeezing the wash bottle, the fumes that are produced can be directed from the nozzle toward the surface under investigation. Using either of these methods, marks can be developed on both porous and nonporous surfaces. Mashiko and coworkers (1991) reported good results with the RTX technique on a variety of surfaces including paper, plastic, and human skin. The method is simple and relatively rapid, and no special lighting is required to record developed marks.

Mashiko and Miyamoto (1998) subsequently proposed a modification to the RTX procedure that employs a developing solution made up of RTX dissolved in a HFC solvent (such as tetradecafluorohexane) at a concentration of 0.25% w/v. The result is a deep yellow, transparent, nonflammable reagent that does not dissolve any of the sebaceous components in the fingermark deposit. The fumes from the solution have an ozone-like odor. The solution is sprayed directly onto the surface of interest, and treated latent marks soon appear as brownish-black images (Figure 4.56). Where contrast is insufficient, the reagent can be reapplied. As an alternative to spraying, items can be treated by direct immersion in the solution. Regardless of the application method, RTX must be used with great care, as it is reported to be toxic by inhalation or skin contact (Blackledge 1998).

(a)   (b)

FIGURE 4.56 Ruthenium tetroxide–developed fingermarks on (a) normal paper and (b) thermal paper. (Images courtesy of S. Moret.)

RTX spray was evaluated by Flynn et al. (2004) on surfaces likely to be encountered at the crime scene. It was found to be effective for the development of fresh marks (up to 1 day old) on a range of substrates including wallpaper and painted surfaces. However, powdering was more effective on older marks. Sequencing work showed that RTX treatment was incompatible with powdering and CA fuming (with a rhodamine 6G stain). Due to the expense of the commercial RTX spray, more cost-effective alternatives were investigated. A formulation was developed that gave comparable development to the commercial version but at a reduced cost and with a shelf life of up to 2 months.

4.7.4 SILVER NITRATE

Silver nitrate reacts with the chloride component of the latent fingermark (eccrine secretion) to form light-sensitive silver chloride. Upon exposure to light, silver chloride, which is white in color, is decomposed to silver metal (Figure 4.57), producing a dark brown-to-black image of the fingermark (Figure 4.58). The technique is effective on most paper surfaces and untreated wood. However, loss of fingermark detail tends to be observed with relatively old marks (>1 week) developed with silver nitrate due to the diffusion of chlorides through the substrate. This phenomenon was proposed by Angst (1962) as a method for determining the age of a fingermark on paper. Although simple to apply, the method is destructive, causing a strong background reaction that results in a darkening of the substrate with time. Silver nitrate is also an expensive chemical reagent.

$$NaCl \; + \; AgNO_3 \; \longrightarrow \; AgCl \; + \; NaNO_3$$

$$\downarrow h\nu$$

$$Ag$$

FIGURE 4.57 Silver nitrate reacts with chloride in the fingermark deposit to form silver chloride. In the presence of light ($h\nu$), silver chloride decomposes to silver metal.

FIGURE 4.58   Fingermark on raw wood developed with silver nitrate. (Image courtesy of S. Moret.)

A typical working solution is 2% (w/v) silver nitrate in methanol. The solution may be applied by immersion or with a spray. After treatment, the article is exposed to a UV light source (sunlight, arc lamp, or UV lamp) until the best contrast between the developed fingermarks and the substrate is observed. Developed marks should be photographed immediately and treated items stored in the dark. Price and Stow (1998) have recommended the use of a stopping solution to slow down the background discoloration that occurs on items processed with silver nitrate. The silver nitrate technique can sometimes be effective for improving the contrast in weak ninhydrin-developed fingermarks. This can be particularly effective on raw wood provided that the fingermarks are relatively fresh. Dilute PD can be used to intensify weak silver nitrate–developed marks (Lennard and Margot 1988).

Nic Daéid et al. (2009) considered a number of techniques, including silver nitrate, for the detection of latent fingermarks on untreated plywood surfaces. Of the 13 detection methods evaluated, only four successfully recovered marks that were more than 1 day old: iodine–benzoflavone, ninhydrin, silver nitrate, and PD. On simulated casework samples, the application of PD→bleach resulted in more identifiable fingermarks than either ninhydrin→PD→bleach or silver nitrate→dilute PD.

Schwarz and Hermanowski (2011a) recently confirmed that silver nitrate is capable of developing relatively fresh fingermarks on modern paper substrates. However, the method is not recommended for routine use due to the background discoloration that intensifies on treated items over time.

4.7.5   SUDAN BLACK

Sudan black (solvent black 3) is a fat-soluble dye that was first applied to fingermark detection by Mitsui and coworkers (1980). They demonstrated that a solution of sudan black could recover fingermarks on paper that had been submerged in water for 10 days. The application of sudan black for fingermark detection on both porous and nonporous substrates was further explored by the Home Office Central Research Establishment (Pounds et al. 1982; Pounds and Strachan 1986). Subsequent research by the Home Office PSDB led to the finding that sudan black had potential for developing fingermarks on nonporous surfaces that were contaminated and powdering was not possible (Home Office 1998). The original ethanol-based dye solution was ultimately replaced with a less flammable formulation containing 1-methoxy-2-propanol that was proposed for operational use (Home Office 2005a). While not recommended as a primary treatment for any particular surface, sudan black can be effective on nonporous surfaces contaminated with greasy or sticky substances (as may be encountered on kitchen surfaces, fast food containers, etc.). The solution can be applied by immersion or via a wash bottle, followed by thorough rinsing with water. Developed marks are dark blue to black in color and the staining process can be repeated if necessary.

Cadd and coworkers (2013) compared the relative effectiveness of two formulations of sudan black—the original ethanol-based formulation and one based on 1-methoxy-2-propanol—for the enhancement of natural, sebaceous, and grease-contaminated fingermarks across a range of surfaces. In general, the dye formulation containing 1-methoxy-2-propanol was found to be significantly better on most surfaces for both natural and sebaceous marks, and at least as good as the ethanol-based formulation for contaminated marks. The surfaces tested included ceramic tiles, glass, PVC, laminated wood, and gloss-painted wood.

Garrett and Bleay (2013) studied the fundamental interactions between sebaceous components in fingermarks and the three lipophilic stains sudan black, gentian violet (basic violet 3), and new fuchsin (basic violet 2). It was found that these stains interact with fingermarks in different ways at a microscopic level, with variations observed in terms of the sebaceous components of a fingermark and greasy contaminants that are targeted by each process. There is therefore the potential to use such methods in sequence to maximize the enhancement of marks where sebaceous material and/or greasy contaminants are present. New fuchsin exhibited a stronger luminescence emission in treated marks compared to gentian violet, suggesting that it may be worthy of consideration in future studies.

Various fingermark enhancement processes, including sudan black, may be considered where a greasy contamination is present on a substrate. Gaskell and coworkers (2013b) considered a range of greasy contaminants and undertook an evaluation of several enhancement methods. They found that there are benefits in conducting sequential processing to maximize the recovery of marks from grease-contaminated surface. For example, where latent and contaminated marks may be present in combination on a light-colored nonporous surface, the authors recommended the sequential application of a powder suspension followed by gentian violet and sudan black. For dark nonporous surfaces, the naturally occurring dye curcumin (natural yellow 3) was found to be a suitable replacement for sudan black due to the luminescence produced in treated marks (Gaskell et al. 2013a).

4.8 NOVEL APPROACHES TO FINGERMARK DETECTION

4.8.1 Upconverters

Modern fingermark detection methods rely heavily on luminescence detection, where a luminescent material in the fingermark emits light of a longer wavelength than that of the excitation source. For single-photon processes, where one photon absorbed results in one photon emitted, the emission is at a lower energy (longer wavelength) and the difference in energy between the excitation and emission maxima is referred to as the Stokes shift (Figure 4.59a). All common luminescent substances, including the materials responsible for the substrate luminescence that can sometimes interfere with fingermark visualization, behave in this manner. Anti-Stokes luminescence, however, is where the emitted photons are of higher energy (shorter wavelength) than the excitation radiation (Figure 4.59b). Materials that exhibit this property are commonly referred to as "upconverters" or "upconverting phosphors" (UCPs). The absorption of two (or more) photons is followed by the emission of a single photon of higher energy (Figure 4.60). UCPs are typically submicron-sized, inorganic crystals that are excited with NIR radiation and emit photons in the

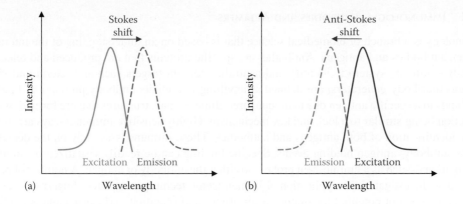

FIGURE 4.59 Schematic representation of (a) Stokes and (b) anti-Stokes luminescence.

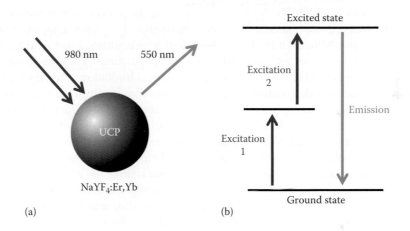

FIGURE 4.60 Example of (a) an upconverting phosphor (NaYF$_4$:Er,Yb) with (b) long-wavelength double-photon excitation resulting in short-wavelength single-photon emission.

visible range at a wavelength that depends on the ion composition of the material. Given that anti-Stokes luminescence is a rare property, the use of UCPs for fingermark detection can potentially result in significant enhancement due to the prospect of recording images in the luminescence mode that are free of background interference.

Ma and coworkers (2011) used sodium yttrium tetrafluoride doped with erbium and ytterbium (NaYF$_4$:Er,Yb), as both a dry powder and a wet powder suspension, to develop latent fingermarks on a number of luminescent and nonluminescent substrates. This commercially available UCP has an excitation maximum at 980 nm, with an emission in the green at approximately 550 nm. The results illustrated, for the first time, the potential of upconverters to develop fingermarks with high contrast on substrates that would otherwise prove difficult. In subsequent work (Ma et al. 2012), the UCP YVO$_4$:Er,Yb (yttrium vanadate doped with ytterbium and erbium) was evaluated for fingermark detection on a range of nonporous and semiporous substrates, including Australian polymer banknotes. Again, promising results were demonstrated when the UCP was applied as either a dry powder or a wet powder suspension.

Drabarek et al. (2012) developed fingermarks on strongly luminescent surfaces via powdering with an upconverting pigment, referred to as UP54, both on its own and mixed with conventional white fingerprint powder (1:1 ratio). The advantages offered by this approach were confirmed, although the powders evaluated lacked the adhesive properties necessary for the effective development of aged fingermarks.

4.8.2 Immunology: Antibodies and Aptamers

Immunology is a branch of biomedical science that is based on an understanding of the interactions between antibodies and antigens. Antibodies are specific proteins that are produced and released by the body's immune system to identify and neutralize foreign targets such as bacteria and viruses. Antigens (*anti*body *gen*erators) are defined as anything that elicits antibody production. Each antibody binds to a specific antigen due to unique three-dimensional structures that are formed, with this interaction being similar to a lock and key mechanism. Highly sensitive immunoassays are available for the identification of both antigens and antibodies. These immunoassays rely on the detection of specific antibody–antigen binding events. Specific binding can be readily visualized by attaching a tag or marker—such as a luminescent probe—to either the antibody or antigen. A number of research groups have investigated the application of immunogenic techniques to latent fingermark detection given the significant potential for improved sensitivity and specificity (Hazarika and Russell 2012; Wood et al. 2013).

The earliest use of immunology for fingermark development was reported by Japanese researchers in 1997 (Ishiyama et al. 1977). A mixed cell agglutination reaction was used to detect the presence of ABH blood group material in latent fingermarks. The general approach was further explored by Pounds and Allman in the United Kingdom who confirmed that both fresh and aged fingermarks deposited by "secretors"—around 80% of the population—could be revealed (Hussain and Pounds 1985; Pounds and Hussain 1987). Despite practical limitations, the very high sensitivity of the antibody approach was demonstrated, with the authors commenting that if antibodies to major fingermark constituents such as triglycerides or wax esters were available, then detection sensitivity might be considerably improved. In subsequent work, Allman and Pounds (1992a) successfully applied antibody-based techniques to the enhancement of fingermarks in blood. While highly luminescent impressions could be obtained, the authors concluded that, due to complex methodology, expense, and impracticality, the method was unlikely to find routine use at that point in time.

More recently, immunogenic techniques have been reinvestigated as an approach for fingermark detection and enhancement. Using an antibody-based approach, drug metabolites within latent fingermarks have been successfully targeted for fingermark detection by Russell and coworkers in the United Kingdom (Leggett et al. 2007; Hazarika et al. 2008, 2009, 2010; Boddis and Russell 2012). The methods established by this research group show great promise both for the visualization of latent fingermarks and for gaining information on the drug use of the donors. However, the targeting of drug metabolites limits the use of this approach as such compounds are not universal in latent fingermark deposits.

Reinholz (2008) targeted the plasma protein albumin, present in eccrine gland secretions, to develop latent fingermarks on porous substrates. An immunoblot procedure was employed, which involves the antibody-based staining of the target protein. The method proved to be effective on a range of paper types, with the development of clear ridge detail for samples aged for up to 130 days.

Drapel et al. (2009) investigated the use of antibodies to visualize latent fingermarks by targeting certain skin proteins. Keratins 1 and 10, cathepsin-D, and dermcidin were all chosen as potential antigenic components due to their various roles in skin regeneration and eccrine perspiration. Latent fingermarks placed on polyvinylidene fluoride (PVDF) membranes and paper substrates were treated with antibodies against each of the selected proteins using a standard immunodetection protocol. Fingermark development was observed on all of the substrates tested; however, the ridge detail was weaker and less sharp on the paper samples, presumably due to partial diffusion of the target compounds.

Spindler and coworkers (2011a) successfully targeted amino acids in the fingermark deposit using anti–amino acid antibodies conjugated to gold nanoparticles. This antibody-based system was found to be particularly effective for the detection of aged and dried fingermarks on nonporous surfaces. As noted by the authors, an immunogenic approach targeting amino acids on nonporous surfaces broadens the potential for detecting fingermarks on substrates that have typically been reserved for nonspecific physical and physicochemical detection techniques.

The simultaneous immunolabeling of multiple components in a single fingermark was demonstrated by van Dam and coworkers (2013). The concept was demonstrated via the selective targeting of two antigens of interest, dermcidin and albumin. The authors concluded that the multiple labeling approach could be used to identify, in a single labeling session, specific components in a fingermark deposit to obtain donor information concerning gender, lifestyle, and drug consumption. In addition, such methods could be used to enhance fingermarks that are poorly developed by conventional techniques.

Aptamers are oligonucleic acid or peptide molecules that bind to specific target compounds due to the formation of complex and stable three-dimensional structures. They are usually created by selecting them from a large random sequence pool. The term "aptamer" is derived from the Latin word "aptus" (meaning to fit) and the Greek word "meros" (meaning part). Aptamers can be considered to be synthetic antibodies; in fact, the affinity and specificity shown by some aptamer–target binding complexes has been found to be higher than that of typical antibody–antigen complexes. Aptamers can be produced against a broad range of target compounds and offer significant advantages over antibodies (Wood et al. 2013). Antibody production requires the use of an animal host, while aptamers are produced by chemical synthesis. As a result, antibodies suffer from batch-to-batch variations while specifically selected aptamers are consistent in performance. Aptamers are now beginning to rival antibodies for both diagnostic and therapeutic applications because of such advantages.

The first-ever use of aptamers for fingermark detection purposes was reported by Wood et al. (2012). In this proof-of-concept work, the authors produced aptamer-based reagents using aptamers selected against lysozyme. The reagents demonstrated high sensitivity and specificity and were able to develop latent fingermarks on a PVDF test substrate that were strongly luminescent and easy to visualize. Research is ongoing to investigate the use of aptamers to target other latent fingermark components and for application on common substrates.

More recently, Li and coworkers (2013) demonstrated the use of cocaine-specific aptamers bound to gold nanoparticles to image latent fingermarks and to detect the presence of cocaine. The aptamer-bound gold nanoparticles therefore act as a probe with dual functionality: fingermark imaging and molecular recognition. The authors concluded that, taking into account the wide availability of aptamer libraries, the strategy could become a generic platform for the detection and identification of a broad range of small molecules and proteins in latent fingermarks.

4.8.3 Mass Spectrometric Imaging

MS is an analytical technique for the separation and detection of ionized molecules and molecular fragments, with a measurement of the mass-to-charge ratio (m/z) of these ions. The ionization of a molecule can be induced by a number of means, including bombardment with a stream of electrons, a stream of small molecules, or with a laser. An ionized molecule—referred to as a molecular ion or parent ion—may remain intact or may fragment into characteristic daughter ions, which may themselves further fragment or react with other daughter ions. Provided that the ionization conditions are kept constant, the fragmentation of a particular molecule (i.e., the nature and relative concentration of parent and daughter ions) will be reproducible. The m/z separation and detection of these ions by MS results in the generation of a mass spectrum that can be used for compound identification.

Conventional MS is a destructive process; however, recent advances have permitted not only the nondestructive MS analysis of fingermarks but the generation of images that represent the distribution of specific chemical species across a fingermark. For example, desorption electrospray ionization (DESI) MS has been used to image fingermarks through the detection of molecular ions associated with both endogenous and exogenous species (Ifa et al. 2008). With DESI, charged solvent droplets are sprayed onto the sample causing the release and ionization of surface analytes, which are subsequently detected by MS. To image a fingermark, a mass spectrum is recorded at each point on the item by scanning (or "rastering") the stream of charged droplets across the surface.

False-color fingermark images with a spatial resolution of 150 µm can be generated by monitoring particular *m/z* ions that are characteristic of the compounds of interest.

Wolstenholme and coworkers (2009) used matrix-assisted laser desorption/ionization MS (MALDI-MS) to image endogenous lipids in fresh and aged fingermarks. The ionization process requires the initial application of a UV-absorbing MALDI matrix, which can be applied as a powder via dusting. The purpose of the matrix is to assist desorption and ionization of the target analytes using a UV laser. In the initial study, fingermark patterns were reconstructed by retrieving the *m/z* values of oleic acid and its degradation products. Importantly, the research group demonstrated that the matrix could be subsequently removed, using a simple washing step, thus allowing the underlying fingermark to be processed using standard detection methods such as conventional fingerprint powder. In subsequent work, the researchers demonstrated that the approach could be used to separate overlapping fingermarks using ion signals that were characteristic of each fingermark and that may be endogenous or exogenous in nature (Bradshaw et al. 2012). The methodology could be applied using either manual inspection of the spectral profiles or the application of multivariate statistical analyses. MALDI-MS profiling and imaging can be used to determine the presence of blood in fingermarks by specifically detecting heme and hemoglobin molecules through their mass-to-charge ratios (Bradshaw et al. 2014). The potential integration of MALDI-MS imaging techniques into current fingermark examination workflows has also been investigated (Bradshaw et al. 2013; Francese et al. 2013).

Secondary ion MS (SIMS) is a technique used to analyze the composition of solid surfaces by directing a focused primary ion beam onto the sample and collecting and analyzing ejected secondary ions. Sisco et al. (2013) demonstrated that SIMS was capable of detecting a number of compounds commonly encountered in latent fingermarks, including both eccrine and sebaceous components, and that chemical imaging using SIMS could provide complementary information to that obtained with conventional fingerprint examination methods. Bailey et al. (2013) demonstrated that SIMS could be used to improve the quality of partially recovered fingermarks. They provided examples of how SIMS imaging was able to offer additional enhancement of fingermarks deposited on aluminum foil, glass, and the handle of a hand grenade compared with conventional development methods. Chemical mapping with SIMS has also been shown to be capable of determining the deposition order of overlapping latent fingermarks and inks on documents (Bright et al. 2012; Attard Montalto et al. 2013).

Bailey and coworkers (2012) undertook an extensive investigation of a range of analytical methods for the chemical characterization of endogenous compounds in latent fingermark deposits. Results obtained using time-of-flight secondary ion MS (ToF-SIMS), high-energy SIMS, and x-ray photoelectron spectroscopy were compared to those from more established techniques (gas chromatography MS and attenuated total reflection Fourier transform infrared [ATR-FTIR] spectroscopy), with good overall agreement observed across these methods. Of the newer techniques evaluated, ToF-SIMS was found to be the most selective, showing reproducible differences between the deposits from all three fingermark donors used in the study.

The application of analytical techniques such as MS to fingermark detection can not only assist in the identification of an individual via the images generated, but can also provide additional information such as whether the person has recently consumed particular licit or illicit drugs, or if they have recently handled substances such as drugs or explosives. Investigative information of this nature cannot be obtained using conventional detection methods. However, at this point in time, the analytical instrumentation required is expensive, lacks portability, is time consuming to apply, and is not routinely available to fingerprint examiners.

4.9 FINGERMARK DETECTION ON SEMIPOROUS SURFACES

Fingermark detection techniques generally fall into two groups: those that work best on porous surfaces (e.g., DFO, IND-Zn, ninhydrin) and those that work best on nonporous surfaces (e.g., fingerprint powder, CA fuming, VMD). Intermediate, semiporous surfaces are sometimes problematic.

Such surfaces include waxed paper, glossy paper, matte-painted substrates, and rubber/latex gloves. Single techniques that may be successful on such surfaces include iodine–benzoflavone spray and MMD. For example, Jones et al. (2003b) found that MMD II was particularly effective on problematic surfaces such as latex and nitrile gloves, expanded polystyrene, and waxed paper. Otherwise, the best general approach is to use a combination of techniques applied in a logical sequence. One such sequence is depicted in Figure 4.61. Given the unusual nature of some semiporous surfaces, tests should be conducted on a similar surface before proceeding with the treatment of an evidential item.

Note that the application of a luminescent CA stain can be problematic on some semiporous surfaces as the substrate itself may absorb the stain to produce high background luminescence.

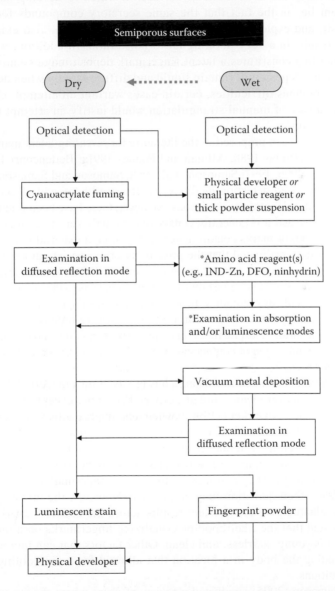

FIGURE 4.61 Possible sequence of methods for the detection of latent fingermarks on wet and dry semiporous surfaces (e.g., wax paper, glossy paper). Where possible, wet surfaces should be allowed to dry at room temperature before proceeding. Note that cyanoacrylate fuming may be less effective if the item has been wet. (*Skip if item has been wet.)

In such circumstances, the enhancement of CA-developed marks using a fingerprint powder may be preferred. Alternatively, consideration should be given to the use of a one-step luminescent CA fuming process such as Lumicyano™ (Prete et al. 2013). For some semiporous surfaces, such as polymer banknotes, the use of VMD after CA fuming and before the application of a luminescent stain may give the best results.

4.10 FINGERMARK DETECTION ON HUMAN SKIN

4.10.1 GENERAL

Human skin is probably the most difficult surface on which to develop latent fingermarks. The major problem lies in the fact that the same secretory compounds found in the latent fingermark deposit, and exploited for latent fingermark detection, also exist on the surface of the skin. This results in a very poor signal-to-noise ratio. In addition, while the eccrine/ sebaceous emulsion that constitutes a latent fingermark deposit may essentially solidify on a cold surface, this same deposit will remain liquid and diffuse rapidly when deposited on warm skin. Despite these obvious difficulties, certain cases warrant an attempt to detect marks on skin. For example, a case of manual strangulation would justify an attempt to develop marks on the neck of the victim.

Many techniques have been proposed in the literature for revealing latent marks on human skin (Shin and Argue 1976; Delmas 1988; Allman and Pounds 1991a; Bettencourt 1991; Hébrard and Donche 1994; Sampson 1996, 1997; Sampson et al. 1998; Sampson and Sampson 2005; Wilkinson 2011). Some of the suggested detection methods are described here, and all have been shown to produce results under ideal laboratory conditions. However, there have been relatively few reported successes in actual cases, and it is generally considered that only very fresh marks of good quality (less than a few hours old) or marks contaminated with a foreign material have any real chance of being detected. It has been estimated that the probability of recovering an identifiable fingermark on the skin of a cadaver is around 1 in 15 million (Sampson 1996). While certain cases justify a search for fingermarks on skin, it is important to remain realistic as to the chances of success on this surface. Human skin will always remain a difficult substrate for fingermark detection and, despite the research that has already been undertaken, further studies are required if higher success rates are to be obtained in the future. Despite inherent difficulties, it should be noted that, even if no ridge detail is developed, any indication of contact can be useful to direct the collection of potential trace DNA for profiling purposes.

Most of the research undertaken in this area has involved the controlled deposition of good-quality latent fingermarks on clean, cooled cadaver skin. One exception is the 2-year study reported by Wilkinson and coworkers (1996a) where test impressions were deposited on warm, unwashed skin close to the time of death. This is a scenario that more closely represents the typical situation encountered in actual casework. It was encouraging that the authors were able to demonstrate that fingermarks on warm cadaver skin can sometimes persist for several hours in an identifiable form. They commented that, if the fingermarks survive the initial cooling period after death, then detection may be possible. However, the majority of the development techniques evaluated give inconsistent results across the cadavers available in the study. The research indicated that the likelihood of visualizing fingermarks on a murder victim will improve if the skin is young, hairless, and clean. Other factors that can increase the chance of success include finding the body in a location that allowed for rapid cooling of the skin and low-humidity conditions.

Sampson and Sampson (2005) conducted a review of cases where the successful recovery of latent marks from human skin had been reported. Of the techniques employed, direct transfer methods appeared to be the most effective. This involves transferring the latent marks from the skin surface onto a clean substrate, such as a sheet of glass or stiff plastic, prior to development. The next most successful method was the direct application of magnetic powder to the skin surface. Other methods of detection that had yielded results included CA fuming, chemical development, and visualization of fingermarks using forensic light sources. The authors indicated that there is no one perfect method for obtaining fingermarks from skin and that method selection must be based on conditions—such as temperature, humidity, and surface moisture—and the examiner's experience, skill, and judgment.

4.10.2 POWDERING

The direct application of a fingerprint powder, such as magnetic powder, to the skin surface has been successful in a number of reported cases (e.g., Haslett 1983). The skin surface needs to be relatively dry otherwise high background development will occur. If necessary, prior to applying the powder, a small battery-operated fan (for example) can be used to assist in evaporating excess moisture from the skin surface (Sampson and Sampson 2005). Any developed marks are then photographed before being lifted using fingerprint lifting tape or silicone casting material.

Trapecar and Balazic (2007) evaluated a range of powders for the development of latent fingermarks on both living subjects and dead bodies. Of the powders tested, Swedish Black powder and Magnetic Jet Black powder gave the best results on both types of skin surface. In a subsequent study, Trapecar (2009) evaluated a number of lifting techniques for fingermarks on live skin developed with Swedish Black powder up to 4 hours after deposition. Of the lifting techniques evaluated (white instant lifter, white gelatin lifter, black gelatin lifter, silicone, and transparent adhesive tape), the best results were obtained with silicone and white gelatin lifters. Baran (2009) reported that it was possible to develop fingermarks on skin after up to 43 hours using magnetic powder followed by lifting with silicone.

An extensive European trial directed at the recovery of latent fingermarks and DNA from the skin of corpses was described by Farber et al. (2010). In each of the four participating countries—Austria, Denmark, Germany, and the United Kingdom—250 fingermarks were placed on and recovered from 10 corpses, giving a total of 1000 marks analyzed. Marks were treated between 30 and 60 minutes after deposition with either magnetic powder or black fingerprint powder and then lifted with either silicone casting material (Isomark®) or gelatin foils. Fingermarks suitable for elimination or identification were developed by direct powdering in 16% of cases, with magnetic powder (18.4%) outperforming black fingerprint powder (13.6%). The number of fingermarks suitable for elimination or identification decreased in the associated lifts (12.7%), with Isomark® (14.9%) being the preferred lifting material in comparison with gelatin foils (10.1%). The authors subsequently recommended the sequence magnetic powder→photography→Isomark® for the recovery of fingermarks from skin.

4.10.3 TRANSFER TECHNIQUES

One approach to developing marks on skin is to transfer the latent fingermarks onto another surface before processing. A commonly cited technique is the transfer of latent marks onto glossy paper (e.g., Kromekote® cards; Reichardt et al. 1978). Unexposed but fixed photographic paper can also be used. After transfer, the marks can be processed with magnetic powder (or any other suitable powder or development technique). The advantage of transferring latent marks onto a clean surface is that this removes the skin background that typically causes problems when direct development is attempted.

Glass is one of the best surfaces on which to detect latent fingermarks. For this reason, Sampson (1992, 1995) proposed the use of a clean glass sheet as a support for the lifting of latent fingermarks from skin (glass recovery investigative technique [GRIT]). After the transfer procedure, various techniques (physical or chemical) can be applied to reveal any ridge detail (episcopic coaxial illumination, fingerprint powder, CA fuming, etc.).

Hoyser (1992) suggested an alternative GRIT technique. In this case, marks are lifted from the skin surface onto a sheet of plastic film. The sheet should be relatively thick but pliable enough to easily conform to most body contours. The transferred marks can then be fumed with CA or dusted with conventional powder. Guo and Xing (1992) indicated that latent marks can be lifted from human skin using a semirigid PET sheet. The plastic sheet is electrostatically charged by vigorous rubbing and then pressed onto the surface of interest. Any dust present in the latent mark will be attracted by the static electricity in the charged sheet. The transferred marks are visualized on the plastic sheet by oblique lighting. Using this method, the authors reported good results for the detection of latent marks over a week old on skin.

Hébrard and Donche (1994) found that transfer techniques onto glass, PET, or photographic paper gave only limited results on live subjects due to rapid fingermark diffusion on the skin surface. Limited results were also obtained on cadavers due to postmortem discharge phenomena and high moisture levels on the skin caused by condensation when the bodies were removed from the cold room prior to processing. However, more optimistic results have been reported in other studies. For example, Reichardt et al. (1978) suggested that latent impressions on living skin can be transferred using the Kromekote lift technique and subsequently developed using fingerprint powder up to 1.5 hours after deposition. In addition, the lift technique may be repeated several times on the same latent impression. These subsequent lifts may be of better quality due to the removal of excess background secretions by the previous lifts. The authors reported the successful application of the Kromekote process on a murder victim, with an identifiable palm impression developed. Sampson and Sampson (2005) also indicated that there have been more successes in actual cases with the direct transfer method than with any other single method. In addition, the technique can be readily applied at the crime scene and it can be followed up with any other appropriate detection method (i.e., after the transfer process, the skin surface can be treated with methods such as fingerprint powdering or CA fuming). For living subjects, the transfer process is less intrusive than, for example, the direct application of a powder. With any lift technique, care must be exercised to ensure that the transfer medium is meticulously clean and free of any latent marks prior to use. Hamm (1988) reported a case where a fingermark developed on a Kromekote lift turned out to have been from a technician who had prepared the lift cards more than 12 months earlier.

When ridge detail is visibly impressed into the skin—in the case of manual strangulation, for example—then this can be photographed using oblique lighting. A silicone casting material can then be used to "lift" the mark in a similar way as for toolmarks. Other detection methods can then be applied to the impression in order to obtain additional ridge detail. Immamura and Asahida (1981) cite a case where this casting procedure was successfully applied on a person murdered by strangulation.

4.10.4 Iodine Fuming

Iodine fuming combined with silver plate transfer has been reported as a viable detection method for fingermarks on skin (Adcock 1977; Gray 1978). A portion of the skin is fumed with iodine vapor over approximately 30 seconds. The possible presence of a latent fingermark is indicated by the formation of a brownish stain (no ridge detail can normally be discerned at this stage). A highly polished silver plate is then pressed directly against this processed area. The plate is removed after 5–10 seconds and exposed to strong light (direct sunlight, UV lamp, incandescent lamp, etc.). A dark brown image of the lifted mark is formed on the silver plate. The results are variable, and contradictory opinions are expressed in the literature concerning the performance of this technique. It has been reported that results can be obtained on live skin up to 2 hours after deposition while, on cadavers, impressions have been developed that were from 2 to 5 days old (Adcock 1977). Hébrard and Donche (1994) found that fingermarks on live subjects were difficult to detect by this procedure after 15 minutes or after 4 hours on warm cadavers. However, they were able to develop latent fingermarks up to 16 hours after deposition on cadavers that had been kept in a cold room (6°C).

Wilkinson and coworkers (1996a) compared the iodine/silver plate transfer process with iodine fuming followed by treatment of the skin surface with a solution of 7,8-benzoflavone (applied with a spray). This latter treatment produces a dark blue reaction product that can be clearly seen against the skin. The iodine/silver plate transfer process only developed partial ridges and proved very awkward when searching for marks on bony regions of the body. On the other hand, the iodine/benzoflavone technique showed great promise. The technique demonstrated excellent selectivity, providing that care was taken to ensure that excess iodine was allowed to evaporate from the background skin before the application of the benzoflavone solution. The authors reported that iodine fuming followed by benzoflavone treatment consistently developed fresh marks deposited on skin and that field testing of the technique was recommended (Wilkinson et al. 1996a).

4.10.5 CYANOACRYLATE

Skin fragments or body parts can be treated with CA using a conventional fuming chamber. If a complete body must be processed, then this can be placed in a tent constructed from plastic sheeting and subsequently fumed with heat-generated CA vapor (commercially available CA pads can also be used). After CA processing and photography of any ridge detail, the skin surface can be treated with a luminescent stain (rhodamine 6G or BY40, for example). The skin is then examined using a suitable light source. If necessary, after stain application, the surface can be washed with water or methanol to reduce background luminescence. As an alternative to the application of a luminescent stain, marks developed by CA fuming can be enhanced by the application of black magnetic powder (Fortunato and Walton 1998).

An advantage of the CA fuming technique is that any latent marks that may be present can be rapidly fixed at the crime scene before the cadaver is transported and placed in a cold room. Secondary treatment can then be conducted at a later stage under controlled conditions in the laboratory. In the case of a body that has already been kept in a cold room, water condensation over the skin surface normally precludes CA processing. Delmas (1988) reported the use of CA fuming followed by luminescent magnetic powder and obtained identifiable fingermarks on four bodies (out of five) for test impressions up to several hours old; Hamilton and Dibattista (1985) cited successful fingermark development in a case involving a 5-year-old child; Misner and coworkers (1993) presented positive results for the detection of test fingermarks on cadavers using CA fuming followed by the application of a novel luminescent stain. In contrast, experiments conducted on cadavers where latent fingermarks had been deposited on warm, unwashed skin close to the time of death gave inconsistent results (Wilkinson et al. 1996a). The researchers concluded that, under these conditions, the CA fuming method exhibits poor sensitivity due to polymer development on the background skin.

Hébrard and Donche (1994) found that the fuming of cadavers in a plastic tent was a relatively efficient process; developed fingermarks could be subsequently treated with a luminescent stain, such as BY40, to aid visualization and photography. However, they indicated that the chance of success with CA fuming depended on a number of factors, including the presence of moisture on the skin, ambient conditions, and whether or not the body had been stored in a cold room. Best results were obtained on cadavers that had not been placed in a cold room and where it was less than 24 hours since death. Otherwise, water condensation on the skin, in addition to moisture naturally dispelled by the body after death, resulted in very high background development. Surface moisture appeared to be an important limiting factor for fingermark detection on skin using the CA fuming method. Trapecar and Balazic (2007) confirmed this observation and reported poor results using the CA technique. The cadavers used in their experiments had been stored in a cold room and the authors concluded that the poor CA results may have been due to moisture condensation on the skin surface due to the temperature difference between the cold room and the laboratory.

Wilgus (2002) presented a casework example involving a female homicide victim. The body, which had not been placed in a cold room, was kept overnight in an examination area at approximately 21°C prior to processing for fingermarks. After examination with a forensic light source, the body was treated with CA vapor using an improvised plastic fuming tent (15 minutes of fuming time) and then black magnetic powder applied. A single palm mark was revealed on the stomach area and, after photography, this was lifted using silicone casting material. A suspect in the investigation was subsequently identified as being the source of the palm impression. This case example is also notable in terms of emphasizing the importance of placing a control fingermark on the body to ensure that the fuming time is adequate and that the process is working effectively.

4.10.6 RUTHENIUM TETROXIDE

Mashiko and coworkers reported good results on skin using RTX applied as a vapor or as a solution (Mashiko et al. 1991; Mashiko and Miyamoto 1998). Tests conducted by Dolci (1992) indicated that the technique can successfully develop latent marks on skin up to at least 8 hours after deposition. However, the results obtained by Hébrard and Donche (1994) indicated that adequate ridge detail could only be obtained for fingermarks deposited using light fingertip pressure on the skin. This observation clearly restricts the usefulness of the technique in actual casework. The RTX fuming method can be applied in sequence after the iodine/silver plate transfer method.

Wilkinson and coworkers (1996a) evaluated commercial RTX solution by spraying it directly onto the skin where latent fingermarks had been deposited. While ridge detail was obtained on freshly deposited marks, the authors found that the resulting impressions lacked contrast compared to similar marks visualized with iodine–benzoflavone.

Trapecar and Balazic (2007) compared CA fuming with the use of commercial RTX solution, applied by spraying or by fuming. They achieved more consistent results with RTX, with 90% of initially deposited test marks being developed using the reagent. However, as indicated previously, they obtained poor CA results; this was most likely due to excessive surface moisture.

4.10.7 FINGERMARKS IN BLOOD ON SKIN

The likelihood of visualizing ridge detail on skin increases if there are fingermarks present that are contaminated with a substance that is not normally found on the skin surface. An example of this is fingermarks in blood, which may be targeted for enhancement provided that the skin surface itself is relatively clean.

Clements (1983) described a case where a hand impression in blood was located on the back of a female murder victim. After photography, the impression was enhanced using the blood reagent orthotolidine (o-tolidine). Ridge detail visualized in the enhanced mark led to the identification and conviction of the offender. In another report, the body of the 53-year-old white female, the victim of a fatal stabbing, had been examined approximately 30–34 hours after death (Anon. 1993). While no visible fingermarks were observed using optical examination with a forensic light source, amido black treatment of the skin surface revealed ridge detail on the victim's inner right thigh. Comparison against reference impressions from a suspect yielded positive results.

A more recent case example was provided by Lawley (2003), involving a murder victim with multiple stab wounds and blood smears on the ankles, legs, and wrists. Examination with a forensic light source revealed the possibility of fingermarks on the inner thigh region. However, fuming of the body with CA followed by the application of a luminescent powder failed to reveal any ridge detail. Subsequent processing of the skin surface with the protein stain amido black resulted in the visualization of previously undetected ridge detail on the inner right thigh of the body. While this was inadequate for identification purposes, it demonstrated the value of this enhancement process for fingermarks in blood.

Beaudoin (2012b) compared the performance of o-tolidine and amido black for the enhancement of fingermarks in blood on pig skin, which was used as a simulant for human skin. Treatment with o-tolidine, despite the reagent's high toxicity and potentially carcinogenic nature, gave the best results and was recommended for use as the preferred technique.

4.10.8 Recommended Detection Sequence

The processing of a cadaver for potential fingermark evidence should ideally be conducted where the body is found, as any movement or unnecessary time delay is likely to reduce any chance of success. Where examination at another location is required (due to poor environmental conditions at the scene, for example), the body should be transported as quickly as possible in cotton sheets, without a plastic cover, to minimize moisture condensation on the skin surface. Prior to fingermark processing, the body should not be stored in a cold room. If the body has been refrigerated, it should be left to warm to room temperature over several hours and surface moisture allowed to dissipate before proceeding. The use of a fan may assist with this process. On live subjects, the rapid diffusion of latent fingermarks into the hydro-lipid film on the skin surface, combined with elevated skin temperature and the fact that the skin is continuing to exude natural secretions, normally precludes successful detection. If fingermark detection on live skin is to be attempted, then this will generally be restricted to targeted areas using nonhazardous methods such as direct transfer (e.g., onto a glass plate, stiff plastic, or glossy card) and/or the direct application of a fingerprint powder, such as black magnetic powder.

The best chance of success will be on relatively smooth, hairless, and clean areas of skin and, for cadavers, where the body is relatively "fresh"—less than 24 hours since death—and has not been refrigerated (Hébrard and Donche 1994). A delay of more than 24 hours since death generally precludes the application of CA fuming due to the body's natural elimination of water through the pores in the skin. Similarly, a body kept in a cold room will tend to be excessively moist due to water condensation, which can lead to high background development when CA fuming is applied.

The casework circumstances should be considered to determine the possibility that fingermarks of interest were deposited on the skin surface and where these fingermarks are likely to be located. For example, a body that has been relocated may have been dragged by the wrists or ankles. When significant finger pressure has been employed by the aggressor (strangulation, for example), fingermarks may be visible on the cadaver. Such areas should be targeted for fingermark detection. Whatever detection methods are selected, the examination sequence should always commence with a meticulous examination of the skin surface under different lighting conditions (white light, UV, monochromatic light [laser, LED or filtered light source], absorption mode, luminescence mode, etc.) in order to detect any weakly visible or luminescent marks (caused by contamination of the fingers, for example). This initial examination may also indicate whether or not fingermarks in blood may be present, in which case blood enhancement reagents should be considered at the end of the detection sequence. Any visible ridge detail should be recorded photographically before proceeding with any other treatment. A possible examination sequence for the detection of latent fingermarks on skin is depicted in Figure 4.62.

As for the other detection sequences presented in this chapter, the proposed sequence in Figure 4.62 is a general guide only—one of the many possible combinations that may be effective depending on the situation. The sequence of detection methods used in any specific case will depend on casework circumstances, examiner experience, and the resources/techniques available.

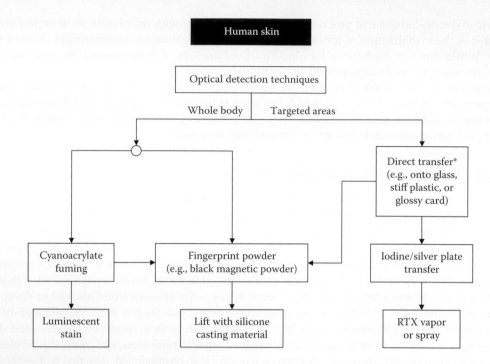

FIGURE 4.62 Possible sequence of methods for the detection of latent fingermarks on human skin. If the body has been stored in a cold room, then it should be allowed to warm to room temperature with the evaporation of excess moisture facilitated (e.g., body uncovered and a fan employed). (*Develop transferred marks using a suitable method [e.g., powdering or cyanoacrylate fuming].)

4.11 FINGERMARK DETECTION ON ADHESIVE SURFACES

Adhesive surfaces, such as the sticky side of self-adhesive tape or labels, can be very productive for fingermark detection due to their receptive nature—essentially pulling secretions and skin debris off the fingertip surface when touched—and the fact that it is difficult to manipulate adhesive materials while wearing gloves. In addition, fingermarks trapped in the adhesive layer will be protected from environmental degradation when the tape or label is applied to a substrate. Various techniques have been proposed for treating adhesives surfaces, the most notable being gentian violet (crystal violet) staining solutions and, more recently, thick powder suspensions referred to as "sticky-side" powder (Midkiff 1994; Midkiff and Codell 1995; Midkiff et al. 1997; Brzozowski et al. 2005; Home Office 2006a).

Adhesive tapes can be categorized into two main types: (1) those with a rubber-based adhesive and (2) those with an acrylic-based adhesive. The type of adhesive can affect the choice of fingermark development method. The majority of tapes use rubber-based adhesives that perform well with most development methods, with minimal background development resulting. However, a small minority of tapes use adhesives that are acrylic based and these can be problematic, with poor contrast in developed fingermarks due to heavy background coloration (Brzozowski et al. 2005; Home Office 2006a).

One of the operational difficulties associated with the treatment of adhesive surfaces such as adhesive tape is the fact that such materials often have to be separated from another surface, or themselves, before processing. Methods recommended for removing or unraveling sections of adhesive tape include freezing (Varnon 1988), heating (Campbell 1991a; Perez-Avila 2008), and the application of a solvent (Choudhry and Whritenour 1990). Care should be exercised with the application of such methods to limit any unnecessary damage to the latent marks that may be present. Usually, one of these proposed methods will work for a particular type of tape or adhesive label. In any given situation, tests should be conducted to determine the best method before proceeding.

Depending on the adhesive, placement of the item in a freezer (e.g., below −20°C) may assist subsequent separation or removal. Cooling with liquid nitrogen (−196°C) has also been reported to be successful (Stephens et al. 1999; Bergeron 2009; Bailey and Crane 2011). However, extreme care must be exercised when using liquid nitrogen in terms of ensuring adequate skin and eye protection, and some adhesive tapes become fragile and fracture easily when cooled to such a low temperature. An easier and safer alternative is to use a commercially available aerosol freezer spray, such as the one marketed by RS Components Ltd (Home Office 2006a).

As an alternative to freezing, gentle heating, such as directing warm hair from a hair dryer onto the adhesive material, may be effective in some circumstances. Solvent treatment can be conducted using a commercial adhesive remover such as Un-Du® (a heptane-based formulation), which has been reported to be effective for the removal or separation of adhesive tapes and labels while not compromising the subsequent detection of latent fingermarks (Stimac 2000; Schwartz et al. 2003; Molina 2007). Good results have also been reported using the solvent AK-225 (Stoilovic and Lennard 2012). Given that the role of the solvent is to at least partially dissolve the adhesive, there is always the risk of damage to any latent fingermarks that may be on the adhesive layer. However, solvent treatment is generally the only effective method in some situations, such as removing tapes and labels from porous surfaces and separating adhesive surfaces that are stuck to each other (Home Office 2006a).

When adhesive tape or an adhesive label is applied to a nonporous nonadhesive substrate such as glass or plastic, there is the possibility of latent fingermarks being transferred from the substrate to the adhesive layer of the tape or label. Fingermarks transferred in this manner and subsequently developed on the adhesive surface will be a mirror image of the original fingermarks. Similarly, with adhesive tapes or adhesive labels applied to a porous substrate such as paper or cardboard, there is the possibility of latent fingermarks being transferred from the adhesive layer of the tape or label to the substrate (Maceo and Wertheim 2000). Examiners need to be aware of these possibilities when examining such items.

4.11.1 Gentian Violet

Gentian violet (crystal violet; basic violet 3) is a lipid stain that can be effective for the detection of latent fingermarks on the adhesive side of self-adhesive tapes and labels. Historically, the procedure involved the treatment of the adhesive side of these items with a solution of gentian violet that contains phenol to assist the absorption of the stain by the sebaceous material in the fingermark deposit. Phenol-free formulations are now recommended given that phenol is highly toxic and carcinogenic. Treatment can be by dipping, by floating the item (adhesive side down) on the stain solution, or by application with a pipette. Excess reagent is then removed by washing with water. The sebaceous component of the fingermark deposit is stained dark purple by this process, and therefore marks become visible as dark purple ridges against a lightly stained background. The degree of background staining is dependent on the nature of the adhesive material and any contamination present. The procedure can be extended to darkly colored tapes using a lifting technique in which marks developed with gentian violet are transferred to a clean gelatin surface. This is achieved by firmly pressing the adhesive surface of the tape, after treatment with the stain, onto a fixed and washed sheet of photographic paper; diffusion of the stain into the gelatin occurs rapidly (Wilson and McCloud 1982; Home Office 1998).

The phenol-free gentian violet formulation proposed by the HOSDB (now CAST) contains the anionic surfactant dioctyl sodium sulfosuccinate, also referred to as Aerosol OT or AOT. This formulation has been shown to perform well in comparison with the original phenol-based solution, particular when used on acrylic-based adhesives (Home Office 2006a).

Gentian violet staining produces a dark purple coloration; therefore, observation of treated marks is generally conducted in the absorption mode under white light. However, Ziv and Springer (1993) reported that coaxial illumination can sometimes be a useful optical enhancement procedure for marks developed with gentian violet on the adhesive side of self-adhesive tape. Bramble and coworkers (2000) studied the deep red to NIR luminescence characteristics of gentian violet–treated latent marks. The luminescence data recorded in their study were used to optimize a relatively inexpensive viewing system for the observation and capture of the luminescence emission. Given the additional sensitivity offered by the luminescence mode, the authors found that the system permitted the visualization of both treated marks on dark surfaces and weakly developed marks on light surfaces.

As an alternative to gentian violet, Menzel (1989) proposed the use of basic fuchsin (rosaniline hydrochloride). This stain was evaluated by Howard (1993) for the processing of black electrical tape. The staining procedure is similar to that of gentian violet, but the developed marks are luminescent when visualized under a forensic light source, with observation conditions as for rhodamine 6G. Using both water- and methanol-based stain formulations, results were found to be comparable to those produced using gentian violet or CA/rhodamine 6G. Midkiff and Codell (1995) used an aqueous solution of basic fuchsin and reported good results on a range of adhesive tapes. A detection method based on the use of a phase transfer catalyst and rose bengal dye has also been proposed (Jasuja et al. 2007).

4.11.2 POWDER SUSPENSIONS

A process referred to as "sticky-side powder," based on a thick suspension of black fingerprint powder in a detergent solution, was developed in Japan in the early 1990s for the detection of latent fingermarks on the sticky side of adhesive tape (Yamashita et al. 1993; Burns 1994). The suspension can be readily prepared by mixing a suitable detergent solution (such as equal parts of Kodak Photoflo® detergent and water) with a black powder until a consistency similar to thin paint is achieved. This suspension is then painted onto the adhesive surface using a soft brush (e.g., camel-hair fingerprint brush). After 10–15 seconds, the adhesive surface is gently rinsed under running tap water. Treated marks are dark gray to black in color. The process can be repeated if development is weak. Burns (1994) reported good results on a range of adhesive surfaces including the adhesive side of duct tape, masking tape, surgical tape, paper-backed labels, clear plastic tapes, and reinforced packing tapes. Gray (1996) evaluated the sticky-side powder technique and found that it generally outperformed gentian violet on the adhesive surfaces tested.

Bratton and Gregus (1996, 1997) evaluated a number of detergent/powder combinations and found that a formulation based on Lightning Black™ Powder and Liquinox™ glassware detergent was the most effective on a broad range of adhesive tapes. It was determined that this method was superior to both the original sticky-side powder formulation and conventional gentian violet processing. The authors suggest that this should be the method of choice for adhesive surfaces and that attempts to apply other methods first may render the powder method ineffective. Sneddon (1999) explored the use of the Liquinox/black powder method for processing the adhesive side of duct tape. It was confirmed that excellent results could be obtained and that the powder suspension produced better overall results on this surface compared with results obtained with gentian violet.

The standard sticky-side powder method yields poor results on dark adhesive surfaces due to insufficient contrast. Martin (1999) reported that white or ash gray powder could be used instead of black powder in the sticky-side formulation for use on black electrical tape. This simple alternative was found to produce excellent results on the adhesive side of this tape. Parisi (1999) also reported success using powder suspensions produced by mixing fluorescent or white fingerprint powders with Liquinox and water. This approach has obvious advantages on dark adhesive surfaces, where black powder gives poor contrast. As suggested by Kimble (1996), a range of conventional fingerprint powders can be used in suspension to develop latent marks on adhesive surfaces. Wade (2002) proposed the use of titanium dioxide (TiO_2) for the preparation of white sticky-side powder for the detection of latent marks on dark adhesive surfaces. This was further explored by Williams and Elliott (2005) using both prepared TiO_2 suspensions and commercially available white SPR. The authors reported that such suspensions could produce useful fingermark contrast on the adhesive side of dark or transparent tapes, particularly electrical and duct tape.

The nanoscale analysis of commercially available titanium dioxide–based materials demonstrated varying levels of effectiveness for fingermark development, with some powders adhering to the background as well as the mark itself (Reynolds et al. 2008; Jones et al. 2010b). SEM images of fingermarks developed with different powders showed a range of levels of particle aggregation, with no preferential deposition of a particular particle size contributing to background development. Differences in structure and chemical composition were used to elucidate possible mechanisms behind the varying performance of TiO_2-based powder suspensions.

Brzozowski and coworkers (2005) evaluated two formulations of gentian violet—one with and one without phenol—and two commercial powder suspensions (Sticky-Side Powder™ and Wetwop™; Lightning Powder Co.) for their ability to develop latent fingermarks on the adhesive side of a range of different adhesive tapes. They determined that Wetwop™ was the most effective and the most universal method of those tested. The gentian violet stains were much less efficient than the powder suspensions, especially when applied to older fingermarks.

Formulations for black and white powder suspensions (WPSs) were proposed and evaluated by the HOSDB (Home Office 2006a). These suspensions perform well on the adhesive side of rubber-based adhesive tapes; however, they are generally ineffective on acrylic-based adhesive tapes due to high background coloration that precludes useful fingermark contrast. Figure 4.63 shows examples of fingermarks developed using a commercial BPS on the adhesive side of tape.

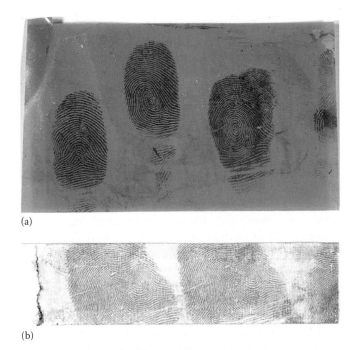

(a)

(b)

FIGURE 4.63 Fingermarks developed using a commercial black powder suspension on the adhesive side of (a) brown packaging tape and (b) masking tape.

4.11.3 Cyanoacrylate Fuming

Morris (1992) proposed the use of CA fuming followed by staining with BY40 as an alternative to gentian violet for processing the adhesive side of tape. Similarly, Isaac (1993) compared a number of techniques and reported that CA fuming, followed by either rhodamine 6G or MBD staining, can be very effective for developing marks on a range of self-adhesive tapes. Midkiff and Codell (1995) evaluated several techniques and found that CA fuming alone gives highly variable results, depending on the type of tape. Differences in the type, thickness, or consistency of the adhesive are believed to account for the observed variability in fingermark development. Some tapes were found to be easily overdeveloped, resulting in a loss of fingermark detail and poor contrast.

Steele and Ball (2003) proposed a two-step process for visualizing fingermarks on the adhesives side of tape: CA fuming followed by fuming with a disperse dye (such as disperse yellow 211). The authors reported that this sequential process yielded excellent resolution, even on the difficult substrate of black electrical tape.

CA fuming plus application of a luminescent stain (such as BY40) can be effective for the development of fingermarks on both sides of plastic-backed adhesive tape. However, high background development may result on acrylic-based adhesives (Home Office 2006a).

4.11.4 Miscellaneous Techniques

Hollars et al. (2000) proposed the use of "Liqui-Drox"—a solution composed of Ardrox® P-133D (a fluorescent dye penetrant), Liquinox® (an industrial detergent), and water—for the detection of fingermarks on the adhesive side of tape. The adhesive surface is painted with the solution using a small brush and the solution left on the tape for around 10 seconds. After rinsing with water, the adhesive surface is viewed in the luminescence mode under a long-wave UV lamp. Developed marks exhibit a green–yellow emission under these conditions. TapeGlo™ is a commercial fluorescent dye solution that works in a similar fashion but with excitation at 500 nm preferred for the visualization of treated marks (Ong et al. 2004).

MMD can be effective for the detection of fingermarks on a wide range of adhesive and nonadhesive surfaces. As such, its use may be considered in situations where more routine detection methods are ineffective. Other nanoparticle solutions and suspensions have been proposed for the detection of fingermarks on adhesive surfaces, for example, CdS/PAMAM (Yang et al. 2008), CdSe (Wang et al. 2009), CdTe (Yang et al. 2011), and PAMAM dendrimers (Jin et al. 2012).

4.11.5 Recommended Detection Sequence

Detection techniques applied to an adhesive surface must be used in sequence with methods that will also develop latent marks on any nonadhesive surfaces that are also present. For example, the processing of adhesive tape must take into consideration the detection of latent fingermarks on both the nonadhesive and adhesive sides of the tape. Typically, any latent marks present on the nonadhesive side of the tape should be developed and photographed before proceeding with the treatment of the adhesive surface. For tape or labels stuck down on an object (such as packaging tape and labels on a cardboard box), it is prudent to develop and record fingermarks on the nonadhesive upper surface before attempting to remove the tape or label to treat the adhesive side.

A recommended sequence for the detection of latent fingermarks on adhesive surfaces is given in Figure 4.64. While MMD (or SMD) is not included in this sequence, its use may be considered in some cases, as it is capable of developing marks on both adhesive and nonadhesive surfaces as well as for both porous and nonporous backings. The choice of a technique for the adhesive surface

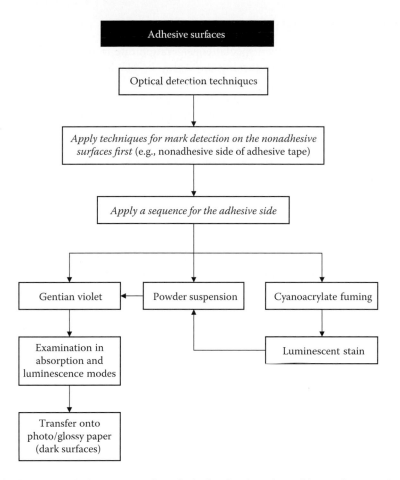

FIGURE 4.64 Recommended sequence of methods for the detection of latent fingermarks on adhesive surfaces.

itself (e.g., adhesive side of adhesive tape) will depend on experience and experimentation. Certain adhesive tapes, for example, respond better to a particular technique. No one technique performs better than the others on all adhesive surfaces. For any given case, therefore, tests should be conducted in a systematic manner to determine the most appropriate method to apply.

The Home Office recommends spot testing the adhesive surface with a powder suspension, prior to processing for fingermarks, to determine the type of adhesive (Home Office 2006a). Powder suspensions typically work well on rubber-based adhesives but are problematic on acrylic-based adhesives due to high background development. Rubber-based adhesives can be treated with powder suspensions or by CA fuming followed by the application of a luminescent stain. Note that CA fuming may adversely affect the performance of powder suspensions when these methods are used in sequence. For acrylic-based adhesives, powder suspensions and CA fuming are generally ineffective and the use of a nonphenolic formulation of gentian violet has been proposed in such cases (Home Office 2006a).

Schiemer and coworkers (2005) investigated a range of methods for the detection of latent fingermarks on black electrical tape. The following sequence of techniques was subsequently proposed: (1) optical examination, (2) CA fuming followed by the application of a luminescent stain, (3) WPS, and, if necessary, (4) processing with gentian violet stain and transferring of developed marks to photographic paper.

4.12   FINGERMARK DETECTION ON THERMAL PAPER

Thermal and carbonless papers need special consideration due to the risk that the development method will result in the substrate turning dark gray or black (Stimac 2003a). The sensitive layer of thermal paper, which typically contains dye capsules, sensitizers, and stabilizers, can be activated by polar solvents (such as some of the solvent mixtures used to formulate fingermark reagents) or by the heat required for some detection protocols. Various approaches have been proposed to overcome these difficulties, including (1) modification of reagent formulations to avoid the use of solvents that cause discoloration, (2) deactivation of the thermosensitive layer prior to the application of a conventional development method (Home Office 2006c), (3) chemical reversal of the substrate darkening after fingermark development, and (4) use of development techniques that do not darken the substrate (such as solvent-free or water-based methods or the controlled application of heat).

Alternatives to conventional ninhydrin processing, which is problematic on thermal paper, include the use of modified formulations (Stimac 2003a) and the use of ninhydrin hemiketals that have increased solubility in nonpolar solvents (Takatsu et al. 1991). The solvent-free application of ninhydrin, via sublimation under reduced pressure, has also been proposed (Schwarz and Frerichs 2002). The amino acid reagent IND can be used effectively on thermal paper as either a modified formulation (Stimac 2003b) or a solventless, dry-transfer process (Patton et al. 2010). Schwarz and coworkers proposed a method to decolorize the thermosensitive layer of thermal paper after fingermark detection using ninhydrin, DFO, or IND-Zn (Schwarz and Klenke 2007; Schwarz and Hermanowski 2011b). A similar process was reported by Fitzi et al. (2014). A one-step treatment using a ninhydrin solution containing polyvinylpyrrolidones has also been suggested (Schwarz and Klenke 2010). DMAC, applied as a vapor-based reagent or via a dry-transfer process, can also be effective for fingermark detection on thermal paper as previously discussed in Section 4.7.2.

Gentle heating using a hair dryer was proposed as a novel, reagent-free method for developing fingermarks on thermal paper (Wakefield and Armitage 2005). The addition of humidity was found to improve the results obtained using this technique (Scott 2008). Bissonnette et al. (2010) proposed a steam technique that was found to be effective on a range of different thermal paper samples and for latent fingermarks aged for up to 4 weeks. The authors proposed that the observed development was due to a reaction with unsaturated lipids from the sebaceous secretions, such as unsaturated fatty acids and squalene. Kusenthiran and coworkers (2010) compared the performance of the steam technique with that of VMD and found that both methods have the ability to develop fingermarks on thermal paper without causing background discoloration. Both techniques were effective at developing identifiable fingermarks 3 weeks after deposition. An apparatus designed for fingermark detection on thermal paper via the controlled application of heat has also been described (Bond 2013, 2015). Other methods proposed for the processing of thermal paper include exposing the substrate to hydrochloric acid or acetic acid vapor (Broniek and Knaap 2002; Ma and Wei 2006).

Solvent pretreatment of the thermal paper can be used to remove all printed text and deactivate the thermosensitive layer. For example, predipping in ethanol followed by the application of standard ninhydrin or DFO formulations may be effective on some thermal paper substrates (Home Office 2006c; Lee et al. 2009). However, this method may result in blurred marks (Fitzi et al. 2014) and the removal of the printed text may not be desirable, in which case the other options discussed earlier need to be considered.

Fitzi and coworkers (2014) undertook a comprehensive assessment of 19 detection techniques adapted for the processing of thermal paper. Based on the results obtained, a recommended detection sequence was proposed that incorporates modified formulations for IND-Zn and ninhydrin, with SMD at the end of the sequence (Figure 4.65). Note that SMD could be replaced with PD in the proposed sequence.

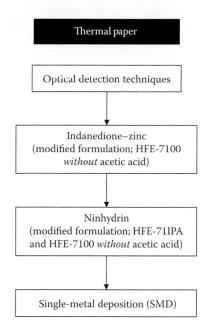

FIGURE 4.65   Sequence of methods recommended by Fitzi et al. (2014) for the detection of latent finger-marks on thermal paper.

4.13   FINGERMARK DETECTION ON FABRICS

Fingermark detection on fabric substrates is possible using a range of techniques, depending on the fabric type; however, usable ridge detail is only possible with very-fine-weave patterns. Some fabrics, such as 100% cotton, behave as a porous surface and hence fingermark detection methods suitable for such surfaces should be applied. Examples include the amino acid reagents IND-Zn and ninhydrin. Synthetic fabrics such as polyester and nylon, however, behave more like nonporous substrates and should be treated accordingly (e.g., CA fuming followed by the application of a luminescent stain). When in doubt, a range of methods should be applied in an appropriate sequence and preliminary tests conducted on similar fabric before proceeding with casework items. If fingermarks in blood are present, then blood enhancement methods such as amido black can be used at the end of the detection sequence.

There have been relatively few systematic studies conducted on fabrics. Fraser and coworkers (2011) undertook a study to determine if conventional Au/Zn VMD could recover fingermark ridge detail on different fabric types, namely, cotton, nylon, polyester, and polycotton (polyester/cotton blend). They found that there was consistently greater ridge detail developed on the shinier, tighter weave nonporous textiles such as nylon. When VMD was applied to the duller, more porous fabrics such as cotton, only empty fingermarks or grab marks, rather than ridge detail, resulted. However, as indicated by the authors, such grab impressions are still useful as they can indicate a sequence of events and highlight regions of the fabric that should be targeted for DNA. In a subsequent study, silver VMD was applied to the visualization of fingermarks and grab impressions on four different dark fabrics: black satin, black polyester, dark blue cotton, and black polycotton (Knighting et al. 2013). The best results were obtained on satin and polyester, with excellent ridge detail observed on the polyester samples. However, the Ag VMD treatment did not result in any ridge detail on the cotton and polycotton fabrics. Compared to Au/Zn VMD, Ag VMD proved to be a viable fingermark detection method on certain dark fabrics as treated marks are light in color, which contrasts well against the dark background.

A direct comparison of Au/Zn VMD and CA fuming, followed by staining with BY40, for fingermark detection on fabrics was reported by Fraser et al. (2014). Four different fabrics—nylon, polyester, polycotton, and cotton—were utilized, with the smoother fabrics such as nylon consistently producing greater ridge detail. The duller, porous fabrics such as cotton tended to produce only empty fingermarks or touch impressions without ridge detail. Of the two detection methods, the VMD process proved to be around five times more effective than CA fuming in terms of providing some form of visualization.

4.14 FINGERMARK DETECTION ON FIREARMS AND CARTRIDGE CASES

The detection of latent fingermarks on fired cartridge cases is problematic, and low success rates are generally encountered in actual casework. The cartridge case surface itself is not the cause, as marks can be developed on unfired rounds using a range of techniques. The possible reasons for low success rates on fired rounds have been reviewed by Wiesner and coworkers (1996) and include the following:

- Friction between the surface of the cartridge case and surfaces of the firearm at different stages of the firing process (e.g., loading of the magazine, the introduction of the live round into the chamber, and the ejection of the empty case after firing)
- High temperature and pressure generated within the cartridge case at the moment of firing
- Exposure of the surface of the cartridge case to the combustion gases and discharge residues generated at the moment of firing

Studies conducted on each of these effects indicated that, while each factor plays a role, the main cause of fingermark deterioration is the friction between the surface of the cartridge case and the chamber at the moment of ejection (Wiesner et al. 1996). At the moment of firing, the diameter of the cartridge case increases due to the high internal pressure that is generated. As a result, friction is more pronounced on ejection of the fired round rather than upon introduction of the live round prior to firing. Given the smearing of latent marks that can result from this friction, low success rates will tend to be encountered regardless of the detection techniques employed.

While a range of detection techniques can be applied, it should be appreciated that latent marks on brass cartridge cases may sometimes spontaneously develop over time due to a process of differential tarnishing (Saunders and Cantú 1996). A careful visual examination should therefore be conducted, and any ridge detail recorded, before proceeding with any other treatment.

Fingermark detection on the firearms themselves can also present difficulties, depending on factors such as the nature of the surface (e.g., metal, wood, or plastic), any surface finish or pattern, surface contamination (e.g., gun oil and discharge residues), and how the firearm has been handled and packaged. Barnum and Klasey (1997) have reviewed the reasons why it can be difficult to obtain identifiable marks from firearms. Despite the inherent problems, the authors claim that, in their experience, identifiable marks are encountered almost 10% of the time. Johnson (2010) examined the data from a single U.S. laboratory, generated over a 12-month period, and found that identifiable fingermarks were obtained on approximately 12% of all firearms processed. However, over the same period, no results were reported on unfired cartridges and only one success on discharged cartridge cases (with the one success being attributed to a fingermark deposited after firing of the weapon). Similar results were reported by Pratt (2012), who looked at success rates over a 3-year period achieved by the U.S. Bureau of Alcohol, Tobacco, Firearms and Explosives Forensic Science Laboratory in San Francisco. Identifiable fingermarks were obtained on 13% of all firearms processed, while the success rate on ammunition cartridges was only 0.12%. Maldonado (2012) compiled 2 years of data from the

Denver Police Department and found that recovery rates were less than 4% on firearms, 0.25% on unfired cartridges, and 0% on spent cartridge cases.

4.14.1 CYANOACRYLATE FUMING

Sampson (1993) investigated the application of CA fuming for the detection of latent marks on both brass and nickel cartridge cases. Nickel cartridge cases were found to yield good overall results, while the results achieved on brass cartridge cases were generally poor. Donche and Musy (1994) found that the results obtained with CA on plastic shotgun cartridges were generally satisfactory, while the technique gave limited results on metallic casings.

Bentsen and coworkers (1996) evaluated a range of techniques on fired cartridge cases, including both atmospheric-pressure and VCA fuming followed by treatment with a luminescent stain. It was determined that both CA systems were effective, although the vacuum method gave sharper ridge definition. Of the luminescent stains evaluated, BY40 was found to give better overall results.

Klasey and Barnum (2000) evaluated VCA fuming for fingermark detection on a range of different firearms. Marks developed with the vacuum process were found to be not as white as those developed under atmospheric conditions. However, overdevelopment of fingermarks was avoided, making this a good first choice for processing firearms. Virtually none of the test marks in this study were enhanced by a second treatment by VCA fuming. However, subsequent atmospheric-pressure CA fuming enhanced some of these marks.

4.14.2 GUN BLUE

While most fingermark detection techniques are dependent on a reaction with the fingermark deposit, the gun blueing process involves a reaction with the substrate. The principal active ingredients in gun blue include selenious acid (H_2SeO_3) and a cupric salt in an acid solution. Both selenious acid and cupric ions can oxidize certain metals (e.g., zinc, aluminum, and iron). When these two components are reduced in the presence of such metals, a black copper-selenide coating is formed (Migron and Mandler 1997; Cantú et al. 1998). This coating will only form on a clean metal surface; no deposit will occur if the surface is contaminated with a greasy or oily material, as is the case when a sebaceous fingermark is present. Dilute gun blue solution can therefore be used to treat certain metal surfaces, such as brass cartridge cases, to reveal latent marks as transparent images against a dark background.

A selenious acid process reported by Bentsen and coworkers (1996) involved the immersion of cartridge cases in a 0.4% aqueous solution of selenious acid until optimum ridge detail is observed. Treated cartridge cases are then rinsed thoroughly with water and dried. Developed marks can be preserved by dipping the cartridge cases in clear varnish to prevent further surface oxidation (alternatively, the surface can be coated with protective oil). Developed marks should be photographed immediately, as further oxidation can destroy ridge detail. The results are dependent on the composition of the cartridge case; selenious acid treatment was reported to be ineffective on aluminum- and nickel-coated brass cases. While the method is highly sensitive, propellant by-product contamination can limit results on some spent cases (Bentsen et al. 1996).

Saunders and Cantú (1996) evaluated several techniques for developing latent marks on both unfired and fired cartridge cases. Treatment with dilute gun blue solution gave better overall results compared with CA fuming. However, superior results were obtained with CA fuming followed by gun blue treatment compared with gun blue solution alone. (This suggests that a possible sequence for processing cartridge cases would be as follows: CA fuming → selenious acid → luminescent stain.) The authors were unable to develop any ridge detail on oily or dirty cartridges, even after the application of degreasing or washing techniques.

Both etching and blueing techniques were evaluated by Schütz and coworkers (1999) and the results compared with those obtained with MMD. (Etching involves the acid-based dissolution of the metal surfaces, whereas blueing involves both an acid-based dissolution and the formation of a dark metal complex.) The best efficiency for latent fingermark detection on brass cartridge cases was generally observed with gun blue treatment, particularly for sebaceous fingermarks. However, on aluminum cartridge cases, better results were obtained with MMD. Only the modified PD step of the MMD treatment appeared to contribute to the fingermark detection. Lacquered steel cartridge cases were problematic, and the authors recommended CA fuming for this surface.

Cantú and coworkers (1998) determined that a mixture of acetic acid and hydrogen peroxide could be used to remove excess gun blue deposit from metal cartridge cases that had been overdeveloped by gun blue treatment. It was also found that the acidified hydrogen peroxide solution could be used to visualize latent marks on cartridge cases by an etching process and that such marks could be enhanced by subsequent gun blue treatment. The acidified hydrogen peroxide method was further explored by Swofford et al. (2013), who found that it was an effective processing technique but that it should be applied after CA fuming and dye staining.

Vouk (1996) has warned that the use of gun blue solution for the detection of latent marks can result in a loss of detail in the individual toolmarks left on the cartridge case by the firearm. Such markings on a cartridge case should therefore be recorded by a firearms examiner before proceeding with the gun blue treatment. Similar detrimental effects were reported for the acidified hydrogen peroxide method; therefore, firearms examiners should be consulted prior to the application of such techniques on cartridge cases (Swofford et al. 2013).

4.14.3 MISCELLANEOUS TECHNIQUES

Migron and coworkers investigated palladium deposition techniques for the development of latent fingermarks on brass cartridge cases (Migron et al. 1996, 1998; Migron and Mandler 1997). The treatment is by immersion in an aqueous solution of either dipotassium hexachloropalladate or disodium tetrachloropalladate for 40 seconds, followed by rinsing in distilled water. The reaction with the metal surface is a displacement process that involves the oxidation of zinc and, to a lesser extent, copper, resulting in the deposition of palladium. A dark metallic deposit forms on the exposed metal surface (including the fingermark valleys), while the ridges remain golden-brass in color (Migron and Mandler 1997). A number of experiments were also conducted where iodine was used to etch the metal surface of the cartridge to sensitize it for subsequent palladium deposition. This etching step was found to significantly improve fingermark visualization (Migron et al. 1996; Migron and Mandler 1997).

Overall, the palladium deposition technique was found to be a very promising method for fingermark detection on unfired cartridge cases. The technique is relatively simple to apply, producing good fingermark detail in a reproducible fashion. However, while application of the method on spent cartridge cases gave an indication that latent fingermarks were still present after firing, the developed images were rarely of good quality. It was confirmed in a further study that, under laboratory conditions, substantial parts of latent fingermarks on some cartridge cases could remain intact after firing. In such cases, metal vapor deposition and the careful use of illumination can enable fingermark visualization. The authors also proposed a model for the structural changes to latent fingermarks due to the firing process (Migron et al. 1998).

Williams and coworkers (2001) reported that electrochemical interactions between metallic substrates and latent fingerprints, specifically inorganic salts present in eccrine secretions, result in Volta (electrostatic) potential differences across the surface. The Volta potential patterns that are formed can be mapped and displayed using a Scanning Kelvin Probe (SKP) technique. Using this method, latent fingermarks deposited on a range of polished and roughened metallic surfaces can be effectively imaged (Williams and McMurray 2007). The authors also demonstrated that the SKP technique could visualize fingermarks obscured beneath an opaque film of soot or fingermarks physically removed by rubbing. While the method shows promise for the detection of fingermarks on difficult substrates such as cartridge cases, it suffers from a number of limitations. It is only effective on conductive surfaces and for relatively small scan areas, commercial instrumentation is not currently available, and long scan times are required.

The chemical reactions between latent fingermarks and various metallic surfaces, at temperatures up to 600°C, have been investigated by Bond (2008), who found that corrosive effects can result in fingermark images that are durable in nature. Furthermore, the author reported that the electrostatic charging of metal substrates can enable the preferential adherence of conductive powder to the areas of corrosion caused by the latent fingermark deposit. This was proposed as a technique for addressing the problem of fingermark detection on fired cartridge cases. In a subsequent article, Bond and Heidel (2009) presented a case study where fingermark ridges were developed on a brass cartridge case from a 14-year-old homicide investigation using conducting carbon powder after the application of a 2.5 kV potential to the casing.

4.14.4 Recommended Detection Sequence

Edmiston and Johnson (2009) investigated a number of detection sequences and reported that, of the sequences tested, the best overall sequence for nickel and brass cartridge cases and shotgun shells was as follows: CA fuming → rhodamine 6G → acidified hydrogen peroxide → powder. Dominick and Laing (2011) compared the effectiveness of six different detection methods on a range of brass cartridge cases. The methods compared were CA fuming followed by staining with BY40, gun blue (GB), CA fuming followed by GB followed by BY40, palladium (Pd) deposition, CA fuming followed by Pd deposition, and BPS. Two sequences were found to give the best results, with no statistical difference observed with respect to their relative effectiveness for fingermark detection on brass: (1) CA fuming → GB → BY40 (Figure 4.66) and (2) CA fuming → Pd deposition. Similar results were reported by Girelli and coworkers (2015), who evaluated a range of methods and found that the best results for both fired and unfired cartridge cases were obtained by the sequential application of CA fuming, gun blueing solution, and BY40.

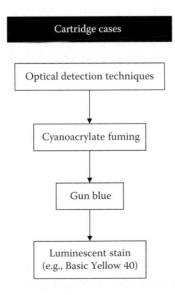

FIGURE 4.66 Possible sequence for the detection of latent fingermarks on brass cartridge cases. (From Dominick, A.J. and Laing, K., *J. Forensic Ident.*, 61, 155, 2011.)

4.15   ENHANCEMENT OF FINGERMARKS IN BLOOD

Fingermarks in blood are often encountered in cases of violent crime where the offender's hands are contaminated with the blood of the victim. A fingermark identified as being from the suspect but deposited in the blood of the victim (as suggested by DNA profiling results) may constitute very powerful forensic information. Every effort should therefore be made to enhance any fingermark in blood, for fingermark identification purposes, without compromising the possibility of obtaining a DNA profile from the blood (see Section 4.17.2). Nondestructive optical enhancement procedures should be employed before proceeding with another treatment. Where possible, heavily blood-stained areas that are unlikely to yield ridge detail should be sampled for DNA profiling purposes before processing the surface for fingermarks.

There are a number of blood- or protein-specific enhancement techniques (e.g., diamino-benzidine [DAB] and amido black) that will not develop any latent fingermarks that may be present and are likely, in fact, to destroy such marks. This must be taken into consideration when processing an item for potential fingermark evidence. An appropriate sequence of methods is required that will both develop any latent fingermarks that are present and enhance any fingermarks in blood. A sequence that exploits only the blood-contaminated marks will be to the detriment of any latent marks that may also be present on the evidential item. An excellent overview of blood enhancement techniques and their use in sequence with other methods has been published by Sears (2012).

In some cases, it may be of interest to determine whether a blood-contaminated fingermark is from a finger contaminated with blood or is a latent fingermark that was already on the surface but subsequently exposed to liquid blood. The distinction is an important one in terms of determining if the suspect had the victim's blood on their hands at the time of the incident versus latent fingermarks that may have been previously deposited under legitimate circumstances. Creighton (1997) conducted a number of experiments where blood was allowed to flow over a series of latent impressions. The results suggested that preexisting latent impressions would not develop into visible fingermarks in blood by incidental or direct contact with blood. The observed effect was that the latent deposit tended to repel the blood. Further studies were conducted by Huss and coworkers (2000), who confirmed that (1) blood will not visualize a previously deposited eccrine fingermark and (2) blood may reveal a previously deposited sebaceous (greasy) fingermark, although the mark will be reversed, as blood will tend to be repelled by the ridges and hence accumulate in the furrows. The correct interpretation, however, may actually be far more complex according to Praska and Langenburg (2013), who explored whether a latent fingermark exposed to blood and later developed with a blood enhancement reagent could appear as a genuine blood mark. They found that an interaction may occur between a latent fingermark and diluted blood to produce what may be referred to as a "faux" blood mark. However, this was found to be inconsistent and predictable patterns were not established. Faux blood marks were sometimes observed when latent residue was exposed to whole blood, but it was more likely to occur with diluted blood and when the latent residue was allowed to dry over an extended period of time. While faux blood marks could be distinguished from genuine blood marks prior to chemical enhancement, this was increasingly difficult after enhancement. The authors commented that

- Crime scene officers and fingerprint examiners need to be aware of the effects that may occur,
- Potential fingermarks in blood need to be carefully examined and photographed in their original state prior to chemical enhancement,
- Attention must be paid to the appearance of the ridge detail after chemical enhancement,
- Crime scene specialists and fingerprint examiners need to be precise with their terminology when describing *latent* fingermarks, *patent* (visible) fingermarks, and fingermarks that have been revealed as a result of chemical treatment.

4.15.1 OPTICAL TECHNIQUES

Although blood has a broad absorption spectrum in the entire light region (UV–visible–IR), it exhibits a strong and narrow absorption maximum at 415 nm (Figure 4.67a) (Stoilovic 1991). The enhancement of untreated blood marks can be performed in either the absorption or reflection modes. The absorption mode is recommended for lightly colored or luminescent surfaces, while the diffused reflection mode is recommended for dark or shiny surfaces. Optical enhancement techniques are generally nondestructive, and therefore their use is strongly recommended before proceeding with any chemical treatment.

To employ the absorption mode for blood enhancement, a forensic light source is required that provides a strong band of light at around 415 nm (HBW approximately 40 nm) (Figure 4.67b). Under dark conditions, blood marks will appear almost black under such illumination due to the strong absorption of dry blood at this wavelength. Good contrast will therefore be obtained on lightly colored or luminescent surfaces (Figure 4.68). Note that the human eye is relatively insensitive in the violet region (400–420 nm) and any perceived enhancement will generally be much better when captured on film or via a digital camera. If enhancement is required in full daylight (or artificial light), then the camera needs to be fitted with a 415 nm bandpass filter.

While dry blood strongly absorbs violet light, other wavelengths tend to be diffusely reflected. It is this characteristic that can be employed for enhancing blood marks on dark or shiny surfaces. An illumination wavelength is chosen that is outside the violet region; for example, strong blue light at 450 nm produces good results in most cases. Working under dark conditions, the blood mark is observed perpendicular to the surface, without any barrier filter, while the incident light angle

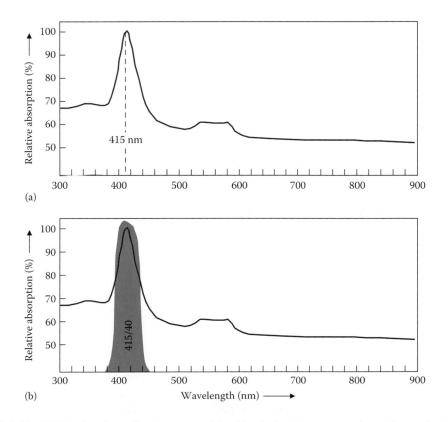

FIGURE 4.67 (a) Relative absorption spectrum of dry blood, showing a strong absorption peak at 415 nm. (b) Recommended bandpass filter for observation in the absorption mode.

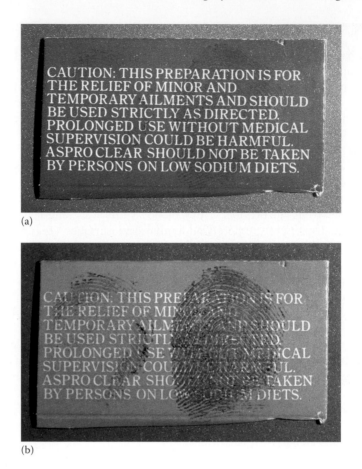

(a)

(b)

FIGURE 4.68 Fingermarks in blood on printed cardboard imaged (a) under white light and (b) in the absorption mode at 415 nm.

is varied until the best contrast is obtained. The incident light will either be strongly absorbed or reflected by the surface, depending on whether the surface is dark or shiny. The blood mark will diffusely reflect the light, and hence the mark will appear as a light image against a dark background. In the case of a colored substrate, selecting an illumination band that is opposite to the substrate color will generally enhance the contrast.

Springer and colleagues reported that UV luminescence techniques (shortwave UV excitation; observation in the long-wave UV region) can be effective for detecting and enhancing marks in blood, semen, and saliva (Springer et al. 1994). Care must be exercised with such techniques, however, due to the danger associated with the use of shortwave UV light and the possible detrimental effect that it may have on subsequent DNA profiling. For blood marks on dark or multicolored substrates, imaging in the NIR may also be beneficial (Lin et al. 2007).

4.15.2 Protein Stains

Before proceeding with any chemical treatment such as the application of a protein stain, blood marks need to be "fixed" to prevent the blood from washing away or diffusing. Two effective blood-fixing agents are methanol and 5-sulfosalicylic acid solution (Hussain and Pounds 1988; Sears and Prizeman 2000). The average fixing time is generally 5 minutes, although heavy deposits should be fixed for longer periods, 15 minutes or more, before applying the enhancement process.

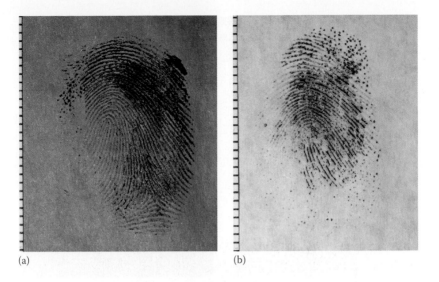

(a)   (b)

FIGURE 4.69 Fingermarks in blood on white paper after enhancement with (a) amido black and (b) diaminobenzidine. (Images courtesy of S. Moret.)

The protein stain amido black (naphthol blue black B; acid black 1) has long been a recommended treatment for fingermarks in blood on both porous and nonporous surfaces (Hussain and Pounds 1989; Home Office 1998; Sears and Prizeman 2000). Such marks are generally treated by immersion in a solution of amido black. After approximately 30 seconds in the staining solution, the sample is washed successively in three different solutions to clear (destain) the background, thereby improving the fingermark contrast. Treated marks are visible as dark blue ridges against a light blue or colorless background depending on the nature of the support (Figure 4.69a). The conventional amido black formulation is methanol based and may not be suitable on some surfaces or as a crime scene technique. Sears and Prizeman (2000) investigated alternative formulations and proposed a new ethanol/water-based system. This new formulation is suitable for application both in the laboratory and in the field. Warrick (2000) has described a case where marks in blood on cotton fabric were stained with amido black and then digitally enhanced, ultimately leading to the identification of a suspect in a murder investigation.

Coomassie blue is also a protein stain, giving results comparable to amido black. The same staining procedure is employed, and treated marks are blue but of a lighter color than that obtained with amido black. McCarthy and Grieve (1989) compared amido black with both Crowle's stain and coomassie blue. It was concluded that, of the three protein stains evaluated, amido black is generally the best choice for treating fingermarks in blood and that CA preprocessing is not deleterious for most substrates that are subsequently processed with amido black.

Sears and coworkers (2001) conducted a systematic evaluation of a range of protein stains—including fuchsin acid (Hungarian red) (Velders 1997)—for the enhancement of fingermarks in blood on surfaces typically encountered at crime scenes. Of the stains tested, two were found to show potential and warrant further investigation through operational trials. The first of these, acid violet 17 (coomassie brilliant violet), is an absorbing stain that produces a visible enhancement of blood marks; this stain may serve as a possible replacement for amido black. The second candidate, benzoxanthene yellow, was found to induce a luminescence in weak blood deposits on nonporous surfaces. This property may be an advantage on dark, nonluminescent, nonporous surfaces, where absorbing stains such as amido black are less effective. In further work, Sears et al. (2005) investigated the use of AY7 (brilliant sulfoflavine) as a replacement for benzoxanthene yellow, given that the latter is now unavailable and having it specially manufactured would be problematic. Weak blood deposits stained with AY7 exhibit a green–yellow luminescence emission when excited using

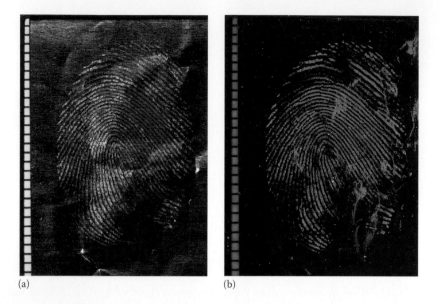

(a)   (b)

FIGURE 4.70 Fingermark in blood on aluminum foil enhanced with acid yellow 7 and visualized (a) under white light and (b) in the luminescence mode (excitation at 445 nm with a 565 nm bandpass barrier filter). (Images courtesy of S. Moret.)

violet–blue radiation (Figure 4.70). On heavy blood deposits, however, luminescence can be very weak unless extended dyeing times are employed (up to several hours). As AY7 is impossible to remove from porous substrates, it is only suitable for use on nonporous surfaces.

Phloxine B (acid red 92) has also been applied as a protein stain for the enhancement of blood marks, particularly on dark or multicolored surfaces. Treated marks are reddish-orange in color. Agarwal et al. (2010) undertook a comparative study on dark-colored substrates using phloxine B and AY7. They found that, in many cases, both techniques were effective. However, they found that the luminescence properties of AY7 were an advantage, particularly on textured substrates.

A study on the recovery of fingermarks in blood from fire scenes was reported by Moore and coworkers (2008). It was determined that the protein stains amido black, acid violet 17, and AY7 were capable of enhancing blood marks on various surfaces exposed to temperatures of around 200°C. However, no single stain was found to be more effective than the others across the full range of substrates tested. Aronson (2011) evaluated a number of techniques for the enhancement of blood marks on the adhesive side of duct tape. While amido black produced the best results, a powder suspension method was also successful on both bloody impressions and latent fingermarks. The results achieved with the powder suspension were only slightly degraded when used as a secondary process after amido black processing. Protein stains such as amido black have also been demonstrated to be effective for the enhancement of fingermarks in blood on fruit and vegetables (Rae et al. 2013).

Alginate casting material is typically used in the field of dentistry but it can also be applied to the lifting of footwear marks and fingermarks in blood. Lifted impressions can then be enhanced, using amido black, for example, and the original blood marks remain largely unchanged. Munro et al. (2013) evaluated this method across a range of porous, semiporous, and nonporous and found that alginate was not compatible with certain substrates. In addition, on compatible substrates, the enhanced fingermarks on the alginate cast were generally inferior to direct enhancement of the blood marks without the use of alginate. More promising results were obtained by mixing the protein stain with the alginate, which provided direct enhancement of the original mark on the substrate as well as simultaneously enhancing the lifted impression.

4.15.3 DIAMINOBENZIDINE

Work by Allman and Pounds (1991b, 1992c) indicated that the reagent DAB is a sensitive alternative to protein stains for the enhancement of blood marks both in the laboratory and at the crime scene. The reaction between DAB and hydrogen peroxide is catalyzed by the peroxidase-like activity of blood (heme) to give a dark brown insoluble product. In contrast to protein staining, the reaction shows good specificity for blood and produces little background coloration; no destaining of the surface is required. Before treatment, the blood marks are first fixed with a solution of 5-sulfosalicylic acid over several minutes. After being rinsed with water, the marks are then developed with a buffered solution of DAB over approximately 4 minutes. The revealed impressions are then rinsed with water and allowed to dry (Figure 4.69b). The method is therefore quite rapid, with blood enhancement achieved in less than 10 minutes. The technique is particularly effective on porous surfaces, where protein stains tend to give a high background coloration. As a crime scene technique, application of DAB can be via reagent-saturated paper towels. This can be effective on a variety of surfaces, including doors and painted or wallpapered walls. However, DAB must be used with caution as the compound is a possible carcinogen (Sigma-Aldrich 2014).

Sahs (1992) evaluated DAB for the enhancement of blood marks and also proposed a DAB–MBD combined process. In this modified procedure, MBD (a luminescent stain that can be used for the enhancement of CA-developed marks) is added to the sulfosalicylic acid fixing solution. While Sahs reported that results were inconsistent, luminescence was induced in some blood marks after treatment with the modified fixing solution. The addition of MBD to the fixing solution did not have any observable detrimental effect on the subsequent DAB reaction. However, marks enhanced with DAB were no longer luminescent; intermediate results must therefore be recorded before proceeding.

4.15.4 MISCELLANEOUS TECHNIQUES

In addition to DAB, a number of other heme-reacting chemicals have been proposed for the enhancement of blood marks. These include reagents such as leucomalachite green (LMG), phenolphthalein, fluorescein, and tetramethylbenzidine (Lee 1984; Shipp et al. 1994; Cheeseman and DiMeo 1995). In general, heme-reacting chemicals demonstrate high sensitivity, being able to detect blood down to extremely low concentrations. This added sensitivity may be an advantage in some circumstances. Caldwell and coworkers (2000) proposed the use of ABTS [2,2′-azino-bis(3-ethylbenzothiazoline-6-sulfonic acid) diammonium salt] as an effective and safe alternative to DAB for the enhancement of fingermarks in blood on porous surfaces. As is the case with DAB, ABTS undergoes oxidation to a colored form in the presence of hydrogen peroxide and hemoglobin. However, unlike DAB, ABTS is considered to be nontoxic and safe to use. The authors found that the bright green color of the oxidized ABTS was an advantage on certain colored surfaces where the dark brown color of DAB-treated marks showed poor contrast. For blood marks on glass, better results were obtained with DAB. Treatment with ABTS did not interfere with subsequent DAB processing, indicating that the two techniques can be used in sequence if desired.

The transfer of fingermarks in blood, enhanced by either LMG, leucocrystal violet (LCV), or DAB, has been investigated (Jaret et al. 1997). It was found that fixed black-and-white photographic paper could be successfully used to transfer blood marks treated with LMG or LCV. This may be an advantage on dark surfaces, where contrast is poor, or for marks located in areas that are difficult to photograph. The transfer of DAB-enhanced impressions was not successful.

A comparison of four different blood enhancement methods—amido black, coomassie blue, ABTS, and fluorescein—was reported by Marchant and Tague (2007). Of the techniques evaluated, they found that a methanol-based amido black formulation gave the best overall results (with a water-based formulation being largely ineffective), but that the ABTS method could be considered as an option for use under certain circumstances. ABTS is a more expensive and more complicated technique to apply.

The amino acid reagents commonly used for the detection of latent fingermarks—ninhydrin, DFO, and IND-Zn—are also effective for the enhancement of weak fingermarks in blood as blood also contains amino acids and amino acid reagents will also react with the terminal amine groups in proteins. Both DFO and IND-Zn can produce highly luminescent marks in such cases; however, they are less effective for fingermarks heavily loaded with blood due to quenching effects. Compared to protein stains, amino acid reagents can produce superior results on highly porous surfaces such as paper. On less porous surfaces such as glossy magazine paper, however, protein stains may be more effective (Sears et al. 2005). Amino acid reagents have the advantage that they will also develop latent fingermarks, and their use does not preclude the later application of a protein stain such as amido black. As such, for porous substrates, processing with amino acid reagents (e.g., IND-Zn followed by ninhydrin) is always recommended, as latent marks not contaminated with blood will not be revealed by a staining procedure alone.

Thomas and Farrugia (2013) investigated the ability of genipin and lawsone, two naturally occurring amino acid reagents, to enhance fingermarks in blood on a range of paper substrates. Their performance was compared to that of ninhydrin and DFO. The results indicated that neither genipin nor lawsone were suitable reagents for blood mark enhancement, with ninhydrin proving to be the most successful reagent of those tested. DFO enhancement was limited largely due to fluorescence quenching.

Dark surfaces can pose a significant challenge for the detection of bloody fingermarks. Bergeron (2003) reported good success using a methanol-based suspension of titanium dioxide as a development method, without any detrimental effects on subsequent DNA profiling. The use of powder suspensions as a technique for the enhancement of blood marks was further explored by Au and coworkers (2011). The results indicated that commercial WPS, used alone or in conjunction with a protein stain such as AY7, can be effective for the enhancement of blood marks on dark-colored, smooth nonporous surfaces. However, preliminary data indicated a decrease in DNA yield following WPS enhancement.

Bécue and coworkers (2009) proposed the use of highly luminescent cadmium telluride (CdTe) QDs in aqueous solution for the enhancement of weak fingermarks in blood on nonporous surfaces. When the performance was compared with that of AY7, the QD method was found to be equally efficient on glass, polyethylene, and propylene surfaces and superior on aluminum foil. However, the use of cadmium-based techniques of this nature raises significant health and safety concerns. In subsequent work, the authors proposed the replacement of CdTe QDs with zinc sulfide QDs doped with copper (ZnS/Cu) as a safer alternative (Moret et al. 2013). When applied to the enhancement of blood marks on nonporous surfaces, the ZnS/Cu QDs proved to be better than AY7 and at least as effective as CdTe QDs on most of the substrates tested.

4.15.5 Recommended Detection Sequence

The range of techniques available for the detection and enhancement of blood-contaminated fingermarks has been reviewed by Bossers et al. (2011). In any given situation where blood marks may be present, an optimized sequence of techniques needs to be applied that will target both latent marks and fingermarks in blood. This sequence logically commences with optical visualization and recording techniques, which can be applied in a nondestructive manner prior to the application of more destructive methods. Even if blood marks are visible on the substrate under examination, the sequence needs to include techniques for the detection and enhancement of latent (nonbloody) fingermarks. Using certain blood enhancement reagents exclusively may preclude the detection of any latent marks that may also be present.

Sears and coworkers (2005) evaluated a number of techniques that can target blood marks on various surfaces, both porous and nonporous. The use of these techniques in an optimized sequence—to maximize the development of fingermarks that may be present (both latent and blood marks)—was also investigated. For blood marks on porous surfaces such as paper, the amino acid reagents DFO and ninhydrin were found to be particularly effective, with the advantage that they will also develop latent marks. However, on less porous surfaces, protein stains were the favored treatment.

On porous surfaces, amino acid reagents must be used before any blood enhancement method that may diffuse amino acids, which includes amido black and DAB. Sears et al. (2005) found that prior treatment with DFO or ninhydrin did not affect the performance of amido black on porous surfaces but there was some loss of performance when this sequence was applied to semiporous surfaces such as lacquer-coated wallpaper. DAB can be used after DFO without a problem; however, reduced performance may be observed after ninhydrin treatment. On nonporous surfaces, the careful application of a fingerprint powder should not interfere with subsequent blood enhancement treatment. CA fuming, on the other hand, can be detrimental to the performance of blood enhancement methods such as AY7. The resulting layer of CA polymer over the blood marks reduces the effectiveness of these methods (Sears et al. 2005). Therefore, while CA fuming is a favored technique for the detection of latent marks on nonporous surfaces, it must be used with caution if fingermarks in blood are important to the case.

A recommended sequence of methods for the detection and enhancement of fingermarks in blood is provided in Figure 4.71. The sequences proposed by Sears (2012) should also be considered.

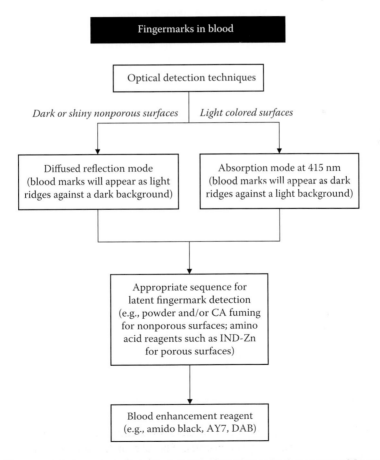

FIGURE 4.71 Recommended sequence of methods for the detection and enhancement of fingermarks in blood.

4.16 FINGERMARK DETECTION AT THE CRIME SCENE

Fingermark detection at the crime scene should logically begin with a detailed visual examination of all appropriate surfaces. The application of different optical techniques, using various light sources (strong white light, UV lamp, laser or filtered arc lamp, etc.), can reveal latent fingermarks or enhance weakly visible marks. Small objects or pieces of evidence should be removed from the crime scene, with all the normal precautions (proper packaging, labeling, etc.), for optimum fingermark treatment back at the laboratory. Nontransportable objects and fixed surfaces should then be processed using a suitable detection sequence.

Allman and Pounds (1992b) expounded a sequence of reagents for developing both latent and blood marks on various surfaces (porous, semiporous, and nonporous) at the crime scene. The authors performed experiments on a range of different surfaces that may be encountered at a crime scene, including wallpaper, wood, gloss paint, emulsion or matt paint, glass, polyethylene, and metal. They found that the iodine–benzoflavone solution, applied with an air brush or paint spray, was an effective detection method for crime scene use on a range of surfaces and for marks up to around 2 weeks of age (Pounds et al. 1992). For nonporous/semiporous surfaces, conventional fingerprint powder can be applied before or after the iodine–benzoflavone spray. For surfaces that are more porous in nature, such as certain types of wallpaper, the iodine–benzoflavone spray can be employed prior to ninhydrin treatment. The authors reported that the iodine–benzoflavone spray could reveal marks equal in quality to those developed with aluminum powder, and it was consistently better than ninhydrin at detecting relatively fresh marks on porous/semiporous surfaces such as wallpaper.

A study reported by Flynn and coworkers (2004) confirmed that the iodine–benzoflavone treatment can be successfully employed either before or after powdering across a range of surfaces at the crime scene. They found that the iodine–benzoflavone spray was the best technique on wallpaper, vinyl, brick, and raw wood, while powder was more effective on treated wood and glass. If CA fuming is envisaged, then prior treatment of the surface with iodine–benzoflavone is not recommended as it can interfere with CA development. For certain cases (such as serious crimes), the use of iodine–benzoflavone at the scene may be justified; however, health and safety precautions must be considered, including a thorough cleanup of the scene to remove chemical residues before it is released from police control.

CA fuming at the crime scene may also be a consideration in some cases. This may be possible using an improvised fuming system or a commercially available alternative such as the SUPERfume® (Foster + Freeman Ltd., United Kingdom). For fixed surfaces at the crime scene, studies have shown that powdering may perform better on some substrates while on-site CA fuming may be more effective on others (Bandey and Kent 2003; Fieldhouse 2011). For items that are transportable, CA fuming back in the laboratory should be the favored option.

After the sequence of methods for the detection of latent fingermarks, blood marks—if present—can be enhanced using techniques such as protein stains (e.g., amido black) or DAB. If blood is known to be present, fingerprint powder should be applied with care: excessive brushing may affect the integrity of a blood mark and excessive powder may decrease the effectiveness of the blood reagent. CA fuming may also adversely affect the performance of some blood enhancement methods.

For the processing of wet or heavily contaminated nonporous surfaces, the use of powder suspensions should be considered. Such suspensions can be effective on various surfaces at a fire scene (Bleay et al. 2006; Bradshaw et al. 2008; Dominick et al. 2011) and on grease-contaminated substrates (Gaskell et al. 2013b). Where a greasy contaminant is present, the use of a lipophilic stain such as sudan black should be included at the end of the detection sequence on nonporous and semiporous substrates.

A recommended sequence of methods for the exploitation of latent and bloody fingermarks at the crime scene is provided in Figure 4.72.

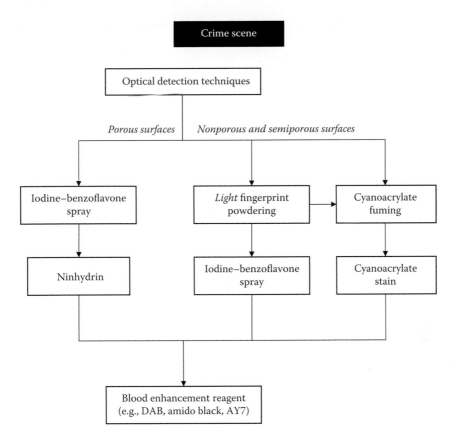

FIGURE 4.72 Recommended sequence of methods for the exploitation of latent and bloody fingermarks at the crime scene. For the processing of wet or heavily contaminated nonporous surfaces (such as grease-contaminated substrates and various surfaces at a fire scene), the use of powder suspensions should be considered. If a greasy contaminant is present, then the application of a lipophilic stain (such as sudan black) should also be included at the end of the detection sequence for nonporous and semiporous substrates. (Note: Light fingerprint powdering refers to the use of a minimum amount of powder to avoid overly contaminating the surface with excess powder.)

4.17 EFFECTS OF FINGERMARK DETECTION TECHNIQUES ON SUBSEQUENT FORENSIC ANALYSES

4.17.1 DOCUMENT EXAMINATION

Documents submitted for forensic examination may carry, in addition to latent fingermarks and DNA, indented impressions and inked inscriptions that can be subjected to handwriting or signature comparisons. Indented impressions are latent indentations on a sheet of paper that are formed when writing is fashioned on a second sheet of paper resting upon the first. For example, when writing on the top sheet of a notepad, indented impressions will be formed in the subsequent sheets. In cases involving anonymous correspondence (e.g., ransom notes or extortion letters), decipherable indentations can provide valuable information for the investigation. These indentations are typically revealed using electrostatic detection with a device such as the Electrostatic Detection Apparatus (ESDA; Foster + Freeman Ltd., United Kingdom). Given that indented impressions can be compromised by excessive handling or the application of fingermark detection reagents (Moore 1988), the ESDA examination of documents should be conducted prior to any processing for fingermarks. Documents are exposed to high humidity (60%–80% RH) prior to ESDA treatment as this can enhance the detection of indented impressions (D'Andrea et al. 1996). However, as high humidity can diffuse amino acids in latent fingermarks, the duration of this humidification step should be minimized. Excessive humidification can have detrimental effects on subsequent fingermark development (Moore 1988; Azoury et al. 2003).

Amino acid reagents such as DFO, IND-Zn, and ninhydrin are typically formulated using nonpolar carrier solvents to minimize ink diffusion on treated documents. Despite this, some ink diffusion may still result, potentially interfering with the examination of any inked inscriptions that may be present. For this reason, the examination of such inscriptions by a questioned document examiner should be conducted prior to processing for fingermarks. If the chemical analysis of ink samples is envisaged, then consideration should be given to the removal of subsamples prior to fingerprint treatment. Such subsamples should be taken from areas of the document least likely to have been handled (and, hence, least likely to carry latent fingermarks).

LaPorte and Ramotowski (2003) undertook a study to determine the effects of fingermark development techniques (specifically ninhydrin and PD, with bleach enhancement) on the physical and chemical examination of documents produced from inkjet printers, laser printers, and photocopiers. While the application of ninhydrin did not impede the general microscopic examination of such documents, there were significant changes in the optical properties of the inkjet samples when viewed in the luminescence mode. PD treatment resulted in significant macro- and microscopic changes due to silver deposition and extreme color fading was noted for the inkjet samples. Bleach enhancement virtually obliterated the three processing colors (cyan, magenta, yellow), with no significant effect on the black ink. The authors concluded that, while some examinations may still be possible, caution is warranted when analyzing documents that have been treated with fingermark development reagents.

For any items where document examination may be required, a questioned document examiner should be consulted before processing the items for potential fingermark evidence or DNA (see following section). The standard protocol is for the questioned document examination to be undertaken first as valuable information may otherwise be sacrificed.

4.17.2 DNA Profiling

DNA profiling techniques have become increasingly more sensitive and are now an integral component of the criminal investigation process. The recovery and analysis of DNA is not only possible when there is visible biological material present, such as blood and semen stains, but also where items may have been touched and trace amounts of DNA deposited (van Oorschot and Jones 1997; Lowe et al. 2002; van Oorschot et al. 2010). In this latter case, the deposited DNA is as a result of the skin cells that are naturally shed from the epidermis. The valuable information that may be obtained via DNA profiling cannot be ignored, and the fingerprint technician must therefore take into consideration the possible effects that fingermark detection techniques may have on subsequent DNA analysis. Fingermark identification and DNA profiling are complementary approaches that should be used in sequence where possible and where justified based on case circumstances (Ferraro 2012). For example, even if a fingermark detection method does not reveal identifiable impressions, the location of touch marks can highlight areas that should be swabbed for possible trace DNA. Similarly, an identifiable fingermark may not necessarily contain sufficient DNA to produce a useful genetic profile (Dominick et al. 2009). As well as considering how different fingermark detection processes may impact on any DNA that may be present, the fingerprint practitioner must also be cautious to avoid contaminating an item under examination with DNA from another source.

Polymerase chain reaction (PCR)-based short tandem repeat (STR) DNA typing was performed by Stein and coworkers (1996) on bloodstains and saliva on various supports after treatment with common fingermark detection techniques, including black powder, ninhydrin, CA fuming, and gentian violet. It was determined that the fingermark treatments did not adversely affect DNA extraction, quality, or profiling. Andersen and Bramble (1997) described a study designed to investigate the effects of different light sources used for fingermark enhancement on the subsequent PCR-STR analysis of bloodstains. While four out of the five light sources evaluated had no significant effect on subsequent quadruplex PCR analysis, exposure of the bloodstains to shortwave UV for more than 30 seconds precluded successful DNA typing. A study reported by Roux and coworkers (1999) investigated the effects of a range of common fingermark detection techniques on bloodstains deposited on a number of surfaces. DNA typing performed using PCR amplification (D1S80 and CTT primers) was adversely affected by magnetic fingerprint powder, MMD, and UV radiation. The remaining fingermark detection techniques evaluated had no significant effect.

A study reported by von Wurmb and coworkers (2000) investigated whether or not CA fuming had an effect on the relative efficiency of three different forensic PCR systems: mtDNA, Y-STR determination, and the Profiler Plus® STR profiling kit. Results obtained from blood and saliva stains on glass slides indicated that the amount of specific PCR products is reduced when typing CA-treated items. However, no difference in genotyping results was observed. Frégeau and coworkers (2000) evaluated a range of blood enhancement reagents (amido black, Crowle's double stain, DFO, Hungarian red, LMG, luminol, and ninhydrin) to determine their effect on the subsequent Profiler Plus analysis of fresh and aged blood marks on various porous and nonporous substrates. The study revealed that while DNA typing was still reliable after fingermark processing, some loss of biological material can take place, particularly with techniques that require destaining steps, such as amido black, Crowle's double stain, and Hungarian red. Caution is therefore recommended in cases where the amount of biological material is limited. A more recent study by Fox et al. (2014) explored the recovery and detection of messenger RNA (mRNA) and DNA from fingermarks in blood enhanced with long-wave UV light, amido black, AY7, and LCV. The results confirmed that genetic profiling can be successful after chemical enhancement; however, some reduction in the effectiveness of subsequent mRNA profiling was observed, particularly with depleted marks where limited biological material was available.

Studies reported by Zamir and coworkers (2000a,b) looked at the effects of different fingermark detection techniques on subsequent STR profiling. Previous treatment of envelopes and stamps with DFO was found to have no adverse effect on subsequent DNA analysis after phenol–chloroform extraction. DNA was successfully extracted from adhesive tapes and profiled after the tapes had undergone fingermark processing using a forensic light source, CA fuming, BY40 staining, and crystal violet staining. SPR treatment has also been shown to have no adverse effect on subsequent DNA profiling (Zamir et al. 2002). STR profiles have been successfully obtained from envelopes and stamps previously treated with IND but it is recommended that the DNA extraction is conducted as soon as possible after the fingermark treatment (Azoury et al. 2002). PCR-STR profiling was also found to be successful on IND-developed fingermarks on thermal and carbonless paper (Yu and Wallace 2007). Schulz et al. (2004) reported on a murder case where STR profiling was successfully applied to fingermarks that had previously been developed with ninhydrin.

A comprehensive study reported by Grubwieser et al. (2003) investigated the influence of a range of fingermark detection methods—optical, physical, and chemical—on the subsequent STR profiling of blood and saliva traces on various substrates. As a general finding, none of the fingermark enhancement methods included in the study impeded subsequent STR profiling of the biological material. It was also demonstrated that the use of a sequence consisting of an optical method (UV lamp operating at 350 nm) and two chemical enhancement methods was not detrimental after purification of the extracted DNA.

Raymond et al. (2004) investigated the effect of fifteen common fingermark detection techniques on the DNA typing of fingermarks that had been previously deposited on five different surface types. The results indicated that it is possible in many circumstances to obtain a DNA profile from fingermarks after such processing. It was found that DNA recovery was more dependent on the surface type than on the enhancement technique applied. No DNA profiles were obtained from treated or untreated fingermarks on the paper and aluminum foil substrates that were tested, but profiling was successful on marks deposited on three other surfaces. Sewell and coworkers (2008) found that while certain paper types allowed for good recovery of DNA—such as newspaper, magazine, and filter paper—common office paper and white card strongly interfered with DNA recovery, resulting in poor-quality profiles. They also observed a significant decrease in the amount of DNA recovered following treatment with DFO and/or ninhydrin; however, this did not have an adverse effect on the quality of the DNA profile obtained. Contrasting with this, Balogh et al. (2003) reported that, on average, fingermarks on paper gave 88% of a full DNA profile but that this dropped to an average of 47% of a full profile for fingermarks that had been previously developed using a chemical or physical treatment (although only a limited number of samples and detection methods were assessed in the study).

Bhoelai and coworkers (2011) reported that full STR profiles can be obtained from single latent fingermarks even after application of various fingermark detection methods such as CA fuming and VMD. However, large variations in fingermark DNA quantity were observed between donors and other factors that play a role include the duration and intensity of contact between the finger and the substrate, and the surface type. Treatments that involve washing steps, such as the staining of CA-developed marks with BY40, reduce the amount of DNA recovered. Detection methods that involve immersion, such as DFO and ninhydrin, did not impact on the profile obtained from the fingermark but did increase the risk of introducing DNA contamination. PD was found to be deleterious for DNA profiling, most likely due to the successive washing steps, including the maleic acid prewash. Au et al. (2011) evaluated powder suspensions for the enhancement of fingermarks in blood. While the technique did not interfere with subsequent presumptive tests on blood, treatment with a powder suspension was shown to reduce the amount of recoverable DNA leading to a decrease in the quality of the DNA profiles obtained.

In a study reported by Norlin and coworkers (2013), more than 200 latent fingermarks were deposited on various surfaces under controlled conditions and then treated using nine different detection methods, including fingerprint powder, powder suspension, CA fuming, ninhydrin, PD, and silver nitrate. DNA was then extracted from the fingermarks and quantified using real-time PCR. The results indicated that some detection methods had no adverse impact on DNA (e.g., black fingerprint powder and powder suspension on adhesive tape), while others were problematic (e.g., PD and silver nitrate). DNA was recovered from most of the surfaces tested, but there were large variations in the quantities obtained depending on the donor, the surface, and the fingermark detection method applied. The general observation from the DNA quantitation data was that DNA profiling is possible for many fingermarks visualized by different techniques.

Many systems have been implemented by operational laboratories for the automated extraction of DNA from biological samples, with one of these based on the use of DNA IQ™ paramagnetic beads (Promega Corporation). Laurin and coworkers (2015) investigated the compatibility of a range of fingerprint enhancement reagents/methods with the DNA IQ chemistry. The fingermark enhancement treatments that were considered included CA fuming, CA stains, VMD, DFO, IND-Zn, ninhydrin, PD, silver nitrate, ORO, TapeGlo™, and a range of fingerprint powders (both magnetic and nonmagnetic). For the majority of these treatments, no detrimental impact on DNA recovery was noted. However, Magna™ Jet Black was found to inhibit DNA extraction. Sample centrifugation or filtration prior to DNA extraction was recommended to improve DNA yields when this powder has been employed. The authors found that, regardless of the fingermark enhancement treatment applied, the DNA profiles obtained from the DNA extracts were of high quality, suggesting that DNA integrity was not compromised and that PCR inhibitors were not present in the DNA extracts.

From the published studies, it is possible to conclude that DNA profiling may still be successful after the application of most common fingermark detection methods provided that sufficient

DNA can be recovered from the developed fingermarks. However, each detection method applied is likely to remove some of the available DNA, particularly if washing steps are involved. As more techniques are applied in the detection sequence, an increasing amount of DNA will be lost. Methods that involve a significant number of washing steps, such as PD, may remove all available DNA and should therefore be used with caution if subsequent DNA recovery and profiling is envisaged. Because the success rate of DNA profiling may be reduced by fingermark enhancement procedures, consideration should be given to the collection of DNA samples prior to processing for fingermarks or early in the detection sequence. Such samples could be taken from areas unlikely to carry identifiable fingermarks. For example, the mouthpiece of a drink bottle or the rim of a drinking glass can be swabbed for DNA with little risk of damaging any fingermarks that may be present provided that the item is handled appropriately. In addition, a latent mark or biological stain revealed early in a detection sequence that is clearly unsuitable for fingerprint identification purposes could be swabbed for DNA before proceeding with other techniques in the sequence.

Another means by which fingermark detection methods may compromise subsequent DNA profiling is via the introduction of DNA contamination, being DNA transferred from other items under examination—either directly or via an intermediate—or DNA introduced by the DNA practitioners themselves. Van Oorschot and colleagues (2005) raised the potential of fingerprint brushes collecting and transferring DNA during powdering. The risk of this occurring was increased when powdering very fresh fingermarks or biological stains such as blood or saliva. DNA on a contaminated brush may be redeposited on subsequently powdered objects. While it is unlikely that detectable quantities of DNA will be transferred under normal circumstances using current techniques, the possibility of detecting transferred DNA will increase as more sensitive DNA profiling methods are introduced. Proff et al. (2006) analyzed 51 used fingerprint brushes and found that 86% were contaminated with DNA, mostly as DNA mixtures. A secondary transfer study was then undertaken with used and artificially contaminated brushes, with profiling results indicating that there was a limited risk of DNA transfer via this means. Consideration should be given to the frequent cleaning of fingerprint brushes or periodic treatment within a UV cabinet to remove DNA contamination, or the use of inexpensive, disposable brushes that can be regularly replaced. In addition to brushes being a potential contamination medium, the continued use of a single container of fingerprint powder may result in the accumulation of DNA in the powder itself. The use of separate small aliquots of fresh powder would reduce the associated risks (van Oorschot et al. 2005).

Various surfaces within a fingerprint laboratory, such as examination tables, can be contaminated with DNA via direct or indirect means. Direct transfer includes the touching of a surface with the bare hands or DNA deposition via speaking, coughing, or sneezing over the surface. The indirect transfer of DNA is via an intermediate, such as DNA falling off one evidentiary item onto an examination surface and being picked up by another item subsequently placed on that surface. Gibb and coworkers (2012) reported that DNA can accumulate on the internal and external surfaces of a CA fuming chamber and that DNA can be transferred from one item to another during the fuming process. Recommendations to avoid DNA contamination include the use of fuming cabinets that incorporate UV lamps (switched on between fuming cycles to degrade any DNA that may be present) and the regular cleaning of internal and external surfaces of the cabinet (including any accessories such as pegs or clips). More generally across the fingerprint lab, staff should wear appropriate protective equipment (such as a lab coat, face mask, and gloves), all surfaces should be thoroughly cleaned using methods known to remove or destroy DNA, environmental monitoring swabs should be frequently collected to check for DNA accumulation, and staff should undergo DNA awareness training (Gibb et al. 2012). Meakin and Jamieson (2013) reviewed the factors affecting the deposition, persistence, transfer, and recovery of trace DNA, with casework implications discussed.

4.17.3 Recovery and Analysis of Explosive Residues

Counterterrorism initiatives rely heavily on the detection and identification of explosive material found at scenes related to individuals or incidents under investigation. The analysis of explosive substances can involve (1) the detection and identification of explosives in *preblast* scenarios (i.e., unexploded bulk material and location where a device was constructed) and (2) the identification of explosive residues in *postblast* environments (i.e., after detonation). The location where an explosive device may have been constructed could hold many other forms of trace material to assist an examiner in identifying possible suspects. Latent fingermarks are an example of potential evidence of this type. Not only could these fingermarks link an individual to a particular scene, they may also contain exogenous material—such as explosive residues— that is relevant to the investigation. If the explosive residues found in these fingermarks are identified as being the same as those associated with a planned or actual bombing, then this may become crucial evidence.

Various studies have been published on the direct analysis of endogenous materials (including explosives) in fingermarks. Examples include the following:

- The in situ detection and identification of trace explosives in fingermarks by Raman spectroscopy (Cheng et al. 1995)
- The detection and identification of drugs of abuse and adulterants, present as contaminants in both latent fingermarks and fingermarks developed by CA fuming, using Raman spectroscopy (Day et al. 2004a,b)
- The simultaneous chemical analysis and imaging of fingermarks using Raman chemical imaging (Emmons et al. 2009; Tripathi et al. 2011; Guicheteau et al. 2013)
- The use of mass spectrometric methods, including surface-assisted laser desorption/ionization time-of-flight MS (SALDI-ToF-MS) and direct analysis in real-time MS, to detect common explosives in latent fingermarks and in fingermarks developed using black powder (Ifa et al. 2008; Rowell et al. 2012)
- The detection and identification of explosive residues in fingermarks using ATR-FTIR microspectroscopy (Mou and Rabalais 2009)
- The use of infrared spectroscopic imaging techniques and multivariate analysis for fingermarks that reflect a specific chemical history, such as exposure to explosives (Chen et al. 2009)
- The detection of microscopic particles, including high explosives, present as contaminants in latent fingermarks by means of synchrotron radiation-based Fourier transform infrared microimaging (Banas et al. 2012)
- The analysis of explosive residues in fingermarks using optical catapulting laser-induced breakdown spectroscopy (Abdelhamid et al. 2011)

These studies have generally ignored either the way latent fingermarks are routinely detected and enhanced by fingerprint examiners or how a forensic chemist typically processes items submitted for explosive residue analysis. However, recent research published by King and coworkers (2014) investigated the effects that common fingermark detection techniques could have on the subsequent detection of any explosive residues that may be present in latent fingermarks. 2,4,6-Trinitrotoluene (TNT) was chosen as a representative nitroaromatic, pentaerythritol tetranitrate (PETN) as a representative nitrate ester, and hexahydro-1,3,5-trinitro-1,3,5-triazine (RDX) as a representative nitramine. Sodium chlorate and ammonium nitrate were selected as representative inorganic compounds relevant to explosive residue analysis. These compounds were chosen as they are commonly encountered in either military, commercial, or improvised explosives. They also possess low volatility (low vapor pressure) and would therefore result in residues remaining for significant periods in contaminated fingermarks. The first phase of the project was to determine the likely mass of explosive residues that would be present in latent fingermarks deposited by an individual who had recently handled a bulk amount of explosive material. This was intended to simulate a scenario in which an individual responsible for assembling an explosive device handled bulk explosive material and subsequently touched other surfaces, depositing fingermarks contaminated with explosive residues. Once specific values were determined via handling experiments, these were used in the second phase to determine realistic starting amounts of each target compound that would be subjected to selected fingermark detection techniques; these amounts were 15 μg for TNT, PETN, and RDX, 30 μg for sodium chlorate, and 60 μg for ammonium nitrate. In the second phase, quantitative methods were applied to determine any loss of target material that resulted from the action of each fingermark detection method on each test substrate. The test substrates consisted of one porous surface (paper) and three nonporous surfaces (glass, clear polyethylene, and aluminum foil). Routine fingermark detection methods were applied individually and in sequence; IND-Zn, ninhydrin, and PD were selected for the paper substrate and black magnetic fingerprint powder, CA fuming, and rhodamine 6G staining for the nonporous surfaces.

For the nonporous substrates tested, the application of a fingerprint powder had, in general, no significant effect on the subsequent recovery of the target compounds. While CA fuming had minimal effect on the percent recoveries from the glass substrate, some losses were observed from plastic and aluminum foil. It is likely that these losses were due to the target compound being trapped in the deposited CA polymer. The inorganic target compounds (chlorate and nitrate) did not survive the water-based rhodamine 6G treatment applied in the study. To minimize such losses, the use of a nonaqueous stain solution and the avoidance of a final water rinse are recommended.

For the paper substrate, some losses were observed as a result of ninhydrin treatment. Such losses may be the result of physical removal of the target compounds due to the action of dipping the paper in the ninhydrin solution (resulting in the washing off of loose particles and/or via dissolution in the solvent mixture that makes up the ninhydrin formulation). While not tested in this research, it may be possible to reduce these losses by using a fine spray to apply a minimal quantity of reagent. Care would need to be taken to only apply enough solution to wet the surface. With the IND-Zn treatment, percent recoveries were significantly lower for nitrate and all three organic explosives tested compared to the control samples. While some of these losses may have been due to the action of dipping the paper samples in the solution (as for ninhydrin), losses may also be due to the use of a heat press for development (160°C for 10 seconds). To minimize such losses, it is recommended to apply the reagent as a fine spray and to either conduct the development at room temperature over several days or use an oven rather than a heat press (e.g., 100°C for 30 minutes) to avoid physical contact with the surfaces that may carry residues of interest.

The PD technique involves a significant number of water washes and treatments with an aqueous solution of maleic acid and the aqueous PD reagent itself. It was assumed from the outset that the two inorganic salts (chlorate and nitrate) would not survive this treatment so this was not specifically tested. For the organic target compounds, only PETN could be detected after PD application. This persistence of PETN is in agreement with the observations made by Kamyshny and colleagues (2003) who found that the detection of PETN on high-density polyethylene, linoleum, glass, and aluminum remained possible even after a month of soaking in seawater. They reported that traces of PETN were consistently more persistent in water than the other organic explosives that were tested. TNT and RDX were not detected after the PD treatment. Given this observed impact and the loss of inorganic residues, the use of PD should be avoided if it is intended that any explosive residues that may be present will be recovered and analyzed.

The results reported by King et al. (2014) suggest that, with most of the fingermark detection methods tested, it will still be possible to recover and analyze any explosives residues that may have been originally present in the fingermarks when they were deposited. However, each detection method applied in a sequence is likely to reduce the amount of residue remaining. To minimize such losses, it is recommended that only a limited number of techniques be applied in the detection sequence, that certain methods are avoided (e.g., PD on porous surfaces and water-based CA stains on nonporous surfaces), and that methods are applied in a certain way (e.g., application of amino acid reagents in the form of a fine spray rather than by immersion). The adoption of such recommendations would provide the greatest chance of success with respect to the detection and identification of explosive residues in fingermarks from individuals who have recently handled bulk explosives. While not tested, it is likely that similar observations would result from a study applied to other exogenous contaminants in fingermarks, such as illicit drug residues.

4.18 STANDARDS FOR FINGERMARK DETECTION RESEARCH

Early methods for the detection of latent fingermarks resulted from chance observations rather than structured and fundamental research. More recent studies have relied on an understanding of chemical composition and physicochemical interactions that might favor the generation of an adequate signal-to-noise ratio (i.e., the generation of contrast between the fingermark ridges and the substrate on which the fingermark was deposited). Fundamental research was stimulated in the United Kingdom in the 1970s and 1980s by researchers at the AWRE, the Home Office Central Research Establishment, and the Home Office Police Scientific Development Branch (now CAST). This prompted fingerprint research in other countries, with many contributions in the 1980s from groups in Australia, Canada, Israel, and Switzerland. Contributors to the scientific literature in this field were subsequently invited to join what is now referred to as the International Fingerprint Scientific Research Group (IFRG; https://ips-labs.unil.ch/ifrg/, last accessed February 7, 2016) that meets every 2 years. The contributions of all these researchers are acknowledged throughout this book.

There are many publications that claim the superiority of a new or modified fingermark detection method where such claims could not be confirmed when scrutinized. The IFRG also noted that there is significant variability with respect to the evaluation protocols employed by fingerprint research groups worldwide, including significant variability in the number and types of fingermarks collected for testing purposes. As a result, the IFRG has developed and published *best practice* guidelines to promote rigorous and objective evaluations of any detection method under consideration, from initial concept through to final casework implementation (International Fingerprint Research Group 2014). The guidelines consider four research phases from pilot studies (Phase 1), to optimization and comparison studies (Phase 2), to validation (Phase 3), and to operational evaluations and casework trials (Phase 4). Research methodology for each phase is discussed and key relevant variables are described such as environmental conditions (temperature, RH, etc.), fingermark age and composition (whether groomed and enriched with sebaceous material, limited to eccrine secretions, or *natural*), substrates (given that substrates within the same class can differ widely in chemical and physical properties), development and evaluation conditions (heating, fuming, humidity, light sources, etc.) and, finally, research implications (such as independent assessments and regulatory needs). The guidelines make detailed recommendations for each of the identified research phases and present evaluation scales as currently employed by the prominent research groups in the field.

The IFRG recommendations, which include a flow chart depicting the evaluation phases (Figure 4.73), serve as a useful guide for current and prospective researchers in this field. Any publication making claims that a particular new or modified fingermark detection method shows advantages over existing techniques should be able to demonstrate, in a rigorous manner, that this is indeed the case.

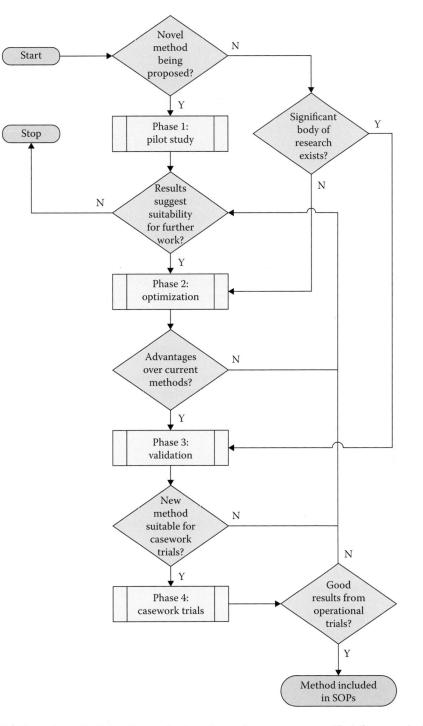

FIGURE 4.73 Flow chart depicting the evaluation phases for a new or modified fingermark detection method. (From International Fingerprint Research Group, *J. Forensic Ident.*, 64, 174, 2014.)

4.19 HEALTH AND SAFETY CONSIDERATIONS

4.19.1 HAZARDOUS SUBSTANCES

During any work involving the manipulation of chemicals, all reasonable precautions should be taken to prevent accidental or long-term exposure. Appropriate training must be provided to staff to ensure that there is general knowledge in the workplace regarding the hazards associated with particular chemicals and the safe work practices to be adopted. The laboratory itself must also be properly equipped with appropriate storage and handling facilities for any hazardous materials in use. Protective clothing (laboratory coats, safety glasses, and disposable gloves, for example) must also be provided, with usage enforced.

Occupational Health and Safety checklists are available in the specialized literature and should be used in the course of regular safety audits. Typical requirements include the following:

- An up-to-date inventory is maintained for all chemicals stored in the facility.
- Safety Data Sheets (SDSs) are available for all hazardous substances in storage or use.
- All chemicals and containers are clearly labeled (with hazard warning symbols where appropriate).
- Chemicals are stored in compatible containers.
- Leakage of chemicals onto storage shelving is controlled.
- Storage of flammable material in domestic refrigerators is prohibited (specialized laboratory refrigerators or cold rooms must be employed).
- Storage areas are separated depending on chemical compatibility (e.g., solvents separated from corrosives, strong acids separated from strong bases, and fuels separated from oxidizing materials).
- Procedures are in place for handling hazardous materials.
- Personnel handling chemicals are required to wear protective equipment (gloves, glasses, aprons, etc.) when needed, in accordance with the appropriate SDS.
- Personnel are trained in the operation and use of safety and emergency equipment where provided.
- Occupants of the laboratory are aware of what to do in the event of an emergency involving a chemical spill.
- Dry-powder fire extinguishers are readily available.
- Chemical spill kits are readily available.
- Emergency eye wash and safety showers are readily available.
- Basic first-aid kits are readily available.
- The laboratory has adequate ventilation.
- Fume cupboards are available for the handling of hazardous volatile substances.
- Biohazard cabinets are available for the handling of items contaminated with biological material.
- Eating, drinking, smoking, and the application of makeup is prohibited in the laboratory area.
- Appropriate hand-washing facilities are available for staff.
- Chemical waste is disposed of in a responsible manner and in accordance with local legislation.

SDSs for hazardous chemicals can be obtained directly from the manufacturer or distributor (e.g., may be available via a download from the manufacturer's website). The laboratory should have a complete collection of these documents, representing all hazardous materials stored and used in the workplace. The SDS collection must be current and must be accessible to all laboratory users; staff should be encouraged to review the data sheets before handling any hazardous substance.

Any given chemical should be considered as being toxic unless there is reliable information, such as an SDS, that indicates otherwise. Each SDS should contain the following information (Masters 2002):

- Name and contact details of the manufacturer
- Identity of the substance (the chemical name, chemical formula, and common name for each component of the material)
- Physical and chemical properties
- Physical hazards (including any potential for fire and explosion)
- Reactivity and incompatibility data
- Health hazards (including routes of entry, symptoms of exposure, permissible exposure or threshold limits, acute and chronic effects of exposure, and first-aid procedures)
- Precautions related to safe handling and storage (recommended personal protective equipment, ventilation requirements, procedures for dealing with a leak or spill, and waste disposal information)

All chemicals, including purchased or prepared reagents, must be stored in appropriate containers that are clearly labeled. Labels should include the chemical name and any appropriate hazard warning symbols and/or hazard warning keywords (e.g., *flammable*, *toxic*, and *corrosive*). For prepared reagents (e.g., ninhydrin solution), the label should give the name of each component, the concentration of each component, the name of the person who prepared the reagent, the date of preparation, any required storage conditions, and the expiry date. A standard classification scheme for dangerous goods is provided in Table 4.4 (United Nations Economic Commission for Europe 2014).

The following nonexhaustive list includes materials that may be encountered (or considered for use) in the fingerprint laboratory, and the specific hazards listed should be noted:

Acetic acid: Causes burns; avoid inhalation of vapor and contact with the skin; flammable.
Cadmium salts: Extremely toxic; use should be avoided.
Chemical reagents used for fingermark development: Generally stain the skin; may cause inflammations; harmful if swallowed (e.g., ninhydrin, IND, DFO).
CA vapor: Avoid prolonged exposure; long-term effects of exposure to this vapor are not well documented; avoid overheating large quantities of CA (monomer or polymer) as highly toxic cyanide gas may be generated.
Cyclohexane, diethyl ether, petroleum ether, and *ethyl acetate*: Highly flammable solvents; vapors can create explosive mixtures with air.
Dichloromethane and *chloroform*: Chlorinated organic solvents are toxic by inhalation and carcinogenic.
Ethanol and *methanol*: Flammable; methanol is toxic.
Fingerprint powders: Prolonged inhalation should be avoided; use a dust mask, particularly when using powders over extended periods.
Gentian violet (crystal violet): Toxic by inhalation and contact with the skin.
Halogenated carrier solvents (e.g., HFE, HFC, CFC, HCFC): Create a heavy vapor that can displace air in enclosed spaces; risk of asphyxiation; good ventilation required.
Iodine: Toxic by inhalation; corrosive.
Liquid nitrogen: Cryogenic material with a temperature of −196°C; skin and eye protection required; do not pour down the sink.
Nanoparticles (including dry nanopowders and suspensions): Use with caution as the short- and long-term health effects associated with exposure to these substances are largely unknown.
Phenol: Toxic by inhalation, contact with the skin, and ingestion; causes burns; carcinogenic; use should be avoided.
Silver nitrate: Toxic and corrosive.

TABLE 4.4

Example of a Dangerous Goods Classification Scheme

Class	Description
1. Explosive substances	Solid or liquid substances capable, by chemical reaction, of producing gases at such a temperature and pressure and at such a speed as to cause damage to the surroundings Pyrotechnic substances: substances designed to produce an effect by heat, light, sound, gas, or smoke as the result of nondetonating self-sustaining exothermic chemical reactions
2. Gases	
2.1. Flammable gases	Gases that that are ignitable
2.2. Nonflammable, nontoxic gases	Gases that do not come under the other divisions but may be asphyxiants (dilute or replace oxygen normally in the air) or oxidizing (cause or contribute to the combustion of other materials more than air does)
2.3. Toxic gases	Gases that are known to be so toxic or corrosive to humans as to pose a hazard to health (or are presumed to be toxic or corrosive to humans based on available data)
3. Flammable liquids	Liquids (including solutions or suspensions) that give off a flammable vapor
4. Flammable solids	Readily combustible solids and solids that may cause fire through friction (including substances prone to spontaneous combustion or substances that emit flammable gases when in contact with water)
5. Oxidizing agents and organic peroxides	
5.1. Oxidizing substances	Substances that, while not necessarily combustible themselves, may cause, or contribute to, the combustion of other material
5.2. Organic peroxides	Organic substances that contain the bivalent -O–O- structure; may react dangerously with other substances, may be sensitive to impact or friction, and may burn rapidly or explosively decompose
6. Toxic and infectious substances	
6.1. Toxic substances	Substances that are liable to cause death or serious injury or to harm human health if swallowed or inhaled, or by skin contact
6.2. Infectious substances	Substances known, or reasonably expected, to contain pathogens that are microorganisms (including bacteria, viruses, parasites, and fungi) that can cause disease in humans or animals
7. Radioactive material	Any material containing radionuclides that can spontaneously emit radiation
8. Corrosive substances	Substances that, by chemical action, will cause severe damage when in contact with living tissue or will damage or destroy other materials
9. Miscellaneous dangerous substances	Substances that present a danger not covered by other classes; includes environmentally hazardous substances

Source: United Nations Economic Commission for Europe, *European Agreement Concerning the International Carriage of Dangerous Goods by Road*, Volume I, United Nations, New York, available from: http://www.unece.org/trans/danger/publi/adr/adr_e.html, accessed 7 February 2016, 2014.

4.19.2 LIGHT SOURCES

Lasers and other high-intensity light sources (such as filtered arc lamps and UV systems) are now an integral part of fingermark detection and enhancement procedures. While the different forensic light sources on the market vary in output power and operating wavelength, they all pose potential health hazards that must be taken into consideration. Direct or reflected beams can cause permanent skin and eye damage, and appropriate safety measures must be employed. Adequate skin and eye protection must be enforced when working with these systems, with particular reference to any recommendations provided by the manufacturer.

Damage to the eye can be avoided through the use of appropriate viewing filters, safety glasses, goggles, or face shields. Most light source manufacturers provide such equipment. High-intensity light should never be viewed directly at short distances, even for a fraction of a second, without eye protection. In addition, high-intensity light can burn the skin, so gloves and long-sleeve laboratory coats should always be worn.

UV radiation poses a particular hazard due to its high energy and the fact that it is invisible to the naked eye. It is the UV component of sunlight that causes sunburn and skin cancer. When working with UV lamps, safety goggles/glasses that filter UV wavelengths must be employed. For the examination of reflective surfaces, use of a UV-protective face shield is recommended.

REFERENCES

Abdelhamid, M., Fortes, F. J., Harith, M. A., and Laserna, J. J. (2011), Analysis of explosive residues in human fingerprints using optical catapulting-laser-induced breakdown spectroscopy, *J. Anal. Atom. Spectrom.*, 26, 1445–1450.

Adcock, J. M. (1977), The development of latent fingerprints on human skin: The iodine silver plate method, *J. Forensic Sci.*, 22, 599–605.

Agarwal, M., Herlihy, R., and Reitnauer, A. (2010), A comparative study of the development of blood impressions on dark-colored substrates using phloxine b and acid yellow 7, *Fingerprint Whorld*, 36(140), 98–111.

Akiba, N., Saitoh, N., and Kuroki, K. (2007), Fluorescence spectra and images of latent fingerprints excited with a tunable laser in the ultraviolet region, *J. Forensic Sci.*, 52, 1103–1106.

Allman, D. S., Maggs, S. J., and Pounds, C. A. (1992), The use of colloidal gold/multi-metal deposition for the detection of latent fingerprints—A preliminary evaluation, HOCRE Report No. 747, Home Office Central Research Establishment, Aldermaston, U.K.

Allman, D. S. and Pounds, C. A. (1991a), Detection of fingerprints on skin, *Forensic Sci. Rev.*, 3, 83–89.

Allman, D. S. and Pounds, C. A. (1991b), Diaminobenzidine: A simple, safe and sensitive method for the enhancement of blood marks at scene of crime and in the laboratory, HOCRE Report No. 733, Home Office Central Research Establishment, Aldermaston, U.K.

Allman, D. S. and Pounds, C. A. (1992a), The detection of finger marks by use of antibody techniques, HOCRE Report No. 752, Home Office Central Research Establishment, Aldermaston, U.K.

Allman, D. S. and Pounds, C. A. (1992b), The sequence of reagents to be used to develop fingerprints at a scene of crime, HOCRE Report No. 748, Home Office Central Research Establishment, Aldermaston, U.K.

Allman, D. S. and Pounds, C. A. (1992c), The specificity of diaminobenzidine for the detection of blood, HOCRE Report No. 771, Home Office Central Research Establishment, Aldermaston, U.K.

Almog, J. (2001), Fingerprint development by ninhydrin and its analogues, in *Advances in Fingerprint Technology*, 2nd ed., eds., H. C. Lee and R. E. Gaensslen, Boca Raton, FL: CRC Press, pp. 177–209.

Almog, J. (2012), Ninhydrin and ninhydrin analogues: Recent developments, in *Lee and Gaensslen's Advances in Fingerprint Technology*, 3rd ed., ed. R. Ramotowski, Boca Raton, FL: CRC Press, pp. 293–305.

Almog, J., Azoury, M., Elmaliah, Y., Berenstein, L., and Zaban, A. (2004), Fingerprints' third dimension: The depth and shape of fingerprints penetration into paper—Cross section examination by fluorescence microscopy, *J. Forensic Sci.*, 49, 981–985.

Almog, J., Cohen, Y., Azoury, M., and Hahn, T.-R. (2004), Genipin—A novel fingerprint reagent with colorimetric and fluorogenic activity, *J. Forensic Sci.*, 49, 255–257.

Almog, J. and Hirshfeld, A. (1988), 5-Methoxyninhydrin: A reagent for the chemical development of latent fingerprints that is compatible with the copper-vapor laser, *J. Forensic Sci.*, 33, 1027–1030.

Almog, J., Hirshfeld, A., Frank, A., Grant, H., Harel, Z., and Ittah, Y. (1992), 5-Methylthio ninhydrin and related compounds: A novel class of fluorogenic fingerprint reagents, *J. Forensic Sci.*, 37, 688–694.

Almog, J., Hirshfeld, A., Frank, A., Sterling, J., and Leonov, D. (1991), Aminoninhydrins: Fingerprint reagents with direct fluorogenic activity—Preliminary studies. *J. Forensic Sci.*, 36, 104–110.

Almog, J., Hirshfeld, A., and Klug, J. T. (1982), Reagents for the chemical development of latent fingerprints: Synthesis and properties of some ninhydrin analogues, *J. Forensic Sci.*, 27, 912–917.

Almog, J., Klein, A., Davidi, I., Cohen, Y., Azoury, M., and Levin-Elad, M. (2008), Dual fingerprint reagents with enhanced sensitivity: 5-methoxy- and 5-methylthioninhydrin, *J. Forensic Sci.*, 53, 364–368.

Almog, J., Levinton-Shamuilov, G., Cohen, Y., and Azoury, M. (2007), Fingerprint reagents with dual action: Color and fluorescence, *J. Forensic Sci.*, 52, 330–334.

Almog, J., Sears, V. G., Springer, E., Hewlett, D. F., Walker, S., Wiesner, S., Lidor, R., and Bahar, E. (2000), Reagents for the chemical development of latent fingerprints: Scope and limitations of benzo[f]ninhydrin in comparison to ninhydrin, *J. Forensic Sci.*, 45, 538–544.

Almog, J., Springer, E., Wiesner, S., Frank, A., Khodzhaev, O., Lidor, R., Bahar, E., Varkony, H., Dayan, S., and Rozen, S. (1999), Latent fingerprint visualization by 1, 2-indanedione and related compounds: Preliminary results, *J. Forensic Sci.*, 44, 114–118.

Andersen, J. and Bramble, S. (1997), The effects of fingermark enhancement light sources on subsequent PCR-STR DNA analysis of fresh bloodstains, *J. Forensic Sci.*, 42, 303–306.

Anon. (1993), Amido black treatment of a murder victim, *Fingerprint Whorld*, 19(73), 55.

Antoine, K. M., Mortazavi, S., Miller, A. D., and Miller, L. M. (2010), Chemical differences are observed in children's versus adults' latent fingerprints as a function of time, *J. Forensic Sci.*, 55, 513–518.

Arndt, C. B. (1985), Iodine silver plate transfer method, *RCMP Gaz.*, 47(5), 19–21.

Aronson, C. K. (2011), Development of bloody prints on the adhesive side of duct tape, *J. Forensic Ident.*, 61, 250–259.

Asano, K. G., Bayne, C. K., Horsman, K. M., and Buchanan, M. V. (2002), Chemical composition of fingerprints for gender determination, *J. Forensic Sci.*, 47, 805–807.

Attard Montalto, N., Ojeda, J. J., and Jones, B. J. (2013), Determining the order of deposition of natural latent fingerprints and laser printed ink using chemical mapping with secondary ion mass spectrometry, *Sci. Justice*, 53, 2–7.

Au, C., Jackson-Smith, H., Quinones, I., Jones, B. J., and Daniel, B. (2011), Wet powder suspensions as an additional technique for the enhancement of bloodied marks, *Forensic Sci. Int.*, 204, 13–18.

Aubert, P.-F. (1878), Des modifications subies par la sécrétion de la sueur dans les maladies de la peau, *Ann. derm. syph.*, 9, 359–373.

Azoury, M., Gabbay, R., Cohen, D., and Almog, J. (2003), ESDA processing and latent fingerprint development: The humidity effect, *J. Forensic Sci.*, 48, 564–570.

Azoury, M., Zamir, A., Oz, C., and Wiesner, S. (2002), The effect of 1,2-indanedione, a latent fingerprint reagent on subsequent DNA profiling, *J. Forensic Sci.*, 47, 586–588.

Bailey, J. A. and Crane, J. S. (2011), Use of nitrogen cryogun for separating duct tape and recovery of latent fingerprints with a powder suspension method, *Forensic Sci. Int.*, 210, 170–173.

Bailey, M. J., Bright, N. J., Croxton, R. S., Francese, S., Ferguson, L. S., Hinder, S., Jickells, S. et al. (2012), Chemical characterization of latent fingerprints by matrix-assisted laser desorption ionization, time-of-flight secondary ion mass spectrometry, mega electron volt secondary mass spectrometry, gas chromatography/mass spectrometry, x-ray photoelectron spectroscopy, and attenuated total reflection Fourier transform infrared spectroscopic imaging: An intercomparison, *Anal. Chem.*, 84, 8514–8523.

Bailey, M. J., Ismail, M., Bleay, S., Bright, N., Elad, M. L., Cohen, Y., Geller, B. et al. (2013), Enhanced imaging of developed fingerprints using mass spectrometry imaging, *Analyst*, 138, 6246–6250.

Balogh, M. K., Burger, J., Bender, K., Schneider, P. M., and Alt, K. W. (2003), STR genotyping and mtDNA sequencing of latent fingerprint on paper, *Forensic Sci. Int.*, 137, 188–195.

Banas, A., Banas, K., Breese, M. B. H., Loke, J., Heng Teo, B., and Lim, S. K. (2012), Detection of microscopic particles present as contaminants in latent fingerprints by means of synchrotron radiation-based Fourier transform infra-red micro-imaging, *Analyst*, 137, 3459–3465.

Bandey, H., Bleay, S., Bowman, V., Fitzgerald, L., Gibson, A., Hart, A., and Sears, V. (2006), Fingerprint imaging across EM spectrum, *Imaging Sci. J.*, 54, 211–218.

Bandey, H. L., Bleay, S. M., and Gibson, A. P. (2012), Powders for fingerprint development, in *Lee and Gaensslen's Advances in Fingerprint Technology*, 3rd ed., ed., R. Ramotowski, Boca Raton, FL: CRC Press, pp. 191–217.

Bandey, H. and Kent, T. (2003), Superglue treatment of crime scenes: A trial of the effectiveness of the Mason Vactron SUPERfume process, Publication No. 30/03, Home Office Police Scientific Development Branch, Sandridge, U.K.

Baran, M. (2009), Lifting fingerprints from skin using silicone, *Can. Soc. Forensic Sci. J.*, 42, 121–131.

Barnum, C. A. and Klasey, D. R. (1997), Factors affecting the recovery of latent prints on firearms, *J. Forensic Ident.*, 47, 141–149.

Batey, G. W., Copeland, J., Donnelly, D. L., Hill, C. L., Laturnus, P. L., McDiarmid, C. H., Miller, K. J., Misner, A. H., Tario, A., and Yamashita, A. B. (1998), Metal deposition for latent print development, *J. Forensic Ident.*, 48, 165–175.

Beaudoin, A. (2004), New technique for revealing latent fingerprints on wet, porous surfaces: Oil Red O, *J. Forensic Ident.*, 54, 413–421.

Beaudoin, A. (2011), Oil Red O: Fingerprint development on a 21-year-old cold case, *J. Forensic Ident.*, 61, 50–59.

Beaudoin, A. (2012a), Fingerprint staining technique on dark and wetted porous surfaces: Oil Red O and rhodamine 6G, *J. Forensic Ident.*, 62, 315–329.

Beaudoin, A. (2012b), Comparison of ortho-tolidine and amido black for development of blood-based fingerprints on skin, *J. Forensic Ident.*, 62, 588–601.

Bécue, A. and Cantú, A. A. (2012), Fingermark detection using nanoparticles, in *Lee and Gaensslen's Advances in Fingerprint Technology*, 3rd ed., ed., R. Ramotowski, Boca Raton, FL: CRC Press, pp. 308–379.

Bécue, A., Champod, C., and Margot, P. (2007), Use of gold nanoparticles as molecular intermediates for the detection of fingermarks, *Forensic Sci. Int.*, 168, 169–176.

Bécue, A., Moret, S., Champod, C., and Margot, P. (2009), Use of quantum dots in aqueous solution to detect blood fingermarks on non-porous surfaces, *Forensic Sci. Int.*, 191, 36–41.

Bécue, A., Moret, S., Champod, C., and Margot, P. (2011), Use of stains to detect fingermarks, *Biotechn. Histochem.*, 86, 140–160.

Bécue, A., Scoundrianos, A., Champod, C., and Margot, P. (2008), Fingermark detection based on the in situ growth of luminescent nanoparticles—Towards a new generation of multimetal deposition, *Forensic Sci. Int.*, 179, 39–43.

Bécue, A., Scoundrianos, A., and Moret, S. (2012), Detection of fingermarks by colloidal gold (MMD/SMD)—Beyond the pH 3 limit, *Forensic Sci. Int.*, 219, 39–49.

Bentolila, A., Totre, J., Zozulia, I., Levin-Elad, M., and Domb, A. J. (2013), Fluorescent cyanoacrylate monomers and polymers for fingermark development, *Macromolecules*, 46, 4822–4828.

Bentsen, R. K., Brown, J. K., Dinsmore, A., Harvey, K. K., and Kee, T. G. (1996), Post-firing visualisation of fingerprints on spent cartridge cases, *Sci. Justice*, 36, 3–8.

Ben-Yosef, N., Almog, J., Frank, A., Springer, E., and Cantú, A. A. (1998), Short UV luminescence for forensic applications: Design of a real-time observation system for detection of latent fingerprints and body fluids, *J. Forensic Sci.*, 43, 299–304.

Berdejo, S., Rowe, M., and Bond, J. W. (2012), Latent fingermark development on a range of porous substrates using ninhydrin analogs—A comparison with ninhydrin and 1,8-diazofluoren, *J. Forensic Sci.*, 57, 509–514.

Bergeron, J. (2003), Development of bloody prints on dark surfaces with titanium dioxide and methanol, *J. Forensic Sci.*, 53, 149–161.

Bergeron, J. W. (2009), Use of liquid nitrogen to separate adhesive tapes, *J. Forensic Ident.*, 59, 7–25.

Bessman, C. W., Nelson, E., Lipert, R. J., Coldiron, S., and Herrman, T. R. (2005), A comparison of cyanoacrylate fuming in a vacuum cabinet to a humidity fuming chamber, *J. Forensic Ident.*, 55, 10–27.

Bettencourt, D. S. (1991), A compilation of techniques for processing deceased human skin for latent prints, *J. Forensic Ident.*, 41, 111–120.

Bhoelai, B., de Jong, B. J., de Puit, M., and Sijen, T. (2011), Effect of common fingerprint detection techniques on subsequent STR profiling, *Forensic Sci. Int.: Gen.*, 3, e429–e430.

Bicknell, D. E. and Ramotowski, R. S. (2008), Use of an optimized 1,2-indanedione process for the development of latent prints, *J. Forensic Sci.*, 53, 1108–1116.

Bissonnette, M., Knaap, W., and Forbes, S. L. (2010), Steam development of latent fingerprints on thermal paper, *J. Forensic Ident.*, 60, 619–638.

Blackledge, R. D. (1998), Re: Latent print processing by the ruthenium tetroxide method [letter plus editor's reply], *J. Forensic Ident.*, 48, 557–559.

Blasdell, R. (2001), The longevity of the latent fingerprints of children vs adults, *Policing*, 24, 363–370.

Bleay, S. M., Bradshaw, G., and Moore, J. E. (2006), Fingerprint development and imaging newsletter: Special edition, Publication No. 26/06, Home Office Scientific Development Branch, Sandridge, U.K.

Bleay, S. M. and Kent, T. (2005), The use of infra-red filters to remove background patterns in fingerprint imaging, *Fingerprint Whorld*, 31(122), 225–238.

Bleay, S. M., Sears, V. G., Bandey, H. L., Gibson, A. P., Bowman, V. J., Downham, R., Fitzgerald, L., Ciuksza, T., Ramadani, J., and Selway, C. (2013), Finger mark development techniques within scope of ISO 17025, Chapter 3 in *Fingerprint Source Book*, Home Office Centre for Applied Science and Technology, Sandridge, U.K.

Bobev, K. (1995), Fingerprints and factors affecting their condition, *J. Forensic Ident.*, 45, 176–183.

Boddis, A. M. and Russell, D. A. (2012), Development of aged fingermarks using antibody-magnetic particle conjugates, *Anal. Methods*, 4, 637–641.

Bohanan, A. M. (1998), Latents from pre-pubescent children versus latents from adults, *J. Forensic Ident.*, 48, 570–573.

Bond, J. W. (2008), Visualization of latent fingerprint corrosion of metallic surfaces, *J. Forensic Sci.*, 53, 812–822.

Bond, J. W. (2013), Development of latent fingerprints on thermal paper by the controlled application of heat, *J. Forensic Sci.*, 58, 767–771.

Bond, J. W. (2015), Response assessment of thermal papers from four continents to fingerprint development by heat, *J. Forensic Sci.*, 60, 1331–1336.

Bond, J. W. and Heidel, C. (2009), Visualization of latent fingerprint corrosion on a discharged brass shell casing, *J. Forensic Sci.*, 54, 892–894.

Bossers, L. C. A. M., Roux, C., Bell, M., and McDonagh, A. M. (2011), Methods for the enhancement of fingermarks in blood, *Forensic Sci. Int.*, 210, 1–11.

Braasch, K., de la Hunty, M., Deppe, J., Spindler, X., Cantú, A. A., Maynard, P., Lennard, C., and Roux, C. (2013), Nile red: Alternative to physical developer for the detection of latent fingermarks on wet porous surfaces? *Forensic Sci. Int.*, 230, 74–80.

Bradshaw, G., Bleay, S., Deans, J., and Nic Daéid, N. (2008), Recovery of fingerprints from arson scenes: Part 1—Latent fingerprints, *J. Forensic Ident.*, 58, 54–82.

Bradshaw, R., Bleay, S., Clench, M. R., and Francese, S. (2014), Direct detection of blood in fingermarks by MALDI MS profiling and imaging, *Sci. Justice*, 54, 110–117.

Bradshaw, R., Bleay, S., Wolstenholme, R., Clench, M. R., and Francese, S. (2013), Towards the integration of matrix assisted laser desorption ionisation mass spectrometry imaging into the current fingermark examination workflow, *Forensic Sci. Int.*, 232, 111–124.

Bradshaw, R., Rao, W., Wolstenholme, R., Clench, M. R., Bleay, S., and Francese, S. (2012), Separation of overlapping fingermarks by matrix assisted laser desorption ionisation mass spectrometry imaging, *Forensic Sci. Int.*, 222, 318–326.

Bramble, S. K., Cantú, A. A., Ramotowski, R. S., and Brennan, J. S. (2000), Deep red to near infrared (NIR) fluorescence of gentian violet-treated latent prints, *J. Forensic Ident.*, 50, 33–49.

Bramble, S. K., Creer, K. E., Gui Qiang, W., and Sheard, B. (1993), Ultraviolet luminescence from latent fingerprints, *Forensic Sci. Int.*, 59, 3–14.

Bratton, R., Gregus, J., and Juhala, J. (1996), A black powder method to process adhesive tapes, in *Proceedings of the International Symposium on Fingerprint Detection and Identification*, Ne'urim, Israel: eds. J. Almog and E. Springer, Israel National Police, June 26–30, 1995, pp. 143–147.

Bratton, R. and Gregus, J. (1997), Development of a black powder method to process adhesive tapes, *Fingerprint Whorld*, 23(87), 21–23.

Bratton, R. M. and Juhala, J. A. (1995), DFO-dry, *J. Forensic Ident.*, 45, 169–172.

Brennan, J. S. (1996), The development of fingerprints by fuming with dimethylamino-cinnamaldehyde (DMAC), in *Proceedings of the International Symposium on Fingerprint Detection and Identification*, Ne'urim, Israel: eds. J. Almog and E. Springer, Israel National Police, June 26–30, 1995, pp. 85–90.

Brennan, J., Bramble, S., Crabtree, S., and Wright, G. (1995), Fuming of latent fingerprints using dimethyl-aminocinnamaldehyde, *J. Forensic Ident.*, 45, 373–380.

Bright, N. J., Webb, R. P., Bleay, S., Hinder, S., Ward, N. I., Watts, J. F., Kirkby, K. J., and Bailey, M. J. (2012), Determination of the deposition order of overlapping latent fingerprints and inks using secondary ion mass spectrometry, *Anal. Chem.*, 84, 4083–4087.

Broniek, B. and Knaap, W. (2002), Latent fingerprint development on thermal paper using muriatic (hydrochloric) acid, *J. Forensic Ident.*, 52, 427–432.

Brzozowski, J., Bialek, I., and Subik, P. (2005), Visualisation of fingerprints on sticky side of adhesive tapes, *Prob. Forensic Sci.*, 64, 333–342.

Buchanan, M. V., Asano, K., and Bohanan, A. (1997), Chemical characterization of fingerprints from adults and children, in *Proceedings of SPIE—The International Society for Optical Engineering*, Orlando, FL, Vol. 2941, pp. 89–95.

Bullock, K. M., Harris, J. S., and Latumus, P. L. (1994), Use of a simple coaxial lighting system to enhance fingerprint and handwriting evidence, *Can. Soc. Forensic Sci. J.*, 27, 69–80.

Burns, D. S. (1994), Sticky-side powder: The Japanese solution, *J. Forensic Ident.*, 44, 133–138.

Burns, T. B., Brown, J. K., Dinsmore, A., and Harvey, K. K. (1998), Base-activated latent fingerprints fumed with a cyanoacrylate monomer. A quantitative study using Fourier-transform infra-red spectroscopy, *Anal. Chim. Acta*, 362, 171–176.

Cadd, S., Islam, M., Manson, P., and Bleay, S. (2015), Fingerprint composition and aging: A literature review, *Sci. Justice*, 55, 219–238.

Cadd, S. J., Bleay, S. M., and Sears, V. G. (2013), Evaluation of the solvent black 3 fingermark enhancement reagent: Part 2—Investigation of the optimum formulation and application parameters, *Sci. Justice*, 53, 131–143.

Cai, K., Yang, R., Wang, Y., Yu, X., and Liu, J. (2013), Super fast detection of latent fingerprints with water soluble CdTe quantum dots, *Forensic Sci. Int.*, 226, 240–243.

Caldwell, J. P., Henderson, W., and Kim, N. D. (2000), ABTS: A safe alternative to DAB for the enhancement of blood fingerprints, *J. Forensic Sci.*, 45, 785–794.

Campbell, B. M. (1991a), Separation of adhesive tapes, *J. Forensic Ident.*, 41, 102–106.

Campbell, B. M. (1991b), Vacuum chamber cyanoacrylate technique evolution, *RCMP Gaz.*, 53(12), 12–16.

Cantú, A. A. (2001), Silver physical developers for the visualization of latent prints on paper, *Forensic Sci. Rev.*, 13, 29–64.

Cantú, A. A. (2014), The physical principles of the reflected ultraviolet imaging systems, *J. Forensic Ident.*, 64, 123–141.

Cantú, A. A. and Johnson, J. L. (2001), Silver physical development of latent prints, in *Advances in Fingerprint Technology*, 2nd ed., eds., H. C. Lee and R. E. Gaensslen, Boca Raton, FL: CRC Press, pp. 241–274.

Cantú, A. A., Leben, D. A., Joullié, M. M., Heffner, R. J., and Hark, R. R. (1993), A comparative examination of several amino acid reagents for visualizing amino acid (glycine) on paper, *J. Forensic Ident.*, 43, 44–66.

Cantú, A. A., Leben, D. A., Ramotowski, R., Kopera, J., and Simms, J. R. (1998), Use of acidified hydrogen peroxide to remove excess gun blue from gun blue-treated cartridge cases and to develop latent prints on untreated cartridge cases, *J. Forensic Sci.*, 43, 294–298.

Chadwick, S. (2013), Near infrared laser dyes for the detection of latent fingermarks, Ph.D. thesis, University of Technology Sydney, Sydney, Australia.

Chadwick, S., Maynard, P., Kirkbride, P., Lennard, C., McDonagh, A., Spindler, X., and Roux, C. (2012), Styryl dye coated metal oxide powders for the detection of latent fingermarks on non-porous surfaces, *Forensic Sci. Int.*, 219, 208–214.

Chadwick, S., Maynard, P., Kirkbride, P., Lennard, C., Spindler, X., and Roux, C. (2011), Use of Styryl 11 and STaR 11 for the luminescence enhancement of cyanoacrylate-developed fingermarks in the visible and near-infrared regions, *J. Forensic Sci.*, 56, 1505–1513.

Chan, J., Shimmon, R., Spindler, X., Maynard, P., Lennard, C., Roux, C., and Stuart, B. H. (2010), An investigation of isatin as a potential reagent for latent fingermark detection on porous surfaces, *J. Forensic Ident.*, 60, 320–336.

Charlton, D. T., Bleay, S. M., and Sears, V. G. (2013), Evaluation of the multimetal deposition process for fingermark enhancement in simulated operational environments, *Anal. Methods*, 5, 5411–5417.

Cheeseman, R. and DiMeo, L. A. (1995), Fluorescein as a field-worthy latent bloodstain detection system, *J. Forensic Ident.*, 45, 631–646.

Chen, T., Schultz, Z. D., and Levin, I. W. (2009), Infrared spectroscopic imaging of latent fingerprints and associated forensic evidence, *Analyst*, 134, 1902–1904.

Cheng, C., Kirkbride, T. E., Batchelder, D. N., Lacey, R. J., and Sheldon, T. G. (1995), In situ detection and identification of trace explosives by Raman microscopy, *J. Forensic Sci.*, 40, 31–37.

Cheng, K. H., Ajimo, J., and Chen, W. (2008), Exploration of functionalized CdTe nanoparticles for latent fingerprint detection, *J. Nanosci. Nanotechnol.*, 8(3), 1170–1173.

Choi, M. J., McBean, K. E., Ng, P. H. R., McDonagh, A. M., Maynard, P. J., Lennard, C., and Roux, C. (2008), An evaluation of nanostructured zinc oxide as a fluorescent powder for fingerprint detection, *J. Mater. Sci.*, 43, 732–737.

Choi, M. J., McBean, K. E., Wuhrer, R., McDonagh, A. M., Maynard, P. J., Lennard, C., and Roux, C. (2006), Investigation into the binding of gold nanoparticles to fingermarks using scanning electron microscopy, *J. Forensic Ident.*, 56, 24–32.

Choi, M. J., McDonagh, A. M., Maynard, P., and Roux, C. (2008), Metal-containing nanoparticles and nanostructured particles in fingermark detection, *Forensic Sci. Int.*, 179, 87–97.

Choi, M. J., McDonagh, A. M., Maynard, P. J., Wuhrer, R., Lennard, C., and Roux, C. (2006), Preparation and evaluation of metal nanopowders for the detection of fingermarks on nonporous surfaces, *J. Forensic Ident.*, 56, 756–768.

Choi, M. J., Smoother, T., Martin, A. A., McDonagh, A. M., Maynard, P. J., Lennard, C., and Roux, C. (2007), Fluorescent TiO_2 powders prepared using a new perylene diimide dye: Applications in latent fingermark detection, *Forensic Sci. Int.*, 173, 154–160.

Choudhry, M. Y. and Whritenour, R. D. (1990), A new approach to unraveling tangled adhesive tape for potential detection of latent prints and recovery of trace evidence, *J. Forensic Sci.*, 35, 1373–1383.

Clements, W. W. (1983), Blood print on human skin, *Ident. News*, 33(8), 4, 6.

Conn, C., Ramsay, G., Roux, C., and Lennard, C. (2001), The effect of metal salt treatment on the photoluminescence of DFO-treated fingerprints, *Forensic Sci. Int.*, 116, 117–123.

Crane, N. J., Bartick, E. G., Perlman, R. S., and Huffman, S. (2007), Infrared spectroscopic imaging for noninvasive detection of latent fingerprints, *J. Forensic Sci.*, 52, 48–53.

Creer, K. E. (1993), Detection and photography of latent marks using specialised lighting and imaging techniques, in *International Symposium on the Forensic Aspects of Latent Prints*, FBI Academy, Quantico, VA.

Creer, K. E. (1996), Detection and enhancement of latent marks using specialised lighting and imaging techniques, in *International Symposium in Fingerprint Detection and Identification*, Ne'urim, Israel: eds. J. Almog and E. Springer, Israel National Police, June 26–30, 1995, pp. 25–35.

Creighton, J. T. (1997), Visualization of latent impressions after incidental or direct contact with human blood, *J. Forensic Ident.*, 47, 534–541.

Cummings, H., Hollars, M., Peigare, F., and Trozzi, T. (1990), BBD and MBD: Multipurpose reagents for latent print detection, *J. Forensic Ident.*, 40, 334–340.

Cummings, H., Hollars, M., and Trozzi, T. (1993), Getting the most from cyanoacrylate dyes, *J. Forensic Ident.*, 43, 37–43.

Czekanski, P., Fasola, M., and Allison, J. (2006), A mechanistic model for the superglue fuming of latent fingerprints. *J. Forensic Sci.*, 51, 1323–1328.

Dadmun, M. D. (2014), *Developing Methods to Improve the Quality and Efficiency of Latent Fingermark Development by Superglue Fuming*, National Institute of Justice, Washington, DC. https://www.ncjrs.gov/pdffiles1/nij/grants/248637.pdf (accessed February 6, 2016).

Dalrymple, B. and Almog, J. (2012), Comparison of latent print detection using semiconductor laser and LED light sources with three chemical reagents, *J. Forensic Ident.*, 62, 14–27.

Dalrymple, B. E., Duff, J. M., and Menzel, E. R. (1977), Inherent fingerprint luminescence—Detection by laser, *J. Forensic Sci.*, 22, 106–115.

D'Andrea, F., Mazzella, W. D., Khanmy, A., and Margot, P. (1996), Effects of the relative humidity and temperature on the efficiency of the ESDA (electrostatic detection apparatus) process, *Int. J. Forensic Document Examiners*, 2, 209–213.

Davies, P. J., Kobus, H. J., Taylor, M. R., and Wainwright, K. P. (1995), Synthesis and structure of the zinc(II) and cadmium(II) complexes produced in the photoluminescent enhancement of ninhydrin developed fingerprints using Group 12 metal salts, *J. Forensic Sci.*, 40, 565–569.

Day, J. S., Edwards, H. G. M., Dobrowski, S. A., and Voice, A. M. (2004a), The detection of drugs of abuse in fingerprints using Raman spectroscopy I: Latent fingerprints, *Spectrochim. Acta A*, 60, 563–568.

Day, J. S., Edwards, H. G. M., Dobrowski, S. A., and Voice, A. M. (2004b), The detection of drugs of abuse in fingerprints using Raman spectroscopy II: Cyanoacrylate-fumed fingerprints, *Spectrochim. Acta A*, 60, 1725–1730.

Day, K. and Bowker, W. (1996), Enhancement of cyanoacrylate developed latent prints using nile red, *J. Forensic Ident.*, 46, 183–187.

de la Hunty, M., Spindler, X., Chadwick, S., Lennard, C., and Roux, C. (2014), Synthesis and application of an aqueous nile red microemulsion for the development of fingermarks on porous surfaces, *Forensic Sci. Int.*, 244, e48–e55.

de Puit, M., Koomen, L., Bouwmeester, M., de Gijt, M., Rodriguez, C., van Wouw, J., and de Haan, F. (2011), Use of physical developer for the visualization of latent fingerprints, *J. Forensic Ident.*, 61, 166–170.

Delmas, B. J. (1988), Postmortem latent print recovery from skin, *J. Forensic Ident.*, 38, 49–56.

Deppe, J., Braasch, K., Cantú, A. A., Spindler, X., Shimmon, R., Maynard, P., Lennard, C., and Roux, C. (2010), Nile red: Alternative to physical developer for the detection of latent fingermarks on wet non-porous surfaces, presented at the *Australian and New Zealand Forensic Science Society 20th International Symposium on the Forensic Sciences*, Sydney, Australia, September 5–9, 2010.

Didierjean, C., Debart, M.-H., and Crispino, F. (1998), New formulation of DFO in HFE7100, *Fingerprint Whorld*, 24(94), 163–167.

Dilag, J., Kobus, H., and Ellis, A. V. (2009), Cadmium sulfide quantum dot/chitosan nanocomposites for latent fingermark detection, *Forensic Sci. Int.*, 187, 97–102.

Dilag, J., Kobus, H. J., and Ellis, A. V. (2011), Nanotechnology as a new tool for fingermark detection: A review, *Current Nanosci.*, 7, 153–159.

Dilag, J., Kobus, H., and Ellis, A. V. (2013), CdS/polymer nanocomposites synthesized via surface initiated RAFT polymerization for the fluorescent detection of latent fingermarks, *Forensic Sci. Int.*, 228, 105–114.

Dolci, D. (1992), Révélation des empreintes digitales sur la peau, technical report, Institut de police scientifique et de criminologie, University of Lausanne, Lausanne, Switzerland.

Dominick, A. J. and Laing, K. (2011), A comparison of six fingerprint enhancement techniques for the recovery of latent fingerprints from unfired cartridge cases, *J. Forensic Ident.*, 61, 155–165.

Dominick, A. J., Nic Daéid, N., and Bleay, S. M. (2011), The recoverability of fingerprints on nonporous surfaces exposed to elevated temperatures, *J. Forensic Ident.*, 61, 520–536.

Dominick, A. J., Welch, L. A., Nic Daéid, N., and Bleay, S. M. (2009), Is there a relationship between fingerprint donation and DNA shedding? *J. Forensic Ident.*, 59, 133–143.

Donche, A. and Musy, C. (1994), Development of latent fingerprints on cartridge casings, *Fingerprint Whorld*, 20(75), 13–19.

Donnelly, E. F., Johnston, D. S., Pepper, D. C., and Dunn, D. J. (1977), Ionic and zwitterionic polymerization of n-alkyl 2-cyanoacrylates, *J. Polym. Sci. Pol. Lett.*, 15, 399–405.

Downham, R. P., Mehmet, S., and Sears, V. G. (2012), A pseudo-operational investigation into the development of latent fingerprints on flexible plastic packaging films, *J. Forensic Ident.*, 62, 661–682.

Drabarek, B., Siejca, A., Moszczynski, J., and Konior, B. (2012), Applying anti-stokes phosphors in development of fingerprints on surfaces characterized by strong luminescence, *J. Forensic Ident.*, 62, 28–35.

Drapel, V., Bécue, A., Champod, C., and Margot, P. (2009), Identification of promising antigenic components in latent fingermark residues, *Forensic Sci. Int.*,184, 47–53.

Durussel, P., Stauffer, E., Bécue, A., Champod, C., and Margot, P. (2009), Single-metal deposition: Optimization of this fingermark enhancement technique, *J. Forensic Ident.*, 59, 80–96.

Edmiston, K. E. and Johnson, J. (2009), Determining an optimal sequence for chemical development of latent prints on cartridge casings and shotgun shells, *J. Forensic Sci.*, 54, 1327–1331.

Edwards, H. G. M. and Day, J. S. (2006), Anomalies in polycyanoacrylate formation studied by raman spectroscopy: Implications for the forensic enhancement of latent fingerprints for spectral analysis, *Vib. Spectrosc.*, 41, 155–159.

Elkayam, R., Rhima, I., and Shelef, R. (1996), II. Optimization of small particle reagent for the development of latent fingerprints from glass surfaces washed in accelerant fluids, *J. Forensic Ident.*, 46, 561–565.

Emmons, E. D., Tripathi, A., Guicheteau, J. A., Christesen, S. D., and Fountain, A. W. (2009), Raman chemical imaging of explosive-contaminated fingerprints, *Appl. Spectrosc.*, 63, 1197–1203.

Exline, D. L., Wallace, C., Roux, C., Lennard, C., Nelson, M. P., and Treado, P. J. (2003), Forensic applications of chemical imaging: Latent fingerprint detection using visible absorption and luminescence, *J. Forensic Sci.*, 48, 1047–1053.

Fairley, C., Bleay, S. M., Sears, V. G., and Nic Daéid, N. (2012), A comparison of multi-metal deposition processes utilising gold nanoparticles and an evaluation of their application to 'low yield' surfaces for finger mark development, *Forensic Sci. Int.*, 217, 5–18.

Farber, D., Seul, A., Weisser, H.-J., and Bohnert, M. (2010), Recovery of latent fingerprints and DNA on human skin, *J. Forensic Sci.*, 55, 1457–1461.

Farrugia, K. J., Deacon, P., and Fraser, J. (2014), Evaluation of Lumicyano™ cyanoacrylate fuming process for the development of latent fingermarks on plastic carrier bags by means of a pseudo operational comparative trial, *Sci. Justice*, 54, 126–132.

Ferguson, L. S., Wulfert, F., Wolstenholme, R., Fonville, J. M., Clench, M. R., Carolan, V. A., and Francese, S. (2012), Direct detection of peptides and small proteins in fingermarks and determination of sex by MALDI mass spectrometry profiling, *Analyst*, 137, 4686–4692.

Ferraro, J. (2012), DNA versus fingerprints, *J. Forensic Ident.*, 62, 405–408.

Fieldhouse, S. J. (2011), An investigation into the use of a portable cyanoacrylate fuming system (SUPERfume®) and aluminum powder for the development of latent fingermarks, *J. Forensic Sci.*, 56, 1514–1520.

Fitzi, T., Fischer, R., Moret, S., and Bécue, A. (2014), Fingermark detection on thermal papers: Proposition of an updated processing sequence, *J. Forensic Ident.*, 64, 329–350.

Flynn, J., Stoilovic, M., and Lennard, C. (1999), Detection and enhancement of latent fingerprints on polymer banknotes: A preliminary study, *J. Forensic Ident.*, 49, 594–613.

Flynn, K., Maynard, P., Du Pasquier, E., Lennard, C., Stoilovic, M., and Roux, C. (2004), Evaluation of iodine-benzoflavone and ruthenium tetroxide spray reagents for the detection of latent fingermarks at the crime scene, *J. Forensic Sci.*, 49, 707–715.

Fortunato, S. L. and Walton, G. (1998), Development of latent fingerprints from skin, *J. Forensic Ident.*, 48, 704–717.

Fox, A., Gittos, M., Harbison, S. A., Fleming, R., and Wivell, R. (2014), Exploring the recovery and detection of messenger RNA and DNA from enhanced fingermarks in blood, *Sci. Justice*, 54, 192–198.

Francese, S., Bradshaw, R., Ferguson, L. S., Wolstenholme, R., Clench, M. R., and Bleay, S. (2013), Beyond the ridge pattern: Multi-informative analysis of latent fingermarks by MALDI mass spectrometry, *Analyst*, 138, 4215–4228.

Frank, A. and Almog, J. (1993), Modified SPR for latent fingerprint development on wet, dark objects, *J. Forensic Ident.*, 43, 240–244.

Fraser, J., Deacon, P., Bleay, S., and Bremner, D. H. (2014), A comparison of the use of vacuum metal deposition versus cyanoacrylate fuming for visualisation of fingermarks and grab impressions on fabrics, *Sci. Justice*, 54, 133–140.

Fraser, J., Sturrock, K., Deacon, P., Bleay, S., and Bremner, D. H. (2011), Visualisation of fingermarks and grab impressions on fabrics. Part 1: Gold/zinc vacuum metal deposition, *Forensic Sci. Int.*, 208, 74–78.

Frégeau, C. J., Germain, O., and Fourney, R. M. (2000), Fingerprint enhancement revisited and the effects of blood enhancement chemicals on subsequent Profiler Plus™ fluorescent short tandem repeat DNA analysis of fresh and aged bloody fingerprints, *J. Forensic Sci.*, 45, 354–380.

Frick, A. A., Busetti, F., Cross, A., and Lewis, S. W. (2014), Aqueous nile blue: A simple, versatile and safe reagent for the detection of latent fingermarks, *Chem. Commun.*, 50, 3341–3343.

Frick, A. A., Fritz, P., Lewis, S. W., and van Bronswijk, W. (2012), A modified Oil Red O formulation for the detection of latent fingermarks on porous substrates, *J. Forensic Ident.*, 62, 623–641.

Frick, A. A., Fritz, P., Lewis, S. W., and van Bronswijk, W. (2013), Sequencing of a modified Oil Red O development technique for the detection of latent fingermarks on paper surfaces, *J. Forensic Ident.*, 63, 369–385.

Fritz, P., van Bronswijk, W., and Lewis, S. W. (2015), A new p-dimethylaminocinnamaldehyde reagent formulation for the photoluminescence detection of latent fingermarks on paper, *Forensic Sci. Int.*, 257, 20–28.

Froude, J. H. (1996), The super glue fuming wand: A preliminary evaluation, *J. Forensic Ident.*, 46, 19–31.

Fung, T. C., Grimwood, K., Shimmon, R., Spindler, X., Maynard, P., Lennard, C., and Roux, C. (2011), Investigation of hydrogen cyanide generation from the cyanoacrylate fuming process used for latent fingermark detection, *Forensic Sci. Int.*, 212, 143–149.

Gamboe, M. and O'Daniel, L. (1999), Substitute Ardrox formula, *J. Forensic Ident.*, 49, 134–141.

Gao, D., Li, F., Song, J., Xu, X., Zhang, Q., and Niu, L. (2009), One step to detect the latent fingerprints with gold nanoparticles, *Talanta*, 80, 479–483.

Gao, F., Han, J., Zhang, J., Li, Q., Sun, X., Zheng, J., Bao, L., Li, X., and Liu, Z. (2011), The synthesis of newly modified CdTe quantum dots and their application for improvement of latent fingerprint detection, *Nanotechnology*, 22, art. no. 075705.

Gardner, E. (2010), Using a reflected ultraviolet imaging system to recover friction ridge impressions on post-blast material, *J. Forensic Ident.*, 60, 104–118.

Gardner, S. J. and Hewlett, D. F. (2003), Optimization and initial evaluation of 1,2-indandione as a reagent for fingerprint detection, *J. Forensic Sci.*, 48, 1288–1292.

Garrett, H. J. and Bleay, S. M. (2013), Evaluation of the solvent black 3 fingermark enhancement reagent: Part 1—Investigation of fundamental interactions and comparisons with other lipid-specific reagents, *Sci. Justice*, 53, 121–130.

Gaskell, C., Bleay, S. M., and Ramadani, J. (2013a), Natural yellow 3: A novel fluorescent reagent for use on grease-contaminated fingermarks on nonporous dark surfaces, *J. Forensic Ident.*, 63, 274–285.

Gaskell, C., Bleay, S. M., Willson, H., and Park, S. (2013b), The enhancement of fingermarks on grease-contaminated, nonporous surfaces: A comparative assessment of processes for light and dark surfaces, *J. Forensic Ident.*, 63, 286–319.

Geller, B., Springer, E., and Almog, J. (1998), Field devices for cyanoacrylate fuming: A comparative analysis, *J. Forensic Ident.*, 48, 442–450.

German, E. R. (1987), Computer image enhancement of latent print and hard copy output devices, in *Proceedings of the International Forensic Symposium on Latent Prints*, FBI Academy, Quantico, VA, pp. 151–152.

Gibb, C., Gutowski, S. J., and van Oorschot, R. A. H. (2012), Assessment of the possibility of DNA accumulation and transfer in a superglue chamber, *J. Forensic Ident.*, 62, 409–424.

Gibson, A. P., Bannister, M., and Bleay, S. M. (2012), A comparison of three ultraviolet searching and imaging systems for the recovery of fingerprints, *J. Forensic Ident.*, 62, 349–367.

Girelli, C. M. A., Lobo, B. J. M., Cunha, A. G., Freitas, J. C. C., and Emmerich, F. G. (2015), Comparison of practical techniques to develop latent fingermarks on fired and unfired cartridge cases, *Forensic Sci. Int.*, 250, 17–26.

Girod, A., Ramotowski, R., and Weyermann, C. (2012), Composition of fingermark residue: A qualitative and quantitative review, *Forensic Sci. Int.*, 223, 10–24.

Goode, G. C. and Morris, J. R. (1983), Latent fingerprints: A review of their origin, composition and methods for detection, AWRE Report No. 022/83, Atomic Weapons Research Establishment, Aldermaston, U.K.

Grady, D. P. (1999), Cyanoacrylate fuming: Accelerated by heat within a vacuum, *J. Forensic Ident.*, 49, 377–387.

Grant, H., Springer, E., and Ziv, Z. (1996), Vacuum metal deposition inhibition on polythene bags, in *Proceedings of the International Symposium on Fingerprint Detection and Identification*, Ne'urim, Israel: eds. J. Almog and E. Springer, Israel National Police, June 26–30, 1995, pp. 203–215.

Gray, C. (1978), The detection and persistence of latent fingerprints on human skin: An assessment of the iodine–silver plate method, *J. Forensic Sci. Soc.*, 18, 47–52.

Gray, M. L. (1996), Sticky-side powder versus gentian violet: The search for the superior method for processing the sticky side of adhesive tape, *J. Forensic Ident.*, 46, 268–272.

Grigg, R., Malone, J. F., Mongkolaussavaratana, T., and Thianpatanagul, S. (1986), Cycloaddition reactions relevant to the mechanism of the ninhydrin reaction: X-ray crystal structure of protonated Ruhemann's purple, a stable 1,3-dipole, *J. Chem. Soc.: Chem. Commun.*, 421–422.

Grigg, R., Mongkolaussavaratana, T., Pounds, C. A., and Sivagnanam, S. (1990), 1,8-Diazafluorenone and related compounds—A new reagent for the detection of alpha-amino acids and latent fingerprints, *Tetrahedron Lett.*, 31, 7215–7218.

Groeneveld, G., Kuijer, S., and de Puit, M. (2014), Preparation of cyanoacrylate derivatives and comparison of dual action cyanoacrylate formulations, *Sci. Justice*, 54, 42–48.

Grubwieser, P., Thaler, A., Köchl, S., Teissl, R., Rabl, W., and Parson, W. (2003), Systematic study on STR profiling on blood and saliva traces after visualization of fingerprint marks, *J. Forensic Sci.*, 48, 733–741.

Guicheteau, J. A., Swofford, H., Tripathi, A., Wilcox, P. G., Emmons, E. D., Christesen, S. D., Wood, J., and Fountain, A. W. (2013), Sequential Raman chemical imaging and biometric analysis on fingerprints for rapid identification of threat materials and individuals, *J. Forensic Ident.*, 63, 90–101.

Guigui, K. and Beaudoin, A. (2007), The use of Oil Red O in sequence with other methods of fingerprint development, *J. Forensic Ident.*, 57, 550–581.

Gunaratne, A., Knaggs, C., and Stansbury, D. (2007), Vacuum metal deposition: Comparing conventional gold/zinc VMD to aluminium VMD, *Ident. Can*, 30, 40–62.

Guo, Y.-C. and Xing, L.-P. (1992), Visualization method for fingerprints on skin by impression on a polyethylene terephthalate (PET) semirigid sheet, *J. Forensic Sci.*, 37, 604–611.

Hahn, W. and Ramotowski, R. (2012), Evaluation of a novel one-step fluorescent cyanoacrylate fuming process for latent print visualization, *J. Forensic Ident.*, 62, 279–298.

Hamilton, J. and Dibattista, J. (1985), Cyanoacrylate ester—Latent print from murdered body, *Fingerprint Whorld*, 11(41), 18–19.

Hamilton, P. B. (1965), Amino acids on hands, *Nature*, 205, 284–285.

Hamm, E. D. (1988), A latent from human skin or is it? *Fingerprint Whorld*, 14(54), 56–58.

Hansen, D. B. and Joullié, M. M. (2005), The development of novel ninhydrin analogues, *Chem. Sci. Rev.*, 34, 408–417.

Haque, F., Westland, A. D., and Kerr, F. M. (1983), An improved non-destructive method for detection of latent fingerprints on documents with iodine–7,8-benzoflavone, *Forensic Sci. Int.*, 21, 79–83.

Haque, F., Westland, A. D., Milligan, J., and Kerr, F. M. (1989), A small particle (iron oxide) suspension for detection of latent fingerprints on smooth surfaces, *Forensic Sci. Int.*, 41, 73–82.

Hardwick, S., Kent, T., Sears, V., and Winfield, P. (1993), Improvements to the formulation of DFO and the effects of heat on the reaction with latent fingerprints, *Fingerprint Whorld*, 19(73), 65–69.

Hardwick, S. A. (1981), User guide to physical developer—A reagent for detecting latent fingerprints, User guide No. 14/81, Home Office Police Scientific Development Branch, Sandridge, U.K.

Hardwick, S. A., Kent, T., and Sears, V. G. (1990), Fingerprint detection by fluorescence examination: A guide to operational implementation, Home Office Police Scientific Development Branch, Sandridge, U.K.

Hark, R. R. (1996), Synthesis of ninhydrin analogues, PhD thesis, University of Pennsylvania, Philadelphia, PA.

Hark, R. R., Hauze, D. B., Petrovskaia, O., Joullié, M. M., Jaouhari, R., and McComiskey, P. (1994), Novel approaches toward ninhydrin analogs, *Tetrahedron Lett.*, 35, 7719–7722.

Hartzell-Baguley, B., Hipp, R. E., Morgan, N. R., and Morgan, S. L. (2007), Chemical composition of latent fingerprints by gas chromatography-mass spectrometry: An experiment for an instrumental analysis course, *J. Chem. Educ.*, 84, 689–691.

Hauze, D. B., Petrovskaia, O., Taylor, B., Joullié, M. M., Ramotowski, R., and Cantú, A. A. (1998) 1,2-Indanediones: New reagents for visualizing the amino acid components of latent prints, *J. Forensic Sci.*, 43, 744–747.

Hazarika, P., Jickells, S. M., and Russell, D. A. (2009), Rapid detection of drug metabolites in latent fingermarks, *Analyst*, 134, 93–96.

Hazarika, P., Jickells, S. M., Wolff, K., and Russell, D. A. (2008), Imaging of latent fingerprints through the detection of drugs and metabolites, *Angew. Chem. Int. Ed.*, 47, 10167–10170.

Hazarika, P., Jickells, S. M., Wolff, K., and Russell, D. A. (2010), Multiplexed detection of metabolites of narcotic drugs from a single latent fingermark. *Anal. Chem.*, 82, 9150–9154.

Hazarika, P. and Russell, D. A. (2012), Advances in fingerprint analysis, *Angew. Chem. Int. Ed.*, 51, 3524–3531.

Hébrard, J. and Donche, A. (1994), Fingerprint detection methods on skin: Experimental study on 16 live subjects and 23 cadavers, *J. Forensic Ident.*, 44, 623–631.

Heffner, R. J. and Joullié, M. M. (1991a), A synthesis of two novel benzo[f]ninhydrin analogs: 6-Methoxybenzo[f] ninhydrin and thieno[f]ninhydrin, *Synthetic Commun.*, 21, 1055–1069.

Heffner, R. J. and Joullié, M. M. (1991b), Synthetic routes to ninhydrins. Preparation of ninhydrin, 5-methoxyninhydrin, and 5-(methylthio)ninhydrin, *Synthetic Commun.*, 21, 2231–2256.

Herod, D. W. and Menzel, E. R. (1982), Laser detection of latent fingerprints: Ninhydrin followed by zinc chloride, *J. Forensic Sci.*, 27, 513–518.

Hewlett, D. F. and Sears, V. G. (1997), Replacements for CFC113 in the ninhydrin process: Part 1, *J. Forensic Ident.*, 47, 287–299.

Hewlett, D. F. and Sears, V. G. (1999), An operational trial of two non-ozone depleting ninhydrin formulations for latent fingerprint detection, *J. Forensic Ident.*, 49, 388–396.

Hewlett, D. F., Sears, V. G., and Suzuki, S. (1997), Replacements for CFC113 in the ninhydrin process: Part 2, *J. Forensic Ident.*, 47, 300–306.

Hollars, M. L., Trozzi, T. A., and Barron, B. L. (2000), Development of latent fingerprints on dark colored sticky surfaces using Liqui-Drox, *J. Forensic Ident.*, 50, 357–362.

Home Office (1998), *Manual of Fingerprint Development Techniques*, 2nd ed. (revised January 2001), Home Office Police Scientific Development Branch, Sandridge, U.K.

Home Office (2003), What is the oldest fingerprint that you have developed? Fingerprint Development and Imaging Update, Publication No. 26/2003, Home Office Police Scientific Development Branch, Sandridge, U.K.

Home Office (2005a), Solvent Black 3 for scenes of crime, Fingerprint Development and Imaging Newsletter, Publication No. 20/05, Home Office Scientific Development Branch, Sandridge, U.K.

Home Office (2005b), Current programme of work, Fingerprint Development and Imaging Newsletter, Publication No. 47/05, Home Office Scientific Development Branch, Sandridge, U.K.

Home Office (2006a), Additional fingerprint development techniques for adhesive tapes, Publication No. 23/06, Home Office Scientific Development Branch, Sandridge, U.K.

Home Office (2006b), Fingerprint development on car surfaces treated with WD40, Fingerprint Development and Imaging Newsletter, Publication No. 34/06, Home Office Scientific Development Branch, Sandridge, U.K.

Home Office (2006c), Use of DMAC on thermal papers. HOSDB Fingerprint and Footwear Forensics Newsletter, Publication No. 58/06, Home Office Scientific Development Branch, Sandridge, U.K.

Home Office (2014), *Fingermark Visualisation Manual*, Home Office Centre for Applied Science and Technology, Sandridge, U.K.

Houlgrave, S., Andress, M., and Ramotowski, R. (2011), Comparison of different physical developer working solutions—Part I: Longevity studies, *J. Forensic Ident.*, 61, 621–639.

Houlgrave, S., and Ramotowski, R. (2011), Comparison of different physical developer working solutions—Part II: Reliability studies, *J. Forensic Ident.*, 61, 640–651.

Howard, S. (1993), Basic fuchsin—A guide to a one-step processing technique for black electrical tape, *J. Forensic Sci.*, 38, 1391–1403.

Hughes, J. G. (1993), Under the COSHH, *Fingerprint Whorld*, 19(72), 4.

Huss, K., Clark, J., and Chisum, W. J. (2000), Which was first—fingerprints or blood? *J. Forensic Ident.*, 50, 344–350.

Hussain, J. I. and Pounds, C. A. (1985), The detection of latent fingerprints by antibodies: Progress in the detection of ABH blood group material by the mixed agglutination technique, HOCRE Report No. 554, Home Office Central Research Establishment, Aldermaston, U.K.

Hussain, J. I. and Pounds, C. A. (1988), The enhancement of marks in blood, Part I, 5-sulphosalicyclic acid: A convenient and effective fixative for marks made in blood, HOCRE Report No. 649, Home Office Central Research Establishment, Aldermaston, U.K.

Hussain, J. I. and Pounds, C. A. (1989), The enhancement of marks in blood, Part II, A modified amido black staining technique, HOCRE Report No. 685, Home Office Central Research Establishment, Aldermaston, U.K.

Ifa, D. R., Manicke, N. E., Dill, A. L., and Cooks, R. G. (2008), Latent fingerprint chemical imaging by mass spectrometry, *Science*, 321, 805.

Immamura, M. and Asahida, M. (1981), Fingerprints lifted from cadaver skin surface, *Ident. News*, 31, 13–14.

International Fingerprint Research Group (2014), Guidelines for the assessment of fingermark detection techniques, *J. Forensic Ident.*, 64, 174–200.

Isaac, K. L. (1993), A review on detection of latent prints on self-adhesive tapes, *Fingerprint Whorld*, 19(74), 89–96.

Ishiyama, I., Orui, M., Ogawa, K., and Kimura, T. (1977), The determination of isoantigenic activity from latent fingerprints: Mixed cell agglutination reaction in forensic serology, *J. Forensic Sci.*, 22, 365–375.

Jaber, N., Lesniewski, A., Gabizon, H., Shenawi, S., Mandler, D., and Almog, J. (2012), Visualization of latent fingermarks by nanotechnology: Reversed development on paper—A remedy to the variation in sweat composition, *Angew. Chem. Int. Ed.*, 51, 12224–12227.

James, J. D., Pounds, C. A., and Wilshire, B. (1991a), Flake metal powders for revealing latent fingerprints, *J. Forensic Sci.*, 36, 1368–1375.

James, J. D., Pounds, C. A., and Wilshire, B. (1991b), Magnetic flake fingerprint technology, *J. Forensic Ident.*, 41, 237–247.

James, J. D., Pounds, C. A., and Wilshire, B. (1991c), Obliteration of latent fingerprints, *J. Forensic Sci.*, 36, 1376–1386.

James, J. D., Pounds, C. A., and Wilshire, B. (1992), New magnetic applicators and magnetic flake powders for revealing latent fingerprints, *J. Forensic Ident.*, 42, 531–542.

James, J. D., Pounds, C. A., and Wilshire, B. (1993), Magnetic flake powders for fingerprint development, *J. Forensic Sci.*, 38, 391–401.

Jaret, Y., Heriau, M., and Donche, A. (1997), Transfer of bloody fingerprints, *J. Forensic Ident.*, 47, 38–41.

Jasuja, O. P., Singh, G. D., and Sodhi, G. S. (2007), Development of latent fingerprints on the sticky side of adhesive tapes: Phase transfer catalyst-based formulation, *Can. Soc. Forensic Sci. J.*, 40, 1–13.

Jasuja, O. P., Singh, G. D., and Sodhi, G. S. (2008), Small particle reagents: Development of fluorescent variants, *Sci. Justice*, 48, 141–145.

Jelly, R., Lewis, S. W., Lennard, C., Lim, K. F., and Almog, J. (2008), Lawsone: A novel reagent for the detection of latent fingermarks on paper surfaces, *Chem. Commun.*, 3513–3515.

Jelly, R., Lewis, S. W., Lennard, C., Lim, K. F., and Almog, J. (2010), Substituted naphthoquinones as novel amino acid sensitive reagents for the detection of latent fingermarks on paper surfaces, *Talanta*, 82, 1717–1724.

Jelly, R., Patton, E. L. T., Lennard, C., Lewis, S. W., and Lim, K. F. (2009), The detection of latent fingermarks on porous surfaces using amino acid sensitive reagents: A review, *Anal. Chim. Acta*, 652, 128–142.

Jin, Y.-J., Luo, Y.-J., Li, G.-P., Li, J., Wang, Y.-F., Yang, R.-Q., and Lu, W.-T. (2008), Application of photoluminescent CdS/PAMAM nanocomposites in fingerprint detection, *Forensic Sci. Int.*, 179, 34–38.

Jin, Y.-J., Luo, Y.-J., Li, G.-P., and Zhang, W.-L. (2012), Application of PAMAM dendrimers for detecting latent fingerprints on adhesive tapes, *Imaging Sci. Photochem.*, 30, 228–236.

Johnson, S. (2010), Development of latent prints on firearms evidence, *J. Forensic Ident.*, 60, 148–151.

Jones, B. J., Downham, R., and Sears, V. G. (2010a), Effect of substrate surface topography on forensic development of latent fingerprints with iron oxide powder suspension, *Surf. Interface Anal.*, 42, 438–442.

Jones, B. J., Downham, R., and Sears, V. G. (2012), Nanoscale analysis of the interaction between cyanoacrylate and vacuum metal deposition in the development of latent fingermarks on low-density polyethylene, *J. Forensic Sci.*, 57, 196–200.

Jones, B. J., Reynolds, A. J., Richardson, M., and Sears, V. G. (2010b), Nano-scale composition of commercial white powders for development of latent fingerprints on adhesives, *Sci. Justice*, 50, 150–155.

Jones, N. (2002), Metal deposition techniques for the detection and enhancement of latent fingerprints on semi-porous surfaces, Ph.D. thesis, University of Technology Sydney, Sydney, Australia.

Jones, N., Kelly, M., Stoilovic, M., Lennard, C., and Roux, C. (2003a), The development of latent fingerprints on polymer banknotes, *J. Forensic Ident.*, 53, 50–77.

Jones, N., Lennard, C., Stoilovic, M., and Roux, C. (2003b), An evaluation of multimetal deposition II, *J. Forensic Ident.*, 53, 444–488.

Jones, N., Mansour, D., Stoilovic, M., Lennard, C., and Roux, C. (2001a), The influence of polymer type, print donor and age on the quality of fingerprints developed on plastic substrates using vacuum metal deposition, *Forensic Sci. Int.*, 124, 167–177.

Jones, N., Stoilovic, M., Lennard, C., and Roux, C. (2001b), Vacuum metal deposition: Factors affecting normal and reverse development of latent fingerprints on polyethylene substrates, *Forensic Sci. Int.*, 115, 73–88.

Jones, N., Stoilovic, M., Lennard, C., and Roux, C. (2001c), Vacuum metal deposition: Developing latent fingerprints on polyethylene substrates after the deposition of excess gold, *Forensic Sci. Int.*, 123, 5–12.

Jonker, H., Molenaar, A., and Dippel, C. J. (1969), Physical development recording systems: III. Physical development, *Photo. Sci. Eng.*, 13, 38–44.

Joullié, M. M., Thompson, T. R., and Nemeroff, N. H. (1991), Ninhydrin and ninhydrin analogs. Syntheses and applications, *Tetrahedron*, 47, 8791–8830.

Jungbluth, W. O. (1992), Replacement for Freon 113, *Fingerprint Whorld*, 18(67), 26–29.

Jungbluth, W. O. (1993), Replacement for Freon 113, *J. Forensic Ident.*, 43, 226–233.

Kamyshny, A., Magdassi, S., Avissar, Y., and Almog, J. (2003), Water-soaked evidence: Detectability of explosive traces after immersion in water, *J. Forensic Sci.*, 48, 312–317.

Keith, L. V. and Runion, W. (1998), Short-wave UV imaging casework applications, *J. Forensic Ident.*, 48, 563–569.

Kent, T. (1996), Two new solvents for ninhydrin, *Fingerprint Whorld*, 22(85), 108.

Kent, T. (2005), Re: A comparison of cyanoacrylate fuming in a vacuum cabinet to a humidity fuming chamber [letter plus author's reply], *J. Forensic Ident.*, 55, 681–684.

Kent, T., Thomas, G. L., Reynoldson, T. E., and East, H. W. (1976), A vacuum coating technique for the development of latent fingerprints on polythene, *J. Forensic Sci. Soc.*, 16, 93–101.

Kent, T. and Winfield, P. (1996), Superglue fingerprint development—Atmospheric pressure and high humidity, or vacuum evaporation? in *Proceedings of the International Symposium on Fingerprint Detection and Identification*, Ne'urim, Israel: eds. J. Almog and E. Springer, Israel National Police, June 26–30, 1995, pp. 59–66.

Kerr, V., Stringer, K., Thompson, G., Scott, N. W., and Fowler, M. (2008), Testing latent fingerprint longevity on glass after exposure to water, *Fingerprint Whorld*, 34(131), 86–95.

Kimble, G. W. (1996), Powder suspension processing, *J. Forensic Ident.*, 46, 273–280.

King, S., Benson, S., Kelly, T., and Lennard, C. (2014), Determining the effects of routine fingermark detection techniques on the subsequent recovery and analysis of explosive residues on various substrates, *Forensic Sci. Int.*, 233, 257–264.

Klasey, D. R. and Barnum, C. A. (2000), Development and enhancement of latent prints on firearms by vacuum and atmospheric cyanoacrylate fuming, *J. Forensic Ident.*, 50, 572–580.

Knighting, S., Fraser, J., Sturrock, K., Deacon, P., Bleay, S., and Bremner, D. H. (2013), Visualisation of fingermarks and grab impressions on dark fabrics using silver vacuum metal deposition, *Sci. Justice*, 53, 309–314.

Knowles, A. M. (1978). Aspects of physicochemical methods for the detection of latent fingerprints, *J. Physics Ser. E: Sci. Instrum.*, 11, 713–721.

Kobus, H. J., Pigou, P. E., Jahangiri, S., and Taylor, B. (2002), Evaluation of some oxygen, sulfur, and selenium substituted ninhydrin analogues, nitrophenylninhydrin and benzo[f]furoninhydrin, *J. Forensic Sci.*, 47, 254–259.

Kobus, H. J., Stoilovic, M., and Warrener, R. N. (1983), Simple luminescent post-ninhydrin treatment for the improved visualisation of fingerprints on documents in cases where ninhydrin alone gives poor results, *Forensic Sci. Int.*, 22, 161–170.

Kupferschmid, E., Schwarz, L., and Champod, C. (2010), Development of standardized test strips as a process control for the detection of latent fingermarks using physical developers, *J. Forensic Ident.*, 60, 639–655.

Kusenthiran, S. G. V., Rogers, T., and Knaap, W. (2010), Latent fingerprint detection on thermal paper using vacuum metal deposition and steam, *J. Forensic Ident.*, 60, 34–44.

Lam, R. (2014), Recommended protocols for fingerprint detection on Canadian polymer banknotes—Part II: Photography, lighting, and digital enhancement techniques, *J. Forensic Ident.*, 64, 402–422.

Lam, R. and Wilkinson, D. (2011), Forensic light source and environmental effects on the performance of 1,2-indanedione-zinc chloride and 1,8-diazafluoren-9-one for the recovery of latent prints on porous substrates, *J. Forensic Ident.*, 61, 607–620.

Lam, R., Wilkinson, D., Tse, T., and Pynn, B. (2014), Recommended protocols for fingerprint detection on Canadian polymer banknotes—Part I: Chemical development, *J. Forensic Ident.*, 64, 375–401.

Lamothe, P. J. and McCormick, P. G. (1972), Influence of acidity on the reaction of ninhydrin with amino acids, *Anal. Chem.*, 44, 821–825.

LaPorte, G. M. and Ramotowski, R. S. (2003), The effects of latent print processing on questioned documents produced by office machine systems utilizing inkjet technology and toner, *J. Forensic Sci.*, 48, 658–663.

Laurin, N., Célestin, F., Clark, M., Wilkinson, D., Yamashita, B., and Frégeau, C. (2015), New incompatibilities uncovered using the Promega DNA IQ™ chemistry, *Forensic Sci. Int.*, 257, 134–141.

Lawley, R. (2003), Application of amido black mixture for the development of blood-based fingerprints on human skin, *J. Forensic Ident.*, 53, 404–408.

Lee, H. C. (1984), TMB as an enhancement reagent for bloody prints, *Ident. News*, 34(3), 10–11.

Lee, H. C. and Gaensslen, R. E. (1984), Cyanoacrylate fuming, *Ident. News*, 34(6), 8–14.

Lee, H. C. and Gaensslen, R. E. (2001), Methods of latent fingerprint development, in *Advances in Fingerprint Technology*, 2nd ed., eds., H. C. Lee and R. E. Gaensslen, Boca Raton, FL: CRC Press, pp. 105–175.

Lee, J. L., Bleay, S. M., Sears, V. G., Mehmet, S., and Croxton, R. (2009), Evaluation of the dimethylaminocinnamaldehyde contact transfer process and its application to fingerprint development on thermal papers, *J. Forensic Ident.*, 59, 545–568.

Leggett, R., Lee-Smith, E. E., Jickells, S. M., and Russell, D. A. (2007), Intelligent fingerprinting: Simultaneous identification of drug metabolites and individuals by using antibody functionalized nanoparticles, *Angew. Chem. Int. Ed.*, 46, 4100–4103.

Lennard, C. J. (1986), New amino acid specific fingerprint reagents, PhD thesis, Australian National University, Canberra, Australia.

Lennard, C. J. and Margot, P. A. (1988), Sequencing of reagents for the improved visualization of latent fingerprints, *J. Forensic Ident.*, 38, 197–210.

Lennard, C. J., Margot, P. A., Sterns, M., and Warrener, R. N. (1987), Photoluminescent enhancement of ninhydrin developed fingerprints by metal complexations: Structural studies of complexes formed between Ruhemann's purple and Group IIb metal salts, *J. Forensic Sci.*, 32, 597–605.

Lennard, C. J., Margot, P. A., Stoilovic, M., and Warrener, R. N. (1986), Synthesis of ninhydrin analogues and their application to fingerprint development: Preliminary results, *J. Forensic Sci. Soc.*, 26, 323–328.

Lennard, C. J., Margot, P. A., Stoilovic, M., and Warrener, R. N. (1988), Synthesis and evaluation of ninhydrin analogues as reagents for the development of latent fingerprints on paper surfaces, *J. Forensic Sci. Soc.*, 28, 3–23.

LeRoy, H. (1993), Metal vacuum deposition and vacuum cyanoacrylate development of latent prints, in *International Symposium on the Forensic Aspects of Latent Prints*, FBI Academy, Quantico, VA.

Levinton-Shamuilov, G., Cohen, Y., Azoury, M., Chaikovsky, A., and Almog, J. (2005), Genipin, a novel fingerprint reagent with colorimetric and fluorogenic activity, part II: Optimization, scope and limitations, *J. Forensic Sci.*, 50, 1367–1371.

Lewis, L. A., Smithwick, R. W., Devault, G. L., Bolinger, B., and Lewis, S. A. (2001), Processes involved in the development of latent fingerprints using the cyanoacrylate fuming method, *J. Forensic Sci.*, 46, 241–246.

Li, H., Cao, J., Niu, J., and Huang, Y. (2013), Study of UV imaging technology for noninvasive detection of latent fingerprints, in *Proceedings of SPIE 8905, International Symposium on Photoelectronic Detection and Imaging*, Beijing China, 89051L.

Li, K., Qin, W., Li, F., Zhao, X., Jiang, B., Wang, K., Deng, S., Fan, C., and Li, D. (2013), Nanoplasmonic imaging of latent fingerprints and identification of cocaine, *Angew. Chem. Int. Ed.*, 52, 11542–11545.

Lin, A. C.-Y., Hsieh, H.-M., Tsai, L.-C., Linacre, A., and Lee, J. C.-I. (2007), Forensic applications of infrared imaging for the detection and recording of latent evidence, *J. Forensic Sci.*, 52, 1148–1150.

Liu, L., Gill, S. K., Gao, Y., Hope-Weeks, L. J., and Cheng, K. H. (2008), Exploration of the use of novel SiO_2 nanocomposites doped with fluorescent Eu^{3+}/sensitizer complex for latent fingerprint detection, *Forensic Sci. Int.*, 176, 163–172.

Lock, E. R. A., Mazzella, W. D., and Margot, P. A. (1995), A new Europium chelate as a fluorescent dye for cyanoacrylate pretreated fingerprints—EuTTAPhen: Europium thenoyltrifluoro-acetenone ortho-phenanthroline, *J. Forensic Sci.*, 40, 354–358.

Lowe, A., Murray, C., Whitaker, J., Tully, G., and Gill, P. (2002), The propensity of individuals to deposit DNA and secondary transfer of low level DNA from individuals to inert surfaces, *Forensic Sci. Int.*, 129, 25–34.

Ma, R., Bullock, E., Maynard, P., Reedy, B., Shimmon, R., Lennard, C., Roux, C., and McDonagh, A. (2011), Fingermark detection on non-porous and semi-porous surfaces using $NaYF_4$:Er,Yb up-converter particles, *Forensic Sci. Int.*, 207, 145–149.

Ma, R., Shimmon, R., McDonagh, A., Maynard, P., Lennard, C., and Roux, C. (2012), Fingermark detection on non-porous and semi-porous surfaces using YVO_4:Er,Yb luminescent upconverting particles, *Forensic Sci. Int.*, 217, e23–e26.

Ma, R. and Wei, Q. (2006), Chemical fuming: A practical method for fingerprint development on thermal paper, *J. Forensic Ident.*, 56, 364–373.

Maceo, A. V. and Wertheim, K. (2000), Use of ninhydrin in the recovery of latent prints on evidence involving adhesive surfaces attached to porous surfaces, *J. Forensic Ident.*, 50, 581–594.

Maldonado, B. (2012), Study on developing latent fingerprints on firearm evidence, *J. Forensic Ident.*, 62, 425–429.

Marchant, B. and Tague, C. (2007), Developing fingerprints in blood: A comparison of several chemical techniques, *J. Forensic Ident.*, 57, 76–93.

Marriott, C., Lee, R., Wilkes, Z., Comber, B., Spindler, X., Roux, C., and Lennard, C. (2014), Evaluation of fingermark detection sequences on paper substrates, *Forensic Sci. Int.*, 236, 30–37.

Martin, B. L. (1999), Developing latent prints on the adhesive side of black electrical tapes, *J. Forensic Ident.*, 49, 127–129.

Mashiko, K., German, E. R., Motojima, K., and Colman, C. D. (1991), RTX: A new ruthenium tetroxide fuming procedure, *J. Forensic Ident.*, 41, 429–436.

Mashiko, K. and Hizaki, M. I. (1977), Latent fingerprint processing: Iodine 7,8-benzoflavone method, *Ident. News*, 27(11), 3–5.

Mashiko, K. and Miyamoto, T. (1998), Latent fingerprint processing by the ruthenium tetroxide method, *J. Forensic Ident.*, 48, 279–290.

Masters, N. E. (1990), Rhodamine 6G: Taming the beast, *J. Forensic Ident.*, 40, 265–269.

Masters, N. E. (1992), Rhodamine 6G: Disarming the beast, *Fingerprint Whorld*, 18(68), 62–75.

Masters, N. E. (2002), *Safety for the Forensic Identification Specialist*, 2nd ed., Jacksonville, FL: Lightning Powder Co.

Masters, N. E. and DeHaan, J. D. (1996), Vacuum metal deposition and cyanoacrylate detection of older latent prints, *J. Forensic Ident.*, 46, 32–45.

Masters, N. E., Morgan, R., and Shipp, E. (1991), DFO, its usage and results, *J. Forensic Ident.*, 41, 3–10.

Maynard, P., Jenkins, J., Edey, C., Payne, G., Lennard, C., McDonagh, A., and Roux, C. (2009), Near infrared imaging for the improved detection of fingermarks on difficult surfaces, *Aust. J. Forensic Sci.*, 41, 43–62.

Mazzella, W. D. and Lennard, C. J. (1995), An additional study of cyanoacrylate stains, *J. Forensic Ident.*, 45, 5–18.

McCarthy, M. M. (1990), Evaluation of Ardrox as a luminescent stain for cyanoacrylate processed latent impressions, *J. Forensic Ident.*, 40, 75–80.

McCarthy, M. M. and Grieve, D. L. (1989), Preprocessing with cyanoacrylate ester fuming for fingerprint impressions in blood, *J. Forensic Ident.*, 39, 23–32.

McComiskey, P. (1990), DFO: A simple and quick method for the development of latent fingerprints, *Fingerprint Whorld*, 16(62), 64–65.

McGraw, A. C. (1984), Casting, another means of identification, *J. Forensic Sci.*, 29, 1212–1222.

McMullen, L. and Beaudoin, A. (2013), Application of Oil Red O following DFO and ninhydrin sequential treatment: Enhancing latent fingerprints on dry, porous surfaces, *J. Forensic Ident.*, 63, 387–423.

Meakin, G. and Jamieson, A. (2013), DNA transfer: Review and implications for casework, *Forensic Sci. Int.: Gen.*, 7, 434–443.

Menzel, E. R. (1980), *Fingerprint Detection with Lasers*, New York: Marcel Dekker.

Menzel, E. R. (1985), Comparison of argon-ion, copper-vapor, and frequency-doubled neodymium:yttrium aluminum garnet (ND:YAG) lasers for latent fingerprint development, *J. Forensic Sci.*, 30, 383–397.

Menzel, E. R. (1989), Pretreatment of latent prints for laser development, *Forensic Sci. Rev.*, 1, 43–66.

Menzel, E. R. (1999), *Fingerprint Detection with Lasers*, 2nd ed., New York: Marcel Dekker.

Menzel, E. R. (2001), Fingerprint detection with photoluminescent nanoparticles, in *Advances in Fingerprint Technology*, 2nd ed., eds., H. C. Lee and R. E. Gaensslen, Boca Raton, FL: CRC Press, pp. 211–240.

Menzel, E. R., Savoy, S. M., Ulvick, S. J., Cheng, K. H., Murdock, R. H., and Sudduth, M. R. (2000), Photoluminescent semiconductor nanocrystals for fingerprint detection, *J. Forensic Sci.*, 45, 545–551.

Merrick, S., Gardner, S. J., Sears, V. G., and Hewlett, D. F. (2002), An operational trial of ozone-friendly DFO and 1,2-indanedione formulations for latent fingerprint detection, *J. Forensic Ident.*, 52, 595–605.

Midkiff, C. R. (1994), Development of prints on tape, *Fingerprint Whorld*, 20(75), 5–7.

Midkiff, C. R. and Codell, D. E. (1995), Development of latent prints on tape, Part II, *Fingerprint Whorld*, 21(79), 21–26.

Midkiff, C. R., Codell, D., and Chapman, J. (1997), Development of prints on tape, Part III, *Fingerprint Whorld*, 23(89), 83–86.

Migron, Y., Hocherman, G., Springer, E., Almog, J., and Mandler, D. (1998), Visualization of sebaceous fingerprints on fired cartridge cases: A laboratory study, *J. Forensic Sci.*, 43, 543–548.

Migron, Y. and Mandler, D. (1997), Development of latent fingerprints on unfired cartridges by palladium deposition: A surface study, *J. Forensic Sci.*, 42, 986–992.

Migron, Y., Mandler, D., Frank, A., Springer, E., and Almog, J. (1996), Is a fingerprint left on a fired cartridge? The development of latent fingerprints on metallic surfaces by palladium deposition, in *Proceedings of the International Symposium on Fingerprint Detection and Identification*, Ne'urim, Israel: eds. J. Almog and E. Springer, Israel National Police, June 26–30, 1995, pp. 217–225.

Milne, R. (1996), Magnetic fingerprint powder—A field trial of K9 magneta flake powder, *Fingerprint Whorld*, 22(85), 113–116.

Mink, T., Voorhaar, A., Stoel, R., and de Puit, M. (2013), Determination of efficacy of fingermark enhancement reagents; the use of propyl chloroformate for the derivatization of fingerprint amino acids extracted from paper, *Sci. Justice*, 53, 301–308.

Misner, A. H. (1992), Latent fingerprint detection on low density polyethylene comparing vacuum metal deposition to cyanoacrylate fuming and fluorescence, *J. Forensic Ident.*, 42, 26–33.

Misner, A., Wilkinson, D., and Watkin, J. (1993), Thenoyl europium chelate: A new fluorescent dye with a narrow emission band to detect cyanoacrylate developed fingerprints on non-porous substrates and cadavers, *J. Forensic Ident.*, 43, 154–165.

Mitsui, T., Katho, H., Shimada, K., and Wakasugi, Y. (1980), Development of latent prints using a Sudan black B solution, *Ident. News*, 30(8), 9–10.

Mock, J. P. (1985), Cyanoacrylates and heat—A word of caution, *Fingerprint Whorld*, 11(41), 16–17.

Molina, D. (2007), The use of un-du to separate adhesive materials, *J. Forensic Ident.*, 57, 688–696.

Mong, G., Walter, S., Cantú, A. A., and Ramotowski, R. S. (2001), The chemistry of latent prints from children and adults, *Fingerprint Whorld*, 27(104), 66–69.

Montgomery, L., Spindler, X., Maynard, P., Lennard, C., and Roux, C. (2012), Pretreatment strategies for the improved cyanoacrylate development of dry latent fingerprints on nonporous surfaces, *J. Forensic Ident.*, 62, 517–542.

Moorcroft, B. (1996), K9 powder, *Fingerprint Whorld*, 22(85), 109–112.

Moore, D. S. (1988), The electrostatic detection apparatus (ESDA) and its effects on latent prints on paper, *J. Forensic Sci.*, 33, 357–377.

Moore, J., Bleay, S., Deans, J., and Nic Daéid, N. (2008), Recovery of fingerprints from arson scenes: Part 2—Fingerprints in blood, *J. Forensic Ident.*, 58, 83–108.

Moret, S. (2013), Application de nanoparticules luminescentes pour la détection de traces papillaires, Ph.D. thesis, Ecole des sciences criminelle, Institut de police scientifique, University of Lausanne, Lausanne, Switzerland.

Moret, S. and Bécue, A. (2015), Single-metal deposition for fingermark detection—A simpler and more efficient protocol, *J. Forensic Ident.*, 65, 118–137.

Moret, S., Bécue, A., and Champod, C. (2013), Cadmium-free quantum dots in aqueous solution: Potential for fingermark detection, synthesis and an application to the detection of fingermarks in blood on nonporous surfaces, *Forensic Sci. Int.*, 224, 101–110.

Morris, A. D. (1992), Superglue as an option to gentian violet on adhesive side of tape, *Fingerprint Whorld*, 18(69), 101–102.

Morris, J. R. and Goode, G. C. (1975), NFN—An improved ninhydrin reagent for detection of latent fingerprints, *Police Res. Bull.*, 1974, 45–53.

Mou, Y. and Rabalais, J. W. (2009), Detection and identification of explosive particles in fingerprints using attenuated total reflection-Fourier transform infrared spectromicroscopy, *J. Forensic Sci.*, 54, 846–850.

Munro, M., Deacon, P., and Farrugia, K. J. (2013), A preliminary investigation into the use of alginates for the lifting and enhancement of fingermarks in blood, *Sci. Justice*, 54, 185–191.

Murphy, M. (1991), A vacuum metal identification, *J. Forensic Ident.*, 41, 318–320.

Nag, K., Liu, X., Scott, A., and Sandling, G. (2010), Production and evaluation of a dark magnetic flake powder for latent fingerprint development, *J. Forensic Ident.*, 60, 395–407.

Nakamura, A., Okuda, H., Nagaoka, T., Akiba, N., Kurosawa, K., Kuroki, K., Ichikawa, F., Torao, A., and Sota, T. (2015), Portable hyperspectral imager with continuous wave green laser for identification and detection of untreated latent fingerprints on walls, *Forensic Sci. Int.*, 254, 100–105.

Nic Daéid, N., Buchanan, H. A. S., and Laing, K. (2009), Evaluation of available techniques for the recovery of latent fingerprints from untreated plywood surfaces, *J. Forensic Ident.*, 59, 441–465.

Nic Daéid, N., Carter, S., and Laing, K. (2008a), Comparison of three types of white powder suspensions for the recovery of fingerprints on wetted nonporous surfaces, *J. Forensic Ident.*, 58, 590–599.

Nic Daéid, N., Carter, S., and Laing, K. (2008b), Comparison of vacuum metal deposition and powder suspension for recovery of fingerprints on wetted nonporous surfaces, *J. Forensic Ident.*, 58, 600–613.

Nolan, P. J., Brennan, J. S., Keeley, R. H., and Pounds, C. A. (1984), The imaging of developed fingerprints using the scanning electron microscope, *J. Forensic Sci. Soc.*, 24, 419.

Norlin, S., Nilsson, M., Heden, P., and Allen, M. (2013), Evaluation of the impact of different visualization techniques on DNA in fingerprints, *J. Forensic Ident.*, 63, 189–204.

Odén, S. and von Hofsten, B. (1954), Detection of fingerprints by the ninhydrin reaction, *Nature*, 173, 449–450.

Olenik, J. H. (1992), Ardrox: An alternate solvent system, *J. Forensic Ident.*, 42, 513–516.

Olenik, J. H. (1997), A simple three dye blend, *J. Forensic Ident.*, 47, 530–533.

Ong, S. K., Seah, L. K., Murukeshan, V. M., and Ong, L. S. (2004), Visualization of latent prints on adhesive surfaces, *J. Forensic Ident.*, 54, 203–215.

Paine, M., Bandey, H. L., Bleay, S. M., and Willson, H. (2011), The effect of relative humidity on the effectiveness of the cyanoacrylate fuming process for fingermark development and on the microstructure of the developed marks, *Forensic Sci. Int.*, 212, 130–142.

Patton, E. L. T., Brown, D. H., and Lewis, S. W. (2010), Detection of latent fingermarks on thermal printer paper by dry contact with 1,2-indanedione, *Anal. Methods*, 2, 631–637.

Payne, G., Reedy, B., Lennard, C., Comber, B., Exline, D., and Roux, C. (2005), A further study to investigate the detection and enhancement of latent fingerprints using visible absorption and luminescence chemical imaging, *Forensic Sci. Int.*, 150, 33–51.

Perez-Avila, J. (2008), Latent print development under a self-adhesive stamp, *J. Forensic Ident.*, 58, 429–431.

Petrovskaia, O., Taylor, B. M., Hauze, D. B., Carroll, P. J., and Joullié, M. M. (2001), Investigations of the reaction mechanisms of 1,2-indanediones with amino acids, *J. Org. Chem.*, 66, 7666–7675.

Petruncio, A. V. (2000), A comparative study for the evaluation of two solvents for use in ninhydrin processing of latent print evidence, *J. Forensic Ident.*, 50, 462–469.

Pfister, R. (1985), The optical revelation of latent fingerprints, *Fingerprint Whorld*, 10(39), 64–70.

Philipson, D. and Bleay, S. (2007), Alternative metal processes for vacuum metal deposition, *J. Forensic Ident.*, 57, 252–273.

Phillips, C. E., Cole, D. O., and Jones, G. W. (1990), Physical developer: A practical and productive latent print developer, *J. Forensic Ident.*, 40, 135–147.

Pleckaitis, J. (2007), Developing friction ridge detail on the interior of latex and nitrile gloves, *J. Forensic Ident.*, 57, 230–239.

Plese, C. A., Exline, D. L., and Stewart, S. D. (2010), Improved methods of visible hyperspectral imaging provide enhanced visualization of untreated latent fingerprints, *J. Forensic Ident.*, 60, 603–618.

Porpiglia, N., Bleay, S., Fitzgerald, L., and Barron, L. (2012), An assessment of the effectiveness of 5-methylthioninhydrin within dual action reagents for latent fingerprint development on paper substrates, *Sci. Justice*, 52, 42–48.

Pounds, C. A. and Allman, D. S. (1991), The use of 1,8-diazafluoren-9-one for the fluorescent detection of latent fingerprints on paper: Results of laboratory and operational trials, HOCRE Report No. 740, Home Office Central Research Establishment, Aldermaston, U.K.

Pounds, C. A. and Allman, D. S. (1992), A preliminary assessment of thienoninhydrin, 5-methylthioninhydrin and 5-aminoninhydrin for revealing latent fingerprints as fluorescent images, HOCRE Report No. 750, Home Office Central Research Establishment, Aldermaston, U.K.

Pounds, C. A., Allman, D. S., and Wild, F. M. (1992), The development of latent fingerprints using an iodine spray technique, HOCRE Report No. 746, Home Office Central Research Establishment, Aldermaston, U.K.

Pounds, C. A., Griggs, R., and Mongkolaussavaratana, T. (1990), The use of 1,8-diazafluoren-9-one (DFO) for the fluorescent detection of latent fingerprints on paper: A preliminary evaluation, *J. Forensic Sci.*, 35, 169–175.

Pounds, C. A. and Hussain, J. J. (1987), Biologic and chemical aspects of latent fingerprint detection, in *Proceedings of the International Forensic Symposium on Latent Prints*, FBI Academy, Quantico, VA, pp. 9–13.

Pounds, C. A., Jones, R. J., and Hall, S. (1982) The use of biological dyes for revealing latent fingerprints. Part 1—Selection of suitable dye and laboratory comparison with metal deposition on plastic surfaces, HOCRE Report No. 9, Home Office Central Research Establishment, Aldermaston, U.K.

Pounds, C. A. and Strachan, J. M. (1986) The use of biological dyes for revealing latent fingerprints. Part 2—Operational trials to compare performance of sudan black B with metal deposition and small particle reagent on plastic surfaces, HOCRE Report No. 595, Home Office Central Research Establishment, Aldermaston, U.K.

Praska, N. and Langenburg, G. (2013), Reactions of latent prints exposed to blood, *Forensic Sci. Int.*, 224, 51–58.

Pratt, A. (2012), Fingerprints and firearms, *J. Forensic Ident.*, 62, 234–242.

Prete, C., Galmiche, L., Quenum-Possy-Berry, F.-G., Allain, C., Thiburce, N., and Colard, T. (2013), Lumicyano™: A new fluorescent cyanoacrylate for a one-step luminescent latent fingermark development, *Forensic Sci. Int.*, 233, 104–112.

Price, D. and Stow, K. (1998), A method for stopping overdevelopment of silver nitrate treated finger and footwear marks, *Fingerprint Whorld*, 24(93), 107–110.

Proff, C., Schmitt, C., Schneider, P. M., Foerster, G., and Rothschild, M. A. (2006), Experiments on the DNA contamination risk via latent fingerprint brushes, *Int. Cong. Ser.*, 1288, 601–603.

Quinche, N. and Margot, P. (2010), Coulier, Paul-Jean (1824–1890): A precursor in the history of fingermark detection and their potential use for identifying their source (1863), *J. Forensic Ident.*, 60, 129–134.

Rae, L., Gentles, D., and Farrugia, K. J. (2013), An investigation into the enhancement of fingermarks in blood on fruit and vegetables, *Sci. Justice*, 53, 321–327.

Rajtar, P. E. (2000), 3M Novec engineered fluid HFE-7100, *Fingerprint Whorld*, 26(102), 143–152.

Ramotowski, R. S. (1996a), Fluorescence visualization of latent fingerprints on paper using p-dimethylaminocinnamaldehyde (pDMAC), in *Proceedings of the International Symposium on Fingerprint Detection and Identification*, Ne'urim, Israel: eds. J. Almog and E. Springer, Israel National Police, June 26–30, 1995, pp. 91–97.

Ramotowski, R. S. (1996b), Importance of an acid prewash prior to the use of physical developer, *J. Forensic Ident.*, 46, 673–677.

Ramotowski, R. S. (2000), A comparison of different physical developer systems and acid pre-treatments and their effects on developing latent prints, *J. Forensic Ident.*, 50, 363–384.

Ramotowski, R. S. (2001), Composition of latent print residue, in *Advances in Fingerprint Technology*, 2nd ed., eds., H. C. Lee and R. E. Gaensslen, Boca Raton, FL: CRC Press, pp. 63–104.

Ramotowski, R. S., Cantú, A. A., Joullié, M. M., and Petrovskaia, O. (1997), 1,2-Indanediones: A preliminary evaluation of a new class of amino acid visualizing compounds, *Fingerprint Whorld*, 23(90), 131–140.

Ramotowski, R. S. (2012), Amino acid reagents, in *Lee and Gaensslen's Advances in Fingerprint Technology*, 3rd ed., ed. R. Ramotowski, Boca Raton, FL: CRC Press, pp. 17–54.

Rawji, A. and Beaudoin, A. (2006), Oil Red O versus physical developer on wet papers: A comparative study, *J. Forensic Ident.*, 56, 33–54.

Raymond, J. J., Roux, C., Du Pasquier, E., Sutton, J., and Lennard, C. (2004), The effect of common fingerprint detection techniques on the DNA typing of fingerprints deposited on different surfaces, *J. Forensic Ident.*, 54, 22–44.

Reichardt, G. J., Carr, J. C., and Stone, E. G. (1978), A conventional method for lifting latent fingerprints from human skin surfaces, *J. Forensic Sci.*, 23, 135–141.

Reinholz, A. D. (2008), Albumin development method to visualize friction ridge detail on porous surfaces, *J. Forensic Ident.*, 58, 524–539.

Reynolds, A. J., Jones, B. J., Sears, V., and Bowman, V. (2008), Nano-scale analysis of titanium dioxide fingerprint-development powders, *J. Phys. Conf. Ser.*, 126, art. no. 012069.

Roux, C., Gill, K., Sutton, J., and Lennard, C. (1999), A further study to investigate the effect of fingerprint enhancement techniques on the DNA analysis of bloodstains, *J. Forensic Ident.*, 49, 357–376.

Roux, C., Jones, N., Lennard, C. J., and Stoilovic, M. (2000), Evaluation of 1,2-indanedione and 5,6-dimethoxy-1,2-indanedione for the detection of latent fingerprints on porous surfaces, *J. Forensic Sci.*, 45, 761–769.

Rowell, F., Seviour, J., Lim, A. Y., Elumbaring-Salazar, C. G., Loke, J., and Ma, J. (2012), Detection of nitro-organic and peroxide explosives in latent fingermarks by DART- and SALDI-TOF-mass spectrometry, *Forensic Sci. Int.*, 221, 84–91.

Saferstein, R. and Graf, S. L. (2001), Evaluation of a reflected ultraviolet imaging system for fingerprint detection, *J. Forensic Ident.*, 51, 385–393.

Sahs, P. T. (1992), DAB: An advancement in blood print detection, *J. Forensic Ident.*, 42, 412–420.

Salama, J., Aumeer-Donovan, S., Lennard, C., and Roux, C. (2008), Evaluation of the fingermark reagent Oil Red O as a possible replacement for physical developer, *J. Forensic Ident.*, 58, 203–237.

Salares, V. R., Eves, C. R., and Carey, P. R. (1979), On the detection of fingerprints by laser excited luminescence, *Forensic Sci. Int.*, 14, 229–237.

Sametband, M., Shweky, I., Banin, U., Mandler, D., and Almog, J. (2007), Application of nanoparticles for the enhancement of latent fingerprints, *Chem. Commun.*, 1142–1144.

Sampson, W. C. (1992), Glass recovery investigative technique: G.R.I.T., *J. Forensic Ident.*, 42, 96–100.

Sampson, W. C. (1993), An inquiry into the methodology of preserving and developing latent prints on expended cartridge casings, *J. Forensic Ident.*, 43, 4–12.

Sampson, W. C. (1995), Glass recovery investigative technique: G.R.I.T., *Fingerprint Whorld*, 21(80), 55–56.

Sampson, W. C. (1996), Latent fingerprint evidence on human skin, Part 1, *J. Forensic Ident.*, 46, 188–195.

Sampson, W. C. (1997), Sequential applications in the development and recovery of latent fingerprint evidence from human skin, *Fingerprint Whorld*, 23(89), 94–97.

Sampson, W. C. and Sampson, K. L. (2005), Recovery of latent prints from human skin, *J. Forensic Ident.*, 55, 362–385.

Sampson, W. C., Sampson, K. L., and Shonberger, F. (1998), *Recovery of Latent Fingerprint Evidence from Human Skin: Causation, Isolation and Processing Techniques*, Salem, OR: Lightning Powder Co. and Lynn Peavey Co.

Sasson, Y. and Almog, J. (1978), Chemical reagents for the development of latent fingerprints, 1: Scope and limitations of the reagent 4-dimethylaminocinnamaldehyde, *J. Forensic Sci.*, 23, 852–855.

Saunders, G. C. (1989), Multimetal deposition technique for latent fingerprint development, in *74th IAI Educational Conference Proceedings*, Pensacola, FL, June 1989.

Saunders, G. C. (1993), Notes on the use of nile red, dansyl chloride, a modified physical developer, and the ITEK RS process for visualizing latent prints, presented at the U.S. Secret Service Forensic Laboratory, May 1993.

Saunders, G. C. and Cantú, A. A. (1996), Evaluation of several techniques for developing latent prints on expended cartridge casings, in *Proceedings of the International Symposium on Fingerprint Detection and Identification*, Ne'urim, Israel: eds. J. Almog and E. Springer, Israel National Police, June 26–30, 1995, pp. 155–160.

Sauzier, G., Frick, A. A., and Lewis, S. W. (2013), Investigation into the performance of physical developer formulations for visualizing latent fingerprints on paper, *J. Forensic Ident.*, 63, 70–89.

Schiemer, C., Lennard, C., Maynard, P., and Roux, C. (2005), Evaluation of techniques for the detection and enhancement of latent fingermarks on black electrical tape, *J. Forensic Ident.*, 55, 214–238.

Schnetz, B. (1999), La révélation des empreintes digitales par l'or colloïdal: l'amplification par des techniques biochimiques, Ph.D. thesis, Institut de police scientifique, University of Lausanne, Lausanne, Switzerland.

Schnetz, B. and Margot, P. A. (2001), Technical note: Latent fingermarks, colloidal gold and multimetal deposition (MMD): Optimisation of the method, *Forensic Sci. Int.*, 118, 21–28.

Schulz, M. M., Wehner, H.-D., Reichert, W., and Graw, M. (2004), Ninhydrin-dyed latent fingerprints as a DNA source in a murder case, *J. Clin. Forensic Med.*, 11, 202–204.

Schütz, F., Bonfanti, M., and Champod, C. (1999), La révélation des traces papillaires sur les douilles par les techniques de etching et de blueing et comparaison avec la déposition multimétallique, *J. Can. Forensic Sci. Soc.*, 33, 65–81.

Schwartz, R. L., Higginbotham, L. C., and Smith, D. R. (2003), The effect of Un-Du® on latent print development, *Fingerprint Whorld*, 29(112), 66–73.

Schwarz, L. and Frerichs, I. (2002), Advanced solvent-free application of ninhydrin for detection of latent fingerprints on thermal paper and other surfaces, *J. Forensic Sci.*, 47, 1274–1277.

Schwarz, L. and Hermanowski, M.-L. (2011a), Detection of latent fingerprints by the use of silver nitrate [Daktyloskopische Spurensicherung mit Silbernitrat], *Archiv fur Kriminologie*, 227, 111–123.

Schwarz, L., and Hermanowski, M.-L. (2011b), Using indanedione-zinc, heat, and G3 solution sequentially to detect latent fingerprints on thermal paper, *J. Forensic Ident.*, 61, 30–37.

Schwarz, L. and Klenke, I. (2007), Enhancement of ninhydrin- or DFO-treated latent fingerprints on thermal paper, *J. Forensic Sci.*, 52, 649–655.

Schwarz, L. and Klenke, I. (2010), Improvement in latent fingerprint detection on thermal paper using a one-step ninhydrin treatment with polyvinylpyrrolidones (PVP), *J. Forensic Sci.*, 55, 1076–1079.

Scott, M. (2008), Improved results in the development of latent fingerprints on thermal paper, *J. Forensic Ident.*, 58, 424–428.

Sears, V. G. (2012), Enhancement techniques for fingerprints in blood, in *Lee and Gaensslen's Advances in Fingerprint Technology*, 3rd ed., ed., R. Ramotowski, Boca Raton, FL: CRC Press, pp. 219–239.

Sears, V. G., Batham, R., and Bleay, S. (2009), The effectiveness of 1,2-indandione-zinc formulations and comparison with HFE-based 1,8-diazafluoren-9-one for fingerprint development, *J. Forensic Ident.*, 59, 654–678.

Sears, V. G., Butcher, C. P. G., and Prizeman, T. M. (2001), Enhancement of fingerprints in blood—Part 2: Protein dyes, *J. Forensic Ident.*, 51, 28–38.

Sears, V. G., Butcher, C. P. G., and Fitzgerald, L. A. (2005), Enhancement of fingerprints in blood—Part 3: Reactive techniques, acid yellow 7, and process sequences, *J. Forensic Ident.*, 55, 741–763.

Sears, V. G. and Hewlett, D. (2003), DFO formulations in non-ozone depleting substances, *Ident. Canada*, 26, 4–12.

Sears, V. G. and Prizeman, T. M. (2000), Enhancement of fingerprints in blood—Part 1: The optimization of amido black, *J. Forensic Ident.*, 50, 470–480.

Sewell, J., Quinones, I., Ames, C., Multaney, B., Curtis, S., Seeboruth, H., Moore, S., and Daniel, B. (2008), Recovery of DNA and fingerprints from touched documents, *Forensic Sci. Int.: Gen.*, 2, 281–285.

Shelef, R., Levy, A., Rhima, I., Tsaroom, S., and Elkayam, R. (1996), Development of latent fingerprints from unignited incendiary bottles, *J. Forensic Ident.*, 46, 556–569.

Shenawi, S., Jaber, N., Almog, J., and Mandler, D. (2013), A novel approach to fingerprint visualization on paper using nanotechnology: Reversing the appearance by tailoring the gold nanoparticles' capping ligands, *Chem. Commun.*, 49, 3688–3690.

Shin, D. H. and Argue, D. G. (1976), Identification of fingerprints left on human skin, *J. Can. Soc. Forensic Sci.*, 9, 81–84.

Shipp, E., Fassett, M., Wright, R., and Togneri, E. (1994), Tetramethylbenzidine to the rescue, *J. Forensic Ident.*, 44, 159–164.

Sigma-Aldrich (2014), Product Information for 3,3'-Diaminobenzidine Tetrahydrochloride, Product No. D5637, http://www.sigmaaldrich.com/content/dam/sigma-aldrich/docs/Sigma/Product_Information_Sheet/d5637pis.pdf (accessed February 7, 2016).

Sisco, E., Demoranville, L. T., and Gillen, G. (2013), Evaluation of C60 secondary ion mass spectrometry for the chemical analysis and imaging of fingerprints, *Forensic Sci. Int.*, 231, 263–269.

Sneddon, N. (1999), Black powder method to process duct tape, *J. Forensic Ident.*, 49, 347–356.

Sodhi, G. S. and Kaur, J. (2001), Powder method for detecting latent fingerprints: A review, *Forensic Sci. Int.*, 120, 172–176.

Sodhi, G. S. and Kaur, J. (2010), Fluorescent small particle reagent, Part 1: A novel composition for detecting latent fingerprints on wet non-porous items, *Fingerprint Whorld*, 36(141), 150–153.

Spindler, X., Hofstetter, O., McDonagh, A. M., Roux, C., and Lennard, C. (2011a), Enhancement of latent fingermarks on non-porous surfaces using anti-L-amino acid antibodies conjugated to gold nanoparticles, *Chem. Commun.*, 47, 5602–5604.

Spindler, X., Shimmon, R., Roux, C., and Lennard, C. (2011b), The effect of zinc chloride, humidity and the substrate on the reaction of 1,2-indanedione-zinc with amino acids in latent fingermark secretions, *Forensic Sci. Int.*, 212, 150–157.

Spindler, X., Stoilovic, M., Lennard, C., and Lennard, A. (2009), Spectral variations for reaction products formed between different amino acids and latent fingermark detection reagents on a range of cellulose-based substrates, *J. Forensic Ident.*, 59, 308–324.

Springer, E., Almog, J., Frank, A., Ziv, Z., Bergman, P., and Gui Qiang, W. (1994), Detection of dry body fluids by inherent short wavelength UV luminescence, *Forensic Sci. Int.*, 66, 89–94.

Springer, E. and Bergman, P. (1995), A fluorescent small particle reagent (SPR), *J. Forensic Ident.*, 45, 164–168.

Stauffer, E., Bécue, A., Singh, K. V., Thampi, K. R., Champod, C., and Margot, P. (2007), Single-metal deposition (SMD) as a latent fingermark enhancement technique: An alternative to multimetal deposition (MMD), *Forensic Sci. Int.*, 168, e5–e9.

Steele, C. A., and Ball, M. S. (2003), Enhancing contrast of fingerprints on plastic tape, *J. Forensic Sci.*, 48, 1314–1317.

Steele, C. A., Hines, M., Rutherford, L., and Wheeler, A. W. (2012), Forced condensation of cyanoacrylate with temperature control of the evidence surface to modify polymer formation and improve fingerprint visualization, *J. Forensic Ident.*, 62, 335–348.

Stein, C., Hyeck, S. H., and Henssge, C. (1996), DNA typing of fingerprint reagent treated biological stains, *J. Forensic Sci.*, 41, 1012–1017.

Stephens, B. G., Nazareno, G., Block, M., and Hnatow, P. (1999), Use of liquid nitrogen to remove duct tape from a homicide victim, *Am. J. Forensic Med. Path.*, 20, 154–157.

Stimac, J. T. (2000), Adhesive tape separation with Un-Du®, *Fingerprint Whorld*, 26(102), 153–157.

Stimac, J. T. (2003a), Thermal and carbonless papers: A fundamental understanding for latent friction ridge development, *J. Forensic Ident.*, 53, 185–197.

Stimac, J. T. (2003b), Thermal paper: Latent friction ridge development via 1,2-indanedione. *J. Forensic Ident.*, 53, 265–271.

Stoilovic, M. (1991), Detection of semen and blood stains using Polilight as a light source, *Forensic Sci. Int.*, 51, 289–296.

Stoilovic, M. (1993), Improved method for DFO development of latent fingerprints, *Forensic Sci. Int.*, 60, 141–153.

Stoilovic, M., Kobus, H. J., Margot, P. A., and Warrener, R. N. (1986), Improved enhancement of ninhydrin developed fingerprints by cadmium complexation using low temperature photoluminescence techniques, *J. Forensic Sci.*, 31, 432–445.

Stoilovic, M. and Lennard, C. (2012), *Fingermark Detection and Enhancement*, 6th edn., National Centre for Forensic Studies, Canberra, Australia.

Stoilovic, M., Lennard, C., Wallace-Kunkel, C., and Roux, C. (2007), Evaluation of a 1,2-indanedione formulation containing zinc chloride for improved fingermark detection on paper, *J. Forensic Ident.*, 57, 4–18.

Suzuki, S., Suzuki, Y., and Ohta, H. (2002), Detection of latent fingerprints on newly developed substances using the vacuum metal deposition method, *J. Forensic Ident.*, 52, 573–578.

Swofford, H. J. and Kovalchick, A. T. (2012), Fingerprint powders: Aerosolized application revisited, *J. Forensic Ident.*, 62, 109–128.

Swofford, H. J., Paul, L. S., Steffan, S. M., and Bonar, D. (2013), Development of latent fingerprints on fired brass cartridge cases: Impact of latent print development using acidified hydrogen peroxide on forensic firearm and toolmark examinations, *J. Forensic Ident.*, 63, 359–368.

Tahtouh, M., Despland, P., Shimmon, R., Kalman, J. R., and Reedy, B. J. (2007), The application of infrared chemical imaging to the detection and enhancement of latent fingerprints: Method optimization and further findings, *J. Forensic Sci.*, 52, 1089–1096.

Tahtouh, M., Kalman, J. R., Roux, C., Lennard, C., and Reedy, B. J. (2005), The detection and enhancement of latent fingermarks using infrared chemical imaging, *J. Forensic Sci.*, 50, 64–72.

Takatsu, M., Kageyama, H., Hirata, H., Akashi, S., Yoko Ta, T., and Shiitana, M. (1991), Development of a new method to detect latent fingerprint on thermal paper with o-alkyl derivatives of ninhydrin, *Rep. Natl. Inst. Police Sci. (Jpn.)*, 44, 1–6.

Takatsu, M., Shimoda, O., and Teranishi, H. (2012), Vapor-phase staining of cyanoacrylate-fumed latent fingerprints using p-dimethylaminobenzaldehyde, *J. Forensic Sci.*, 57, 515–520.

Taroni, F., Lennard, C. J., and Margot, P. A. (1990), Latent fingerprint detection on non-porous surfaces: Comparison between metal deposition and cyanoacrylate fuming, in *12th Meeting of the International Association of Forensic Sciences*, Adelaide, South Australia, Australia.

Theys, P., Turgis, Y., Lepareux, A., Chevet, G., and Ceccaldi, P. F. (1968), Nouvelle technique de révélation de traces papillaires latentes (sur le papier) par métallisation sous vide, *Revue Internationale Police Criminelle*, 23(217), 106–108.

Thomas, G. L. (1973), The physics of fingerprints, *Criminology*, 8, 21–38.

Thomas, G. L. (1975), The resistivity of fingerprints, *J. Forensic Sci. Soc.*, 15, 133–135.

Thomas, G. L. (1978), The physics of fingerprints and their detection, *J. Phys. Ser. E: Sci. Instrum.*, 11, 722–731.

Thomas, P. and Farrugia, K. (2013), An investigation into the enhancement of fingermarks in blood on paper with genipin and lawsone, *Sci. Justice*, 53, 315–320.

Tissier, P., Didierjean, C., Prud'Homme, C., Pichard, J., and Crispino, F. (1999), A "cyanoacrylate case" for developing fingerprints in cars, *Sci. Justice*, 39, 163–166.

Trapecar, M. (2009), Lifting techniques for finger marks on human skin previous enhancement by Swedish Black powder—A preliminary study, *Sci. Justice*, 49, 292–295.

Trapecar, M. and Balazic, J. (2007), Fingerprint recovery from human skin surfaces, *Sci. Justice*, 47, 136–140.

Tripathi, A., Emmons, E. D., Wilcox, P. G., Guicheteau, J. A., Emge, D. K., Christesen, S. D., and Fountain, A. W. (2011), Semi-automated detection of trace explosives in fingerprints on strongly interfering surfaces with Raman chemical imaging, *Appl. Spectrosc.*, 65, 611–619.

United Nations Economic Commission for Europe (2014), *European Agreement Concerning the International Carriage of Dangerous Goods by Road*, Volume I, United Nations, New York, available from: http://www.unece.org/trans/danger/publi/adr/adr_e.html (accessed February 7, 2016).

United Nations Environment Programme (2015), The Montreal Protocol on Substances that Deplete the Ozone Layer, http://ozone.unep.org/en/treaties-and-decisions/montreal-protocol-substances-deplete-ozone-layer (accessed 6 February 2016).

van Dam, A., Aalders, M. C. G., van de Braak, K., Hardy, H. J. J., Van Leeuwen, T. G., and Lambrechts, S. A. G. (2013), Simultaneous labeling of multiple components in a single fingermark, *Forensic Sci. Int.*, 232, 173–179.

van Oorschot, R. A. H., Ballantyne, K. N., and Mitchell, R. J. (2010), Forensic trace DNA: A review, *Investig. Gen.*, 1, art. no. 14.

van Oorschot, R. A. H. and Jones, M. K. (1997), DNA fingerprints from fingerprints, *Nature*, 387, 767.

van Oorschot, R. A. H., Treadwell, S., Beaurepaire, J., Holding, N. L., and Mitchell, R. J. (2005), Beware of the possibility of fingerprinting techniques transferring DNA, *J. Forensic Sci.*, 50, 1417–1422.

Varnon, J. H. (1988), Latent fingerprint development: Special techniques for obtaining latent fingerprints on duct tape and similar tapes, *FDIAI News*, September 4–5, 1988.

Velders, M. J. M. (1997), Blutspuren, *Kriminalistik*, 51, 349–352.

Velthuis, S. and de Puit, M. (2011), Studies toward the development of a positive control test for the cyanoacrylate fuming technique using artificial sweat, *J. Forensic Ident.*, 61, 16–29.

von Wurmb, N., Meissner, D., and Wegener, R. (2000), Influence of cyanoacrylate on the efficiency of forensic PCRs, *Forensic Sci. Int.*, 124, 11–16.

Voss-De Haan, P. (2006), Physics and fingerprints, *Contemp. Phys.*, 47, 209–230.

Vouk, D. M. (1996), The effects of cold gun blue on individual characteristics on cartridge casings, *AFTE J.*, 28, 256–257.

Wade, D. C. (2002), Development of latent prints with titanium dioxide (TiO_2), *J. Forensic Ident.*, 52, 551–559.

Wakefield, M. and Armitage, S. (2005), The development of latent fingerprints on thermal paper using a novel, solvent-free method, *J. Forensic Ident.*, 55, 202–213.

Wallace-Kunkel, C., Lennard, C., Stoilovic, M., and Roux, C. (2007), Optimisation and evaluation of 1,2-indanedione for use as a fingermark reagent and its application to real samples, *Forensic Sci. Int.*, 168, 14–26.

Wang, G. Q. (1996), Detecting and enhancing latent fingerprints with short wave UV reflection photography, in *Proceedings of the International Symposium on Fingerprint Detection and Identification*, Ne'urim, Israel: eds. J. Almog and E. Springer, Israel National Police, June 26–30, 1995, pp. 37–49.

Wang, Y. F., Yang, R. Q., Wang, Y. J., Shi, Z. X., and Liu, J. J. (2009), Application of CdSe nanoparticle suspension for developing latent fingermarks on the sticky side of adhesives, *Forensic Sci. Int.*, 185, 96–99.

Wargacki, S. P., Lewis, L. A., and Dadmun, M. D. (2007), Understanding the chemistry of the development of latent fingerprints by superglue fuming, *J. Forensic Sci.*, 52, 1057–1062.

Wargacki, S. P., Lewis, L. A., and Dadmun, M. D. (2008), Enhancing the quality of aged latent fingerprints developed by superglue fuming: Loss and replenishment of initiator, *J. Forensic Sci.*, 53, 1138–1144.

Warrick, P. (2000), Identification of blood prints on fabrics using amido black and digital enhancement, *J. Forensic Ident.*, 50, 20–32.

Watkin, J. E. and Misner, A. H. (1990), Fluorescence and crime scenes in the 90's, *RCMP Gaz.*, 52(9), 1–5.

Watkin, J. E., Wilkinson, D., Misner, A. H., and Yamashita, A. B. (1994), Cyanoacrylate fuming of latent prints: Vacuum versus heat/humidity, *J. Forensic Ident.*, 44, 545–556.

Watling, W. J. and Smith, K. O. (1993), Heptane: An alternative to the Freon/ninhydrin mixture, *J. Forensic Ident.*, 43, 131–134.

Weaver, D. E. and Clary, E. J. (1993), A one-step fluorescent cyanoacrylate fingerprint development technology, *J. Forensic Ident.*, 43, 481–492.

West, M. H., Brasley, R. E., Frair, J., and Hall, F. (1990), Reflective ultraviolet imaging system (RUVIS) and the detection of trace evidence and wounds on human skin, *J. Forensic Ident.*, 40, 249–255.

Wiesner, S., Springer, E., and Argaman, U. (1996), A closer look at the effects of the shooting process on fingerprint development on fired cartridge cases, in *Proceedings of the International Symposium on Fingerprint Detection and Identification*, Ne'urim, Israel: eds. J. Almog and E. Springer, Israel National Police, June 26–30, 1995, pp. 161–178.

Wiesner, S., Springer, E., Sasson, Y., and Almog, J. (2001), Chemical development of latent fingerprints: 1,2-indanedione has come of age, *J. Forensic Sci.*, 46, 1082–1084.

Wightman, G., Emery, F., Austin, C., Andersson, I., Harcus, L., Arju, G., and Steven, C. (2015), The interaction of fingermark deposits on metal surfaces and potential ways for visualisation, *Forensic Sci. Int.*, 249, 241–254.

Wilgus, G. (2002), Latent print recovery from human skin, *J. Forensic Ident.*, 52, 133–135.

Wilkinson, D. (2000a), Spectroscopic study of 1,2-indanedione, *Forensic Sci. Int.*, 114, 123–132.

Wilkinson, D. (2000b), Study of the reaction mechanism of 1,8-diazafluoren-9-one with the amino acid l-alanine, *Forensic Sci. Int.*, 109, 87–103.

Wilkinson, D. (2011), A review of fingerprints from human skin, *Ident. Can.* 34, 48–60.

Wilkinson, D. and Watkin, J. E. (1993), Europium aryl-β-diketone complexes as fluorescent dyes for the detection of cyanoacrylate developed fingerprints on human skin, *Forensic Sci. Int.*, 60, 67–79.

Wilkinson, D., Watkin, J. E., and Misner, A. H. (1996a), A comparison of techniques for the visualization of fingerprints on human skin including the application of iodine and α-naphthoflavone, *J. Forensic Ident.*, 46, 432–453.

Wilkinson, D., Watkin, J. E., and Misner, A. H. (1996b), A comparison of techniques for the visualization of fingerprints on human skin including the application of iodine and α-naphthoflavone [correction], *J. Forensic Ident.*, 46, 663.

Williams, G., McMurray, H. N., and Worsley, D. A. (2001), Latent fingerprint detection using a scanning Kelvin microprobe, *J. Forensic Sci.*, 46, 1085–1092.

Williams, G. and McMurray, N. (2007), Latent fingermark visualisation using a scanning Kelvin probe, *Forensic Sci. Int.*, 167, 102–109.

Williams, N. H. and Elliott, K. T. (2005), Development of latent prints using titanium dioxide (TiO_2) in small particle reagent, white (SPR-W) on adhesives, *J. Forensic Ident.*, 55, 292–305.

Wilson, B. L. and McCloud, V. D. (1982), Development of latent prints on black plastic tape using crystal violet dye and photographic paper, *Ident. News*, 32, 3–4.

Wilson, J. D., Cantú, A. A., Antonopoulos, G., and Surrency, M. J. (2007), Examination of the steps leading up to the physical developer process for developing fingerprints, *J. Forensic Sci.*, 52, 320–329.

Wolstenholme, R., Bradshaw, R., Clench, M. R., and Francese, S. (2009), Study of latent fingermarks by matrix-assisted laser desorption/ionisation mass spectrometry imaging of endogenous lipids, *Rapid Commun. Mass Spectrom.*, 23, 3031–3039.

Wood, L. W. (1991), The discovery of Super Glue fuming, *Fingerprint Whorld*, 16(64), 117–118.

Wood, M., Maynard, P., Spindler, X., Lennard, C., and Roux, C. (2012), Visualization of latent fingermarks using an aptamer-based reagent, *Angew. Chem. Int. Ed.*, 51, 12272–12274.

Wood, M., Maynard, P., Spindler, X., Roux, C., and Lennard, C. (2013), Selective targeting of fingermarks using immunogenic techniques, *Aust. J. Forensic Sci.*, 45, 211–226.

Wood, M. A. and James, I. T. (2009), Latent fingerprint persistence and development techniques on wet surfaces, *Fingerprint Whorld*, 35(135), 90–100.

Yamashita, K., Oishi, M., Okiura, T., Shirakami, A., and Ohue, M. (1993), A new method for detection of latent fingerprints on a craft adhesive tape by using SP-Black® powder, *Rep. Natl. Res. Inst. Police Sci. (Jpn.)*, 46, 189–191.

Yang, R., Wang, Y., Xia, B., Wang, Y., and Liu, J. (2011), Application of CdTe quantum dots to development fingerprints on adhesive surfaces, *Mater. Sci. Forum*, 694, 874–880.

Yang, R.-Q., Zhou, Q.-Y., Wang, Y.-F., and Jin, Y.-J. (2008), Nano meter CdS/PAMAM G5.0 for developing oil latent fingerprints on adhesive side of common tapes, *Chin. J. Inorg. Chem.*, 24, 1874–1879.

Yong, A. S. J. (1986), Detection of latent fingerprints with cyanoacrylates: New techniques involving coloured and photoluminescent compounds, Ph.D. thesis, National Australian University, Canberra, Australia.

Yong, A. S. J., Margot, P. A., and Warrener, R. N. (1986), Visual enhancement of superglue developed fingerprints, in *Ninth Australian International Forensic Science Symposium*, Melbourne, Australia.

Yu, I.-H., Jou, S., Chen, C.-M., Wang, K.-C., Pang, L.-J., and Liao, J. S. (2011), Development of latent fingerprint by ZnO deposition, *Forensic Sci. Int.*, 207, 14–18.

Yu, P.-H. and Wallace, M. M. (2007), Effect of 1,2-indanedione on PCR-STR typing of fingerprints deposited on thermal and carbonless paper, *Forensic Sci. Int.*, 168, 112–118.

Yu, X., Liu, J., Zuo, S., Yu, Y., Cai, K., and Yang, R. (2013), Application of mercaptosuccinic acid capped CdTe quantum dots for latent fingermark development, *Forensic Sci. Int.*, 231, 125–130.

Zamir, A., Oz, C., and Geller, B. (2000a), Threat mail and forensic science: DNA profiling from items of evidence after treatment with DFO, *J. Forensic Sci.*, 45, 445–446.

Zamir, A., Oz, C., Leifer, A., and Geller, B. (2002), The effect of small particle reagent employed as a fingerprint enhancement technique on subsequent STR typing from bloodstains, *J. Forensic Ident.*, 52, 691–695.

Zamir, A., Springer, E., and Glattstein, B. (2000b), Fingerprints and DNA: STR typing of DNA extracted from adhesive tape after processing of fingerprints, *J. Forensic Sci.*, 45, 687–688.

Zhang, X., Tang, X., and Bowen, K. (2013), Photoelectron spectroscopic study of the ethyl cyanoacrylate anion, *Chem. Phys. Lett.*, 582, 21–23.

Ziv, Z. and Springer, E. (1993), More applications of coaxial illumination in fingerprint detecting and photography, *J. Forensic Ident.*, 43, 362–367.

5 Issues Related to the Exploitation of Fingerprints and Fingermarks

Technical issues related to automated fingerprint identification systems (AFISs) and associated computer technologies for database searching are important, but they need separate treatment. Such systems, for the extraction of relevant information from a large amount of data, are technical tools that rely on pattern recognition and complex computerized systems outside the scope of this book (see, for example, the book chapters by Komarinski [2005], Maltoni et al. [2009], and Moses [2011]). The operational performance of automated systems and probabilistic models have been the subject of recent research (for example, de Jongh and Rodriguez [2012], Rodriguez et al. [2012], and Haraksim et al. [2015]). Further, the most recent systems include images (mug shots, tattoos, scars) and criminal records, as well as other classical anthropometric features (height, weight, eye, and hair color, etc.). There is a welcome trend to ask more from biometric research and apply it to forensic science issues, and we can expect that AFIS installations will benefit from these developments in the near future (Jain and Ross 2015). This includes automatic tattoo recognition and facial recognition of mugshots, surveillance images, or facial composite sketches. Systems were, until recently, devoted to criminal and specific populations only (defined legally, such as crime investigation personnel, military, and emergency services), but they are now becoming part of a universal identification system such as that developed in India (www.uidai.gov.in; accessed January 29, 2016), which has already recorded data from over 870 million individuals with a 12-digit unique identification number based on biometric features in a system called "aadhaar." The various associated factors (political, legal, ethical), although essential, fall outside the scope of this book, and we focus here on many professional issues that directly affect dactyloscopists in their activities. This includes semantics and terminology, the information content (not simply the identification potential) of friction ridge skin impressions, the relevancy of traces (their age, the potential for forgeries and their detection), identification errors, and training and education requirements for fingerprint specialists. These issues, which are rarely covered in any detail in the general literature, are addressed in this chapter. Some of these issues are difficult to address, and some are controversial, but they are introduced to show that the field is not stale and that there is room for further discussion and advancement. Many questions raised may not have complete or satisfactory answers, but we hope that the mere fact of raising the issues will prompt relevant research and development efforts.

5.1 TERMINOLOGY

The use of ridge skin patterns for the purpose of identification has gone through rapid developments throughout the twentieth century, resulting in conflicting opinions as to who preceded whom and what the proper terminology was supposed to be. Practitioners developed a working terminology for their own purpose, and the lack of a common vocabulary introduced different words for the same concept and different concepts for the same word. Although it might be clear what is meant within the specialist language in a given geographical/sociocultural environment, differences have led to inconsistent uses and abuses, misunderstandings, and a flourishing of words to express or specify aspects of the *science of fingerprinting*. The terminology has ranged from *fingerprints* (Galton 1892) to *icnophalangometry* (Vucetich 1904 [reported by Locard 1931]); *dactyloscopy* (Latzina [reported by Locard 1931]); *lophoscopy* (Lambert 1990); *cretoscopy*, *ridgeoscopy*, and *ridgeology* (Ashbaugh 1982); *edgeoscopy* (Chatterjee 1962); *poroscopy* (Locard 1913); *chiroscopy* and *pelmatoscopy* (referred to by Locard [1931]); *friction ridge skin* (Cowger 1983), etc. In addition, terms such as *stains*, *prints*, *traces*, or *marks* could be used without distinction to express the cause of the trace (pattern, details) and the trace itself (marks and their characteristics). These terms have mostly been created (neologisms) and are based on descriptive aspects of the subject matter, sometimes even without reference to a more or less universal etymological root. In scientific circles (botany, zoology, etc.), it is habitual to use a Greek or Latin descriptive root that can have universal acceptance and will give a general key for similarly constructed words. The further advantage of this is that these roots are found in all modern Indo-European languages and can be readily translated.

The most general and universal term is therefore *lophoscopy*, from the Greek root *lophos*, meaning "crest" or "ridge," and *skopein*, meaning "study" or "examination." Both roots are commonly encountered, the first in the naming (taxonomy) of plants (e.g., **Lophophora**, a kind of cactus with crests) and animals (e.g., **Bilophosauria**, a dinosaur with two crests), the second to describe instruments used to observe or examine (e.g., *micro**scope***, used to study small objects). In use in France and Belgium (according to Interpol), *lophoscopy* is translated (official European Council translation) into "ridge pattern analysis" in English and would correspond to the "ridgeoscopy" of Ashbaugh. *Ridgeoscopy* as a term has the merit of clarity in English, but it is etymologically heterogeneous, mixing both English and Greek roots, as is *edgeoscopy* as proposed by Chatterjee (Chatterjee 1962). It is therefore advocated that *lophoscopy* should be the generic term defining the study of ridges. The International Criminal Police Organisation adopted this terminology (Lambert 1990).

Similarly, *dactyloscopy* has been coined from *dactylos* (a Greek root meaning "digit" or "finger") and was proposed by Dr. Francisco Latzina, who published a report in the journal *La Nacion* (Buenos Aires [reported by Locard 1931]) after visiting Vucetich. He used the term *dactiloscopia* (in Spanish), referring to what Vucetich was calling *icnophalangometria* from the Greek root *iknos* (meaning the trace), *phalank* (the finger joint), and *metria* (measure). *Dactyloscopy* has since been adopted in most languages (*la dactyloscopie* [Spanish and French], *die Daktyloskopie* [German], etc.), but English has remained faithful to the "fingerprint" of Galton. Unfortunately, with the advent of modern analytical chemistry, DNA technology, biochemistry, etc., the term *fingerprint* is widely employed to describe the highly selective nature of a technique, feature, or method. It is impossible to perform a database search (the Internet, scientific indexes, etc.) for *fingerprint* without finding thousands of references that have nothing to do with the study of fingers (or of fingerprints, for that matter). In June 2015, a search through Scopus (www.scopus.com) with the keyword "fingerprint" showed 297 papers for the first 6 months of 2015 that have fingerprints in their title or keywords of which only 22 concern the subject of this book (more than 92% of the papers concern biology, chemistry, statistics, etc.). It is time to adopt a unique identifier, *dactyloscopy* being the obvious choice due to its wide distribution across languages and geographically (even if formally it would exclude ridges from palms and the plant of feet, indicating the prevalence of fingermarks or fingerprints). Some fingerprint specialists erroneously use the term *dactylography* ("writing with fingers"), which is widely used for "typewriting." The latter word introduces additional confusion and should be avoided. *Dactyloscopy* has such a wide usage that it covers all aspects of detection, comparison, and identification of finger impressions and is equated in many countries with the misnomer of *fingerprint science*. A dactyloscopic file/card is a ten-print card, and a monodactyloscopic file is a classification based on a one-finger-specific print file (e.g., right thumb prints only).

Finally, ridge skin is not found only on fingers, and *chiroscopy* is the proper descriptor for the study of palms (the root *chiros* is found in ***chiro**practic*, meaning "healing by using palms" or "massages," and in ***chiromancy***, meaning "divination using the crease lines of palms" or "palmistry"). Crease or flexion lines of the palm can also be used for comparison or identification, and these belong in the realm of chiroscopy, even if few reports exist since the work of Claps in 1931 (referred to by Locard [1931]). Specialists mostly use crease lines as landmarks for orienting palm prints. Similarly, "pelmatoscopy" is the study of the soles of the feet. (There are few widely used words with *pelmatos* as a root, except in the area of foot medicine [podiatry].)

Poroscopy (from the root *poros*, meaning "pore"), first described by Locard (1912), is usually discussed in relation to ridge skin, and rightly so, since pores protrude and open on the surface of ridges. Nevertheless, it may have wider application, as pores are present everywhere on the skin surface, and it may be possible to map (like an astronomical map, using the expression of Locard) other skin surfaces that have been in contact with an object (see discussion of *dermatoglyphics*). In fact, cases are known where such a mapping has been used as evidence in court, although this is fraught with difficulties and remains rather an academic exercise.

This nomenclature, which defines the object of study (ridges) and its localization (fingers, palms, or soles of the feet), was already established at the beginning of the twentieth century. Such a nomenclature should be widely adopted to avoid further confusion. The proposed terminology is listed in Table 5.1.

The term *dermatoglyphics* (from the roots *derma*, meaning "skin," and *gluphein*, meaning "engrave") was introduced by Cummins (1926) (Cummins and Midlo 1926) as the science of the study of skin patterns as a clinical instrument. Used commonly at the time in the study of the morphogenesis of skin patterns, this term is not quite synonymous with *lophoscopy*. Other skin patterns, such as the netlike arrangements seen at the back of the hands, are incidentally being researched in China for their identification potential and a documented case has been published (Harrison et al. 2014).

A further confusion in terminology concerns the distinction between a "fingerprint" and a "fingermark." The first term should be employed for a record or comparison print taken for identification, exclusion, or database purposes (sometimes referred to as a "known" print), whereas the second should only concern traces left (unknowingly) by a person on an object (sometimes referred to as the "unknown," "latent," or "questioned" mark). The mark generally implies a lesser quality impression that includes latent, partial, distorted, reversed (tonally or laterally), or superimposed impressions, even if sloppy print taking will result in lesser ridge information than many marks. The lexical

TABLE 5.1
Proposed Terminology

Proposed Terminology	Equivalent	To Avoid
Chiroscopy	Ridge pattern analysis of palms	—
Dactyloscopy	Ridge pattern analysis from fingers; fingerprinting	Science of fingerprinting
Dactyloscopist	Fingerprint specialist	—
Dermatoglyphics	Friction ridge skin pattern analysis	—
Fingerprint	"A plain impression obtained by placing the bulb of the finger on the inked slab and then impressing it on paper" (p. 24) (Henry 1900); by extension, a control impression taken from a finger	
Fingermark	Trace impression by ridged skin of uncontrolled quality, which may be visible or latent	Latent fingerprint
Lophoscopy	Cretoscopy, ridgeology, ridge pattern analysis, ridgeoscopy	Science of fingerprinting
Pelmatoscopy	Ridge pattern analysis from the soles of the feet	—
Edgeoscopy	Study of the edges of friction ridges	—
Poroscopy	Study of pores of friction ridges	—

and colloquial use of "latent fingerprint," even for patent marks, is common in North America; elsewhere, the distinction between print (reference) and mark (trace impression) is made. It follows an unwritten rule that had already appeared in Henry's book and its last chapter written by Collins (New Scotland Yard) (Henry 1900). This distinction avoids some confusion that appears in many publications.

5.2   USE OF FINGERPRINTS

Fingerprints have not traditionally been recorded for the systematic identification of the population, although this has been advocated in the past. For example, the gathering of systematic records for a full national register (national database) was first introduced by law in Argentina on July 20, 1916, but this led to violent opposition, and the law was suspended on May 28, 1917, and the register destroyed. Ecuador introduced a national register in 1924 without apparent opposition, and such registers were advocated throughout the world but were rejected on the basis of human rights (privacy laws, individual rights, etc.). This has changed with tighter identification controls introduced after terrorist attacks in the early twenty-first century and the development of biometric-based identity systems (biometric passports and identity cards). Controversies have arisen as to whether a central repository should exist and be available for law enforcement and criminal investigation purposes. It appears that India will be the first country with a full biometric identification system for its whole population. As of 2015, over 870 million people are registered in the system but legislation is still pending and concerns regarding privacy will become an issue.

On the other hand, registers of offenders are widely employed. Other registers, restricted to certain sections of the population, exist in some countries (e.g., migrant/refugee registers, military personnel, investigation and emergency services). Typically, access to these databases is narrowly defined for specific purposes, such as to avoid multiple requests for refugee status under false pretense at different border entry points. Many countries also have registers for military, security, special agents, and law enforcement personnel to aid in the identification of casualties in military actions or for the identification of marks inadvertently left on the scene of a crime. (It is not uncommon for up to 30% of marks found at crime scenes to have been made by police officers, according to Mark [1996], but the question is not addressed in the scientific literature.) All such registers are subject to specific laws within the frameworks of local legal systems. Similar laws have been introduced for DNA records and, in some instances, the laws regulating the taking of fingerprint records have been extended to include other biometric markers such as DNA, offender photographs, and descriptive characteristics (remnants of the anthropometric system of Bertillon [1885]). Systematic records of newborn babies and other such practices have not found wide support and are mostly not applied.

Other uses cover the proof of identity by the application of a fingerprint (usually a thumb or an index print) on identification documents such as passports and identity cards (there is always a legal basis for these applications) or, in the last few years, as a morphometric or biometric means of identification in access control systems for computers, doors, safes, etc. Recent interest in automatic access control is leading to the creation of records or files whose legality is often not established. Such database construction occurs on the basis of agreement or consensus decision only. Registers of this type may become the source of prints useful for identification purposes in large-scale disaster victim identification (DVI) or for the investigation of specific computer crimes (unauthorized access, fraudulent file modifications, etc.).

Fingerprints have been suggested as a replacement for signatures on civil documents, bank checks, or works of art, but reports of such applications are mostly anecdotal. Historically, this usage of finger impressions was widespread in Asia (China, India) (Xiang-Xin and Chun-Ge 1988), leading to later developments by both Herschel (1887 letter from India referred to as the Hooghly Letter) and Faulds (1880) following his experience in Japan.

Modern artists such as Chuck Close are using fingerprints to paint portraits, and Jennifer Hannaford, a forensic scientist and artist, has made forensic science–related portraits using fingerprints on canvas.

5.2.1 PRINT-TO-PRINT COMPARISON

Print-to-print or print-to-record comparisons are the bases of recognition of persons previously recorded and needing to be identified. This is the principle of biometric access controls and was the basis of the proposal initially made by Herschel for the state to be able to recognize habitual criminals after their release from prisons (Herschel 1880). This is the principle of administrative databases recording fingerprints, DNA, or other physical features (early Bertillonage). A useful distinction is made between *verification* and *identification*. When prints of an individual claiming a given identity are compared to a record corresponding to that identity, then it is a 1:1 *verification* task. Searching a corresponding print against a database of size N (number of prints or of individuals) is the usual 1:N *identification* process.

Print-to-print or print-to-record comparisons do not generally create special difficulties. The quality of prints and the amount of information available (finger number, position, central pattern, deltas, ridge counts, not to mention a multitude of minutiæ) make the process of exclusion easy, with often only a cursory glance at the comparison prints being required. The process of identification is hardly more difficult for the trained observer, even if this is now largely machine processed using AFIS, with remote operation possible using live-scan input stations. Such a comparison is mostly required in a procedure of confirmation (e.g., that the print on an identification document, or in a register of habitual offenders, corresponds to the print of the person under control, going through customs, or arrested in the course of an investigation). It must be noted that the quality of the print is mostly not at issue here, and sometimes this leads to sloppy print taking; the amount of information available is generally such that even if parts of the prints are not clear, or are obliterated, the identification process is not significantly impeded. Unfortunately, this is often a neglected aspect of print taking that affects the identification process when comparison is made with imperfect impressions found at crime scenes. Quality control in the taking of reference prints should therefore be an essential part of specialist training, and utmost care should be taken to have the highest standard prints for storage in AFIS databases.

5.2.2 TRACE-TO-RECORD OR TRACE-TO-PRINT COMPARISON

The trace-to-record or trace-to-print comparison came from the observation that fingermarks were deposited on handled objects or touched items and their fine detail could be identified to their source. This was the development published by Faulds that was the fundamental step in changing identification from an administrative task to one of investigation (Faulds 1880).

Forensic science is the art of working with imperfect data/samples/information. A trace is by essence a mark or material indicative of a source and/or action. The production of the trace is a limiting process: imperfections can be minimal to the point where the trace is deemed comparable to the reference material, or they can be great enough that it is difficult to even identify the possible source type for the trace. In dactyloscopy, a trace could be a smudge that may or may not be the mark of a finger, or it may be possible to identify the trace as a fingermark but without ridge detail. The position of a fingermark may give information on the event, probable handedness of the donor, etc. A general ridge pattern may be visible, with an approximate indication of ridge count, or ridge detail may be visible without knowing from which part of the ridge skin it originated (e.g., a partial mark that could be from a finger, a palm, a foot sole, or even an animal). There may be sufficient information to determine which finger is responsible for a mark (e.g., the right index in a normal anatomical sequence), but with little detail other than a possible pattern and approximate ridge count. Finally, it may be possible to identify which finger is responsible for the mark and, with sufficient ridge detail, to decide upon the identity of the person whose finger made the trace.

Whatever specimen or information is available at the crime scene, however imperfect, there may still be exclusion value important in the resolution of the case. The process of identification is discussed elsewhere (Chapter 2), but there is always a need to evaluate—at the scene—the pertinence or the relevance of the mark to the case or to the investigation or to the activity of the criminal who the investigator is trying to identify. The question of activity is rarely the focus for fingerprint practitioners since the apparent question is always: "is this trace from this person or from a person recorded in the database?" when the position of the trace may be just as relevant as its ridge features and may be much more important in various case situations. To have an indication that an object was seized using a left hand rather than a right hand (using ridge flow and/or anatomical sequences) may be an indication as to the way a weapon may have been used. Position indicating using a weapon or lifting a weapon from the ground gives quite different stories. The value of fingermarks for potential case reconstruction purposes should be part of the initial evaluation of these traces. The precise location of a fingermark may also limit the search to a specific hand/finger in large databases, thus reducing the potential population. A "strange" position may also be a telltale indicator for fabricated or planted fingermarks. The absence of fingermarks on some objects/items may also help reduce the propositions concerning the events under investigation.

Finally, the capacity of specialists across the profession to reliably detect and identify fingermark features has come under recent scrutiny. The question remained largely unexplored in the past as the identification process was an accessory for the overall criminal investigation process that was used to support other elements of the case. With "cold hits" or the identification of a source that is neither suspected nor apparently linked to specific events, practitioner overconfidence and resolute trust in one's abilities have led to the tragic decisions discussed in the following section concerning errors. This also has a fundamental impact on training, education, validation, and verification as addressed at the end of this chapter.

5.2.3 Trace-to-Trace Comparison

Problems linked with the quality of the traces are compounded in this case because each trace can suffer from all the faults that a single trace may have. Depending on position and pattern types, it may be possible to determine whether one or more authors committed the crime, which part of the action can be associated with one author, and a partial reconstruction of the events. This is the usual primary observation made at the scene. More importantly, a trace may be observed at more than one crime scene, thereby creating a link between otherwise separate events. This provides the investigator with one of the strongest pieces of information one could obtain in the analysis of serial and high-volume crimes. Trace-to-trace comparisons therefore have a very high operational value when investigating such crimes (e.g., serial burglaries [Ribaux et al. 2010a,b]) and should be considered as a potential investigative tool (Morelato et al. 2014; Baechler et al. 2015). However, preliminary results show that, unlike with DNA—where each trace initially contains a wealth of information from the source—the number of instances with partial-print matches is usually low (Aguzzi 2002; Anthonioz et al. 2003).

Out of 1001 identifications (of 867 individuals) using AFIS in Switzerland in 2001, only 11 criminals (mostly burglars) were associated to multiple crime scenes through fingermarks. Ten of these cases were checked, and no mark-to-mark match was found. It must be noted that, in practice, not all marks found are submitted for AFIS searching. Typically, only the best mark in an anatomical sequence or good-quality marks—only about half the marks obtained—are filed in the database, thus reducing the potential use of fingermarks in serial and volume crime investigation.

5.2.4 COMBINING EVIDENCE TYPES

One issue that is bound to influence the work of fingerprint experts is the advent of extremely sensitive DNA-based methods (Ostojic et al. 2014; Kumar et al. 2015; Steadman et al. 2015) that can be successfully applied to generate a DNA profile from smudged or superimposed marks. Such marks may be identified to be from the criminal because of their positions at the crime scene, but they may lack ridge characteristics of sufficient quality for dactyloscopic treatment. The first reported successes in obtaining a DNA profile from a fingermark go back almost 20 years (van Oorschot and Jones 1997).

Increased sensitivity in DNA technology creates the risk of profiling nonpertinent biological traces (background noise) (Lowe et al. 2002; Wickenheiser 2002); but, applied to traces such as smudged fingermarks, it is bound to bring about valuable results for a reasonable percentage of marks (Schulz and Reichert 2002). One requirement, however, is that the fingerprint detection and enhancement process does not adversely affect the DNA analysis (see Section 4.17.2). It must be stressed that research on contact DNA and contamination issues has to be considered very carefully (Meakin and Jamieson 2013; Szkuta et al. 2013, 2015).

One issue might become the comparison of marks of less than perfect quality combined with incomplete DNA profiles to give an overall value for the evidence collected. This is an issue that most fingerprint specialists view with suspicion. Their skepticism is focused on the loss of the "positivity" that has pervaded the field for almost a century, rather than seeing new potential lifeblood for a whole range of marks that were otherwise deemed insufficient to be used in evidence. The issue of combining less than perfect fingerprint evidence with other evidence types has already been raised (Champod 1995), but without much support from fingerprint specialists. The resistance probably arises from a perceived loss of control over one's discipline through the introduction of new dimensions that may require a different and more complex training and education program for identification specialists than in the past.

5.2.5 IDENTIFICATION DECISION IN OTHER FORUMS THAN THE COURT

The identification process described in Chapter 2 is mostly linked to a decision made by a court, based on an expert opinion. In most DVI situations, including tragedies such as tsunamis and earthquakes, the identification decision is not taken by the courts but by the specialists involved in the identification. Identifications may be based on factors that are less stringent than those required in a decision that is "beyond reasonable doubt" and may combine a number of circumstantial factors to help families start their mourning. This decision process has been thoroughly researched by Gremaud (2010) and further discussed after a tsunami DVI investigation by an Australian team (Gremaud 2010; Wright et al. 2015).

5.3 RELEVANCE

The determination of relevance usually comes from proper documentation of where the mark was found in relation to the event, on which surface, and when and how the scene was preserved. This aspect of proper trace evidence management and documentation has an essential impact in criminal investigations. If the trace (a fingermark) is associated to a person that had no reason to be at the crime scene at the time of the incident, it becomes essential to know if it was on a mobile or a fixed surface, whether the location, orientation, and position could fit the perceived event. Allegations questioning the validity of the evidence—that the trace was not found where it is alleged to have been found, that case notes were mixed from two or more scenes by overworked personnel, or that the mark was placed there before (or after) the event under investigation—can usually be laid to rest through proper case management and documentation. Poorly handled contested cases can create massive amounts of work to reconstitute the source of a trace (e.g., going back to the scene, documenting surface patterns to match with lifted marks). If the relevance of a mark is contested and unsuccessfully demonstrated, doubts can be cast on the value of the evidence.

There are three very important aspects that have to be discussed in relation to the relevance of evidence based on lophoscopy: the first concerns the date or the age of the evidence; the second concerns false traces (forged, fabricated, planted, etc.); and the third concerns the errors, or error rates, in deciding on an identification or an exclusion. The remainder of this chapter focuses on these three aspects.

5.4   AGE ESTIMATION OF MARKS

An estimation of the age of a particular trace is of both theoretical and practical importance, as it can indicate whether or not that trace is related to the offence under investigation. Time factors suffer from the fundamental issue of asymmetry, i.e., one generally cannot go back to witness and document a situation. This leads to the difficulty of knowing the initial status and to the relative fuzziness of duration and succession, and whether two events were simultaneous or sequential.

Some external factors or time markers may be useful, like the date and time recordings on a video, metadata in electronic devices, or indications of the initial existence of an item (date of manufacture or birth). Other factors may be seen in sequences establishing a chronology. Finally, analytical studies may give indications on the aging kinetics (chemical, physical modifications over time) of an item; a fingermark in this instance.

Numerous studies have been carried out aimed at developing techniques capable of determining the absolute (true) age, or at least the relative age, of particular items of evidence (Margot 2000). Examples include the dating of inks and documents, blood samples, footwear and tool marks, firearm discharge residues, and, of course, fingermarks. For all of these traces, attempts at determining an approximate age can be both a difficult and controversial matter (Howorka 1989; Baniuk 2000). Following the review published by Wertheim (2003), work has been conducted by Weyermann's group (Girod et al. 2012; Girod and Weyermann 2013; Girod et al. 2014; Girod and Weyermann 2014) showing some dynamic features of fingermark composition that may be used in the study of aging. A critical review highlighting what is known about fingerprint composition, how composition may affect aging, the variables that need to be addressed, and research possibilities was recently published (Cadd et al. 2015).

Intuitively, a fresh fingermark will show better ridge detail than an equivalent fingermark that has been exposed to environmental conditions over a certain period of time. One must consider, however, the parameters that influence this loss in fingermark detail. The aging process involves the drying out of the latent mark, resulting in

- Dulling of the sweat–grease deposit
- Loss of stickiness
- Narrowing of the fingerprint ridges
- Loss of continuity along the fingerprint ridges

The rate of dehydration of the latent mark will depend on many factors, including the amount of fatty material contained in the deposit, the temperature and relative humidity, air currents, exposure to the sun, and the nature of the surface (porous or nonporous, rough or smooth) (Figure 5.1) (Holyst 1987). In addition to the dehydration of the latent mark, a loss of legibility may result from the effects of dust, atmospheric pollution, precipitation, bacterial action, oxidation and decomposition of the deposit, diffusion of the fingerprint material through the surface, and so on.

As far as the age of fingermarks is concerned, there are very few systematic studies published in the literature. In 1961, Angst proposed a technique for determining the age of latent fingermarks on paper (Angst 1961). His method was based on the use of silver nitrate (Section 4.6.4) to evaluate the diffusion of the chloride component of the fingermark through the paper support. He claimed that

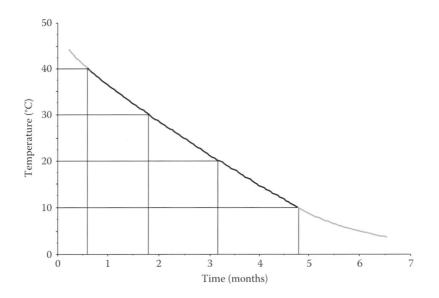

FIGURE 5.1 A typical fingerprint dehydration curve relating temperature to average drying time (in months) under controlled conditions (relative humidity = 50%). (From Holyst, B., *Archiv für Kriminologie*, 179, 94, 1987.)

an age could be estimated by studying the fingerprint images produced both on the recto and verso sides of the document after silver nitrate treatment, and then comparing these images with those produced under controlled conditions. Despite his detailed study of fingermark aging on paper, the technique suffers from obvious drawbacks, notably those related to the use of silver nitrate as a detection technique. The diffusion of chlorides through a document will obviously depend on the structure and composition of the paper and the degree of humidity. It would be impossible to reproduce the exact conditions under which a document has been stored. In addition, as with all fingermark age determination techniques, *the quality and composition of a particular latent mark at the time of its deposition is unknown*. More recent aging studies on fingermark residues using thin-layer and high-performance liquid chromatography (Duff and Menzel 1978; Dikshitulu et al. 1986) were of academic interest but did not propose at the time a realistic solution to the age determination problem.

One of the most complete early studies on fingermark aging was probably that described by Holyst (1987), used to estimate such age in the dactyloscopy department in Warsaw some 25 years ago (Baniuk 1990). In this study, extensive tests were carried out on fingermarks deposited on various nonporous surfaces (glass, metal, and plastic) that were subsequently aged both indoors and outdoors. A large number of factors, including temperature, humidity, dust concentration, and exposure to water, were taken into account. The studies revealed that traces keep longest on glass, whereas their survival on plastics is short because of the material's electrostatic charge, which attracts dust. A distinction was made between sweat marks (i.e., high eccrine component) and sweat–grease marks (i.e., high sebaceous component), with the latter preserving about five times as long. The publication shows that temperature, humidity, dust content in the air, and the type of substrate carrying the trace are factors of considerable impact on the aging process. Hence, such factors would need to be considered in any attempt to estimate the date of deposition for a given mark.

Additional information concerning the estimation of the age of a latent fingermark can be found in the form of case reports, some of which have been published in the literature. These are mostly based on limited empirical experiments that do not allow for a general estimation and are often designed without much knowledge of fingerprint chemistry and/or physics. For example, O'Brien (1984) describes the case of a double murder that occurred in New Zealand in 1981. A young couple was murdered while asleep in their bedroom. At the scene, fingerprint evidence was collected from 71 different locations. A suspect was apprehended, and his fingerprints were found to correspond with marks collected from eight different locations at the murder scene, including a mark on the outside of the back door. In the opinion of the fingerprint experts involved, this mark was "very fresh." The defense's explanation for the fingerprint evidence was that the suspect had left these marks when he was an occupant of the property over 6 months before the murders had been committed. Extensive tests were subsequently carried out on good-quality test marks deposited on both the inside and the outside of the back door in question. It was concluded that fingermarks placed on the outside of the back door would not remain in good condition for more than a few weeks. On the other hand, some test marks on the inside of the door remained in excellent condition even after 40 days! Via the painstaking comparison of nearly all the marks from the 71 locations, it was possible to show that none of the marks belonged to any of the persons known to have been in the house up to the end of the suspect's occupancy (with the exception of the suspect himself). Experimentation showed that the chances of the offender's marks surviving from his previous occupation, while those of his family and friends did not, were almost nil. The chances of eight marks surviving such a time were claimed to be impossible. The accused was found not guilty of murder on grounds of insanity.

Schwabenland (1992) described a case of double murder where a suspect's thumb mark had been developed on an empty aluminum beer can using black magnetic powder. The beer can had been found in an open field, close to the bodies of the two victims. Both victims appeared to have died within the previous 24 hours. The suspect admitted to having been at the scene with the two victims (where they had eaten fried chicken and drank some beers) but claimed that the occurrence had been 1 week previously. It, therefore, appeared important to determine the age of the thumb mark found on the beer can in question. Testing was subsequently conducted on marks deposited on similar beer cans. Control marks were aged under conditions chosen to simulate those presumed to have influenced the evidential mark (for example, the amount of sunlight exposure and the fact that the suspect's fingers had probably been contaminated with grease from the fried chicken). Schwabenland had concluded, from the results of his experiments, that clear marks, comparable to the evidential thumb mark, could only be detected up to 48 hours after deposition. He stated that marks of this quality could not have resulted after outdoor exposure for 1 week. The results therefore refuted the suspect's version of the events. Schwabenland claimed that his experiment was a major factor in California's Fifth District Court of Appeal trial that led to the defendant being found guilty on two counts of second-degree murder.

The case report, described by Schwabenland, was subsequently reviewed by McRoberts and Kuhn (1992), who concluded as follows:

> Conceptually, what the author was attempting to accomplish is worthwhile. Unfortunately, the guidance he followed and the approach he utilised lacked a thorough consideration of all the recognized factors for a complete and integrated study. Any examiner considering similar experiments should be cautioned to consider all relevant factors, follow scientific protocols, and limit conclusions to the extent supported by the study. *The scientific certainty and acceptability must be gained within the field of Friction Ridge Skin Identification prior to presenting testimony in a court of law* [emphasis added].

In addition to these criticisms, it was also determined that Schwabenland's experiment had never been mentioned in the trial under discussion, despite what the author had claimed in his article (Anon. 1992).

Almog (1992) has also reported a case in Israel where a fingermark age estimation was required. A lady was found dead in her Jerusalem apartment, and the pathologist estimated that she had been murdered the day before she was found. The principal suspect had had a romantic relationship with the deceased, and his fingermarks were found in two places in the apartment where the murder took place: on a porcelain tile in the kitchen and on a white painted door in the laundry. The suspect claimed that these fingermarks had been left there from his last visit, which had been 7 or 8 months prior to the murder. According to the accused, he had not visited the apartment or seen the deceased since that time. The field technician, based on his experience, estimated that the evidential marks (that he had developed with aluminum powder) were "fresh." In addition, it was stated that the victim was obsessively clean and that it was not plausible that fingermarks would be left in such prominent places for 7 or 8 months. The Jerusalem Division of Identification and Forensic Science conducted laboratory tests on fingermarks deposited on a clean porcelain tile and on a door, both taken from the victim's apartment. It was found that good-quality marks deteriorated to a point that no detail remained after 4 months. The evidential marks, however, showed good contrast and resolution of the ridge patterns as well as a high adherence of powder, all indicating the "freshness" of the marks. On the basis of the fingerprint evidence, in addition to evidence relating to bite marks found on the back of the victim, the accused was found guilty.

Despite these documented cases and recent studies into the effects of aging on latent deposits, validated scientific tools for determining the age of a fingermark remain elusive. Additional case studies published more recently showed the exceptional and unexpected capability for fingermarks to be detected months or even years after the incident (Cohen et al. 2012a,b; Bunter 2015).

Midkiff (1993) reviewed what little information was available concerning fingermark aging, and he underlined the need for continued research in this area. He even went so far as to suggest that attorneys should contest the value of fingermarks as a means of proving the "guilt" (sic) of an individual. One of the easiest ways of countering dactyloscopic evidence is to establish previous legitimate access to the place at which the fingermarks were found. This leads to the worrying statement that experts have been testifying in courts about the age of fingermarks based on uncontrolled parameters and little research.

An age estimation should never be based solely on the quality of a developed mark (for example, Involdstad [1976] reported developing a good-quality fingermark on one page of a book that had not been touched for over 30 years). In some cases, however, it may be conceivable to put limits on the age of a particular mark using results from well-designed aging experiments. In order to justify such an estimation, aging studies should be conducted corresponding as closely as possible to the case under investigation (type of surface, temperature, humidity, sunlight, etc.). Obviously, the same fingermark detection technique should be employed as was used to develop the evidential mark. As some parameters are impossible to determine and control (for example, the quality and composition of the latent fingermark at the moment of deposition), these should be critically evaluated. In addition, and as an indirect method of age determination, best use should be made of various types of background information that may identify the time a trace was formed. In this way, it may be possible to identify the maximum age of a particular fingermark (Cowger 1983). For example, if it can be shown that a particular surface is thoroughly cleaned at least once a week and that such cleaning would have removed any fingermarks that may have been present, then a mark found on that surface could not be more than a week old. In the case of a fingermark on a manufactured item, the date of manufacture (if it can be determined) will obviously indicate an upper limit for the age of the mark. This relies on the search for anachronisms (as is done in questioned documents examination)—material evidence that precludes the possibility of an evidential item being placed outside a certain time frame. Any allegation to the contrary must then be false.

Ongoing research on the chemical composition of fingerprint residues (Bramble 1995; Jacquat 1999; Jones et al. 2000) and their chemical degradation over time, such as the kinetics of decomposition and oxidation, should help determine useful aging markers, although surface effects may play a more significant role than originally expected. As part of a broad project on age determination issues in forensic science financed by the Swiss National Science Foundation and led by Weyermann, fingermark age estimation based on chemical composition was considered. Girod and Weyermann (2013) subsequently undertook an extensive critical review of all approaches described to answer the question "how old is this fingermark?" highlighting the lack of methods

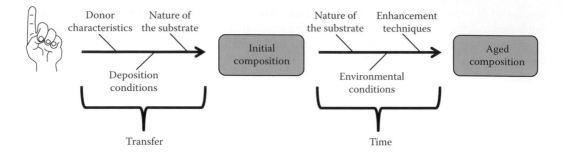

FIGURE 5.2 Factors affecting the composition of a latent fingermark. Donor characteristics, deposition conditions, and the nature of the substrate will affect the nature of the transferred residues; then changes will depend on a number of factors that include environmental conditions. (From Girod, A., *Etude de la composition initiale et du vieillissement des traces digitales: vers le développement d'une méthode de datation?*, Université de Lausanne, Ecole des sciences criminelles, Lausanne, Switzerland, 2015, Figure 1; Courtesy of the author.)

and many contradictory statements in the literature. One approach that was seen as promising focuses on the detection and measurement of specific target compounds in fingermark residues. This led to the review of the state of knowledge as to the qualitative and quantitative composition of fingermark residues, with Ramotowski as an additional author (Girod et al. 2012). This paper covers the initial composition of fingermark residues at the time of deposition and the composition of the aged fingermark deposit. Five factors further affecting the complex nature of the deposit are discussed: (1) donor characteristics, (2) deposition conditions, (3) the nature of the substrate, (4) environmental conditions, and (5) the detection and enhancement techniques applied (Figure 5.2). The lack of quantitative data, aging kinetics, and influence factors was the basis of further research and the formulation of a formal research framework in association with Roux (Girod et al. 2014). Lipid aging kinetics in fingermark residues was the first step in the methodological development. One hundred and four lipid compounds were found in fingerprint residues from 25 donors (of which 43 were reported for the first time in fingermark deposits) (Girod and Weyermann 2014). The research investigated the extent of variation of these lipids over time for one donor (intravariability) and the variation between fingermarks from different donors (intervariability). Ten compounds were selected as promising target compounds showing a lower intravariability than intervariability, with donors classified as either "poor" or "rich" lipid donors. Analytical developments allowed useful observations and kinetic studies using GC/MS, FTIR, and FTIR combined with chemical imaging (Girod et al. 2015, 2016a,b). Various statistical models (univariate and multivariate) could separate and describe the aging of target compounds, but, overall, these kinetic models were very much influenced by the donor (i.e., the initial composition), the substrate, whether exposed to light or not, and the application of detection techniques, thus hindering the reliability of the age estimation. Figure 5.3 illustrates the effect of light on aging of fingermarks under standardized conditions. Many other factors were thoroughly researched by Girod (2015).

Blind studies showed correct age estimations in 60% of the cases (which may be good or bad, depending on the point of view) using a controlled experimental setup. Although still far from a satisfactory answer to the initial question "how old is this fingermark?" such research offers considerable new knowledge that may narrow down a timeframe and help resolve certain aging issues. The same group of authors is offering a current view on legal issues given our current state of knowledge (Girod et al. 2016c). The whole experimental design and some answers to the questions posed can be found in Girod's thesis 2015. Research in this area is continuing but offering an age estimation as potential evidence, at this point in time, should still be regarded with suspicion.

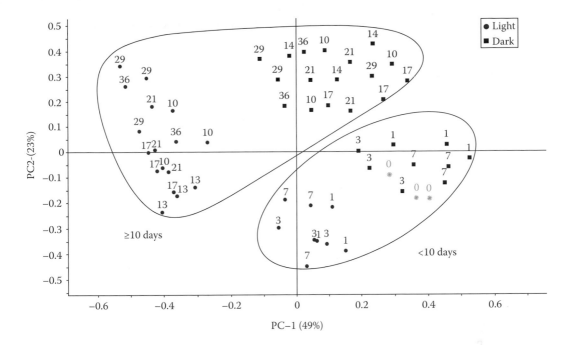

FIGURE 5.3 Principal component analysis applied to the composition of marks deposited by one donor under standardized conditions and analyzed by GC/MS, with the fingermark age (in days) indicated above each data point. (From Girod, A., *Etude de la composition initiale et du vieillissement des traces digitales: vers le développement d'une méthode de datation?*, Université de Lausanne, Ecole des sciences criminelles, Lausanne, Switzerland, 2015, Figure 10; Courtesy of the author.) Gray markers indicate fresh marks, black indicates marks aged in the dark, and red indicates marks exposed to light. Light exposure has clearly impacted on the results, with a separation between exposed/nonexposed samples and between aged (≥10 days) and relatively fresh (<10 days).

5.5   FORGED AND FABRICATED FINGERPRINT EVIDENCE

Planted or fabricated evidence can completely divert, slow down, or change police conclusions concerning the scenario of a crime. Documented cases of fingermark forgery are known since the beginning of the twentieth century. Now DNA is being subjected to the same threat with the blind trust given to this type of evidence. There is an obvious resistance to admit the possibility of police investigators and the courts being fooled. Little research has been done to establish the extent of the phenomenon and how to detect it. Forgery covers reproduction, modification, or alteration with the intent to deceive. It includes counterfeiting, which is imitating with the intention that the imitation will be deceptively believed to be genuine.

Some fingerprint experts consider the phenomenon of fingerprint forgery only as an annoying curiosity; others, however, see it as a serious potential problem. The cases that do exist are few and far between, and documentation is rarely comprehensive, with many unsubstantiated allegations. When describing cases of this type of forgery, some sources omit important details, while the reliability of other sources raises questions. Information retrieval and evidence collection on this subject are not simple. Although the number of well-recorded and properly documented cases of fingerprint forgery is relatively small, there are reasons to believe that the real number of cases is higher and probably cannot be accurately estimated.

Cases of fingermark forgery fall into two main groups:

1. Forgery committed by law enforcement officers, police specialists, and fingerprint experts
2. Forgery committed by criminals (or on behalf of criminals)

In both instances, the intent is to frame or direct the attention on a person that has not left fingermarks where they were reportedly recorded. There is a third category of fingerprint imitation/modification, where scientists and experts attempt to reproduce alleged or admitted modus operandi by forgers. This is generally for research purposes or in order to detect forgeries and determine ways to avoid being fooled by them.

5.5.1 FORGERIES COMMITTED BY LAW ENFORCEMENT PERSONNEL

In the early days of dactyloscopy, publications on the topic of fingerprint forgery were rare. The field was still fairly novel with, very often, passionate experts, and it had not yet developed to the industrial level we have today. Fingerprint identification was a craft, rewarding when successful, and acknowledged as a help for police investigators, but still marginal compared with traditional policing and evidence gathering. The earliest reported case of forgery is one made by a government official in 1903 to link a suspect with a crime scene, but the manner of forgery is not documented (Gupta 1976; Geller et al. 1999).

This highlights the temptation for officials who deal with finger traces on a daily basis to *help* solve difficult or high-profile, emotive cases to demonstrate one's own importance, for reward. This is observed throughout the century, the world over, with cases in America, Europe, and Asia. It is telling that the first report comes from India, where fingerprints had been used extensively in contracts, official deals, etc. (Hooghly Letter [Herschel 1887] addressed to the General Inspector of prisons in Bengal, whose content was reproduced by Herschel [1916]). Probably a longer history of forgery could be found in China, since fingerprints had been used to prove authorship, as "official" and judicial seals/signatures, since the sixth century (at least) under the T'ang Dynasty. It would be rather strange if no instances of forgery were found in historical documents there, even if there was a certain "magical" dimension given to the act of signing by fingerprint.

With more recent reports (Wertheim 1998; Geller et al. 2001) and the multiplication of documented cases, it is difficult to know whether more forgeries are occurring, or simply more are being reported. What can be safely said is that technical evidence is required more often than ever. Pressure on officers/experts is thus increasing, and a lack of ethics and control might lead the weakest to "prove" their worth and demonstrate their efficiency by helping put "good" suspects behind bars (much like the fireman who sets a fire so that he can demonstrate courage and self-sacrifice in putting it out). It makes for rewarding statistics and promotion opportunities, and obvious "bad characters" are kept in check. It may also be a (bad) response to the increased political pressure on police to obtain results while following "human rights" principles in their investigations, thus resulting in fewer admissions of guilt by suspects.

Champod and Espinoza (2014) have published a comprehensive review of fingerprint forgeries in forensic science with a discussion of experimental research in this area. The authors considered various options available to produce forgeries (Figure 5.4) and then studied features/defects that may affect these fabrications and help identify the *modus operandi*.

Reported cases from the United States have had a significant impact among dactyloscopists because of the openness with which these cases were discussed and because of the wide audience the relevant professional journals have across the world. The De Palma case and the Trooper Harding case are sensational stories that have left traces within the profession (Geller et al. 1999) and led to integrity-assurance measures focused on personnel requirements (selection, hiring and retention, dismissal of problem employees, and a commitment to ethics and integrity), structural adjustments (independence of the identification unit to avoid external and operational pressure), and the need for proper documentation and continuity of evidence (Wertheim 1998).

5.5.2 FORGERIES COMMITTED BY CRIMINALS

The number of documented cases of forgeries committed by criminals is extremely small. This may be due to the successful stratagems adopted by criminals or, more probably, due to the lack of preparation, time, and perhaps intelligence to adopt a successful strategy of fooling investigators.

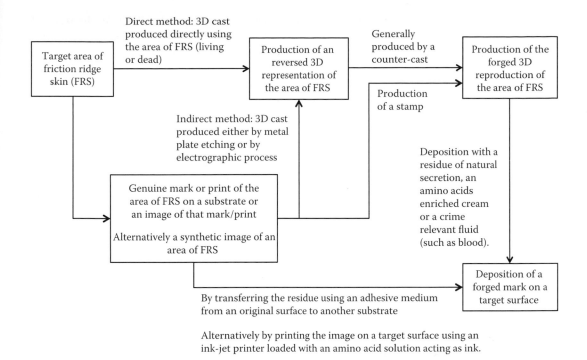

FIGURE 5.4 Experimentally tested forgery methods reported by Champod and Espinoza (2014). (With kind permission from Springer Science+Business Media: Champod, C., and Espinoza, M. (2014), Forgeries of fingerprints in forensic science, in Handbook of biometric anti-spoofing, eds. S. Marcel, M. S. Nixon and S. Z. Li, London: Springer Verlag, pp. 13–34, Fig. 2.1.)

The majority of cases concern confidence tricks or illusion-based trickery used to obtain financial gains. The planting of evidence to incriminate an innocent person is exceedingly rare due to the lack of opportunities to obtain a "model" for the forgery (unless there is a spontaneous opportunity). Any attempt at forgery would likely remain largely undetected, as was shown through limited experiments with specialists (Cummins 1938), and especially because, in many countries, the trust in fingerprint evidence is so high that it is almost never disputed.

5.5.3 Detection of Forged Marks

Most forged marks will be found on smooth, plain, and easily accessible surfaces. The aim of the forger is for the mark to be readily found and for it to be of good quality, so that it is used as evidence. Performed by law enforcement personnel, the staging is relatively easy, with improperly documented lifts either mislabeled or taken from known prints allegedly lifted from the crime scene. Such activities can be difficult to even suspect let alone detect. High print quality— forgeries are almost always present as a single, clean mark—and a lack of proper photographic documentation could raise suspicion. The key issue here is that photographic documentation of the scene should be systematic, with illustrations of the marks prior to lifting, thus documenting the material on which the mark was found and ensuring a proper chain of evidence (labeling of lifts, use of proper case management, bar codes, etc.). Professional practices such as these should make forgery a difficult and risky activity with a high chance of discovery if contested.

The criminal who would like to direct suspicion toward another individual will have less opportunity to access good-quality prints. The temptation will therefore be to employ some form of cast as a template (Hildebrandt et al. 2012). This can give surprisingly good results, as was shown by Groenendal (1996) and, more recently, by Matsumoto (2002) and Champod and Espinoza (2014), who demonstrated that this technique can fool biometric access systems. The development of imaging and printing technologies provides the opportunity to replace the ink with a fingerprint-like mix of amino acids in an inkjet printer and the use of an image of a given ridge pattern as a template (Hildebrandt et al. 2012). While Hildebrandt et al. demonstrated that even marks produced using high resolution printers may be easily detected as forgeries, vigilance was required.

Telltale signs of forgeries were listed by Champod and Espinoza (2014) and are reproduced here:

General features observed on forgeries:

- Background noise (a type of halo effect) around the mark itself or in areas without ridges. This is due to an interaction on the surface of the mould material bearing no ridge and the substrate.
- An overall shape of the mark that is inconsistent with the natural deposition of a finger.
- Clear and well-defined external contours of the mark, either partially or entirely, as a function of their deposition. Ridges will end abruptly at the boundaries of the forged mark whereas, comparatively, ridges coming to the border of the mark will tend to fade gently on genuine marks.
- Missing section of ridges, or section of ridges that are of lower clarity compared to the highest quality of the neighboring (adjacent) ridges.
- Smudged or distorted friction ridges in areas that are not compatible with the dynamics of natural deposition of a finger on a surface.
- Unexpected appearance of the ridges following the detection technique used. For example, amino-acid reagents tend to develop genuine marks as a series of dots leading to the appearance of papillary lines. Forged marks are laid down with a film of residue that hardly mimics the succession of rich-residue pores.

Particular features observed on forgeries (when clarity of the mark allows):

- The presence of air bubbles and defects due to the casting. Note that a careful choice of the casting material can diminish the occurrence of artefacts due to air bubbles.
- The absence of visible sweat pores. Some authors give a lot of weight to the presence of pores attesting the authenticity of a mark (e.g., Senay 1990), but again an adequate choice of the casting materials allows reproducing pores.
- Very narrow valleys compared to the ridges or uneven widths of ridges and valleys.
- The presence of reproducible artefacts on multiple marks from the same area of Fiction Ridge Skin (FRS).

Forged marks may present some specific extrinsic features [very well described as early as 1933 by Lee (1933) and Harper (1937), and reaffirmed in the subsequent forensic literature]. They are:

- The detection of the mark from one finger in situations where an associated detection of the marks left by the other fingers or palm would also be expected.
- The detection of multiple appositions of marks representing the same area of friction ridge skin, at times even to the point that they overlap completely and share the same shapes of pores or ridge edges.
- The detection of a mark in an anatomical position that is not consistent with the natural pre-emption of the receiving object.
- The forensic evidence in the case is based only on these fingermarks.

Despite all these potential signs, the detection of forgeries, when unsuspected, remains elusive at best. This implies a heavier role and impact of the overall crime scene investigation that should help identify potential fabrication through a questioning of the genuineness of detected and collected marks.

The advent of electronic biometric systems for security controls is introducing a new dimension to the problem of fooling the identification process. The question of "spoofing" such systems has become a current hot topic with the development of technical countermeasures. The vulnerability of fingerprint readers used in biometric access systems is an ongoing issue. A comprehensive review may be quickly outdated with technological developments. An excellent review covering the state of affairs regarding spoofing has been published by Galbally et al. (2014).

5.6 ERRORS

To err is human, but humans hate to be found at fault. Fingerprint specialists are no different, and the usual stance is to lay the responsibility for a mistake on individuals rather than identifying the risks that everyone faces when confronted with evidence requiring an interpretation. Reports of errors in the fingerprint field were few, demonstrating that fingerprint evidence was reliable and has helped satisfactorily resolve many criminal cases. This has been demonstrated time and again throughout the last century of practice, and it is difficult to cast doubt on the value of fingerprint evidence. The doctrine of infallibility became the hallmark of fingerprint identification, which in turn became the icon for all other types of identification evidence with a high power of discrimination (approaching 100%). This has led to the misnomers "DNA fingerprinting," the "fingerprint" region of an infrared spectrum, "voiceprints," and "shoeprints," to name just a few. Many of the scientists who handled fingerprints at the beginning were well aware of the risks of matching a mark to a print when the mark was less than perfect, and they recognized the probabilistic nature of identifying the source of a mark as being the same as the source of a print. This is the basis of Locard's third rule and the arguments discussed in Chapter 2 concerning the process of identification and its subjectivity in determining identity. Court acceptance without much scrutiny in adversarial legal systems has led to an almost blind faith in fingerprint evidence (Saks 1998). Judges in inquisitorial systems can use one of the major principles of European continental law—"la libre appréciation" or "freedom of appreciation," which implies that judges have a completely free hand in determining the value of each piece of evidence submitted to them. Further, they have an obligation to review and integrate—in order to critically accept or reject, even what might be seen as rock-solid evidence by specialists.

Nevertheless, mistakes have been documented, and results from proficiency testing have shown less than satisfactory performance, stupefying a profession that, in most cases, still preferred to single out black sheep rather than admit that mistakes are an integral part of all human activities. The year 2004 was a turning point with the occurrence of terrorist attacks on trains in Madrid, Spain, that resulted in an error that led to question the whole identification process and the value of forensic science evidence as a whole (National Research Council 2009). A partial fingermark found on a plastic wrapping was circulated around the world and its source was identified by the FBI as being an Oregon lawyer, Brandon Mayfield, when in fact it was a North African member of a terrorist group identified by the Spanish police. The error was admitted although three specialists as well as an independent expert had confirmed the identification at the time. This was an opportunity for psychologists, sociologists, and lawyers to attack the basis of the identification process (Koehler 2008; Haber and Haber 2014; Kellman et al. 2014). They raised a number of potential sources of errors (biases, lack of error rate, reliability) often proposing self-serving research studies or diverging perspectives (Mnookin et al. 2011) that have been questioned (Margot 2011). Nevertheless, valid criticisms led to research methodological improvements (dealt with in Chapter 2) as well as the abandonment of dogmatic views regarding the identification paradigm, the so-called leap of faith behind the decision of identification. The IAI moved away from the concept of identification certainty (and infallibility) and was faced with the necessary probabilistic assessment and interpretation of the identification.

Errors have occurred and will continue to occur; the rarer the occurrence of error, the more difficult it is to detect. Admission of this paves the way for the establishment of control mechanisms that should limit the number of errors, detect errors before their release, and correct those that are identified. This is a sign of maturity for any human endeavor. Recently, closer attention has been given to erroneous identifications, and these are documented and discussed on the Internet (http://www.onin.com/fp/problemidents.html and http://www.cplex.com/, accessed January 18, 2016). We recommend that all fingerprint examiners study these cases carefully.

There have been many important changes in the last 30 years that have brought to the fore the possibility of mistakes in the field of dactyloscopy. For most of the twentieth century, with manual searches and local offender collections, identification bureaus were rarely at the forefront of the investigation, and cold hits were infrequent occurrences. Identification was generally a matter of confirming the results of an investigation by bringing physical evidence to otherwise mostly circumstantial combinations of elements collected from witnesses, observations, and other traditional police sources, thus feeding the potential for confirmation biases. At the beginning, most specialists were also enthusiasts, confident in the value of their trade and quite happy, in some cases, to demonstrate that the investigation had gone astray by showing that the evidence marks were not made by the main suspect! Also, early dactyloscopists needed a trained eye to classify and subclassify prints in order to have efficient searches to facilitate the association of a mark to a potential source. This brought about stories of specialists with photographic memory that would spot and attribute a mark at first sight. But, as files became more complex and criminals became more mobile, cold hits became the exception and investigative confirmation became the stock of the trade. This meant mostly routine identification procedures, confirming or consolidating cases. In many instances, this also led to a lackluster situation for dactyloscopists, who were perceived as secondary assistants of "true" or "real" investigators. This situation reached the point that, in some instances, bad investigators were "punished," by placing them in fingerprint bureaus, where they might make good technicians after some intensive reskilling. This was never formally acknowledged and was certainly not the case overall, but it had a significant impact on the work of many identification services. This situation, combined with the almost certain confirmation that the suspect presented as the probable culprit is the source of marks, was the sure grounds for systematic confirmation bias. This was further nourished by the infallibility paradigm that we already questioned in the first edition of this book. Current experiments using PiAnoS (Chapter 2) in collaborative exercises show some spectacular discrepancies concerning the evaluation of marks and the need to train and test specialists on the basis of marks whose source is known (ground truth).

What brought about change was the introduction of AFIS. Suddenly, access to large national collections was possible even for very small operational units. Cold hits became common, and the trade changed from a backroom craft to an industrial production line that created new pressure and new approaches. What came out is also the possibility of close nonmatches (as in the Brandon Mayfield case) that may be difficult to differentiate especially if the mark is partial or of poor quality. From a handful of potential sources, the profession is now faced with millions of potential sources, some of which may be difficult to separate on the sole basis of their intrinsic features, but perhaps by circumstantial exclusion information (such as geographical distance). The same phenomenon of close nonmatches is also appearing with DNA databases. The problem of close nonmatches is a current hot research topic (Dror and Mnookin 2010; Langenburg 2012; Srihari 2012; Taylor et al. 2012; Abraham et al. 2013; Busey et al. 2014; Neumann et al. 2015). This situation is not bad in itself since the AFIS excludes millions of fingerprints in the system, keeping sometimes only a handful of potential sources that may be further investigated or checked either through detailed analyses of prints or using circumstantial discrepancies, accepting the probabilistic nature of the identification. The change in the profession has been huge at the end of the twentieth century and acknowledging this change must bring a change of culture. Pinpointing the problem of bias is looking at an important but marginal problem considering the current revolution.

The development of new detection methods also brought in more marks over a broad quality range. This increase in scale created a need for a change in organization, for more checks and controls, and for new training schemes. Proficiency tests, which were mostly resisted by the profession until the first reports of errors came out in the open, and surveys, such as those discussed in Chapter 2, demonstrated the subjectivity of the process of identification using fingerprint patterns and ridge detail. This also reinforces the need for training and continuous education, and a proper research culture has to start with an appropriate academic culture with forensic science as the academic focus (Margot 2011).

The awareness and acceptance of the possibility of errors, even if limited in occurrence, is already a sign of progress and is an insurance against more widespread errors. In the future, we hope to see disputes handled and resolved in a framework of agreed procedures, specified at the outset of the comparison process rather than through the use of post hoc empty statements such as "fingerprint comparison is a matter of opinion."

5.6.1 ERROR TYPES

One always imagines errors whereby a person is identified as the author of a mark found at a crime scene when in fact the mark was made by someone else's finger. This is the dreaded false identification, such as those reported at the UK National Fingerprint Conference in October 2001 (Ritchie 2002) and those that have occurred over the last 25 years on both sides of the Atlantic. This is the most feared error because it can have serious consequences for the identified person whether innocent or not, who may have difficulty defending their innocence, especially in view of possible past criminal records.

There is a second type of error that deserves much more scrutiny because of the "no harm done" attitude toward it. This is the mark that can be used for exclusion purposes but is errone-ously discounted or marks that have been erroneously excluded. The recent studies on examiners' performance have all shown that the rate of false exclusion is much higher than the rate of errone-ous association (e.g., Ulery et al. 2011, 2012; Langenburg et al. 2015). The profession needs to put substantial efforts into trying to minimize that type of error as well, even if it is generally perceived (fallaciously) as bearing less adverse consequences. A more systematic use of AFIS may help to reduce the number of misses as recently shown by Langenburg et al. (2015).

It is also our contention that there are many marks that have exclusion power (i.e., capable of excluding the possibility that it was made by a certain individual's fingers) but are branded as incon-clusive, when indeed they have much value in exonerating potential suspects. This is one of the values attributed to DNA but is equally valid for fingerprints. Proficiency testing has shown that this error is not uncommon, and it is our contention that such errors are just as serious as the false identifications. Such errors demonstrate a certain lack of understanding of the principles of identi-fication, as they should be applied within the profession (as proposed in Chapter 2). This is an issue that rests with the education and training of specialists.

Other errors, considered administrative by some, are improper case documentation or manage-ment (not labeling at scenes, documenting at a later date, etc.), even if one cannot totally eliminate the risk of mislabeling or otherwise incorrect documentation, for example. This is a concern for any manager of an identification service even if current computerized case management systems can help reduce this risk. No system is ever foolproof and healthy scrutiny plus quality insurance mechanisms remains the best safeguards against errors.

5.6.2 QUALITY ASSURANCE

The changes of perspective from a craft to an industry, and from a confirmatory role to an investiga-tive- and intelligence-led activity, introduce new demands on the overall quality of the service provided by dactyloscopy. A large number of laboratories have now implemented quality assurance programs. A convergence is currently seen toward the adoption of the EN ISO/IEC 17020 or 17025 standards. In 2009, the Council of the European Union issued a decision (Council Framework Decision 2009/905/JHA) requiring all forensic laboratories dealing with friction ridge skin impressions to gain accredita-tion under EN ISO/IEC 17025 by 2018. Article 7 of the Council's Act (Council of the European Union 2009) stipulates that "It is particularly important to introduce common standards for forensic service providers relating to such sensitive personal data as DNA profiles and dactyloscopic data."

This was followed by statutory documents in the United Kingdom and in the United States introducing critical recommendations based on ISO 17025 or ASCLD-LAB standards (Gray 2011; Forensic Science Regulator 2015). These standards stipulate that all examiners should be trained and found to be competent to perform casework (i.e., competence assessment) and all decisions made by an examiner must be verified by another competent examiner (verification). Processing, case documentation, report writing, and communication all follow ISO 17025 recommendations as are procedures for instances of nonconformity.

The Prüm Convention signed in 2005 by seven European countries (Austria, Belgium, France, Germany, Luxembourg, Spain, and the Netherlands) includes the obligation of ISO 17025 accreditation by participating laboratories and service providers. This is a treaty that enables the signatories to exchange data regarding DNA, fingerprints, and vehicle registrations in a cooperation against terrorism (Council of the European Union 2005). In 2015, 14 countries (adding Bulgaria, Estonia, Finland, Hungary, Romania, Slovakia, and Slovenia) had ratified the Treaty; further European Union countries are in the process of joining (Greece, Italy, Portugal, and Sweden) as are a number of nonmember countries (Iceland, Norway, and Switzerland). The United Kingdom has currently opted out but will assess its potential participation.

The quality standards cover three main areas that need to be considered:

1. Fingerprint examiners/specialists
2. Processes
3. Results or products

All three aspects need periodic review, both internally and externally.

5.6.2.1 Fingerprint Examiner

5.6.2.1.1 Recruitment

Little has been done in the past to consider specific recruitment requirements for dactyloscopists. Even now, in most countries and jurisdictions, the recruitment of future sworn police officers is made on the basis of standard police work rather than on identification skills or, for civilians, on the basis of standard administrative skills. Initial recruitment should be based on two important skills:

1. *Observation skills*: The capacity to extract shapes and forms from complex designs, to connect similar patterns and details, and to discriminate dissimilar ones. Although this is something that can be trained, individuals with such qualities can rapidly become dependable identification specialists. Good observers of nature such as artists, biologists trained in taxonomy (classifying observed features), and medical doctors trained in identifying signs of illnesses may be professions that offer guidance on observation skills.
2. *Technical skills*: Efficiently detecting and recording traces and marks requires a basic knowledge of chemistry and physics, as well as aptitudes at image treatment (e.g., photography and digital imaging). This requires a certain level of education, at least at laboratory technician or basic scientific degree level, which can be reached through an appropriate education program.

Certain qualities such as patience, curiosity, and critical thinking should also be favored instead of the error-free paradigm that used to circulate among fingerprint practitioners. The current consideration of cognitive abilities following studies on cognitive bias issues has led to a discussion around perception, similarity judgments, memory, and decision making, and how these can be improved with training and experience (Busey and Dror 2011). This dialog, and most other papers in this area, calls for further research but is short on propositions, with some exceptions (Dror 2013).

Clearly, there is a need to set up tests based on the aforementioned selection criteria. Then, as a standard procedure in law enforcement structures, selected candidates can be further checked for personality, honesty, integrity, commitment, and pride. Various agencies have developed selection criteria along the aforementioned lines, such as the image-recognition recruitment test as used by the National Identification Bureau in the Netherlands. Bertram and colleagues propose form blindness testing as a selection tool for the recruitment of fingerprint specialists (Bertram et al. 2010).

5.6.2.1.2 Education and Training

There is no unique or fail-safe education model valid for all circumstances; human diversity and nature help develop new skills and create new knowledge and working methodologies. However, an ideal education model would include sound foundations in science and technology (chemistry, physics, mathematics, computing), both theoretical and practical, in order to understand detection methods and the recording of evidence using advanced techniques. A strong component of the education program should, as a priority, deal with probabilities and inference. Additional requirements include a basic knowledge of the laws of the country—and those of neighboring countries—and a thorough knowledge on the use of physical evidence in the legal system (criminal law, criminal procedure, laws of evidence) in order to understand the requirements of the courts. Specific education should cover crime types (criminology, criminal psychology), methods of investigation starting from the scene of the crime, the evidence types that can be collected, systematic methods for crime scene investigation, documentation requirements, and the systematic stepwise and professional treatment of detected evidence. Training should be imparted through multiple full-scale mock investigations, starting with simple collection and documentation of evidence to the full treatment of complex scenes. Each case should be fully completed by the individual. By controlling the evidence before (setting up the scenario) and after the investigation (check completeness, quality, and recording), it is possible at all stages to evaluate the progress of candidates and ensure a competence level that satisfies the highest expectations. In the past, most specialists did not have to face tests against fellow trainees where the ground truth was known. It is now possible to use tools such as PiAnoS for full-scale control of the process involved.

A basic knowledge of general forensic science ensures that identification procedures are not applied to the detriment of other evidence types. By having full control over collection, the trainee is made aware of the relative position of traces; the way marks were placed; and the handedness, position, and finger type that made each mark. This evaluation is essential, and adequate documentation provides a comprehensive chain of custody, with scene images recording the surface type on which the evidence has been collected. Such training provides good insurance against tampering, mixing, or mislabeling traces, or even planting evidence.

The correct application of laboratory techniques, enhancement procedures, and imaging methods—with specific care taken to have the highest sensitivity and the highest selectivity for a particular situation—ensure that the best possible marks are documented. Only then does the identification process begin, i.e., searching through databases and comparing marks with suspects' prints. It is not sufficient to be able to observe comparable features; the specialist has to be able to highlight them, make them evident to others (judges, juries, lawyers), and discuss the weight that is attributed to these features and why. The specialist must be able to describe the whole identification process starting from initial observations through to the appraisal and decision-making described in Chapter 2.

Such an education and training program may take several years to complete, but it ensures a solid foundation upon which the identification process and the courts can rely. This is the basis, for example, of the training program developed at the University of Lausanne in Switzerland, which is further completed with an additional year of training on other evidence types. Specialists trained in this manner quickly adapt to real-life cases and are highly regarded in their professional environments and by the courts. Lophoscopy needs professionals who have a sound foundation and knowledge well above the strict drills and experience that are the key elements of most training programs. Mustonen and Himberg (2011) describe a novel approach developed in Finland to educate fingerprint experts.

5.6.2.1.3 Portfolio and Competency Assessment

Each examiner should have a personal portfolio highlighting career development and achievements, internal assessments, and periodic evaluations, both internal and external, to demonstrate competence and potential for career advancement.

5.6.2.2 Processes

This section addresses the internal management structures to be set up in agreement with local regulations and organizational needs. The following are necessary requirements to guarantee transparent quality assurance measures.

A set of written case-handling procedures should detail basic requirements for scene work (documentation, detection, photographic records, evidence collection, labeling rules, chain-of-custody requirements), laboratory work (enhancement, imaging, documenting), identification and checking procedures, and reporting (including the necessity for written statements of exclusion).

Concerning verification procedures, over 90% of identifications are generally not problematic. Consequently, we do not believe that systematic double-blind checks are necessary; they are time consuming and unnecessarily consume significant personnel resources. More important is that potentially problematic marks be checked routinely, and the verification structure should cater to this need. That applies to both side of the coin: toward identifications or exclusions. The primary responsibility lies with the specialists themselves to have these marks checked independently (i.e., the supervisor chooses another examiner to go through the whole identification procedure, without knowledge of conclusions reached by the first examiner). All contested conclusions should also be checked and analyzed independently as a matter of principle. Any mark in the "complex" zone (Chapter 2, Figure 2.7, SWGFAST sufficiency graph) should be analyzed independently using available tools (e.g., GYRO, PiAnoS) to evaluate the quality of the mark and its potential value in the identification process. This may lead to consensus meetings and a documented decision process.

Proficiency tests should ensure that the general quality is up to the standards required. This avoids the systematic, time-consuming, routine double checks that introduce bad working habits (such as complacency). Proficiency tests also reinforce individual responsibility and increase the motivation of each specialist. The occasional errors should only arise from problematic traces, and these should be identified through the independent verification process. Failures will happen, but it is a bad management to exclude those that have failed rather than encourage continuing training and education. In this way, some services have lost valuable personnel by eliminating them rather than offering the possibility to demonstrate their skills and abilities as well as an understanding that errors can be part of the whole process… and should be viewed critically.

Managers should be ready for a full audit if doubts are cast on any one aspect of the work produced by the service and should be amenable to changes due to weaknesses identified by this process. Any identified error should lead to such an audit, with corrective measures proposed when the problem is identified. Rather than systematically identifying a scapegoat or a black sheep for good conscience and convenience, efforts should be made to identify and rectify the root cause (e.g., reviewing the staff selection process, education requirements, training and competency-testing program, adapting to current technologies developed to help the processes).

5.6.2.3 The Product

Various measures of performance have been proposed in the past, mostly coming from the industrial management of processes (number of marks collected, number of marks identified, number of exclusions). Such measurements are useful management tools but may introduce undue pressure that could have serious consequences in the judicial process. Meaningful performance indicators are usually more difficult to set up than simply calculating numerical values. For example, a difficult but pertinent mark identified in a complex case may not change the numbers dramatically, but it may be a significant event (and a significant performance indicator) for a given specialist.

Identification is not an industrial item; it requires competence, qualifications, trust, and responsibility. External pressure may introduce bias and encourage sloppy work to fit requested target numbers while decreasing job satisfaction and generating negative attitudes toward work. There is a delicate balance that relies heavily on the personalities of the individuals chosen to manage such service delivery. Audits or reviews may show deficiencies in this respect, and corrective measures may include a change of manager.

REFERENCES

Abraham, J., Champod, C., Lennard, C., and Roux, C. (2013), Spatial analysis of corresponding fingerprint features from match and close non-match populations, *Forensic Sci. Int.*, 230, 87–98.

Aguzzi, A. (2002), Le potentiel des traces digitales pour lier les cas, Technical Report, Institut de Police Scientifique et de Criminologie, Université de Lausanne, Switzerland.

Almog, J. (1992), Personal communication.

Angst, E. (1961), Untersuchungen zur Bestimmung des Alters von daktyloskopischen Spuren auf Papier, *Kriminalistik*, 15, 1–12.

Anon. (1992), Editorial comment, *J. Forensic Ident.*, 42, 218.

Anthonioz, A., Aguzzi, A., Girod, A., Egli, N., and Ribaux, O. (2003), Potential use of fingerprint in forensic intelligence: Crime scene linking, *Z Zagadnien Nauk Sadowych—Prob. Forensic Sci.*, 51, 166–170.

Ashbaugh, D. R. (1982), Edgeology/poroscopy/ridgeology—Our next evaluative step, *RCMP Gaz.*, 44(2), 4–6; 45(2), 12–17; 45(3), 10–14.

Baechler, S., Morelato, M., Ribaux, O., Beavis, A., Tahtouh, M., Kirkbride, K. P., Esseiva, P., Margot, P., and Roux, C. (2015), Forensic intelligence framework. Part II: Study of the main generic building blocks and challenges through the examples of illicit drugs and false identity documents monitoring, *Forensic Sci. Int.*, 250, 44–52.

Baniuk, K. (2000), Importance of laboratory experiment in fingerprint age determination, *Problemy Kryminalistyki*, 228, 69–72.

Bertillon, A. (1885), *Instructions signalétiques*, Melun, France: Imprimerie administrative.

Bertram, D. J., Carlan, P. E., Byrd, J. S., and White, J. L. (2010), Screening potential latent fingerprint examiner trainees: the viability of form blindness testing, *J. Forensic Ident.*, 60, 460–476.

Bramble, S. K. (1995), Separation of latent fingermark residue by thin-layer chromatography, *J. Forensic Sci.*, 40, 969–975.

Bunter, S. (2015), How long can a fingerprint persist on an external surface? A case study, *Fingerprint Whorld*, 40, 5–14.

Busey, T., Silapiruti, A., and Vanderkolk, J. (2014), The relation between sensitivity, similar non-matches and database size in fingerprint database searches, *Law Probab. Risk*, 13, 151–168.

Busey, T. A. and Dror, I. E. (2011), Chapter 15: Special abilities and vulnerabilities in forensic expertise, in *The Fingerprint Sourcebook*, ed., A. McRoberts, Washington, DC: National Institute of Justice, http://www.ncjrs.gov/pdffiles1/nij/225335.pdf (last accessed January 29, 2016).

Cadd, S., Islam, M., Manson, P., and Bleay, S. (2015), Fingerprint composition and aging: A literature review, *Sci. Justice*, 55, 219–238.

Champod, C. (1995), Locard, numerical standards and probable identification, *J. Forensic Ident.*, 45, 132–159.

Champod, C. and Espinoza, M. (2014), Forgeries of fingerprints in forensic science, in *Handbook of Biometric Anti-Spoofing*, eds., S. Marcel, M. S. Nixon, and S. Z. Li, London, U.K.: Springer-Verlag, pp. 13–34.

Chatterjee, S. K. (1962), Edgeoscopy, *Fingerprint Ident. Mag.*, 44, 3–13.

Cohen, Y., Azoury, M., and Elad-Levin, M. (2012a), Survivability of latent fingerprints. Part II: The effect of cleaning agents on the survivability of latent fingerprints, *J. Forensic Ident.*, 62, 54–61.

Cohen, Y., Rozen, E., Azoury, M., Attias, D., Gavrielli, B., and Elad-Levin, M. (2012b), Survivability of latent fingerprints. Part 1: Adhesion of latent fingerprints to smooth surfaces, *J. Forensic Ident.*, 62, 47–53.

Council of the European Union (2005), Convention Between the Kingdom of Belgium, the Federal Republic of Germany, the Kingdom of Spain, the French Republic, the Grand Duchy of Luxembourg, the Kingdom of the Netherlands and the Republic of Austria on the Stepping up of Cross-Border Cooperation, Particularly in Combating Terrorism, Cross-Border Crime and Illegal Migration (Prüm Convention), May 2005.

Council of the European Union (2009), Council Framework Decision 2009/905/JHA of 30 November 2009 on Accreditation of Forensic Service Providers Carrying Out Laboratory Activities, L322/14.

Cowger, J. F. (1983), *Friction Ridge Skin: Comparison and Identification of Fingerprints*, New York: Elsevier Science Publishing.

Cummins, H. H. (1926), Epidermal ridge configurations in developmental defects, with particular references to the ontogenetic factors which condition ridge direction, *Am. J. Anat.*, 38, 89–151.

Cummins, H. H. (1938), Experimental work of fingerprint forgery, *J. Criminal Law Criminol. Police Sci.*, 28, 666–671.

Cummins, H. and Midlo, C. (1926), Palmar and plantar epidermal ridge configurations (dermatoglyphics) in European-Americans, *Am. J. Phys. Anthropol.*, 9, 471–502.

de Jongh, A. and Rodriguez, C. M. (2012), Performance evaluation of automated fingerprint identification systems for specific conditions observed in casework using simulated fingermarks, *J. Forensic Sci.*, 57, 1075–1081.

Dikshitulu, Y. S., Prasad, L., Pal, J. N., and Rao, C. V. N. (1986), Aging studies on fingerprint residues using thin layer and high performance liquid chromatography, *Forensic Sci. Int.*, 31, 261–266.

Dror, I. E. (2013), Practical solutions to cognitive and human factor challenges in forensic science, *Forensic Sci. Policy Manage.*, 4, 1–9.

Dror, I. E. and Mnookin, J. L. (2010), The use of technology in human expert domains: Challenges and risks arising from the use of automated fingerprint identification systems in forensic science, *Law Probability Risk*, 9, 47–67.

Duff, J. M. and Menzel, E. R. (1978), Laser-assisted thin-layer chromatography and luminescence of fingerprints: An approach to fingerprint age determination, *J. Forensic Sci.*, 23, 129–134.

Faulds, H. (1880), On the skin-furrows of the hand, *Nature*, 22, 605.

Forensic Science Regulator (2015), *Codes of Practice and Conduct: Fingerprint Comparison (FSR-C-128)*, Birmingham, U.K.: UK Government, https://www.gov.uk/government/uploads/system/uploads/attachment_data/file/415108/128_FSR_fingerprint_appendix__Issue1.pdf (last consulted January 29, 2016).

Galbally, J., Fierrez, J., Ortega-Garcia, J., and Cappelli, R. (2014), Fingerprint anti-spoofing in biometric systems, in *Handbook of Biometric Anti-Spoofing*, eds., S. Marcel, M. S. Nixon and S. Z. Li, London, U.K.: Springer, pp. 35–64.

Galton, F. (1892), *Finger Prints*, London, U.K.: MacMillan and Co.

Geller, B., Almog, J., Margot, P., and Springer, E. (1999), A chronological review of fingerprint forgery, *J. Forensic Sci.*, 44, 963–968.

Geller, B., Almog, J., and Margot, P. (2001), Fingerprint forgery—A survey, *J. Forensic Sci.*, 46(3), 731–733.

Girod, A. (2015), *Etude de la composition initiale et du vieillissement des traces digitales: vers le développement d'une méthode de datation?*, Université de Lausanne, Ecole des sciences criminelles, Lausanne, Switzerland.

Girod, A., Ramotowski, R., Lambrechts, S., Misrielal, P., Aalders, M., and Weyermann, C. (2016c), Fingermark dating: Legal considerations, review of the literature and practical propositions, *Forensic Sci. Int.*, 262, 212–226.

Girod, A., Ramotowski, R., and Weyermann, C. (2012), Composition of fingermark residue: A qualitative and quantitative review, *Forensic Sci. Int.*, 223, 10–24.

Girod, A., Reedy, B., Xiao, L., Roux, C., and Weyermann, C. (2016b), Can FTIR-chemical imaging be used to investigate differences in the residue distribution of natural fingermarks due to pressure and time?, *Forensic Sci. Int.*, in press.

Girod, A., Roux, C., and Weyermann, C. (2014), Fingermark dating (Part II): Proposition of a formal framework, *Rev. Intern. Crim. Pol. Tech. Sci.*, 67, 226–249.

Girod, A., Spyratou, A., Holmes, D., and Weyermann, C. (2016a), Aging of target lipid parameters in fingermark residue using GC/MS: Effects of influence factors and perspective for dating purposes, *Sci. Justice*, in press.

Girod, A. and Weyermann, C. (2013), Dating fingermarks (Part I): Critical review (in French), *Rev. Intern. Crim. Pol. Tech. Sci.*, 66, 364–377.

Girod, A. and Weyermann, C. (2014), Lipid composition of fingermark residue and donor classification using GC/MS, *Forensic Sci. Int.*, 238, 68–82.

Girod, A., Xiao, L., Reedy, B., Roux, C., and Weyermann, C. (2015), Fingermark initial composition and aging using Fourier transform infrared microscopy (μ-FTIR), *Forensic Sci. Int.*, 254, 185–196.

Gray, M. L. (2011), Chapter 12: Quality assurance, in *The Fingerprint Sourcebook*, ed., A. McRoberts, Washington, DC: National Institute of Justice, http://www.ncjrs.gov/pdffiles1/nij/225332.pdf (last accessed January 29, 2016).

Gremaud, J.-L. (2010), *Processus de reconnaissance et d'identification de personnes décédées*, PhD thesis, Université de Lausanne, Ecole des sciences criminelles, Lausanne.

Groenendal, H. (1996), Forged latent prints, in *Proceedings of the International Symposium on Fingerprint Detection and Identification*, Ne'urim, Israel: eds., J. Almog and E. Springer, Israel National Police, June 26–30, 1995, pp. 373–379.

Gupta, R. S. (1976), Forgeries in fingerprints, *Revue Internationale Police Criminelle*, 133–139.

Haber, R. N. and Haber, L. (2014), Experimental results of fingerprint comparison validity and reliability: A review and critical analysis, *Sci. Justice*, 54, 375–389.

Haraksim, R., Ramos, D., Meuwly, D., and Berger, C. E. H. (2015), Measuring coherence of computer-assisted likelihood ratio methods, *Forensic Sci. Int.*, 249, 123–132.

Harper, W. W. (1937), Fingerprint "forgery"—Transferred latent fingerprints, *J. Criminal Law Criminol.*, 28, 573–580.

Harrison, A., Smith, K., and Bleay, S. M. (2014), Case study: The enhancement, comparison, and matching of a skin texture mark from the back of a hand, *J. Forensic Ident.*, 64, 105–121.

Henry, E. R. (1900), *Classification and Uses of Finger Prints*, 4th ed., London, U.K.: Georges Routledge.

Herschel, W. J. (1916), The origin of finger-printing, London, Humphrey Milford: Oxford University Press.

Herschel, W. (1880), Skin furrows of the hand, *Nature*, 23, 76.

Hildebrandt, M., Kiltz, S., Sturm, J., Dittmann, J., and Vielhauer, C. (2012), High-resolution printed amino acid traces: A first-feature extraction approach for fingerprint forgery detection, in *Proceedings of SPIE—The International Society for Optical Engineering*, Burlingame, California, USA, 83030J.

Holyst, B. (1987), Kriminalistische Abschätzung des Spurenalters bei Fingerpapillarlinien, *Archiv für Kriminologie*, 179, 94–103.

Howorka, H. (1989), Questions relating to the determination of the age of objects assuming relevance in criminal investigations, *Fingerprint Whorld*, 15, 23–28.

Involdstad, H. (1976), How long will a fingerprint last? *Fingerprint Ident. Mag.*, 57 (9), 4–5.

Jacquat, A. (1999), Evolution des substances grasses des empreintes digitales au cours du temps—Analyse par TLC et GC-MS, Technical Report, Institut de Police Scientifique et de Criminologie, Université de Lausanne, Lausanne, Switzerland.

Jain, A. K. and Ross, A. (2015), Bridging the gap: From biometrics to forensics, *Philos. Trans. Roy. Soc. B: Biol. Sci.*, 370 (1674). DOI: 10.1098/rstb.2014.0254.

Jones, N., Davies, L. M., Brennan, J. S., and Bramble, S. K. (2000), Separation of visibly excited fluorescent components in fingerprint residue by thin-layer chromatography, *J. Forensic Sci.*, 45, 1286–1293.

Kellman, P. J., Mnookin, J. L., Erlikhman, G., Garrigan, P., Ghose, T., Mettler, E., Charlton, D., and Dror, I. E. (2014), Forensic comparison and matching of fingerprints: Using quantitative image measures for estimating error rates through understanding and predicting difficulty, *PLOS ONE*, 9 (5), e94617.

Koehler, J. J. (2008), Fingerprint error rates and proficiency tests: What they are and why they matter, *Hastings Law J.*, 59, 1077–1100.

Komarinski, P. (2005), *Automated Fingerprint Identification Systems (AFIS)*, New York: Elsevier Academic Press.

Kumar, P., Gupta, R., Singh, R., and Jasuja, O. P. (2015), Effects of latent fingerprint development reagents on subsequent forensic DNA typing: A review, *J. Forensic Legal Med.*, 32, 64–69.

Lambert, J. L. F. (1990), *International Illustrated Vocabulary of French-English Fingerprint Terminology with a Short Index in Six Languages (Serbian, Japanese, Dutch, Italian, Spanish, German)*, 2nd ed., Ottawa, Ontario, Canada: Ministry of the Solicitor General, Royal Canadian Mounted Police.

Langenburg, G. (2012), *A Critical Analysis and Study of the ACE-V Process*, PhD thesis, Université de Lausanne, Ecole des sciences criminelles, Lausanne, Switzerland.

Langenburg, G., Hall, C., and Quincy, R. (2015), Utilizing AFIS searching tools to reduce errors in fingerprint casework, *Forensic Sci. Int.*, 257, 123–133.

Lee, C. D. (1933), Further discussion of the evidentiary value of fingerprints, *Univ. Penn. Law Rev. Am. Law Register*, 81, 320–323.

Locard, E. (1912), Les pores et l'identification des criminels, *Biologica—Journal scientifique du médecin*, 2, 357–365.

Locard, E. (1913), La poroscopie—Identification par les orifices sudoripares, *Archives d'anthropologie criminelle de médecine légale et de psychologie normale et pathologique*, 28, 528–546.

Locard, E. (1931), *Traité de criminalistique*, Vol. I to VII, Lyon, France: J. Desvigne et fils.

Lowe, A. L., Murray, C., Whitaker, J. P., Tully, G., and Gill, P. (2002), The propensity of individuals to deposit DNA and secondary transfer of low level DNA from individuals to inert surfaces, *Forensic Sci. Int.*, 129, 25–34.

Maltoni, D., Maio, D., Jain, A. K., and Prabhakar, S. (2009), *Handbook of Fingerprint Recognition*, 2nd ed., London, U.K.: Springer-Verlag.

Margot, P. (2000), A question of time, *Sci. Justice*, 40, 64–71.

Margot, P. (2011), Commentary on the need for a research culture in the forensic sciences, *UCLA Law Rev.*, 58, 795–801.

Mark, Y. (1996), Policemen's fingerprints at the scene of crime, in *Proceedings of the International Symposium on Fingerprint Detection and Identification*, Ne'urim, Israel: eds. J. Almog and E. Springer, Israel National Police, June 26–30, 1995, pp. 411–417.

Matsumoto, T. (2002), Importance of open discussion on adversarial analyses for mobile security technologies—A case study for user identification, in *ITU-T Workshop on Security*, Seoul, Korea.

McRoberts, A. L. and Kuhn, K. E. (1992), A review of the case report—"Determining the evaporation rate of latent impressions on the exterior surfaces of aluminum beverage cans," *J. Forensic Ident.*, 42, 213–218.

Meakin, G. and Jamieson, A. (2013), DNA transfer: Review and implications for casework, *Forensic Sci. Int.: Genet.*, 7, 434–443.

Midkiff, C. R. (1993), Lifetime of a latent: How long? Can you tell? *J. Forensic Ident.*, 43, 386–392.

Mnookin, J. L., Cole, S. A., Dror, I. E., Fischer, B. A. J., Houck, M. M., Inman, K., Kaye, D. H. et al. (2011), The need for a research culture in the forensic sciences, *UCLA Law Rev.*, 58, 725–779.

Morelato, M., Baechler, S., Ribaux, O., Beavis, A., Tahtouh, M., Kirkbride, P., Roux, C., and Margot, P. (2014), Forensic intelligence framework—Part I: Induction of a transversal model by comparing illicit drugs and false identity documents monitoring, *Forensic Sci. Int.*, 236, 181–190.

Moses, K. R. (2011), Automatic fingerprint identification systems (AFIS), in *The Fingerprint Sourcebook*, ed., A. McRoberts, Washington, DC: National Institute of Justice, pp. 6.1–6.33.

Mustonen, V. and Himberg, K. (2011), A novel approach to the education of fingerprint experts, *Forensic Sci. Policy Manage.*, 2, 28–35.

National Research Council (2009), *Strengthening Forensic Science in the United Sates: A Path Forward*, Washington, DC: National Academies Press.

Neumann, C., Champod, C., Yoo, M., Genessay, T., and Langenburg, G. (2015), Quantifying the weight of fingerprint evidence through the spatial relationship, directions and types of minutiae observed on fingermarks, *Forensic Sci. Int.*, 248, 154–171.

O'Brien, W. J. (1984), My fingerprints? Of course, I lived there! *Austr. Police J.*, October–December, 142–147.

Ostojic, L., Klempner, S. A., Patel, R. A., Mitchell, A. A., Axler-Diperte, G. L., and Wurmbach, E. (2014), Qualitative and quantitative assessment of single fingerprints in forensic DNA analysis, *Electrophoresis*, 35, 3165–3172.

Ribaux, O., Baylon, A., Roux, C., Delémont, O., Lock, E., Zingg, C., and Margot, P. (2010a), Intelligence-led crime scene processing. Part I: Forensic intelligence, *Forensic Sci. Int.*, 195, 10–16.

Ribaux, O., Baylon, A., Lock, E., Delémont, O., Roux, C., Zingg, C., and Margot, P. (2010b), Intelligence-led crime scene processing. Part II: Intelligence and crime scene examination, *Forensic Sci. Int.*, 199, 63–71.

Ritchie, A. T. (2002), An update on some recent Manchester cases, *Fingerprint Whorld*, 28, 11–17.

Rodriguez, C. M., de Jongh, A., and Meuwly, D. (2012), Introducing a semi-automatic method to simulate large numbers of forensic fingermarks for research on fingerprint identification, *J. Forensic Sci.*, 57, 334–342.

Saks, M. J. (1998), Merlin and Solomon: Lessons from the law's formative encounters with forensic identification science, *Hast. Law J.*, 49, 1069–1141.

Schulz, M. M. and Reichert, W. (2002), Archived or directly swabbed latent fingerprints as a DNA source for STR typing, *Forensic Sci. Int.*, 127, 128–130.

Schwabenland, J. F. (1992), Determining the evaporation rate of latent impressions on the exterior surfaces of aluminum beverage cans, *J. Forensic Ident.*, 42, 84–90.

Senay, P. (1990), Empreintes digitales falsifiées (counterfeit fingerprints), *La Gazette de la Gendarmerie Royale du Canada* (Royal Canadian Mounted Police Gazette), 52, 6–7.

Srihari, S. (2012), *Quantitative Measures in Support of Latent Print Comparison*, Washington, DC: National Institute of Justice https://www.ncjrs.gov/pdffiles1/nij/grants/241288.pdf (last accessed January 29, 2016).

Steadman, S. A., Hoofer, S. R., Geering, S. C., King, S., and Bennett, M. A. (2015), Recovery of DNA from latent fingerprint tape lifts archived against matte acetate, *J. Forensic Sci.*, 60, 777–782.

Szkuta, B., Harvey, M. L., Ballantyne, K. N., and van Oorschot, R. A. H. (2013), The potential transfer of trace DNA via high risk vectors during exhibit examination, *Forensic Sci. Int. Genet.*, 4, e55–e56.

Szkuta, B., Harvey, M. L., Ballantyne, K. N., and Van Oorschot, R. A. H. (2015), DNA transfer by examination tools—A risk for forensic casework?, *Forensic Sci. Int. Genet.*, 16, 246–254.

Taylor, S. J., Dutton, E. K., Aldrich, P. R., and Dutton, B. E. (2012), *Application of Spatial Statistics to Latent Print Identifications: Towards Improved Forensic Science Methodologies*, Washington, DC: National Institute of Justice https://www.ncjrs.gov/pdffiles1/nij/grants/240590.pdf (last accessed January 29, 2016).

Ulery, B. T., Hicklin, R. A., Buscaglia, J., and Roberts, M. A. (2011), Accuracy and Reliability of Forensic Latent Fingerprint Decisions, in *Proc. Natl. Acad. Sci. USA*, 108, 7733–7738.

Ulery, B. T., Hicklin, R. A., Buscaglia, J., and Roberts, M. A. (2012), Repeatability and reproducibility of decisions by latent fingerprint examiners, *PLOS ONE*, 7 (3), e32800.

van Oorschot, R. A. H. and Jones, M. K. (1997), DNA fingerprints from fingerprints, *Nature*, 387, 767.

Wertheim, K. (2003), Fingerprint age determination: Is there any hope? *J. Forensic Ident.*, 53, 42–49.

Wertheim, P. A. (1998), Integrity assurance: Policies and procedures to prevent fabrication of latent print evidence, *J. Forensic Ident.*, 48, 431–441.

Wickenheiser, R. A. (2002), Trace DNA: A review, discussion of theory, and application of the transfer of trace quantities of DNA through skin contact, *J. Forensic Sci.*, 47, 442–450.

Wright, K., Mundorff, A., Chaseling, J., Forrest, A., Maguire, C., and Crane, D. I. (2015), A new disaster victim identification management strategy targeting "near identification-threshold" cases: Experiences from the Boxing Day tsunami, *Forensic Sci. Int.*, 250, 91–97.

Xiang-Xin, Z. and Chun-Ge, L. (1988), The historical application of hand prints in Chinese litigation, *J. Forensic Ident.*, 38, 277–284.

6 Conclusions

To conclude this book, we have outlined what we believe will be the future of fingermark detection and fingerprint identification and the associated challenges that are likely to be faced by the practitioners and agencies providing these services. We borrow here, in part, from a chapter entitled "Fingerprints and fingermarks: where to from here?" that was prepared, with a number of coauthors, for a recent book edited by a collective of contributors as a tribute to Professor Pierre Margot (Collective 2015).

We concentrate first on the detection side of the equation and then we address identification. For the latter, we reiterate some of the recommendations made by Sir Anthony Campbell following the Fingerprint Inquiry in the case of Shirley McKie (Campbell 2011) and the SWGFAST response (2011) to the Research, Development, Testing and Evaluation Interagency Working Group (under the White House National Science and Technology Council, Committee on Science, Subcommittee on Forensic Science) set up following the release of the NRC report (2009).

6.1 FINGERMARK DETECTION

Based on current research efforts, the following technologies are expected to play an important role in the future:

- Imaging systems and detection methods that work over much broader wavelength ranges than is currently the case (e.g., incorporating the ultraviolet and near-infrared regions) and using technologies such as upconversion (anti-Stokes luminescence) and hyperspectral imaging
- Functionalized nanoparticles that target either particular components of the fingermark deposit—possibly as a multiplexed reagent employing antibodies and/or aptamers—or the substrate itself (where the latent fingermark can act as a mask as is the case with VMD)
- Optimized nanopowders to replace existing fingerprint powders (as dry powders or in wet powder suspensions), providing better sensitivity and specificity for targeting fingermark deposits
- One-step luminescent cyanoacrylate fuming techniques to avoid the need for the secondary application of luminescent stains, particularly on surfaces where this can be detrimental (e.g., semiporous surfaces such as glossy or wax paper or varnished wood)

These directions, however, can present some major challenges. Nanostructured materials have not yet provided the success that was originally envisaged and producing specificity for selected fingermark components has been difficult. In fact, component specificity has really only been achieved with amino acid reagents; the targeting of specific lipid constituents has been somewhat elusive. The application of nanopowders and other nanoparticle-based systems raises significant health and safety concerns, and this aspect of their use needs to be further investigated. Modifying molecules to improve specificity and/or performance has had only limited success and can result in the loss of other properties that are important for fingermark detection. For example, attempts to functionalize the cyanoacrylate monomer to produce a luminescent one-step reagent have generally resulted in a loss of volatility and reactivity due to increasing the compound's molecular weight.

One of the challenges for the operational application of fingermark development methods remains the ever-increasing range of detection techniques that are available. Arguably, the number of fingermark detection techniques is already too large for routine police work, creating confusion for practitioners. The choice of a detection method, or sequence of methods, often relies as much on personal preference as it does on underpinning scientific justifications. The future should see a focus on the more effective methods rather than on a greater selection of methods. It would be desirable to have a reduced number of optimized, validated, and generally accepted techniques.

In addition to research directed at improved fingermark detection, a better understanding of how components in the latent deposit degrade over time, combined with an ability to undertake nondestructive chemical analyses on fingermarks (e.g., using mass spectrometric imaging methods), may provide methodologies for the reliable estimation of fingermark age (i.e., time since deposition). In addition, in situ chemical profiling brings with it the possibility of obtaining donor information such as gender, materials recently handled (e.g., explosives or illicit drugs), and substances recently consumed (e.g., certain foodstuffs, illicit drugs, performance-enhancing drugs, or prescription pharmaceuticals).

6.2 FINGERPRINT IDENTIFICATION

Over the years, the fingerprint community has fostered a state of *laissez-faire* that left most of the debate to the personal informed decisions of the examiner. This state manifests itself in the dubious terminology and semantics that are used by the profession at large, and we have endeavored to address this in the book. We also believe that general attitudes within the discipline have not been conducive to the elaboration of a structured research strategy on the weight that ought to be assigned to fingerprint features and the inferences that can be drawn from the observations made. For example, we often hear that all fingerprint features (up to the shape of an individual ridge unit) can contribute to the decision-making process, leaving the discussion of their respective merits to the training and experience of the examiners. A simple hierarchy among features has been lost and we believe that the discipline should reinstate what is obvious to us: Level 2 features (especially minutiæ) are the driving force in terms of specificity and reproducibility; Level 1 features are fundamental class characteristics but their overall contribution in terms of weight of the findings is rather limited for the individual finger; and Level 3 features may bring complementary information and provide an indicator for the quality of the impression, but their contribution is limited due to a high potential for variability and lack of reproducibility. With that hierarchy in mind, research objectives are easier to set. These should concentrate more on the specificity of Level 2 features, in the context of Level 1 features (meaning that the studies should account for the general pattern of the ridges while exploring the selectivity of these features). Level 2 features encompass here more than minutiæ, and attention should also be given to white lines, creases, and scars. Results from the earlier discussion will increase the examiner's ability to assign weight to similarities. However, as part of the balanced approach we advocate, efforts should also be devoted to the weight to be assigned to dissimilarities. Hence, another priority should be a focus on an understanding of the reproducibility of features from mark to mark. Only limited studies are available that tackle the issues of distortion, double touch, movement, pressure, and the effects of substrates or media (such as blood). The assessment of reproducibility is currently left to the examiner's judgment. Data in this area will certainly be welcome to support that assessment. Hence, considering jointly the aforementioned reproducibility and specificity questions, we refer here to research on statistical modeling. At present, no published models have been subjected to extensive validation and implementation exercises from an operational perspective. This would require deploying a model in operational practice, defining its scope of operations, monitoring its rates of misleading evidence, and defining the standard operating procedures. Any statistical output will generally be based on features identified as such by the examiners, hence the importance of taking these inputs into account when undertaking statistical research of this nature. The output of the mathematical models could be as robust as one desires but no more reliable than the inputs.

All data available regarding the features annotated by examiners during the analysis and comparison stages show that there are no consensual procedures adopted by examiners and that the quantity of features reported for the same images may vary extensively between individuals. However, strict training regimes—as seen in the Netherlands—are a valid response to minimize variability. So, there is a need to refocus the training of fingerprint examiners on Level 2 features and promote transparency and consistency in their detection, interpretation, and annotation in the analysis and comparison stages. There is significant merit in constituting teams of examiners working on the same case—particularly for *difficult* fingermarks—who will agree on a consensus set of features on which the comparison will be based. This will depersonalize the work and avoid examiners measuring themselves against the "eagle" eye of the senior examiner in the office.

Throughout the book, we have insisted on the need to rank marks and prints as a function of their *complexity*. Technology can assist in that task by providing robust and examiner-independent measures. These efforts should be pursued because of their positive impact, not only on the way examiners conduct examinations, but also on the whole AFIS operation.

Indeed, we foresee significant improvements in AFIS software algorithms that are likely to lead to automated *easy* (non-complex) associations and automated *easy* exclusions. The problem will be that the work left for the fingerprint examiner will consist of the harder, more complex comparisons, with an associated increased risk of error. Mechanisms to mitigate this risk will be required. In addition, as fingerprint databases get larger and more widely interconnected, the probability of finding close nonmatches increases. The situation will require different procedures and protocols, and statistical support tools will become of greater importance. The fingerprint identification profession will need to accept this transition in response to increasing pressure to apply more scientifically defensible methods for interpreting and presenting fingerprint evidence. Mathematical models can play an important role here and they are likely to be embedded in the AFIS software so that relevant statistical tools are readily available to the fingerprint examiners when comparisons are being undertaken. The model will initially be operated side by side with the examiner, acting as a quality control measure and backup. Ultimately, it may be the case that the model will replace the human expert in some situations (e.g., pristine marks of low complexity).

A strong emphasis is currently put on research aimed at measuring the impact of human factors in the decision-making process and, in particular, mitigating the risk posed by contextual bias. High-profile cases, such as in the Mayfield case, provide fertile ground for these initiatives that are now under the umbrella of *cognitive forensics*. We believe that such efforts should be rightly pursued but not to the detriment of the research priorities outlined previously (Champod 2014). It is indeed desirable to maintain a set of procedures that control the examiners' activities (acting as black boxes) and prevent any undesired side effects, but it is also necessary to provide them with structured and objective data to support their endeavors.

Identifications and exclusions that are considered by the examiner as beyond reasonable doubt, based on the magnitude of the associated likelihood ratios, may well continue to be reported as such, as long as the examiner remains transparent as to the exact nature of the opinion reached. We would recommend, however, a much more humble way of reporting this type of evidence to the decision maker. Fingerprint examiners should be encouraged to report all their associations by indicating the degree of support the mark provides in favor of an association. In that situation, the terms "identification" or "individualization" may disappear from reporting practices as we have suggested in this book. Alternatively, examiners may choose to continue reporting identifications but they will have to be prepared to justify the now implicit steps taken to reach these decisions. At the moment, the logical foundation of these decisions is either unknown or flawed. Appropriate training in decision theory is the only way to be able to articulate the current decision process. The route will be opened when the profession adopts a transparent decision-making process and, at that point, the nature of the reported conclusions will inevitably be reviewed. For example, where there are potential identifications that do not reach the required threshold, the evidence will be reported as the degree to which the evidence supports the proposition that the questioned fingermark and reference fingerprint are from the same individual. This will more closely align fingerprint practices with those employed in other forensic disciplines such as DNA profiling. By logical extension, examiners will refrain from claiming identity or individualization (a conclusion coming with an undeserved and dangerous aura of infallibility) but will simply state the amount of support their findings provide to the proposition of identification versus the alternative. It will bring fingerprint evidence back to the status that it should never have lost despite its direct and undisputed strength: as for any other type of forensic evidence, fingermarks remain corroborative in nature and no case should be based solely on fingerprint information. Regardless, the reporting practices of fingerprint examiners must change drastically if they are to comply with the requirements of logic and candor.

REFERENCES

Campbell, S. A. (2011), *The Fingerprint Inquiry Report*, Edinburgh, Scotland: APS Group Scotland.

Champod, C. (2014), Research focused mainly on bias will paralyse forensic science, *Sci. Justice*, 54, 107–109.

Collective (2015), *La science forensique*, Lausanne, Switzerland: Presses polytechniques et universitaires romandes.

National Research Council (2009), *Strengthening Forensic Science in the United States: A Path Forward*, Washington, DC: The National Academies Press.

Scientific Working Group on Friction Ridge Analysis Study and Technology (SWGFAST) (2011), SWGFAST response to the research, development, testing & evaluation inter-agency working group of the national science and technology council, committee on science, subcommittee on forensic science, http://www.swgfast.org/Resources/111117-ReplytoRDT&E-FINAL.pdf (accessed January 25, 2016).

Appendix A: Statistical Data for General Fingerprint Patterns, Ridge Widths, and Gender

Data obtained from the FBI fingerprint collection have been collated by the National Institute of Standards and Technology in 1993. The collection has been sorted according to the finger number (finger #1 to finger #5 for the right hand [thumb to auricular—the little finger, as the one most easily inserted in the ear (*Oxford English Dictionary*)] and finger #6 to finger #10 for the left hand) and the National Crime Information Center (NCIC) classification. These data can be found at http://www.dermatoglyphics.com (last accessed January 29, 2016). An explanation of the NCIC codes is given in Table A.1.

The rules for the general pattern classification, ridge count, and ridge tracing can be found in the description of the Galton/Henry classification used by the FBI (U.S. Department of Justice and FBI 1984).

For each finger, the distribution of the general patterns in terms of total counts and relative frequencies (rounded to three decimal places) is given in Tables A.2 and A.3 for male and female fingerprint forms, respectively. The data in Table A.2 are based on 17,951,192 10-print forms from male donors. The data in Table A.3 are based on 4,313,521 10-print forms from female donors.

In Table A.4, we provide an overview of the studies dealing with ridge width and gender from 1999.

TABLE A.1
National Crime Information Center Classification Scheme

Pattern Type	Subgroup	NCIC Fingerprint Code
Arches	Plain and tented	AA and TT
Loops	Ulnar loop	Two numbers indicating the actual ridge count; an ulnar loop with ridge count of 7 will be entered as 07
Loops	Radial loop	50 + actual ridge count of the loop; if the ridge count is 13, the radial loop will be classified as 63
Plain whorl	Inner, meeting, and outer ridge tracing	PI, PM, and PO
Central pocket loop whorl	Inner, meeting, and outer ridge tracing	CI, CM, and CO
Double loop whorl	Inner, meeting, and outer ridge tracing	DI, DM, and DO
Accidental whorl	Inner, meeting, and outer ridge tracing	XI, XM, and XO
Missing/amputated finger	Preexisting condition	XX
Scarred/mutilated pattern	Preexisting condition	SR

TABLE A.2

National Crime Information Center Classification Statistics Based on 17,951,192 10-Print Forms from Male Donors

NCIC Code	Finger #1	Finger #2	Finger #3	Finger #4	Finger #5	Finger #6	Finger #7	Finger #8	Finger #9	Finger #10
1	24067 (0.001)	158059 (0.009)	157907 (0.009)	68636 (0.004)	47762 (0.003)	33360 (0.002)	117626 (0.007)	140339 (0.008)	69760 (0.004)	61146 (0.003)
2	62517 (0.003)	338978 (0.019)	373189 (0.021)	181419 (0.01)	175609 (0.01)	90434 (0.005)	261799 (0.015)	318948 (0.018)	175942 (0.01)	193283 (0.011)
3	82889 (0.005)	351074 (0.02)	444137 (0.025)	234080 (0.013)	314759 (0.018)	123926 (0.007)	284801 (0.016)	361747 (0.02)	218048 (0.012)	297660 (0.017)
4	105770 (0.006)	368689 (0.021)	546771 (0.03)	318187 (0.018)	464229 (0.026)	167079 (0.009)	330925 (0.018)	434885 (0.024)	290656 (0.016)	438976 (0.024)
5	126605 (0.007)	327820 (0.018)	560614 (0.031)	337307 (0.019)	569537 (0.032)	203479 (0.011)	334989 (0.019)	436625 (0.024)	305718 (0.017)	501943 (0.028)
6	153326 (0.009)	288084 (0.016)	540178 (0.03)	307786 (0.017)	637564 (0.036)	246464 (0.014)	328542 (0.018)	421280 (0.023)	284086 (0.016)	517440 (0.029)
7	176251 (0.01)	287364 (0.016)	571383 (0.032)	302458 (0.017)	653399 (0.036)	293372 (0.016)	361131 (0.02)	467143 (0.026)	298106 (0.017)	552264 (0.031)
8	211197 (0.012)	332561 (0.019)	717548 (0.04)	350515 (0.02)	687023 (0.038)	357762 (0.02)	448326 (0.025)	625069 (0.035)	381809 (0.021)	668161 (0.037)
9	232763 (0.013)	441989 (0.025)	736208 (0.041)	353698 (0.02)	709543 (0.04)	401993 (0.022)	638400 (0.036)	672635 (0.037)	428482 (0.024)	752895 (0.042)
10	248063 (0.014)	456414 (0.025)	1023382 (0.057)	363533 (0.02)	815229 (0.045)	422325 (0.024)	666734 (0.037)	977053 (0.054)	474840 (0.026)	899485 (0.05)
11	387467 (0.022)	396499 (0.022)	1141366 (0.064)	388231 (0.022)	893517 (0.05)	705494 (0.039)	545141 (0.03)	1147239 (0.064)	538838 (0.03)	1041116 (0.058)
12	446969 (0.025)	509524 (0.028)	1112046 (0.062)	475976 (0.027)	1046780 (0.058)	803142 (0.045)	689361 (0.038)	1127595 (0.063)	677736 (0.038)	1306708 (0.073)
13	391622 (0.022)	483877 (0.027)	1161866 (0.065)	701306 (0.039)	1136957 (0.063)	642662 (0.036)	618289 (0.034)	1208000 (0.067)	1029935 (0.057)	1412833 (0.079)
14	473206 (0.026)	397575 (0.022)	1091501 (0.061)	706338 (0.039)	1200693 (0.067)	742321 (0.041)	460725 (0.026)	1163214 (0.065)	1022666 (0.057)	1425599 (0.079)
15	449216 (0.025)	325842 (0.018)	917488 (0.051)	565269 (0.031)	1181509 (0.066)	641954 (0.036)	347853 (0.019)	997113 (0.056)	765277 (0.043)	1334172 (0.074)
16	739801 (0.041)	287887 (0.016)	754109 (0.042)	735237 (0.041)	1146558 (0.064)	1077461 (0.06)	273928 (0.015)	840126 (0.047)	970744 (0.054)	1299848 (0.072)
17	783533 (0.044)	190010 (0.011)	509285 (0.028)	638563 (0.036)	969442 (0.054)	981777 (0.055)	160624 (0.009)	587600 (0.033)	813071 (0.045)	1009457 (0.056)
18	644161 (0.036)	114041 (0.006)	305864 (0.017)	532778 (0.03)	766724 (0.043)	626307 (0.035)	86041 (0.005)	367962 (0.02)	677042 (0.038)	724781 (0.04)
19	626882 (0.035)	66117 (0.004)	171652 (0.01)	408056 (0.023)	537438 (0.03)	589675 (0.033)	44192 (0.002)	214698 (0.012)	507728 (0.028)	467305 (0.026)
20	627174 (0.035)	40952 (0.002)	99377 (0.006)	355759 (0.02)	374011 (0.021)	506460 (0.028)	24161 (0.001)	130555 (0.007)	425906 (0.024)	306769 (0.017)
21	491480 (0.027)	19701 (0.001)	45581 (0.003)	238450 (0.013)	217598 (0.012)	377280 (0.021)	10462 (0.001)	62725 (0.003)	287645 (0.016)	163324 (0.009)
22	539102 (0.03)	9022 (0.001)	19627 (0.001)	140756 (0.008)	116987 (0.007)	266693 (0.015)	4515 (0)	27971 (0.002)	173234 (0.01)	78816 (0.004)
23	403673 (0.022)	4175 (0)	8268 (0)	88458 (0.005)	58164 (0.003)	178924 (0.01)	1999 (0)	12656 (0.001)	111008 (0.006)	37439 (0.002)
24	234212 (0.013)	1995 (0)	3574 (0)	61569 (0.003)	27195 (0.002)	112330 (0.006)	1008 (0)	5731 (0)	78068 (0.004)	17468 (0.001)
25	175812 (0.01)	842 (0)	1373 (0)	34368 (0.002)	11974 (0.001)	67262 (0.004)	476 (0)	2294 (0)	45174 (0.003)	7564 (0)
26	115284 (0.006)	321 (0)	580 (0)	17256 (0.001)	4819 (0)	38363 (0.002)	262 (0)	946 (0)	24212 (0.001)	3215 (0)
27	70387 (0.004)	147 (0)	215 (0)	9639 (0.001)	1930 (0)	20226 (0.001)	128 (0)	392 (0)	14474 (0.001)	1420 (0)

(Continued)

TABLE A.2 (Continued)
National Crime Information Center Classification Statistics Based on 17,951,192 10-Print Forms from Male Donors

NCIC Code	Finger #1	Finger #2	Finger #3	Finger #4	Finger #5	Finger #6	Finger #7	Finger #8	Finger #9	Finger #10
28	42255 (0.002)	76 (0)	103 (0)	5441 (0)	781 (0)	10588 (0.001)	99 (0)	175 (0)	9179 (0.001)	637 (0)
29	22933 (0.001)	41 (0)	50 (0)	2829 (0)	294 (0)	5230 (0)	48 (0)	91 (0)	5352 (0)	353 (0)
30	13558 (0.001)	26 (0)	27 (0)	1949 (0)	162 (0)	2660 (0)	36 (0)	66 (0)	4220 (0)	193 (0)
31	6363 (0)	16 (0)	21 (0)	906 (0)	51 (0)	1107 (0)	36 (0)	49 (0)	2122 (0)	100 (0)
32	3193 (0)	12 (0)	11 (0)	608 (0)	21 (0)	506 (0)	17 (0)	36 (0)	1613 (0)	69 (0)
33	1503 (0)	3 (0)	9 (0)	341 (0)	13 (0)	190 (0)	14 (0)	30 (0)	995 (0)	33 (0)
34	719 (0)	2 (0)	7 (0)	210 (0)	7 (0)	104 (0)	6 (0)	9 (0)	599 (0)	19 (0)
35	310 (0)	1 (0)	4 (0)	125 (0)	6 (0)	48 (0)	7 (0)	13 (0)	412 (0)	21 (0)
36	150 (0)	1 (0)	0 (0)	73 (0)	1 (0)	23 (0)	5 (0)	11 (0)	227 (0)	15 (0)
37	73 (0)	0 (0)	3 (0)	21 (0)	1 (0)	12 (0)	5 (0)	4 (0)	106 (0)	14 (0)
38	29 (0)	1 (0)	3 (0)	16 (0)	0 (0)	5 (0)	1 (0)	4 (0)	77 (0)	10 (0)
39	17 (0)	2 (0)	2 (0)	12 (0)	1 (0)	3 (0)	3 (0)	4 (0)	35 (0)	4 (0)
40	9 (0)	3 (0)	1 (0)	11 (0)	1 (0)	5 (0)	3 (0)	7 (0)	22 (0)	10 (0)
>40	7 (0)	10 (0)	11 (0)	9 (0)	16 (0)	15 (0)	13 (0)	22 (0)	33 (0)	30 (0)
51	331 (0)	93833 (0.005)	17043 (0.001)	2644 (0)	824 (0)	413 (0)	129475 (0.007)	36341 (0.002)	3364 (0)	847 (0)
52	773 (0)	215260 (0.012)	30187 (0.002)	6309 (0)	1958 (0)	915 (0)	293857 (0.016)	60305 (0.003)	5986 (0)	1473 (0)
53	1010 (0)	239894 (0.013)	27236 (0.002)	8432 (0)	2734 (0)	1284 (0)	325475 (0.018)	49237 (0.003)	5831 (0)	1382 (0)
54	1331 (0)	251618 (0.014)	21498 (0.001)	11358 (0.001)	3527 (0)	1727 (0)	343812 (0.019)	35091 (0.002)	6080 (0)	1344 (0)
55	1541 (0)	198586 (0.011)	15687 (0.001)	14017 (0.001)	4056 (0)	2083 (0)	272173 (0.015)	21011 (0.001)	6098 (0)	1324 (0)
56	1818 (0)	138233 (0.008)	12639 (0.001)	16496 (0.001)	4561 (0)	2595 (0)	187531 (0.01)	12801 (0.001)	6233 (0)	1322 (0)
57	2288 (0)	112261 (0.006)	12261 (0.001)	18734 (0.001)	4588 (0)	3085 (0)	141516 (0.008)	9164 (0.001)	6117 (0)	1329 (0)
58	2829 (0)	107113 (0.006)	13205 (0.001)	20410 (0.001)	4749 (0)	3730 (0)	120903 (0.007)	7409 (0)	6234 (0)	1368 (0)
59	3148 (0)	128890 (0.007)	13018 (0.001)	20296 (0.001)	4531 (0)	4052 (0)	120141 (0.007)	6017 (0)	5603 (0)	1236 (0)
60	3460 (0)	127130 (0.007)	17836 (0.001)	19607 (0.001)	4386 (0)	4545 (0)	93601 (0.005)	7157 (0)	5205 (0)	1177 (0)
61	4577 (0)	116128 (0.006)	17759 (0.001)	17028 (0.001)	3353 (0)	5935 (0)	70295 (0.004)	6853 (0)	4413 (0)	996 (0)
62	5162 (0)	165309 (0.009)	15228 (0.001)	13998 (0.001)	2865 (0)	6282 (0)	91803 (0.005)	5570 (0)	3622 (0)	901 (0)
63	4667 (0)	185107 (0.01)	15233 (0.001)	14543 (0.001)	2064 (0)	5387 (0)	98320 (0.005)	5585 (0)	3523 (0)	754 (0)
64	5065 (0)	185107 (0.01)	14103 (0.001)	10142 (0.001)	1447 (0)	5804 (0)	98692 (0.005)	5410 (0)	2597 (0)	566 (0)

(Continued)

TABLE A.2 (*Continued*)
National Crime Information Center Classification Statistics Based on 17,951,192 10-Print Forms from Male Donors

NCIC Code	Finger #1	Finger #2	Finger #3	Finger #4	Finger #5	Finger #6	Finger #7	Finger #8	Finger #9	Finger #10
65	4958 (0)	187306 (0.01)	11968 (0.001)	5914 (0)	899 (0)	5390 (0)	101298 (0.006)	4933 (0)	1548 (0)	419 (0)
66	5966 (0)	201744 (0.011)	10619 (0.001)	4595 (0)	573 (0)	6853 (0)	116638 (0.006)	4679 (0)	1231 (0)	288 (0)
67	5609 (0)	176202 (0.01)	8523 (0)	2847 (0)	295 (0)	5969 (0)	105947 (0.006)	3840 (0)	834 (0)	186 (0)
68	4677 (0)	142483 (0.008)	7113 (0)	1802 (0)	144 (0)	4882 (0)	87465 (0.005)	3306 (0)	498 (0)	113 (0)
69	4278 (0)	110548 (0.006)	5568 (0)	1055 (0)	83 (0)	4403 (0)	69385 (0.004)	2611 (0)	339 (0)	59 (0)
70	4005 (0)	90926 (0.005)	4310 (0)	668 (0)	63 (0)	4198 (0)	59959 (0.003)	2195 (0)	230 (0)	52 (0)
71	3129 (0)	62405 (0.003)	3225 (0)	358 (0)	29 (0)	3456 (0)	40177 (0.002)	1703 (0)	117 (0)	29 (0)
72	2583 (0)	40856 (0.002)	2446 (0)	198 (0)	15 (0)	2886 (0)	25508 (0.001)	1304 (0)	69 (0)	21 (0)
73	1908 (0)	25992 (0.001)	1734 (0)	100 (0)	10 (0)	2174 (0)	15632 (0.001)	874 (0)	49 (0)	10 (0)
74	1306 (0)	16854 (0.001)	1208 (0)	47 (0)	5 (0)	1610 (0)	10250 (0.001)	619 (0)	30 (0)	7 (0)
75	887 (0)	10461 (0.001)	799 (0)	38 (0)	6 (0)	1111 (0)	5943 (0)	466 (0)	14 (0)	7 (0)
76	601 (0)	6278 (0)	538 (0)	14 (0)	3 (0)	764 (0)	3240 (0)	325 (0)	11 (0)	4 (0)
77	345 (0)	3858 (0)	397 (0)	14 (0)	6 (0)	493 (0)	1882 (0)	225 (0)	9 (0)	5 (0)
78	217 (0)	2533 (0)	278 (0)	11 (0)	3 (0)	324 (0)	1096 (0)	99 (0)	5 (0)	3 (0)
79	121 (0)	1579 (0)	174 (0)	5 (0)	1 (0)	184 (0)	628 (0)	91 (0)	4 (0)	0 (0)
80	86 (0)	1290 (0)	154 (0)	8 (0)	0 (0)	108 (0)	496 (0)	82 (0)	4 (0)	5 (0)
81	34 (0)	676 (0)	82 (0)	6 (0)	5 (0)	80 (0)	212 (0)	28 (0)	6 (0)	3 (0)
82	21 (0)	487 (0)	56 (0)	1 (0)	0 (0)	25 (0)	155 (0)	19 (0)	0 (0)	1 (0)
83	14 (0)	306 (0)	40 (0)	3 (0)	0 (0)	24 (0)	94 (0)	13 (0)	0 (0)	0 (0)
84	5 (0)	209 (0)	25 (0)	1 (0)	0 (0)	13 (0)	49 (0)	11 (0)	0 (0)	1 (0)
85	12 (0)	142 (0)	18 (0)	0 (0)	0 (0)	5 (0)	56 (0)	8 (0)	1 (0)	1 (0)
86	5 (0)	82 (0)	14 (0)	0 (0)	1 (0)	5 (0)	34 (0)	1 (0)	1 (0)	0 (0)
87	1 (0)	43 (0)	9 (0)	0 (0)	0 (0)	4 (0)	13 (0)	1 (0)	0 (0)	0 (0)
88	3 (0)	35 (0)	5 (0)	0 (0)	0 (0)	2 (0)	13 (0)	2 (0)	0 (0)	1 (0)
89	3 (0)	18 (0)	3 (0)	1 (0)	1 (0)	1 (0)	4 (0)	0 (0)	0 (0)	0 (0)
90	2 (0)	21 (0)	1 (0)	0 (0)	0 (0)	3 (0)	5 (0)	1 (0)	0 (0)	2 (0)
>90	4 (0)	8 (0)	8 (0)	1 (0)	1 (0)	15 (0)	26 (0)	9 (0)	5 (0)	7 (0)

(*Continued*)

TABLE A.2 (Continued)
National Crime Information Center Classification Statistics Based on 17,951,192 10-Print Forms from Male Donors

NCIC Code	Finger #1	Finger #2	Finger #3	Finger #4	Finger #5	Finger #6	Finger #7	Finger #8	Finger #9	Finger #10
AA	454125 (0.025)	1022300 (0.057)	755815 (0.042)	200535 (0.011)	127095 (0.007)	829907 (0.046)	1035510 (0.058)	961491 (0.054)	281194 (0.016)	166404 (0.009)
TT	66787 (0.004)	1464143 (0.082)	599484 (0.033)	176441 (0.01)	114881 (0.006)	99534 (0.006)	1447009 (0.081)	793601 (0.044)	238104 (0.013)	171547 (0.01)
XX	15748 (0.001)	42580 (0.002)	39766 (0.002)	29586 (0.002)	25582 (0.001)	18727 (0.001)	44513 (0.002)	42640 (0.002)	34615 (0.002)	27968 (0.002)
SR	4482 (0)	33463 (0.002)	24367 (0.001)	11508 (0.001)	10542 (0.001)	6753 (0)	27731 (0.002)	23543 (0.001)	11923 (0.001)	10469 (0.001)
PI	1046615 (0.058)	2601211 (0.145)	787299 (0.044)	997497 (0.056)	94061 (0.005)	2407512 (0.134)	1074206 (0.06)	1296150 (0.072)	3567425 (0.199)	1163027 (0.065)
CI	66614 (0.004)	551942 (0.031)	123766 (0.007)	180728 (0.01)	35151 (0.002)	147798 (0.008)	277035 (0.015)	362973 (0.02)	1482915 (0.083)	567567 (0.032)
DI	82436 (0.005)	488927 (0.027)	81429 (0.005)	17197 (0.001)	1139 (0)	2206636 (0.123)	266744 (0.015)	256940 (0.014)	297877 (0.017)	171900 (0.01)
XI	2379 (0)	48364 (0.003)	3584 (0)	4302 (0)	343 (0)	1998 (0)	16032 (0.001)	3619 (0)	5120 (0)	616 (0)
PM	1234283 (0.069)	1001221 (0.056)	774319 (0.043)	1733535 (0.097)	300817 (0.017)	434288 (0.024)	784084 (0.044)	533591 (0.03)	551268 (0.031)	94491 (0.005)
CM	1954 (0)	32999 (0.002)	15804 (0.001)	55616 (0.003)	18318 (0.001)	1017 (0)	40927 (0.002)	13149 (0.001)	25495 (0.001)	5874 (0)
DM	105401 (0.006)	58523 (0.003)	26302 (0.001)	18043 (0.001)	3106 (0)	67116 (0.004)	56294 (0.003)	19270 (0.001)	6444 (0)	1912 (0)
XM	1098 (0)	20264 (0.001)	2180 (0)	3737 (0)	553 (0)	1172 (0)	21848 (0.001)	3162 (0)	1702 (0)	309 (0)
PO	3962126 (0.221)	735116 (0.041)	985263 (0.055)	3908637 (0.218)	1728667 (0.096)	780220 (0.043)	2105657 (0.117)	506971 (0.028)	211295 (0.012)	20543 (0.001)
CO	123232 (0.007)	201011 (0.011)	322305 (0.018)	1348378 (0.075)	600842 (0.033)	40379 (0.002)	367016 (0.02)	53857 (0.003)	41469 (0.002)	8181 (0)
DO	1589114 (0.089)	93328 (0.005)	90598 (0.005)	120034 (0.007)	73117 (0.004)	74704 (0.004)	260399 (0.015)	27801 (0.002)	2445 (0)	471 (0)
XO	1470 (0)	8236 (0)	1322 (0)	5538 (0)	887 (0)	1591 (0)	49643 (0.003)	3976 (0)	793 (0)	75 (0)

TABLE A.3
National Crime Information Center Classification Statistics Based on 4,313,521 10-Print Forms from Female Donors

NCIC Code	Finger #1	Finger #2	Finger #3	Finger #4	Finger #5	Finger #6	Finger #7	Finger #8	Finger #9	Finger #10
1	9304 (0.002)	47886 (0.011)	44982 (0.01)	25112 (0.006)	21403 (0.005)	12406 (0.003)	39362 (0.009)	47795 (0.011)	27818 (0.006)	29720 (0.007)
2	23876 (0.006)	98841 (0.023)	103227 (0.024)	62741 (0.015)	74681 (0.017)	33517 (0.008)	83424 (0.019)	103235 (0.024)	66149 (0.015)	88610 (0.021)
3	31518 (0.007)	100427 (0.023)	120687 (0.028)	76997 (0.018)	121633 (0.028)	44724 (0.01)	86464 (0.02)	111189 (0.026)	78239 (0.018)	126046 (0.029)
4	39800 (0.009)	103419 (0.024)	140961 (0.033)	94907 (0.022)	162749 (0.038)	57822 (0.013)	92544 (0.021)	122504 (0.028)	93035 (0.022)	161398 (0.037)
5	46910 (0.011)	97944 (0.023)	146025 (0.034)	96144 (0.022)	184848 (0.043)	68697 (0.016)	93017 (0.022)	121560 (0.028)	92146 (0.021)	170009 (0.039)
6	57109 (0.013)	95773 (0.022)	151430 (0.035)	91247 (0.021)	196070 (0.045)	83870 (0.019)	96177 (0.022)	122643 (0.028)	87007 (0.02)	171784 (0.04)
7	65274 (0.015)	99889 (0.023)	165017 (0.038)	89769 (0.021)	193963 (0.045)	97153 (0.023)	104401 (0.024)	135457 (0.031)	90501 (0.021)	175561 (0.041)
8	77218 (0.018)	108181 (0.025)	199216 (0.046)	100876 (0.023)	200233 (0.046)	115325 (0.027)	114696 (0.027)	166534 (0.039)	108873 (0.025)	196787 (0.046)
9	85057 (0.02)	150105 (0.035)	202730 (0.047)	103696 (0.024)	203809 (0.047)	126463 (0.029)	162617 (0.038)	171769 (0.04)	119493 (0.028)	210672 (0.049)
10	90499 (0.021)	160259 (0.037)	299721 (0.069)	112958 (0.026)	230174 (0.053)	129840 (0.03)	167705 (0.039)	261756 (0.061)	133352 (0.031)	243413 (0.056)
11	135005 (0.031)	135869 (0.031)	333261 (0.077)	121114 (0.028)	242246 (0.056)	199104 (0.046)	127022 (0.029)	295934 (0.069)	147174 (0.034)	262831 (0.061)
12	154482 (0.036)	158784 (0.037)	288862 (0.067)	134541 (0.031)	272526 (0.063)	214351 (0.05)	141932 (0.033)	250181 (0.058)	161591 (0.037)	302531 (0.07)
13	134441 (0.031)	146358 (0.034)	300551 (0.07)	204884 (0.047)	282707 (0.066)	166701 (0.039)	118346 (0.027)	262490 (0.061)	251220 (0.058)	308311 (0.071)
14	157148 (0.036)	118402 (0.027)	272750 (0.063)	210571 (0.049)	284717 (0.066)	179102 (0.042)	84839 (0.02)	240687 (0.056)	245728 (0.057)	295957 (0.069)
15	143972 (0.033)	92467 (0.021)	215778 (0.05)	158690 (0.037)	267954 (0.062)	147260 (0.034)	58461 (0.014)	192088 (0.045)	166947 (0.039)	260734 (0.06)
16	217956 (0.051)	72893 (0.017)	162367 (0.038)	192451 (0.045)	248317 (0.058)	215863 (0.05)	40234 (0.009)	146830 (0.034)	196021 (0.045)	237221 (0.055)
17	212146 (0.049)	45470 (0.011)	103792 (0.024)	167713 (0.039)	198424 (0.046)	174719 (0.041)	21965 (0.005)	95715 (0.022)	162210 (0.038)	173126 (0.04)
18	160462 (0.037)	26552 (0.006)	60474 (0.014)	144309 (0.033)	149107 (0.035)	101972 (0.024)	10897 (0.003)	56990 (0.013)	134988 (0.031)	119335 (0.028)
19	145229 (0.034)	14499 (0.003)	31868 (0.007)	109338 (0.025)	97567 (0.023)	85341 (0.02)	5263 (0.001)	30968 (0.007)	100232 (0.023)	72705 (0.017)
20	130014 (0.03)	8030 (0.002)	16557 (0.004)	89707 (0.021)	64651 (0.015)	65169 (0.015)	2554 (0.001)	16754 (0.004)	79543 (0.018)	45011 (0.01)
21	93898 (0.022)	3717 (0.001)	7232 (0.002)	61093 (0.014)	35356 (0.008)	43130 (0.01)	1042 (0)	7836 (0.002)	53933 (0.013)	22888 (0.005)
22	83984 (0.019)	1641 (0)	3131 (0.001)	38196 (0.009)	17249 (0.004)	26732 (0.006)	478 (0)	3360 (0.001)	34360 (0.008)	10671 (0.002)
23	55421 (0.013)	749 (0)	1262 (0)	24433 (0.006)	8081 (0.002)	15705 (0.004)	205 (0)	1405 (0)	22304 (0.005)	4901 (0.001)
24	29297 (0.007)	290 (0)	493 (0)	15660 (0.004)	3583 (0.001)	8610 (0.002)	111 (0)	563 (0)	14767 (0.003)	2096 (0)
25	18808 (0.004)	144 (0)	209 (0)	8905 (0.002)	1497 (0)	4421 (0.001)	69 (0)	200 (0)	9360 (0.002)	885 (0)
26	10556 (0.002)	61 (0)	77 (0)	4900 (0.001)	529 (0)	2093 (0)	26 (0)	94 (0)	5355 (0.001)	343 (0)
27	5590 (0.001)	26 (0)	41 (0)	2650 (0.001)	206 (0)	971 (0)	19 (0)	38 (0)	3213 (0.001)	151 (0)
28	2905 (0.001)	19 (0)	25 (0)	1632 (0)	88 (0)	511 (0)	22 (0)	33 (0)	2088 (0)	52 (0)

(Continued)

TABLE A.3 (Continued)
National Crime Information Center Classification Statistics Based on 4,313,521 10-Print Forms from Female Donors

NCIC Code	Finger #1	Finger #2	Finger #3	Finger #4	Finger #5	Finger #6	Finger #7	Finger #8	Finger #9	Finger #10
29	1373 (0)	8 (0)	14 (0)	845 (0)	36 (0)	211 (0)	11 (0)	15 (0)	1227 (0)	34 (0)
30	692 (0)	3 (0)	9 (0)	603 (0)	22 (0)	85 (0)	7 (0)	16 (0)	999 (0)	17 (0)
31	277 (0)	3 (0)	5 (0)	217 (0)	2 (0)	40 (0)	4 (0)	4 (0)	444 (0)	5 (0)
32	141 (0)	2 (0)	1 (0)	169 (0)	2 (0)	12 (0)	2 (0)	5 (0)	330 (0)	4 (0)
33	56 (0)	2 (0)	2 (0)	80 (0)	1 (0)	8 (0)	0 (0)	5 (0)	181 (0)	2 (0)
34	20 (0)	1 (0)	2 (0)	51 (0)	0 (0)	1 (0)	1 (0)	4 (0)	115 (0)	0 (0)
35	9 (0)	2 (0)	2 (0)	30 (0)	1 (0)	2 (0)	0 (0)	2 (0)	69 (0)	1 (0)
36	7 (0)	0 (0)	0 (0)	15 (0)	0 (0)	0 (0)	1 (0)	2 (0)	31 (0)	0 (0)
37	1 (0)	0 (0)	0 (0)	8 (0)	0 (0)	0 (0)	2 (0)	0 (0)	17 (0)	1 (0)
38	0 (0)	0 (0)	1 (0)	1 (0)	0 (0)	0 (0)	1 (0)	1 (0)	5 (0)	2 (0)
39	0 (0)	0 (0)	0 (0)	4 (0)	0 (0)	0 (0)	0 (0)	0 (0)	4 (0)	0 (0)
40	3 (0)	2 (0)	1 (0)	2 (0)	1 (0)	1 (0)	5 (0)	2 (0)	1 (0)	1 (0)
>40	0 (0)	2 (0)	4 (0)	3 (0)	3 (0)	0 (0)	7 (0)	4 (0)	1 (0)	3 (0)
51	111 (0)	20323 (0.005)	2860 (0.001)	693 (0)	238 (0)	183 (0)	33950 (0.008)	10467 (0.002)	1627 (0)	415 (0)
52	264 (0)	40729 (0.009)	4521 (0.001)	1712 (0)	615 (0)	462 (0)	70212 (0.016)	16264 (0.004)	2935 (0.001)	740 (0)
53	412 (0)	40455 (0.009)	3561 (0.001)	2248 (0.001)	841 (0)	727 (0)	71439 (0.017)	12474 (0.003)	2988 (0.001)	768 (0)
54	541 (0)	36039 (0.008)	2400 (0.001)	2714 (0.001)	936 (0)	912 (0)	66130 (0.015)	8271 (0.002)	3268 (0.001)	781 (0)
55	660 (0)	27682 (0.006)	1717 (0)	3260 (0.001)	993 (0)	1198 (0)	49740 (0.012)	4998 (0.001)	3413 (0.001)	692 (0)
56	846 (0)	19742 (0.005)	1437 (0)	3826 (0.001)	1062 (0)	1519 (0)	35089 (0.008)	3278 (0.001)	3261 (0.001)	756 (0)
57	961 (0)	16295 (0.004)	1399 (0)	4040 (0.001)	1021 (0)	1883 (0)	27015 (0.006)	2431 (0.001)	3191 (0.001)	719 (0)
58	1168 (0)	14925 (0.003)	1460 (0)	4190 (0.001)	979 (0)	2165 (0.001)	22413 (0.005)	2170 (0.001)	3256 (0.001)	696 (0)
59	1325 (0)	18771 (0.004)	1421 (0)	3938 (0.001)	840 (0)	2397 (0.001)	24951 (0.006)	2015 (0)	2882 (0.001)	665 (0)
60	1563 (0)	19951 (0.005)	1831 (0)	3487 (0.001)	769 (0)	2720 (0.001)	23181 (0.005)	2273 (0.001)	2610 (0.001)	602 (0)
61	1790 (0)	18371 (0.004)	1797 (0)	3040 (0.001)	568 (0)	3408 (0.001)	18876 (0.004)	2114 (0)	2153 (0)	542 (0)
62	1931 (0)	24006 (0.006)	1503 (0)	2203 (0.001)	450 (0)	3635 (0.001)	24435 (0.006)	1949 (0)	1676 (0)	410 (0)
63	1664 (0)	26108 (0.006)	1459 (0)	1994 (0)	302 (0)	3174 (0.001)	27081 (0.006)	1822 (0)	1630 (0)	306 (0)
64	1640 (0)	26655 (0.006)	1263 (0)	1332 (0)	196 (0)	3170 (0.001)	28059 (0.007)	1720 (0)	1147 (0)	219 (0)
65	1463 (0)	26146 (0.006)	1032 (0)	724 (0)	96 (0)	2899 (0.001)	27956 (0.006)	1529 (0)	685 (0)	131 (0)

(Continued)

TABLE A.3 (Continued)
National Crime Information Center Classification Statistics Based on 4,313,521 10-Print Forms from Female Donors

NCIC Code	Finger #1	Finger #2	Finger #3	Finger #4	Finger #5	Finger #6	Finger #7	Finger #8	Finger #9	Finger #10
66	1675 (0)	26197 (0.006)	924 (0)	509 (0)	67 (0)	3484 (0.001)	30114 (0.007)	1421 (0)	523 (0)	85 (0)
67	1349 (0)	22390 (0.005)	743 (0)	322 (0)	32 (0)	3075 (0.001)	26613 (0.006)	1200 (0)	321 (0)	56 (0)
68	975 (0)	18314 (0.004)	601 (0)	185 (0)	24 (0)	2338 (0.001)	22038 (0.005)	999 (0)	202 (0)	30 (0)
69	793 (0)	13858 (0.003)	405 (0)	99 (0)	7 (0)	2070 (0)	17137 (0.004)	778 (0)	119 (0)	21 (0)
70	722 (0)	11293 (0.003)	364 (0)	59 (0)	7 (0)	1783 (0)	14105 (0.003)	678 (0)	74 (0)	17 (0)
71	529 (0)	7900 (0.002)	263 (0)	37 (0)	9 (0)	1318 (0)	9072 (0.002)	446 (0)	47 (0)	4 (0)
72	353 (0)	5298 (0.001)	169 (0)	18 (0)	1 (0)	1037 (0)	5938 (0.001)	345 (0)	23 (0)	5 (0)
73	266 (0)	3336 (0.001)	109 (0)	11 (0)	1 (0)	726 (0)	3577 (0.001)	238 (0)	11 (0)	2 (0)
74	160 (0)	2139 (0)	77 (0)	10 (0)	1 (0)	469 (0)	2295 (0.001)	174 (0)	12 (0)	1 (0)
75	110 (0)	1393 (0)	83 (0)	6 (0)	2 (0)	342 (0)	1355 (0)	105 (0)	6 (0)	0 (0)
76	52 (0)	881 (0)	46 (0)	7 (0)	1 (0)	215 (0)	704 (0)	78 (0)	3 (0)	0 (0)
77	32 (0)	526 (0)	24 (0)	1 (0)	0 (0)	126 (0)	430 (0)	55 (0)	6 (0)	2 (0)
78	21 (0)	306 (0)	29 (0)	0 (0)	0 (0)	72 (0)	247 (0)	34 (0)	2 (0)	1 (0)
79	13 (0)	234 (0)	12 (0)	1 (0)	0 (0)	31 (0)	157 (0)	15 (0)	3 (0)	0 (0)
80	6 (0)	182 (0)	12 (0)	2 (0)	1 (0)	32 (0)	108 (0)	10 (0)	1 (0)	0 (0)
81	5 (0)	69 (0)	8 (0)	0 (0)	0 (0)	12 (0)	37 (0)	6 (0)	1 (0)	0 (0)
82	4 (0)	62 (0)	3 (0)	0 (0)	0 (0)	7 (0)	30 (0)	4 (0)	1 (0)	1 (0)
83	3 (0)	26 (0)	3 (0)	0 (0)	0 (0)	4 (0)	20 (0)	1 (0)	0 (0)	0 (0)
84	0 (0)	29 (0)	2 (0)	0 (0)	0 (0)	1 (0)	6 (0)	3 (0)	0 (0)	0 (0)
85	0 (0)	17 (0)	3 (0)	0 (0)	0 (0)	1 (0)	11 (0)	0 (0)	0 (0)	0 (0)
86	0 (0)	8 (0)	1 (0)	0 (0)	0 (0)	1 (0)	5 (0)	0 (0)	0 (0)	0 (0)
87	0 (0)	2 (0)	1 (0)	0 (0)	0 (0)	0 (0)	1 (0)	0 (0)	0 (0)	0 (0)
88	0 (0)	6 (0)	1 (0)	0 (0)	0 (0)	0 (0)	1 (0)	0 (0)	0 (0)	1 (0)
89	1 (0)	3 (0)	0 (0)	0 (0)	0 (0)	0 (0)	2 (0)	0 (0)	0 (0)	0 (0)
90	0 (0)	2 (0)	0 (0)	0 (0)	0 (0)	2 (0)	1 (0)	0 (0)	0 (0)	0 (0)
>90	0 (0)	2 (0)	2 (0)	0 (0)	0 (0)	2 (0)	3 (0)	3 (0)	2 (0)	1 (0)

(Continued)

TABLE A.3 (*Continued*)
National Crime Information Center Classification Statistics Based on 4,313,521 10-Print Forms from Female Donors

NCIC Code	Finger #1	Finger #2	Finger #3	Finger #4	Finger #5	Finger #6	Finger #7	Finger #8	Finger #9	Finger #10
AA	226462 (0.053)	354903 (0.082)	249975 (0.058)	80551 (0.019)	65882 (0.015)	344675 (0.08)	386139 (0.09)	369727 (0.086)	121814 (0.028)	91403 (0.021)
TT	23597 (0.005)	300826 (0.07)	137833 (0.032)	58682 (0.014)	46731 (0.011)	32443 (0.008)	362593 (0.084)	243941 (0.057)	93831 (0.022)	76408 (0.018)
XX	824 (0)	2447 (0.001)	2277 (0.001)	1789 (0)	1684 (0)	935 (0)	2307 (0.001)	2219 (0.001)	1824 (0)	1693 (0)
SR	857 (0)	4433 (0.001)	3374 (0.001)	1598 (0)	1494 (0)	1023 (0)	3901 (0.001)	3373 (0.001)	1645 (0)	1448 (0)
PI	176056 (0.041)	516946 (0.12)	102657 (0.024)	131562 (0.03)	11562 (0.003)	513877 (0.119)	226992 (0.053)	249219 (0.058)	733130 (0.17)	241970 (0.056)
CI	12180 (0.003)	103400 (0.024)	14569 (0.003)	33061 (0.008)	6059 (0.001)	33603 (0.008)	61533 (0.014)	80154 (0.019)	355477 (0.082)	132491 (0.031)
DI	12893 (0.003)	75349 (0.017)	7942 (0.002)	1763 (0)	120 (0)	467944 (0.108)	49061 (0.011)	38013 (0.009)	41593 (0.01)	19485 (0.005)
XI	369 (0)	7935 (0.002)	469 (0)	463 (0)	30 (0)	551 (0)	2324 (0.001)	601 (0)	1157 (0)	145 (0)
PM	249538 (0.058)	264070 (0.061)	130160 (0.03)	286478 (0.066)	45842 (0.011)	138410 (0.032)	189608 (0.044)	121402 (0.028)	145809 (0.034)	31994 (0.007)
CM	473 (0)	8000 (0.002)	2544 (0.001)	14582 (0.003)	4634 (0.001)	448 (0)	9464 (0.002)	4409 (0.001)	11504 (0.003)	3516 (0.001)
DM	27868 (0.006)	14337 (0.003)	3858 (0.001)	2424 (0.001)	566 (0)	25295 (0.006)	11948 (0.003)	3464 (0.001)	1112 (0)	409 (0)
XM	242 (0)	3554 (0.001)	260 (0)	670 (0)	83 (0)	537 (0)	4537 (0.001)	721 (0)	474 (0)	102 (0)
PO	739816 (0.172)	197879 (0.046)	177728 (0.041)	768509 (0.178)	244097 (0.057)	244236 (0.057)	500646 (0.116)	125241 (0.029)	56460 (0.013)	6228 (0.001)
CO	27018 (0.006)	53649 (0.012)	57656 (0.013)	321550 (0.075)	102323 (0.024)	16434 (0.004)	102705 (0.024)	18030 (0.004)	17877 (0.004)	3656 (0.001)
DO	371200 (0.086)	25023 (0.006)	15716 (0.004)	20763 (0.005)	7785 (0.002)	23021 (0.005)	50008 (0.012)	5013 (0.001)	475 (0)	61 (0)
XO	262 (0)	1379 (0)	190 (0)	1146 (0)	134 (0)	557 (0)	11288 (0.003)	958 (0)	189 (0)	24 (0)

TABLE A.4

Studies on the Predictive Capability of Epidermal Friction Ridge Density to Infer Gender

Study	Population Considered (50% Males/50% Females)	Fingers Considered, Location(s) of the 25 mm² Area and Type of Inking	Male Mean (SD)	Female Mean (SD)
Acree (1999)	200 Caucasians	All 10 fingers jointly	11.14 (1.31)	13.32 (1.24)
	200 African-Americans	Upper part of the core on the radial side	10.90 (1.15)	12.61 (1.43)
		Rolled prints		
Gungadin (2007)	500 individuals from the Karnataka province in India	All 10 fingers jointly	12.8 (0.90)	14.6 (0.085)
		Upper part of the core on the radial side		
		Plain prints		
Gutiérrez-Redomero et al. (2008)	200 Spanish Caucasians	10 fingers separately	Ulnar, 15.31 (1.32)	Ulnar, 16.38 (1.46)
		Three areas, i.e., on the upper part of the core on the radial and ulnar side and on the lower part of the core	Radial, 16.23 (1.39)	Radial, 17.91 (1.47)
		Rolled prints		
Nayak et al. (2010b)	200 Chinese	All 10 fingers jointly	11.73 (1.07)	14.15 (1.04)
	50 Malaysians	Upper part of the core on the radial side	11.44 (0.98)	13.63 (0.91)
		Plain prints		
Nayak et al. (2010a)	200 individuals from South India	All 10 fingers jointly	11.05 (0.11)	14.20 (0.02)
		Upper part of the core on the radial side		
		Plain prints		
Singh (2012)	2 × 50 individuals from two populations (Khatri and Bania)	All 10 fingers jointly	12.05 (0.97)	14.14 (0.72)
		Upper part of the core on the radial side		
		Rolled prints		
Jowaheer et al. (2013)	200 Indo-Mauritians	R1, R2, and R3	R1, 10.56 (0.95)	R1, 12.71 (1.00)
		Results for all 10 fingers given by Agnihotri et al. (2012)	R2, 11.08 (0.87)	R2, 13.43 (1.17)
		Upper part of the core on the radial side	R3, 11.91 (0.93)	R3, 14.92 (1.54)
		Plain prints		
Krishan et al. (2013)	194 young individuals from North India	10 fingers separately	Ulnar, 15.51 (1.08)	Ulnar, 17.11 (1.21)
		Three areas, i.e., on the upper part of the core on the radial and ulnar side and on the lower part of the core	Radial, 15.84 (1.23)	Radial, 17.94 (1.23)
		Rolled prints		
Kapoor and Badiye (2015a)	200 individuals from a Marathi population (central India)	Thumbprints only	Left, 11.58 (1.46)	Left, 14.60 (1.69)
		Upper part of the core on the left and right side	Right, 11.82 (1.37)	Right, 14.56 (1.54)
		Rolled prints		

REFERENCES

Acree, M. A. (1999), Is there a gender difference in fingerprint ridge density, *Forensic Sci. Int.*, 102, 35–44.

Agnihotri, A. K., Jowaheer, V., and Allock, A. (2012), An analysis of fingerprint ridge density in the Indo-Mauritian population and its application to gender determination, *Med. Sci. Law*, 52, 143–147.

Gungadin, S. (2007), Sex determination from fingerprint ridge density, *Internet Journal of Medical Update*, 2, 4–7.

Gutiérrez-Redomero, E., Alonso, C., Romero, E., and Galera, V. (2008), Variability of fingerprint ridge density in a sample of Spanish caucasians and its application to sex determination, *Forensic Sci. Int.*, 180, 17–22.

Jowaheer, V., Pardassee, D., and Agnihotri, A. K. (2013), Comparison of the quantitative models for predicting gender using fingerprint ridge counts, *J. Forensic Ident.*, 63, 320–331.

Kapoor, N., and Badiye, A. (2015), Sex differences in the thumbprint ridge density in a central Indian population, *Egyptian Journal of Forensic Sciences*, 5, 23–29.

Krishan, K., Kanchan, T., and Ngangom, C. (2013), A study of sex differences in fingerprint ridge density in a North Indian young adult population, *J. Forensic Leg. Med.*, 20, 217–222.

Nayak, V. C., Rastogi, P., Kanchan, T., Lobo, S. W., Yoganarasimha, K., Nayak, S., Rao, N. G., Pradeep Kumar, G., Suresh Kumar Shetty, B., and Menezes, R. G. (2010a), Sex differences from fingerprint ridge density in the Indian population, *J. Forensic Leg. Med.*, 17, 84–86.

Nayak, V. C., Rastogi, P., Kanchan, T., Yoganarasimha, K., Kumar, G. P., and Menezes, R. G. (2010b), Sex differences from fingerprint ridge density in Chinese and Malaysian population, *Forensic Sci. Int.*, 197, 67–69.

Singh, G. (2012), Determination of gender differences from fingerprints ridge density in two northern Indian population of Chandigarh region, *J. Forensic Res.*, 3, 145, doi:10.4172/2157-7145.1000145.

United States Department of Justice, and Federal Bureau of Investigation. *The Science of Fingerprints.* Washington DC: U.S. Government Printing Office, 1984.

Appendix B: Statistical Data on Minutiæ

The main statistical findings from the study by Champod are presented in this appendix (Champod 1996; Champod and Margot 1996).

B.1 MODEL

The study aimed at exploring the validity of a statistical model to compute match probabilities associated with level 2 features reduced to minutiæ. The postulated model suggests that the probability of a configuration of minutiæ, Pr(C), can be computed using the following equation:

$$\Pr(C) = \Pr(N) \cdot \Pr(T) \cdot \Pr(S) \cdot \Pr(D) \cdot \Pr(A)$$

where
Pr(N) is the probability of a given number of minutiæ on the surface considered
Pr(T) is the probability of the observed types of minutiæ (obtained by the multiplication of the probability of each minutia type)
Pr(S) is the probability of the orientations of the minutiæ (obtained by the multiplication of the probability of the orientation for each minutia)
Pr(D) is the probability of the length of minutiæ (when applicable, obtained by the multiplication of the probability of each minutia length)
Pr(A) is the probability of the arrangement of the minutiæ

Only the probabilities for the number, type, orientation, and length of minutiæ—Pr(N), Pr(T), Pr(S), and Pr(D), respectively—have been studied.

We are not suggesting using the aforementioned model for any calculation of Pr(C). Indeed, likelihood ratio–based models should be preferred. However, the following data can help examiners in assessing the specificity of the given type (Tables B.4 and B.5), direction (Tables B.6 and B.7), or length (Tables B.8 and B.9) of the minutiæ or the mere presence or absence of the minutiæ.

B.2 MINUTIÆ CONSIDERED

Two types of minutiæ are considered as fundamental points: ridge endings and bifurcations. From these two basic forms, it is possible to consider compound minutiæ resulting from the specific arrangement of these two fundamental points. Compound minutiæ are described in Table B.1. For each instance of combined minutiæ, maximum distance is used as a threshold to distinguish between the combined type and two distinct fundamental points.

B.3 SAMPLE AND DATA ACQUISITION

The sample available for the study breaks down in Table B.2. The algorithms used (fully described by Champod [1996]) involved the following steps:

1. From an 8-bit grayscale image of the fingerprint scanned at 800 dpi, a binary image is obtained by applying an adaptive threshold.
2. The image is then reduced to a skeleton and checked by an operator for its reliability.

TABLE B.1
Minutiæ Considered in the Study

Minutiae	Illustration	Particular Case
Ridge ending		
Bifurcation		
Island (short ridge) and point or dot (particular case)		
Lake (enclosure)		
Opposed bifurcations and cross		
Bridge		
Double bifurcation and trifurcation		
Hook (or spur)		
Bifurcation opposed with an ending		

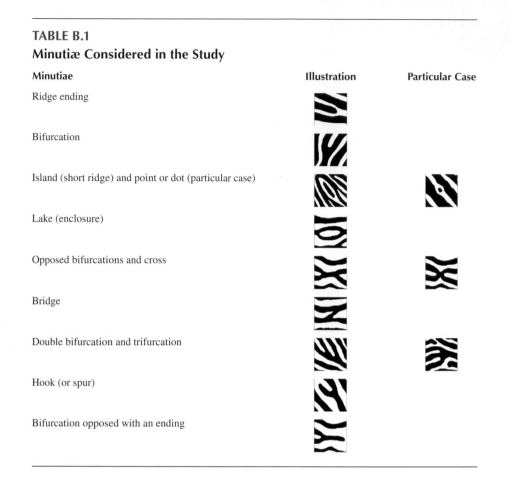

TABLE B.2
Breakdown of the Sample according to the General Pattern and Ridge Count

Description	Number
Ulnar loops from right index finger (ridge count i: RC = 3–6)	217
Ulnar loops from right index finger (ridge count o: RC = 12–16)	104
Ulnar loops from right middle finger (ridge count i: RC = 3–6)	185
Ulnar loops from right middle finger (ridge count o: RC = 12–16)	180
Ulnar loops from left middle finger (ridge count i: RC = 3–6)	118
Whorls from right middle finger (ridge tracing meet)	173

3. The skeleton is then searched (walked through) for basic and combined minutiæ. Decisions on categories are deterministically based on the number of branches and leaves and their angles.

4. For each detected minutia, its Cartesian coordinates from the core and the number of ridges from the core are recorded as well as the orientation defined relative to the vertical axis and the length of the minutiæ (for combined minutiæ only).

B.4 STATISTICAL FINDINGS

B.4.1 Minutiæ Density

It was found that the density of minutiæ on the prints varied considerably—consistent with latent fingerprint examiner's expectations—the delta and core area being more dense in terms of minutiæ than the rest of the pattern. The process was modeled using a Poisson distribution of parameter λ being based on the density and depending only on the position of the minutiæ on the print. Table B.3 shows the average density estimations according to the main positioning on the print.

This may seem obvious to fingerprint examiners, but this is the first time that the extent of this variation has been quantified. Also, modeling this distribution through a Poisson process allows us to predict the probability $Pr(N)$ and, hence, not only the chance of a positive number of minutiæ in a given area but also the absence of minutiæ in a given area. This highlights the fact that the absence of minutiæ over an extensive surface (an open field of uninterrupted ridges) also provides selectivity.

B.4.2 Localized Relative Frequencies of Minutiæ Types

From the core of the fingerprint pattern, minutiæ frequencies were analyzed within a ridge count radius of about 13. Further zones in the periphery (ridge counts from 11 to 25 from the core) were investigated above the core. It was observed that regions corresponding to the core or the delta presented more compound minutiæ than the periphery of the print. So, when assessing the relative frequency of minutiæ, the location on the fingerprint pattern has to be considered. The frequencies were shown not to vary with finger number, depending instead on the complexity of the pattern (presence of one or two deltas). The independence assumptions postulated in the model were shown to be robust for the most minutiæ types except the short ridge.

Tables B.4 and B.5 summarize the findings for the 804 loops and the 173 whorls, respectively.

TABLE B.3

Average Minutiæ Densities on the Core/Delta Area and Outside These Focal Points

Region Considered	Density of Minutiæ per mm²
Core/delta area	0.49
Out of core/delta area	0.18

TABLE B.4

Actual Counts and Relative Proportions of the Various Types of Minutiæ Recorded in Three Areas of 804 Loops

Minutiæ Type	Within Delta Zone		Outside Delta Zone		Periphery	
Ridge ending	2763	(0.374)	6842	(0.455)	7070	(0.584)
Bifurcation	1002	(0.135)	3301	(0.22)	2515	(0.208)
Island	993	(0.134)	2313	(0.154)	1667	(0.138)
Lake	331	(0.045)	518	(0.034)	146	(0.012)
Opposed bifurcations	40	(0.005)	208	(0.014)	49	(0.004)
Bridge	523	(0.071)	231	(0.015)	121	(0.01)
Double bifurcation	688	(0.093)	716	(0.048)	52	(0.004)
Hook	665	(0.09)	579	(0.039)	451	(0.037)
Bifurcation opposed with ridge ending	390	(0.053)	321	(0.021)	39	(0.003)

TABLE B.5

Actual Counts and Relative Proportions of the Various Types of Minutiæ Recorded in Three Areas of 173 Whorls

Minutiæ Type	Within Delta Zone		Outside Delta Zone		Periphery	
Ridge ending	1383	(0.422)	1308	(0.529)	1371	(0.635)
Bifurcation	595	(0.181)	521	(0.211)	393	(0.182)
Island	482	(0.147)	354	(0.143)	274	(0.127)
Lake	193	(0.059)	30	(0.012)	18	(0.008)
Opposed bifurcations	49	(0.015)	25	(0.01)	8	(0.004)
Bridge	62	(0.019)	18	(0.007)	17	(0.008)
Double bifurcation	197	(0.06)	105	(0.042)	7	(0.003)
Hook	223	(0.068)	79	(0.032)	62	(0.029)
Bifurcation opposed with ridge ending	96	(0.029)	33	(0.013)	10	(0.005)

B.4.3 Relative Orientation of Minutiæ

Relative orientations were studied in 45° sectors around the core, excepting the delta areas (where the relative orientation was ill defined). Orientation was defined with reference to the vertical axis; minutiæ creating ridges to the right were defined as positive, and minutiæ creating ridges to the left were classified as negative. The results showed that negative orientation was more frequent for ulnar loops on the right hand and that the reverse was true for the ulnar loops on the left hand. In fact, the relative orientations depend crucially on the presence of one or more deltas. As soon as this mirroring effect was taken into account for the loops, the orientation results were shown to depend slightly on the minutiæ type but were not affected by the finger number. Orientation results were obtained for 804 ulnar loops (Table B.6) and 173 whorls (Table B.7).

TABLE B.6

Actual Counts and Relative Proportions of the Orientations of Minutiæ Recorded in Three Areas of 804 Loops

Minutiæ Type	Above Delta	Opposite Delta	Beside Delta
Ridge ending +	661 (0.31)	486 (0.33)	429 (0.17)
Ridge ending −	1461 (0.69)	967 (0.67)	2038 (0.83)
Bifurcation +	427 (0.41)	224 (0.21)	197 (0.22)
Bifurcation −	619 (0.59)	847 (0.79)	710 (0.78)
Other minutiæ +	126 (0.39)	23 (0.21)	83 (0.22)
Other minutiæ −	200 (0.61)	89 (0.79)	297 (0.78)

TABLE B.7

Actual Counts and Relative Proportions of the Orientations of Minutiæ Recorded in Three Areas of 173 Whorls

Minutiæ Type	Above Left Delta	Above Right Delta
Ridge ending +	113 (0.16)	407 (0.7)
Ridge ending −	612 (0.84)	176 (0.3)
Bifurcation +	47 (0.18)	185 (0.71)
Bifurcation −	215 (0.82)	74 (0.29)
Other minutiæ +	21 (0.38)	14 (0.27)
Other minutiæ −	35 (0.63)	37 (0.73)

B.4.4 Length of Combined Minutiæ

The length (in millimeters) of combined minutiæ was studied for given intervals (D1 to D5) defined in Table B.8, depending on their type. The results in Table B.9 show that as soon as some conditioning was adopted for the short ridges (a function of their position within the delta pattern area), the length showed good independence behavior in the face of the number or orientation of the points.

TABLE B.8
Definition of the Interval D1 to D5 in Function of the Type of Combined Minutiæ

	D1	D2	D3	D4	D5
Island	0–0.65	0.66–1.27	1.28–1.90	1.91–2.54	2.55–3.18
Lake	0–0.96	0.96–1.90	1.91–2.85	2.86–3.81	3.82–4.76
Other combined minutiæ	0–0.44	0.45–0.89	0.90–1.33	1.34–1.79	1.80–2.22

TABLE B.9
Actual Counts and Relative Proportions of the Length of Minutiæ according to Their Type

	D1		D2		D3		D4		D5	
Island (outside delta zone)	2563	(0.76)	333	(0.1)	211	(0.06)	142	(0.04)	143	(0.04)
Island (within delta zone)	442	(0.59)	96	(0.13)	75	(0.1)	79	(0.11)	58	(0.08)
Lake	272	(0.25)	418	(0.39)	195	(0.18)	116	(0.11)	71	(0.07)
Other combined minutiæ	267	(0.11)	497	(0.21)	517	(0.22)	530	(0.23)	536	(0.23)

REFERENCE

Champod, C. (1996), *Reconnaissance automatique et analyse statistique des minuties sur les empreintes digitales*, PhD Thesis, Université de Lausanne, Institut de Police Scientifique et de Criminologie, Lausanne, Suisse.

Champod, C., and Margot, P. A. (1996), Computer assisted analysis of minutiæ occurrences on fingerprints, in *Proceedings of the international symposium on fingerprint detection and identification*, eds. J. Almog and E. Springer, Ne'urim, Israel, June 26–30, 1995: Israel National Police, pp. 305–318.

Appendix C: Fingermark Detection Sequences

C.1 GENERAL

The application of more than one method or reagent for the detection of latent fingermarks can often increase the number of marks found or improve the quality of those already developed. However, it is imperative that detection and enhancement methods are applied in a systematic, predetermined order. The incorrect choice or application of one method can preclude the later use of another technique or lessen its effectiveness.

A comprehensive range of fingermark detection sequences was proposed by the Home Office Police Scientific Development Branch in their Manual of Fingerprint Development Techniques (Home Office 1998). Now called the Centre for Applied Science and Technology, they have released their Fingermark Visualisation Manual as an interactive PDF that is an excellent resource for any casework or research facility involved in the detection and enhancement of fingermarks on various surfaces (Home Office 2014). Systematic approaches to fingermark development have also been extensively covered in textbooks edited by Lee and Gaensslen (2001) and Ramotowski (2012).

A fingermark detection sequence should, in all cases, commence with a nondestructive optical examination (such as with a forensic light source) before the application of any other treatment. Standard safeguards should be employed, with marks developed at any stage in the sequence photographed under optimum conditions before proceeding. In this respect, the possibilities offered by modern digital image recording and enhancement should be taken into consideration.

The proposed sequences for fingermark detection and enhancement on particular surfaces, as presented in this book, should be considered as general recommendations only that will give satisfactory results in 70%–80% of cases. Different situations and surfaces will necessitate the consideration of modified sequences or the application of other methods. Operational laboratories should adapt sequences of this type to their own needs, based on available resources and casework circumstances (techniques and instruments at hand, time limitations, etc.).

In serious cases, where all possible means must be exploited regardless of cost or time, extensive detection sequences are recommended, with more sophisticated enhancement methods employed where available (e.g., vacuum metal deposition, advanced digital image processing). In these instances, a relevant sequence should be followed until no further possibilities remain. The correct application of an optimized and validated reagent sequence will provide the greatest chance of latent fingermark detection on an item or surface under examination.

C.2 RECOMMENDED FINGERMARK DETECTION SEQUENCES

C.2.1 POROUS SURFACES

Examples are paper, cardboard, and raw (untreated) wood (Figure C.1).

C.2.2 NONPOROUS SURFACES

Examples are glass, plastic, metal, and gloss-painted surfaces (Figure C.2).

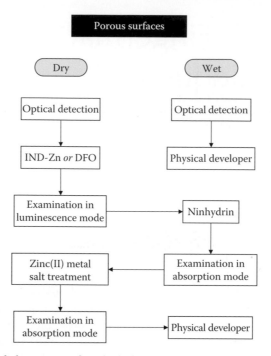

FIGURE C.1   Recommended sequence of methods for the detection of latent fingermarks on wet and dry porous surfaces (e.g., paper, cardboard). A porous surface that has been wet, even if received dry, should be treated as a wet surface. Depending on the substrate, single-metal deposition (particularly SMD II) may be used as an alternative to physical developer.

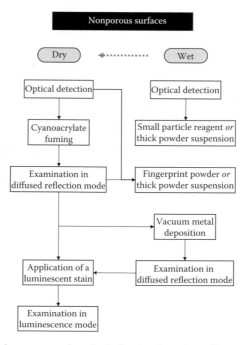

FIGURE C.2   Recommended sequence of methods for the detection of latent fingermarks on wet and dry nonporous substrates (e.g., plastic, glass, gloss-painted surfaces). Where possible, wet surfaces should be allowed to dry at room temperature before being processed. Note that cyanoacrylate fuming may be less effective if the item has been wet. The use of single-metal deposition (particularly SMD II) may also be considered at the end of the sequence.

C.2.3 Semiporous Surfaces

Examples are glossy paper, wax paper, and matte-painted surfaces (Figure C.3).

C.2.4 Human Skin

Examples are fingermarks deposited on human skin—generally cadavers, as the chance of success on warm skin is extremely low (Figure C.4).

C.2.5 Adhesive Surfaces

Examples are the adhesive side of self-adhesive tapes and adhesive labels (Figure C.5).

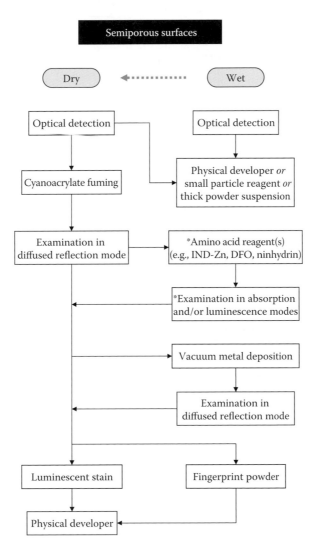

FIGURE C.3 Possible sequence of methods for the detection of latent fingermarks on wet and dry semiporous surfaces (e.g., wax paper, glossy paper). Where possible, wet surfaces should be allowed to dry at room temperature before proceeding. Note that CA fuming may be less effective if the item has been wet. Depending on the substrate, single-metal deposition (particularly SMD II) may be used as an alternative to physical developer. (*Skip if item has been wet.)

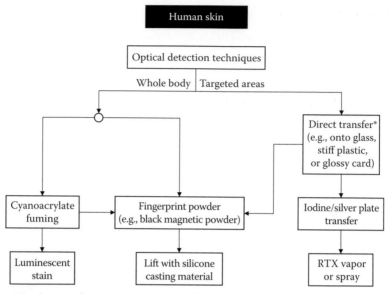

*Develop transferred marks using a suitable method (e.g., powdering or CA fuming).

FIGURE C.4 Possible sequence of methods for the detection of latent fingermarks on human skin. If the body has been stored in a cold room, then it should be allowed to warm to room temperature with the evaporation of excess moisture facilitated (e.g., body uncovered and a fan employed).

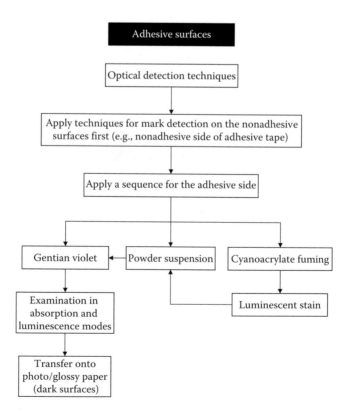

FIGURE C.5 Recommended sequence of methods for the detection of latent fingermarks on adhesive surfaces.

C.2.6 THERMAL PAPER

Examples are tickets and receipts printed on thermal paper (Figure C.6).

C.2.7 CARTRIDGE CASES

Examples are brass cartridge cases (Figure C.7).

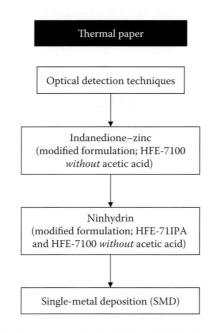

FIGURE C.6   Sequence of methods recommended by Fitzi et al. (2014) for the detection of latent fingermarks on thermal paper.

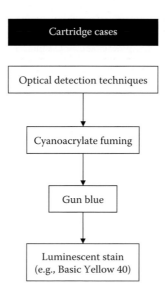

FIGURE C.7   Possible sequence for the detection of latent fingermarks on brass cartridge cases. (From Dominick and Laing 2011.)

C.2.8   FINGERMARKS IN BLOOD

Examples are fingermarks in blood, deposited on porous, semiporous, and nonporous surfaces (Figure C.8).

C.2.9   CRIME SCENE

Examples are fingermarks on fixed surfaces (porous, semiporous, and nonporous) at the crime scene (Figure C.9).

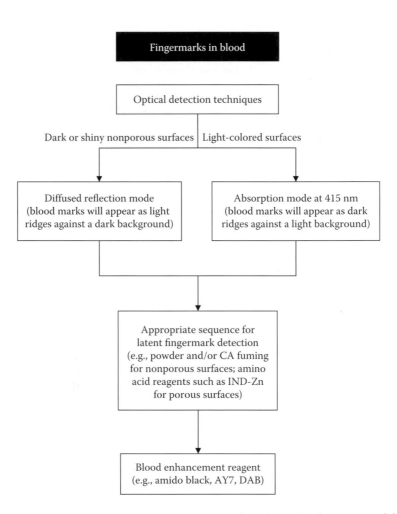

FIGURE C.8 Recommended sequence of methods for the detection and enhancement of fingermarks in blood. The use of single-metal deposition (particularly SMD II) may also be considered at the end of the sequence.

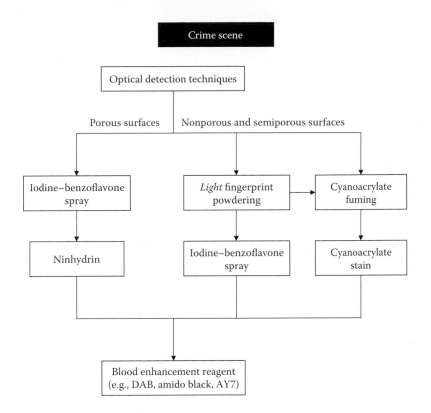

FIGURE C.9 Recommended sequence of methods for the exploitation of latent and bloody fingermarks at the crime scene. For the processing of wet or heavily contaminated nonporous surfaces (such as grease-contaminated substrates and various surfaces at a fire scene), the use of powder suspensions should be considered. If a greasy contaminant is present, then the application of a lipophilic stain (such as sudan black) should also be included at the end of the detection sequence for nonporous and semiporous substrates.

REFERENCES

Dominick, A.J. and Laing, K. (2011), A comparison of six fingerprint enhancement techniques for the recovery of latent fingerprints from unfired cartridge cases, *J. Forensic Identification*, 61, 155–165.

Fitzi, T., Fischer, R., Moret, S., and Bécue, A. (2014), Fingermark detection on thermal papers: Proposition of an updated processing sequence, *J. Forensic Identification*, 64, 329–350.

Home Office. (1998), *Manual of Fingerprint Development Techniques*, 2nd ed. (revised January 2001), Sandridge, U.K.: Home Office Police Scientific Development Branch.

Home Office. (2014), *Fingermark Visualisation Manual*, Sandridge, U.K.: Home Office Centre for Applied Science and Technology.

Lee, H. C. and Gaensslen, R. E., Eds. (2001), *Advances in Fingerprint Technology*, 2nd ed., Boca Raton, FL: CRC Press.

Ramotowski, R., Ed. (2012), *Lee and Gaensslen's Advances in Fingerprint Technology*, 3rd ed., Boca Raton, FL: CRC Press.

Appendix D: Reagent Preparation and Application*

D.1 SAFETY CONSIDERATIONS

During any work involving the handling of chemicals, all reasonable precautions should be taken to minimize exposure. Some general guidelines are as follows:

- Cleanliness is the most important general safety rule, with even minor spills cleaned up immediately.
- All chemicals should be considered dangerous unless reliable scientific information indicates otherwise.
- If you are unfamiliar with a particular chemical, then consult the relevant Safety Data Sheet before proceeding.
- Suitable clothing and footwear should be worn for all laboratory work (e.g., laboratory coat [or overalls], disposable gloves, safety glasses, face mask [if appropriate]).
- Adequate skin and eye protection is required when working with high-intensity light sources—if in doubt, refer to the recommendations provided by the light source manufacturer.
- No eating, drinking, or smoking in the laboratory and hands should be washed thoroughly before leaving the laboratory area.
- Ventilation hoods (fume cupboards) should be employed, where available, for all reagent preparation and use.
- Chemicals should be stored appropriately (e.g., flammable liquids stored in flammable liquid cabinets, acids stored separately from bases, fuels stored separately from oxidizers).
- All prepared reagents are to be labeled and stored appropriately.
- Chemical waste should never be washed down the sink or thrown out with normal rubbish—it should be disposed of in accordance with local procedures/regulations.

D.2 ACID YELLOW 7

D.2.1 USE

Acid Yellow 7 (brilliant sulfoflavine) is a protein dye for the enhancement of blood marks on nonporous surfaces. As the treatment produces luminescent marks, it can be used on dark nonporous surfaces, such as black plastic, where protein stains such as amido black suffer from poor contrast.

Acid Yellow 7 is unsuitable for porous surfaces as the dye cannot be removed from the background. Note that Acid Yellow 7 will not develop latent fingermarks.

D.2.2 MATERIALS/CHEMICALS REQUIRED

- Acid Yellow 7 (brilliant sulfoflavine)
- 5-Sulfosalicylic acid
- Ethanol
- Deionized/distilled water
- Acetic acid

---

* Every effort has been made to reproduce accurate reagent formulations in this appendix. However, the reader should refer to the referenced sources where necessary. In addition, as reagent formulations tend to change over time (for example, as a result of ongoing optimization and validation studies), updated formulations will be made available via the website associated with the book (http://esc-app.unil.ch/blogs/forsi/).

D.2.3   PREPARATION

Working solution (1 L)

20 g	5-sulfosalicylic acid, dissolved in a mixture of
700 mL	water,
250 mL	ethanol, and
50 mL	acetic acid, then add
1 g	Acid Yellow 7, and mix well until dissolved

Note: The working solution is orange in color when it is first made but it will turn yellow over time. This color change does not affect its performance.

D.2.4   STORAGE AND SHELF LIFE

Store the solution at room temperature in an appropriately labeled clear or dark bottle. The shelf life is 12 months.

D.2.5   APPLICATION

1. Apply the Acid Yellow 7 working solution and leave for 3–5 minutes.
2. Rinse well with water and allow item to dry.

The staining process can be repeated if visualization (see Section D.2.6) indicates weak results. Longer treatment times may be required depending on the nature of the substrate and the amount of blood present.

D.2.6   RECORDING RESULTS

The application of Acid Yellow 7 does not produce any significant enhancement of fingermarks in blood when viewed under white light, although some "yellowing" of the blood may occur after extended dyeing times. However, treated marks are luminescent and should be viewed in the luminescence mode. Excitation can be achieved using a narrow band at 430–450 nm, with observation using yellow goggles or an OG495/OG515 long-pass barrier filter (i.e., same conditions as for Basic Yellow 40).

On heavy deposits of blood, luminescence may be weak (unless extended dyeing times are employed—e.g., several hours) due to the quenching effect of hemoglobin.

References

- Sears et al. (2005)
- Stoilovic and Lennard (2012)
- Home Office (2014)

D.3   AMIDO BLACK

D.3.1   USE

Amido black (naphthol blue black) is a protein stain that can be used to enhance fingermarks on blood on both porous and nonporous surfaces. The method is suitable for light-colored surfaces but cannot be used on dark surfaces as insufficient contrast results. For dark, nonporous surfaces, Acid Yellow 7 is preferred.

The ethanol-/water-based formulation is nonflammable and nontoxic, making it suitable for use on all surfaces at the crime scene.

D.3.2   MATERIALS/CHEMICALS REQUIRED

For methanol formulation:

- Amido black (naphthol blue black)
- Methanol
- Acetic acid
- Deionized/distilled water

For ethanol/water formulation:

- Amido black (naphthol blue black)
- 5-Sulfosalicylic acid
- Ethanol
- Acetic acid
- Deionized/distilled water

D.3.3   PREPARATION: METHANOL FORMULATION

Stain solution (1 L)

2 g	amido black, dissolved in
900 mL	methanol, then add
100 mL	acetic acid

Wash solution A (1 L)

900 mL	methanol, mixed with
100 mL	acetic acid

Wash solution B (1 L)

50 mL	acetic acid, mixed with
950 mL	water

D.3.4   PREPARATION: ETHANOL/WATER FORMULATION

Fixing solution (1 L)

20 g	5-sulfosalicylic acid, dissolved in
1000 mL	water

Stain solution (1 L)

1 g	amido black, dissolved in
250 mL	ethanol,
50 mL	acetic acid, and
700 mL	water

Wash solution (1 L)

250 mL	ethanol, mixed with
50 mL	acetic acid, and
700 mL	water

D.3.5   STORAGE AND SHELF LIFE

The solutions should be stored at room temperature in appropriately labeled clear or dark bottles. The shelf life is 2 years.

D.3.6   Application: Methanol Formulation

1. Blood marks should be fixed by treatment with methanol for 5 minutes prior to staining.
2. Treat with stain solution for 3–4 minutes.
3. Rinse the exhibit in wash solution A.
4. Rinse the exhibit in wash solution B.
5. Rinse the exhibit in water.
6. Allow it to dry.

D.3.7   Application: Ethanol/Water Formulation

1. Immerse the exhibit in the fixing solution or apply the solution with a pipette. For large exhibits or fixed surfaces, apply using a spray. Treat for 5 minutes.
2. Treat with the stain solution for 3–4 minutes.
3. Destain with the wash solution (several changes of solution may be required to remove all excess stain).
4. Rinse the exhibit in water.
5. Allow it to dry.

D.3.8   Recording Results

Treated marks are dark blue in color and these can be recorded under white light. In some cases, improved contrast can be achieved using an orange long-pass (e.g., KV550) or orange bandpass barrier filter (e.g., 590 nm) in front of the camera.

References

- Sears and Prizeman (2000)
- Home Office (2014)

D.4   BASIC YELLOW 40

D.4.1   Use

Basic Yellow 40 is a luminescent dye that can be used to stain fingermarks developed by cyanoacrylate fuming.

D.4.2   Materials/Chemicals Required

- Basic Yellow 40
- Methanol
- Deionized/distilled water
- Filter paper

D.4.3   Preparation

Stain solution (1 L)
    2 g   Basic Yellow 40, dissolved in
    1000 mL   methanol
Filter the solution through filter paper if cloudy.

D.4.4 STORAGE AND SHELF LIFE

The stain solution should be stored at room temperature in an appropriately labeled clear or dark bottle. The shelf life is 2 years.

D.4.5 APPLICATION

Note: It is recommended that cyanoacrylate-fumed exhibits are left overnight before treatment with a stain solution.

1. Immerse the cyanoacrylate exhibit in the stain solution for 10–20 seconds.
2. Rinse thoroughly in water and allow it to air-dry.

D.4.6 RECORDING RESULTS

Examine stained fingermarks in the luminescence mode. Best results are obtained using a narrow excitation band at 430–450 nm and yellow goggles. For photography, an OG495 or OG515 long-pass barrier filter should be employed (or a 490–520 nm bandpass barrier filter).

References

- Hardwick et al. (1990)
- Home Office (2014)

D.5 DIAMINOBENZIDINE

D.5.1 USE

Diaminobenzidine (DAB) is a sensitive reagent for the enhancement of faint blood marks. It produces a dark-brown coloration in treated blood marks and is suitable for both porous and nonporous surfaces. The working solution is unstable and must be prepared just prior to use.

D.5.2 MATERIALS/CHEMICALS REQUIRED

- DAB tetrahydrochloride dihydrate
- 5-Sulfosalicylic acid
- Potassium dihydrogen phosphate
- Sodium hydrogen phosphate
- 30% hydrogen peroxide solution
- Deionized/distilled water

D.5.3 PREPARATION

Fixing solution (1 L)

20 g	5-sulfosalicylic acid, dissolved in
1000 mL	water

Phosphate buffer (1 L)

26.8 g	potassium dihydrogen phosphate, and
142.9 g	sodium hydrogen phosphate, dissolved in
1000 mL	water

DAB stock solution (100 mL)
  1 g   DAB tetrahydrochloride dehydrate, dissolved in
  100 mL   water

Note: The DAB solution is unstable at room temperature and should be decanted into vials (10 mL of DAB solution in each vial) that are sealed and kept in a freezer at −20°C.

DAB working solution (100 mL)
  10 mL   phosphate buffer, diluted with
  80 mL   water, then add
  10 mL   DAB stock solution, then add
  0.5 mL   30% hydrogen peroxide solution

D.5.4 STORAGE AND SHELF LIFE

The fixing solution and phosphate buffer can be stored at room temperature in appropriately labeled clear or dark bottles. The shelf life is 2 years.

The DAB stock solution should be stored at −20°C (in labeled plastic vials). The shelf life at this temperature is 12 months.

The DAB working solution is unstable and must be prepared just prior to use.

D.5.5 APPLICATION

1. Immerse (spray) the exhibit in the 5-sulfosalicylic acid solution for 2 minutes.
2. Wash the exhibit with water.
3. Immerse (spray) the exhibit in the DAB working solution for 4 minutes.
4. Rinse well in water.
5. Allow it to dry.

For fixed surfaces at the crime scene, or on large objects, a paper towel can be overlaid on the surface to be treated to act as a reagent reservoir. After application of each solution, the paper towel is removed and discarded. A fresh paper towel is used for each treatment.

D.5.6 RECORDING RESULTS

Blood will be stained dark brown by this treatment and should be photographed under white light.

Reference

- Allman and Pounds (1991b, 1992c)

D.6 DIAZAFLUORENONE

D.6.1 USE

Diazafluorenone (DFO) is suitable for porous and semiporous surfaces that have a low-to-moderate luminescent background. It is not recommended for highly luminescent substrates. DFO reacts with amino acids and proteins to produce a pale pink–purple colored compound that exhibits strong luminescence at room temperature.

D.6.2 MATERIALS/CHEMICALS REQUIRED

- 1,8-Diazafluoren-9-one (DFO)
- Dichloromethane
- Methanol

- Acetic acid
- HFC-4310mee (1,1,1,2,2,3,4,5,5,5-decafluoropentane)
- Dry heat press (e.g., ironing press)

D.6.3 PREPARATION

DFO stock solution (1 L)

8 g	DFO, dissolved in
300 mL	dichloromethane, then add
640 mL	methanol, then add
60 mL	acetic acid

DFO working solution (1 L)

90 mL	DFO stock solution, diluted with
910 mL	HFC carrier solvent

DFO working solution (2.5 L)

225 mL	DFO stock solution, diluted with
2275 mL	HFC carrier solvent

D.6.4 STORAGE AND SHELF LIFE

DFO solutions should be stored at room temperature in appropriately labeled dark bottles (tightly sealed to ensure no loss of volatile solvent). The shelf life is 12 months.

D.6.5 APPLICATION

1. Preheat a dry heat press (e.g., ironing press) to 180°C.
2. Working in a fume cupboard, pour a small amount of DFO working solution into a tray, sufficient to treat up to 10 documents.
3. Put one document at a time through the working solution, long enough to soak through; then take it out, allowing the excess working solution to run back into the tray. Hang the document to air-dry (or place on clean absorbent paper to air-dry). Repeat this procedure for each document. *Never treat more than 10 documents per tray load of DFO.* If you notice that the working solution becomes cloudy, stop using it and discard it into a waste recovery bottle.
4. Discard leftover DFO working solution into a waste recovery bottle.
5. Repeat steps 2 through 4 for the remaining items.
6. Treated items, once dry, should be heated for 10 seconds at 180°C in the dry heat press between clean sheets of absorbent paper.

Note: DFO working solution can also be applied using a spray (e.g., handheld garden spray). Items should be sprayed until wet and then allowed to air-dry prior to heating.

D.6.6 RECORDING RESULTS

Developed fingermarks will be pale pink–purple in color and will be luminescent at room temperature without any further treatment. Note that weak fingermarks may not be visible to the naked eye under white light so all items must be examined in the luminescence mode (under darkened conditions) as indicated here:

1. To screen items, use excitation at 500–510 nm while wearing orange goggles. An alternative is to use an excitation at around 530 or 550 nm while wearing red goggles.
2. For photography, several filter combinations are possible and a number of combinations should be assessed to find the one that is the best for the particular substrate

being examined. An excitation band at around 550 nm, in conjunction with a red OG590 long-pass barrier filter, is recommended for general photography of DFO developed fingermarks.

3. If there is interference due to red background luminescence, a bandpass barrier filter should be used instead of a long-pass barrier filter. For example, with excitation at around 550 nm, use a 600 or 610 nm bandpass barrier filter. An alternative is to use excitation at 530 nm in conjunction with a 590 nm bandpass barrier filter.

References

- Stoilovic (1993)
- Marriott et al. (2014)
- Home Office (2014)

D.7 DIMETHYLAMINOCINNAMALDEHYDE

D.7.1 Use

A dry-transfer method based on dimethylaminocinnamaldehyde (DMAC) transfer sheets can be used to develop latent fingermarks on thermal paper. Developed marks exhibit room-temperature luminescence that tends to improve over 24 hours.

D.7.2 Materials/Chemicals Required

- DMAC
- Methanol
- Sheets of filter paper or copy paper
- Cold press

D.7.3 Preparation

DMAC solution (100 mL)
     0.25 g   DMAC, dissolved in
     100 mL   methanol

Dry-transfer sheets

1. Pour a small amount of DMAC solution in a tray suitable in size for the transfer sheets.
2. Soak clean sheets of paper (e.g., filter or copy paper) in the DMAC solution.
3. Take the sheets, one at the time, out of the solution, and let the excess solution drip back into the tray.
4. Hang the sheets to air-dry.
5. Store each sheet in a sealed plastic bag in a refrigerator.

D.7.4 Storage and Shelf Life

The DMAC solution should be stored at room temperature in an appropriately labeled dark bottle. The shelf life is 2 years.

The shelf life of the dry-transfer sheets is 12 months, provided that they are kept in sealed plastic bags in a refrigerator.

D.7.5 APPLICATION

1. Place the exhibit (e.g., thermal paper receipt) between two transfer sheets.
2. Place aluminum foil on each side of this "sandwich."
3. Place the lot in a cold press for 30 minutes to 1 hour.

Note: Dry-transfer sheets can be reused several times and then discarded.

D.7.6 RECORDING RESULTS

Developed fingermarks must be examined in the luminescence mode (under darkened conditions) as indicated here:

1. To screen items, use excitation in the range 400–450 nm while wearing yellow goggles.
2. For photography, use excitation in the range 400–450 nm with a suitable bandpass (500–570 nm) or long-pass (GG490/OG515) barrier filter.
3. Reexamine the items in the luminescence mode after 24 hours (as the luminescence intensity may have improved).

References

- Ramotowski (1996)
- Lee et al. (2009)
- Stoilovic and Lennard (2012)

D.8 GENTIAN VIOLET FOR ADHESIVE SURFACES

D.8.1 USE

Gentian violet (GV) stains the sebaceous material and dead skin cells that have been pulled off the skin surface by an adhesive material (e.g., sticky side of adhesive tape), producing a purple image of the latent fingermark. Weakly stained marks may also exhibit a red luminescence emission when excited in the green–yellow region.

D.8.2 MATERIALS/CHEMICALS REQUIRED

- GV—also referred to as Crystal Violet or Basic Violet 3
- Dioctyl sodium sulfosuccinate (DOSS)—also referred to as Aerosol OT or AOT
- Ethanol
- Deionized/distilled water
- Kodak Photoflo 200 (for the transfer process)
- Dry fixed and washed photographic paper or glossy inkjet paper (for the transfer process)
- Cold press (for the transfer process)

D.8.3 PREPARATION

GV stock solution for adhesive tape (50 mL)

5 g	GV, dissolved in
50 mL	ethanol

DOSS stock solution for adhesive tape (500 mL)
>   5 g   DOSS, dissolved in
>   500 mL   water

GV working solution for adhesive tape (260 mL)
>   10 mL   GV stock solution
>   250 mL   DOSS stock solution

Note: Cloudy DOSS stock solution should not be used. The GV working solution should be discarded if a reddish-gold film is persistent on the surface of the solution after mixing for several minutes.

D.8.4   STORAGE AND SHELF LIFE

The GV stock solution should be stored at room temperature in an appropriately labeled dark bottle. The shelf life is 12 months.

The DOSS stock solution should be stored at room temperature in an appropriately labeled clear or dark bottle. The shelf life is 12 months.

The GV working solution should be stored at room temperature in an appropriately labeled dark bottle. The shelf life is 1 month.

D.8.5   APPLICATION

1. Treat the item with the adhesive side facing down on the surface of the working solution for 10–30 seconds. The tape *must not be immersed* in the solution in the case of an absorbing substrate, e.g., paper or fabric backing.
2. After removing the tape from the working solution, wash it immediately in water for 20–30 seconds (or until the purple background is removed).
3. If weak fingermark staining with no background staining is observed, then steps 1 and 2 can be repeated (increased contrast may be achieved in some cases).
4. Leave the tape, adhesive side up, to air-dry.
5. The developed marks can be protected by applying the tape to a sheet of thick, clear plastic, or a sheet of glass.

In the case of dark-colored tape (e.g., black electrical tape), the transfer of developed fingermarks onto fixed photographic paper or glossy inkjet paper is recommended (see below; D.8.6). *The transfer process should only be applied after examination and recording of any developed marks in the absorption and luminescence modes.*

D.8.6   TRANSFER TO PHOTO/GLOSSY PAPER

1. After washing the stained tape in water, rinse it in dilute "Photoflo" wetting agent (1 mL of Kodak Photoflo® 200 diluted to 100 mL with water), and then apply the tape to dry fixed photographic paper or glossy inkjet paper with the adhesive side toward the paper, ensuring that no water or air bubbles are trapped between the tape and the paper.
2. Place the photo/glossy paper plus tape between two sheets of absorbent paper and mount in a cold press for 1 hour (several hours may be required in some cases).
3. Carefully peel off the tape from the photo/glossy paper after removing it from the cold press. The developed purple fingermarks will be transferred onto the paper.
4. If necessary, the staining and transfer processes can be repeated.

D.8.7   RECORDING RESULTS

Developed fingermarks will be dark purple in color. Photography can be carried out in daylight, using any white light source, with an orange barrier filter in front of the camera (e.g., 590 nm bandpass filter or KV550 long-pass filter). Weakly stained marks may exhibit a red luminescence emission when excited in the green–yellow region. This may be beneficial on dark surfaces such as black electrical tape. For the luminescence mode, use excitation in the range 550–590 nm with a suitable red long-pass barrier filter on the camera.

References

- Home Office (1998)
- Home Office (2014)

D.9   GENTIAN VIOLET AS A CYANOACRYLATE STAIN

D.9.1   USE

GV can be used as a colored stain to enhance cyanoacrylate-developed fingermarks on light-colored surfaces. This may be a suitable alternative to luminescent stains (such as rhodamine 6G [R6G]) in instances where the substrate is highly luminescent or when a suitable light source for luminescence enhancement is unavailable.

D.9.2   MATERIALS/CHEMICALS REQUIRED

- GV—also referred to as Crystal Violet or Basic Violet 3
- Acetonitrile
- Methanol
- HFE-7100 (methoxynonafluoroisobutane/methoxynonafluorobutane)

D.9.3   PREPARATION

Working solution (100 mL)

0.1 g	GV, dissolved in
10 mL	acetonitrile, then add
5 mL	methanol, then dilute with
85 mL	HFE-7100 carrier solvent

D.9.4   STORAGE AND SHELF LIFE

The working solutions should be stored at room temperature in an appropriately labeled clear or dark bottle. The shelf life is 12 months.

D.9.5   APPLICATION AND RECORDING

Note: It is recommended that cyanoacrylate-fumed exhibits are left overnight before treatment with a stain solution.

The stain solution can be applied to cyanoacrylate-developed fingermarks using a pipette or by immersion. Excess reagent must be immediately removed by washing with water.

Stained fingermarks will be dark purple in color and can be recorded under white light or, for transparent substrates (such as clear plastic film), using transmitted light. An orange barrier filter in front of the camera (e.g., 590 nm bandpass filter or KV550 long-pass filter) may improve contrast on some substrates.

Reference

- Stoilovic and Lennard (2012)

D.10   GUN BLUE

D.10.1   Use

Dilute gun blue solution can be used to develop latent fingermarks on brass cartridge cases. The process can be applied after cyanoacrylate fuming and before the application of a luminescent stain.

D.10.2   Materials/Chemicals Required

- Commercial gun blue solution (e.g., Birchwood Casey "Super Blue")
- Deionized/distilled water

D.10.3   Preparation

A working solution is prepared by diluting commercial gun blue solution with water. The dilution factor will depend on the brand and strength of the commercial reagent. As a guide, Birchwood Casey "Super Blue" has been successfully used as a 1-in-40 dilution (e.g., 1 mL of "Super Blue" diluted with 39 mL water). Experiments should be conducted with different dilutions before processing the evidential items.

D.10.4   Storage and Shelf Life

The working solution should be stored at room temperature in an appropriately labeled dark bottle. The shelf life is 12 months.

D.10.5   Application and Recording

Immerse the cartridge case in the gun blue working solution and remove when sufficient fingermark contrast is observed (typically up to several minutes). After treatment, the cartridge case is rinsed thoroughly with water and air-dried. Developed marks should be photographed immediately as the surface may continue to darken through oxidation.

References

- Dominick and Laing (2011)
- Girelli et al. (2015)

D.11   INDANEDIONE–ZINC FOR NORMAL PAPER

D.11.1   Use

Indanedione–zinc (IND-Zn) treatment is suitable for porous and semiporous surfaces that have a low-to-moderate photoluminescent background. The technique will generally be ineffective on highly luminescent substrates. IND-Zn reacts with amino acids and proteins producing a pale pink–purple colored compound that is highly luminescent at room temperature.

Note: The following procedure is not suitable for thermal paper. Refer to the modified IND-Zn treatment in this instance.

D.11.2 Materials/Chemicals Required

- 1,2-Indanedione
- Zinc chloride
- Ethyl acetate
- Acetic acid
- Ethanol (absolute)
- HFE-7100 (methoxynonafluoroisobutane/methoxynonafluorobutane)
- Dry heat press (e.g., ironing press)

D.11.3 Preparation

IND stock solution (500 mL)

2.3 g	indanedione, dissolved in
480 mL	ethyl acetate, then add
20 mL	acetic acid

Zinc chloride stock solution (200 mL)

8 g	zinc chloride, dissolved in
200 mL	ethanol (absolute)

IND-Zn working solution (1 L)

130 mL	IND stock solution, diluted with
870 mL	HFE-7100 carrier solvent, then add
4 mL	Zinc chloride stock solution

D.11.4 Storage and Shelf Life

The solutions should be stored at room temperature in appropriately labeled dark bottles (tightly sealed to ensure no loss of volatile solvent).

The shelf life for the IND stock solution is 12 months.

The shelf life for the zinc chloride stock solution is 2 years.

The shelf life for the working solution is 3 months.

D.11.5 Application

1. Preheat a dry heat press (e.g., ironing press) to 155°C–160°C.
2. Working in a fume cupboard, pour a small amount of IND-Zn working solution into a tray, sufficient to treat up to 10 documents.
3. Put one document at a time through the working solution, long enough to soak through, and then take it out, allowing the excess working solution to run back into the tray. Hang the document to air-dry (or place on clean absorbent paper to air-dry). Repeat this procedure for each document. *Never treat more than 10 documents per tray load of working solution.* If you notice that the working solution becomes cloudy, stop using it and discard it into a waste recovery bottle.
4. Discard leftover IND-Zn working solution into a waste recovery bottle.
5. Repeat steps 2 through 4 for remaining items.
6. Treated items, once dry, should be heating for 10 seconds at 155°C–160°C in the dry heat press between clean sheets of absorbent paper.

Note: IND-Zn working solution can also be applied using a spray (e.g., handheld garden spray). Items should be sprayed until wet and then allowed to air-dry prior to heating.

Note: For optimum results, items should be left to air-dry for no more than 2 minutes and then heat-developed immediately.

D.11.6 Recording Results

Developed fingermarks will be pale pink in color and will be luminescent at room temperature without any further treatment. Note that weak fingermarks may not be visible to the naked eye under white light so all items must be examined in the luminescence mode (under darkened conditions) as indicated here:

1. To screen items, use excitation at 500–510 nm while wearing orange goggles.
2. For photography, several filter combinations are possible and a number of combinations should be assessed to find the one that is the best for the particular substrate being examined. A 500–510 nm excitation band can be used in conjunction with a KV550 long-pass barrier filter or a 560–570 nm bandpass barrier filter. A 530 nm excitation band can be used in conjunction with a 590 nm bandpass barrier filter.
3. If the substrate exhibits a red luminescent background, the use of a bandpass barrier filter is recommended.

References

- Stoilovic et al. (2007)
- Stoilovic and Lennard (2012)
- Marriott et al. (2014)

D.12 INDANEDIONE–ZINC FOR THERMAL PAPER

D.12.1 Use

A modified IND-Zn treatment can be used to develop latent fingermarks on thermal paper. The modified formulation does not contain acetic acid and development is allowed to proceed at room temperature (i.e., no heat applied to accelerate development).

D.12.2 Materials/Chemicals Required

- 1,2-Indanedione
- Zinc chloride
- Ethyl acetate
- Ethanol (absolute)
- HFE-7100 (methoxynonafluoroisobutane/methoxynonafluorobutane)

D.12.3 Preparation

Zinc chloride stock solution (200 mL)
     8 g   zinc chloride, dissolved in
     200 mL   ethanol (absolute)

Thermal IND-Zn working solution (1 L)
     0.35 g   indanedione, dissolved in
     40 mL   ethyl acetate, then diluted with
     960 mL   HFE-7100 carrier solvent, then add
     4 mL   zinc chloride stock solution

D.12.4 Storage and Shelf Life

The solutions should be stored at room temperature in appropriately labeled dark bottles (tightly sealed to ensure no loss of volatile solvent).

The shelf life for the zinc chloride stock solution is 2 years.

The shelf life for the working solution is 3 months.

D.12.5 Application

1. Working in a fume cupboard, pour a small amount of IND-Zn working solution into a tray, sufficient to treat up to 10 documents.
2. Put one document at a time through the working solution, long enough to soak through, and then take it out, allowing the excess working solution to run back into the tray. Hang the document to air-dry (or place on clean absorbent paper to air-dry). Repeat this procedure for each document. *Never treat more than 10 documents per tray load of working solution.* If you notice that the working solution becomes cloudy, stop using it and discard it into a waste recovery bottle.
3. Discard leftover IND-Zn working solution into a waste recovery bottle.
4. Repeat steps 1 through 3 for the remaining items.
5. Treated items, once dry, should be stored in the dark and allowed to develop at room temperature for at least 24 hours.

D.12.6 Recording Results

Results should be recorded in the luminescence mode using the same conditions as for normal IND-Zn treatment.

References

- Stoilovic and Lennard (2012)
- Fitzi et al. (2014)

D.13 IODINE FUMING + BENZOFLAVONE TREATMENT

D.13.1 Use

Iodine fuming is one of the oldest methods for latent fingermark development. The exhibit is exposed to iodine vapor (in a chamber or via an iodine fuming gun) for a short period of time until yellowish-brown fingermarks are developed. Developed marks must be recorded or fixed immediately due to the transient nature of absorbed iodine. While the technique can detect fingermarks on a wide range of porous, semiporous, and nonporous surfaces, it lacks sensitivity and will generally only detect very fresh, good-quality latent marks (less than about 3 days old).

Note: Iodine vapor is toxic and corrosive!

D.13.2 Materials/Chemicals Required

- Iodine crystals
- Fuming chamber or iodine fuming gun
- 7,8-Benzoflavone
- Dichloromethane
- Carrier solvent (e.g., HFC-4310mee or AK-225)

D.13.3 PREPARATION

Benzoflavone solution (100 mL)

0.3 g	benzoflavone, dissolved in
10 mL	dichloromethane, then dilute with
90 mL	carrier solvent (e.g., HFC-4310mee or AK-225)

D.13.4 STORAGE AND SHELF LIFE

The benzoflavone solution should be stored at room temperature in an appropriately labeled clear or dark bottle. The shelf life is 12 months.

D.13.5 APPLICATION

Items should be fumed with iodine vapor until yellowish-brown fingermarks are observed. The benzoflavone reagent is applied dropwise to any visible marks immediately after iodine development, producing a permanent dark-blue image.

D.13.6 RECORDING RESULTS

Photography can be done under white light with an orange (e.g., KV550 long-pass or 590 nm band-pass) barrier filter in front of the camera.

References

- Haque et al. (1983)
- Home Office (2014)

D.14 IODINE–BENZOFLAVONE COMBINED REAGENT

D.14.1 USE

A combined reagent, based on a mixture of iodine and 7,8-benzoflavone, can be used at the crime scene for developing relatively fresh latent marks (up to about 2 weeks of age) on a range of nonporous, semiporous, and porous surfaces (e.g., matte- and gloss-painted surfaces, smooth brickwork/concrete, wallpaper). The technique requires separate iodine and benzoflavone stock solutions. The working solution is prepared just before use due to its short life (up to about 30 minutes).

D.14.2 MATERIALS/CHEMICALS REQUIRED

- Iodine
- 7,8-Benzoflavone
- AK-225 (3,3-dichloro-1,1,1,2,2-pentafluoropropane/1,3-dichloro-1,1,2,2,3-pentafluoropropane)
- Dichloromethane
- Filter paper
- Spray system (e.g., paint sprayer or handheld garden spray)

D.14.3 PREPARATION

Iodine stock solution (1 L)

1 g	iodine, dissolved with stirring in
1000 mL	AK-225

Benzoflavone stock solution (100 mL)

      12 g   benzoflavone, dissolved in

      100 mL   dichloromethane

Iodine–benzoflavone working solution (100 mL)

      2 mL   benzoflavone stock solution, mixed well with

      100 mL   iodine stock solution

Prepare the working solution just prior to use. Allow to stand for 5 minutes and then filter through filter paper. Use filtered solution immediately.

D.14.4 STORAGE AND SHELF LIFE

The stock solutions should be stored at room temperature in appropriately labeled clear or dark bottles. The shelf life is 2 years.

D.14.5 APPLICATION

Spray the working solution on the area of interest. Latent fingermarks are developed as dark-blue images as the solvent evaporates.

Note: The spraying of any chemical reagent should only be employed in a well-ventilated area and with appropriate protective equipment (charcoal filter mask, goggles, gloves, etc.).

D.14.6 RECORDING RESULTS

Photography can be done under white light with an orange (e.g., KV550 long-pass or 590 nm band-pass) barrier filter in front of the camera.

Note that developed marks will fade over time, particularly if the surface is exposed to direct sunlight. Developed fingermarks should therefore be recorded as soon as possible.

References

- Pounds et al. (1992)
- Flynn et al. (2004)
- Stoilovic and Lennard (2012)

D.15 LEUCO CRYSTAL VIOLET

D.15.1 USE

Leuco Crystal Violet (LCV) can be used for the enhancement of weak blood marks on almost any surface. It is a very sensitive technique and very simple to apply. A reaction between LCV and hydrogen peroxide, catalyzed by the hemoglobin in blood, results in the formation of a purple–violet colored product.

D.15.2 MATERIALS/CHEMICALS REQUIRED

- LCV
- 5-Sulfosalicylic acid
- 3% hydrogen peroxide solution
- Sodium acetate

Note: If the LCV is yellow instead of white, obtain fresh LCV.

D.15.3   PREPARATION

LCV working solution (500 mL)

10 g	5-sulfosalicylic acid, dissolved in
500 mL	3% hydrogen peroxide solution, then add
3.7 g	sodium acetate, then add
1 g	LCV and stir until dissolved

D.15.4   STORAGE AND SHELF LIFE

The LCV working solution should be stored in a refrigerator in an appropriately labeled clear or dark bottle. The shelf life is 2 months.

D.15.5   APPLICATION AND RECORDING

Although the solution includes 5-sulfosalicylic acid as a fixative for blood, some running of blood stains may occur, particular if the blood is fresh. It is strongly recommended to fix the blood with methanol or 2% (w/v) 5-sulfosalicylic acid solution prior to LCV treatment. LCV is applied in the form of a light spray or by immersion. The reaction is instantaneous and blood marks will turn purple–violet in color.

Developed marks can be photographed under white light.

References

- Stoilovic and Lennard (2012)
- Home Office (2014)

D.16   MULTIMETAL DEPOSITION I

D.16.1   USE

Multimetal deposition (MMD) is based on a very sensitive protein detection technique used in biochemistry. The two-step method—colloidal gold treatment followed by modified physical developer (PD)—can be applied to fingermark detection on a wide range of porous, semiporous, and nonporous surfaces. For successful application of the technique, glassware must be scrupulously clean (free of any contaminants, including detergent) and only ultrapure distilled or deionized water used for reagent preparation and application.

For common substrates, MMD is generally no more sensitive than routine detection methods. However, MMD may be an advantage on difficult substrates where routine techniques fail to give satisfactory results (e.g., some semiporous surfaces).

Note: The following method is based on the original MMD technique (MMD I). A more sensitive and more reliable version of this technique, referred to as MMD II, has been developed and evaluated; however, this is more complicated and more time-consuming to apply.

D.16.2   MATERIALS/CHEMICALS REQUIRED

- Gold chloride (tetrachloroauric acid)
- Sodium citrate
- Citric acid
- Ferric nitrate
- Ammonium ferrous sulfate (ferrous ammonium sulfate)
- Tween 20

- Silver nitrate
- Ultrapure deionized/distilled water
- pH meter

D.16.3 PREPARATION: COLLOIDAL GOLD

Gold chloride stock solution (10 mL)
1 g	gold chloride (tetrachloroauric acid), dissolved in
10 mL	water

Sodium citrate stock solution (100 mL)
1 g	sodium citrate, dissolved in
100 mL	water

Citric acid stock solution (500 mL)
48 g	citric acid, dissolved in
500 mL	water

Colloidal gold working solution (1 L)
1 mL	gold chloride stock solution, added to
1000 mL	water, bring to the boil and then add
10 mL	sodium citrate stock solution and boil gently for
10 min	(solution should be port-wine in color)

While still hot, add 5 mL of Tween 20, mix well, and allow the solution to cool.

Adjust the pH to 3.0 using the citric acid stock solution (generally around 1 mL will be required). Restore the volume to 1000 mL, if necessary, by the addition of water.

D.16.4 STORAGE AND SHELF LIFE: COLLOIDAL GOLD

The stock solutions can be stored at room temperature in appropriately labeled clear or dark bottles. The shelf life is 12 months.

The colloidal gold working solution should be stored in a refrigerator in a scrupulously clean and appropriately labeled glass bottle. The shelf life is 6 months.

D.16.5 PREPARATION: MODIFIED PHYSICAL DEVELOPER

Tween 20 stock solution (100 mL)
1 mL	Tween 20
99 mL	water

Redox solution (1 L)
16 g	ferric nitrate, dissolved in
1000 mL	water, then add
44 g	ammonium ferrous sulfate, then add
11 g	citric acid, then add
0.25 mL	Tween 20 stock solution (1% v/v)

Silver nitrate stock solution (100 mL)
10 g	silver nitrate, dissolved in
100 mL	water

Modified PD working solution (100 mL)
2 mL	silver nitrate stock solution, added slowly with stirring to
100 mL	redox solution

Note: The modified PD working solution should be prepared just prior to use as it is only stable for around 10 minutes.

D.16.6 Storage and Shelf Life: Modified Physical Developer

The Tween 20 and redox stock solutions should be stored at room temperature in appropriately labeled clear or dark bottles. The shelf life is 2 years.

The silver nitrate stock solution must be stored in the dark at room temperature in an appropriately labeled dark bottle. The shelf life is 12 months.

The modified PD working solution is unstable and must be used immediately after preparation.

D.16.7 Application

Note: Just prior to use, the pH of the colloidal gold solution should be checked and adjusted if necessary (by adding citric acid stock solution).

1. Prepare five scrupulously clean glass dishes and arrange these as shown here.

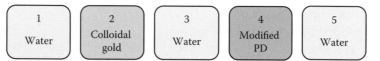

2. For porous substrates, soak in several changes of deionized/distilled water for 20–30 minutes. For nonporous surfaces, rinse briefly (5–10 minutes) in deionized/distilled water.
3. Immerse the exhibit in the colloidal gold solution for 30–120 minutes (generally 30–60 minutes for nonporous surfaces and up to 120 minutes for porous surfaces). Some fingermarks may already be visible after this step.
4. Rinse the exhibit in deionized/distilled water.
5. Prepare the modified PD working solution.
6. Immerse the exhibit in the PD working solution until good contrast is achieved, usually 1–5 minutes.
7. Thoroughly rinse the exhibit in several changes of deionized/distilled water.
8. Air-dry at room temperature, and then record any developed marks.

D.16.8 Recording Results

Developed fingermarks are dark gray to black in color and can be photographed under white light.

References

- Allman et al. (1992)
- Schnetz and Margot (2001)

D.17 MULTIMETAL DEPOSITION II

D.17.1 Use

MMD is based on a very sensitive protein detection technique used in biochemistry. The two-step method—colloidal gold treatment followed by modified PD—can be applied to fingermark detection on a wide range of porous, semiporous, and nonporous surfaces. MMD may be an advantage on difficult substrates where routine techniques fail to give satisfactory results (e.g., some semiporous surfaces).

Note: MMD II—the method described as follows—is generally considered to be more sensitive and more reliable than the original MMD protocol (MMD I). Silanization is recommended for all glassware used to prepare and employ the MMD II reagents.

D.17.2 Materials/Chemicals Required

- Gold chloride (tetrachloroauric acid)
- Sodium citrate
- Citric acid
- Tannic acid
- Tween 20
- Silver acetate
- Hydroquinone
- Ultrapure deionized/distilled water
- pH meter
- Photographic fixer

For glassware silanization:

- Extran® (universal cleaning agent)
- 3-Aminopropyltriethoxysilane (APTES)
- Acetone

D.17.3 Glassware Silanization

1. Soak glassware overnight in a bath of 10% Extran®.
2. Rinse well in hot water and then cold water.
3. Dry in an oven at 100°C.
4. Remove from oven and cool to room temperature.
5. Soak for 5 seconds in a treatment solution prepared from 4 mL of APTES in 200 mL acetone.
6. Rinse twice in acetone.
7. Rinse twice in distilled/deionized water.
8. Dry in an oven overnight at 42°C.

Glassware that is silanized in this manner is resistant to numerous washings.

D.17.4 Preparation: Colloidal Gold

Gold chloride stock solution (10 mL)
     1 g   gold chloride (tetrachloroauric acid), dissolved in
     10 mL   water

Sodium citrate stock solution (100 mL)
     1 g   sodium citrate, dissolved in
     100 mL   water

Tannic acid stock solution (100 mL)
     1 g   tannic acid, dissolved in
     100 mL   water

Citric acid stock solution (100 mL)
     9.6 g   citric acid, dissolved in
     100 mL   water

Colloidal gold working solution (500 mL)
    1. 0.5 mL   gold chloride stock solution, added to
      400 mL   water, and the solution heated to 60°C

2. 20 mL   sodium citrate solution, mixed with
   75 mL   water and
   0.1 mL   tannic acid solution, and the solution heated to 60°C
3. With the two solutions at 60°C, quickly add the second solution to the first while mixing vigorously.
4. Bring the mixture to boiling point; the solution should turn ruby red.
5. Allow to cool to room temperature.
6. Adjust the volume to 500 mL by the addition of water.
7. Add 0.5 mL of Tween 20 with stirring.
8. Using a pH meter, adjust the pH to 2.7 via the addition of citric acid solution.

D.17.5   STORAGE AND SHELF LIFE: COLLOIDAL GOLD

The stock solutions should be stored in a refrigerator in appropriately labeled clear or dark bottles. The shelf life is 6 months.

The colloidal gold working solution should be stored in a refrigerator in a scrupulously clean and appropriately labeled plastic bottle. The shelf life is 6 months.

The colloidal gold solution should be restored to room temperature immediately before use.

D.17.6   PREPARATION: MODIFIED PHYSICAL DEVELOPER

Citric acid stock solution (1 L)
      255 g   citric acid, dissolved in
      1000 mL water

Sodium citrate stock solution (1 L)
      235 g   sodium citrate, dissolved in
      1000 mL water

Citrate buffer (960 mL)
      240 mL   citric acid solution, mixed with
      220 mL   sodium citrate solution and
      500 mL   water

The buffer should have a pH of 3.8; add citric acid solution or sodium citrate solution to adjust the pH if necessary.

Silver acetate stock solution (100 mL)
      0.2 g   silver acetate, dissolved in
      100 mL   water

Hydroquinone stock solution (200 mL)
      1 g   hydroquinone, dissolved in
      200 mL   citrate buffer

Hydroquinone rinse (200 mL)
      100 mL   hydroquinone stock solution, diluted with
      100 mL   water

Modified PD working solution (200 mL)
      100 mL   sodium acetate stock solution, mixed with
      100 mL   hydroquinone stock solution

Note: The modified PD working solution should be prepared just prior to use.

D.17.7   STORAGE AND SHELF LIFE: MODIFIED PHYSICAL DEVELOPER

The silver acetate and hydroquinone solutions are not stable for more than 1 day, so these should be prepared just prior to use.

The modified PD working solution is unstable and must be used immediately after preparation. The remaining solutions can be stored at room temperature in appropriately labeled clear or dark bottles. The shelf life is indefinite.

D.17.8 APPLICATION

Note: Just prior to use, the pH of the colloidal gold solution should be checked and adjusted if necessary (by adding citric acid stock solution).

1. Prepare six scrupulously clean glass dishes.

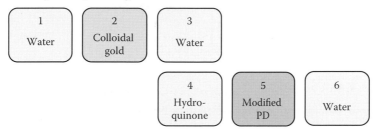

2. Rinse the item in deionized/distilled water (dish 1) for 2–3 minutes.
3. Treat the exhibit in the colloidal gold solution (dish 2) for 5–15 minutes with gentle agitation.
4. Thoroughly rinse the exhibit in deionized/distilled water (dish 3) for several minutes.
5. Soak for 2–5 minutes in the hydroquinone rinse (dish 4).
6. Transfer the item to freshly prepared PD solution (dish 5) and soak for approximately 18 minutes with gentle agitation; the solution will become dark gray after 10–20 minutes, but this will not affect results.
7. Thoroughly rinse the exhibit in several changes of deionized/distilled water (dish 6).
8. Fix with photographic fixer (diluted 1:9 with water) for 2–5 minutes.
9. Rinse in deionized/distilled water.
10. Air-dry at room temperature, and then record any developed marks.

D.17.9 RECORDING RESULTS

Developed fingermarks are dark gray to black in color and can be photographed under white light.

References

- Schnetz and Margot (2001)
- Jones et al. (2003)

D.18 NILE RED

D.18.1 USE

Nile red is a luminescent lipid dye that can be used to develop latent fingermarks on porous surfaces that have been wet. In such cases, it is recommended that nile red be used in sequence after PD.

Nile red treatment may result in high background luminescence on some substrates, particular highly recycled paper and cardboard.

D.18.2 MATERIALS/CHEMICALS REQUIRED

- Nile red
- Methanol
- Sodium hydroxide
- Deionized/distilled water

D.18.3 Preparation

Nile red stock solution (1 L)
      100 mg   nile red, dissolved in
      1000 mL methanol

Sodium hydroxide solution (1 L)
      100 mg   sodium hydroxide, dissolved in
      1000 mL water

Working solution (400 mL)
      230 mL   nile red stock solution, added slowly with stirring to
      170 mL   sodium hydroxide solution

Note: The working solution should be prepared just prior to use.

D.18.4 Storage and Shelf Life

The stock solutions should be stored in labeled dark bottles at room temperature. The shelf life is 6 months.

The working solution is unstable and should be discarded after use.

D.18.5 Application

1. Rinse items in deionized/distilled water for 5–10 minutes.
2. Replace the water with the working solution and leave the item in the stain, with agitation, until ridges appear or until 60 minutes has elapsed.
3. Rinse several times with water and allow items to dry.

D.18.6 Recording Results

Developed marks should be observed in the luminescence mode, using excitation at 480–500 nm and either a KV550 long-pass or a 550–570 nm bandpass barrier filter.

Reference

• Braasch et al. (2013)

D.19 NINHYDRIN

D.19.1 Use

Ninhydrin is an amino acid–sensitive reagent for the development of latent fingermarks on porous surfaces. More sensitive alternatives, such as DFO and IND-Zn, are now available and these have advantages on porous substrates that are not highly luminescent. However, ninhydrin can still be applied after these treatments and may reveal additional ridge detail, particularly on highly luminescent substrates where luminescence visualization may be problematic.

D.19.2 Materials/Chemicals Required

• Ninhydrin (2,2-dihydroxy-1,3-indandione)
• Ethanol (absolute)
• Ethyl acetate
• Acetic acid
• HFE-7100 (methoxynonafluoroisobutane/methoxynonafluorobutane)

D.19.3 Preparation

Stock solution (500 mL)

35 g	ninhydrin, dissolved in
425 mL	ethanol, then add
35 mL	ethyl acetate, then add
40 mL	acetic acid

Working solution (1 L)

65 mL	stock solution, diluted with
935 mL	HFE-7100 carrier solvent

Note: The working solution should be clear. If the working solution is cloudy, add a small amount of absolute ethanol and then shake well. Repeat this procedure till a clear solution is obtained.

D.19.4 Storage and Shelf Life

The stock solution should be stored in a well-sealed, appropriately labeled dark bottle at room temperature. The shelf life is 12 months.

The working solution should be stored in a well-sealed, appropriately labeled dark bottle at room temperature. The shelf life is 12 months.

D.19.5 Application

1. Shake the bottle of ninhydrin working solution. If the solution is cloudy, add a small amount of absolute ethanol and then shake again. If the solution remains cloudy, repeat the addition of ethanol until the solution is clear.
2. Working in a fume cupboard, pour a small amount of ninhydrin working solution into a tray, just enough for about 10 documents.
3. Put one document at a time through the working solution, long enough to soak through, and then take it out, allowing the excess working solution to run back into the tray. Hang the document to air-dry (or place on clean absorbent paper to air-dry). Repeat this procedure for each document. *Never treat more than 10 documents per tray load of working solution.* If you notice that the working solution becomes cloudy, stop using it and discard it into a waste recovery bottle.
4. Discard leftover working solution into a waste recovery bottle.
5. Repeat steps 2 through 4 for the remaining items.
6. Store treated items in the dark and allow development to proceed at room temperature over 24–48 hours. (Alternatively, special-purpose ninhydrin development cabinets—with controlled temperature and humidity—may be used to accelerate the reaction.)

Note: For large objects (e.g., cardboard boxes), the ninhydrin working solution may be applied with a brush or spray.

Note: With room temperature development, development will be retarded under dry atmospheric conditions (i.e., low relative humidity). In such cases, treated objects may need to be briefly exposed to steam to enhance development.

D.19.6 Recording Results

Developed fingermarks will be dark purple in color and should be photographed under white light with a green–yellow filter (e.g., 560–580 nm bandpass filter) in front of the camera.

As ninhydrin-developed fingermarks may fade over time, examination, photography, and enhancement (metal salt posttreatment, if employed) should be done within a week of treating the items with ninhydrin.

References

- Marriott et al. (2014)
- Home Office (2014)

D.20 NINHYDRIN + ZINC CHLORIDE TREATMENT

D.20.1 Use

Ninhydrin-developed fingermarks can be posttreated with a zinc chloride solution. This changes the color from dark purple to orange due to the formation of a coordination complex. The treatment can sometimes improve contrast when results are observed in the absorption mode. The complex is also luminescent when cooled with liquid nitrogen (although this enhancement method is somewhat redundant given the superior results generally obtained with other reagents such as DFO and IND-Zn).

Note: While posttreatment with a cadmium salt solution is also possible, this is not recommended due to cadmium's toxicity.

D.20.2 Materials/Chemicals Required

- Zinc chloride
- Ethanol (absolute)
- HFE-7100 (methoxynonafluoroisobutane/methoxynonafluorobutane)
- Liquid nitrogen (only required for enhancement in the luminescence mode)

D.20.3 Preparation

Working solution (250 mL)

0.4 g	zinc chloride, dissolved in
15 mL	ethanol, then diluted with
235 mL	HFE-7100 carrier solvent

D.20.4 Storage and Shelf Life

The solution should be stored at room temperature in an appropriately labeled clear or dark bottle. The shelf life is 12 months.

D.20.5 Application

Individual ninhydrin-developed fingermarks can be treated by applying the zinc chloride solution drop-wise. Alternatively, the item may be briefly immersed in the zinc chloride solution. Allow it to air-dry.

Treated marks should be orange in color once the solvent has evaporated.

If no color change occurs, then the zinc chloride solution may need to be reapplied and/or the fingermarks briefly exposed to steam.

D.20.6 Recording Results

Ninhydrin-developed and zinc chloride posttreated fingermarks should be examined and recorded in the absorption mode at 490 nm. This can be achieved using a light source operating at this wavelength or by using a suitable barrier filter in front of the camera.

For enhancement in the luminescence mode, cooling with liquid nitrogen (−196°C) is required. Optimum excitation is at 490 nm with observation using either a KV550 long-pass or a 560–570 nm bandpass barrier filter.

References

- Stoilovic et al. (1986)
- Stoilovic and Lennard (2012)
- Home Office (2014)

D.21 OIL RED O

D.21.1 USE

Oil Red O (ORO) is a dark-red lipid dye that can be used to develop latent fingermarks on porous surfaces that have been wet. It can be used in a sequence before PD; however, it is generally only effective on fingermarks up to about 4 weeks of age. It can be used in a detection sequence after amino acid reagents provided that these reagents do not employ a hydrocarbon-based carrier solvent (as such solvents can interfere with the sebaceous fraction that is targeted by ORO).

D.21.2 MATERIALS/CHEMICALS REQUIRED

- ORO
- Sodium hydroxide
- Methanol
- Sodium carbonate
- Nitric acid (concentrated)
- Deionized/distilled water

D.21.3 PREPARATION

ORO stain solution (1 L)

9.2 g	sodium hydroxide, dissolved in
230 mL	water and this solution then added to a solution of
1.54 g	ORO, dissolved in
770 mL	methanol

Buffer solution (pH 7; 2.5 L)

26.5 g	sodium carbonate, dissolved in
2 L	water, then slowly add (with stirring)
18.3 mL	nitric acid (concentrated), then add
	water, to give a final volume of 2.5 L

D.21.4 STORAGE AND SHELF LIFE

The ORO stain solution should be stored out of direct light in an appropriately labeled dark bottle at room temperature. The shelf life is 6 months.

The buffer solution can be stored at room temperature in an appropriately labeled clear or dark bottle. The shelf life is 12 months.

D.21.5 APPLICATION

1. The sample is placed in a glass tray and immersed in the ORO stain solution.
2. With constant shaking/agitation (e.g., using an automatic shaker), treatment should be allowed to proceed for 60–90 minutes or until sufficient fingermark/background contrast is observed.

3. Remove the sample from the stain solution, drain, and transfer to a second glass tray containing the buffer solution.
4. Leave the sample in the buffer solution for several minutes (to soak the item thoroughly and to ensure that a neutral pH is obtained).
5. Rinse the item thoroughly in at least two changes of deionized/distilled water.
6. Allow it to air-dry.

Note: The ORO stain solution can be reused but the used buffer solution should be discarded.

D.21.6 RECORDING RESULTS

Stained marks will be red against a pink background and can be photographed under white light. In some cases, contrast may be improved using illumination with blue–green light (e.g., 500–510 nm) or by using a blue–green barrier filter on the camera.

References

- Beaudoin (2004)
- Salama et al. (2008)
- Frick et al. (2012, 2013)

D.22 PHYSICAL DEVELOPER

D.22.1 USE

The PD reagent—similar to a photographic developer—contains silver ions, a buffered ferrous/ferric redox system, and a detergent–surfactant in an aqueous solution. PD reacts with non-water-soluble material in the latent fingermark deposit, resulting in the deposition of metallic silver along the fingermark ridges. The technique can develop fingermarks on porous surfaces even if the substrate has been wet. As it is a destructive procedure, it should only be applied at the end of a detection sequence. PD may develop fingermarks that are not detected by amino acid reagents such as indanedione and ninhydrin.

Certain paper substrates may trigger the precipitation of silver, leading to heavy background development. A maleic acid prewash is recommended to help avoid this.

Note: High-purity chemicals and good-quality distilled or deionized water must be used for PD preparation and use.

D.22.2 MATERIALS/CHEMICALS REQUIRED

- *N*-dodecylamine acetate
- Synperonic N *or* Tween 20
- Ferric nitrate
- Ammonium ferrous sulfate (ferrous ammonium sulfate)
- Citric acid
- Silver nitrate
- Deionized/distilled water

D.22.3 PREPARATION

Surfactant stock solution (500 mL)

2 g	*N*-dodecylamine acetate and
2 g	Synperonic N *or* Tween 20, dissolved by prolonged stirring in
500 mL	water

Maleic acid solution (1 L)
>   25 g   maleic acid, dissolved in
>   1000 mL   water

Silver nitrate solution (50 mL)
>   10 g   silver nitrate
>   50 mL   water

Redox solution (940 mL)
>   30 g   Ferric nitrate, dissolved by stirring in
>   900 mL   water, then add
>   80 g   ammonium ferrous sulfate, then add
>   20 g   citric acid, and continue stirring until dissolved, then add
>   40 mL   surfactant stock solution

PD working solution (990 mL)
>   50 mL   silver nitrate solution, added slowly with stirring to
>   940 mL   redox solution

Note: The glassware must be scrupulously clean (free of any contaminants, including detergent) and preferably kept only for use with this process. After washing, the glassware should be thoroughly rinsed under cold running tap water, followed by a final rinse with distilled or deionized water.

Note: The Synperonic N formulation can be used immediately after preparation, whereas the Tween 20 formulation should be allowed to age for 24–48 hours prior to use.

D.22.4 Storage and Shelf Life

The surfactant stock solution can be stored at room temperature in an appropriately labeled clear or dark bottle. The shelf life is 2 years. The solution can be filtered if it becomes cloudy.

The redox stock solution can be stored at room temperature in an appropriately labeled clear or dark bottle. The shelf life is 12 months.

The silver nitrate solution is light sensitive and it must be stored out of direct light at room temperature in an appropriately labeled dark bottle. The shelf life is 12 months.

The maleic acid solution can be stored at room temperature in an appropriately labeled clear or dark bottle. The shelf life is 2 years.

The PD working solution is light sensitive and relatively unstable. It should be kept out of direct light in an appropriately labeled dark bottle. For the Synperonic N formulation, the shelf life is from a few days up to around 2 weeks. For the Tween 20 formulation, the shelf life is 2–3 months.

The PD working solution must be tested just prior to use to ensure that it is working correctly. A solution that fails this test should be discarded and a new solution prepared.

D.22.5 Application

To test the PD working solution, use at least 1-month-old latent fingermarks from a good donor on good-quality white paper known to produce good PD results. Only use the PD working solution on casework items if satisfactory results are obtained with these test impressions.

Prepare a minimum of five clean glass dishes as indicated here:

1. Half fill the first dish with distilled/deionized water.
2. Half fill the second dish with maleic acid solution.

3. Half fill the third dish with distilled/deionized water
4. Pour some PD into the fourth dish. The amount of PD depends on the number of exhibits to be treated. The PD solution should be brownish yellow in color and should be clear (*not* cloudy).
5. Half fill the fifth dish with distilled/deionized water
6. Wash the test sample in distilled/deionized water (dish 1) for 10–15 minutes. Discard the water, replace with fresh distilled/deionized water, and wash for a further 10–15 minutes. Repeat with a third wash.
7. Immerse the test sample in the maleic acid solution (dish 2) for 5 minutes.
8. Rinse the test sample in distilled/deionized water (dish 3) for 5–10 minutes.
9. Immerse the test sample in the PD solution (dish 4) and gently rock the dish. Silver will start to deposit onto the paper surface causing the paper to darken. Latent fingermarks will generally cause a higher rate of deposition so they will appear dark gray against a light gray background.
10. When good contrast between the paper background and the fingermarks is obtained, take the test sample out and rinse it in distilled/deionized water (dish 5) for 10–15 minutes. *Do not overdevelop the fingermarks as the PD process cannot be reversed.* Discard the water, replace with fresh distilled/deionized water, and wash for a further 10–15 minutes. At least three water washes are required to remove unreacted PD from the paper.
11. Dry the test sample on clean paper towel at room temperature. Store developed fingermarks in the dark.

If the PD works satisfactorily on the test sample, the exhibits can then be processed (steps 6 through 11). Additional washing steps (step 6) are required for dirty items or items previously treated with an amino acid reagent. If only weak PD development is observed, the process may be repeated (with the omission of the maleic acid treatment).

Note: Development time in the PD working solution depends on the paper substrate, on the silver concentration in the PD, and on the quality of any fingermarks that are present. Good development can take anywhere from 5 minutes to 1 hour.

Note: After each exhibit is processed, the silver concentration decreases and development time increases. When the development time increases substantially (e.g., to more than 1 hour), the PD solution should be discarded.

D.22.6 BLEACH TREATMENT

The contrast in PD developed fingermarks on dark surfaces (e.g., brown paper or dark cardboard) can be improved in some cases by immersing the exhibits in dilute bleach solution (50% household bleach and 50% water). PD developed fingermarks should be photographed before the bleaching process is applied. Exhibits are kept in the bleach solution until good contrast is achieved (generally 2–3 minutes). After the bleach treatment, the items should be thoroughly rinsed in water then allowed to dry.

D.22.7 RECORDING RESULTS

Developed fingermarks are dark gray to black in color and can be photographed under white light.

For paper samples containing optical brighteners, contrast may be improved in some cases using photography in the luminescence mode under UV excitation. Alternatively, the treatment of the paper sample with a luminescent stain, such as Basic Yellow 40, with observation in the luminescence mode may be beneficial. Developed fingermarks will be dark against a bright background.

References

- Phillips et al. (1990)
- Houlgrave et al. (2011)
- Home Office (2014)

D.23 POWDER SUSPENSION

D.23.1 Use

Thick powder suspensions were originally proposed for the development of latent fingermarks on the sticky side of adhesive tape, with the method referred to as sticky-side powder. More recently, however, it was determined that such suspensions can also be effective on nonadhesive substrates such as plastic packaging film. The method is simple to apply and can develop excellent ridge detail on a range of adhesive and nonadhesive surfaces.

The following procedure describes the preparation of a black powder suspension. A white powder suspension based on titanium dioxide, for use on dark surfaces, can be prepared in a similar manner (see, for example, Nic Daéid et al. 2008a). As an alternative, premixed black and white powder suspensions are commercially available.

D.23.2 Materials/Chemicals Required

- Iron (II/III) oxide powder (particle size 0.2–1.0 μm)
- Triton X-100
- Ethylene glycol
- Deionized/distilled water
- Soft brush (e.g., squirrel-hair fingerprint brush)

D.23.3 Preparation

Detergent stock solution (100 mL)

25 mL	Triton X-100, mixed well with
35 mL	ethylene glycol, then add
40 mL	water

Black powder suspension

20 g	iron oxide powder, mixed well with
20 mL	detergent stock solution

D.23.4 Storage and Shelf Life

The detergent stock solution can be stored at room temperature in an appropriately labeled clear or dark bottle. The shelf life is 12 months.

The powder suspension can be stored at room temperature in an appropriately labeled container. The shelf life is 1 month. Mix well just prior to use.

D.23.5 Application

1. Paint the surface with the powder suspension using a soft brush.
2. Leave for 10–20 seconds.
3. Rinse gently under slow running cold water until excess powder suspension has been removed from the background.
4. Repeat steps 1 through 3 if necessary.
5. Allow the item to air-dry.

D.23.6 Recording Results

Developed fingermarks should be photographed in the absorption mode as for marks developed using conventional fingerprint powder.

References

- Bratton and Gregus (1997)
- Downham et al. (2012)
- Home Office (2014)

D.24   RHODAMINE 6G

D.24.1   Use

R6G is an efficient luminescent dye that can be used as a general-purpose stain for cyanoacrylate-developed marks. Care should be taken to ensure that the surface itself does not absorb the stain to produce a luminescent background. This is a water-based R6G formulation that can produce excellent results on a range of substrates.

D.24.2   Materials/Chemicals Required

- R6G
- Isopropanol
- Methyl ethyl ketone (MEK)
- Deionized/distilled water

D.24.3   Preparation

Stock solution (500 mL)

0.2 g	R6G, dissolved in
200 mL	isopropanol, then add
300 mL	MEK

Working solution (1 L)

250 mL	stock solution, diluted with
750 mL	water

It is recommended to prepare a large quantity of staining solution (e.g., bucket full) in order to totally immerse exhibits rather than pouring the staining solution in a tray just for one use.

D.24.4   Storage and Shelf Life

The stock and working solutions should be stored at room temperature in an appropriately labeled clear or dark bottle (or sealed plastic bucket for the working solution).

The shelf life for both solutions is 2 years.

D.24.5   Application

Note: It is recommended that cyanoacrylate-fumed exhibits are left overnight before treatment with a stain solution.

1. Immerse the cyanoacrylate-fumed exhibit in the stain solution for 10–20 seconds. (Alternatively, the stain solution can be applied locally using a pipette.)
2. Rinse thoroughly in water and allow it to air-dry.
3. In the case of poor photoluminescence in treated marks, repeat the staining procedure (steps 1 and 2).

Note: If the working solution becomes contaminated and dirty, it should be replaced immediately.

D.24.6 Recording Results

Examine stained fingermarks in the luminescence mode using excitation at 505 nm while wearing orange goggles.

Photography can be conducted using either

1. Excitation at 500–510 nm and either a KV550 long-pass or 560–570 nm bandpass barrier filter
2. Excitation at 530 nm and an OG590 long-pass or 580–600 nm bandpass barrier filter

Reference

- Stoilovic and Lennard (2012)

D.25 RUTHENIUM TETROXIDE

D.25.1 Use

Ruthenium tetroxide (RTX) vapor, generated by the mixing of two stock solutions, can be used to develop relatively fresh fingermarks on a wide range of nonporous, semiporous, and porous surfaces. RTX reacts with the unsaturated fats (sebaceous deposit) in the latent fingermarks. The method is simple to use and developed fingermarks are permanent in nature, with a dark-gray coloration resulting. While RTX is generally not as sensitive as routine techniques on conventional surfaces, it may be considered for certain problematic surfaces, such as paper banknotes, expanded polystyrene cups, wax paper surfaces, or thermal paper. It may also produce results on leather and human skin.

As an alternative to the procedure described here, commercial RTX kits are available that include a developer (RTX solution), a fumer, and a portable air pump. The kit can be used to generate RTX vapor. Alternatively, items can be dipped directly in the developer or the developer applied with a spray.

D.25.2 Materials/Chemicals Required

- Ruthenium (III) chloride hydrate
- Ceric ammonium nitrate
- Deionized/distilled water

D.25.3 Preparation

Ruthenium chloride stock solution (100 mL)
    0.1 g   ruthenium (III) chloride hydrate, dissolved in
    100 mL   water

Ceric ammonium nitrate stock solution (100 mL)
    11.3 g   ceric ammonium nitrate, dissolved in
    100 mL   water

D.25.4 Storage and Shelf Life

The stock solutions should be stored at room temperature in appropriately labeled clear or dark bottles.

The shelf life for both solutions is 12 months.

D.25.5 Application

Equal amounts of ruthenium chloride and ceric ammonium nitrate stock solutions are mixed together in a small open dish (e.g., Petri dish). The dish is then placed in an enclosed space (e.g., glass fuming cabinet) containing the exhibits. The exhibits are exposed to the RTX fumes that are slowly generated from the mixed solution.

Latent fingermarks are developed as dark gray images over several minutes (10–20 minutes in larger chambers).

Note: Treatment should be done in a fume cupboard as RTX vapor is irritating to the eyes and respiratory tract.

Note: RTX treatment may preclude any subsequent fingermark development by techniques such as cyanoacrylate fuming or IND-Zn. If necessary, tests should be conducted on a similar substrate before treatment of the evidential item.

D.25.6 Recording Results

Developed fingermarks are dark gray in color and should be photographed under white light.

References

- Mashiko et al. (1991)
- Mashiko and Miyamoto (1998)

D.26 SILVER NITRATE

D.26.1 Use

Silver nitrate solution reacts with the chloride (salt) component of latent fingermarks on porous surfaces. The technique can only be used on relatively fresh latent marks (up to 2 weeks old) since the chloride component diffuses rapidly with time. It is not a sensitive technique, but is simple to apply and can produce results with fresh latent fingermarks on some surfaces, e.g., cardboard and untreated wood.

Note: The silver nitrate method is destructive. It should be the last technique in any sequential reagent application. All fingermarks developed by other techniques must be photographed prior to the silver nitrate method being applied.

D.26.2 Materials/Chemicals Required

- Silver nitrate
- Methanol

D.26.3 Preparation

Silver nitrate working solution (2% w/v; 100 mL)
     2 g   silver nitrate, dissolved in
     100 mL   methanol

D.26.4 Storage and Shelf Life

The solution should be kept in an appropriately labeled dark bottle, out of direct light. The shelf life is up to 6 months.

D.26.5 APPLICATION

The solution can be applied as for other liquid reagents, i.e., by dipping the item in a tray of solution or by application with a brush, spray, or pipette. After application, exhibits should be left to air-dry. Exhibits should then be exposed to an UV-rich light source, e.g., sunlight or light from a mercury lamp. The UV band on a filtered light source can also be used for this purpose. The development should be continuously monitored. When good ridge detail is obtained, UV exposure should cease.

D.26.6 RECORDING RESULTS

Photography must be carried out *immediately* since the ongoing development of a dark background over time may obliterate any developed fingermarks. Treated exhibits remain light sensitive and must be stored in total darkness.

The contrast in weakly developed marks may be improved, in some cases, via treatment with dilute PD followed by thorough rinsing with water.

References

- Lennard and Margot (1988)
- Nic Daéid et al. (2009)

D.27 SINGLE-METAL DEPOSITION

D.27.1 USE

Single-metal deposition (SMD) has been proposed as a simpler alternative to MMD. While MMD offers good sensitivity across a range of surface, it is time-consuming and requires the use of many reagents. SMD replaces the silver enhancement of the gold colloids by a gold enhancement procedure. This reduces the number of baths by one as well as the number of reagents and their cost. The SMD process is less labor intensive and offers quasi-identical results to MMD, thus making it an attractive alternative to MMD.

Note: Silanization is recommended for all glassware used to prepare and employ SMD. Refer to the entry for MMD II.

D.27.2 MATERIALS/CHEMICALS REQUIRED

- Gold chloride (tetrachloroauric acid)
- Sodium citrate
- Citric acid
- Tannic acid
- Tween 20
- Hydroxylamine hydrochloride
- Ultrapure deionized/distilled water
- pH meter

D.27.3 PREPARATION: COLLOIDAL GOLD

Gold chloride stock solution (10 mL)
    1 g   gold chloride (tetrachloroauric acid), dissolved in
    10 mL   water

Sodium citrate stock solution (100 mL)
    1 g   sodium citrate, dissolved in
    100 mL water

Tannic acid stock solution (100 mL)

    1 g   Tannic acid, dissolved in
    100 mL Water

Citric acid stock solution (100 mL)

    9.6 g   citric acid, dissolved in
    100 mL water

Colloidal gold working solution (500 mL)

1. 0.5 mL   gold chloride stock solution, added to
   400 mL water and the solution heated to 60°C
2. 20 mL   sodium citrate stock solution, mixed with
   75 mL   water and
   0.1 mL   tannic acid stock solution, and the solution heated to 60°C
3. With the two solutions at 60°C, quickly add the second solution to the first while mixing vigorously.
4. Bring the mixture to boiling point; the solution should turn ruby red.
5. Allow to cool to room temperature.
6. Adjust the volume to 500 mL by the addition of water.
7. Add 0.5 mL of Tween 20 with stirring.
8. Using a pH meter, adjust the pH to 2.7 via the addition of citric acid solution.

D.27.4 STORAGE AND SHELF LIFE: COLLOIDAL GOLD

The stock solutions should be stored in a refrigerator in appropriately labeled clear or dark bottles. The shelf life is 6 months.

The colloidal gold working solution should be stored in a refrigerator in a scrupulously clean and appropriately labeled plastic bottle. The shelf life is 6 months.

The colloidal gold solution should be restored to room temperature just prior to use.

D.27.5 PREPARATION: GOLD ENHANCEMENT

Hydroxylamine hydrochloride stock solution (100 mL)

    2 g   hydroxylamine hydrochloride, dissolved in
    100 mL water

Gold enhancement working solution (200 mL)

    0.2 mL   gold chloride stock solution (used in colloidal gold preparation), diluted with
    200 mL water, then add (with intense stirring)
    0.2 mL   hydroxylamine hydrochloride stock solution

Note: The gold enhancement working solution should be prepared just prior to use.

D.27.6 STORAGE AND SHELF LIFE: GOLD ENHANCEMENT

The hydroxylamine hydrochloride stock solution can be stored at room temperature in an appropriately labeled clear or dark bottle. The shelf life is 6 months.

The gold enhancement working solution is unstable and must be used immediately after preparation.

D.27.7 APPLICATION

Note: Just prior to use, the pH of the colloidal gold working solution should be checked and adjusted if necessary (by adding citric acid stock solution).

1. Prepare five scrupulously clean glass dishes arranged as follows.

2. Rinse the item in deionized/distilled water (dish 1) for 2–3 minutes.
3. Treat the item in the colloidal gold solution (dish 2) for 5–15 minutes with gentle agitation.
4. Thoroughly rinse the item in deionized/distilled water (dish 3) for several minutes.
5. Transfer the item to freshly prepared gold enhancement solution (dish 4) and treat for at least 20 minutes using intense agitation. Additional time can be used if necessary.
6. Thoroughly rinse the item in several changes of deionized/distilled water (dish 5).
7. Air-dry at room temperature, and then record any developed marks.

D.27.8 RECORDING RESULTS

Developed fingermarks are dark gray and can be photographed under white light.

Reference

- Stauffer et al. (2007)
- Durussel et al. (2009)

D.28 SINGLE-METAL DEPOSITION II

D.28.1 USE

Further optimization of the SMD technique has led to the development of SMD II, which is simpler and faster to apply as it does not require the monitoring of temperature and pH. Compared to the original SMD method, SMD II is also a more effective fingermark development method and more robust for the processing of porous substrates such as paper.

Note: The use of silanized glassware is no longer required in the SMD II protocol.

D.28.2 MATERIALS/CHEMICALS REQUIRED

- Gold chloride (tetrachloroauric acid)
- Sodium citrate
- Sodium hydroxide
- L-Aspartic acid
- Citric acid monohydrate
- Hydroxylamine hydrochloride
- Tween 20
- Ultrapure deionized/distilled water

D.28.3 PREPARATION: COLLOIDAL GOLD

Gold chloride stock solution (10 mL)
    1 g   gold chloride (tetrachloroauric acid), dissolved in
    10 mL water

Sodium citrate stock solution (100 mL)
    2 g   sodium citrate, dissolved in
    100 mL water

Aspartic acid stock solution (50 mL)

      0.24 g   sodium hydroxide, and
      0.76 g   aspartic acid, dissolved with intense stirring in
      50 mL   water

Citric acid stock solution (50 mL)

      10.5 g   citric acid monohydrate, dissolved in
      50 mL   water

Colloidal gold working solution (2.5 L)

1. 1 mL   gold chloride stock solution, added with stirring to
   460 mL   water and the solution heated to boiling point
2. 42 mL   sodium citrate solution, mixed with
   0.42 mL aspartic acid solution
3. When the first solution is boiling, quickly add the second solution.
4. Keep heating the combined solution until it turns deep ruby red.
5. Adjust the volume to 2.5 L by the addition of water.
6. Add 2.5 mL of Tween 20 with stirring.

D.28.4   STORAGE AND SHELF LIFE: COLLOIDAL GOLD

The stock solutions should be stored in a refrigerator in appropriately labeled clear or dark bottles. The shelf life is 6 months.

The colloidal gold working solution should be stored in a refrigerator in a scrupulously clean and appropriately labeled polypropylene bottle. The shelf life is 6 months.

The colloidal gold solution should be restored to room temperature just prior to use.

D.28.5   PREPARATION: GOLD ENHANCEMENT

Hydroxylamine hydrochloride stock solution (50 mL)

      1 g   hydroxylamine hydrochloride, dissolved in
      50 mL   water

Gold enhancement working solution (200 mL)

      0.2 mL   gold chloride stock solution (used in colloidal gold preparation), diluted with
      200 mL   water, then add (with intense stirring)
      0.2 mL   hydroxylamine hydrochloride solution

Note: The gold enhancement working solution should be prepared just prior to use.

D.28.6   STORAGE AND SHELF LIFE: GOLD ENHANCEMENT

The hydroxylamine hydrochloride stock solution can be stored at room temperature in an appropriately labeled clear or dark bottle. The shelf life is 6 months.

The gold enhancement working solution is unstable and must be used immediately after preparation.

D.28.7   APPLICATION

Note: Before processing samples, the pH of the colloidal gold working solution must be adjusted using the recommended amount of citric acid stock solution as indicated here.

1. Prepare five scrupulously clean glass dishes arranged as follows.

2. Remove the required amount of colloidal gold working solution from the refrigerator and allow it to warm to room temperature.
3. Adjust the pH by adding, with constant stirring, 3 mL of citric acid stock solution for every 100 mL of colloidal gold working solution.
4. Rinse the item in deionized/distilled water (dish 1) for 2–5 minutes.
5. Treat the item in the colloidal gold solution (dish 2) for 20 minutes with gentle agitation.
6. Thoroughly rinse the item in deionized/distilled water (dish 3) for several minutes.
7. Transfer the item to freshly prepared gold enhancement solution (dish 4) and treat for at least 20 minutes using intense agitation. Immersion time can be extended if necessary.
8. Thoroughly rinse the item in several changes of deionized/distilled water (dish 5).
9. Air-dry at room temperature, and then record any developed marks.

D.28.8 RECORDING RESULTS

Developed fingermarks are dark gray and can be photographed under white light.

Reference

- Moret and Bécue (2015)

D.29 SMALL PARTICLE REAGENT

D.29.1 USE

Small particle reagent (SPR) is a wet powdering technique that can be used to develop latent fingermarks on wet nonporous surfaces. Conventional gray SPR is prepared as a suspension of molybdenum disulfide powder in dilute detergent solution. Alternatively, commercially available SPR kits—available as dark, white, and fluorescent versions—can be employed.

Note: Where possible, the surface should be allowed to dry so that conventional detection techniques can be applied.

D.29.2 MATERIALS/CHEMICALS REQUIRED

- Molybdenum disulfide powder (*must be fine grade*)
- Tergitol 8
- Deionized/distilled water
- Spray system (e.g., handheld garden spray)

D.29.3 PREPARATION

Detergent stock solution (500 mL)
      4 mL   Tergitol 8, dissolved by mixing with
      500 mL water

Powder stock suspension (100 mL)
      15 g   molybdenum disulfide powder, suspended in
      100 mL detergent stock solution

Powder working suspension (1 L)
      100 mL powder stock suspension, mixed well with
      900 mL water

D.29.4 STORAGE AND SHELF LIFE

The solutions/suspensions can be stored at room temperature in appropriately labeled clear or dark bottles. The shelf life is 12 months but the suspensions must be mixed well just prior to use.

D.29.5 Application

The best method for application of SPR is by spraying.

The spray bottle must be shaken well before application (to resuspend the powder). After treatment, the surface is rinsed with water to remove excess SPR. The treatment may be repeated several times if necessary in order to obtain sufficient contrast.

D.29.6 Recording Results

Fingermarks developed using SPR should be left to dry and then photographed and lifted as for marks developed using conventional fingerprint powder.

References

- Goode and Morris (1983)
- Stoilovic and Lennard (2012)
- Home Office (2014)

D.30 SUDAN BLACK

D.30.1 Use

Sudan black is a dye that stains sebaceous/greasy material to produce a blue–black image. The method can be applied at the crime scene—on nonporous and semiporous surfaces—at the end of the examination sequence. Sudan black may be useful on surfaces contaminated with foodstuffs, oils, and other greasy substances.

D.30.2 Materials/Chemicals Required

- Sudan black (solvent black 3)
- 1-Methoxy-2-propanol (propylene glycol monomethyl ether; PGME)
- Deionized/distilled water
- Filter paper
- Plastic wash bottle (for scene application)

D.30.3 Preparation

Sudan black working solution (1 L)
  10 g   sudan black, dissolved by stirring in
  500 mL   1-methoxy-2-propanol, then dilute with
  500 mL   water

Continue to stir for at least an hour and then filter through filter paper.

D.30.4 Storage and Shelf Life

Store at room temperature in an appropriately labeled clear or dark bottle.

The shelf life is 1 month (after which the staining intensity produced will decrease).

D.30.5 Application

Treat the item by immersion for between 10 seconds and 1 minute (depending on the surface and the degree of background staining). For fixed surfaces, the sudan black solution can be applied using a wash bottle. Rinse with water and allow to dry.

D.30.6 RECORDING RESULTS

Stained marks will be blue–black in color and can be photographed under white light. In some cases, improved contrast may be achieved using an orange barrier filter.

References

- Cadd et al. (2013)
- Home Office (2014)

REFERENCES

Allman, D. S., Maggs, S. J., and Pounds, C. A. (1992), *The Use of Colloidal Gold/Multi-Metal Deposition for the Detection of Latent Fingerprints—A Preliminary Evaluation*, HOCRE Report No. 747, Aldermaston, U.K.: Home Office Central Research Establishment.

Allman, D. S. and Pounds, C. A. (1991), *Diaminobenzidine: A Simple, Safe and Sensitive Method for the Enhancement of Blood Marks at Scene of Crime and in the Laboratory*, HOCRE Report No. 733, Aldermaston, U.K.: Home Office Central Research Establishment.

Allman, D. S. and Pounds, C. A. (1992), *The Specificity of Diaminobenzidine for the Detection of Blood*, HOCRE Report No. No. 771, Aldermaston, U.K.: Home Office Central Research Establishment.

Beaudoin, A. (2004), New technique for revealing latent fingerprints on wet, porous surfaces: Oil red O, *J. Forensic Ident.*, 54, 413–421.

Braasch, K., de la Hunty, M., Deppe, J., Spindler, X., Cantú, A.A., Maynard, P., Lennard, C., and Roux, C. (2013), Nile red: Alternative to physical developer for the detection of latent fingermarks on wet porous surfaces? *Forensic Sci. Int.*, 230, 74–80.

Bratton, R. and Gregus, J. (1997), Development of a black powder method to process adhesive tapes, *Fingerprint Whorld*, 23(87), 21–23.

Cadd, S. J., Bleay, S. M., and Sears, V. G. (2013), Evaluation of the solvent black 3 fingermark enhancement reagent: Part 2—Investigation of the optimum formulation and application parameters, *Sci. Justice*, 53, 131–143.

Dominick, A. J. and Laing, K. (2011), A comparison of six fingerprint enhancement techniques for the recovery of latent fingerprints from unfired cartridge cases, *J. Forensic Ident.*, 61, 155–165.

Downham, R. P., Mehmet, S., and Sears, V. G. (2012), A pseudo-operational investigation into the development of latent fingerprints on flexible plastic packaging films, *J. Forensic Ident.*, 62, 661–682.

Fitzi, T., Fischer, R., Moret, S., and Bécue, A. (2014), Fingermark detection on thermal papers: Proposition of an updated processing sequence, *J. Forensic Ident.*, 64, 329–350.

Flynn, K., Maynard, P., Du Pasquier, E., Lennard, C., Stoilovic, M., and Roux, C. (2004), Evaluation of iodine-benzoflavone and ruthenium tetroxide spray reagents for the detection of latent fingermarks at the crime scene, *J. Forensic Sci.*, 49, 707–715.

Frick, A. A., Fritz, P., Lewis, S. W., and van Bronswijk, W. (2012), A modified oil red O formulation for the detection of latent fingermarks on porous substrates, *J. Forensic Ident.*, 62, 623–641.

Frick, A. A., Fritz, P., Lewis, S. W., and van Bronswijk, W. (2013), Sequencing of a modified oil red O development technique for the detection of latent fingermarks on paper surfaces, *J. Forensic Ident.*, 63, 369–385.

Girelli, C. M. A., Lobo, B. J. M., Cunha, A. G., Freitas, J. C. C., and Emmerich, F. G. (2015), Comparison of practical techniques to develop latent fingermarks on fired and unfired cartridge cases, *Forensic Sci. Int.*, 250, 17–26.

Goode, G. C. and Morris, J. R. (1983), *Latent Fingerprints: A Review of Their Origin, Composition and Methods for Detection*, AWRE Report No. 022/83, Aldermaston, U.K.: Atomic Weapons Research Establishment.

Haque, F., Westland, A. D., and Kerr, F. M. (1983), An improved non-destructive method for the detection of latent fingerprints on documents with iodine–7,8-benzoflavone, *Forensic Sci. Int.*, 21, 79–83.

Hardwick, S. W., Kent, T., and Sears, V. G. (1990), *Fingerprint Detection by Fluorescence Examination: A Guide to Operational Implementation*, Sandridge, U.K.: Home Office Police Scientific Development Branch.

Herod, D. W. and Menzel, E. R. (1982), Laser detection of latent fingerprints: Ninhydrin followed by zinc chloride, *J. Forensic Sci.*, 27, 513–518.

Home Office. (1998), *Manual of Fingerprint Development Techniques*, 2nd ed. (revised January 2001), Sandridge, U.K.: Home Office Police Scientific Development Branch.

Home Office. (2014), *Fingermark Visualisation Manual*, Sandridge, U.K.: Home Office Centre for Applied Science and Technology.

Houlgrave, S., Andress, M., and Ramotowski, R. (2011), Comparison of different physical developer working solutions—Part I: Longevity studies, *J. Forensic Ident.*, 61, 621–639.

Jones, N., Lennard, C., Stoilovic, M., and Roux, C. (2003), An evaluation of multimetal deposition II, *J. Forensic Ident.*, 53, 444–488.

Lee, J. L., Bleay, S. M., Sears, V. G., Mehmet, S., and Croxton R. (2009), Evaluation of the dimethylaminocinnamaldehyde contact transfer process and its application to fingerprint development on thermal papers, *J. Forensic Ident.*, 59, 545–568.

Lennard, C. J. and Margot, P. A. (1988), Sequencing of reagents for the improved visualization of latent fingerprints, *J. Forensic Ident.*, 38, 197–210.

Marriott, C., Lee, R., Wilkes, Z., Comber, B., Spindler, X., Roux, C., and Lennard, C. (2014), Evaluation of fingermark detection sequences on paper substrates, *Forensic Sci. Int.*, 236, 30–37.

Mashiko, K., German, E. R., Motojima, K., and Colman, C. D. (1991), RTX: A new ruthenium tetroxide fuming procedure, *J. Forensic Ident.*, 41, 429–436.

Mashiko, K. and Miyamoto, T. (1998), Latent fingerprint processing by the ruthenium tetroxide method, *J. Forensic Ident.*, 48, 279–290.

Moret, S. and Bécue, A. (2015), Single-metal deposition for fingermark detection—A simpler and more efficient protocol, *J. Forensic Ident.*, 65, 118–137.

Nic Daéid, N., Carter, S., and Laing, K. (2008a), Comparison of three types of white powder suspensions for the recovery of fingerprints on wetted nonporous surfaces, *J. Forensic Ident.*, 58, 590–599.

Nic Daéid, N., Buchanan, H.A.S., and Laing, K. (2009), Evaluation of available techniques for the recovery of latent fingerprints from untreated plywood surfaces, *J. Forensic Ident.*, 59, 441–465.

Phillips, C. E., Cole, D. O., and Jones, G. W. (1990), Physical developer: A practical and productive latent print developer, *J. Forensic Ident.*, 40, 135–147.

Pounds, C. A., Allman, D. S., and Wild, F. M. (1992), *The Development of Latent Fingerprints Using an Iodine Spray Technique*, HOCRE Report No. 746, Aldermaston, U.K.: Home Office Central Research Establishment.

Ramotowski, R. S. (1996), Fluorescence visualization of latent fingerprints on paper using p-Dimethylaminocinnamaldehyde (PDMAC), in *Proceedings of the International Symposium on Fingerprint Detection and Identification*, Israel National Police, Ne'urim, Israel, June 26–30, 1995, pp. 91–97.

Salama, J., Aumeer-Donovan, S., Lennard, C., and Roux C. (2008), Evaluation of the fingermark reagent oil red O as a possible replacement for physical developer, *J. Forensic Ident.*, 58, 203–237.

Schnetz, B. and Margot, P. A. (2001), Technical note: Latent fingermarks, colloidal gold and multimetal deposition (MMD): Optimisation of the method, *Forensic Sci. Int.*, 118, 21–28.

Sears, V. G., Butcher, C. P. G., and Fitzgerald, L. A. (2005), Enhancement of fingerprints in blood. Part 3: Reactive techniques, acid yellow 7, and process sequences, *J. Forensic Ident.*, 55, 741–763.

Sears, V. G. and Prizeman, T. M. (2000), Enhancement of fingerprints in blood, Part 1: The optimization of amido black, *J. Forensic Ident.*, 50, 470–480.

Stauffer, E., Bécue, A., Singh, K.V., Thampi, K.R., Champod, C., and Margot, P. (2007), Single-metal deposition (SMD) as a latent fingermark enhancement technique: an alternative to multimetal deposition (MMD), *Forensic Sci. Int.*, 168, e5–e9.

Stoilovic, M. (1993), Improved method for DFO development of latent fingerprints, *Forensic Sci. Int.*, 60, 141–153.

Stoilovic, M., Kobus, H. J., Margot, P. A., and Warrener, R. N. (1986), Improved enhancement of ninhydrin developed fingerprints by cadmium complexation using low temperature photoluminescence techniques, *J. Forensic Sci.*, 31, 432–445.

Stoilovic, M. and Lennard, C. (2012), *Fingermark Detection and Enhancement*, 6th ed., Canberra, Australian Capital Territory, Australia: National Centre for Forensic Studies.

Stoilovic, M., Lennard, C., Wallace-Kunkel, C., and Roux, C. (2007), Evaluation of a 1,2-indanedione formulation containing zinc chloride for improved fingermark detection on paper, *J. Forensic Ident.*, 57, 4–18.

Appendix E: Abbreviations*

5MTN	5-Methylthioninhydrin
[A]	Ampere
[Å]	Angström
AAFS	American Academy of Forensic Sciences
ABTS	2,2′-Azino-bis(3-ethylbenzothiazoline-6-sulfonic acid)
ACE-V	Analysis, comparison, evaluation, and verification
ADC	Analog-to-digital converter
AFIS	Automated fingerprint identification system
AFM	Atomic force microscopy
a.k.a.	Also known as
ALS	Alternate light source, a nonlaser FLS
amu	Atomic mass unit
Anon.	Anonymous
ANSI	American National Standards Institute
AOT	Aerosol OT (dioctyl sodium sulfosuccinate; DOSS)
APTES	3-Aminopropyltriethoxysilane
ASA	American Standards Association
ASCLD	American Society of Crime Laboratory Directors
ATR	Attenuated total reflectance
atto	A decimal fraction of international (SI) units (e.g., an attogram is 10^{-18} g)
AWRE	Atomic Weapons Research Establishment (UK)
AY7	Acid yellow 7
BMP	Bitmap
BN	Bayesian network
BPS	Black powder suspension
BW	Bandwidth
BY40	Basic yellow 40
c	Speed of light, approximately 300 million m/s
CA	Cyanoacrylate
CAST	Centre for Applied Science and Technology (UK)
CCD	Charged-coupled device
[cd]	Candela
CD	Compact disc
CFC	Chlorofluorocarbon
CMOS	Complementary metal-oxide semiconductor
CR	Crown rump
CW	Central wavelength
DAB	Diaminobenzidine
DART-MS	Direct analysis in real-time mass spectrometry
DESI	Desorption electrospray ionization
DFO	1,8-Diazafluoren-9-one
DMAC	Dimethylaminocinnamaldehyde
DNA	Deoxyribonucleic acid
DOSS	Dioctyl sodium sulfosuccinate (Aerosol OT; AOT)

---

* Square brackets are used to indicate physical units.

dpi	Dots per inch
DSLR	Digital single-lens reflex (camera)
DSP	Digital signal processor
DVD	Digital video disc
DVI	Disaster victim identification
DZ	Dizygotic
EDTA	Ethylenediaminetetraacetic acid
EESAG	Electronic Evidence Specialist Advisory Group (Australia)
EFS	Extended feature set
EGA	Estimated gestational age
EM	Expectation maximization
ENFSI	European Network of Forensic Science Institutes
ε	Greek letter epsilon for energy
ESDA	Electrostatic detection apparatus
EV	Exposure value
EW	Edge wavelength
EWCA	England and Wales Court of Appeal
EXIF	Exchangeable image file
FBI	Federal Bureau of Investigation (USA)
femto	A decimal fraction of international (SI) units (e.g., a femtogram is 10^{-15} g)
FFT	Fast Fourier transform
FLS	Forensic light source (an ALS if not laser-based)
FRS	Friction ridge skin
FT	Fourier transform
FTIR	Fourier transform infrared
[g]	Gram (1000 g = 1 kg)
GB	Gun blue
GC	Gas chromatography
GIF	Graphic interchange format
giga	A unit prefix in the international (SI) units denoting a factor of one billion (10^9) as in memory capacity in informatics expressed as gigabytes (GB)
GPS	Global positioning system
GRIT	Glass recovery investigative technique
GV	Gentian violet
GYRO	Green, yellow, red, and orange system to annotate marks and prints
H	Height
HBW	Half bandwidth
HCFC	Hydrochlorofluorocarbon
HDPE	High-density polyethylene
HFC	Hydrofluorocarbon
HFE	Hydrofluoroether
HOCRE	Home Office Central Research Establishment (UK)
HOPSDB	Home Office Police Scientific Development Branch (UK)
HOSDB	Home Office Scientific Development Branch (UK)
HSI	Hyperspectral imaging
I	Intensity
IAFIS	Integrated automated fingerprint identification system
IAI	International Association for Identification
ICPO	International Criminal Police Organization
ID	Identification
IEEGFI	Interpol European Expert Group on Fingerprint Identification

IFRG	International Fingerprint Research Group
INC	Inconclusive
IND	1,2-Indanedione
IND-Zn	Indanedione–zinc
IR	Infrared
ISO	International Organization for Standardization
JEIDA	Japan Electronic Industry Development Association
JPEG (JPG)	Joint Photographic Experts Group file interchange format
[K]	Kelvin (0 K = –273°C)
kilo	A unit prefix in the international (SI) units denoting a factor of one thousand as in kilogram (kg = 1000 g) and kilometer (km = 1000 m)
[kg]	Kilogram (1 kg = 1000 g)
[L]	Liter (1 L = 1000 mL)
λ	Greek letter lambda for wavelength
Laser	Light amplification by stimulated emission of radiation
LCD	Liquid crystal display
LDPE	Low-density polyethylene
LED	Light-emitting diode
LCV	Leucocrystal violet
LMG	Leucomalachite green
LR	Likelihood ratio
[m]	Meter
MALDI	Matrix-assisted laser desorption/ionization
MBD	7-(p-Methoxybenzylamino)-4-nitrobenz-2-oxa-1,3-diazole
mega	A unit prefix in the international (SI) units denoting a factor of one million as in megapixels (1,000,000 pixels)
MEK	Methyl ethyl ketone
micro	A decimal fraction of international (SI) units of one million (e.g., a microgram is 10^{-6} g a micrometer 10^{-6} m)
milli	A decimal fraction of international (SI) units of one thousand (e.g., a milligram is 10^{-3} g, 1 millimeter is 10^{-3} m)
[mL]	Milliliter (1000 mL = 1 L)
MMD	Multimetal deposition
[mol]	Mole
MP	Megapixels (1,000,000 pixels)
MPD	Modified physical developer
mRNA	Messenger RNA
MS	Mass spectrometry
μ	Greek letter mu for micro
MZ	Monozygotic
nano	A decimal fraction of international (SI) units of one billion (e.g., a nanogram is 10^{-9} g, 1 nanometer = 10^{-9} m)
NCIC	National Crime Information Center (FBI, USA)
NFSTC	National Forensic Science Technology Center (USA)
NIH	National Institutes of Health (USA)
NIJ	National Institute of Justice (USA)
NIN	Ninhydrin
NIR	Near-infrared
NIST	National Institute of Standards and Technology (USA)
NMR	Nuclear magnetic resonance
NR	Nile red

NRC	National Research Council (USA)
ν	Greek letter nu for frequency
NV	No value
NWSD	Non water-soluble deposit
OC-LIBS	Optical catapulting laser-induced breakdown spectroscopy
ODP	Ozone depletion potential
OH&S	Occupational health and safety
OIG	Office of the Inspector General (USA)
ORO	Oil Red O
PAMAM	Poly(amidoamine)
PCA	Principal component analysis
PCR	Polymerase chain reaction
PD	Physical developer
PDR	Primary dermal ridge
PER	Primary epidermal ridge
PET	Polyethylene terephthalate
PETN	Pentaerythritol tetranitrate
PGME	Propylene glycol monomethyl ether (1-methoxy-2-propanol)
PiAnoS	Picture annotation system
pico	A decimal fraction of international (SI) units of one trillion (e.g., a picogram is 10^{-12} g, 1 picometer = 10^{-12} m)
pixel	Picture element
POI	Person of interest
ppi	Pixels per inch
PSDB	Police Scientific Development Branch (UK)
PVC	Polyvinyl chloride
PVDF	Polyvinylidene fluoride
PVP	Polyvinylpyrrolidone
QD	Quantum dot
R6G	Rhodamine 6G
RCMP	Royal Canadian Mounted Police
RDX	Hexahydro-1,3,5-trinitro-1,3,5-triazine
RGB	Red, green, and blue
RH	Relative humidity
RMED	Rate of misleading evidence in favor of the defense proposition (H_d)
RMEP	Rate of misleading evidence in favor of the prosecution proposition (H_p)
RNA	Ribonucleic acid
ROI	Region of interest
RP	Ruhemann's purple (ninhydrin reaction product)
RTX	Ruthenium tetroxide
RUVIS	Reflected ultraviolet imaging system
SALDI	Surface-assisted laser desorption/ionization
SCRO	Scottish Criminal Records Office
SCU	Serious crimes unit
SDS	Safety data sheet
[sec]	Second
SEM	Scanning electron microscope
SI	Système International (International System of Units = SI units)
SIMS	Secondary ion mass spectrometry
SKP	Scanning Kelvin probe
SLR	Single-lens reflex (camera)

SMANZFL	Senior Managers of Australian and New Zealand Forensic Laboratories
SMD	Single-metal deposition
S/N	Signal-to-noise ratio
SNP	Spanish National Police
spi	Samples per inch
SPR	Small particle reagent
SR-FTIR	Synchrotron radiation–based Fourier transform infrared
STR	Short tandem repeat
SWGFAST	Scientific Working Group on Friction Ridge Analysis, Study and Technology (USA)
SWGIT	Scientific Working Group on Imaging Technology (USA)
tera	A unit prefix in the international (SI) units denoting a factor of one trillion (used in informatics as in terabytes = 10^{12} bytes)
TGA	Thioglycolic acid (also referred to as mercaptoacetic acid)
TIFF (TIF)	Tagged image file format
TNT	2,4,6-Trinitrotoluene
ToF	Time-of-flight
UCP	Upconverting phosphor
ULW	Universal latent workstation
UV	Ultraviolet
VCA	Vacuum cyanoacrylate
VEO	Value for exclusion only
VID	Value for identification
VIS	Visible
VMD	Vacuum metal deposition
[W]	Watt
W	Width
WoE	Weight of evidence
WPS	White powder suspension
WSD	Water-soluble deposit

Index

A

Abnormal friction ridge skin
  congenital malformations, 17
  flexion creases, 17, 19
  hand malformations, 19
Absorption mode
  color wheel, 145–146
  ninhydrin-developed fingermark, 147–148
  schematic representation, 146–147
  selective, 144–145
ACE-V methodology
  fingerprint patterns, three levels of, 35–38
  Mairs' family tree, 38
  scientific method, 34–35
  simple flow diagram, 34
Acid yellow 7 (AY7), 275–276, 373–374
Adhesive tape/label
  cyanoacrylate, 264
  gentian violet formulation, 261–262
  Liqui-Drox solution, 264
  operational difficulties, 260–261
  powder suspensions, 262–263
  recommended detection sequence, 264–265
  types, 260
Adobe Photoshop, 173
Age estimation
  case study, 324–325
  dehydration, 322
  factors, 326
  latent fingermark, 323–324
Alginate, 276
Amido black, 275–276, 374–376
Analysis process, fingerprint identification
  conclusion variability, 53–55
  decision process
    assessment, 51 52
    schematic representation, 52
    suitability approaches, 51, 53
  documentation
    GYRO, 45–46
    PiAnoS, 46–47
    SWGFAST guidance, 46–47, 49
    systematical, 49
    ULW, 46
  influencing factors
    clarity bridge transition, 44
    reproducibility questions, 43–44
    third-level detail, reproducibility of, 45
  probabilities, 41
  purpose, 39–40
  quality metrics, 50
  reproducibility, 40
  specificity and quality, 41
  tolerances, 40–41
Anatomical positioning, 56
Antibodies, 250–251
Aptamers, 251

Ardrox®, 227–228
Atomic weight/mass, 129–131
Automated fingerprint identification systems (AFISs)
  auto-classification algorithm, 61
  comparison process, 67
  evaluation process, 102
  finger number, 56
  improvements, 345
  probability, 111–112
  quality metrics, 50
  technical issues, 315
  trace-to-trace comparison, 320
AY7, *see* Acid yellow 7
2,2′-Azino-bis(3-ethylbenzothiazoline-6-sulfonic acid)
  diammonium salt (ABTS), 277–278

B

Base measurement units, 128
Basic Yellow 40, 228–229, 233, 376–377
Bayesian networks (BNs), 33, 56–61, 63, 67, 86, 102
Bayes theorem, 57, 59, 81–83, 87, 116
Benzene ring, graphical representations for, 132
Bitmap (BMP), 170
Blind verification, 105
Blood-contaminated fingermark
  absorption spectrum, 273–274
  amino acid reagents, 278
  blood fixing agents and time, 274
  CdTe QDs, 278
  DAB, 277
  DNA profiling, 272
  faux blood marks *vs.* genuine blood marks, 272
  heme-reacting chemicals, 277–278
  protein stains
    alginate casting material, 276
    amido black, 275–276
    AY7, 275–276
    blood fixing agents and time, 274
    coomassie blue, 275
    phloxine B, 276
  recommended detection sequence, 278–279
  UV luminescence techniques, 274

C

Cadmium telluride (CdTe) QDs, 240, 278
CA fuming, *see* Cyanoacrylate fuming
Carbon isotopes, atomic structures for, 130
Carbonless paper, 266–267
Case pre-assessment, 42–43
CdS/dendrimer nanocomposites, 239–240
CdSe/ZnS QDs, 239
CdTe QDs, *see* Cadmium telluride QDs
Chemical elements, 128–129
Chemistry theory
  atomic weight, 129–131
  benzene ring, graphical representations for, 132

empirical and structural formulas, 132
isotopes, atomic structures for, 130
matter, 133
Chiroscopy, 316–317
Cocaine-specific aptamers, 251
Colored light, 136
Comparison process, fingerprint identification
   AFIS systems, 67
   documentation, 69–70
   prior knowledge, 68
   reverse reasoning, 68
   target group, 68–69
Conditional probabilities, 44
Coomassie blue, 275
Copper-doped zinc sulfide (ZnS:Cu) QDs, 240
Cyanoacrylate (CA) fuming
   adhesive tape, 264
   crime scene, 280
   fabrics, 267–268
   fired cartridge cases, 269
   human skin, 257–258
   nonporous surfaces
      conventional, 221–224
      enhancement, 226–231
      portable fuming, 225
      VCA method, 225–226

D

DAB, *see* Diaminobenzidine
Dactylography, 316
Dactyloscopy, 316–317
Dangerous goods classification scheme, 291–292
Data, definition of, 35
Decision process
   assessment, 51–52
   schematic representation, 52
   suitability approaches, 51, 53
Dermal papillae, 12–14
Dermatoglyphics, 7–8, 67, 317
Desorption electrospray ionization (DESI) MS, 251–252
Detailed quality metrics, 50
DFO-developed fingermarks, *see* Diazafluorenone-
      developed fingermarks
Diaminobenzidine (DAB), 277, 377–378
Diazafluorenone-developed fingermarks, 378–380
   advantage, 200
   vs. IND-Zn developed fingermarks, 205–207
   luminescence spectra, 200–201
   vs. ninhydrin, 202–203
   reaction scheme, 200
   weak fingermarks, 202
Diffused reflection, 138, 148–149
Digital cameras
   camera settings, 165–167
   DSLR cameras, 164–165
   image sensors, 162–164
   lenses, 165
   selection, 168
   sensitivity and noise, 167–168
Digital imaging
   compression, 170
   file formats, 170–171
   image processing, 171–173

legal requirements, 173–175
   workflow, 175
Digital single-lens reflex (DSLR) cameras,
      164–165
Dimethylaminocinnamaldehyde-developed fingermark,
      380–381
   latent fingermarks, 243
   luminescence spectra, 244
   palm impression, 245
Disaster victim identification (DVI), 96
DNA profiling techniques
   combining evidence types, 321
   forensic examination
      automated extraction, 284
      fingerprint brushes, 285
      PCR analysis, 282–283
      recovery and analysis, 282
      STR profiles, 283–284
Documentation process
   examination, 281–282
   GYRO, 45–46
   PiAnoS, 46–47
   SWGFAST guidance, 46–47, 49
   systematical, 49
   ULW, 46
Dry contact method, 207
DSLR cameras, *see* Digital single-lens reflex cameras

E

Edgeoscopy, 316–317
Electromagnetic spectrum, 133–134
Electromagnetic wave, 134
Electrostatic Detection Apparatus (ESDA), 281
Episcopic coaxial illumination, 149–150, 186–187
Errors, 331–333
   education and training, 335
   portfolio and competency assessment, 335
   processes, 336
   product, 336
   recruitment, 334
   types, 333
European Network of Forensic Science Institutes (ENFSI),
      35, 44
Evaluation phase, fingerprint identification
   exclusion
      decision theory framework, 97
      definition, 96–97
      wrong exclusion, 97
   hierarchy of propositions
      activity level and offence level issues, 100, 102
      missing evidence, 101–102
      schematic representation, 100
   identification
      Bayesian network, 86, 88–91
      conclusion of certainty, 79
      conditional probability table, 87
      consequences, 80, 92
      decision theory analysis, 96
      definition, 78, 80
      Neumann case study, 85–86
      opinion, 79
      schematic representation, 81
      utilities and losses, 93–95

inconclusive, 97–99
reliability
    black box studies, 102
    false exclusions, 103
    Miami-Dade police department
        test, 103–104
Exchangeable image file (EXIF), 169
Exclusion, 96–97
Expert knowledge elicitation, 44
Expert Working Group on Human Factors in Latent Print
        Analysis
    ACE-V methodology, 34
    comparison, 68
    documentation, 47
    identification, 79–80
Explosive residue analysis
    direct analysis, 286
    nonporous substrates, 287
    paper substrate, 287
    PD technique, 287–288
    TNT, PETN, and RDX, 286–287

F

Fast Fourier transform (FFT) methods, 172
Faux blood marks, 272
Fingermark detection
    absorption, 185
    adhesive surfaces, 260–265, 368
    age determination
        case study, 324–325
        dehydration, 322
        factors, 326
        latent fingermark, 323–324
    blood, 370
        absorption spectrum, 273–274
        amino acid reagents, 278
        blood fixing agents and time, 274
        CdTe QDs, 278
        DAB, 277
        DNA profiling, 272
        faux blood marks vs. genuine blood
            marks, 272
        heme-reacting chemicals, 277–278
        protein stains, 274–276
        recommended detection sequence,
            278–279
        UV luminescence techniques, 274
    brass cartridge cases, 369
    challenges, 343–344
    crime scene, 280–281, 371
    detection research standards, 288–289
    DFO, 200–203
    diffused reflection, 186
    DMAC, 243–245
    fabric substrates, 267–268
    fired cartridge cases
        CA fuming, 269
        difficulties, 268
        electrochemical interactions,
            270–271
        gun blue solution, 269–270
        low success rates, reasons for, 268
        palladium deposition techniques, 270

flow chart, for detection phases, 289
forensic examination
    DNA profiling techniques, 282–285
    documents, 281–282
    explosive residue analysis, 286–288
genipin, 207
health and safety considerations
    checklists, 290
    dangerous goods classification scheme, 291–292
    light sources, 292–293
    nonexhaustive list, 291
    SDSs, 290–291
historical milestones, 105–106
holistic approaches, 108–111
human skin, 254–255, 368
    blood, 258–259
    CA fuming, 257–258
    iodine fuming, 256–257
    powdering, 255
    recommended detection sequence, 259–260
    RTX fuming, 258
    transfer techniques, 255–256
immunology
    antibodies, 250–251
    aptamers, 251
indanedione, 203–207
iodine–benzoflavone solution, 388–389
    application, 242
    vs. powdering, 243
isatin, 208
latent fingermarks, 179–180
    antibodies, 250
    blood, 272
    chemical composition, influencing
        factors for, 182
    DFO, 202
    diffused reflection, 186–187
    human skin, 254–260
    iodine treatment, 241–242
    natural secretions, 180–181
    secretory glands, 180–181
lawsone, 207–208
lipid stains, 211–214
LR-based reporting scheme, 114–116
luminescence, 185–186
mass spectrometric imaging, 251–252
nanoparticle-based detection methods
    health and safety concerns, 241
    MMD, 237–238, 390–395
    nanopowders, 236–237
    QDs, 239–240
    silica-based nanocomposites, 240–241
    SMD, 238–239, 407–411
near-infrared imaging, 188–189
nonporous surfaces, 184, 216–236, 366
physical developer, 208–211
porous surfaces, 183–184, 190–216, 366
predetermined numerical standard, 106–108
probability models, 111–114
relevance, 321–322
RTX spray, 245–246
semiporous surfaces, 185, 252–254, 367
silver nitrate, 246–247
sudan black, 247–248

thermal paper, 266–267, 369
upconverters, 248–249
usage cornerstones, 27
visible, 179
visible hyperspectral imaging, 189–190
Finger number prediction
    anatomical positioning, 56, 64
    Bayesian network, 60, 63
    gender and finger number nodes, 60
    general pattern and ridge tracing nodes, 61
    minutiæ loop tendencies, 65
    NCIC data, 56, 59
Fingerprint(s), 318–319
    combining evidence types, 321
    definition, 316–317
    detection of forged marks, 329–330
    errors, 331–333
        education and training, 335
        portfolio and competency assessment, 335
        processes, 336
        product, 336
        recruitment, 334
        types, 333
    forgeries committed by criminals, 328–329
    forgeries committed by law enforcement
            personnel, 328
    identification process, 321
    print-to-print comparison, 319
    trace-to-record/trace-to-print comparison, 319–320
    trace-to-trace comparison, 320
    twins, 9
Fingerprint Inquiry report
    identification, 79
    McKie case, 48
Fingerprint Inquiry in Scotland, 35, 69
FLSs, *see* Forensic light sources
Forensic examination
    DNA profiling techniques
        automated extraction, 284
        fingerprint brushes, 285
        PCR analysis, 282–283
        recovery and analysis, 282
        STR profiles, 283–284
    documents, 281–282
    explosive residue analysis
        direct analysis, 286
        nonporous substrates, 287
        paper substrate, 287
        PD technique, 287–288
        TNT, PETN, and RDX, 286–287
Forensic light sources (FLSs)
    barrier filters and goggles, 159
    LEDs, 156–158
    nonlaser, 155–156
    recommended output bands, 159
    schematic diagram, 156
Forged fingermarks
    by criminals, 328–329
    by law enforcement personnel, 328
Friction ridge identification procedures
    analysis
        decision process, 51–53
        documentation, 45–49

        factors, 43–45
        purpose, 39–43
        quality metrics, 50
        variability, 53–55
    challenges, 344–346
    comparison phase, 67–70
    evaluation phase
        exclusion, 96–97
        identification, 78–82
        inconclusive, 97–99
        propositions, 99–102
        reliability, 102–104
    search heuristics
        finger number, 56–65
        gender prediction, 67
        source area prediction, 65–66
    verification process, 104–105
Friction ridge skin morphogenesis, 22–27
    abnormal prints, 17–19
    alterations
        AFIS systems, 27
        epidermal fingerprint, 25
        left thumb, 23
        right thumb, 22
        scarring, 23–24
        skin diseases, 26
    diagrammatic representation, 20
    epidermis, 1–2
    estimated gestational age (EGA), 3
    incipient ridges, 14–15
    minutiæ, general pattern of
        diagnostic and genetic study, 7
        Merkel cells, 10
        SFinGe Demo v. 4.1 program image, 11
        twins, 8–9
        whorl pattern, 10
    permanency, 20–22
    primary dermal ridge development, 3–5
    secondary dermal ridge development, 12–14
    selectivity, 27
    uniqueness, 27
    white lines, 15–16

G

Gabor filtering techniques, 11
Genipin, 207
Gentian violet (GV) staining, 261–262,
            381–384
Genuine blood marks, 272
Gold nanopowder, 236
Graphics interchange format (GIF), 170
Green, yellow, red, orange (GYRO), 45–46
Gun blue solution, 269–270, 384

H

Hierarchy of propositions, 99–100
Highly sensitive immunoassays, 250
HSI, *see* Hyperspectral imaging
Hydrogen isotopes, atomic structures for, 130
2-Hydroxy-1,4-naphthoquinone, *see* Lawsone
Hyperspectral imaging (HSI) system, 175–176, 189

I

IAI, *see* International Association for Identification
Identification process
    Bayesian network, 86, 88–91
    conclusion of certainty, 79
    conditional probability table, 87
    consequences, 80, 92
    decision theory analysis, 96
    definition, 78, 80
    Neumann case study, 85–86
    opinion, 79
    schematic representation, 81
    utilities and losses, 93–95
IFRG, *see* International Fingerprint Scientific
        Research Group
Image program, 173
Immunogenic techniques
    antibodies, 250–251
    aptamers, 251
Incipient ridges, 14–15
Inconclusive conclusion, 97–99
Indanedione (IND)-developed fingermarks
    amino acids, 203–204
    vs. DFO, 203–204
    vs. IND-Zn developed fingermarks, 204–205
    1,2-Indanedione–Zn developed fingermarks, 384–387
        vs. conventional IND reagent, 204–205
        vs. DFO, 205–207
    luminescence spectra, 205–206
    solventless "dry contact" method, 207
IND-developed marks, *see* Indanedione-developed
        fingermarks
Indented fingermarks, 179, 281–282
Individual characteristic, 74
Individualization, *see* Identification
1H-Indole-2,3-dione, *see* Isatin
International Association for Identification
        (IAI), 78, 98, 108–109
International Fingerprint Scientific Research Group
        (IFRG), 288
International System of Units (SI units), 127
Interpol European Expert Group on Fingerprint
        Identification (IEEGFI), 106
Iodine–benzoflavone solution, 241–243, 388–389
Iodine fuming, 256–257, 387–388
Isatin, 208

J

Joint Photographic Experts Group (JPEG) format, 171

L

Latent fingermarks, 179–180
    antibodies, 250
    blood, 272
    chemical composition, influencing factors for, 182
    DFO, 202
    diffused reflection, 186–187
    human skin, 254–255, 368
        blood, 258–259
        CA fuming, 257–258

    iodine fuming, 256–257
    powdering, 255
    recommended detection sequence, 259–260
    RTX fuming, 258
    transfer techniques, 255–256
    iodine treatment, 241–242
    luminescence, 185–186
    natural secretions, 180–181
    secretory glands, 180–181
Lawsone, 207–208
Leuco Crystal Violet (LCV), 389–390
Light
    absorption mode, 137, 144–148
    colored light, 136
    diffused reflection mode, 148–149
    electromagnetic spectrum, 134
    episcopic coaxial illumination, 149–150
    filters, 140–144
    human eye, spectral sensitivity of, 136–137
    particle theory, 134–135
    photoluminescence emission
        excitation and emission curves, 150–151
        experiment setup, 152
        indanedione–zinc, 151
        phenomenon, 139–140
    polarization
        enhancement setup, 152–153
        phenomenon, 138–139
    reflection mode, 137–138
    role, 133
    ultraviolet illumination techniques, 153–155
    wave theory, 133–134
    white light, 135–136
Light-emitting diodes (LEDs)-based light sources, 156–158
Likelihood ratio (LR)
    following analysis, 42–43
    missing evidence, 101
    posterior odds and prior odds, 82–84
Lipophilic stain-developed fingermarks
    NR, 213–214
    ORO, 211–213
Liqui Drox solution, 264
Locard's third directive, 98
Lophoscopy, 316–317
LR, *see* Likelihood ratio
Luminescent fingermark, 185–186

M

Mairs' family tree of transitional fingerprint patterns, 38
Mass spectrometric imaging (MS), 251–252
Matrix-assisted laser desorption/ionization MS
        (MALDI-MS), 252
Matter, 128, 133, 135, 139, 142, 145
Merkel cells, 9–10
Miami-Dade police department, 103–104
Minutiæ
    general pattern of
        diagnostic and genetic study, 7
        Merkel cells, 10
        SFinGe Demo v. 4.1 program image, 11
        twins, 8–9
        whorl pattern, 10

statistical data on
  compound minutiæ, 359–360
  densities, 361
  length, 363
  localized relative frequencies, 361–362
  model, 359
  relative orientation, 362
  sample and data acquisition, 359–360
MMD, *see* Multimetal deposition
Montreal Protocol on Substances that Deplete the Ozone
      Layer, 243
MS, *see* Mass spectrometric imaging
Multimetal deposition (MMD), 237–238, 390–395

N

Nanoparticle-based fingermark detection methods
  health and safety concerns, 241
  MMD, 237–238, 390–395
  nanopowders, 236–237
  QDs, 239–240
  silica-based nanocomposites, 240–241
  SMD, 238–239, 407–411
Nanopowders, 236–237
National Crime Information Center (NCIC) Classification
      Scheme, 56, 60–61, 347–355
Near-infrared (NIR) imaging, 188–189
Negative visible fingermark, 179–180
Nile red-developed fingermarks, 395–396
  chemical structures, 211
  vs. PD treatment, 213–214
  revised formulation, 214
  use of, 214
Ninhydrin-developed fingermarks, 190–193,
      396–399
  vs. DFO, 202–203
  formulations, 193–195
  secondary metal salt treatment, 195–198
  synthesized analogs, 198–200
NIR imaging, *see* Near-infrared imaging
Nitrogen isotopes, atomic structures for, 130
Non-blind verification, 105
Nonporous surface-developed fingermarks,
      184, 366
  CA fuming, 221–231
  fingerprint powders, 216–218
  recommended detection sequence, 235–236
  SPR, 218–219, 411–412
  thick powder suspensions, 219–221, 403–404
  VMD, 231–235
NR-developed fingermarks, *see* Nile red-developed
      fingermarks

O

Occupational Health and Safety checklists, 290
Oil Red O-developed fingermarks, 399–400
  chemical structures, 211
  vs. PD treatment, 212–213
Optical techniques
  blood-contaminated fingermark, 179, 273–274
  crime scene, 280
  dry nonporous surface, 235
  visible marks, 179

ORO-developed fingermarks, *see* Oil Red O-developed
      fingermarks
Oxygen isotopes, atomic structures for, 130

P

Particle theory, 134–135
Patent fingermarks, *see* Visible fingermarks
PD, *see* Physical developer
PDRs, *see* Primary dermal ridges
Pelmatoscopy, 316–317
Periodic table, 129
Person of interest (POI), 71, 73, 85, 87, 101, 115–116
Phloxine B, 276
Photography
  digital cameras
    camera settings, 165–167
    DSLR cameras, 164–165
    image sensors, 162–164
    lenses, 165
    selection, 168
    sensitivity and noise, 167–168
  image formation
    chromatic aberration, 161
    lens, 160
    pinhole, 160
    spherical aberration, 161
  luminescence mode, 168–169
Photoluminescence emission
  excitation and emission curves, 150–151
  experiment setup, 152
  indanedione–zinc, 151
  phenomenon, 139–140
Physical developer (PD), 400–402
  acid prewash step study, 211
  vs. amino acid reagents, 210
  enhancement techniques, 210
  inconveniences, 210
  positively charged micelles, 208–209
  redox reaction, 209
  schematic fingermark, 208
  test strips, 211
Picture Annotation System (PiAnoS) version 4, 46–47, 70
Polarized light
  enhancement setup, 152–153
  phenomenon, 138–139
Poroscopy, 317
Porous surface-developed fingermarks,
      183–184, 366
  genipin, 207
  IND, 203–207
  isatin, 208
  lawsone, 207–208
  lipid stains, 211–214
  ninhydrin, 190–193
    vs. DFO, 202–203
    formulations, 193–195
    secondary metal salt treatment, 195–198
    synthesized analogs, 198–200
  PD, 208–209
  recommended detection sequence, 214–216
Positive visible fingermark, 179
Primary dermal ridges (PDRs), 3, 6, 12
Print-to-print comparison, 319

Probabilities
    conditional, 44
    subjective, 44
Prum Convention, 334

Q

Quantum dots (QDs), 239–240

R

Reflected UV imaging system (RUVIS), 154
Rhodamine 6G, 227, 404–405
Ridgeoscopy, 316
Ridge widths and gender, statistical data for, 356
Royal Canadian Mounted Police (RCMP)
    ACE-V methodology, 34
    IND-Zn, 207
    VMD, 232
Ruthenium tetroxide (RTX)-developed fingermarks,
    245–246, 258, 405–406

S

Safety data sheets (SDSs), 290–291
Scale of dimensions, 128
Scanning Kelvin probe (SKP) technique, 270–271
Scientific Working Group on Friction Ridge Analysis,
    Study and Technology (SWGFAST), 46–47, 49,
    51, 80, 97
SDSs, see Safety data sheets
Search heuristics
    finger number prediction
        anatomical positioning, 56, 64
        Bayesian network, 60, 63
        gender and finger number nodes, 60
        general pattern and ridge tracing nodes, 61
        minutiæ loop tendencies, 65
        NCIC data, 56, 59
    gender prediction, 67
    source area prediction, 65–66
Secondary dermal ridge development, 12–14
Secondary ion MS (SIMS), 252
Semiporous surface-developed fingermarks, 185,
    252–254, 367
Silica (SiO$_2$)-based nanocomposites, 240–241
Silver nitrate-developed fingermarks, 406–407
    plywood surfaces, 247
    raw wood fingermark, 246–247
    reaction, 246
Single-metal deposition (SMD), 238–239, 407–411
SKP technique, see Scanning Kelvin probe technique
Small particle reagent (SPR), 218–219,
    411–412
SMD, see Single-metal deposition
Spectral sensitivity, of human eye, 136–137
Specular reflection, 138

SPR, see Small particle reagent
STaR 11 magnetic powder, 237
Sticky-side powder method, 262–263
Subjective probability, 44
Sudan black, 247–248, 412–413
SWGFAST, see Scientific Working Group on Friction
    Ridge Analysis, Study and Technology

T

Tagged image file format (TIF/TIFF), 170
Thermal paper, 266–267
Thumbs Plus program, 173
Time-of-flight secondary ion MS (ToF-SIMS), 252
Trace-to-record/trace-to-print comparison, 319–320
Trace-to-trace comparison, 320

U

UK forensic science regulator, 80
Ultraviolet illumination techniques, 153–155
Universal Latent Workstation (ULW) version 6.4.1, 46, 50
U.S. Scientific Working Group on Imaging
    Technology (SWGIT), 174

V

Vacuum cyanoacrylate (VCA) fuming,
    225–226, 269
Vacuum metal deposition (VMD), 231–236
    fabrics, 267–268
    semiporous surfaces, 254
    vs. WPS, 220–221
Value for identification (VID), 51
VCA fuming, see Vacuum cyanoacrylate fuming
Verification process, fingerprint identification
    blind and non-blind types, 105
    merits, 105
    peer review, 104
Visible fingermarks
    absorption, 185
    blood, 258, 272
    lawsone, 208
    purple–brown, 208
    types, 179
    white light examination, 214
VMD, see Vacuum metal deposition
V++ program, 173

W

Wave theory, 133–134
Weight of evidence (WoE), 43
White light, 135–136
White lines, 15–16
William Blackstone ratio, 104
Wrong exclusion, 97